American Casebook Series
Hornbook Series and Basic Legal Texts
Nutshell Series

of

WEST PUBLISHING COMPANY
P.O. Box 64526
St. Paul, Minnesota 55164–0526

ACCOUNTING

Faris' Accounting and Law in a Nutshell, 377 pages, 1984 (Text)

Fiflis, Kripke and Foster's Teaching Materials on Accounting for Business Lawyers, 3rd Ed., 838 pages, 1984 (Casebook)

Siegel and Siegel's Accounting and Financial Disclosure: A Guide to Basic Concepts, 259 pages, 1983 (Text)

ADMINISTRATIVE LAW

Davis' Cases, Text and Problems on Administrative Law, 6th Ed., 683 pages, 1977 (Casebook)

Davis' Basic Text on Administrative Law, 3rd Ed., 617 pages, 1972 (Text)

Davis' Police Discretion, 176 pages, 1975 (Text)

Gellhorn and Boyer's Administrative Law and Process in a Nutshell, 2nd Ed., 445 pages, 1981 (Text)

Mashaw and Merrill's Cases and Materials on Administrative Law–The American Public Law System, 2nd Ed., approximately 1125 pages, 1985 (Casebook)

Robinson, Gellhorn and Bruff's The Administrative Process, 2nd Ed., 959 pages, 1980, with 1983 Supplement (Casebook)

ADMIRALTY

Healy and Sharpe's Cases and Materials on Admiralty, 875 pages, 1974 (Casebook)

Maraist's Admiralty in a Nutshell, 390 pages, 1983 (Text)

Sohn and Gustafson's Law of the Sea in a Nutshell, 264 pages, 1984 (Text)

AGENCY—PARTNERSHIP

Fessler's Alternatives to Incorporation for Persons in Quest of Profit, 258 pages, 1980 (Casebook)

AGENCY—PARTNERSHIP—Continued

Henn's Cases and Materials on Agency, Partnership and Other Unincorporated Business Enterprises, 2nd Ed., 733 pages, 1985 (Casebook)

Reuschlein and Gregory's Hornbook on the Law of Agency and Partnership, 625 pages, 1979, with 1981 pocket part (Text)

Seavey, Reuschlein and Hall's Cases on Agency and Partnership, 599 pages, 1962 (Casebook)

Selected Corporation and Partnership Statutes and Forms, approximately 560 pages, 1985

Steffen and Kerr's Cases and Materials on Agency-Partnership, 4th Ed., 859 pages, 1980 (Casebook)

Steffen's Agency-Partnership in a Nutshell, 364 pages, 1977 (Text)

AGRICULTURAL LAW

Meyer, Pedersen, Thorson and Davidson's Agricultural Law: Cases and Materials, approximately 925 pages, 1985 (Casebook)

AMERICAN INDIAN LAW

Canby's American Indian Law in a Nutshell, 288 pages, 1981 (Text)

Getches, Rosenfelt and Wilkinson's Cases on Federal Indian Law, 660 pages, 1979, with 1983 Supplement (Casebook)

ANTITRUST LAW

Gellhorn's Antitrust Law and Economics in a Nutshell, 2nd Ed., 425 pages, 1981 (Text)

Gifford and Raskind's Cases and Materials on Antitrust, 694 pages, 1983 with 1985 Supplement (Casebook)

Hovenkamp's Economics and Federal Antitrust Law, Student Ed., approximately 375 pages, 1985 (Text)

List current as of January, 1985

I

LAW SCHOOL PUBLICATIONS—Continued

ANTITRUST LAW—Continued

Oppenheim, Weston and McCarthy's Cases and Comments on Federal Antitrust Laws, 4th Ed., 1168 pages, 1981 with 1985 Supplement (Casebook)

Posner and Easterbrook's Cases and Economic Notes on Antitrust, 2nd Ed., 1077 pages, 1981, with 1984–85 Supplement (Casebook)

Sullivan's Hornbook of the Law of Antitrust, 886 pages, 1977 (Text)

See also Regulated Industries, Trade Regulation

ART LAW

DuBoff's Art Law in a Nutshell, 335 pages, 1984 (Text)

BANKING LAW

Lovett's Banking and Financial Institutions in a Nutshell, 409 pages, 1984 (Text)

Symons and White's Teaching Materials on Banking Law, 2nd Ed., 993 pages, 1984 (Casebook)

BUSINESS PLANNING

Epstein and Scheinfeld's Teaching Materials on Business Reorganization Under the Bankruptcy Code, 216 pages, 1980 (Casebook)

Painter's Problems and Materials in Business Planning, 2nd Ed., 1008 pages, 1984 (Casebook)

Selected Securities and Business Planning Statutes, Rules and Forms, 470 pages, 1985

CIVIL PROCEDURE

Casad's Res Judicata in a Nutshell, 310 pages, 1976 (text)

Cound, Friedenthal, Miller and Sexton's Cases and Materials on Civil Procedure, 4th Ed., approximately 1147 pages, 1985 with 1985 Supplement (Casebook)

Ehrenzweig, Louisell and Hazard's Jurisdiction in a Nutshell, 4th Ed., 232 pages, 1980 (Text)

Federal Rules of Civil-Appellate-Criminal Procedure—West Law School Edition, approximately 457 pages, 1984

Friedenthal, Kane and Miller's Hornbook on Civil Procedure, Student Edition, approximately 750 pages, 1985 (Text)

Hodges, Jones and Elliott's Cases and Materials on Texas Trial and Appellate Procedure, 2nd Ed., 745 pages, 1974 (Casebook)

Hodges, Jones and Elliott's Cases and Materials on the Judicial Process Prior to Trial in Texas, 2nd Ed., 871 pages, 1977 (Casebook)

Kane's Civil Procedure in a Nutshell, 271 pages, 1979 (Text)

CIVIL PROCEDURE—Continued

Karlen's Procedure Before Trial in a Nutshell, 258 pages, 1972 (Text)

Karlen, Meisenholder, Stevens and Vestal's Cases on Civil Procedure, 923 pages, 1975 (Casebook)

Koffler and Reppy's Hornbook on Common Law Pleading, 663 pages, 1969 (Text)

Park's Computer-Aided Exercises on Civil Procedure, 2nd Ed., 167 pages, 1983 (Coursebook)

Siegel's Hornbook on New York Practice, 1011 pages, 1978 with 1981–82 Pocket Part (Text)

See also Federal Jurisdiction and Procedure

CIVIL RIGHTS

Abernathy's Cases and Materials on Civil Rights, 660 pages, 1980 (Casebook)

Cohen's Cases on the Law of Deprivation of Liberty: A Study in Social Control, 755 pages, 1980 (Casebook)

Lockhart, Kamisar and Choper's Cases on Constitutional Rights and Liberties, 5th Ed., 1298 pages plus Appendix, 1981, with 1984 Supplement (Casebook)—reprint from Lockhart, et al. Cases on Constitutional Law, 5th Ed., 1980

Vieira's Civil Rights in a Nutshell, 279 pages, 1978 (Text)

COMMERCIAL LAW

Bailey's Secured Transactions in a Nutshell, 2nd Ed., 391 pages, 1981 (Text)

Epstein and Martin's Basic Uniform Commercial Code Teaching Materials, 2nd Ed., 667 pages, 1983 (Casebook)

Henson's Hornbook on Secured Transactions Under the U.C.C., 2nd Ed., 504 pages, 1979 with 1979 P.P. (Text)

Murray's Commercial Law, Problems and Materials, 366 pages, 1975 (Coursebook)

Nordstrom and Clovis' Problems and Materials on Commercial Paper, 458 pages, 1972 (Casebook)

Nordstrom and Lattin's Problems and Materials on Sales and Secured Transactions, 809 pages, 1968 (Casebook)

Nordstrom, Murray and Clovis' Problems and Materials on Sales, 515 pages, 1982 (Casebook)

Selected Commercial Statutes, approximately 1379 pages, 1985

Speidel, Summers and White's Teaching Materials on Commercial and Consumer Law, 3rd Ed., 1490 pages, 1981 (Casebook)

Stockton's Sales in a Nutshell, 2nd Ed., 370 pages, 1981 (Text)

Stone's Uniform Commercial Code in a Nutshell, 2nd Ed., 516 pages, 1984 (Text)

Uniform Commercial Code, Official Text with Comments, 994 pages, 1978

COMMERCIAL LAW—Continued

UCC Article 9, Reprint from 1962 Code, 128 pages, 1976

UCC Article 9, 1972 Amendments, 304 pages, 1978

Weber and Speidel's Commercial Paper in a Nutshell, 3rd Ed., 404 pages, 1982 (Text)

White and Summers' Hornbook on the Uniform Commercial Code, 2nd Ed., 1250 pages, 1980 (Text)

COMMUNITY PROPERTY

Mennell's Community Property in a Nutshell, 447 pages, 1982 (Text)

Verrall and Bird's Cases and Materials on California Community Property, 4th Ed., 549 pages, 1983 (Casebook)

COMPARATIVE LAW

Barton, Gibbs, Li and Merryman's Law in Radically Different Cultures, 960 pages, 1983 (Casebook)

Glendon, Gordon, and Osakwe's Comparative Legal Traditions in a Nutshell, 402 pages, 1982 (Text)

Langbein's Comparative Criminal Procedure: Germany, 172 pages, 1977 (Casebook)

COMPUTERS AND LAW

Mason's An Introduction to the Use of Computers in Law, 223 pages, 1984 (Text)

CONFLICT OF LAWS

Cramton, Currie and Kay's Cases-Comments-Questions on Conflict of Laws, 3rd Ed., 1026 pages, 1981 (Casebook)

Scoles and Hay's Hornbook on Conflict of Laws, Student Ed., 1085 pages, 1982 (Text)

Scoles and Weintraub's Cases and Materials on Conflict of Laws, 2nd Ed., 966 pages, 1972, with 1978 Supplement (Casebook)

Siegel's Conflicts in a Nutshell, 469 pages, 1982 (Text)

Engdahl's Constitutional Power in a Nutshell: Federal and State, 411 pages, 1974 (Text)

Lockhart, Kamisar and Choper's Cases-Comments-Questions on Constitutional Law, 5th Ed., 1705 pages plus Appendix, 1980, with 1984 Supplement (Casebook)

Lockhart, Kamisar and Choper's Cases-Comments-Questions on the American Constitution, 5th Ed., 1185 pages plus Appendix, 1981, with 1984 Supplement (Casebook)—reprint from Lockhart, et al. Cases on Constitutional Law, 5th Ed., 1980

Manning's The Law of Church-State Relations in a Nutshell, 305 pages, 1981 (Text)

CONFLICT OF LAWS—Continued

Miller's Presidential Power in a Nutshell, 328 pages, 1977 (Text)

CONSTITUTIONAL LAW

Nowak, Rotunda and Young's Hornbook on Constitutional Law, 2nd Ed., Student Ed., 1172 pages, 1983 (Text)

Rotunda's Modern Constitutional Law: Cases and Notes, 2nd Ed., approximately 1055 pages, 1985 (Casebook)

Williams' Constitutional Analysis in a Nutshell, 388 pages, 1979 (Text)

See also Civil Rights

CONSUMER LAW

Epstein and Nickles' Consumer Law in a Nutshell, 2nd Ed., 418 pages, 1981 (Text)

McCall's Consumer Protection, Cases, Notes and Materials, 594 pages, 1977, with 1977 Statutory Supplement (Casebook)

Selected Commercial Statutes, approximately 1379 pages, 1985

Spanogle and Rohner's Cases and Materials on Consumer Law, 693 pages, 1979, with 1982 Supplement (Casebook)

See also Commercial Law

CONTRACTS

Calamari & Perillo's Cases and Problems on Contracts, 1061 pages, 1978 (Casebook)

Calamari and Perillo's Hornbook on Contracts, 2nd Ed., 878 pages, 1977 (Text)

Corbin's Text on Contracts, One Volume Student Edition, 1224 pages, 1952 (Text)

Fessler and Loiseaux's Cases and Materials on Contracts, 837 pages, 1982 (Casebook)

Freedman's Cases and Materials on Contracts, 658 pages, 1973 (Casebook)

Friedman's Contract Remedies in a Nutshell, 323 pages, 1981 (Text)

Fuller and Eisenberg's Cases on Basic Contract Law, 4th Ed., 1203 pages, 1981 (Casebook)

Hamilton, Rau and Weintraub's Cases and Materials on Contracts, 830 pages, 1984 (Casebook)

Jackson and Bollinger's Cases on Contract Law in Modern Society, 2nd Ed., 1329 pages, 1980 (Casebook)

Keyes' Government Contracts in a Nutshell, 423 pages, 1979 (Text)

Reitz's Cases on Contracts as Basic Commercial Law, 763 pages, 1975 (Casebook)

Schaber and Rohwer's Contracts in a Nutshell, 2nd Ed., 425 pages, 1984 (Text)

COPYRIGHT

See Patent and Copyright Law

LAW SCHOOL PUBLICATIONS—Continued

CORPORATIONS

Hamilton's Cases on Corporations—Including Partnerships and Limited Partnerships, 2nd Ed., 1108 pages, 1981, with 1981 Statutory Supplement and 1984 Supplement (Casebook)

Hamilton's Law of Corporations in a Nutshell, 379 pages, 1980 (Text)

Henn's Cases on Corporations, 1279 pages, 1974, with 1980 Supplement (Casebook)

Henn and Alexander's Hornbook on Corporations, 3rd Ed., Student Ed., 1371 pages, 1983 (Text)

Jennings and Buxbaum's Cases and Materials on Corporations, 5th Ed., 1180 pages, 1979 (Casebook)

Selected Corporation and Partnership Statutes, Regulations and Forms, approximately 560 pages, 1985

Solomon, Stevenson and Schwartz' Materials and Problems on Corporations: Law and Policy, 1172 pages, 1982 with 1984 Supplement (Casebook)

CORPORATE FINANCE

Hamilton's Cases and Materials on Corporate Finance, 895 pages, 1984 (Casebook)

CORRECTIONS

Krantz's Cases and Materials on the Law of Corrections and Prisoners' Rights, 2nd Ed., 735 pages, 1981, with 1982 Supplement (Casebook)

Krantz's Law of Corrections and Prisoners' Rights in a Nutshell, 2nd Ed., 384 pages, 1983 (Text)

Popper's Post-Conviction Remedies in a Nutshell, 360 pages, 1978 (Text)

Robbins' Cases and Materials on Post Conviction Remedies, 506 pages, 1982 (Casebook)

Rubin's Law of Criminal Corrections, 2nd Ed., 873 pages, 1973, with 1978 Supplement (Text)

CREDITOR'S RIGHTS

Bankruptcy Code, Rules and Forms, Law School Ed., 602 pages, 1984

Epstein's Debtor-Creditor Law in a Nutshell, 2nd Ed., 324 pages, 1980 (Text)

Epstein and Landers' Debtors and Creditors: Cases and Materials, 2nd Ed., 689 pages, 1982 (Casebook)

Epstein and Sheinfeld's Teaching Materials on Business Reorganization Under the Bankruptcy Code, 216 pages, 1980 (Casebook)

LoPucki's Player's Manual for the Debtor-Creditor Game, 123 pages, 1985 (Coursebook)

CREDITOR'S RIGHTS—Continued

Riesenfeld's Cases and Materials on Creditors' Remedies and Debtors' Protection, 3rd Ed., 810 pages, 1979 with 1979 Statutory Supplement and 1981 Case Supplement (Casebook)

White's Bankruptcy and Creditor's Rights: Cases and Materials, approximately 820 pages, 1985 (Casebook)

CRIMINAL LAW AND CRIMINAL PROCEDURE

Cohen and Gobert's Problems in Criminal Law, 297 pages, 1976 (Problem book)

Davis' Police Discretion, 176 pages, 1975 (Text)

Dix and Sharlot's Cases and Materials on Criminal Law, 2nd Ed., 771 pages, 1979 (Casebook)

Federal Rules of Civil-Appellate-Criminal Procedure—West Law School Edition, 457 pages, 1984

Grano's Problems in Criminal Procedure, 2nd Ed., 176 pages, 1981 (Problem book)

Israel and LaFave's Criminal Procedure in a Nutshell, 3rd Ed., 438 pages, 1980 (Text)

Johnson's Cases, Materials and Text on Substantive Criminal Law in its Procedural Context, 3rd Ed., approximately 750 pages, 1985 (Casebook)

Kamisar, LaFave and Israel's Cases, Comments and Questions on Modern Criminal Procedure, 5th ed., 1635 pages plus Appendix, 1980 with 1984 Supplement (Casebook)

Kamisar, LaFave and Israel's Cases, Comments and Questions on Basic Criminal Procedure, 5th Ed., 869 pages, 1980 with 1984 Supplement (Casebook)—reprint from Kamisar, et al. Modern Criminal Procedure, 5th ed., 1980

LaFave's Modern Criminal Law: Cases, Comments and Questions, 789 pages, 1978 (Casebook)

LaFave and Israel's Hornbook on Criminal Procedure, Student Ed., approximately 1100 pages, 1985 (Text)

LaFave and Scott's Hornbook on Criminal Law, 763 pages, 1972 (Text)

Langbein's Comparative Criminal Procedure: Germany, 172 pages, 1977 (Casebook)

Loewy's Criminal Law in a Nutshell, 302 pages, 1975 (Text)

Saltzburg's American Criminal Procedure, Cases and Commentary, 2nd Ed., 1193 pages, 1984 with 1984 Supplement (Casebook)

LAW SCHOOL PUBLICATIONS—Continued

**CRIMINAL LAW AND CRIMINAL PRO-
CEDURE**—Continued

Uviller's The Processes of Criminal Justice:
Investigation and Adjudication, 2nd Ed.,
1384 pages, 1979 with 1979 Statutory
Supplement and 1983 Update (Casebook)

Uviller's The Processes of Criminal Justice:
Adjudication, 2nd Ed., 730 pages, 1979.
Soft-cover reprint from Uviller's The
Processes of Criminal Justice: Investiga-
tion and Adjudication, 2nd Ed. (Case-
book)

Uviller's The Processes of Criminal Justice:
Investigation, 2nd Ed., 655 pages, 1979.
Soft-cover reprint from Uviller's The
Processes of Criminal Justice: Investiga-
tion and Adjudication, 2nd Ed. (Case-
book)

Vorenberg's Cases on Criminal Law and
Procedure, 2nd Ed., 1088 pages, 1981
with 1985 Supplement (Casebook)

See also Corrections, Juvenile Justice

DECEDENTS ESTATES

See Trusts and Estates

DOMESTIC RELATIONS

Clark's Cases and Problems on Domestic
Relations, 3rd Ed., 1153 pages, 1980
(Casebook)

Clark's Hornbook on Domestic Relations,
754 pages, 1968 (Text)

Krause's Cases and Materials on Family
Law, 2nd Ed., 1221 pages, 1983 (Casebook)

Krause's Family Law in a Nutshell, 400
pages, 1977 (Text)

Krauskopf's Cases on Property Division at
Marriage Dissolution, 250 pages, 1984
(Casebook)

ECONOMICS, LAW AND

Goetz' Cases and Materials on Law and Economics, 547 pages, 1984 (Casebook)

Manne's The Economics of Legal Relationships—Readings in the Theory of Property
Rights, 660 pages, 1975 (Text)

See also Antitrust, Regulated Industries

EDUCATION LAW

Alexander and Alexander's The Law of
Schools, Students and Teachers in a Nutshell, 409 pages, 1984 (Text)

Morris' The Constitution and American Education, 2nd Ed., 992 pages, 1980 (Casebook)

EMPLOYMENT DISCRIMINATION

Player's Cases and Materials on Employment
Discrimination Law, 2nd Ed., 782 pages,
1984 (Casebook)

EMPLOYMENT DISCRIMINATION—
Continued

Player's Federal Law of Employment Discrimination in a Nutshell, 2nd Ed., 402
pages, 1981 (Text)

See also Women and the Law

ENERGY LAW

Rodgers' Cases and Materials on Energy
and Natural Resources Law, 2nd Ed., 877
pages, 1983 (Casebook)

Selected Environmental Law Statutes, 758
pages, 1984

Tomain's Energy Law in a Nutshell, 338
pages, 1981 (Text)

See also Natural Resources Law, Environmental Law, Oil and Gas, Water Law

ENVIRONMENTAL LAW

Bonine and McGarity's Cases and Materials
on the Law of Environment and Pollution,
1076 pages, 1984 (Casebook)

Findley and Farber's Cases and Materials on
Environmental Law, 2nd Ed., approximately 800 pages, 1985 (Casebook)

Findley and Farber's Environmental Law in
a Nutshell, 343 pages, 1983 (Text)

Rodgers' Hornbook on Environmental Law,
956 pages, 1977 with 1984 pocket part
(Text)

Selected Environmental Law Statutes, 758
pages, 1984

See also Energy Law, Natural Resources
Law, Water Law

EQUITY

See Remedies

ESTATES

See Trusts and Estates

ESTATE PLANNING

Kurtz' Cases, Materials and Problems on
Family Estate Planning, 853 pages, 1983
(Casebook)

Lynn's Introduction to Estate Planning, in a
Nutshell, 3rd Ed., 370 pages, 1983 (Text)

See also Taxation

EVIDENCE

Broun and Meisenholder's Problems in Evidence, 2nd Ed., 304 pages, 1981 (Problem book)

Cleary and Strong's Cases, Materials and
Problems on Evidence, 3rd Ed., 1143
pages, 1981 (Casebook)

Federal Rules of Evidence for United States
Courts and Magistrates, 337 pages, 1984

Graham's Federal Rules of Evidence in a
Nutshell, 429 pages, 1981 (Text)

Kimball's Programmed Materials on Problems in Evidence, 380 pages, 1978 (Problem book)

LAW SCHOOL PUBLICATIONS—Continued

EVIDENCE—Continued

Lempert and Saltzburg's A Modern Approach to Evidence: Text, Problems, Transcripts and Cases, 2nd Ed., 1296 pages, 1983 (Casebook)

Lilly's Introduction to the Law of Evidence, 486 pages, 1978 (Text)

McCormick, Elliott and Sutton's Cases and Materials on Evidence, 5th Ed., 1212 pages, 1981 (Casebook)

McCormick's Hornbook on Evidence, 3rd Ed., Student Ed., 1155 pages, 1984 (Text)

Rothstein's Evidence, State and Federal Rules in a Nutshell, 2nd Ed., 514 pages, 1981 (Text)

Saltzburg's Evidence Supplement: Rules, Statutes, Commentary, 245 pages, 1980 (Casebook Supplement)

FEDERAL JURISDICTION AND PROCEDURE

Currie's Cases and Materials on Federal Courts, 3rd Ed., 1042 pages, 1982 (Casebook)

Currie's Federal Jurisdiction in a Nutshell, 2nd Ed., 258 pages, 1981 (Text)

Federal Rules of Civil-Appellate-Criminal Procedure—West Law School Edition, 457 pages, 1984

Forrester and Moye's Cases and Materials on Federal Jurisdiction and Procedure, 3rd Ed., 917 pages, 1977 with 1981 Supplement (Casebook)

Redish's Cases, Comments and Questions on Federal Courts, 878 pages, 1983 (Casebook)

Vetri and Merrill's Federal Courts, Problems and Materials, 2nd Ed., 232 pages, 1984 (Problem Book)

Wright's Hornbook on Federal Courts, 4th Ed., Student Ed., 870 pages, 1983 (Text)

FUTURE INTERESTS

See Trusts and Estates

IMMIGRATION LAW

Aleinikoff and Martin's Immigration Process and Policy, approximately 800 pages, 1985 (Casebook)

Weissbrodt's Immigration Law and Procedure in a Nutshell, 345 pages, 1984 (Text)

INDIAN LAW

See American Indian Law

INSURANCE

Dobbyn's Insurance Law in a Nutshell, 281 pages, 1981 (Text)

INSURANCE—Continued

Keeton's Cases on Basic Insurance Law, 2nd Ed., 1086 pages, 1977

Keeton's Basic Text on Insurance Law, 712 pages, 1971 (Text)

Keeton's Case Supplement to Keeton's Basic Text on Insurance Law, 334 pages, 1978 (Casebook)

Keeton's Programmed Problems in Insurance Law, 243 pages, 1972 (Text Supplement)

York and Whelan's Cases, Materials and Problems on Insurance Law, 715 pages, 1982 (Casebook)

INTERNATIONAL LAW

Henkin, Pugh, Schachter and Smit's Cases and Materials on International Law, 2nd Ed., 1152 pages, 1980, with Documents Supplement (Casebook)

Jackson's Legal Problems of International Economic Relations, 1097 pages, 1977, with Documents Supplement (Casebook)

Kirgis' International Organizations in Their Legal Setting, 1016 pages, 1977, with 1981 Supplement (Casebook)

Weston, Falk and D'Amato's International Law and World Order—A Problem Oriented Coursebook, 1195 pages, 1980, with Documents Supplement (Casebook)

Wilson's International Business Transactions in a Nutshell, 2nd Ed., 476 pages, 1984 (Text)

INTERVIEWING AND COUNSELING

Binder and Price's Interviewing and Counseling, 232 pages, 1977 (Text)

Shaffer's Interviewing and Counseling in a Nutshell, 353 pages, 1976 (Text)

INTRODUCTION TO LAW

Dobbyn's So You Want to go to Law School, Revised First Edition, 206 pages, 1976 (Text)

Hegland's Introduction to the Study and Practice of Law in a Nutshell, 418 pages, 1983 (Text)

Kinyon's Introduction to Law Study and Law Examinations in a Nutshell, 389 pages, 1971 (Text)

See also Legal Method and Legal System

JUDICIAL ADMINISTRATION

Carrington, Meador and Rosenberg's Justice on Appeal, 263 pages, 1976 (Casebook)

Nelson's Cases and Materials on Judicial Administration and the Administration of Justice, 1032 pages, 1974 (Casebook)

LAW SCHOOL PUBLICATIONS—Continued

JURISPRUDENCE

Christie's Text and Readings on Jurisprudence—The Philosophy of Law, 1056 pages, 1973 (Casebook)

JUVENILE JUSTICE

Fox's Cases and Materials on Modern Juvenile Justice, 2nd Ed., 960 pages, 1981 (Casebook)

Fox's Juvenile Courts in a Nutshell, 3rd Ed., 291 pages, 1984 (Text)

LABOR LAW

Gorman's Basic Text on Labor Law—Unionization and Collective Bargaining, 914 pages, 1976 (Text)

Leslie's Labor Law in a Nutshell, 403 pages, 1979 (Text)

Nolan's Labor Arbitration Law and Practice in a Nutshell, 358 pages, 1979 (Text)

Oberer, Hanslowe and Andersen's Cases and Materials on Labor Law—Collective Bargaining in a Free Society, 2nd Ed., 1168 pages, 1979, with 1979 Statutory Supplement and 1982 Case Supplement (Casebook)

See also Employment Discrimination, Social Legislation

LAND FINANCE

See Real Estate Transactions

LAND USE

Hagman's Cases on Public Planning and Control of Urban and Land Development, 2nd Ed., 1301 pages, 1980 (Casebook)

Hagman's Hornbook on Urban Planning and Land Development Control Law, 706 pages, 1971 (Text)

Wright and Gitelman's Cases and Materials on Land Use, 3rd Ed., 1300 pages, 1982 (Casebook)

Wright and Webber's Land Use in a Nutshell, 316 pages, 1978 (Text)

LEGAL HISTORY

Presser and Zainaldin's Cases on Law and American History, 855 pages, 1980 (Casebook)

See also Legal Method and Legal System

LEGAL METHOD AND LEGAL SYSTEM

Aldisert's Readings, Materials and Cases in the Judicial Process, 948 pages, 1976 (Casebook)

Berch and Berch's Introduction to Legal Method and Process, approximately 460 pages, 1985 (Casebook)

Bodenheimer, Oakley and Love's Readings and Cases on an Introduction to the Anglo-American Legal System, 161 pages, 1980 (Casebook)

LEGAL METHOD AND LEGAL SYSTEM—Continued

Davies and Lawry's Institutions and Methods of the Law—Introductory Teaching Materials, 547 pages, 1982 (Casebook)

Dvorkin, Himmelstein and Lesnick's Becoming a Lawyer: A Humanistic Perspective on Legal Education and Professionalism, 211 pages, 1981 (Text)

Fryer and Orentlicher's Cases and Materials on Legal Method and Legal System, 1043 pages, 1967 (Casebook)

Greenberg's Judicial Process and Social Change, 666 pages, 1977 (Coursebook)

Kelso and Kelso's Studying Law: An Introduction, 587 pages, 1984 (Coursebook)

Kempin's Historical Introduction to Anglo-American Law in a Nutshell, 2nd Ed., 280 pages, 1973 (Text)

Kimball's Historical Introduction to the Legal System, 610 pages, 1966 (Casebook)

Murphy's Cases and Materials on Introduction to Law—Legal Process and Procedure, 772 pages, 1977 (Casebook)

Reynolds' Judicial Process in a Nutshell, 292 pages, 1980 (Text)

See also Legal Research and Writing

LEGAL PROFESSION

Aronson, Devine and Fisch's Problems, Cases and Materials on Professional Responsibility, approximately 710 pages, 1985 (Casebook)

Aronson and Weckstein's Professional Responsibility in a Nutshell, 399 pages, 1980 (Text)

Mellinkoff's The Conscience of a Lawyer, 304 pages, 1973 (Text)

Mellinkoff's Lawyers and the System of Justice, 983 pages, 1976 (Casebook)

Pirsig and Kirwin's Cases and Materials on Professional Responsibility, 4th Ed., 603 pages, 1984 (Casebook)

Schwartz and Wydick's Problems in Legal Ethics, 285 pages, 1983 (Casebook)

Selected Statutes, Rules and Standards on the Legal Profession, 276 pages, Revised 1984

Smith's Preventing Legal Malpractice, 142 pages, 1981 (Text)

Wolfram's Hornbook on Professional Responsibility, Student Edition, approximately 700 pages (Text)

LEGAL RESEARCH AND WRITING

Cohen's Legal Research in a Nutshell, 4th Ed., approximately 425 pages, 1985 (Text)

Cohen and Berring's How to Find the Law, 8th Ed., 790 pages, 1983. Problem book by Foster and Kelly available (Casebook)

Cohen and Berring's Finding the Law, 8th Ed., Abridged Ed., 556 pages, 1984 (Casebook)

LAW SCHOOL PUBLICATIONS—Continued

LEGAL RESEARCH AND WRITING—
Continued

Dickerson's Materials on Legal Drafting, 425 pages, 1981 (Casebook)

Felsenfeld and Siegel's Writing Contracts in Plain English, 290 pages, 1981 (Text)

Gopen's Writing From a Legal Perspective, 225 pages, 1981 (Text)

Mellinkoff's Legal Writing—Sense and Nonsense, 242 pages, 1982 (Text)

Rombauer's Legal Problem Solving—Analysis, Research and Writing, 4th Ed., 424 pages, 1983 (Coursebook)

Squires and Rombauer's Legal Writing in a Nutshell, 294 pages, 1982 (Text)

Statsky's Legal Research, Writing and Analysis, 2nd Ed., 167 pages, 1982 (Coursebook)

Statsky's Legislative Analysis: How to Use Statutes and Regulations, 2nd Ed., 217 pages, 1984 (Text)

Statsky and Wernet's Case Analysis and Fundamentals of Legal Writing, 2nd Ed., 441 pages, 1984 (Text)

Teply's Programmed Materials on Legal Research and Citation, 334 pages, 1982. Student Library Exercises available (Coursebook)

Weihofen's Legal Writing Style, 2nd Ed., 332 pages, 1980 (Text)

LEGISLATION

Davies' Legislative Law and Process in a Nutshell, 279 pages, 1975 (Text)

Nutting and Dickerson's Cases and Materials on Legislation, 5th Ed., 744 pages, 1978 (Casebook)

Statsky's Legislative Analysis: How to Use Statutes and Regulations, 2nd Ed., 217 pages, 1984 (Text)

LOCAL GOVERNMENT

McCarthy's Local Government Law in a Nutshell, 2nd Ed., 404 pages, 1983 (Text)

Michelman and Sandalow's Cases-Comments-Questions on Government in Urban Areas, 1216 pages, 1970, with 1972 Supplement (Casebook)

Reynolds' Hornbook on Local Government Law, 860 pages, 1982 (Text)

Valente's Cases and Materials on Local Government Law, 2nd Ed., 980 pages, 1980 with 1982 Supplement (Casebook)

MASS COMMUNICATION LAW

Gillmor and Barron's Cases and Comment on Mass Communication Law, 4th Ed., 1076 pages, 1984 (Casebook)

Ginsburg's Regulation of Broadcasting: Law and Policy Towards Radio, Television and Cable Communications, 741 pages, 1979, with 1983 Supplement (Casebook)

MASS COMMUNICATION—Continued

Zuckman and Gayne's Mass Communications Law in a Nutshell, 2nd Ed., 473 pages, 1983 (Text)

MEDICINE, LAW AND

King's The Law of Medical Malpractice in a Nutshell, 340 pages, 1977 (Text)

Shapiro and Spece's Problems, Cases and Materials on Bioethics and Law, 892 pages, 1981 (Casebook)

Sharpe, Fiscina and Head's Cases on Law and Medicine, 882 pages, 1978 (Casebook)

MILITARY LAW

Shanor and Terrell's Military Law in a Nutshell, 378 pages, 1980 (Text)

MORTGAGES

See Real Estate Transactions

NATURAL RESOURCES LAW

Laito's Cases and Materials on Natural Resources Law, approximately 900 pages, 1985 (Casebook)

See also Energy Law, Environmental Law, Oil and Gas, Water Law

NEGOTIATION

Edwards and White's Problems, Readings and Materials on the Lawyer as a Negotiator, 484 pages, 1977 (Casebook)

Williams' Legal Negotiation and Settlement, 207 pages, 1983 (Coursebook)

OFFICE PRACTICE

Hegland's Trial and Practice Skills in a Nutshell, 346 pages, 1978 (Text)

Strong and Clark's Law Office Management, 424 pages, 1974 (Casebook)

See also Computers and Law, Interviewing and Counseling, Negotiation

OIL AND GAS

Hemingway's Hornbook on Oil and Gas, 2nd Ed., Student Ed., 543 pages, 1983 (Text)

Huie, Woodward and Smith's Cases and Materials on Oil and Gas, 2nd Ed., 955 pages, 1972 (Casebook)

Lowe's Oil and Gas Law in a Nutshell, 443 pages, 1983 (Text)

See also Energy and Natural Resources Law

PARTNERSHIP

See Agency—Partnership

LAW SCHOOL PUBLICATIONS—Continued

PATENT AND COPYRIGHT LAW

Choate and Francis' Cases and Materials on Patent Law, 2nd Ed., 1110 pages, 1981 (Casebook)

Miller and Davis' Intellectual Property—Patents, Trademarks and Copyright in a Nutshell, 428 pages, 1983 (Text)

Nimmer's Cases on Copyright and Other Aspects of Entertainment Litigation, 3rd Ed., approximately 1000 pages, 1985 (Casebook)

POVERTY LAW

Brudno's Poverty, Inequality, and the Law: Cases-Commentary-Analysis, 934 pages, 1976 (Casebook)

LaFrance, Schroeder, Bennett and Boyd's Hornbook on Law of the Poor, 558 pages, 1973 (Text)

See also Social Legislation

PRODUCTS LIABILITY

Noel and Phillips' Cases on Products Liability, 2nd Ed., 821 pages, 1982 (Casebook)

Noel and Phillips' Products Liability in a Nutshell, 2nd Ed., 341 pages, 1981 (Text)

PROPERTY

Aigler, Smith and Tefft's Cases on Property, 2 volumes, 1339 pages, 1960 (Casebook)

Bernhardt's Real Property in a Nutshell, 2nd Ed., 448 pages, 1981 (Text)

Boyer's Survey of the Law of Property, 766 pages, 1981 (Text)

Browder, Cunningham and Smith's Cases on Basic Property Law, 4th Ed., 1431 pages, 1984 (Casebook)

Bruce, Ely and Bostick's Cases and Materials on Modern Property Law, 1004 pages, 1984 (Casebook)

Burby's Hornbook on Real Property, 3rd Ed., 490 pages, 1965 (Text)

Burke's Personal Property in a Nutshell, 322 pages, 1983 (Text)

Chused's A Modern Approach to Property: Cases-Notes-Materials, 1069 pages, 1978 with 1980 Supplement (Casebook)

Cohen's Materials for a Basic Course in Property, 526 pages, 1978 (Casebook)

Cunningham, Stoebuck and Whitman's Hornbook on the Law of Property, Student Ed., 916 pages, 1984 (Text)

Donahue, Kauper and Martin's Cases on Property, 2nd Ed., 1362 pages, 1983 (Casebook)

Hill's Landlord and Tenant Law in a Nutshell, 319 pages, 1979 (Text)

Moynihan's Introduction to Real Property, 254 pages, 1962 (Text)

Phipps' Titles in a Nutshell, 277 pages, 1968 (Text)

PROPERTY—Continued

Uniform Land Transactions Act, Uniform Simplification of Land Transfers Act, Uniform Condominium Act, 1977 Official Text with Comments, 462 pages, 1978

See also Real Estate Transactions, Land Use

PSYCHIATRY, LAW AND

Reisner's Law and the Mental Health System, Civil and Criminal Aspects, approximately 700 pages, 1985 (Casebooks)

REAL ESTATE TRANSACTIONS

Bruce's Real Estate Finance in a Nutshell, 2nd Ed., approximately 300 pages, 1985 (Text)

Maxwell, Riesenfeld, Hetland and Warren's Cases on California Security Transactions in Land, 3rd Ed., 728 pages, 1984 (Casebook)

Nelson and Whitman's Cases on Real Estate Transfer, Finance and Development, 2nd Ed., 1114 pages, 1981, with 1983 Supplement (Casebook)

Osborne's Cases and Materials on Secured Transactions, 559 pages, 1967 (Casebook)

Osborne, Nelson and Whitman's Hornbook on Real Estate Finance Law, 2nd Ed., approximately 900 pages, 1985 (Text)

REGULATED INDUSTRIES

Gellhorn and Pierce's Regulated Industries in a Nutshell, 394 pages, 1982 (Text)

Morgan, Harrison and Verkuil's Cases and Materials on Economic Regulation of Business, 2nd Ed., approximately 900 pages, 1985 (Casebook)

Pozen's Financial Institutions: Cases, Materials and Problems on Investment Management, 844 pages, 1978 (Casebook)

See also Mass Communication Law, Banking Law

REMEDIES

Dobbs' Hornbook on Remedies, 1067 pages, 1973 (Text)

Dobbs' Problems in Remedies, 137 pages, 1974 (Problem book)

Dobbyn's Injunctions in a Nutshell, 264 pages, 1974 (Text)

Friedman's Contract Remedies in a Nutshell, 323 pages, 1981 (Text)

Leavell, Love and Nelson's Cases and Materials on Equitable Remedies and Restitution, 3rd Ed., 704 pages, 1980 (Casebook)

McCormick's Hornbook on Damages, 811 pages, 1935 (Text)

O'Connell's Remedies in a Nutshell, 2nd Ed., 325 pages, 1985 (Text)

LAW SCHOOL PUBLICATIONS—Continued

REMEDIES—Continued

York and Bauman's Cases and Materials on Remedies, 4th Ed., approximately 1300 pages, 1985 (Casebook)

REVIEW MATERIALS

Ballantine's Problems
Black Letter Series
Smith's Review Series
West's Review Covering Multistate Subjects

SECURITIES REGULATION

Hazen's Hornbook on The Law of Securities Regulation, Student Ed., approximately 520 pages, 1985 (Text)

Ratner's Securities Regulation: Materials for a Basic Course, 2nd Ed., 1050 pages, 1980 with 1982 Supplement (Casebook)

Ratner's Securities Regulation in a Nutshell, 2nd Ed., 322 pages, 1982 (Text)

Selected Securities and Business Planning Statutes, Rules and Forms, approximately 485 pages, 1985

SOCIAL LEGISLATION

Hood and Hardy's Workers' Compensation and Employee Protection Laws in a Nutshell, 274 pages, 1984 (Text)

LaFrance's Welfare Law: Structure and Entitlement in a Nutshell, 455 pages, 1979 (Text)

Malone, Plant and Little's Cases on Workers' Compensation and Employment Rights, 2nd Ed., 951 pages, 1980 (Casebook)

See also Poverty Law

TAXATION

Dodge's Cases and Materials on Federal Income Taxation, approximately 925 pages, 1985 (Casebook)

Dodge's Federal Taxation of Estates, Trusts and Gifts: Principles and Planning, 771 pages, 1981 with 1982 Supplement (Casebook)

Garbis and Struntz' Cases and Materials on Tax Procedure and Tax Fraud, 829 pages, 1982 with 1984 Supplement (Casebook)

Gunn's Cases and Materials on Federal Income Taxation of Individuals, 785 pages, 1981 with 1985 Supplement (Casebook)

Hellerstein and Hellerstein's Cases on State and Local Taxation, 4th Ed., 1041 pages, 1978 with 1982 Supplement (Casebook)

Kahn's Handbook on Basic Corporate Taxation, 3rd Ed., Student Ed., 614 pages, 1981 with 1983 Supplement (Text)

Kahn and Gann's Corporate Taxation and Taxation of Partnerships and Partners, 2nd Ed., approximately 1300 pages, 1985 (Casebook)

TAXATION—Continued

Kragen and McNulty's Cases and Materials on Federal Income Taxation, 4th Ed., approximately 1200 pages, 1985 (Casebook)

McNulty's Federal Estate and Gift Taxation in a Nutshell, 3rd Ed., 509 pages, 1983 (Text)

McNulty's Federal Income Taxation of Individuals in a Nutshell, 3rd Ed., 487 pages, 1983 (Text)

Posin's Hornbook on Federal Income Taxation of Individuals, Student Ed., 491 pages, 1983 with 1985 pocket part (Text)

Rice and Solomon's Problems and Materials in Federal Income Taxation, 3rd Ed., 670 pages, 1979 (Casebook)

Rose and Raskind's Advanced Federal Income Taxation: Corporate Transactions—Cases, Materials and Problems, 955 pages, 1978 (Casebook)

Selected Federal Taxation Statutes and Regulations, 1255 pages, 1983

Soboloff and Weidenbruch's Federal Income Taxation of Corporations and Stockholders in a Nutshell, 362 pages, 1981 (Text)

TORTS

Christie's Cases and Materials on the Law of Torts, 1264 pages, 1983 (Casebook)

Dobbs' Torts and Compensation—Personal Accountability and Social Responsibility for Injury, approximately 1,050 pages, 1985 (Casebook)

Green, Pedrick, Rahl, Thode, Hawkins, Smith and Treece's Cases and Materials on Torts, 2nd Ed., 1360 pages, 1977 (Casebook)

Green, Pedrick, Rahl, Thode, Hawkins, Smith, and Treece's Advanced Torts: Injuries to Business, Political and Family Interests, 2nd Ed., 544 pages, 1977 (Casebook)—reprint from Green, et al. Cases and Materials on Torts, 2nd Ed., 1977

Keeton, Keeton, Sargentich and Steiner's Cases and Materials on Torts, and Accident Law, 1360 pages, 1983 (Casebook)

Kionka's Torts in a Nutshell: Injuries to Persons and Property, 434 pages, 1977 (Text)

Malone's Torts in a Nutshell: Injuries to Family, Social and Trade Relations, 358 pages, 1979 (Text)

Prosser and Keeton's Hornbook on Torts, 5th Ed., Student Ed., 1286 pages, 1984 (Text)

Shapo's Cases on Tort and Compensation Law, 1244 pages, 1976 (Casebook)

See also Products Liability

TRADE REGULATION

McManis' Unfair Trade Practices in a Nutshell, 444 pages, 1982 (Text)

LAW SCHOOL PUBLICATIONS—Continued

TRADE REGULATION—Continued

Oppenheim, Weston, Maggs and Schechter's Cases and Materials on Unfair Trade Practices and Consumer Protection, 4th Ed., 1038 pages, 1983 (Casebook)

See also Antitrust, Regulated Industries

TRIAL AND APPELLATE ADVOCACY

Appellate Advocacy, Handbook of, 249 pages, 1980 (Text)

Bergman's Trial Advocacy in a Nutshell, 402 pages, 1979 (Text)

Binder and Bergman's Fact Investigation: From Hypothesis to Proof, 354 pages, 1984 (Coursebook)

Goldberg's The First Trial (Where Do I Sit?, What Do I Say?) in a Nutshell, 396 pages, 1982 (Text)

Hegland's Trial and Practice Skills in a Nutshell, 346 pages, 1978 (Text)

Herr, Stempel and Haydock's Fundamentals of Pre-Trial Litigation, approximately 700 pages, 1985 (Casebook)

Hornstein's Appellate Advocacy in a Nutshell, 325 pages, 1984 (Text)

Jeans' Handbook on Trial Advocacy, Student Ed., 473 pages, 1975 (Text)

McElhaney's Effective Litigation, 457 pages, 1974 (Casebook)

Nolan's Cases and Materials on Trial Practice, 518 pages, 1981 (Casebook)

Parnell and Shellhaas' Cases, Exercises and Problems for Trial Advocacy, 171 pages, 1982 (Coursebook)

Sonsteng, Haydock and Boyd's The Trialbook: A Total System for Preparation and Presentation of a Case, Student Ed., 404 pages, 1984 (Coursebook)

TRUSTS AND ESTATES

Atkinson's Hornbook on Wills, 2nd Ed., 975 pages, 1953 (Text)

Averill's Uniform Probate Code in a Nutshell, 425 pages, 1978 (Text)

Bogert's Hornbook on Trusts, 5th Ed., 726 pages, 1973 (Text)

Clark, Lusky and Murphy's Cases and Materials on Gratuitous Transfers, 3rd Ed., approximately 1200 pages, 1985 (Casebook)

TRUSTS AND ESTATES—Continued

Gulliver's Cases and Materials on Future Interests, 624 pages, 1959 (Casebook)

Gulliver's Introduction to the Law of Future Interests, 87 pages, 1959 (Casebook)—reprint from Gulliver's Cases and Materials on Future Interests, 1959

McGovern's Cases and Materials on Wills, Trusts and Future Interests: An Introduction to Estate Planning, 750 pages, 1983 (Casebook)

Mennell's Cases and Materials on California Decedent's Estates, 566 pages, 1973 (Casebook)

Mennell's Wills and Trusts in a Nutshell, 392 pages, 1979 (Text)

Powell's The Law of Future Interests in California, 91 pages, 1980 (Text)

Simes' Hornbook on Future Interests, 2nd Ed., 355 pages, 1966 (Text)

Turrentine's Cases and Text on Wills and Administration, 2nd Ed., 483 pages, 1962 (Casebook)

Uniform Probate Code, 5th Ed., Official Text With Comments, 384 pages, 1977

Waggoner's Future Interests in a Nutshell, 361 pages, 1981 (Text)

WATER LAW

Getches' Water Law in a Nutshell, 439 pages, 1984 (Text)

Trelease's Cases and Materials on Water Law, 3rd Ed., 833 pages, 1979, with 1984 Supplement (Casebook)

See also Energy Law, Natural Resources Law, Environmental Law

WILLS

See Trusts and Estates

WOMEN AND THE LAW

Kay's Text, Cases and Materials on Sex-Based Discrimination, 2nd Ed., 1045 pages, 1981, with 1983 Supplement (Casebook)

Thomas' Sex Discrimination in a Nutshell, 399 pages, 1982 (Text)

See also Employment Discrimination

WORKERS' COMPENSATION

See Social Legislation

XII

ECONOMICS AND FEDERAL ANTITRUST LAW

By

Herbert Hovenkamp

Associate Professor of Law,
University of California,
Hastings College of the Law

HORNBOOK SERIES
STUDENT EDITION

WEST PUBLISHING CO.
ST. PAUL, MINN., 1985

COPYRIGHT © 1985 By WEST PUBLISHING CO.
                        50 West Kellogg Boulevard
                        P.O. Box 64526
                        St. Paul, Minnesota 55164–0526

Library of Congress Cataloging in Publication Data

Hovenkamp, Herbert.
  Economics and federal antitrust law.

  (Hornbook series student edition)
  Includes index.
  1. Antitrust law—United States. 2. Antitrust law—
Economic aspects—United States. I. Title. II. Series.
KF1649.H67 1985   343.73'072   84–25783
                      347.30372

ISBN 0–314–86196–3

Hovenkamp Econ. & Antitrust HB

Preface

This book is an introduction to the complex, symbiotic relationship between economic theory and American antitrust policy. It presumes that the reader has no background in economics, and very little in antitrust law. Beginning with that premise, it attempts to integrate elementary price theory, organization economics and the existing body of antitrust case law in a way that has not been done in any single-volume survey.

This book's scope is necessarily limited by its size. Its coverage includes areas of substantive antitrust law in which economic theory plays an important part, and a brief discussion of the rapidly evolving law of private enforcement. It does not include procedure, jurisdiction under the commerce clause, state antitrust laws, the exempt industries, the "state action" exemption, or extraterritorial application of the antitrust laws.

Any discussion of the relationship between economics and antitrust law is necessarily affected with ideology. Economics is an ideological science, and antitrust an ideological and highly political area of law.

Traditionally, antitrust scholars have aligned themselves loosely around three different ideological positions. The liberal, or "Columbia School," which has origins at least as far back as the New Deal, places little confidence in the power of unregulated markets to function competitively, and very little confidence in the ability of economic theory to say anything useful about how real world markets work. Its members are skeptical about claims that antitrust or any other area of the law can either identify or pursue "allocative efficiency." As a result they believe that antitrust is legitimately concerned with distributive goals, such as the protection of small business or the control of large aggregations of economic and political power.

At the other extreme is the "Chicago School," whose name is virtually an epithet to the liberals. Orthodox Chicago economic analysis views antitrust "through the lens of price theory." The Chicago School ideologist believes that unregulated markets generally work quite well, and that most imperfections in markets are caused by interference from the State itself. Implicit in that view is a not-so-tacit suggestion that the antitrust laws have been over-enforced in a way that has done more harm than good to competitive processes.

In the middle is the "Harvard School," whose commitment to economic theory in antitrust is perhaps less than the Chicago School commitment. Traditionally, the Harvard School has expressed at least an abstract willingness to recognize noneconomic values as legitimate, although subordinate, in antitrust policy. The most important distinction between the Chicago and Harvard approaches has not been the amount of economics in antitrust, however, but its nature. While the Chicago School is built on a foundation of price theory, the Harvard School draws more heavily from institutional economics and industrial organization. The traditional Harvard School economist believes that economies of scale and entry barriers have often interfered with the competitive process. He has been much more concerned than the Chicago School economist with the amount but which real world markets appear to deviate from the perfect competition model. As a result the Harvard School analyst has generally found more room for antitrust as a market-correcting mechanism.

The historical existence of three distinct antitrust schools is not as important today as the fact that during the 1970's and 1980's an outpouring of scholarship revealed major defections from the Harvard and Chicago positions, and—perhaps more important—a growing synthesis between the two. Both traditional positions have been widely criticized for employing static models that show little regard for real world markets in movement. This new synthesis suggests, for example, that entry barriers can be knocked down somewhat more easily than Harvard scholars assumed, but that they can be erected more easily than Chicago analysts have believed. Furthermore, each side had pushed its own good ideas to unrealistic extremes. On the one hand, the Chicagoans were right to think that most markets tend to correct themselves; on the other hand, they often overlooked the eminently practical fact that correction takes time, and even temporary monopolies impose a social cost. Likewise, Harvard scholars were correct to observe that economies of scale do not fully explain the level of industrial concentration in the United States; however, in measuring economies Harvard economists traditionally confined themselves to intraplant or multiplant economies, and often overlooked economies of distribution that can be achieved by vertical integration. Finally, and perhaps most importantly, both traditional models failed to account satisfactorily for strategic behavior.

This revisionist economics has made important contributions to antitrust theory. A resulting problem, however, is that economics in antitrust has lost much of the simplicity that kept it within the reach of antitrust lawyers who were not formally trained as economists. This book addresses that problem by giving the serious student of antitrust who has little or no economics training an economic perspective on federal antitrust policy.

I must thank some of the people who have supported my work— Charles Wright, who has helped me so many times I am embarrassed to recall them, Dean Bert Prunty and Dean Wayne Woody for institutional support, Vivien Williamson for research assistance, and Sandi Goodman and Peggie MacDonald and their staff for preparation of the manuscript. I am particularly grateful for the intellectual criticism of Professor Louis B. Schwartz, formerly of Pennsylvania, now a member of the Hastings Sixty-Five Club. Thanks to his persistence I came out of this project

with a somewhat broader view of antitrust policy than I had when I
entered, although Lou and I still find abundant room for disagreement.
Last I thank my wife Beverly for her unwavering intellectual, moral and
emotional support and gratefully dedicate this book to her.

HERBERT HOVENKAMP

San Francisco, California
December, 1984

*

WESTLAW Introduction

Economics and Federal Antitrust Law offers a detailed and comprehensive treatment of the basic rules and principles of the law. However, lawyers frequently need to find additional authority. In an effort to assist with comprehensive research, preformulated WESTLAW references are included after each section of the text in this edition of the hornbook. The WESTLAW references are designed for use with the WESTLAW computer-assisted legal research service. By joining this publication with the extensive WESTLAW databases, the reader is able to move straight from the hornbook into WESTLAW with great speed and convenience.

Some readers may desire to use only the information supplied within the printed pages of this hornbook. Others, however, will encounter issues that require further information. Accordingly, those who opt to go beyond the material contained in the textual format into WESTLAW can rapidly and easily access WESTLAW, an electronic law library that possesses extraordinary currency and magnitude.

Appendix A gives concise, step-by-step instruction on how to coordinate WESTLAW research with this hornbook.

THE PUBLISHER

*

Summary of Contents

*

Table of Contents

CHAPTER 13. PRICE DISCRIMINATION AND THE ROBINSON–PATMAN ACT

CHAPTER 14. PRIVATE ENFORCEMENT

ECONOMICS AND FEDERAL ANTITRUST LAW

*

CHAPTER 1

PRICES, MARKETS AND MONOPOLIES

Table of Sections

§ 1.1 Price Theory: Economic Behavior and Perfect Competition

Market economies are dedicated to the principle that people are best off if they can make voluntary exchanges of goods and services in competitive markets.[1] If all exchanges are voluntary, each person will continue to exchange goods and services until he can make himself no better off by an exchange that is voluntary for both parties to the transaction. If all exchanges take place at a competitive price, society as a whole will be wealthier than it would be if some exchanges occurred at a higher or lower price. An important goal—perhaps the only goal—of antitrust law is to ensure that markets are competitive.

A competitive market is one in which 1) every good is priced at the cost of producing it, giving the producers and sellers only enough

§ 1.1

1. This book undertakes no ethical defense of the free market. For that, see R. Posner, The Economics of Justice (1981). The discussion of price theory that appears in this chapter is very spare—so spare that some may be frustrated by the brevity, the lack of mathematical proof, or the paucity of exam-

ples. Those persons are referred to E. Mansfield, Microeconomics: Theory & Applications (4th ed. 1982) (easy-medium); D. McCloskey, The Applied Theory of Price (1982) (moderately difficult); G. Stigler, The Theory of Price (3d ed. 1966) (more difficult and technical, but highly rewarding).

profit to maintain investment in the industry; and 2) every person willing to pay this price will be able to buy it.

Most customers prefer to purchase things at the lowest possible price—even, if possible, at less than the cost of producing them. Sellers, on the other hand, prefer to sell at a price that will give them the highest possible profits. As a result competition is not an absolutely natural state of affairs; both buyers and sellers must be forced to compete.

The conditions most conducive to competition, and which obtain perfectly in an economic model of "perfect competition," are: 1) All sellers make an absolutely homogenous product, so that customers are indifferent as to which seller they purchase from, provided that the price is the same; 2) each seller in the market is so small in proportion to the entire market that the seller's increase or decrease in output, or even its exit from the market, will not affect the decisions of other sellers in the market; 3) all resources are complete-ly mobile, or alternatively, all sellers have the same access to needed inputs; 4) all participants in the market have perfect knowledge of price, output and other information about the market. As a general rule, the closer a market comes to fulfilling all four of these condi-tions, the more competitively it will perform.

The perfect competition model generally assumes "constant re-turns to scale"—that is, that costs of production per unit remain constant at all practical rates of output. As we shall see in § 1.4, the presence of substantial economies of scale—that is, of costs that decrease on a per unit basis as output increases—can undermine the perfect competition model, particularly if a firm must acquire a large share of the market in order to take advantage of these scale economies.

The most important rule governing price is the law of supply and demand. Price setting in any market, whether competitive or monop-olized, is a function of the relationship between the amount of a product available and the amount that consumers, at the margin, are willing to pay for it. For almost every product different customers are willing to pay different amounts. One effect of a shortage is that the product is sold only to buyers willing to pay a relatively high price. For example, if all the world's steel mills produced only 1000 pounds of steel per year, customers would likely bid a very high price for the steel, which would naturally be sold to the highest bidder. The price would be determined by the marginal customer's willing-ness to pay—that is, by the amount that some buyer would be willing to pay for the 1000th pound. Perhaps orthodontists, who put one-half ounce of steel in a set of $500 braces, would be willing to buy all the steel at $3000 per pound. In that case no steel would be sold at a lower price. If the supply of steel increased 100-fold, however, there might be far more steel than orthodontists could use at a price of

$3000 per pound. In that case the price of steel would drop so that the market could take in additional customers who place a high value on steel but are not willing to pay $3000 per pound.

As more and more steel is produced the market price must drop further and further in order to reach customers who have lower "reservation" prices. A reservation price is the highest amount that a consumer is willing to pay for a product. Importantly, as the price of steel drops those customers with very high reservation prices, such as the orthodontists, will also be able to buy steel at the lower price. In the perfect competition model all sales of a particular good are made at the same price, even though different groups of consumers have vastly different reservation prices. If the seller attempted to sell to different groups of customers at different prices—say, to orthodontists at $3000 per pound but to automakers at $3 per pound—the seller's plan would be frustrated by arbitrage. That is, automakers would buy steel at $3.00 per pound and resell some steel to orthodontists at a price higher than $3.00 per pound but lower than $3000 per pound. If all buyers have complete information about the market, all of them will pay the same price, regardless of their reservation prices.[2]

Assume that the market contains 100 sellers of steel. Each seller wants to make as much money as possible, and every buyer (regardless of her reservation price) wants to purchase steel at the lowest possible price. How much steel will be produced in the market and what will be its price?

Two things seem clear. First, if a firm's cost of making steel is $2.50 per pound, it is not likely to stay in business by persistently selling steel at less than $2.50 per pound. Second, subject to some important limitations, the more steel that is produced, the higher will be the average cost of production. Each producer of steel wants to maximize its net profits, and it does this by minimizing its costs. The first producers of steel will begin producing it from the iron ore that is easiest to obtain and refine. As output increases, however, these firms must turn to more marginal ore. Likewise, as new steel producers enter the market they will buy up the best ore reserves, and firms that come in later will have to take more marginal reserves. As the market grows, increasingly marginal materials will be used and the cost of producing steel will tend to rise. This increase may be barely discernible marketwide in some markets, but it is almost always a factor in the entry and output decisions of a single firm.

Figure One illustrates how a market arrives at "equilibrium"—a point at which supply of a good and demand for it are perfectly

2. In real world markets, however, price discrimination, or obtaining higher profits from one set of customers than from another set, is both possible and common. See Chapter Thirteen below.

balanced and will not change unless the market is disturbed. The figure illustrates the demand curve and the supply curve facing an entire market for a single product. Since both price and output are generally positive numbers, it is common to display only the upper right quadrant of the standard two-axis graph. The vertical axis represents price, which increases from 0 as one moves upward. The horizontal axis represents output (or quantity), which increases from 0 as one moves from the origin to the right.

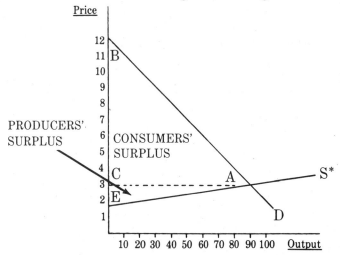

* Supply Curve = Industry Cost Curve = Sum of Marginal Costs of Individual Firms

FIGURE ONE

The graph shows that at low levels of output the cost of production, indicated by the supply curve (S), is quite low. Price, shown by the demand curve (D), is very high, for the good will be sold only to customers who have very high reservation prices. At such levels of output the sellers will be earning enormous profits on their output. Profit, which is price minus cost, is measured by the vertical distance between the supply curve and the demand curve at any point. The supply curve itself includes "competitive" or "normal" profits. As a result, any vertical distance between the supply curve and the demand curve is referred to as "economic" or "monopoly" profits. These are profits in excess of those earned by a competitive industry, and in excess of the amount needed to maintain investment in the industry.

If profits per unit of output are extremely high, as they are when output is very low, two things will happen. First, existing sellers will be encouraged by the very high profits to increase their output. For example, if current output is twenty units, the cost of production is approximately $2.00, but the price is on the order of $10.00: each additional unit that the firm produces will give it economic profits of $8.00. Secondly, and for the same reason, new firms will come into the market. People with money to invest invariably look for opportunities where the expected return is highest.

As existing firms enlarge output and new firms enter the market, total output will increase, or move to the right along the graph. The result will be two-fold: first, the supply price will rise as the new entrants must make use of increasingly marginal (less attractive) resources. Second, the price will fall as the market must reach customers with lower and lower reservation prices. The market will finally stabilize at point A. At any point on the supply curve to the left of A, an increase in output of one unit will generate positive economic profits—that is, more in revenue than the cost of producing the unit. In that case at least one firm will increase its output or at least one new firm will enter the market and start producing. This process will continue until the supply curve rises to the intersection with the demand curve.

On the other hand, if production is at some point on the supply curve to the right of A, then at least some steel is being produced at less than the price than can be obtained for it. In that case the least efficient firms will exit from the market or some firms will close down their least efficient mines and plants until the industry supply curve falls back to the intersection with the demand curve at A. The market constantly moves toward this equilibrium: when supply costs are less than market price output will increase; when supply costs are greater than price output will decline.

As we noted above, in a competitive market all buyers pay the market price, even though their individual reservation prices may be higher. The difference between the buyers' reservation prices and the price they actually pay is called "consumers' surplus." The size of the consumers' surplus in Figure One is represented by triangle ABC. A competitive market tends to maximize the size of the consumers' surplus: the consumers' surplus cannot be larger than ABC without at least one sale being unprofitable.

Some firms in the market are likely to have lower costs than others. They may have the richest veins of ore or the lowest energy, labor, or distribution costs. Triangle ACE represents "producers' surplus:" the difference between total revenue at the competitive price and the sum of the producers' costs. Only at the margin does a firm earn zero profits. Such a marginal firm is the one with the highest costs that is still capable of earning a competitive rate of return when the product is sold at a competitive price. If the market shifts in a way that is unfavorable to sellers, however, this marginal firm is likely to be the first, or one of the first, to go out of business.

The two curves in Figure One can assume an infinite variety of shapes. The figure shows them as straight lines, suggesting that demand increases at a uniform rate as price falls, and that production costs rise at a uniform rate as output increases. Neither happens in real world markets. The two lines are always non-linear, and are frequently quite irregular. Drawing them as straight lines, however, is a useful analytic device that often does not affect analysis of a particular problem.

The relationships expressed by the supply and demand curves can be quantified and expressed in formulas. One formula, for *elasticity of demand*, is simply a short-hand expression for the relationship between a particular change in the price of a product and the corresponding change in demand for it. That formula is:

$$E = \frac{\delta Q}{Q} \div \frac{\delta P}{P}$$

or alternatively,

$$E = \frac{\delta Q}{\delta P} \cdot \frac{P}{Q}$$

in which δQ and δP are equal to changes in quantity demanded and market clearing price, respectively, and Q and P are the base quantity and price from which the changes took place. Since quantity and price change in opposite directions (quantity demanded goes up as price goes down) this number is negative. Economists drop the negative sign, however, as a matter of convention.

If at an output of 200 the market clearing price per unit is $100, and at an output of 240 the market clearing price drops to $90, we can compute market elasticity of demand as follows: change in output = 40; change in price = 10. The elasticity of demand equals:

$$\frac{40}{10} \cdot \frac{100}{200} = \frac{4000}{2000} = 2.$$

A much shorter and simpler way of describing elasticity of demand is to say that it is the relationship between the percentage change in quantity of a good demanded when the price of the good changes by a certain percentage. In the above example a 20% increase in output necessitated a 10% decrease in price, yielding an elasticity of demand of 20%/10%, or 2.

The elasticity of demand along any curve is different than the slope of the curve, which in the case of a straight line is the ratio of the vertical axis to the horizontal axis. While the slope of a linear curve is the same at all points, the elasticity of demand represented by a straight line demand curve is different at all points. If a demand curve stretching from the price axis to the output axis is a straight line, the elasticity of demand will be one at the line's midpoint, higher than one at all points above the midpoint, and lower than one at all points below.[3] Whenever the elasticity of demand in a market is greater than one we term the demand "elastic." In that

3. See Mansfield, note 1, at 112–14.

case a price increase of X% will yield a demand decrease of greater than X%. When the elasticity of demand is less than one we term the demand "inelastic." In that case a price increase of X% yields a demand decrease of less than X%. As you might guess, any seller would prefer to face an inelastic rather than an elastic demand: if demand is inelastic a relatively large price increase will yield a relatively small decrease in demand.

Elasticity of *supply* is a relationship between changes in the price of a product and the amount produced. As the price of a product rises, more of it will be produced because existing firms will increase their output or new firms will enter the market and start producing. The elasticity of supply is measured by the percentage change in the amount supplied that results from a certain percentage change in price. For example, if a 10% price increase yields a 30% increase in supply, the elasticity of supply in the market is 3. If a 30% price increase yields a 15% supply increase, the market's elasticity of supply is .5. Elasticity of supply is a positive number.

For antitrust policy it is important to consider not only the absolute elasticity of supply, but also the amount of time it takes for supply to increase in response to a price increase. Suppose, that the elasticity of supply in a market is 3, which is very high. If price goes up by 10%, the supply in the market will increase by 30%. But suppose that the construction of the additional plants that account for the 30% supply increase takes 10 years. A seller attempting to raise its price to a monopoly level will eventually lose sales to this increased output by its competitors. For ten years, however, while these plants are under construction, it will be able to earn monopoly profits. The expense and time required to build a competing plant may enable the incumbent to engage in certain "strategic" behavior. For example, if prospective competitors know that the incumbent has substantial excess capacity and can increase output and drop price at will, the large investment and long wait for an uncertain return may look unprofitable. Time can also be a factor in antitrust analysis of elasticity of demand, but it is generally not as important. Customers can usually switch to a different seller in response to a price increase much more quickly than suppliers can expand output or enter the market.

The previous discussion of the relationship between supply and demand assumes that the market is in equilibrium, unaffected by any change imposed from outside. If relative consumer income rises or falls, new technology makes a product obsolete or the country goes to war, however, demand for any good may rise or fall regardless of available supply or costs of production. In such cases we talk, not about changes *along* a demand curve, but about *shifts* in the curve. For example, the invention of the electronic calculator had no effect on the cost of production of a slide rule or on the capacity of slide rule factories. Nevertheless, when the electronic calculator was invented the demand for slide rules dropped precipitously. We diagram that change by saying that the demand curve for slide rules shifted to the left. As Figure Two suggests, if a shift to the left is dramatic enough, a product may simply cease to exist. If the lowest possible cost of producing a slide rule by the most efficient producer is $20, but even the consumer with the highest reservation price is unwilling to pay $20 (perhaps because she can obtain an equivalent electronic calculator for $16.00), then no one will be able to make slide rules profitably. They will go the way of the quill pen, the vacuum tube, and hand-blown glass. The shifted demand curve (D2 in Figure Two) illustrates this: it never intersects the supply curve.

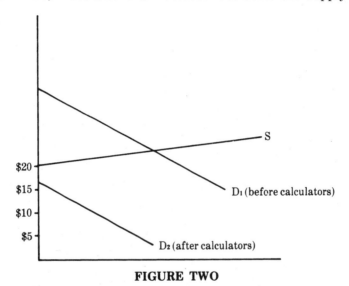

FIGURE TWO

Supply curves, incidentally, may shift just as demand curves do. The invention of the microprocessor in a silicone chip reduced the cost of building computers by a factor of one hundred. The result is that the new supply curve for computers in the 1980's is much lower than the supply curve of the 1960's, and equilibrium output is much higher.

Now that we have considered the competitive, multi-firm market we are ready to examine the behavior of the individual firm in that market. Remember, we are assuming a market with a large number of sellers, into which entry is relatively easy and can be accomplished in a short time. How will an individual firm in that market decide how much to produce and what price to charge?

Even though the steel market's equilibrium price is $3.00 per pound, there are still individual buyers, such as the orthodontists, whose reservation price is far higher than $3.00. Suppose that the individual firm attempts to charge a higher price than $3.00—perhaps $4.00—for a pound of steel. The orthodontists will certainly be willing to pay $4.00, but if they can buy for $3.00 they will do so. When one firm in a 100-firm market attempts to charge $4.00, a buyer who knows that the "going" price is $3.00 will look for a different seller. In a perfectly competitive market in which all buyers have complete price information, all the sellers will be "price takers"—they must simply accept the market price as given. In a competitive market, no single firm is large enough to have an influence either on the total amount produced in the market or on the market price. As a result, the individual firm is able to sell as little or as much as it pleases at the market price; however, it will lose all sales if it attempts to charge more than the market price.

The situation facing the perfect competitor can be described in two ways. First, the firm faces a perfectly horizontal demand curve, as is illustrated in Figure Three. For the perfect competitor the market price is the same at all rates of output. Alternatively, the individual competitor faces an *infinite* firm elasticity of supply and an *infinite* firm elasticity of demand. In response to a very small price increase, alternative suppliers will immediately offer substitute products to the price raiser's customers, and all customers will switch to those substitutes. The firm will lose all of its sales.

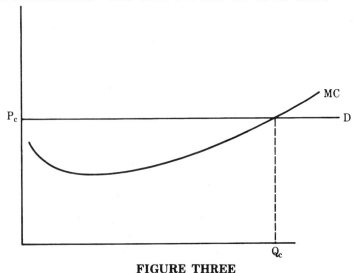

FIGURE THREE

It is therefore important to distinguish between *market* elasticities of supply and demand, and individual *firm* elasticities of supply and demand. Except for the pure monopolist (whose output is the same as the output of the entire market) the individual firm faces higher elasticities of supply and demand than does the market as a whole. This is because *within* a market substitution is easy and quick. If the market contains 100 producers of identical steel, then

A's steel is indistinguishable from B's steel, which is indistinguishable from C's. The fact that customers are indifferent as to whose steel they buy means that they will switch immediately to B or C if A attempts to increase price; conversely, B or C will happily provide the steel.

The firms in a perfectly competitive market have little discretion about what price to charge. They do make individual decisions, however, about the amount to produce. Even in a perfectly competitive market with an established single market price, different firms are of different sizes and produce differing amounts.

The individual competitor's output decision is a function of its marginal costs. Marginal cost is the additional cost that a firm incurs in the production of one additional unit of output. The best way to understand marginal cost is to consider several related cost curves. A firm's costs can be divided into two broad categories, fixed and variable. Fixed costs are those costs that do not change with output over the "short-run," which is some finite period of time, usually less than the lifetime of the plant. Land costs, property taxes, management salaries, plant and durable equipment all generally fall into the category of fixed costs. Importantly, once the money for fixed cost items is invested it must be paid whether or not the plant produces anything, and the costs do not vary with the amount the plant produces.

Variable costs, on the other hand, are costs that change with output. For the steel mill the costs of iron ore and other raw materials are variable costs, as is fuel to burn in the refining furnaces, hourly wages, and transportation. If a firm increases its output by, say 10%, the cost of all these things is likely to rise. The cost of the plant, durable equipment and the president's salary are likely to stay the same. Over the "long-run," however, even these costs must be considered variable. Eventually plant and durable equipment will have to be replaced. The firm will then decide whether to increase capacity, decrease it, or perhaps even go out of business.

Both fixed and variable costs are generally expressed as costs per unit of output. These are illustrated in Figure Four. "Average fixed cost" (AFC) is the amount of fixed cost divided by the amount that the firm produces. Since total fixed costs remain constant, average fixed costs decline as output increases. "Average variable cost" (AVC) is total variable cost divided by the amount the firm produces. The behavior of the average variable cost curve is more complex. Every established plant has some particular range of output in which it is most efficient. For example, a plant properly designed to produce 80–100 units per year will perform at lowest cost when output is in that range. If output drops to 50 the plant will perform less efficiently and costs per unit of output will rise. Blast furnaces, to give just one example, cost the same amount to heat whether they are used at capacity or only at half capacity. The same thing generally holds true for output that exceeds the plant's "optimal capacity." For example, a plant and workforce designed to produce 80 units per week may be able to increase output to 100 units per week only if workers are paid overtime wages, which may be twice their normal wages.

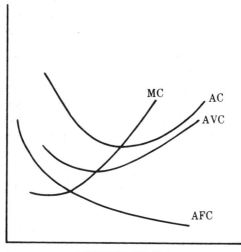

FIGURE FOUR

The average variable cost curve (AVC) of the plant tends to be U-shaped. Average variable cost declines as output increases toward the optimal output for the plant. It is at the lowest point when the plant is producing the optimal output for which it was designed. It increases when the plant's output exceeds optimal capacity. The AVC curve often has a flat bottom, because many plants are efficient over a fairly broad range of output.

Just above the AVC curve in Figure Four is the average total cost curve (AC), usually called the average cost curve, which is nothing more than the *sum* of all fixed and variable costs divided by output. Since all costs are either fixed or variable, the AC curve represents the total costs that a firm incurs in manufacturing one unit of a product. As a result the AC curve is important in determining the firm's profitability. In order to be profitable the firm must obtain an average price per unit equal to or greater than AC.

Once again, *marginal* cost is the additional cost that a firm incurs in producing one additional unit of output. Since a firm incurs no increased *fixed* costs in expanding output, marginal cost is a function of variable costs alone. The marginal cost curve (MC) falls and rises more dramatically than the average variable cost curve does, because the marginal cost curve looks merely at the difference in costs that a change in output produces. AVC, on the other hand, averages that difference over the entire output being produced. Importantly, the marginal cost curve always intersects the AVC curve at its lowest point. A minute's reflection about averages will tell you why. Suppose that you are averaging the height of United States Supreme Court justices and you have managed to gather eight of them, and have computed their average height as 6'0". Now the ninth justice walks in the door and happens to be 5'3" tall. The average will decline. On the other hand, if the ninth justice happens to be 6'7", the average will increase. Whether the average falls or rises is a function of the height of the "marginal" justice.

The relationship between the cost curves is illustrated in Table A. Notice that as output increases total fixed costs remain constant at 120. As a result, average fixed costs decline steadily. Total variable costs increase constantly as output increases; however, they increase more slowly as the plant approaches optimal capacity (in the 3–5 output range), and more rapidly again as the plant exceeds optimal capacity. As a result, *average* variable cost bottoms out at an output of about 5 and then increases.

Output	Total Fixed Cost	Average Fixed Cost	Total Variable Cost	AVC	MC	AC
1	120	120	200	200	200	320
2	120	60	240	120	40	180
3	120	40	270	90	30	130
4	120	30	320	80	50	110
5	120	24	375	75	95	99
6	120	20	510	85	135	105
7	120	17.14	700	100	190	117.14

TABLE A

How will the competitive firm make its output decision? Suppose the market price is $100.00 per unit. At its current rate of production the firm has marginal costs of only $60.00 per unit—that is, if it produced one additional unit it would incur $60.00 in additional costs. Clearly, the production of the additional unit will generate profits of

$40.00. The firm will increase production by one additional unit. However, suppose that the firm's marginal cost at its current rate of output is $120.00. If it produced one fewer unit it would spend $120.00 less. In that case the production of the last unit is generating $20.00 in losses: the firm could make $20.00 more by producing one unit less.

Look back at Figure Three to see the relationship between the competitive firm's marginal cost curve and the demand curve that it faces. The firm will always try to produce at a rate of output at which its marginal cost equals the market price. If it is producing more than that it will be able to increase profits by decreasing production. If it is producing less it will be able to increase profits by increasing production. The competitive rate of output in Figure Three is Q_c.

Two observations are important. First, although economists sometimes say that a firm's efficiency is a function of its marginal costs, all competitive firms have the same marginal cost at current output levels. If the current market price of widgets is $100.00, and the market is perfectly competitive, all firms at their current output rate will have marginal costs of $100.00. (If marginal costs never drop to $100.00, then the firm is so inefficient that it will not produce at all.)

Second, not every firm in a competitive market is necessarily profitable. The fact that every firm has a point on its marginal cost curve which is lower than $100.00 does not tell us anything about the firm's profitability when the market price is $100.00. In order for the firm to be profitable, that point on the marginal cost curve must be at or above the firm's average (total) cost curve. Even if the firm is losing money, however, if it produces at all it will produce at the rate at which price equals marginal cost. In that case that rate of output will be the "loss-minimizing" rather than the "profit-maximizing" rate of output.

Although the market price might be less than a firm's average total cost, the firm will not necessarily cease production. The fixed costs may have been "sunk"—that is, the firm may not be able to recover them if it goes out of business. Further, the fixed costs must be paid whether or not the plant produces. As a general rule, the firm will be able to cut its losses as long as the market price is above its average variable costs, and it will continue to produce. However, when the plant wears out and needs to be replaced, the firm may then decide to go out of business, or else to build a plant of a more efficient size.

Perfectly competitive markets are generally thought to be "efficient" because they do the best job of providing consumers with an ample supply of goods at the cost of producing them. The situation maximizes the total value of goods produced in society. In a competitive market no single firm has the power to reduce the available supply of goods, and no firm has the power profitably to increase the price above the market level.

Unfortunately, there are no perfectly competitive markets in the real world. Many markets do not even come close. Firms often differentiate their products from other firms; as a result, customers are no longer indifferent as to from whom they purchase. Information about market conditions is always less than perfect; as a result many transactions take place at some price other than the market price, and some socially valuable transactions never occur at all.[4] "Economies of scale"—the ability of larger firms to produce at a lower cost than smaller firms—may result in markets that have fewer than the number of sellers required for perfect competition to occur.[5] In short, like all scientific models, the model of perfect competition applies only imperfectly in the real world; nevertheless it is of great service to the antitrust policy maker in predicting the consequences of a certain action or legal rule. That is the way the model is used in this book.

§ 1.2 Monopoly

The monopolist—the only firm selling in a particular market—faces a different array of price and output decisions than those that confront the perfect competitor. For this formal analysis assume that the market contains only one firm, whose demand curve is therefore identical with the market demand curve. Second, assume that the monopolist does not need to worry about new entry by a competitor—that is, it faces an elasticity of supply of zero. These assumptions generally will not apply to the *de facto* monopolist, which is not legally protected from competitive entry. If either assumption is relaxed the monopolist will face a certain amount of "competition" and will vary its behavior accordingly. Assuming, however, that the monopolist has a 100% share of a market and no concern about entry by a competitor, how much will it sell and what price will it charge?

The monopolist has one power that the perfect competitor does not have. If the monopolist reduces output, total market output will be reduced, for the monopolist is the only producer in the market. As total market output goes down, the market-clearing price goes up.

4. In general, the more expensive it is for consumers to search out relevant information about prices and markets, the more likely they will make a less than optimal transaction. As a result, prices tend to vary more in markets in which search costs are high in relation to the value of the product. See Stigler, The Economics of Information, 69 J. Pol. Econ. 213 (1961); G. Stigler, The Theory of Price 2–6 (3d ed. 1966).

5. See § 1.4 below.

As a result, the monopolist, unlike the competitor, can obtain a higher price per unit of output by producing less.

However, the monopolist will not be able to charge an infinite price for its product. Even the orthodontists may be unwilling to pay more than $3000 per pound for steel; if the price goes higher they will change to silver or some other alternative.

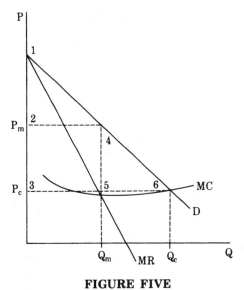

FIGURE FIVE

Figure Five introduces some new curves. One is the marginal revenue curve (MR), which represents the additional revenue that the monopolist obtains when it produces one additional unit of output. As Figure Five shows, the marginal revenue curve is steeper than the demand curve.[1] This is because the monopolist must sell all units of output at the same price, so the marginal revenue curve reflects not only the fact that the market price falls as supply increases (which is what the demand curve shows), but also that less revenue is obtained from sales of all previously made units. This is easy to see in Table B. At output of one unit the price is $20 and the seller's marginal revenue—the difference between the amount it obtains from one unit and the amount it obtains from zero units—is also $20. When output increases to 2 units, price drops to $18. However, the monopolist must sell both the first and the second units for $18.00. While the price drops by $2.00, marginal revenue drops by $4.00—$2.00 for each of the two units. This process continues and yields the MR curve in Figure Five.

§ 1.2

1. If the demand curve is linear the marginal revenue curve will also be linear and will be exactly twice as steep as the demand curve. See D. McCloskey, The Applied Theory of Price 366–67 (1982).

Output	Price	Total Revenue	Marginal Revenue
1	$20	$20	$20
2	$18	$36	$16
3	$16	$48	$12
4	$14	$56	$ 8
5	$12	$60	$ 4
6	$10	$60	0
7	$ 8	$56	$–4
8	$ 6	$48	$–8

TABLE B

The marginal revenue curve for the perfect competitor, incidentally, is identical with the horizontal demand curve that it faces. This is because price remains constant at all rates of output. If the price is $20, each additional sale will generate an additional $20, and marginal revenue will remain constant at $20.

The profit-maximizing monopolist, just as the profit-maximizing competitor, will expand production to the point that one additional unit will produce greater additional costs than additional revenues. It will produce at point Q_m on the graph in Figure Five and charge price P_m. If the monopolist expands output beyond Q_m the additional revenue, shown by the MR curve, will be less than the additional costs, shown by the marginal cost curve (MC). P_m is known as the "monopoly price," or as the monopolist's "profit-maximizing price."

Both the perfect competitor and the monopolist maximize profits by equating marginal revenue and marginal cost. For the competitor the marginal revenue curve is identical with the demand curve, and therefore with the market price. For the monopolist, on the other hand, the marginal revenue curve and marginal cost curve intersect to the left of the marginal cost curve's intersection with the demand curve. The monopolist produces at a lower rate than would a perfect competitor in the same market, and its profit-maximizing price is higher.

The difference between the monopolist's profit-maximizing price, P_m, and the competitor's profit-maximizing price, P_c says something about the degree of power that the monopolist has. If P_c is $1.00, a monopolist whose profit-maximizing price is $1.50 has more monopoly power than one whose profit-maximizing price is $1.02.

A monopolist's market power is a function of the elasticity of demand. If the elasticity of demand for pistachios at the competitive price is high, consumers will be sensitive to the price. If the price goes too high many will buy a substitute, such as almonds or cashews. In that case the "spread" between the competitive price and the monopolist's profit-maximizing price will be relatively small. However, if the elasticity of demand is low, then consumers view the product as having few good substitutes. The monopolist will be able to extract a much higher price without losing too many sales.

Market power as a ratio of a firm's profit-maximizing price to its marginal cost can be quantified precisely, if elasticity of demand is known. The formulas are discussed briefly in § 3.1 below. The formulas are important to the formal analysis of market power and occasionally can offer some guidelines for antitrust policy. In general, however, the formal analysis of market power is of little use to a court because the elasticity of demand a firm faces cannot be computed in litigation.

The mirror image of monopoly is "monopsony." A monopsonist is a monopoly buyer rather than seller. Although most antitrust litigation of market power offenses has involved monopoly sellers rather than monopoly buyers, monopsony can impose social costs on society similar to those caused by monopoly.

By reducing its demand for a product, a monopsonist can force suppliers to sell to it at a lower price than would prevail in a competitive market. Some people are skeptical about this conclusion. No supplier would stay in business if it were forced to sell to the monopsonist at a price lower than its average costs, and price would tend toward average cost in a competitive market. Can a monopsonist actually force suppliers to engage in continuous loss selling?

The answer is no, of course. However, not all suppliers have the same costs, and many suppliers will have lower average costs if they reduce their output. When the price in a competitive market is $1.00, then the average costs of the least efficient, or "marginal," supplier are near $1.00. However, there are likely to be several sellers in the market who have lower costs. If the monopsonist announces that it will pay only 90¢ in the future, then the marginal sellers in the market—those with costs in the 90¢ to $1.00 range—will drop out, at least if the 90¢ price persists and they are unable to reduce their costs. The result is that both price and output will fall below the competitive level. Since the marginal producers will substitute away to some product that would have been their second choice in a competitive market, monopsony produces a deadweight loss triangle similar to the deadweight loss triangle produced by monopoly and discussed in the following section.[2]

The analysis of monopoly in this section was predicated on two assumptions—that the monopolist had 100% of its market and that new entry was impossible. Such monopolies do exist in the real world, but most of them are price-regulated public utilities, such as electric companies. The rationale for the legal recognition of such "natural monopolies" is discussed below in § 1.5. Most antitrust policy concerning monopolies is directed at the *de facto* monopolist, which has no such legal protection. The *de facto* monopolist most generally does not have 100% of its relevant market, although the percentage may be close. Furthermore, the *de facto* monopolist must consider the possibility of entry by new firms.

Once these two assumptions of pure monopoly are relaxed, analyzing the monopolist's output and price decisions becomes far more difficult. The *de facto* monopolist behaves strategically: in making a price or output decision it generally tries to anticipate the response by small competitors or by potential competitors. It may also strategize a price or output decision designed to eliminate a competitor or potential competitor from the market. A great deal of antitrust law is concerned with the strategic decisions of the *de facto* monopolist trying to enlarge or protect its monopoly position. About the only safe generalization that can be made is that the profit-maximizing price for the real life, *de facto* monopolist will be lower than the profit-maximizing price of the pure monopolist. The *de facto* monopolist may deter or delay competitive entry by setting a lower price. In general, the *de facto* monopolist has two choices. On the one hand, it can forget about new entry and establish a "short-run" profit-maximizing price by equating marginal revenue and marginal cost. In that case the monopolist will make maximum monopoly profits now, but its monopoly position will be more quickly eroded by competitors and new entrants who are attracted by the high profits. On the other hand, the monopolist might set a lower "entry deterring" or "limit" price, which will mean lower monopoly profits

---

2. There is some ambiguous legislative history suggesting that Senator Sherman did not intend his bill to apply to monopsony or buyers' cartels.

Senator George (D., Miss.): Upon the formation of [the] bagging trust the cotton farmers * * * agreed that they would not purchase jute bagging, and by that agreement * * * the rich rewards anticipated by the * * * trust were defeated. The fact that the bill * * * applied to all arrangements * * * by whomsoever made, would bring within its reach all defensive agreements made by farmers for the purpose of enhancing the price of their products * * *.

* * *

Senator Sherman: That is a very extraordinary proposition. There is nothing in the bill to prevent a refusal by anybody to buy something. All that it says is that the people producing or selling a particular article shall not make combinations to advance the price of the necessaries of life.

20 Cong.Rec. 1458 (1889).

today; however, the stream of profits will last longer, because new firms will not be as eager or as able to enter the market. Which alternative the monopolist takes varies from case to case, and economists have different opinions about the circumstances under which each will occur. Much of this debate is relevant to antitrust policy, and is discussed in chapters five and six below.

§ 1.3   The Social Cost of Monopoly

A *social cost* is a net loss that society suffers as a result of a particular transaction. A *social benefit* is a net gain. If A gives B $100, B is $100 richer and A is $100 poorer. Disregarding the costs of the transaction itself, such "transfer payments" produce neither a social cost nor a social benefit. On the other hand, if A produces for $100 a widget that B values at $150, society may become $50 richer. B might pay $150 for the widget. In that case B will be neither better nor worse off—he paid $150 for something that he valued at precisely $150. A, on the other hand, will be $50 richer, for his costs were only $100. Alternatively, if A sells the widget at $100, A will be neither better off nor worse off, but B will be $50 better off.

If A holds out for a price of $150 and B is willing to pay only $140, however, the transaction will not occur. In that case no one will be better off. B will then enter into a transaction with C and purchase a substitute that B values at $130, and which costs C, say, $110. The price will be between $110 and $130 if the transaction is to occur. Even if it occurs, however, society will be only $20 better off. The substitute transaction is less favorable to both B and society as a whole than B's preferred transaction would have been.

A social cost can be caused either by a particular transaction or by the failure of a socially beneficial transaction to occur. Some social costs are created when transactions injure someone who was not a party to the transaction. For example, the builder of a factory may not bother to negotiate with neighbors for the right to pollute their air, particularly if he thinks the neighbors have no legal right to protect their air from pollution. However, the neighbors are worse off. The common law of nuisance and the National Environmental Policy Act are both attempts to force the factory to "internalize" and pay at least a part of this cost.[1]

The traditional social cost of monopoly is that monopoly forces some people to forego the transaction that was their first choice and would have produced the largest social benefit. Rather, they take their second choice, which produces a smaller social benefit.

§ 1.3

1. See 42 U.S.C.A. §§ 4321–47; and see Coase, The Problem of Social Cost, 3 J.L. & Econ. 1 (1960); A.M. Polinsky, An Introduction to Law and Economics 11–24 (1983).

Although monopoly imposes a social cost, society is not necessarily poorer because the monopolist exists. For example, society was clearly better off because Alcoa, once the monopoly manufacturer of American aluminum, existed than if no aluminum producer existed at all. Even the monopolist Alcoa produced a product that buyers valued more than the cost of producing it. Otherwise there would have been no market for aluminum. We talk about the "social cost" of the aluminum monopoly in order to underscore the fact that the production and sale of aluminum would have produced even greater social benefits had the market been competitive. The social cost of monopoly is the difference in social value between a monopolized market and a competitive market. It is not the difference in social value between a monopolized market and no market at all. This is why the patent laws are socially valuable, even though they create monopolies.

Consider once again the curves in Figure Five in the preceding section. P_c and Q_c show the price and output in a competitive market. P_m shows the price for the same product in a market dominated by a monopolist, and Q_m shows the monopoly rate of output. Rectangle 2–3–5–4 represents a wealth transfer to the monopolist (the monopolist's output multiplied by the difference between the monopoly and competitive prices). Triangle 1–2–4 at the top of the diagram represents consumers' surplus, which is substantially less than it would be in a competitive market, where it would be triangle 1–3–6.

Finally, triangle 4–5–6 represents the "deadweight loss" of monopoly. Consumers located along the demand curve between points 4 and 6 are not willing to purchase the monopolized product at the monopoly price, even though they would have been willing to buy it at the competitive price. Instead, they substitute to something that would have been their second choice in a competitive market. This inefficient substitution, such as B's substitution from A to C in the preceding illustration, is traditionally spoken of as the social cost of monopoly.[2]

Importantly, the traditional deadweight loss of monopoly does not derive from the fact that consumers pay higher prices. Within the pure monopoly model that loss to consumers is offset by an equal gain to the monopolist and from an efficiency standpoint is a "neutral" transfer of wealth. The deadweight loss arises because the monopoly encourages some customers to engage in an alternative transaction that produces less social value than their first choice would have. A monopoly in the brick market may force a builder to

2. A large literature on the size of the deadweight loss triangle of an individual monopolist and on the total deadweight loss caused by monopoly in the American economy is summarized in F. Scherer, Industrial Market Structure and Economic Performance 459–471 (2d ed. 1980).

switch to aluminum siding, even though he preferred bricks and was willing to pay the competitive price for them.

At one time economists regarded triangle 4–5–6 as the only social cost of monopoly. There is good reason to believe, however, that triangle 4–5–6 substantially understates the social cost of monopoly in real world markets. You will recall that the discussion of monopoly in the previous section assumed that the monopolist did not need to worry about competitive entry. When that assumption is removed, as it is for *de facto* monopolists in real world markets, then the social costs of monopoly are likely to loom larger.[3]

The *de facto* monopolist—the firm that does not have legal protection from new entry—must continually exclude competitors, who would increase output and drive prices down to the competitive level. In fact, the more profitable the monopoly, the more potential entrants will be willing to spend in order to enter the market, and the more the monopolist will be willing to spend to keep them out. Part or perhaps even all of rectangle 2–3–5–4 in Figure Five, which we characterized as a "wealth transfer," may not be a wealth transfer at all because the monopolist uses it up in entrenching its monopoly. At the outer limit the monopolist would spend *all* its expected monopoly profits in protecting its position, and would end up with no more than a competitive rate of return.

In order to quantify the true social cost of monopoly, we must know something about how the monopolist spends these resources. Some attempts by the monopolist to protect its monopoly may have socially useful results and actually reduce the social costs of the monopoly. Others, however, are inefficient or socially harmful and make the total cost of monopoly far larger than the traditional deadweight triangle.

As the previous section observed, one way the monopolist might deter competition is by charging a price lower than its short-run profit-maximizing price. Although full analysis of such entry-deterring pricing is complex,[4] the short-run consequence is to make both the "wealth transfer" rectangle and the "deadweight loss" triangle smaller than they would be under short-run profit-maximizing pricing. Whether such entry-deterring pricing reduces the social cost of monopoly in the long run, however, depends on the effect of the pricing on the duration of the monopoly. A large deadweight loss that lasts for one year may still be less costly than a relatively small deadweight loss that lasts for ten.

A firm might also deter new entry by spending part of its monopoly profits in research and development (R & D), thus constantly keeping ahead of its industry and making it more difficult for

3. See Posner, The Social Costs of Monopoly and Regulation, 83 J.Pol.Econ. 807 (1975); Hovenkamp, Distributive Justice and the Antitrust Laws, 51 Geo. Wash.L.Rev. 1 (1982).

4. See § 6.9 below.

competitors to keep up. Throughout the 1970's, for example, IBM Corp. probably retained a dominant position in the computer market by being an aggressive innovator.[5] R & D may reduce the net deadweight loss of monopoly if society values the product of the R & D by an amount that exceeds its costs plus the increased social costs of any additional monopoly power that the R & D creates. Nevertheless, one effect of R & D will be to make new entry by competitors more difficult.

The relationship between R & D expenditures and monopoly is controversial, and has produced a number of conflicting theories. At one side is Joseph Schumpeter's argument that since research is both expensive and risky firms in competition will not be able to afford it. A large amount of money spent without any return—certainly a possibility—may be enough to sink a competitive firm.[6] A common rebuttal to this argument is that all new investment entails risk. Some research investments are rational and others are not. The consequences for a competitive firm of falling behind other competitors are just as serious as the consequences of spending R & D money unprofitably. Furthermore, competitors research in order to *acquire* market power. If they can somehow distinguish their product and make it more attractive than the product offered by others, the difference may show up as monopoly profits.

The monopolist unconcerned about competitive entry will probably not innovate very much. The public utility protected by law from competitive entry, for example, has little incentive to innovate, particularly if cost-saving technology will reduce the base from which its rate of return is calculated. On the other hand, a monopolist threatened by competitive entry is likely to spend a great deal on innovation, both because it has the funds to spend and because it wants to preserve its position. It has been argued that the monopolist may even engage in inefficient "predatory" innovation—that is, innovation reasonably calculated to preserve the monopolist's dominance, and whose monopoly efficiency losses will exceed any efficiency gains that result from the innovation itself.[7] Whether or not this theory has any economic merit, it has been popular among antitrust plaintiffs. Many monopolization cases in the late 1970's and early 1980's involved allegations that the defendant injured the plaintiff or drove it out of business by predatory product innovation.[8]

5. For a contrary view, however, see Sullivan, Monopolization: Corporate Strategy, the IBM Cases, and the Transformation of the Law, 60 Tex.L.Rev. 587 (1982).

6. See J. Schumpeter, Capitalism, Socialism, and Democracy 106 (3d ed. 1950).

7. See Ordover & Willig, An Economic Definition of Predation: Pricing and Product Innovation, 91 Yale L.J. 8 (1981).

8. For example, Berkey Photo, Inc. v. Eastman Kodak Co., 603 F.2d 263 (2d Cir. 1979), cert. denied, 444 U.S. 1093, 100 S.Ct. 1061 (1980); Calif. Computer Prod., Inc. v. IBM Corp., 613 F.2d 727 (9th Cir. 1979). Both plaintiffs lost on the innovation issue.

Arguments have also been made that large firms can engage in research more cheaply than small firms because the larger firm can distribute the costs of the research and development over a much higher rate of production.[9] Likewise, a firm that operates in many markets might profit more from research and development than a single market firm because often research yields unanticipated or tangential benefits in markets other than the one for which it was undertaken. Neither of these arguments, it should be noted, depends on the firm's market power, but only on its large absolute size or on its operation in many markets. Furthermore, both arguments tend to be undermined by the fact that literally thousands of small firms engage daily and profitably in relatively sophisticated types of research and development. The computer revolution of the late 1970's and early 1980's, for example, involved the research activity of many tiny firms.

The ambiguous relationship between monopoly and innovation has been apparent in the case law since soon after the Sherman Act was passed. In the *American Can* case [10] the court faced the defense that a monopoly created by merger should be preserved because the monopolist could afford research and development activities that had not occurred before the monopoly came into existence. The judge was "reluctant to destroy so finely adjusted an industrial machine * * *." Thirty years later Judge Learned Hand wrote that monopoly was bad because it "deadens initiative * * * and depresses energy," and because "immunity from competition is a narcotic, and rivalry is a stimulant, to industrial progress." In the very same opinion, however, Judge Hand found that Alcoa had illegally monopolized the market because it aggressively "embrace[d] each new opportunity as it opened" and faced "every newcomer with new capacity already geared into a great organization, having the advantage of experience, trade connections and the elite of personnel." [11]

Before criticizing judges for being unclear about the relationship between monopolization and innovation, however, one should simply note that economists have done no better. Even today there is widespread disagreement about whether monopoly encourages or discourages research and development and, if monopoly encourages development, whether that fact increases or decreases the social costs of monopoly.[12] No easy generalizations have been forthcoming.

The monopolist threatened with new entry may also spend part of its monopoly returns in less ambiguous entry-deterring practices

9. See J.K. Galbraith, American Capitalism 86 (Rev.Ed.1956).

10. U.S. v. American Can Co., 230 F. 859, 903 (D.Md.1916), appeal dismissed, 256 U.S. 706, 41 S.Ct. 624 (1921).

11. U.S. v. Aluminum Co. of America (Alcoa), 148 F.2d 416, 427 (2d Cir. 1945).

12. A good discussion of some of the differences among economists is Kamien & Schwartz, Market Structure and Innovation: A Survey, 8 J.Econ.Lit. 1 (1975).

which increase the social costs of monopoly. Properly defined predatory pricing,[13] sabotage, espionage, vexatious litigation, false and misleading advertising can all have the effect of prolonging the period during which a *de facto* monopoly exists and thereby increase the social cost of the monopoly.

Monopoly may also yield certain inefficiencies that are not planned but which appear to accompany the absence of competition in a market. For one thing, the monopolist is a "price maker" rather than a "price taker." The monopolist, unlike the competitor, must calculate its profit-maximizing price by predicting how the market will respond to a price increase of a certain size. If the monopolist predicts incorrectly and sets its price too high, the deadweight loss triangle will become larger and the monopoly profits will become smaller. The effect will be to increase the social cost of the monopoly.

Finally, some economists have attempted to evaluate and quantify Learned Hand's dictum in the *Alcoa* case that monopoly "deadens initiative" and results in less efficient use of resources than would prevail in competitive markets. Monopolists may simply not have the same incentives to reduce costs; their managers may not operate under the same "crisis" conditions that affect competitors; they may become comfortable. Such phenomena undoubtedly exist in many firms. The extent to which they are more prevalent among monopolists than among competitors in an imperfect world, however, is difficult to quantify.[14]

§ 1.4   Industrial Organization and the Limits of Perfect Competition

The field of economics known as industrial organization performs two important functions in antitrust analysis.[1] First, it can help us decide whether the perfect competition model is optimal for a particular market and, if it is not, what role for antitrust exists in that market. Second, industrial organization can help us understand whether a particular firm's activities that affect market structure are efficient and should be encouraged, or inefficient and ought to be condemned.

13. See §§ 6.7–6.12 below.

14. See Leibenstein, Allocative Efficiency vs. "X-Efficiency," 56 Amer. Econ.Rev. 392 (1966); De Alessi, Property Rights, Transaction Costs, and X-Efficiency: An Essay in Economic Theory, 73 Amer.Econ.Rev. 64 (1983).

§ 1.4

1. The classic text on industrial organization is E.A.G. Robinson's The Struc-

ture of Competitive Industry (rev. ed. 1958); the most useful contemporary text is F.M. Scherer, Industrial Market Structure and Economic Performance (2d ed. 1980). An excellent study of the structure of a dozen major American industries is W. Adams, ed., The Structure of American Industry (6th ed. 1982).

Many real world markets do not come very close to the classical model of perfect competition. In some markets this failure is an antitrust problem: the market would perform more efficiently if it approximated the perfect competition model more closely. In other markets, however, competition among large numbers of incumbents producing undifferentiated products is not the optimal structure.

The single largest factor tending to undermine perfect competition is the presence of significant economies of scale. The model of perfect competition is premised on the notion of a market containing many equally efficient firms each indifferent to the output decisions of others. Within the model firm size is not a factor in competitor decisions, because the model assumes constant returns to scale: production and distribution costs do not vary with size. Suppose, however, that one firm in such a market develops a new process that enables it to produce the product at substantially lower cost. In order to take advantage of this new process, however, the firm must build a plant capable of serving one half of the existing market. Now incumbent firms can no longer be indifferent to the price and output decisions of the innovator.

Most economies of scale are not as dramatic as the illustration suggests. However, economies of scale obtain in almost every industry, and they range from the trivial to the very substantial. Technically, an economy of scale exists whenever the costs per unit of some input decrease as volume increases. The following examples illustrate the manifold presence of economies of scale in a wide variety of industries.

1) To drive a truck from point A to point B costs $100, whether the truck is full or half empty. As a result, the full truck can transport its cargo at a lower cost per pound than the half empty truck.

2) A 30–second television commercial advertising automobiles costs $100,000, whether the manufacturer has 10,000 dealerships across the country and produces 10,000,000 cars per year, or has 300 dealerships and produces 90,000 cars per year.

3) To set up an automatic metal lathe to turn out a particular machine part costs $100 in labor. Once the lathe is set up, the costs of turning out the parts is $1.00 each. If the lathe is set up to turn out a single part, its cost will be $101.00. If the lathe is set up to turn out 10,000 parts, their cost will be $1.01 each.

4) A procurement department and legal staff spend $2000 to negotiate and draft a contract to purchase an essential raw material, whether the company is buying 50 units of the material or 5000 units.

5) A manufacturer of essential medical or industrial supplies must always keep one production machine in reserve, so that a breakdown will not interrupt production. If he produces with a single machine operating at a time, he must therefore maintain capacity equal to

twice his actual output. If he produces with eight machines, however, he needs to maintain only nine machines, a capacity equal to 12% more than his output.

6) A production process requires 40 discrete functions. If a firm has ten employees, each must perform, on average, four different functions. If the firm has 4000 employees, no single employee will have to perform more than one function, in which she will be a specialist. If she becomes ill, another specialist in the same function will replace her.

7) The transaction costs of borrowing money (or raising equity capital) are 2% for blocks of $1,000,000; 1% for blocks of $10,000,000; or .5% for blocks of $100,000,000.

8) The development of a new manufacturing process reduces the cost of manufacturing widgets by 50¢ per unit. The research and development costs for inventing the new process were $1,000,000. If the firm produces 1,000,000 units per year, the new process will pay for itself in 2 years and thereafter the firm will save $500,000 per year. If the firm produces 12,000,000 units per year the new process will pay for itself in two months and thereafter the firm will save $6,000,000 per year.

This list is only a tiny sampling of the kinds of economies of scale that can exist, and every industry contains at least one nontrivial economy of scale.[2] Traditionally atomized industries, such as farming, are no exception. An automatic milking machine may greatly reduce the cost of milking dairy cows, but the basic cost of the machine is such that the farmer will not reach the "break-even" point unless he milks at least 100 cows.

Economies of scale are largely a function of technology, which both creates and destroys economies of scale. The invention of the milking machine meant that the large farmer could obtain a cost advantage over the farmer too small to use the machine profitably. As a result dairy farms tended to become larger. On the other hand, the invention of the microprocessor (the tiny silicone chip that is the heart of the modern computer) made it possible for much smaller firms to manufacture computers efficiently.

The above list also reflects that not all economies of scale can be attained within a single plant. Certain "multi-plant" economies give a cost advantage to the operator of multiple plants, if the plants are properly distributed. Other economies, such as advertising, may obtain as output increases whether or not the output comes from a single plant. As a result, it is often impossible to determine the most efficient minimum size of a single plant and conclude that a firm that operates such a plant has attained all available economies of scale. A

2. For a fuller discussion, see Scherer, Id., at 81–150.

firm that operates two or more such plants may have even lower costs.

The term Minimum Optimal Scale (MOS) refers to the smallest production unit capable of achieving all relevant economies of scale. If a firm or plant operates at MOS, no other firm or plant can be more efficient because of its scale of operation (although it may, because of better management, be a more efficient firm).

MOS in any particular industry is difficult to measure. In a multi-step production process, different steps attain MOS at different levels of output. Suppose, for example, that a plant manufactures clocks, which consist of three parts: motor, face and cabinet. The face is printed, and the largest cost of producing faces is drafting the design and setting up the printing press. Once the press is ready to roll it can produce ten million units as easily as ten. As a result MOS in the production of clock faces is very high—say 10,000,000 units per year. The motor is a relatively standard item in which significant economies obtain; a plant of MOS would produce about 100,000 motors per year. Finally, the cabinet involves a great deal of individual work, and economies of scale are less substantial. All available economies in producing the cabinet can be attained at an output of 10,000 units per year. How many clocks will the firm produce?

It probably will not produce 10,000,000 clocks per year, even though at that rate of output it would be taking maximum advantage of the economies available in the printing of the clock faces. In fact, the printing of a particular clock face is likely to be a natural monopoly. Once the face has been designed and the printing press set up, the press will turn out copies of the face until it wears out: the more faces produced, the lower the cost per face. This is frequently true of printed products. The *Kansas City Star* could probably produce 10,000,000 copies of its Wednesday morning news-paper at a lower cost per copy than it could produce 400,000 copies. It produces 400,000 copies, not because of economies of scale, but because the market is not capable of absorbing more than 400,000 copies. Likewise, the market may not be able to absorb 10,000,000 clock faces of a particular style.

The firm will probably be content to manufacture less than the optimal number of clock faces. The problem with motors and cabi-nets is more substantial, however, because they make up a larger percentage of the clock's costs. The firm has some options. It can manufacture both motors and cabinets itself and produce 10,000 units per year. In that case it would achieve all available economies in cabinets, but it would have higher costs in the production of motors. Alternatively, it could manufacture only the cabinets and purchase the motors from an independent motor manufacturing company that is large enough to attain all scale economies. Which choice the firm takes depends on which is cheaper. On one side will be the increased costs of manufacturing motors at an inefficiently low rate. On the other side will be the transaction costs of using the marketplace—of negotiating a contract that covers the motors' detailed specifications, of trusting the motor manufacturer to produce a good product on time, etc. If the clock manufacturer believes that the motor manufacturers are untrustworthy, or that they are charging monopoly prices, it may conclude that it is cheaper to manufacture the motors itself, even at an inefficiently low rate.[3]

The other alternative open to the firm is to expand output to 100,000 units per year, in which case it could manufacture both motors and cabinets at MOS. Then, however, it must discern whether the market will absorb all this increased production. A tenfold increase in output may force the market-clearing price to drop substantially. Any economies achieved by manufacturing both motors and cabinets at MOS might be more than lost in the price decrease.

Even the relatively simple problem of a clockmaker with three inputs (most firms, even clockmakers, have far more) makes MOS difficult to determine. Several economists suggest that there is no reliable way of determining *all* relevant economies of scale in any real world industry. Importantly, a determination that overlooks just one nontrivial economy of scale will understate the minimum optimal size of the firms in that market.[4]

However, in an unrestrained, competitive market successful firms will gravitate upward toward MOS, probably through a long period of trial and error. One firm will grow to a larger size or begin performing for itself a service that it previously purchased in the market. If the change creates no economies, the balance of the market will remain unaffected. If the change gives the firm lower costs, however, the firm will likely expand output and increase its market share at the expense of competitors. These competitors will then be forced to achieve these economies for themselves or eventually be forced out of business. By making a few qualifying assumptions, economists have been able to guess MOS in certain industries by a rule of "natural selection": firms that have attained all important economies of scale tend to survive; those that fail to attain important economies tend not to.[5]

The best way to visualize how firms gravitate toward MOS is by consideration of the long-run average cost curve. The average cost curve discussed in § 1.1 above is the sum of average variable and

3. See Coase, The Nature of the Firm, 4 Economica (n.s.) 386 (1937).

4. See the debate between Professors F.M. Scherer and John S. McGee in H.J. Goldschmid, H.M. Mann, & J. Fred Weston, Industrial Concentration: the New Learning 15–113 (1974).

5. See Stigler, The Economies of Scale, 1 J.L. & Econ. 54 (1958); Weiss, The Survival Technique and the Extent of Suboptimal Capacity, 72 J.Pol.Econ. 246 (1964).

average fixed costs. Over the long run, however, almost all costs are variable. For example, when the plant wears out the firm will have a number of options: it can retire the plant and not replace it, or it can replace the plant with a plant of smaller, equal or greater size. A profit-maximizing firm will select the most profitable option.

The term "long-run average cost" refers to a firm's average costs when the firm is in a position to select the optimum size of a plant or other long-term investment. Once the plant is in place, of course, its costs are sunk and must be considered fixed for the period during which the plant is used.[6]

As a competitive market approaches equilibrium, it will force firms not only to price their products at marginal cost, but also to operate plants of the most efficient size. A moment's thought will bear this out. As noted above, each firm in a perfectly competitive market faces an infinite elasticity of demand. If the prevailing market price is $1.00 and a firm tries to charge a monopoly price of $1.10, it will make no sales. Likewise, if the market price is $1.00 but one firm faces substantial production inefficiencies and must charge $1.10, it will also lose all its sales. Customers are generally indifferent (and probably do not even know) whether a firm's price is too high because it is trying to earn monopoly profits or because it is an inefficient firm. They will buy from someone selling at the competitive price. As one firm attains new economies it will enlarge its output. This will force competitors to copy the cost saving innovation. Competition among the innovators will drive the price down and remaining firms will be forced to copy the innovation as well. Eventually all firms surviving in the market will attain the new cost savings.

The long-run average cost curve determines the *minimum* size a firm must be in order to achieve available economies. We know the curve slopes downward and then levels off at some minimum optimal level of output. Whether the curve eventually slopes upward again— that is, whether there are long-run diseconomies of large size—is debatable and generally irrelevant to antitrust policy. However, the long-run average cost curve in most industries has a flat bottom across a relatively broad range. For example, if MOS in a particular industry is 5% of total market output, it is likely that a much larger firm, producing perhaps 25% of market output, is equally efficient. If this is true, then in any given industry at a certain time we would expect to see plants or firms in a variety of sizes equal to or greater than MOS. This is likely to be true for a number of reasons. First, not all firms of minimum optimal size are equally efficient firms. Some will have better management and grow larger. Others will simply have better luck. If a new industry came into existence today

6. See E. Mansfield, Microeconomics: Theory and Applications 196–98 (4th ed. 1982).

with twenty firms of equal and optimal size and efficiency, we could anticipate a far different market structure a half century from now. Some firms would go out of business. Others would merge. Others would grow internally. The end result might well be two or three firms with 20%–30% of the market, two with 10% of the market, and two or three with 5% each. All of them could be equally efficient.[7]

In addition, if the market is monopolized or cartelized, some fringe firms may be able to survive even if they are not of MOS. For example, suppose that MOS in a particular industry is 20% of the market, and an MOS firm can produce widgets for $1.00 each. A firm with 10% of the market has costs of $1.20. But what if three firms, each with 30% of the market, are engaged in price fixing and charging $1.30? The inefficiently small firm will find it quite easy to compete with the cartel, because its members have created a price "umbrella" which protects the small firm from its inefficiency. If the cartel ever falls apart the small firm may be in trouble.

What role does the notion of economies of scale play in antitrust? First, it suggests that much of antitrust's earlier preoccupation with bigness *per se* was ill-advised, at least if low prices are an important goal of antitrust policy. Firms frequently become big because large firms are more efficient than small firms. The unfortunate result, of course, is that the small firms become unprofitable and are forced either to become big themselves or else to exit the market. Invariably, the minimum optimal *size* of firms in a particular market dictates the optimal maximum *number* of firms in the market. If MOS is 25% of the market, the market will not have room for more than four MOS firms. High market concentration, with all its possible attendant evils, is often a function of economies of scale.

Second, knowledge of economies of scale in a market can help a court evaluate the consequences of certain practices alleged to be monopolistic. Many such practices, such as vertical integration, may be nothing more than a means of attaining economies. Likewise, knowledge of scale economies may help predict the consequences of mergers.

Third, knowledge of scale economies and optimal market structure can help a court determine the appropriateness of "structural" relief in certain cases. If a firm has been found guilty of monopolization or illegal merger, should the court order divestiture—judicially enforced break-up of the defendant into two or more smaller firms? What if

---

7. See Scherer, note 1, at 45–48. It is important to distinguish the question whether the long-run average cost curve rises, and whether the average cost curve does. The average cost curve—which represents the output of an established plant—eventually rises in most industries. That is, when a plant produces more than its optimal capacity it operates inefficiently and incurs higher costs. The long-run average cost curve, however, reflects the fact that the firm has the option of building a different size plant or of operating multiple plants. While the average cost curve in most industries eventually rises, the long-run average cost curve likely does not.

the new firms are too small to achieve important economies of scale? The result might be that prices would be higher in the new "competitive" market than they were in the old "monopolized" market. In such cases a more efficient solution may be to tolerate the highly concentrated, "oligopoly" market and use the antitrust laws to force the firms to compete with each other as much as possible.[8]

§ 1.5   Persistent Economies of Scale, Natural Monopoly, and Contestability

Substantial economies of scale can strain the perfect competition model to the breaking point. For example, if the long-run average cost curve slopes downward to a point equal to one-half of market demand, then the market has room for only two minimum optimal scale firms. Any firm whose output is less than 50% of the market will face higher costs. On the other hand, a market with two or three firms is far more conducive to monopolization or collusion than a market containing dozens of firms.

The extreme example of economies of scale is natural monopoly, which occurs when a firm's costs decline as output increases all the way to the market's saturation point. Figure Six illustrates such a market. The long-run average cost curve (AC) slopes down continuously until it intersects the demand curve. A single plant of MOS would be large enough to satisfy the entire market demand at a price sufficient to cover the firm's costs. Any firm producing a smaller amount would face higher per unit costs.

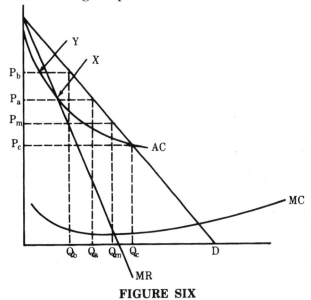

FIGURE SIX

8. The problems of high concentration and oligopoly pricing are discussed in § 4.2 below.

Suppose that the market in Figure Six were divided between two firms of equal size and efficiency, and that each charged a price equal to its average costs (the same as a competitive market in equilibrium). Each firm would fill one-half the demand, so the costs of each would be determined by a point on the AC curve halfway between the vertical axis and the demand curve: point X. At that point each firm would sell one half the market output and recover its costs. However, their joint output would be reduced to Q_a and price would be P_a. If three identical firms shared the market each would have costs equal to that point on the AC curve one-third of the horizontal distance from the vertical axis to the demand curve: point Y. For three firms, combined output would be even lower and price even higher.

The classic example of natural monopoly is the toll bridge. Suppose that a bridge costs $1000 to build and lasts ten years, so fixed costs are $100 per year. Average variable costs are 10¢ per crossing, which include maintenance and the costs of collecting the toll. The bridge is large enough to accommodate any number of crossers. If 1000 people cross the bridge annually, a toll of 20¢ will cover the average total cost of a crossing—10¢ for average variable costs and $100/1000, or 10¢ for average fixed costs.

Suppose that a competitor builds a second toll bridge next to the first. Variable costs for each bridge remain at 10¢ per crossing,[1] but now there are only 500 crossers on each bridge annually. The fixed costs jump from 10¢ per crosser to 20¢ per crosser, and average total costs are 30¢. Worse yet, when the price rises some of the 1000 people willing to cross at a toll of 20¢ opt not to cross at all (or to swim across), rather than pay 30¢. Suppose only 800 people make crossings—400 on each bridge. Then the fixed costs jump to 25¢ per crosser rather than 20¢. As a result of the second bridge 200 fewer people cross, creating a deadweight loss similar to the loss caused by monopoly,[2] and the price of a crossing rises from 20¢ to 35¢. If a third bridge came in, the toll would have to rise even higher before all three bridges could remain profitable.

Natural monopoly markets perform optimally when they are occupied by a single firm that charges a competitive price. The last part of that statement is critical, however. A natural monopolist is a monopolist. Like any monopolist, the natural monopolist will seek out its profit-maximizing price at the intersection of its marginal cost and marginal revenue curves. Sometimes the natural monopolist's profit-maximizing price will be higher than the price charged by multiple competitors in the natural monopoly market and sometimes lower.

§ 1.5

1. Actually, maintenance costs per crosser would also rise, unless maintenance is directly proportional to the number of crossers.

2. See § 1.3 above.

The problem of natural monopoly is easily stated: if the market is occupied by a single firm, the firm will charge a monopoly price. If it is occupied by multiple firms, even assuming that the firms behave competitively,[3] they will have higher costs and will charge higher prices.

The traditional solution to the problem of persistent, recognized natural monopoly is price regulation. A single firm is permitted to occupy the market and is protected by law from competitive entry. In exchange, however, the firm's prices are set by a regulatory agency designed to ensure that pricing approaches P_c in Figure Six rather than P_m. Whether or not the regulation is socially beneficial depends upon the accuracy of the regulatory agency's cost determinations and whether the cost of regulating is greater than or less than the cost of monopoly pricing or of ceding the market to multiple firms.

When a natural monopoly is recognized as such and subjected to price regulation, it acquires a certain amount of immunity from the federal antitrust laws. For some time this has been true of interstate airlines, telecommunications, electric companies, gas companies, and other price regulated utilities. However, many natural monopolies are not recognized as such and are treated no differently than competitive firms. Newspapers, newspaper delivery routes and court reporting services, for example, may be natural monopolies. Failure to recognize this fact has occasionally led courts astray in their analysis of antitrust problems in those markets.[4]

More than any time since the New Deal policy makers in the 1980's have questioned accepted beliefs about the costs, benefits and proper scope of price regulation. In particular, they have become critical of the large costs of operating the regulatory system and of the failure of most regulatory systems to approximate competitive behavior in price-regulated markets.[5] A by-product of this criticism has been a great deal of reinterpretation of the proper scope of the antitrust laws in the price-regulated industries. Neither of these problems is a concern of this volume.[6]

3. Competitors in natural monopoly markets have very strong incentives to collude. In the bridge example, each bridge operator has constant variable costs of 10¢ per crosser—that is, one additional crosser imposes 10¢ in additional costs on the bridge. Each bridge operator will therefore be better off obtaining additional crossers at any price above 10¢. The likely result will be a toll war in which prices are driven to marginal costs without enough remaining to cover fixed costs. One of two things will probably happen: one of the bridges will go out of business or else the two bridges will expressly or tacitly fix prices.

4. For example, see Albrecht v. Herald Co., 390 U.S. 145, 88 S. Ct. 869 (1968), discussed in § 7.2 below. See Hovenkamp, Vertical Integration by the Newspaper Monopolist, 69 Iowa L. Rev. 451 (1984).

5. The best discussion of these problems is S. Breyer, Regulation and its Reform (1982).

6. For discussion, see Baker & Baker, Antitrust and Communications Deregulation, 28 Antitrust Bull. 1 (1983);

One important result of the critical thinking about regulation, however, is a broad attack on the traditional perfect competition model and on the model for natural monopoly. This attack, sometimes called the theory of contestable markets, creates a "competition model" for markets, including natural monopolies, where the given wisdom has been that competition will not work. The theory is opening the way for greater enforcement of the antitrust laws in markets that were once price regulated but are now being deregulated.

The theory of contestable markets believes the perfect competition and natural monopoly models are flawed in one important respect: although they describe competition *in* the market quite well, they ignore the phenomenon of competition *for* the market. Even though a market may have room for only one firm, someone must decide which firm will have the right to enter, how long it may stay, and what price it will charge. Competition can play an important role in this decision process. Furthermore, if the process is constructed properly, a perfectly contestable market with a single seller can perform just as competitively as a traditional perfectly competitive market.[7]

For example, the identity of the firm and the price to be charged can be determined by competitive bidding. The notion that a single firm wins a competitive bid is commonplace. If the city of San Francisco decides to build a sports arena, the "market" for the construction of the arena is probably a natural monopoly—the city would prefer to have a single contractor take charge of the entire project. The city will identify the contractor and the price of the project by taking competitive bids, with the offer generally going to the lowest bidder. Although a single firm ends up building the arena, the process of competitive bidding helps ensure that the firm will not charge a monopoly price.

Competitive, or franchise, bidding in natural monopoly utilities presents some difficult problems, however, because fixed cost items are especially durable. For example, a natural gas pipeline from El Paso to Los Angeles might last fifty years. It would not be practical to ask competing natural gas companies to bid for the right to build the pipeline and supply gas from El Paso to Los Angeles for fifty years. The firms would have to calculate an enormous risk premium

Cohen, The Antitrust Implications of Airline Deregulation, 28 Antitrust Bull. 131 (1983); Breen, Antitrust and Price Competition in the Trucking Industry, 28 Antitrust Bull. 201 (1983).

7. Unlike the perfect competition model, the theory of contestable markets applies equally to natural monopolies and to multi-seller markets. The most comprehensive, but very technical, statement of the theory of contestable markets is W.J. Baumol, J.C. Panzar & R.D. Willig, Contestable Markets and the Theory of Industry Structure (1982); somewhat more approachable is Demsetz, Why Regulate Utilities?, 11 J.L. & Econ. 55 (1968). The theory is criticized in Shepherd, "Contestability" vs. Competition, 74 Am.Econ.Rev. 572 (1984).

into their bids, because they cannot accurately determine the price, supply or demand for gas over such long periods.

One solution to this problem is to divide the period into small intervals and renew the bidding periodically. Suppose bids were taken for the right to build the pipeline and sell natural gas to Los Angeles for a period of one year. After that year the bidding would be renewed. Suppose firm A wins the bid, builds the pipeline and supplies the gas for one year. The original bid will probably yield a price fairly close to the cost of building the pipeline and supplying the gas for one year, assuming there are many bidders and that they do not collude.

But what will happen the second year? A is now in a much different position than other bidders: A already owns a pipeline which has forty-nine years of life remaining. The pipeline cannot costlessly be moved and used for other purposes; so other bidders must calculate its installation costs into their bids. These additional costs, which have already been "sunk" by A, give A considerable latitude for monopolistic pricing. For example, if the pipeline cost $1,000,000 A will be able to add some amount under $1,000,000 to his bid and still underbid all competitors. In general, the higher A's sunk costs—that is, the costs of durable items that can be used throughout the subsequent bid period and that cannot easily be transferred elsewhere—the more latitude A will have to charge a monopoly price.

In some natural monopoly markets sunk costs are far lower and contestability more workable than in the natural gas market. For example, a particular airline route may be a natural monopoly if it has room for only one round trip per day. If two different airline companies tried to offer daily planes on this route each would fly with large numbers of empty seats and average costs would be very high.

The largest expense of establishing an air route between two points is the cost of the plane. The plane itself, however, is easily transferable from route to route. If a potential entrant who already owns a plane moves into the route to compete with the incumbent, the incumbent will not have any particular advantage over the newcomer. Any potential entrant could enter the market cheaply and exit cheaply, taking his plane with him. As a result, natural monopoly airline routes are more practically contestable than natural monopoly pipelines are. In a bidding market we would expect airline routes to behave fairly competitively: if the only airline operating along a route sets a monopoly price, other airlines will quickly bid to come in.[8]

In general, the easier an incumbent can exit the market without abandoning durable and expensive sunk cost items, the more contest-

8. See Brodley, Antitrust Policy Under Deregulation: Airline Mergers and the Theory of Contestable Markets, 61 Boston Univ.L.Rev. 823 (1981).

able the market and the more competitively it will perform, even though it might have room for only one seller at any given time. Airline routes, newspaper delivery routes, bus lines and direct satellite television are relatively contestable. Electric utilities, cable television and natural gas pipelines are not, unless expensive, durable items can be made automatically transferable from one winning bidder to the next. For example, if the pipeline in the above example was publicly owned, and competitive bidding was used to determine only who would deliver the gas and what the price would be, then the market might be contestable. The same result would obtain if the initial winning bidder were forced to transfer the pipeline to the second-term winning bidder at some previously agreed price. Although these methods for awarding natural monopolies on the basis of competitive bidding have been tried, they have not been particularly successful.[9]

The deregulation movement of the 1970's and 1980's has been concentrated in areas in which sunk costs are relatively low, durable and expensive assets are easily transferable, and there are already multiple firms operating in the markets. Long-distance telecommunications by satellite and microwave, trucking, and airline routes are only three important examples. As these industries become governed less by statutory price regulation, and as entry is opened to more firms, antitrust will have an increasingly important role to play.

§ 1.6 Economic Models and Real World Markets

The economic models discussed in the preceding sections are simple, it may seem, in comparison to the state of affairs that exists in the world. Not many markets contain hundreds of small competitors selling indistinguishable products. The real world contains not widgets but automobiles, corn flakes, and stereo sets, and these come in several varieties.

Two very complex theories have been developed to accommodate these relatively simple models to the greater complexities of the real world. These models are called "imperfect competition" [1] and "monopolistic competition." [2] The former has been more useful to practical economics than the latter, although both have had a large influence on economic policy making. Neither formal theory has much explicit effect on antitrust policy, although judges must often consider the degree that competition in the real world appears to deviate from the given models.

9. See Williamson, Franchise Bidding for Natural Monopolies—in General and With Respect to CATV, 7 Bell J. Econ. & Management Science 73 (1976).

§ 1.6

1. See J. Robinson, The Economics of Imperfect Competition (1933).

2. See E. Chamberlin, The Theory of Monopolistic Competition (1933).

The theories are not formally presented in this chapter.[3] Rather, as they are relevant they are discussed in various sections of this book, particularly those on oligopoly and price discrimination.[4]

The following list of imperfections in real world markets is useful to keep in mind, however, for it can often help explain the motive or effect of certain litigated practices.

First, in the real world many products in markets that appear competitive are nevertheless differentiated from one another. Although Ford and Chrysler automobiles compete, some buyers prefer one to the other and are willing to pay somewhat more. To the extent this is true the manufacturer faces a slightly downward sloping demand curve and may charge a price higher than marginal cost. As a result, total output in such markets may be less than optimal. More importantly for antitrust analysis, product differentiation may explain many vertical restrictions on distribution. Such restrictions are discussed in chapter nine below.

Second, in the perfect competition model price discrimination is impossible. In the real world it occurs daily. The two imperfections in real world markets that facilitate most price discrimination are probably information costs and transportation costs. If one group of buyers does not know enough about market conditions or about the contents of the product, they may pay a higher price than other groups of buyers. Likewise, high transportation costs make it possible for firms to earn higher profits from near-by "captive" purchasers than from more remote purchasers.

Third, when markets are highly concentrated, because of economies of scale or for other reasons, a firm cannot reasonably ignore the price and output decisions of competitors. Ford Motor Co., for example, would be unwise *not* to respond to General Motors' price reduction or output increase. These problems are discussed below in § 4.2.

Fourth and perhaps most important, transaction costs—the costs of using the marketplace—can distort our picture of any market. Behavior that appears irrational when transaction costs are ignored becomes rational when they are taken into account.

Last but not least is the problem of "second best." The theory of second best begins with the premise that real world markets never satisfy all the assumptions of the perfect competition model. Economies of scale, cartelization and monopoly, imperfect competition, market imperfections created by the patent system and many other phenomena taint all aspects of the general market system. Given that all markets are imperfect, will improvement of competition in

3. Both theories are discussed in E. Mansfield, Microeconomics: Theory and Application (4th ed. 1982), chaps. 11 & 14.

4. See §§ 4.2 & 13.4.

one market necessarily make the entire system more efficient? The answer is ambiguous, but may be no.[5]

Suppose, for example, that copper and aluminum can both be used to make a particular type of tubing. The competitive price of the copper tubing is $2.00 per foot and the competitive price of the aluminum tubing is $1.50 per foot. At those prices most buyers prefer the aluminum and will buy it. However, both tubing markets are monopolized. The monopoly price of the copper tubing is $3.00 per foot and of the aluminum tubing is $2.50 per foot. In this doubly monopolized market most customers who would buy aluminum in the competitive market continue to buy it.

Suppose the government intervenes under the antitrust laws and destroys the copper monopoly but not the aluminum monopoly. The price of copper drops to $2.00, but the price of aluminum remains at $2.50. Now most of these customers switch to copper. The destruction of only the copper monopoly may actually be inefficient—that is, more inefficient substitutions are made after the monopoly is destroyed than when both products were monopolized. This is because the welfare effects of these two monopolies tended to cancel each other out. The overall welfare effects of monopoly cannot be known unless we have complete information about every market affected by the change from monopoly to competition, or vice-versa.

The theory of second best illustrates one thing well: the model of perfect competition is an artificial model, and the real world satisfies the conditions imposed by the model only imperfectly. However, this fact does not distinguish economics from physics, chemistry or genetics. Model building is endemic in science, and in all cases there is a certain amount of disparity between the technically precise model and the phenomena that observers measure in the real world. Just as the real world contains no perfectly competitive markets, so too it contains no perfectly equilateral triangles. Furthermore, once one line or angle is inaccurate, at least one other line or angle must be inaccurate as well. However, the engineer's imperfect triangle functions very well in most real world applications, from astrodomes to space shuttles.

The value of any model lies not in the absolute fidelity of each element to real world phenomena, but in the model's ability to predict. There the economic model, like most scientific models, has a mixed record. Sometimes it predicts accurately, sometimes not. In general, however, antitrust analysis has confined itself to relatively uncontroversial uses of economic models in which their predictive record is good but not perfect. In those areas second best analysis is

---

5. See F.M. Scherer, Industrial Market Structure and Economic Performance 24–29 (2d ed. 1980); Lipsey & Lancaster, The General Theory of Second Best, 24 Rev.Econ.Stud. 11 (1956).

properly ignored, unless it is obvious that antitrust enforcement in one sector will have adverse consequences in another.[6]

The chief use of second-best analysis in antitrust theory has been ideological. The theory has enabled some scholars to argue for limiting the use of economic analysis in antitrust by presenting the theory of second best as a fatal objection to economic analysis of real world markets.

The use of second best analysis in this way is troublesome. It is impossible to have a little bit of second best: if the theory disqualifies economics as an analytic tool for antitrust, it disqualifies *all* economic analysis. Nevertheless, those who rely on second best as an argument against pervasive economic analysis of antitrust problems continue themselves to give economic justifications for some policies, such as the rules against price fixing. If the implications of second best analysis are accepted however, then even the simple economic argument against price fixing loses its force.[7]

6. The fact that it is logically possible that correction of monopoly in one market will lead to a general welfare loss because of increased imperfections in other markets does not mean that such losses occur very often, or even that they occur at all. Most interrelationships between distinct markets are weak enough to be ignored. If they are strong enough to be considered, the interrelationships will usually be obvious. See Williamson, Assessing Vertical Market Restrictions: Antitrust Ramifications of the Transaction Cost Approach, 127 U.Pa.L.Rev. 953, 987 (1979); Baumol, Informed Judgment, Rigorous Theory and Public Policy, 32 S.Econ.J. 137 (1965).

7. For Example, see L. Sullivan. Handbook of the Law of Antitrust 3–5, 21, 153–54 (1977).

CHAPTER 2

FACTS, VALUES AND ANTITRUST

Table of Sections

§ 2.1 Antitrust Policy: Economics and Other Values

Having a model of price theory and industry structure is one thing. Using the model to guide legal policy (or deciding not to use it) is quite another. Legal analysis is invariably more difficult than the economic model implies it should be. First of all, fact finders are never able to collect all relevant information. Invariably they must fill in gaps, resolve inconsistencies, or deal with facts that do not fit a given paradigm. Sometimes the litigation process yields facts that appear inconsistent with the predictions offered by the economic model. This may be because the process has not generated enough facts, or because one or more of the facts is inaccurate. It may also be because the model itself needs some adjusting to account for "anomalies"—things that the model in its current form is unable to explain.[1]

The antitrust policy maker faces a second, more pervasive problem, however. The model may work perfectly, and the fact finder may be amply supplied with the information necessary for a prediction. However, some value that the model does not take into account may force a different decision than the model suggests. The perfect competition model does one thing quite well: given sufficient data it can predict whether a certain practice is efficient or inefficient, by a

---

§ 2.1

1. For an excellent discussion of the relationship between scientific models, anomalies, and scientific progress, see T. Kuhn, The Structure of Scientific Revolutions (2d ed. 1970).

given definition of efficiency. What the model cannot do, however, is tell us whether efficiency is the only thing that counts.

For example, the legislative history of some antitrust statutes, such as the Robinson-Patman price discrimination statute,[2] or the Celler-Kefauver amendments to the anti-merger statute,[3] promote manifestly bad policy as defined by the economic model. A good case can be made that the Congresses that passed these statutes were willing to tolerate a great deal of allocative *in*efficiency in order to protect certain classes of people, notably small business.[4] Does this mean that merger law today (which is governed by the Celler-Kefauver amendments) should ignore economics; or conversely, that courts should ignore the legislative history of federal merger legislation and read economic efficiency into the statute? § 7 of the Clayton Act, after all, is a democratically passed statute. The United States Code is full of inefficient, democratically passed statutes, many of which are regularly enforced.

There is a principled and viable position that antitrust policy must admit certain noneconomic values.[5] On the other hand, no one believes that efficiency concerns are absolutely irrelevant to antitrust policy. One can go further: no one believes that efficiency concerns are irrelevant in any area of law, even the constitutional law of individual rights.[6]

Today the most important debate about basic principles in antitrust is between those who believe that allocative efficiency should be the exclusive goal of the antitrust laws,[7] and those who believe that antitrust policy should consider certain "competing" values—that is, values that either cannot be accounted for within the economic model, or values that can be asserted only at the cost of a certain amount of efficiency.[8] These competing values include maximization of consumer wealth, protection of small businesses from larger competitors, protection of easy entry into business, concern about large accumulations of economic or political power, prevention of the impersonality

2. See chap. thirteen below.

3. See chap. eleven below.

4. On the Robinson-Patman Act's legislative history, see Hansen, Robinson-Patman Law: A Review and Analysis, 51 Fordham L.Rev. 1113 (1983); on the legislative history of the Celler-Kefauver amendments, see Hovenkamp, Distributive Justice and the Antitrust Laws, 51 Geo.Wash.L.Rev. 1, 24–26 (1982).

5. See Hovenkamp, Id.; Schwartz, "Justice" and Other Non-Economic Goals of Antitrust, 127 U.Pa.L.Rev. 1076 (1979); Pitofsky, The Political Content of Antitrust, 127 U.Pa.L.Rev. 1051

(1979); Sullivan, Book Review, 75 Colum.L.Rev. 1214 (1975).

6. For example, a state can give reasonable aptitude tests to job candidates even though the impact of the test is racially discriminatory. Washington v. Davis, 426 U.S. 229, 245–46, 96 S.Ct. 2040, 2050–51 (1976).

7. The best statements of this position are Posner, The Chicago School of Antitrust Analysis, 127 U.Pa.L.Rev. 925 (1979); and R. Bork, The Antitrust Paradox: A Policy at War With Itself (1978). Following close behind are P. Areeda & D. Turner, Antitrust Law (1978 & 1980).

8. See note 5 above.

or "facelessness" of giant corporations, encouragement of morality or "fairness" in business practice, and perhaps some others.

All these alternative goals can be inconsistent with the goal of maximizing allocative efficiency. In addition, many are inconsistent with each other. If courts adopt any mixture of goals, antitrust is likely to be guided by conflicting policies which must then be balanced against each other. To be sure, this is not a unique phenomenon. Constitutional law is filled with decisions that balance conflicting policies, such as the policy of protecting the free exercise of religion and the policy of limiting government interference with religion.[9] Antitrust could reasonably be expected to balance a policy of low consumer prices against a policy of protecting small businesses from larger competitors, and choose different policies to win in different cases.

On the other hand, those who believe that antitrust should be concerned exclusively with allocative efficiency can offer a relatively consistent policy, provided there is consensus about the relevant elements of the economic model. If vertical integration is efficient, then the "efficiency only" advocate believes it should be legal, even if it injures small businesses, makes big businesses even bigger, and makes it more difficult for newcomers to enter a particular field. She will not attempt to balance these "competing" concerns against economic efficiency, because she does not see them as competing. They are simply ignored.

One thing is clear, however: before someone can "balance" competing values, she must have a fairly good idea of what is being thrown into the scales. This means that the multi-valued policy maker, who believes that antitrust should consider small business welfare as well as economic efficiency, must have a good basic knowledge of prices, markets and industrial organization. There is no basis for the view that the adoption of some "competing" noneconomic policy for antitrust, such as the protection of small business welfare, permits one to do antitrust without knowing economics. Economic theory enables the multi-valued policy maker to estimate the relative costs of protecting certain noneconomic values, and helps her determine whether society should be willing to pay the price. Presumably, it is not worth *any* price to protect small businesses. If that were the policy even price fixing by small businesses would be legal.

Further, economic theory will often help the multi-valued policy maker determine whether a particular legal rule will effectively protect the interest she wants to protect. The history of American antitrust is strewn with the corpses of small businesses who fell victim to antitrust rules designed to protect them. In a dissenting

9. See L. Tribe, American Constitutional Law 815 (1978).

opinion in Standard Oil Co. of California v. U.S.[10] Justice Douglas, who placed a high value on the protection of small business, chastised the court for undermining its own policy. The majority had condemned an exclusive dealing contract imposed by a major oil refiner on its independent retail dealers. The restrictions reduced Standard's distribution costs, but they also restricted the freedom of dealers to make independent choices and made it more difficult for new, independent dealers to enter the market. Justice Douglas predicted the effects of the decision: the need to reduce costs would force Standard to eliminate independent dealers and open its own, company-owned retail outlets. The result would be far more harmful to the independent gasoline station owners than the cost-reducing restrictions struck down by the court. When the dealers' contracts expired, Standard would likely not renew them at all.

The same phenomenon has occurred often in merger law. In the 1950's and 1960's the Supreme Court and the lower courts struck down a number of mergers between major brewers and small regional brewers, generally on the ground that the mergers were destroying the small, locally owned brewery. The major brewers then entered the new markets not by merger, but by building their own competing plants. These new plants were more efficient than those operated by the local brewers, and the national brewers had the advantage of large, well established distribution systems. Many of the local brewers were forced out of business and could not legally sell out to the larger firms. The economics of beer production had determined their fate. The Supreme Court's decisions simply made their painful exit from the market even more painful and expensive than it need have been.[11]

This book generally rejects the view that there can be a principled antitrust policy without a coherent economic model. Absent the model antitrust will fall much too easily to constantly fluctuating interest group politics. Worse yet, there will be a very poor fit between the articulated goals of an adopted antitrust rule and its success in achieving these goals.

Critics of economic analysis in antitrust sometimes argue that the economic approach to antitrust is a function of economists' myopia— their inability to see all the manifold issues that make up value systems in the real world. Economists, it is alleged, are uncomfortable with such competing values, so they create models that purport to account for everything. Nothing is left to chance, politics, or humanitarianism.[12]

10. 337 U.S. 293, 69 S.Ct. 1051 (1949). See § 8.12 below.

11. See Y. Brozen, Concentration, Mergers, and Public Policy 366–67 (1982); FTC, The Brewing Industry 64–65 (1978).

12. For example, Fox, The Modernization of Antitrust: A New Equilibrium, 66 Cornell L.Rev. 1140, 1156 (1981).

Concededly, the world is overrun by myopic economists. However, in this particular instance a far better case can be made for the converse of the above argument: antitrust writers who are untrained in economics rely heavily on noneconomic values because this enables them to have an antitrust policy without undertaking the (sometimes difficult) task of learning how the market system works. That approach may be easier in the short run, but it is calculated to have painful consequences in the long run.

 WESTLAW REFERENCES

antitrust /s competing non-economic** politic** protect*** /6 policy purpose rationale

§ 2.2   Positive and Normative Economics

The author of this book believes that antitrust policy should be concerned principally with economic efficiency. That view is reasonable only if a plausible antitrust policy predicated on efficiency can be constructed. It also implies that competing, noneconomic policy arguments should be ignored unless they are very powerful—as they would be, for example, if Congress expressly overruled a particular judicial decision in order to give effect to some noneconomic value.[1]

The text of this book will not often argue, however, that allocative efficiency should be America's exclusive underlying antitrust policy. It asserts a more modest thesis: that no matter what their ideology, antitrust policy makers who understand the market system can do a better job of reaching their goals than those who do not understand it.

The concern here is more with the *positive* economic analysis of markets and the effects of antitrust rules than it is with the *normative* claim that a given rule should be adopted. The function of *positive*, or descriptive, economic analysis is to examine a certain phenomenon or rule and describe its economic consequences. The statement that a certain instance of vertical integration (for example, a manufacturer's acquisition of a chain of retail stores) will result in lower consumer prices but may force some independent retailers out of business is a positive statement. Importantly, such a statement is at least theoretically verifiable or falsifiable. Someone might be able to conduct an experiment in vertical integration, and measure the resulting effect on consumers and competitors.[2]

On the other hand, the decision whether such a vertical merger should be approved because it lowers consumer prices or condemned because it injures competitors is a normative question. It may involve social concerns that are not addressed by the economic model. Even here, however, economic analysis can perform a useful function.

§ 2.2

1. See § 2.4 below.

2. See R. Posner, Economic Analysis of Law 17–19 (2d ed. 1977).

Although it may not provide a *final* answer to the question whether to approve or condemn the vertical merger, economic analysis may help us evaluate the costs of adopting one rule or the other. That information may help us decide whether society is willing to pay a certain price (higher consumer prices) in order to achieve a certain goal (protection of a certain number of small businesses). Such analysis may also help us determine whether a particular antitrust rule will really have the consequence that we hope it will have.

Positive economic analysis may also indicate that the efficiency consequences of a certain practice are so ambiguous that they cannot be predicted. When efficiency consequences are ambiguous, then noneconomic goals ought to be weighed more heavily. Merger policy may be an example of such preference shifting. Horizontal mergers can create substantial economies of production and distribution, but can also increase the risk of collusive pricing or monopoly. However, no court is capable of measuring these two possibilities and balancing them against each other. The result is that merger policy is much more concerned with the possibility of increased prices (normally a distributive concern) than with the likelihood of post-merger efficiencies. Mergers are often condemned because they pose a risk of increased prices, in spite of the fact that the merger probably creates substantial economies as well. In this case, the relatively clear propensity of a particular merger to cause higher consumer prices "trumps" the ambiguous likelihood that the merger will produce compensating efficiencies.[3]

 WESTLAW REFERENCES
antitrust /p normative

§ 2.3   Allocative Efficiency and Consumer Welfare

The two kinds of efficiency relevant to antitrust analysis are *productive* efficiency and *allocative* efficiency. Productive efficiency is most simply understood as a ratio of a firm's output to its inputs. A firm that produces a product valued at $100 and requires inputs valued at $80 is more efficient than a firm that produces a product valued at $100 but requires inputs valued at $90. Firms achieve higher levels of productive efficiency by building efficient plants, developing cost-saving procedures, using employees more effectively, and a host of other ways. Many acts that arguably violate the antitrust laws are mechanisms by which firms increase their productive efficiency. These include mergers, vertical integration, exclusive dealing or tying arrangements, and even certain agreements among competitors.

3. See § 11.2 below. See Fisher & Lande, Efficiency Considerations in Merger Enforcement, 71 Calif.L.Rev. 1580 (1983).

The attitude of the antitrust laws toward productive efficiency is affirmative but passive. On the one hand, antitrust policy generally permits activities that increase a firm's productive efficiency, unless the activity also enhances the firm's market power. On the other hand, a firm does not generally violate the antitrust laws simply by being inefficient. For example, although vertical integration may reduce a firm's costs and permit it to produce and deliver a product at a lower price, failure to integrate is not illegal under the antitrust laws. The market itself disciplines inefficient firms.

Allocative efficiency is a more theoretical and controversial concept than productive efficiency. Allocative efficiency refers to the welfare of society as a whole. Given a certain amount of inputs or resources, what use and assignment of these resources will make society best off? The concept of allocative efficiency is not self-defining, and different economists and philosophers prefer different definitions. The most influential definition was given by Vilfredo Pareto early in the twentieth century: a given assignment of resources is most efficient ("Pareto-optimal") if no alternative assignment will make at least one person better off without making at least one person worse off as well.[1] In a more limited and realistic framework, any change is "Pareto-superior" if it makes at least one person better off and makes no one worse off. An economist can confidently predict that if a change makes at least one person better off, and if no one is injured in the process, then the change makes society as a whole better off.

Unfortunately, the concept of Pareto-superiority is so rigorous that it would be satisfied by only the most trivial of social changes. A change in a social policy is Pareto-superior only if no one objects to the change. All legal changes—even outrageously good ones—have adverse affects on at least one person. The adoption of a rule condemning robbery, for example, makes robbers worse off. Likewise, the adoption of a legal rule against monopolization or price fixing is not Pareto-superior for the same reason: it makes monopolists and price fixers worse off than they were before the rule was adopted.

For this reason antitrust economists sometimes use a variation of Pareto-efficiency called "potential" Pareto-efficiency. A change is efficient under the potential Pareto measure if the gainers from the change gain enough so that they can fully compensate all losers out of their gains—that is, if the total value placed on the gains exceeds the total value placed on the losses. If those who are made better off by the adoption of a rule against price fixing gain more than those who are made worse off lose, then the rule is efficient under the

§ 2.3

1. See E. Mansfield, Microeconomics: Theory and Applications 440 (4th ed. 1982).

potential Pareto criterion even though its adoption produces some losers. Whether the gainers *actually* compensate the losers out of their gains is irrelevant to the determination of efficiency. For example, it is unlikely that potential price fixers would be compensated for any losses they suffer from the adoption of a rule that makes price fixing illegal.

Figure One suggests why the adoption of a rule against monopolization or price fixing is efficient under the potential Pareto criterion. In a competitive market, with price at marginal cost, consumers' surplus would equal triangle 1–3–6 in the figure. The monopolist or cartel, however, will reduce output to Q_m and raise price to P_m. Consumers' surplus will be reduced to triangle 1–2–4, and the loss to consumers that results from the monopoly pricing will equal quadrilateral 2–3–6–4.

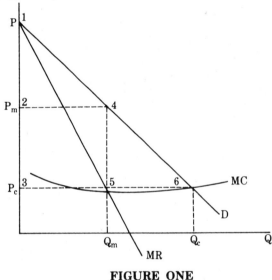

FIGURE ONE

The gain to the monopolist, however, is only rectangle 2–3–5–4.[2] The other part of the consumer loss, triangle 4–5–6, is lost to both the consumers and the monopolist. This is the traditional deadweight loss that is caused by monopoly. Although monopolists are richer as a result of monopolization, consumers are poorer by an even greater amount. For that reason a move from monopoly to competition is efficient by the potential Pareto measure.

The same thing is generally true of actions that increase a firm's productive efficiency without increasing its market power. Cost-reducing vertical integration, for example, makes both consumers and the vertically integrating firm better off, while it makes the firm's competitors worse off. The integrating firm and its customers, however, gain more than the injured competitors lose.

2. Even this rectangle probably overstates the gain to the monopolist. See the discussion of the social cost of monopoly in § 1.3 above.

Potential-Pareto efficiency can be a useful guide for antitrust policy, but it is subject to two important qualifications. First, as with other economic measures of allocative efficiency, potential Pareto analysis is indifferent to how resources are distributed in society. If it could be shown that a certain practice made monopolists richer by exactly the same amount that it made consumers poorer, and no one else was affected, the practice would be judged "neutral" under potential Pareto criteria.[3] However, the legislative history of the Sherman Act shows a great deal of concern for the fact that monopolists transfer wealth away from consumers, but no concern at all for any articulated concept of efficiency.[4]

Second, although the change from orthodox Pareto-efficiency to potential Pareto-efficiency makes an antitrust policy based on efficiency theoretically possible, the change comes with one enormous cost. The efficiency of a social change is relatively easy to measure by the traditional Pareto criterion: if the change produces one identifiable loser, it is inefficient. The potential Pareto criterion, however, requires someone to discover all persons benefited by the change and sum the value of their benefits, and then to identify all losers and sum their losses. The identity of all such people and the amount of their relative gains and losses is generally neither obvious nor easy to calculate. This is particularly true if one admits a problem such as "second best," discussed in § 1.6 above. Even the above demonstration that monopoly is inefficient is necessarily valid only if one considers the single market depicted in the figure. It is possible, however, that the destruction of a monopoly in the market will effectively create monopoly power in other markets. The total allocative losses in those other markets might exceed the gains in the market at hand.

These criticisms aside, the potential Pareto criterion can help us obtain some idea whether the net effect of a practice is a social gain or a social loss. It may help us estimate the gain or loss, even though we likely cannot quantify it precisely. Furthermore, the ambiguities in the potential Pareto criterion are a disabling factor only in relatively close cases. Many cases are not close, and in them it is relatively easy to see that the social gains from a practice outweigh the social losses, or vice-versa.

Although economists often advocate potential Pareto-superiority or some variation of it as the guiding policy for antitrust, you will look a long time to find a judicial opinion articulating antitrust policy in such terms. The term "potential Pareto-efficiency" is an imposing one, carrying with it many implications of technical economic rules and quantification that makes lawyers uncomfortable. Antitrust analysts commonly use a substitute, the "consumer welfare" princi-

3. Perfect price discrimination is such a practice. See § 13.3 below.

4. See § 2.4 below.

ple, which is both less objectionable and somewhat less threatening. Many people who probably believe that maximizing allocative efficiency should be the exclusive goal of antitrust, *state* that the goal of antitrust should be to maximize the welfare of consumers. Spoken in such terms, the goal sounds very attractive and certainly less fearsome than "potential Pareto efficiency."

There is more than a little chicanery in such terminology, however. Although "maximizing consumer welfare" is an appealing term, its content is ambiguous. To say that antitrust should maximize consumer welfare is one thing; to discern an antitrust policy that will do it is quite something else. In fact, the consumer welfare principle is predicated on the observation that *everyone* is a consumer. An antitrust policy of maximizing small business welfare would have to be regarded as distributive, because it would force transfer payments from one group of people (consumers or large businesses) to another group of people (small businesses) even though such a transfer might not make society as a whole better off. Since all of us are consumers, however, an antitrust policy of maximizing consumer welfare is really a policy of maximizing everyone's welfare—at least in their capacity as consumers.[5]

But this observation about the consumer welfare principle brings us right back where we started. *All* definitions of allocative efficiency purport to describe what will make society better off. If "maximizing consumer welfare" is simply a synonym for "maximizing everybody's welfare," then we still do not have a description of an antitrust policy, but only a homily that the best antitrust policy is one that makes everyone better off. Presumably, all of law in a democratic society is designed in furtherance of such a policy.[6]

The consumer welfare principle in use has become identical with the principle that the antitrust laws should strive for optimal allocative efficiency. Perhaps an only slightly cruder alternative is that antitrust policy under the consumer welfare principle chooses that option which leads to highest output and lowest prices in the market which is the subject of the litigation.

 WESTLAW REFERENCES
antitrust /p (allocative pareto +2 efficiency) "consumer welfare"

---

5. There is one important difference between maximization of consumer welfare and maximum allocative efficiency. Allocative efficiency is maximized when the *sum* of consumers' surplus and producers' surplus is maximized. See Figure One in § 1.1 above. Consumer welfare, however, is presumably maximized when the consumers' surplus triangle is maximized. A situation in which the area of the consumers' surplus triangle was ten units and the area of the pro-

ducers' surplus triangle was five units would be more efficient than a situation in which consumers' surplus was twelve units and producers' surplus was one unit. The latter alternative, however, would maximize the welfare of consumers.

6. Hovenkamp, Distributive Justice and the Antitrust Laws, 51 Geo.Wash. L.Rev. 1, 4–7 (1982).

§ 2.4   The Legislative History of the Antitrust Laws

Few elements of statutory interpretation are more difficult and frustrating than the study of legislative history to determine a statute's meaning. Often the debates and compromises leading to a statute's passage contain conflicting statements, made by persons who were elected by disparate interest groups, who have different motives and different perceptions about what a statute will do. Sometimes legislative committees achieve compromises by making statutory language intentionally ambiguous, leaving to the courts to decide when litigation arises which interpretation should prevail.

The legislative histories of the federal antitrust laws are particularly complex and inconsistent. The result is considerable scholarly dispute over Congressional intent. This is particularly true of the Sherman Act, whose language is broad and ambiguous, and whose interpretation has always lain at the root of American antitrust policy. Scholars have argued that the framers of the Sherman Act were concerned almost exclusively with allocative efficiency as measured by the consumer welfare principle.[1] Others have concluded that Congress has often expressed concern with "justice" or fairness in business behavior, but has never articulated any concept of efficiency as such, not even in the antitrust laws.[2] Still others have argued that Congress' chief concern was to arrest wealth transfers away from consumers and toward price fixers or monopolists.[3]

Clearly, the framers of the Sherman Act did not have Pareto-efficiency in mind when they drafted the statute, for Pareto did not develop it until twenty years later.[4] The concept of allocative efficiency and deadweight loss from monopoly is largely a twentieth century phenomenon, and most of the welfare economics of monopoly were developed during the 1930's and after.[5]

The absence of any economic theory of efficiency in the legislative history of the antitrust laws has led some commentators to conclude that the primary goal of the framers was distributive—to transfer wealth away from monopolists and toward consumers or small business.[6] To characterize the concerns of the framers as "distributive," however, is just as anachronistic as to believe that the framers adopted a theory of allocative efficiency that had not yet been invented. All policies, including those motivated solely by concerns for efficiency, affect the distribution of wealth. An antitrust policy

§ 2.4

1. Bork, Legislative Intent and the Policy of the Sherman Act, 9 J.L. & Econ. (1966).

2. Schwartz, "Justice" and other Non-Economic Goals of Antitrust, 127 U.Pa.L.Rev. 1076 (1979).

3. Lande, Wealth Transfers as the Original and Primary Concern of Anti-trust: the Efficiency Interpretation Challenged, 34 Hastings L.J. 65 (1982).

4. V. Pareto, Manual D' Economie Politique (1909).

5. Lande, note 3, at 87–89.

6. Id.

based exclusively on allocative efficiency, for example, may make consumers or large, low-cost businesses richer at the expense of small businesses.

The fact that a policy has certain distributive consequences does not mean that it is "distributive." A policy is purposefully "distributive" only if it is adopted instead of a policy believed to be more efficient, because the adopted policy distributes wealth in a way the policy maker finds more attractive. The fact that the framers of the antitrust laws had no articulated theory of allocative efficiency means that they could not have an articulated theory of distributive justice either. As a result it is unrealistic to look at a particular concern expressed in the legislative history—such as the concern that monopolies might impoverish consumers—and pronounce it either "efficient" or "distributive." [7] The framers of the antitrust laws did not perceive economic policies within such a framework, not even after these terms became an accepted part of economic literature.

One of the great and difficult ironies of the legislative history of the antitrust laws is that as economists' notions of allocative efficiency and the social cost of monopoly became increasingly sophisticated, Congress appeared to become less and less concerned with efficiency and more and more preoccupied with protecting small businesses from larger, more efficient competitors.

Most of the substantive federal antitrust laws were passed in four years: 1890, 1914, 1936, and 1950. The legislative history of the Sherman Act of 1890 contains the best case for the "efficiency" view: that Congress intended the antitrust laws to protect consumers from the high prices and reduced output caused by monopolies and cartels.[8] The legislative history of the Federal Trade Commission Act and Clayton Act of 1914 is somewhat more concerned with the protection of small businesses from the unfair or "exclusionary" practices of bigger firms.[9] The legislative history of the Robinson-Patman Act in 1936,[10] and the Celler-Kefauver Amendments to the antimerger provisions of the Clayton Act in 1950,[11] depart much more radically from any consumer welfare model. In both 1936 and 1950 Congress was concerned chiefly with protecting small businesses from larger competitors who faced lower costs, even though the result of such protection would be lower total output and higher consumer prices.

7. See Hovenkamp, Distributive Justice and the Antitrust Laws, 51 Geo. Wash.L.Rev. 1 (1982).

8. See Bork, note 1.

9. See Fox, The Modernization of Antitrust: A New Equilibrium, 66 Cornell L.Rev. 1140, 1144 (1981). Hovenkamp, note 7, at 19.

10. See Hansen, Robinson-Patman Law: A Review and Analysis, 51 Fordham L.Rev. 1113 (1983). See § 13.6 below.

11. See Bok, Section 7 of the Clayton Act and the Merging of Law and Economics, 74 Harv.L.Rev. 226 (1960). See §§ 11.2–11.3 below.

The trend in the legislative history does not necessarily undermine a general antitrust goal of improving allocative efficiency, however. The legislative history of the Robinson-Patman Act is relevant only in Robinson-Patman Act cases, and the legislative history of the Celler-Kefauver Act is relevant only in merger cases. Cases involving cartels, monopolization and attempt to monopolize are still decided under the 1890 Sherman Act. Nevertheless, Congress' "regression" on the matter of efficiency and consumer welfare is hard to ignore.

The best answer to this argument from legislative history is that the common law nature of antitrust makes the legislative history of the antitrust laws less important than the legislative history of many other federal statutes. The framers of the Sherman Act believed they were federalizing the common law of trade restraints, making the common law more effective by creating a forum with jurisdiction over monopolies or cartels that operated in more than a single state.[12] The earliest judicial decisions interpreting the Sherman Act interpreted the statute in that way: they generally decided cases by reference to common law precedents.[13]

Furthermore, the stated intention was not to "freeze" the common law as it existed in 1890, but rather to regard the common law as an ongoing, ever changing body of rules. As Sherman Act precedent began to accumulate, the courts began to diverge from the nineteenth century common law. The federal antitrust laws took on a life of their own. In short, the Sherman Act can be regarded as "enabling" legislation—an invitation to the federal courts to learn how businesses and markets work and formulate a set of rules that will make them work in socially efficient ways. The standards to be applied always have and probably always will shift as ideology, technology and the American economy changes.

The common law nature of federal antitrust law is not a recent discovery. Federal courts have always interpreted the antitrust statutes in a common law fashion,[14] and the result is a substantial divergence between statutory language and judicial decision. Furthermore, this divergence has been liability expanding as often as liability contracting. Look at the antitrust statutes as long as you please and you will not find anything resembling the distinction between the *per se* rule and the rule of reason, the market power requirements for monopolization cases, the "actual potential entrant"

12. Senator Sherman described his bill as setting "out in the most specific language the rule of the common law which prevails in England and this country * * *." 20 Cong.Rec. 1167 (1889); see Dewey, The Common-Law Background of Antitrust Policy, 41 Va. L.Rev. 759 (1955); Hovenkamp, State Antitrust in the Federal Scheme, 58 Ind. L.J. 375 (1983).

13. For example, U.S. v. Addyston Pipe & Steel Co., 85 F. 271, 278–291 (6th Cir. 1898), affirmed, 175 U.S. 211, 20 S.Ct. 96 (1899); see Baxter, Separation of Powers, Prosecutorial Discretion, and the "Common Law" Nature of Antitrust Law, 60 Tex.L.Rev. 661 (1982).

14. For example, see the discussion in Apex Hosiery Co. v. Leader, 310 U.S. 469, 497–99, 60 S.Ct. 982, 994–996 (1940).

doctrine of potential competition mergers, the "shared monopoly" theory, or the "indirect purchaser" rule.

The common law approach to antitrust analysis is implicit in Congress' use of statutory language. § 1 of the Clayton Act, like the opening sections of many federal statutes, defines the terms used later in the Act.[15] These words include "antitrust laws," "commerce," and "person." Amazingly, however, the list does not include "competition," "monopoly," or "restraint of trade." Congress expressly told the courts what kind of "person" could sue or be sued under the statute but it did not define "competition" or "restraint of trade"—effectively, it yielded to the courts the decision about what substantive standard to apply.[16]

Does this free authorization to the courts mean that the judiciary can usurp the powers of more democratic regulatory institutions? Not in any meaningful sense. After all, when the courts interpret the antitrust laws, they are interpreting federal statutes, and Congress can always respond to an unpopular or ill-conceived decision by revising the statute. Congress has frequently done so, in both liability expanding and liability contracting directions. For example, in 1912 the Supreme Court suggested that the Sherman Act did not condemn tying arrangements.[17] Congress responded in 1914 with § 3 of the Clayton Act,[18] which condemns them if they are anticompetitive (without defining that word). In 1911 the Supreme Court suggested that resale price maintenance was illegal under the Sherman Act,[19] and in 1937 Congress responded by giving the states the right to authorize resale price maintenance for sales within their borders. Forty years later, Congress changed its mind.[20] On many other occasions Congress has either passed or considered legislation that would overrule unpopular antitrust decisions.

Ideology, politics and theory have always changed and undoubtedly always will. American economic and business policy invariably changes with them. The federal antitrust laws were designed in a way that will enable courts to respond to those changes. Congress, if it wants, may rejoin. Perhaps the most isolationistic and regressive of views is that in 1890 or today we have all the right answers.

---

15. 15 U.S.C.A. § 12.

16. Judicial definitions of words such as "competition" have gone through quite an evolution in federal antitrust decisions. See Hovenkamp, Book Review, 33 Hastings L.J. 755, 762 (1982). Judge Bork has identified five distinct meanings of "competition." See R. Bork, The Antitrust Paradox: A Policy at War With Itself 58–61 (1978).

17. Henry v. A.B. Dick Co., 224 U.S. 1, 32 S.Ct. 364 (1912).

18. 15 U.S.C.A. § 14.

19. Dr. Miles Medical Co. v. John D. Park & Sons Co., 220 U.S. 373, 31 S.Ct. 376 (1911).

20. The Miller-Tydings Act of 1937, 50 Stat. 693, permitted states to authorize resale price maintenance. The authorization was withdrawn and the *per se* rule restored for all states by the Consumer Goods Pricing Act of 1975, 89 Stat. 801.

We did not and we do not. The common law nature of antitrust policy permits us to make the best of what we have.

 WESTLAW REFERENCES

antitrust   /p   "common law" "legislative history"   /s   inten!

CHAPTER 3

MEASURING MARKET POWER

Table of Sections

---

§ 3.1 Introduction

Market power is the ability of a firm to increase its profits by reducing output and charging more than a competitive price for its product. In the *du Pont* (cellophane) case the Supreme Court defined market power as "the power to control prices or exclude competition."[1] That definition unfortunately is not very descriptive, and at least one part of it is inaccurate. Market power itself is not an "exclusionary" practice: in fact, the exercise of market power—the sale of products at a supracompetitive price—generally attracts new sellers into the market. Exclusion of competitors is not market power; however, it is an important mechanism by which a firm obtains or maintains market power.

Likewise, to say that market power is the power to "control" prices is not particularly descriptive. Any firm will begin to lose sales when it raises the price of a product. More appropriately, market power is the power to raise prices without losing so many

§ 3.1

1. U.S. v. E.I. du Pont de Nemours & Co., 351 U.S. 377, 391–92, 76 S.Ct. 994, 1005 (1956).

sales that the price increase is unprofitable.[2] A firm that can make more money by selling its output at a higher-than-competitive price has a certain amount of market power.

Many antitrust violations require the plaintiff to show that the defendant has some market power. For example, illegal monopolization under § 2 of the Sherman Act[3] requires that the defendant have monopoly power, which is a high degree of market power.[4] The offense of attempt to monopolize, also a violation of § 2, has a somewhat more ambiguous market power requirement depending on the nature of the activity that is alleged to be an illegal attempt.[5] Establishment of an illegal tying arrangement under § 1 of the Sherman Act[6] or § 3 of the Clayton Act[7] requires a showing that the defendant has a certain amount of market power in the market for the tying product.[8] Courts increasingly require a showing of market power in cases alleging unlawful vertical restrictions or dealer terminations.[9] The law of mergers under § 7 of the Clayton Act[10] does not generally require a showing that either of the merging firms has present market power. Mergers are condemned in part, however, because of their propensity to create market power. As a result market power and market definition analysis is essential in merger cases. Finally, although market power is not a requirement in most *per se* cases, such as price fixing, a private plaintiff seeking damages must generally show that there has been an "overcharge." There will not be an overcharge unless the cartel members collectively wield measurable market power.[11]

The discussion in chapter one suggested why monopoly is bad. The monopolist's price increase and output reduction simultaneously transfer wealth away from consumers and to the monopolist, and produce a certain amount of "deadweight" loss: value that is lost to consumers but is not regained by the monopolist or anyone else.

Creating a deductive model that describes the consequences of market power and monopoly is relatively easy. As the discussion in §§ 1.1–1.2 above shows, a competitor charges a price which tends toward its marginal cost. A monopolist, on the other hand, charges a price determined by the intersection of its marginal cost and marginal revenue curves, and this price is often much higher than marginal cost.

2. Graphic Products Dist., Inc. v. Itek Corp. 717 F.2d 1560, 1570 (11th Cir. 1983) cert. denied, 1984; Valley Liquors, Inc. v. Renfied Importers, Ltd., 678 F.2d 742, 745 (7th Cir. 1982); Landes & Posner, Market Power in Antitrust Cases, 94 Harv.L.Rev. 937 (1981).

3. 15 U.S.C.A. § 2.

4. See chap. five below.

5. See chap. six below.

6. 15 U.S.C.A. § 1.

7. 15 U.S.C.A. § 14.

8. See chap. eight below.

9. For example, *Graphic Products*, note 2 above. See chap. nine below.

10. 15 U.S.C.A. § 18. See chaps. seven, eleven & twelve below.

11. See chap. fourteen below.

Market power can be viewed as the ability of a firm to deviate profitably from marginal cost pricing. Further, marginal cost, or competitive, pricing is an important goal of the antitrust laws. Marginal cost is therefore a useful base from which to measure market power: the greater the ratio of a firm's profit-maximizing price to its marginal cost, the more market power the firm has. The Lerner Index has been developed by economists to quantify a firm's market power: [12]

$$\frac{P_m}{P_c} = \frac{\epsilon}{\epsilon - 1}$$

Where:

ϵ is the price elasticity of demand facing the firm

P_m is the monopoly price (i.e., the price at the firm's most profitable rate of output)

P_c is the competitive price (i.e., the firm's marginal cost at the most profitable rate of output)

The Index is easy to derive [13] and even easier to use. For example, if the elasticity of demand facing a firm is 3, then the ratio of P_m to P_c is 3/(3–1) or 1.5. In that case a firm with marginal costs (P_c) of $1.00 would have a profit-maximizing price (P_m) of $1.50. It would make fifty cents in monopoly profits on each unit that it sold.[14]

The simplicity of the formula is misleading, however. If we knew the elasticity of demand facing any firm we could plug it into the formula and immediately know the ratio of that firm's monopoly price to its competitive price. The higher the ratio, the more market power the firm has. Likewise, if we knew any firm's marginal costs (P_c) we could compare marginal cost with the firm's current price (which is often, but not always, its profit-maximizing price [15]) and then we would also have an immediate, simple "reading" of the firm's market power. From such data we could develop some presumptive legal rules about how high a reading would be necessary to make a merger illegal, or to establish one of the requirements for illegal monopolization.

Unfortunately, marginal cost and firm elasticity of demand are extraordinarily difficult to measure, even by economists operating

---

12. See Landes & Posner, note 2, at 940–41. The formula measures the profit-maximizing price accurately only if the firm's marginal costs are the same at all output levels. If marginal cost rises with output the formula will overstate the difference between the competitive and monopoly prices, because the monopolist will usually have a lower marginal cost at its monopoly price than at the competitive price. The formula as given actually gives the reciprocal of the Lerner Index. Lerner's own version of the Index is $P_m - P_c/P_m$. See Lerner, The Concept of Monopoly and the Measurement of Monopoly Power, 1 Rev.Econ.Stud. 157, 169 (1934).

13. See R. Posner, Antitrust Law: An Economic Perspective 243–48 (1976).

14. A firm has no market power when the elasticity of demand facing it is infinite. In that case the ratio of P_m to P_c approaches 1.

15. See the discussion of limit pricing below in § 6.9.

in the simplest of markets and under the best of laboratory conditions. They cannot be measured directly in the courtroom. Courts rely instead on the fact that there is a positive correlation between market *share* and market power. Suppose that the market for widgets is shared by 10 firms, each with 10% of the market. The marginal cost (and competitive price) of widgets is $1.00. If firm A attempts to raise its price to $1.25, A's customers will look to A's competitors for widgets at the old price. If each of the other nine firms can increase its own output by a little over 10%, A will lose all of its sales.

If A has 80% of the market for widgets, however, A's price increase is much more likely to be profitable. A's customers will still look to A's rivals for lower-priced widgets, but now the rivals will have to increase their own output substantially in order to steal a large percentage of A's customers. To be sure, over the long run A's monopoly profits will encourage the existing rivals to increase their production and new firms to enter the widget market. Eventually A's market share will erode, unless A devises some scheme for excluding its rivals.

All other things being equal, however, a firm with a large market share has a greater ability to increase price profitably than a firm with a smaller share. When A's market share is 10%, the effect of A's unilateral price increase would likely be the *immediate* loss of most sales. When A's market share is 80%, however, A may be able to make sales at the higher price for quite some time. This correlation of market power and market share has permitted courts to use market share as a qualified proxy for market power in antitrust cases.

The word "qualified" is important. Market share is only an imperfect proxy for market power. The correlation between market share and market power can be rigorously expressed in a formula.[16] However, the formula contains *three* relevant variables: market share, market demand elasticity, and the elasticity of supply of competing and fringe firms. If the two elasticity variables remain constant, then market power would be proportional to market share. In the real world, however, market elasticities vary greatly from one market to another. Thus in order to estimate a firm's market power we must gather some information not only about a firm's market

---

16. The formula is:
$$(P_m - P_c) / P_m =$$

$$S_i / (\epsilon_m^d + \epsilon_j^s (1 - S_i)).$$

Where:

P_m = the monopoly price

P_c = the competitive price (marginal cost)

S_i = the firm's market share

ϵ_m^d = the market elasticity of demand

ϵ_j^s = the elasticity of supply of competing or fringe firms

See Landes & Posner, note 2 above, at 945.

share, but also about the demand and supply conditions that it faces.[17]

In most antitrust cases that require proof of market power the court determines whether some "relevant market" exists in which the legally necessary market power requirement can be inferred. In order to do this, the court usually 1) determines a relevant product market, 2) determines a relevant geographic market, and 3) computes the defendant's percentage of the output in the relevant market thus defined. § 2 of the Sherman Act and § 7 of the Clayton Act, the two statutes that most often require analysis of market power, both use language that suggests such an approach. § 2 of the Sherman Act makes it illegal to monopolize "any part of * * * trade or commerce * * *."[18] § 7 of the Clayton Act makes mergers illegal if they tend to lessen competition "in any line of commerce in any section of the country."[19] Both statutes therefore suggest that the court must identify some part or "line" of commerce in which injury to competition is threatened.

WESTLAW REFERENCES

265k12(1.3) /p attempt*** /5 monopol!

digest,synopsis(market /5 power /s tying tied)

market /5 power /s (vertical /10 restrict! restrain***) (dealer
    /10 terminat!)

"market share" /15 "market power"

§ 3.2   Estimating the Relevant Market

The inference is strong that a firm with a high share of a relevant market has market power. Markets do not define themselves, however. The passenger car division of Ford Motor Company makes "Ford cars," "American passenger cars," "passenger cars," "passenger vehicles," and "vehicles." Which of these is a relevant market for antitrust purposes? If the first, Ford Motor Company's share of the relevant market is 100%. If the last, it is trivial, probably less than 1%.

A relevant market is the smallest market for which the elasticity of demand and supply are sufficiently low that a firm with 100% of that market could profitably reduce output and increase its price substantially.[1] Consider first the possibility that the relevant market is "Ford cars." What would happen if Ford raised the price of its cars by, say, $1,000 each. Likely, customers would turn away from

17. See the discussion of elasticities of supply and demand in § 1.1 above.

18. 15 U.S.C.A. § 2. See Standard Oil Co. v. United States, 221 U.S. 1, 61, 31 S.Ct. 502, 516 (1911): "The commerce referred to by the words 'any part' construed in the light of the manifest purpose of the statute * * * includes any portion of the United States and any one of the classes of things forming a part of interstate or foreign commerce."

19. 15 U.S.C.A. § 18.

§ 3.2

1. See § 3.1 above.

Ford cars in droves and go to General Motors, Chrysler, Toyota or some other automobile manufacturer instead. These manufacturers would respond by increasing their production. The almost certain result of Ford's unilateral $1,000 price increase would be that Ford would lose its business. If that is so "Ford cars" is not a relevant market.

Try the market for "American passenger cars" next. Suppose that a single firm made 100% of American passenger cars, and increased the price by $1,000. Once again, many customers would probably attempt to buy Japanese or German cars instead. However, this time we cannot be so certain that these firms will be able to increase their output enough to satisfy this new demand. If they can, however, our "market" is still too small to be a relevant market.

Now consider the market for "passenger cars." Suppose that a single firm manufactured all the world's passenger cars and increased the price by $1,000. This time it would seem that the elasticity of the market on the *demand* side is rather low. Most automobile customers would probably switch from American to foreign cars if the price difference were great enough. But if the price of *all* passenger cars went up, they would have to switch to trucks, bicycles, horses, or do without cars. A far higher percentage of consumers would simply pay the higher price.

How about the supply side? If the passenger car monopolist raised its price by $1,000, the passenger car market would become very attractive to firms in related industries, such as truck manufacturing, and they might switch to production of cars. Eventually enough new firms would enter the passenger car industry to deprive the monopolist of its monopoly. However, this entry could take a long time—perhaps three or four years. During that time the $1,000 price increase might be very profitable. "Passenger cars" is probably a relevant market.

Having determined the smallest relevant market, now we must calculate Ford's share of it. In this case it appears that Ford is not a monopolist. Its share of the world passenger car market is less than 5%.

As the above illustration indicates, it is essential to measure both elasticity of demand *and* elasticity of supply when calculating a relevant market. For example, suppose that an area contained one printer of recipe books and 25 printers of mystery novels. The recipe book printer has 100% of the "recipe book printing" market. Furthermore, the demand for recipe books may be quite inelastic. People need them in order to cook, and neither mystery novels nor anything else provide very good substitutes. Suppose, however, that at very low cost a mystery novel printer can switch production to recipe books. The price of mystery novels is currently competitive, and printers of mystery novels are making only a competitive rate of return. As long as the profitability of mystery books and recipe books is identical and a printer can sell as much as he wants of each, any cost of switching over will discourage a printer from doing so. When the recipe book monopolist attempts to reduce output and obtain monopoly profits on recipe books, however, the high returns will immediately attract the mystery novel printers, who will switch part or all of their capacity from mystery novels to recipe books.

If a firm can costlessly switch from making product A to product B, then as soon as product B is more profitable the firm will switch production to B. In the real world such production changes are seldom costless, but they can be relatively inexpensive. A farmer with standard, unspecialized equipment and 100 acres of tillable soil will decide each spring whether to plant barley or oats. She will plant the one that she predicts will be more profitable. Likewise, a book printer, whose equipment is generally unspecialized, can easily switch from mystery novels to recipe books. On the other hand, it might be quite expensive and time-consuming for a plant currently manufacturing trucks to switch to passenger cars. As a result, a firm that acquired 100% of the market for passenger cars might get away with monopoly pricing for a time, while truck manufacturers retooled their plants to enter the passenger car market. In general it is easier for an existing producer of a similar product to switch to producing some product that has become attractive because of its monopoly price, than it is for a new firm to enter the field. Likewise, elasticity of supply is higher in those industries where plants and equipment are relatively unspecialized. Thus elasticity of supply in the market for recipe books may be very high; elasticity of supply in the market for passenger cars, much lower.

Neither market elasticity of demand nor elasticity of supply can be quantified precisely in litigation.[2] Both, however, can be estimated more accurately than marginal cost or firm elasticity of demand can be. In litigation a court generally tries to identify some market in which there are no close substitutes on the demand side (that is, in which elasticity of demand is low) and for which entry on the supply side is either expensive or time-consuming (that is, in which elasticity of supply is also low).[3] Having identified this relevant market, the court then computes the defendant's share of it, to see if the market share will support an inference that the defendant has the necessary amount of market power.

2. For some attempts at calculating elasticities of demand in a variety of products see H. Houthakker & L. Taylor, Consumer Demand in the United States (1970); Baumol, The Empirical Determination of Demand Relationships, in E. Mansfield, Microeconomics: Selected Readings 55–72 (4th ed. 1982).

3. See Wentz, Mobility Factors in Antitrust Cases: Assessing Market Power in Light of Conditions Affecting Entry and Fringe Expansion, 80 Mich.L. Rev. 1545 (1982).

WESTLAW REFERENCES
"relevant market"   /5   mean defin!
relevant /3 market /s elastic*** /5 demand supply
di relevant market

§ 3.3   Judicial Analysis of Product Demand: "Cross Elasticity of Demand"

When the price of a product rises, some buyers substitute away. The concept of cross elasticity of demand considers the products to which consumers might turn as alternatives. For example, if wheat and corn are close substitutes for many uses when both are sold at a competitive price, a small increase in the price of wheat will encourage many wheat customers to buy corn instead. In that case we would say that the cross elasticity of demand between wheat and corn is quite high. For antitrust purposes the two are in the same relevant market.

Judges are more comfortable estimating cross elasticity of demand than attempting to quantify elasticity of demand directly. The reason is clear. The concept of "cross elasticity" enables the fact-finder to compare two relatively tangible "products" against each other and determine whether one is a good substitute for the other. Even though I may know nothing about economics, my common sense tells me that Fords and Chryslers are often good substitutes for each other. Recipe books and mystery novels, on the other hand, are not.

Unfortunately, judges have often misused the concept of cross elasticity of demand because they have not understood its proper limitations. Used properly, it should help the fact-finder assemble into a single relevant market products that are close substitutes when each is sold at a competitive price. For example, if Ford Motor Company was accused of monopolizing the market for Ford automobiles, the fact-finder should consider whether Chevrolet automobiles, Chrysler automobiles or others ought to be included in the relevant product market. The fact-finder would probably decide that when Fords, Chevrolets and Chryslers are sold at cost many customers regard them as competitive with each other. If the price of Fords went up these customers would switch to Chevrolets or Chryslers. As a result the relevant product market is "automobiles" and not "Fords."

What if the fact-finder were asked to include bicycles and horses in this same relevant market? The effect would be to reduce Ford's share of the "market" even further. In that case the fact-finder would have to make some estimate about the degree to which the demand for horses and bicycles would change in response to a price change in the automobile market. When automobiles and bicycles or horses are all being sold at the competitive price the cross elasticity of demand between them is probably not very high. Not many prospective automobile purchasers would regard a horse or bicycle as a good substitute unless the price of automobiles increased by a very large amount.[1] The fact-finder would probably conclude that bicycles or horses should not be included in the relevant market.

The concept of cross elasticity of demand can lead to mistaken market analysis if it is improperly applied. In United States v. E.I. duPont de Nemours & Co.[2] the defendant duPont was alleged to have monopolized the market for cellophane. duPont produced about 75% of the cellophane sold in the United States. duPont argued, however, that the relevant market was not cellophane, but "flexible packaging materials," which included not only cellophane but also aluminum foil, glassine, pliofilm, greaseproof paper and waxed paper.

Some forms of flexible packaging materials, such as glassine, were cheaper than cellophane. Others, such as polyethylene, were much more expensive. Different wrapping materials had various degrees of acceptance among different buyers, and some buyers were far more cost-conscious than others. For example, virtually all grocery store meats and vegetables had to be wrapped in transparent materials in order to attract grocery consumers. Cellophane occupied about 35% of the market for retail meat wrapping and about half of the market for retail vegetable wrapping. On the other hand, bread was commonly wrapped in opaque paper, and cellophane furnished only 7% of the bakery products market. When a product was expensive in proportion to the amount of wrapping material it needed, cellophane obtained an advantage over cheaper, less transparent packaging materials. For example, 75%–80% of all cigarettes were wrapped in cellophane.[3]

The Supreme Court concluded that the relevant market must include "products that have reasonable interchangeability for the purposes for which they are produced * * *" In the *du Pont* case that was the entire market for flexible packaging materials.[4]

The court's definition of the relevant market was almost certainly wrong. A simple example will illustrate. Suppose that widgets are sold in a competitive market for $1.00, which is also their marginal cost of production. Suppose now that A invents the gizmo, which performs the same functions as a widget, but which can be manufactured for 80¢. A is the only producer of gizmos. At what price will A sell them?

1. However, if the price of an automobile rose from, say, $8,000 to $200,000, then many customers might decide to purchase bicycles instead. Even a monopolist cannot charge an infinite price for its product.

2. 351 U.S. 377, 76 S.Ct. 994 (1956).

3. Id. at 399–400, 76 S.Ct. at 1009–10.

4. Id. at 404, 76 S.Ct. at 1012. The decision is attacked in Turner, Antitrust Policy and the *Cellophane* Case, 70 Harv.L.Rev. 281 (1956).

We would need to know more facts to be sure about A's price. For example, if there were no consumers who preferred gizmos to widgets, then A would be unable to charge more than $1.00 for gizmos. Customers would buy widgets instead. Whether A would sell gizmos at a much lower price—say 90¢—depends on the elasticity of demand. If there is a very large group of potential customers who will buy gizmos at 90¢ but not at $1.00, then A might be better off selling gizmos at 90¢ and attracting that group of marginal customers. If the elasticity of demand in the gizmo market is rather low, however—if there is not a large group of people willing to pay more than 80¢ but unwilling to pay $1.00—then A will worry only about competition from widgets, and A will set the price of gizmos slightly under the widget price. At a price of 99¢ A will sell all the gizmos A can produce to customers who would otherwise buy widgets.[5]

Now suppose A is charged with illegal monopolization. A defends by arguing that he has no market power because the relevant market is not gizmos (in which A's market share is 100%) but rather gizmos plus widgets (in which A's market share is lower). A supports this market definition by providing evidence that the current market price of gizmos is 99¢, while the market price of widgets is $1.00. At those prices there is a high cross elasticity of demand between gizmos and widgets. In fact, if A attempts to raise his price by as little as 1% (1 cent), A will lose large numbers of customers to widgets. If A raises his price by 2%, he may lose all his customers.

Is A's defense good? Clearly not. To be sure, cross elasticity of demand between gizmos and widgets at the *current price* is very high. It is not high, however, because A has no market power in gizmos, but because A *has* market power in widgets *and is already exercising that power*. Every seller, whether monopolist or competitor, sells its output in the high elasticity region of its demand curve. That is to say, every seller sets as high a price as it can without losing so many customers that the price increase is unprofitable.

We would therefore expect the cross elasticity of demand for cellophane and its substitutes to be rather high at the current market price of cellophane. The elasticity of demand facing any seller is high at the current market price unless the seller is not charging its profit-maximizing price. High cross elasticity of demand at the current market price is simply evidence that the seller could not profitably charge an even higher price.[6]

---

5. This discussion assumes that A is not able to price discriminate. See the discussion in chapter thirteen, below.

6. In spite of the substantial, convincing criticism of *du Pont's* analysis, some courts continue to apply it. See, e.g., Satellite Television, Inc. v. Continental Cablevision of Virginia, Inc., 714 F.2d 351, 355 (4th Cir. 1983), cert. denied, ___ U.S. ___, 104 S.Ct. 1285 (1984), holding, without cost analysis, that a relevant market was not cable television, but "cinema, broadcast television, video disks and cassettes and other types of leisure and entertainment-related business * * *."

If the concept of cross elasticity of demand serves a useful function in antitrust analysis, it is to establish whether two products are close substitutes when both are sold at the competitive price. If two things appear to be close substitutes when both are sold at marginal cost, then the two should be included in the same product market. Suppose, for example, that a manufacturer of paper cartons wants to acquire a manufacturer of plastic cartons. A merger between two firms selling in the same relevant market is termed "horizontal" and is subject to a rather strict legal standard. A merger between two firms selling in different markets, however, is a "conglomerate" or "potential competition" merger, and is subject to a generally more lenient standard.[7]

Suppose that the paper carton manufacturer is in competition with five other carton manufacturers, and that its own share of the market is 20%. The plastic carton manufacturer is in competition with eight other plastic carton manufacturers, and its share of the market for plastic cartons is 10%. For nearly all uses plastic cartons and paper cartons compete intensely with each other. In the past customers of paper cartons have responded to a small price increase by switching in large numbers to plastic cartons, and vice-versa.

In this case the high cross elasticity of demand at current market prices tells us more reliably that paper and plastic cartons ought to be included in the same product market. The small market shares and relatively large numbers of firms within a fungible product category suggest that both kinds of cartons are currently being sold at a competitive price. The sensitivity of each to a price change in the other indicates that cross elasticity of demand between the two is high at that price. As a result the presence of the plastic carton manufacturers tends to hold paper carton manufacturers to the competitive price, and vice-versa. The fact-finder should conclude that paper cartons and plastic cartons are a single product and treat the merger as horizontal.[8]

On the other hand, in a monopolization case such as *du Pont*, the concept of cross elasticity of demand is not as helpful unless we know what the competitive price (marginal cost) of the allegedly monopolized product is. In that case, however, we could compute the defendant's market power directly, without the need to determine its share of some relevant market. Alternatively, if the monopolist's product and the products of other firms are so similar in construction that we can infer that their production costs are about the same, then the products should be grouped in the same relevant market. In general, the concept of cross elasticity of demand is more useful in merger cases than in monopolization cases.

---

7. See chapters eleven & twelve below.

8. See United States v. Aluminum Co. of America, 377 U.S. 271, 84 S.Ct. 1283 (1964); United States v. Continental Can Co., 378 U.S. 441, 84 S.Ct. 1738 (1964).

WESTLAW REFERENCES

"cross elasticity" /3 demand

"cross elasticity" /s relevant /3 market

relevant /3 market /s interchang!

horizontal /3 merge* /p "potential competition" conglomerate /3
    merge*

merge* /p elastic*** /5 demand

§ 3.4 Judicial Analysis of Supply Elasticity

Elasticity of supply has been an implicit part of judicial market definition for many years, although courts have begun to recognize it explicitly only recently.[1] A firm with a large share of a proposed market will have little power to increase prices if other firms can immediately flood this market with their own output.

Existing firms already manufacturing a similar product in the same region, or manufacturing the same product some distance away, will often be able to respond to a dominant firm's price increase far more quickly than firms that do not yet exist when the price increase occurs. Often existing firms need merely to increase their output, frequently out of existing capacity. New firms, on the other hand, must still raise capital, build a plant and develop a distribution network. As a result, the best initial question to ask when measuring supply elasticity is whether the defendant's current competitors can increase their own output in response to the defendant's price increase; or alternatively, whether firms making products similar to the defendant's can easily switch to the defendant's product and ship them into the defendant's market if the profits are attractive.

One of the most significant sources of high supply elasticity is therefore the excess capacity of competing firms. Unfortunately, judges have often ignored excess capacity in computing market share. For example, in the *Alcoa*[2] case Judge Learned Hand attempted to determine whether Alcoa had a monopoly in the production of aluminum. Alcoa's market share of virgin aluminum produced in the United States was 100%. Its market share dropped to 90%, however, when Judge Hand included aluminum that was manu-

---

§ 3.4

1. However, see United States v. Columbia Steel Co., 334 U.S. 495, 510, 68 S.Ct. 1107, 1116 (1948), a merger case in which one issue was whether steel plates and shapes should be included in the same product market as other rolled steel products. The Court concluded that if

rolled steel producers can make other products as easily as plates and shapes, then the effect of the removal of Consolidated's demand for plates

and shapes must be measured not against the market for plates and shapes alone, but for all comparable rolled products. The record suggests * * * that rolled steel producers can make other products interchangeably with shapes and plates * * *.

The Court therefore included both in the relevant market.

2. United States v. Aluminum Co. of America, 148 F.2d 416, 424 (2d Cir. 1945).

factured abroad but imported into the United States. Judge Hand refused to include the additional plant capacity of the foreign aluminum producers. Clearly, however, the fact that some aluminum was coming into the United States indicated that foreign aluminum could be sold profitably here. What would have happened if Alcoa had attempted to raise the price of aluminum? The foreign producers would have produced more aluminum and shipped it into the United States, or else they would have diverted some aluminum destined for other markets into the now more profitable American market.[3] Thus assuming that foreign aluminum shipped into the United States and Alcoa's aluminum were price competitive, Judge Hand was wrong to include only foreign aluminum actually imported into the United States in the relevant market. He should have included the entire capacity of the foreign plants. In that case Alcoa's market share would have been substantially lower.

Does this analysis ignore the error that the Supreme Court made in the *Cellophane* case? Perhaps foreign aluminum was entering the United States market because Alcoa was already charging a monopoly price. In this case the fact that *some* aluminum was coming into the United States suggests that Alcoa was unable to exclude the foreign production. Suppose, for example, that Alcoa's costs were $1.00 per unit. It produces all the domestic aluminum there is. Foreign competitors also have costs of $1.00 per unit, but they additionally have 30¢ in transportation costs. In that case Alcoa would be able to charge $1.29 for its aluminum in the United States and exclude all the foreign competition. On the other hand, if it charged $1.31 for aluminum it would have no way of limiting the amount of foreign aluminum that came in. The fact that *some* foreign aluminum was coming in at Alcoa's current market prices suggests that Alcoa did not have sufficiently low costs to exclude these importers. The full capacity of the importers who were actually importing some aluminum into the United States should have been included in the relevant market.[4]

3. Judge Hand noted as much:

While the record is silent, we may therefore assume—the plaintiff having the burden—that, had "Alcoa" raised its prices, more ingot would have been imported. Thus there is a distinction between domestic and foreign competition: the first is limited in quantity, and can increase only by an increase in plant and personnel; the second is of producers who, we must assume, produce much more than they import and whom a rise in price will presumably induce immediately to divert to the American market what they had been selling elsewhere.

148 F.2d at 426.

4. See Landes & Posner, Market Power in Antitrust Cases, 94 Harv.L. Rev. 937, 966–967 (1981); 2 P. Areeda & D. Turner, Antitrust Law ¶ 532 (1978). If there were an absolute quota, however—a legal maximum amount of aluminum that could be imported into the United States in any given year—then only the legal limit should be included in the relevant market.

An important difference between aluminum and the "flexible packaging material" presumed to be the relevant product in the *Cellophane* case is that aluminum is fungible while the packaging material is not. As a result duPont could price its product in such a way as to include one set of buyers (such as

This does not mean that the entire world aluminum capacity should have been included in the relevant market. Suppose that the only foreign aluminum actually sold in the United States came from all parts of Canada and Mexico, but no aluminum was coming in from Europe, even though many plants were located there. We would infer that the Mexican and Canadian plants have lower transportation or production costs, and can compete with Alcoa in the United States market, but that the European producers cannot. In that case the entire capacity of the Mexican and Canadian plants should be included in the relevant market, but not the European plants. The approach taken by the Supreme Court in the *Tampa Electric* case is a more accurate reflection of reality, and *Tampa* may have overruled *Alcoa sub silentio* on this point.[5]

In all cases, once we have decided that the output of a particular plant should be included in the relevant market, we should include that plant's entire capacity and not merely the amount that the plant is currently producing.[6] The unused capacity will act as a significant brake on the ability of any competing firm to raise its prices.

Judges have frequently ignored or misunderstood elasticity of supply, and as a result have miscalculated the defendant's market share. For example, in Telex Corp. v. IBM Corp.,[7] the issue was whether IBM monopolized the market for "plug-compatible peripherals." A peripheral is a unit such as a printer, monitor, or disk drive, that is attached to the central data processing part of a computer. Peripherals are generally designed to work with a particular central processing unit (CPU) and will not work with others. An IBM "plug-compatible" peripheral is one that is capable of easy attachment and use with an IBM CPU. Telex and other plaintiffs alleged that IBM monopolized the market for peripherals that were plug-compatible with its own CPUs. IBM's share of the market for IBM plug-compatible peripherals was quite large. But if *all* peripherals were included in the market, IBM's share was fairly small.

The district judge found that IBM plug-compatible peripherals were a relevant market because the elasticity of demand was low:

retail butchers) but exclude another set (bakers). The producer of a fungible product does not have that choice. Alcoa must price its aluminum low enough to exclude all foreign competition. If it charges a price high enough to admit *some* foreign aluminum, which is identical to its own, then it has no way of controlling the amount of sales it will lose to foreign producers.

5. Tampa Electric Co. v. Nashville Coal Co., 365 U.S. 320, 81 S.Ct. 623 (1961). See § 3.5 below.

6. "Capacity" must be measured with some care, however. A plant can have a very large capacity if cost is not a factor. In this case the relevant capacity is the output capability of a plant at an average cost no higher than average cost at its current output level. See G. Stigler, the Theory of Price 156–158 (3d ed. 1966). In addition, the capacity should be reduced by long-term contractual commitments that will tie up part of the competing firm's output.

7. 510 F.2d 894 (10th Cir.1975), cert. dismissed 423 U.S. 802, 96 S.Ct. 8 (1975).

. customers who already owned IBM CPUs could not use peripherals unless they were compatible.[8]

In reversing, the circuit court noted two things: first, a producer of IBM non-plug-compatible peripherals could easily and cheaply switch to producing plug-compatible peripherals; secondly, by the use of an "interface," which cost as little as $100, a non-compatible peripheral could often be made compatible with the IBM. Because of the degree of "substitutability of production" the circuit court concluded that the relevant market should include all peripherals, and not merely those plug-compatible with IBM central processing units.[9]

Likewise, Calnetics Corp. v. Volkswagen of America[10] involved an allegation that an automobile manufacturer's acquisition of a firm that produced automobile air conditioners was an illegal vertical merger under § 7 of the Clayton Act. If the relevant product market was "Volkswagen air conditioners," then the percentage of the relevant market "foreclosed" by the vertical merger was large enough to be illegal under the legal standard established for vertical acquisitions.[11] On the other hand, if the relevant market was air conditioners for all compact automobiles, then the percentage of the market foreclosed by the merger was not very high. The district judge held that the relevant market was Volkswagen air conditioners and condemned the merger.[12] The circuit court reversed, holding that the lower court had refused to consider "production cross elasticity * * *."[13] Although a Volkswagen air conditioner, once built, would fit only Volkswagens, a plant capable of manufacturing automobile air conditioners could easily shift its production to air conditioners for any model automobile.

8. Telex Corp. v. IBM Corp., 367 F.Supp. 258, 280–82, 336–37 (N.D. Okl. 1973), judgment reversed, 510 F.2d 894 (10th Cir.1975), cert. dismissed, 423 U.S. 802, 96 S.Ct. 8 (1975).

9. 510 F.2d at 919.

10. 348 F.Supp. 606 (C.D.Cal.1972), reversed on this issue, 532 F.2d 674 (9th Cir.1976), cert. denied, 429 U.S. 940, 97 S.Ct. 355 (1976).

11. See § 7.3 below.

12. 348 F.Supp. at 618.

13. 532 F.2d at 691. In Heatransfer Corp. v. Volkswagenwerk, A.G., 553 F.2d 964 (5th Cir. 1977), cert. denied, 434 U.S. 1087, 98 S.Ct. 1282 (1978), the Fifth Circuit decided that Volkswagen air conditioners was a relevant market. See also Twin City Sportservice, Inc. v. Charles O. Finley & Co., 512 F.2d 1264 (9th Cir. 1975), appeal after remand 676 F.2d 1291 (9th Cir. 1982), cert. denied 459 U.S. 1009, 103 S.Ct. 364 (1982), in which the court refused to hold that the defendant possessed market power in the provision of concession services at major league baseball stadiums. "Many aspects of the concession services provided at major league baseball games were identical to the services provided at other public events. The same concessionaries often covered a variety of events and used the same equipment and employees for all of them." The court concluded that the relevant market was concession services for all leisure time activities. A hot dog is a hot dog, even at the opera.

Some courts continue to give little weight to elasticity of supply in defining markets. See Kaiser Alum. & Chem. Corp. v. FTC, 652 F.2d 1324 (7th Cir. 1981).

WESTLAW REFERENCES
elastic*** /3 supply /s market
relevant /3 market /s elastic*** /s substitut!

§ 3.5 The Geographic Market

Someone who has market power does not generally have it everywhere. A relevant market for antitrust purposes includes both a product market and a geographic market.[1] Firms that produce different products are considered not to compete with each other. Likewise, firms that sell the same product in mutually exclusive geographic areas are considered not to compete with each other. The size of the geographic market depends on the nature of the product and of the people who buy and sell it. The relevant geographic market for Alcoa's aluminum, for example, was the entire United States. On the other hand, the owner of the only movie theatre in Ozona, Texas, probably has substantial market power in Ozona, but virtually none 50 miles away.

Elasticity of demand and supply are important to determining the proper geographic market, and most of the discussion in the preceding four sections applies as much to geographic markets as to product markets. For example, assume that widgets are manufactured in Chicago and St. Louis. The owner of Chicago's only widget factory may have no market power if all its customers can costlessly shift their purchases to the St. Louis manufacturers. Likewise, the Chicago widget manufacturer will have no market power in Chicago if the St. Louis manufacturers can flood the Chicago outlets at a price close to the Chicago manufacturer's costs.

The relevant geographic market for antitrust purposes is some "section of the country" in which a firm can increase its price without 1) large numbers of its customers immediately turning to alternative supply sources outside the area; or 2) producers outside the area quickly flooding the area with substitute products. If either of these things happens when the firm attempts to charge a supracompetitive price, then the estimated geographic market has been drawn too narrowly and a larger market must be drawn to include these outside suppliers.[2]

§ 3.5

1. Determination of a relevant product market and of a relevant geographic market both address the same question: is there a grouping of sales in which the defendant has market power? As a result the distinction made between the two markets in antitrust case law is exaggerated. Two economists have noted that "From the standpoint of economic analysis the distinction between product and geographic markets is not particularly useful." Ordover & Willig, The 1982 Department of Justice Merger Guidelines: An Economic Assessment, 71 Calif.L.Rev. 535, 543 (1983).

2. See Landes & Posner, Market Power in Antitrust Cases, 94 Harv.L. Rev. 937, 963–972 (1981); 2 P. Areeda & D. Turner, Antitrust Law, ¶¶ 522–23 (1978).

On the demand side many geographic markets are relatively small, particularly if the market serves retail customers directly. The average grocery store customer, for example, would probably not drive more than 10 or 12 miles to buy groceries.[3] On the supply side, however, competition in the grocery business might cover a wide region, particularly if the competitors are chains that operate in several states. For example, if grocery chains A & B both operate in California and chain A has a store in Sacramento which is earning monopoly profits, chain B will likely regard the Sacramento market as attractive for entry.

The Supreme Court must have had elasticity of supply in mind when it decided that the merger in United States v. Von's Grocery Co.,[4] was a merger between competitors, and therefore should be treated as a horizontal merger. The merger united two grocery store chains, Von's, Inc. and Shopping Bag, Inc., that operated in the Los Angeles area. The Von's stores were located in the southwest part of the city, however, and the Shopping Bag stores were located in the northeast part.[5] Except for a few pairs of stores in the middle of the city, the Von's stores did not compete on the demand side with the Shopping Bag stores. Few consumers would drive half way across Los Angeles to buy groceries. On the other hand, analysis of elasticity of supply might indicate that the market was indeed city-wide. Von's could probably service any store in the city from its warehouses. As a result, if there were supracompetitive profits to be earned in the northeast part of the city, Von's could easily have responded by building its own stores there.[6]

The geographic market definition in United States v. Grinnell Corp.,[7] was a little more problematic. The Supreme Court decided that the defendant had monopolized the business of providing accredited central station protective services, and that the relevant market was the entire United States. An accredited central station protective service involved an electronic hook-up between a building to be protected and a central station that monitored the building for break-ins, fires, or other threatening events. "Accredited" services were approved by insurers and qualified the subscriber for lower premiums. The nature of the central station system meant that people who owned buildings in Chicago had to purchase their services from the Chicago station, people in St. Louis from the St. Louis station, etc. On the demand side the market was quite clearly local.

In explaining why it accepted a nationwide market, rather than a set of individual markets, the Supreme Court observed that the

3. See United States v. Von's Grocery Co., 384 U.S. 270, 296, 86 S.Ct. 1478, 1492 (1966).

4. Id.

5. Id. at 295, 86 S.Ct. at 1492 (J. Stewart, dissenting).

6. In merger cases courts have generally regarded high elasticity of supply as evidence of "potential" rather than actual competition. See chapter twelve below.

7. 384 U.S. 563, 86 S.Ct. 1698 (1966).

defendant had a "national schedule of prices, rates, and terms, though the rates may be varied to meet local conditions."[8] This is merely another way of saying that the defendant charged its profit-maximizing price in each city. Where it faced competition that price was generally lower than it was in cities where it had a monopoly.

On the supply side, however, ADT may have been able to exercise market power on a nationwide basis. For example, it might have used below-cost pricing in one city to "signal" its willingness to engage in predatory pricing to competitors located in many cities.[9] However, the court did not cite any evidence that the defendant was actually engaged in such practices, or even that it was capable of doing so.

The Court ordered Grinnell to divest its stations in some cities.[10] This order is consistent with the decision that the market was nationwide and not citywide. If the court's market definition was incorrect, however, and the defendant really had a large number of citywide monopolies, then the only effect of the divestiture was to give the defendant a smaller number of monopolies than it had before. The court must have thought that if there were two or more nationwide companies competing for the business of providing central station protective services, then any attempt by one to charge monopoly prices in a certain city would invite entry by the competitor. On that basis, the court's decision that the market was nationwide may have been correct. By increasing the number of firms supplying central station services, the court increased the elasticity of supply in the market. The effect would be to reduce the defendant's market power even if the market were completely local on the demand side.

A study of price movements in two different areas will generally help a court determine whether they should be included in the same geographic markets. For example, if over a certain period a price decrease in area A is always followed by a price decrease in area B, and vice-versa, A and B are probably in the same geographic market. Likewise, if producers in A make sales in both areas A and B the two are likely a single geographic market.[11] Thus in Tampa Electric Co. v. Nashville Coal Co.,[12] the Supreme Court decided that the petitioner did not have monopsony power in the market for coal sold in Florida, because coal producers as far away as western Kentucky were eager to sell coal at the competitive price in the Florida market. This

8. 384 U.S. at 575, 86 S.Ct. at 1706. The district court had found that customers of a particular station were located within 25 miles of the station. It nevertheless concluded that the relevant market was national because "financing, selling, advertising, purchasing of equipment, process of management, and overall planning" were conducted by central company headquarters on a national scale. 236 F.Supp. at 253.

9. See Salop, Strategic Entry Deterrence, 69 Amer.Econ.Rev. 335 (1979).

10. 384 U.S. at 577–79, 86 S.Ct. at 1707–08.

11. See L.A. Draper & Son v. Wheelabrator-Frye, Inc., 735 F.2d 414, 422–26 (11th Cir. 1984); and see 2 P. Areeda & D. Turner, Antitrust Law ¶ 522 (1978).

12. 365 U.S. 320, 81 S.Ct. 623 (1961).

suggested to the court that not only the Kentucky producers of coal, but all coal producers closer to Florida than the Kentucky producers should be included in the relevant geographic market.

Furthermore, once we have determined that a remote plant in Kentucky can provide coal to the Florida market at the competitive price, we should include the entire capacity of the Kentucky plant, and not merely the amount that it is shipping into the Florida market. If the Kentucky plant can profitably sell *any* of its coal into the Florida market, then it will probably be able to respond to a price increase in the Florida market by selling even more coal there.[13]

Determining a relevant geographic market means identifying some area such that the firm or firms inside the area have a cost advantage over firms not inside the area. In that case the favored firms will be able to raise the price as much as the cost advantage permits. Frequently the local firms' cost advantage results from transportation costs. For example, if Dallas and Denver producers can both produce widgets at a cost of $1.00, but it costs 25¢ to ship widgets from Dallas to Denver, then a Denver monopolist could charge any price up to $1.25 on the Denver market without worrying about competition from Dallas. The size of the geographic market depends heavily on the relationship between the value of the product and the costs of shipping. Certain products such as cement and gravel have very high transportation costs in proportion to their value. A Dallas producer of cement would probably not worry about competition from Denver producers. On the other hand, the transportation costs of mink coats may be trivial in comparison to their value, and a Denver manufacturer could respond quickly to a price increase in the Dallas market. Other costs such as labor, the costs of state and local regulation, and access to inputs, can also affect the determination of the relevant geographic market.

The availability of price discrimination devices such as delivered or basing point pricing systems should be considered in any definition of the relevant geographic market. Basing-point and delivered pricing systems frequently enable sellers to obtain monopoly returns from nearby "captive" customers, while competing for more remote customers who may be equally close to alternative suppliers. In such circumstances the seller may "compete" in a relatively large geographic area, while continuing to earn significant monopoly profits in a smaller area.[14] Improved competition in the smaller area should be an important concern of the antitrust laws. Accordingly, the smaller area should be considered a relevant geographic market.[15]

13. See the discussion above in § 3.4.

14. See Haddock, Basing-Point Pricing: Competitive vs. Collusive Theories, 72 Amer.Econ.Rev. 289 (1982). Basing point pricing is discussed in § 4.2 below.

15. See Ordover & Willig, The 1982 Dept. of Justice Merger Guidelines: An Economic Assessment, 71 Calif.L.Rev. 535, 548 (1983).

Geographic markets are often asymmetrical. Suppose that A Co. and B Co., which make chocolate cream pies in Manhattan, plan to merge. Each company sells 15% of the pies sold in Manhattan. There are 15 producers of pies in Manhattan, and there is no evidence that they are colluding. However, there are a large number of pie makers in nearby Brooklyn, who have lower labor costs and can produce equally good pies at a lower price. Currently many of the pies retailed in Manhattan are baked and shipped there by the Brooklyn companies.

In this case the Manhattan pie makers operate at a cost disadvantage with respect to the Brooklyn companies. Any attempt by the Manhattan pie makers to charge a supracompetitive price will flood the market with Brooklyn pies. Therefore the full plant capacity of the Brooklyn pie makers must be included in the relevant market. The market shares of A Co. and B Co. may be substantially lower as a result.

It would not follow, however, that Manhattan must be included in the relevant market if two Brooklyn companies planned to merge. In fact, on the above facts it is clear that the Manhattan pie makers will not be able to compete effectively with the Brooklyn pie makers in Brooklyn unless the Brooklyn price rises substantially above the competitive level. In a merger case involving two Brooklyn pie makers, Manhattan should not be included in the relevant geographic market.

 WESTLAW REFERENCES

digest,synopsis(relevant /3 geograph! /3 market)
elastic*** /3 demand supply /p geograph! /3 market
265k20(7)
delivered basing-point /3 pric*** /p compet! & geograph!

§ 3.6 Market Definition in the Justice Department Merger Guidelines

The 1984 Merger Guidelines issued by the United States Department of Justice (DOJ)[1] state the criteria that the DOJ will use to determine whether it will challenge a particular merger. The Guidelines also describe how the DOJ will determine the relevant market in merger cases. The 1984 guidelines define markets exclusively for the purpose of analyzing mergers, in which the chief concern is not exercises of market power by a single firm, but rather increased likelihood of collision.[2] However, many of the economic principles of

§ 3.6

1. 49 Fed.Reg. 26,823 (1984). The 1984 Guidelines are a technical revision of Guidelines that originally appeared in 1982. Most of the law review commentary cited here was written in reference

to the 1982 Guidelines, but is equally applicable to the 1984 Guidelines.

2. See Werden, Market Delineation and the Justice Department's Merger Guidelines, 1983 Duke L.J. 514, which

market delineation developed in the guidelines serve equally well in other antitrust contexts.

The DOJ defines a relevant product market as "a group of products such that a　*　*　*　firm that was the only present and future seller of those products ("monopolist") could profitably impose a 'small but significant and nontransitory' increase in price." In determining such a group of products the DOJ will begin with the product or products of the defendant alone (say, Ford automobiles). Then it will add in the products that the firm's customers view as good substitutes at "prevailing prices." [3]

Next the DOJ will hypothesize a "small but significant and nontransitory" price increase and estimate how many buyers would shift to substitutes. If so many would shift that the price increase would be unprofitable, then the proposed market is too small. The DOJ will redraw the market to include these substitutes and then repeat the process. When it has identified a grouping of products such that large numbers of customers could not substitute away in response to the small but significant price increase, it has defined a relevant product market. The DOJ notes that in most cases a "small but significant and nontransitory" price increase will mean a price increase of five percent which lasts for one year. However, the amount and duration of the price increase will depend on the nature of the industry.[4]

On the supply side the DOJ notes that "if a firm has existing productive and distributive facilities that could easily and economically be used to produce and sell the relevant product within one year in response to a 'small but significant and nontransitory increase in price,' the Department will include that firm in the market." As an exception the DOJ notes that some firms might easily be able to switch production to the product subject to the price increase; however, they may not be able to distribute the new product efficiently. Costs of changing a distribution system or adopting a new one must

gives step-by-step instructions for defining a market under the 1982 guidelines.

Because the Guidelines are heavily concerned with collusion, they regard product differentiation as a mitigating rather than aggravating factor—that is, since collusion is less likely when product differentiation is substantial, the DOJ is less likely to challenge a merger in such a market. 49 Fed.Reg. at 26,832–33. See §§ 4.1–4.2 below. Some critics believe this leniency in differentiated markets overlooks the fact that differentiated markets are more conducive to horizontal product or customer division. See Davidson, The Competitive Significance of Segmented Markets, 71 Calif.L.Rev. 445, 446 (1983). For a generally contrary view, see Maisel, Submarkets in Merger and Monopolization Cases, 72 Geo.L.J. 39 (1983).

3.　49 Fed.Reg. at 26,828. The use of "prevailing prices" is appropriate for market definition in merger cases, although it would not be in monopolization cases. The monopolist would likely price its output at a level where the cross elasticity of demand is high. See the discussion of the *du Pont* case in § 3.3, above. In merger cases, however, the market share of the firms is sufficiently low to create an inference that their current prices are competitive.

4.　49 Fed.Reg. at 26,828.

be considered by any firm contemplating a production change to a product that appears to be more profitable. If these costs would likely make the substitution unprofitable, the firm will not be included in the relevant market.[5]

The Guidelines follow a similar approach for determining a relevant geographic market:

> In general, the Department seeks to identify a geographic area such that a hypothetical firm that was the only present or future producer *or seller* of the relevant product in that area could profitably impose a "small but significant and nontransitory" increase in price. That is, assuming that buyers could respond to a price increase within a tentatively identified area only by shifting to firms located outside the area, what would happen? If firms located elsewhere readily could provide the relevant product to the hypothetical firm's buyers in sufficient quantity at a comparable price, an attempt to raise price would not prove profitable, and the tentatively identified geographic area will prove to have been too narrowly defined.[6]

The DOJ will initially establish a provisional market based on the existing pattern of shipments of the firm and its closest competitors. The Department will then hypothesize a "small but significant and nontransitory increase in price" and consider how many firms outside the area could ship into it. If the addition of these firms is significant enough to suggest that the price increase would be unprofitable, the DOJ will draw a larger geographic circle to include these firms. It will repeat the process until it reaches a geographic market in which the hypothetical price increase would be profitable.

In making this assessment the DOJ will give heavy consideration to the following factors, although it is not clear exactly how they will be weighed:

(1) Shipment patterns of the merging firm and of its actual competitors;

(2) Evidence of buyers actually having considered shifting their purchases among sellers at different geographic locations, especially if the shifts corresponded to changes in relative price or other competitive variables;

(3) Similarities or differences in the price movements of the relative product in different geographic areas over a period of years;

(4) Transportation costs;

(5) Costs of local distribution; and

(6) Excess capacity held by firms outside the location of the merging firm.

5. Id. at 26,829.
6. Id.

The Guidelines are likely to result in larger markets than courts have defined in the past.[7] For example, the inclusion of excess capacity in defined markets will often reduce a firm's market share. Likewise, the "small but significant price increase" rule seems calculated to regard as "competitive" firms that were not considered so when market definition was predicated entirely on current prices.

Perhaps the most substantial criticism of the Guidelines is that, their appearance of economic precision notwithstanding, they add a great deal of uncertainty to market definition. "Hypothesizing" a "small but significant" price increase in a fluctuating market, and then considering how neighboring firms will respond, requires predictive abilities not demanded by the old analysis of current prices and shipments. Furthermore, the predictions must be made in situations in which the variables are manifold and complex. It is by no means clear that the Guidelines' approach to market definition will simplify litigation or produce more consistent rules. If courts choose to follow the Guidelines and if they are up to the task, however, market definition may come closer to reflecting competitive realities.[8]

 WESTLAW REFERENCES
(department /2 justice) d.o.j. /s "merger guidelines"
(department /2 justice) d.o.j. /p "excess capacity" "line of
   commerce" "product market"

§ 3.7 Alternative Methods of Establishing Market Power

Computation of a firm's market share involves a plethora of uncertainties. As a result market share analysis does not always produce a reliable measure of a firm's market power. The exercise

7. The fact that the 1984 Guidelines will yield larger relevant markets does not invariably mean that more mergers will be approved by the DOJ. On the one hand, larger markets will reduce the market shares of the firms in the market. On the other hand, the larger markets may be used to characterize as "horizontal" mergers that under traditional analysis would be characterized as product extension or market extension mergers. See U.S. v. Virginia National Bankshares, Inc., 1982–2 Trade Cases (CCH) ¶ 64,871 (W.D.Va.1982).

8. For criticism of the 1982 Guidelines' approach to market definition, see Shenefield, Market Definition and Horizontal Restraints: A Response to Professor Areeda, 52 A.B.A. Antitrust L.J. 587, 597 (1983); Harris & Jorde, Antitrust Market Definition: An Integrated Approach, 72 Calif.L.Rev. 1 (1984); Harris & Jorde, Market Definition in the Merger Guidelines: Implications for An-

titrust Enforcement, 71 Calif.L.Rev. 464 (1983); Ordover & Willing, The 1982 Dep't of Justice Merger Guidelines: An Economic Assessment, 71 Calif.L.Rev. 535, 543–552 (1983); the latter note that the DOJ's proposals for market definition rest on the assumption that the firms are not practicing price discrimination. Price discrimination by a firm within a single geographic market generally suggests that the firm already has some market power. That should invite close scrutiny of any proposed merger, particularly if it is horizontal. The Guidelines do note that sellers capable of price discriminating might succeed in raising price "only to groups of buyers who cannot easily substitute away." In that case, the DOJ may define a smaller market in which the discriminatory price increase is possible. 49 Fed.Reg. at 26,828. See the discussion of price discrimination below in chap. thirteen.

of the power to raise prices by reducing output leaves certain traces, however, and these can sometimes be used as evidence of market power. In general, courts have not used the following methods exclusively to determine market power; rather, they have been used to supplement market share data and give greater strength to an inference that a firm has or does not have market power.

Persistent Price Discrimination [1]

Not all purchasers of widgets place the same value on them. Suppose that the marginal cost of producing a widget is $1.00. Some buyers will be willing to pay exactly $1.00 for them, others $1.25, others $1.50. A seller can maximize its profits by selling every widget to a customer for the largest price that particular customer is willing to pay. Competition prevents such persistent price discrimination from occurring, however. Even though a particular customer is willing to pay $1.50 for a widget, the customer would prefer to pay $1.00 and will do so if it can find a willing seller. Competition tends to drive all sales to the competitive price.

The monopolist has the power to discriminate, however, provided that it can identify and segregate groups of customers who place different values on the monopolist's product. Not all sellers with market power engage in price discrimination; however, persistent price discrimination is evidence that a seller has market power. It is often much easier to measure price discrimination empirically than it is to determine the difference between a seller's prices and its marginal costs. For example, if we see widely different prices being charged to two groups of customers for whom the cost of service seems to be about the same, we suspect price discrimination, even though we know nothing about the seller's marginal costs.

Only "persistent" price discrimination is evidence of market power. In an imperfect world price discrimination is a common occurrence, even in the most competitive of markets. Prices fluctuate daily as markets are continually shocked by new information and changing supply and demand conditions. Price discrimination is good evidence of market power only when a particular seller has been able systematically to achieve a higher rate of return from one group of customers than it does from another.

A seller with market power can price discriminate in a variety of ways. In the *Alcoa* case for example, Judge Hand noted that Alcoa had different rates of return for aluminum ingot, aluminum sheet, and aluminum cable, depending on the amount of competition it faced in the particular section of the aluminum market.[2] Such differential rates of return would not be possible for a perfect competitor.

§ 3.7

1. For a more complete discussion of price discrimination, see chap. thirteen below.

2. U.S. v. Alum. Co. of America, 148 F.2d 416, 438 (2d Cir. 1945).

Likewise in *United Shoe Machinery* Judge Wyzanski noted that the defendant leased its machinery at different rates of return, depending on the amount of competition that it faced.[3]

A very common price discrimination mechanism is the variable proportion tying arrangement.[4] Often a seller or lessor will grant a customer one product only on the condition that it take another. In the 1936 IBM case, for example, IBM was accused of leasing computing machines only to lessees who also agreed to purchase paper computing cards from IBM. Assuming that IBM's rate of return on paper cards was higher than its rate of return on the machine itself, IBM was in fact price discriminating against lessees who used the computing machines heavily.[5] IBM was taking advantage of the fact that a lessee who made, say, 1000 computations daily requiring one card each, placed a higher value on the machine itself than a lessee who made only 10 computations per day. By charging the same, fairly low rate for the machine to all lessees (say, a 5% rate of return) and a higher rate for the cards (say, 25%) IBM could effectively receive a much higher overall rate of return from high volume users of the machine.

IBM's price discrimination scheme could be successful, however, only if IBM had market power in the market for the computing machines. If there had been significant competition in the computing machine market, then the high volume purchasers—those asked to pay the supracompetitive overall price—would have leased or purchased their computing machines from someone willing to give them a more competitive rate. The law of tie-ins generally requires a plaintiff to show that the defendant has market power in the tying product. Most often, however, that market power can be inferred from the mere existence of the variable proportion tying arrangement.[6]

Persistent price discrimination is fairly good evidence that a seller has *some* market power. It is virtually impossible, however, to quantify a seller's market power on the basis of price discrimination. The success of a price discrimination scheme depends on the seller's market power *and* on its ability to segregate customers and prevent arbitrage. The fact that a seller discriminates in a relatively narrow range may indicate that the seller cannot segregate customers very effectively, not that it has only a small amount of market power. Another seller with far less market power may be much more successful at price discrimination if buyers in its market can more

---

3. U.S. v. United Shoe Machinery, 110 F. Supp. 295, 297 (D.Mass.1953), affirmed, 347 U.S 521, 74 S.Ct. 699 (1954).

4. See § 8.8 below.

5. International Business Machines Corp. v. U.S., 298 U.S. 131, 136, 56 S.Ct. 701, 704 (1936).

6. The existence of a variable proportion tie-in is not necessarily evidence of market power, however. The tie could be a nondiscriminatory metering device that simply measures the wear and tear on the machine. See § 8.8, below.

easily be segregated and arbitrage prevented, perhaps because the buyers are not as well informed. As a result evidence of price discrimination may be fairly useful in tying arrangement cases, where the market power requirements are relatively small. It may also be useful in a cartel case to prove that the defendants are colluding. It is somewhat less useful in a monopolization case, where proof of "monopoly power" is necessary.

Finally, price discrimination in a market may be evidence that the market contains one or more powerful, monopsony *buyers*, rather than monopoly sellers. A monopsonist may be able to reduce its demand for a product and buy at a lower price. A seller who deals with the monopsonist as well as other buyers may be price discriminating even though it has no market power.[7]

Persistent Monopoly Profits

As § 1.3 above indicated, the monopolist does not always make significant monopoly profits. The monopolist may spend most of its anticipated monopoly profits in various exclusionary practices and end up making little more than a competitive rate of return.

The argument has a converse, however. Not all monopolists will spend their entire monopoly profits in protecting their monopoly position. Persistent monopoly profits would appear to be inconsistent with competition and may be fairly good evidence of monopoly power. Both courts and commentators have cited persistent supracompetitive profits as good evidence that a firm has monopoly power.[8]

Such evidence comes with one enormous, potentially disabling qualification, however. The fact-finder must be able to distinguish between monopoly profits and "rents." Not all firms in a competitive market have identical costs. First-comers, for example, are likely to take advantage of the best sites and leave increasingly marginal sites for those who come later.

Figure One illustrates the problem in a competitive market, in which each firm faces a horizontal demand curve. The industry supply curve, however, rises to competitive equilibrium at its intersection with the demand curve. If the price at that point (the competitive market price) is $20, then we know that the least efficient firm (the marginal firm) capable of sustaining itself in the market is a firm whose costs are $20. The market may contain other firms, however,

---

7. See L. Sullivan, Handbook of the Law of Antitrust 89 (1977); see § 1.2 above.

8. See 2 P. Areeda & D. Turner, Antitrust Law ¶¶ 508–13 (1978). In the *du Pont* (cellophane) case, 351 U.S. 377, 76 S.Ct. 994 (1956), discussed above in § 3.3, the evidence indicated that du Pont had an extraordinarily high rate of return on cellophane: 31% before taxes. 351 U.S. at 420, 76 S.Ct. at 1020 (Chief Justice Warren, dissenting). In other markets, such as rayon, du Pont's rate of return was much lower. Id. at 420–21 n. 15, 76 S.Ct. at 1020.

whose costs are much less than $20. These firms may make high profits even though they are not monopolists—that is, they may have a trivial share of the market and no power to charge a higher price by reducing their output.

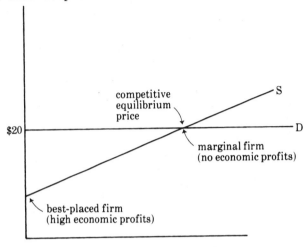

FIGURE ONE

For example, in the 20 years from 1960 to 1980 real estate prices in San Francisco increased as much as twentyfold. San Francisco has approximately 100 Continental restaurants. Some of those restaurants have been in business for more than 20 years, and their owners bought their locations when both real estate prices and interest rates were low. Today those restaurants have mortgage payments of $200 per month, or perhaps no mortgage payments at all. At the other extreme are new entrants who must pay rentals on the order of $4000 per month. No restaurant is a monopolist. Further, the old restaurants generally do not have the power to increase their seating capacity at their original costs—any new space they acquire will be at the same high rate as their newer competitors. However, if the cost of restaurant space is a substantial part of the cost of operating a restaurant, the old restaurants with the low space costs will earn higher profits than the new restaurants which have much higher space costs. Furthermore, the best-placed restaurants' low cost space is protected from new entry: any newcomer will have to pay the higher rental rate. These rents, unlike monopoly profits, are not likely to be consumed by the best-placed restaurants' efforts to retain their monopoly position.

Rents are commonplace in most competitive businesses. Some farmers have fertile soil or ample irrigation supplies, or both; some have neither. Some miners have rich reserves, others marginal. An unusually efficient manager or president can give one firm a cost advantageous over competitors, even though the firm may have no monopoly power.

Persistent, supracompetitive profits are a sign of market power only if the fact-finder can distinguish monopoly profits from rents. Often it will be unable to distinguish the two. As a result the chief function of profit data should be merely to support an inference of market power developed on the basis of conventional market share criteria.

 WESTLAW REFERENCES

(a) Persistent Price Discrimination

"market power" tying   /28   "price discrimination" "variable proportion"

(b) Persistent Monopoly Profits

"market power" monopol***   /p   continu*** persistent   /4   profits

CHAPTER 4

CARTELS, JOINT VENTURES AND OTHER COMBINATIONS OF COMPETITORS

Table of Sections

§ 4.1 Introduction: The Economics of Price Fixing

The simplest cartel is an agreement among perfect competitors to sell all their output at the same, agreed upon price. By entering such an agreement the firms acting in concert can reduce output and earn monopoly profits just as a single-firm monopolist.

Cartels are inherently more volatile than single-firm monopolists. First, they can come into existence far more easily. The formation of a monopoly may take many years of mergers, superior research and development, marketing, predation or simply good luck. A cartel, on the other hand, theoretically can be created overnight.

More importantly, however, even absent legal restraint the cartel is inherently more fragile than the single-firm monopolist. The interests of the cartel as a whole often diverge substantially from the interests of individual members. The nature of a cartel is to invite cheating by members. Often cleverly disguised cheating can impose rather small losses on the cartel as a whole, but give large gains to the individual cheater. If enough cartel members cheat, however, the cartel will fall apart. As a result most cartels go to extraordinary lengths to reduce the opportunities for cheating.

The perfect cartel would contain relatively few members who collectively account for 100% of the production in a relevant market. All members would be the same size and equally efficient, and they would produce identical products. The product would be sold by sealed auction bids made by the sellers in a market containing many, relatively small purchasers, and the winning bids publicly announced.

The cartel would have the most success in raising price by reducing output if its members controlled 100% of the market. If they were equally efficient and produced identical products they would all have the same profit-maximizing price and easily would agree about a cartel price. If they were the same size they would have little trouble allocating the output reduction among members. If the cartel had relatively few members, made its sales by sealed auction bids with publicly announced results, and sold to a large number of small buyers, there would be little opportunity for cheating.[1]

The real world contains few such markets. The products of different competing firms often differ from each other, and the firms vary even more. Few markets make their sales by simple auction bidding. The variations from one market to another are considerable. As a result some markets are more conducive to cartelization than others, and in some markets effective cartelization is impossible.

Theoretically the cartel would determine its profit-maximizing price just as a single-firm monopoly would. For example, if the cartel controlled 100% of the market and new entry was relatively slow, the cartel price would be close to the intersection of the market's marginal revenue curve with the marginal cost curve of the firms.[2] The cartel faces problems that the monopolist does not, however, because individual members of the cartel generally have different costs: some are more efficient than others; different firms may operate on different portions of their average cost curves (for example, some may have excess capacity while others do not); some may produce slightly different products, which cost either a little less or a little more than the product sold by other cartel members.

Figure One illustrates some of these difficulties. Assume for simplicity's sake that three firms are the same size. Operating at optimum capacity each would produce the same number of widgets. Firms 1 and 2 produce identical widgets, but firm 1 is more efficient. Firm 1's marginal costs are MC_1 while firm 2's marginal costs are

§ 4.1

1. For evidence that cartels are most successful in such situations see Hay & Kelley, An Empirical Survey of Price Fixing Conspiracies, 17 J.L. & Econ. 13 (1974).

2. If the monopolist or cartel controlled less than 100% of the market, or if entry was easy and rapid, the fixed price would be less than the short-run profit-maximizing price determined by the intersection of the marginal revenue and marginal cost curves. Otherwise the monopolist's or cartel's market share would erode too quickly. See the discussion in §§ 1.2–1.3 above.

MC_2. Firm 3 has still higher marginal costs, MC_3 but it also produces a higher quality widget that commands a higher price. As a result firm 3 operates on a demand curve, D', which is to the right of demand curve D, the curve that firms 1 and 2 face in a cartelized market. At any given price demand for firm 3's widgets is greater than the demand for widgets produced by firms 1 or 2. Likewise, at any given output level firm 3's widgets will clear the market at a higher price. Because firm 3 faces a different demand curve, it also has a different marginal revenue curve. The marginal revenue curve for firms 1 and 2 is MR, while the marginal revenue curve for firm 3 is MR'.

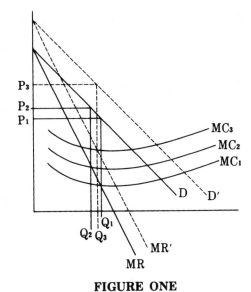

FIGURE ONE

Will the three firms agree about a cartel price? Each firm will want to equate its own anticipated marginal revenue with its own marginal cost. Firm 1 will maximize its profits at a price of P_1, firm 2 at a price of P_2, and firm 3 at a price of P_3. Any cartel price reached by the three firms will be a compromise. A firm whose individual profit-maximizing price deviates substantially from the compromise price is likely to feel cheated, and may be more likely to cheat on the cartel. The wider the variations in the marginal costs or the products produced by the individual cartel members, the less stable the cartel will be.

Incentives to cheat are present, however, even in the most homogeneous of cartels. They are merely exacerbated by heterogeneity. If the cartel is successful each member will be selling its output at a price substantially greater than marginal cost. If a member can secretly make a sale at a lower price it can enlarge its own profits, either by attracting buyers unwilling to pay the cartel price but willing to pay the "shaved" price, or else by stealing buyers from other cartel members.

Cheating is particularly profitable in industries that have relatively high fixed costs. In the railroad industry, for example, short-run marginal costs (the costs of shipping one extra package on a partially loaded train that is already scheduled) are trivial in comparison with the total costs of operating a railroad. As a result the cartel price, which covers total costs plus monopoly profits, will be much higher than the lowest price that is profitable to the railroad. The railroad could give a substantial secret price reduction and still make large profits from the transaction.

A cartel member would not likely be able to make all its sales at a price less than the agreed cartel price. Such pervasive cheating would be quickly detected. It is much more profitable and less risky for the cartel member to honor the cartel price as a general rule, but look for opportunities to make large, secret sales at a lower price.

Cheating by secret price discrimination has been rampant in many cartels, particularly secret cartels that cannot be enforced by law (such as those within the jurisdiction of the American antitrust laws).[3] The cheater will look for opportunities to make large discriminatory sales the terms of which can be concealed. The chance of detection increases with the number of sales, so it is important that the sales be large. More often than not the terms of the sale will be disguised in some way. For example, in the 1911 *Standard Oil* case the defendant was accused of monopolizing the oil market by obtaining "secret rebates" from railroads in exchange for its trade. The secret rebates were used to explain how Standard could undersell its competitors and drive them out of business. In fact, the railroads were engaged in price fixing, and the secret rebates enabled a cheating railroad to make a large sale to Standard at a profitable price. If two or more cartelized railroads had secretly competed for Standard's business, they would have bid the rebates up to the point that the net price equaled their marginal cost. If Standard's competitors made smaller purchases of the railroads' services, however, the railroads' incentive to give them rebates would be much less. The smaller competitor would end up with higher freight costs than Standard had.[4]

---

3. For example, see the discussion of the *Addyston Pipe* cartel in 2 S. Whitney, Antitrust Policies: American Experience in 20 Industries 5 (1958); U.S. v. Addyston Pipe & Steel Co., 85 F. 271 (6th Cir. 1898), modified and affirmed, 175 U.S. 211, 20 S.Ct. 96 (1899). If the cartel is legal, of course, it might enlist the help of the government in prosecuting cheating. For an analysis of cheating in legal cartels, see McGee, Ocean Freight Rate Conferences and the American Merchant Marine, 27 U.Chi.L. Rev. 191 (1960).

4. See Standard Oil Co. v. U.S., 221 U.S. 1, 32–33, 31 S.Ct. 502, 505 (1911), charging Standard with obtaining "large preferential rates and rebates in many and devious ways over [its] competitors from various railroad companies, and * * * by means of the advantage thus obtained many, if not virtually all, competitors were forced either to become members of the combination or were driven out of business * * *."

Cartel members have become ingenious at cheating by this kind of price discrimination, and cartels have had to take elaborate measures to prevent it. For example, a cartel member may price discriminate by designating or labeling a product in such a way that it falls out of the cartel agreement. Suppose that manufacturers of bathroom fixtures have a significant percentage of "seconds"—fixtures that are usable but have slight defects and normally command a lower price. The cartel agrees about price and output of perfect fixtures, but neglects to include seconds in the agreement. If the seconds command a price higher than the cost of producing them,[5] individual cartel members will make money by selling fixtures as seconds, even though they are perfect. The market will then become flooded with these "seconds". As soon as consumers discover this, demand for the cartelized product, designated first quality, will drop. At least one famous cartel was able to solve this problem only by an agreement that all members would destroy their seconds or ship them abroad, so that none would be sold on the domestic market.[6]

A cartel member can cheat on the cartel price in a number of ways. These include secret rebates, reciprocity agreements in which the cartel member buys something back from the customer at a supracompetitive price, and increased services. In fact, often the effect of a price fixing agreement is merely to change the nature of the competition among the cartel members. Before the cartel was formed they competed in price. After they compete by throwing more and more services into the bargain until their marginal costs rise to the cartel price. The cartel members then end up with no more than a competitive rate of return. Customers take the services whether or not they would have been willing to pay their market value in a competitive market.

Some cartels have developed elaborate bookkeeping, reporting or accounting methods so that each member can check the price and output of other members. Such methods are often useless, however, because each member is likely to doubt that other members are providing full and honest disclosure. Most cartels have tried to produce alternative methods of verification—for example, by agreeing on a standard product and the services that can be provided with it, by agreeing to destroy all imperfect merchandise that would be discounted in a competitive market, by making all pricing public, or sometimes by vertically integrating into retailing so that all final output sales are small and public.

The ease of cheating varies considerably with the type of market. Cheating is most difficult (and cartels therefore most successful) in auction markets—where sales are large and relatively few and determined by secret bids with publicly announced results. In such a

5. The cartel's price increase in perfect units will increase demand for the seconds, and their price will rise.

6. See U.S. v. Trenton Potteries Co., 273 U.S. 392, 405, 47 S.Ct. 377, 382 (1927).

market the cartel members will merely pick the "winning" bidder for each prospective sale and determine the bid price. All other members agree to bid a higher price. If a different member wins the bid, the cartel members will know immediately.[7]

On the other hand, if sales are individually negotiated with specifications and terms that vary from one transaction to the next, cheating will be far more difficult to detect. Cheating is also easy to conceal if buyers and the cartel members deal with each other outside the cartelized market. For example, if a manufacturer of widgets and slidgets is involved in a widget cartel, it might cheat by selling widgets to a firm at the cartel price but giving a compensating price reduction in slidgets. Conversely, if a cartel member sells widgets but purchases slidgets from a customer, it might sell the customer widgets at the cartel price, but pay a premium price for slidgets that it buys in return.

Sometimes cartels can reduce the amount of cheating by using alternatives to the simple fixing of prices. For example, some industries may be more conducive to output restriction agreements, in which the members decide how much each should produce and sell, but the market itself determines the price. This kind of agreement generally works well in industries where the government requires detailed reporting of output, or where output or number of units sold is easy to verify.

An alternative to the output reduction agreement is the agreement on market share, with penalties for firms that exceed their assigned shares.[8] Under such an agreement each member promises to reduce its output by a certain, agreed-upon percentage. The result is that the market shares of the respective firms remain constant, although each produces less than it would under competition. Price will rise to reach a new equilibrium with output. Such an agreement can be far more flexible than a strict output reduction agreement, because it enables the parties to deal with sudden changes in demand for the product without consulting each other (which can be dangerous!). In general, market share agreements discourage firms from bidding aggressively for new customers, or from trying to use low bids to steal customers away from other cartel members.

Horizontal territorial division can be an effective method of cartelization, although it works in relatively few markets.[9] For example, four widget manufacturers may divide the country into exclusive zones. The effect of successful horizontal territorial division is to

7. As a result statutes regulating government procurement which require secret competitive bidding and public announcement of the winning bid can actually facilitate cartelization.

8. See G. Stigler, The Organization of Industry 42–43 (1983).

9. Cartelization by territorial division works only if the members are able to divide a relevant market into sections such that each is a monopolist in its own section. An alternative is horizontal customer division, in which the firms agree that each will deal exclusively with certain groups of customers.

give each cartel member a monopoly in its territory, with a promise of no competitive entry from other members. Once each firm has an exclusive territory it is free to estimate its own profit-maximizing price and make its own output decisions. As a result the cartel will be able to circumvent many of the problems of arriving at a compromise cartel price and output. Horizontal territorial division robs the firms of an opportunity to cheat simply by cutting price; however, they can still cheat by making secret sales to customers in the territory of another cartel member. This kind of cheating may be far easier to detect, particularly if the firms are fully integrated to the retail level. One problem with such territorial division, however, is that outsiders can often see what is happening. Firms who deal with the cartel members may learn quickly that each member is a monopolist in its own territory. This may invite prosecution or, perhaps more importantly, new entry by firms looking for an opportunity to make monopoly profits.

The thorn in every cartel's flesh is the firm that refuses to participate. Conversely, the outsider in a cartelized market has the best of all possible situations. First, it suffers no risk of liability. Second, it can ride on the cartel's price increases without reducing its own output. In fact, it can increase output and sell all it wishes at a large profit by charging only slightly less than the cartelized price.[10]

A nonmember who increases output too substantially can destroy a cartel by depriving it of sufficient demand to obtain supracompetitive returns. Cartel members often find it necessary to put various forms of pressure on competitors who refuse to join. Many private actions alleging illegal predatory pricing, concerted refusals to deal or a variety of business torts have been based on the theory that the defendants were attempting to cartelize the market and that the plaintiff was a competitor who refused to participate.[11]

Cartels often encounter the problem that individual members have few incentives for reducing overall costs. The single-firm monopolist generally has such incentives: it must bear the full costs of its own internal inefficiency. On the other hand, each cartel member would prefer to have a certain sale itself, even though it is not the most efficient seller in the cartel. This problem is particularly serious in markets where individual firms have natural advantages with respect to a particular customer—for example, where transportation costs are high.

Suppose that a half dozen manufacturers of heavy pipe are involved in price fixing. The firms generally deliver the pipe to

10. A few plaintiffs have attempted to obtain damages from an illegal cartel for overcharges they paid in purchases from a nonmember. See § 14.4 below.

11. For example, Utah Pie Co. v. Continental Baking Co., 386 U.S. 685, 87 S.Ct. 1326 (1967) (predatory pricing); and see Eastern States Retail Lumber Dealers' Ass'n. v. U.S., 234 U.S. 600, 34 S.Ct. 951 (1914) (boycott).

construction sites, and contractors generally select a seller by taking competitive bids. Different cartel members will be located different distances from any particular construction site, and a competitive market will favor the closest firm. If the firms have equal production costs, the closest firm to the site will be able to deliver the pipe for the lowest total price for pipe plus freight. Even a monopolist who owned all six plants would, other things being equal, deliver the pipe from the plant closest to the delivery point.

A simple price fixing agreement among the pipe manufacturers would destroy the natural advantage of the closest firm. For example, if the contractor received six identical bids for delivered pipe he would have little incentive to select the closest firm. He might be equally likely to choose a firm he has dealt with before, or perhaps even the first firm in alphabetical order. If transportation costs are a high percentage of total costs a substantial part of the monopoly overcharge would go, not to the cartel members, but to the railroad or trucking company that delivered the order.

The cartel as a whole will be best off if each particular sale is made by the cartel member who can make the sale most efficiently— that is, by the firm that would have been most likely to make the sale in a competitive market. Given a pre-fixed price, any reduction in the costs of manufacture and delivery will go to the cartel's members. Sometimes cartels preserve some of this efficiency by holding out a fixed price to customers but engaging in internal competition for the right to make the sale. For example, the cartel condemned by the Supreme Court in U.S. v. Addyston Pipe & Steel Co.[12] used a complex internal bidding arrangement to award the right to sell. First the companies agreed about a bid price that would be presented to the customer as the competitive bid. Then the cartel members bid against each other to see who would transfer the largest amount of the bid price as a "bonus" to the cartel as a whole. Presumably, that would be the firm capable of performing the job at the lowest cost. The winning member would keep the bid price less the bonus; the bonus would be divided among the cartel members in proportion to size.[13]

In spite of all these efforts, cartels are almost never able to operate as efficiently as single-firm monopolists. First of all, the cartel must sustain the significant transaction costs of bargaining, coordinating activities, and investigating and punishing cheating among its own members. To be sure, the monopolist must coordinate

---

12. Note 3 above.

13. The internal bidding scheme created certain frictions among members. Sometimes firms bid up the bonus so their own share would be larger, even though they did not want the job themselves. See G. Stigler, The Theory of Price 230–231 (3d Ed. 1966). An alternative to the internal bidding scheme is "pooling," in which each cartel member's revenues are divided among the members, usually in proportion to their market share. See McGee, Ocean Freight Rates, note 3 above, at 229–230.

as well. However, the costs of such coordination are significantly higher for the cartel, because each member's interests are different. The primary interest of each member is to maximize its own, not the cartel's, profit. Since each member knows that the other members have monopoly profits to look forward to, they will probably be willing to spend much time and resources in bargaining. This generally means a great deal of posturing—threats to pull out of the cartel, to report it to the Justice Department, to exceed quotas, etc. Some public cartels that are not reachable by the antitrust laws, such as OPEC, have nevertheless been unable to arrive at agreements that the members can accept and live with for prolonged periods. For illegal cartels, whose negotiations must be secret and infrequent, the problems are even greater.

Cartels also have far less flexibility than monopolists in coordinating overall production. For example, the monopolist who has five plants and wishes to cut production to 80% of capacity has the option of closing the least efficient plant and running the other four at optimal capacity. As a practical matter a cartel of five firms, each having one plant, does not have that option. The cartel will probably have to settle on some compromise scheme for allocating production among the members, even though the result is not optimal.[14]

As a result of all these difficulties cartels often do not last long, and often their members make little or no monopoly profits. Nevertheless, as long as firms are tempted to fix prices, the strong policy against cartels in the American antitrust laws is a good one. The cost of cartels is not merely the monopoly profits earned by the cartel members and taken from consumers (which is not a true social cost at all); nor is it merely the deadweight loss caused by the cartel's output reduction. The costs include all the wasted resources that the cartel members expend in creating and enforcing their agreement. As a result the total social cost of cartelization is almost certainly higher than the social cost of single-firm monopoly.[15]

 WESTLAW REFERENCES
di cartel
di price fixing

---

14. Cartels sometimes try to improve productive efficiency by giving members transferable production quotas. A firm with lower costs can then "purchase" the right to produce more from a firm with higher costs. For example, if the cartel price is $5.00, one cartel member has costs of $4.00 and another costs of $3.00, the latter firm will purchase production quotas from the former, at a price somewhere between $1.00 and $2.00. Theoretically, an inefficient firm could sell *all* its production quotas to more efficient firms and cease production.

15. See § 1.3 above.

§ 4.2 Express and Tacit Collusion: Proving Cartel Behavior From Economic Performance

§ 1 of the Sherman Act is addressed to "contracts, combinations, or conspiracies" in restraint of trade. The language of § 1 precludes violation by a single entity: before persons can "conspire" there must be two or more of them.[1] In addition, courts generally require evidence of an "agreement" among these two or more firms. In determining whether such an agreement exists, courts have relied heavily on common law contract formulations, such as "meeting of the minds" or "mutual assent."

§ 2 of the Sherman Act, on the other hand, generally applies to conduct by the single firm acting alone.[2] Concerted conduct is inherently suspicious; single-firm conduct is not. As a result the law of § 2 applies to a relatively narrow range of circumstances. For example, § 2 generally requires a showing either that the defendant was a monopolist, or else that there was a dangerous probability it could have become a monopolist.

Some conduct falls through a fairly wide crack in the Sherman Act. Although anticompetitive, there is no evidence that it resulted from explicit agreement among competitors. Nor is it the unilateral conduct of a firm that has or threatens to have monopoly power. For example, firms in highly concentrated, "oligopoly" markets can achieve anticompetitive output reductions and price increases without *explicitly* agreeing among themselves to do anything.

§ 4.2

1. Questions about whether firms related by ownership, such as a parent and its wholly owned subsidiary, can "conspire" within the meaning of the Sherman Act have plagued the courts. However, in Copperweld Corp. v. Independence Tube Corp., ___ U.S. ___, 104 S.Ct. 2731 (1984), the United States Supreme Court overruled older precedents and held that a parent and its wholly owned subsidiary could not be "conspiring entities" under the federal antitrust laws. The Court recognized that a parent and a wholly owned subsidiary are not independent actors but a single firm, which ordinarily achieves a high level of integration with respect to all price and output decisions. The Court held that the existing "intra-enterprise conspiracy doctrine" gave "undue significance to the fact that a subsidiary is separately incorporated and thereby treats as the concerted activity of two entities what is really unilateral behavior flowing from decisions of a single enterprise." 104 S.Ct. at 2739–40. Just

as the "officers of a single firm" are not separate economic actors for the purposes of § 1 of the Sherman Act, so too a parent and its wholly owned subsidiary "have a complete unity of interest." Id. at 2741–42. A corporation's decision whether to create an unincorporated division or an incorporated subsidiary turns almost entirely on tax consequences or questions of law unrelated to competition. A firm cannot enhance its market power simply by separately incorporating a division.

In Hood v. Tenneco Texas Life Ins. Co., 739 F.2d 1012, 1015 (5th Cir. 1984), the Copperweld doctrine was applied to defeat a claim alleging a conspiracy between two wholly owned subsidiaries of a common parent.

For more on the intra-enterprise conspiracy doctrine and its apparent demise, at least with respect to *wholly*-owned subsidiaries, see Areeda, Intraenterprise Conspiracy in Decline, 97 Harv.L.Rev. 451 (1983).

2. See chapters five & six below.

Theories of oligopoly pricing are about 150 years old,[3] although the most influential modern theory was developed in 1933 by Edward Chamberlin, a Harvard University economist.[4] A simplified version of the theory will serve our purpose here.

Suppose that a market contains three equally efficient firms of equal size. They do not need to worry about new entry. They produce widgets, which are sufficiently homogeneous that customers are indifferent whether their widgets come from Firm A, B or C. The firms have costs of $1.00 per widget, and if widgets sold at a competitive price of $1.00, demand for them would be 3000 widgets per year.

Demand for widgets at the competitive price is inelastic, however. If a single firm monopolized the widget market it could maximize its profits by reducing output from 3000 widgets annually to 2400 widgets. In that case the monopolist could clear the market at a price of $1.50 per widget. How many widgets will each of the three firms produce?

Under the Chamberlin model each firm will behave like one-third of a monopolist. Each will produce 800 widgets and sell them at $1.50. Chamberlin reasoned that each firm's price and output decisions will be influenced by the anticipated responses of the other two firms. In a perfectly competitive market containing 100 sellers no one knows or cares whether a single seller increases or reduces its output—the effect as distributed over the remaining 99 firms is imperceptible. In the three-firm market, however, any substantial output increase and price decrease by one firm will result in immediate loss of market share by the other two firms. As a result, they must respond by matching the price reduction. The price cutter will end up with a lower price, but not with the huge gain in market share that it was expecting.

Such a three-firm market may go through a price war or two, but eventually each firm will realize that profits for the group will be maximized when total market output is 2400 widgets, and that no firm will permit one of the others to produce more than its share (800) of that 2400. Since market profits are greatest at an output rate of 2400, and since the three firms divide the profits equally, each firm will realize that it is best off if it produces at the same level that the firms would have established by express agreement, or alternatively, the same amount that a monopolist would produce.

Have the firms "agreed"? They certainly have reached a mutual understanding. However, no firm has done anything that can be

3. See A. Cournot, Studies in the Mathematical Principles of the Theory of Wealth (1838; English translation by N. Bacon, 1897).

4. E. Chamberlin, The Theory of Monopolistic Competition (1933); see also, W. Fellner, Competition Among the Few (1950); G. Stigler, The Organization of Industry 39–63 (1983). The influence of these theories on antitrust policy is discussed in Elzinga, New Developments on the Cartel Front, 29 Antitrust Bull. 3 (1984).

characterized as a "promise" to the other firms. This kind of question caused a great deal of difficulty in the common law of contracts. By its language, Sherman § 1 invited the same problems into antitrust analysis of concerted behavior. Countless Sherman § 1 decisions hold that the statute requires an explicit agreement, although evidence of the agreement may sometimes be circumstantial.[5] Much § 1 case law is preoccupied, not with the defendant's conduct as such, but with whether that conduct was undertaken pursuant to such an agreement. This unfortunate bit of formalism has been the major impediment to effective antitrust action against poor economic performance in oligopoly markets. In such cases the market structure itself produces a "consensus" about how each firm can maximize its own profits by tacitly participating in a strategy to maximize the joint profits of the group.

The emphasis of Sherman § 1 case law on the fact of an explicit agreement has led many commentators to think that price fixing and oligopoly are two quite different things, and that oligopoly is effectively out of reach of the antitrust laws. In an important article Professor Donald Turner once argued that such behavior was beyond the reach of the Sherman Act for an additional reason: it is perfectly rational, given the structure of the market.[6] Each firm in a three firm market is forced by circumstance to consider the response of the others to its own price and output decisions. The structure of the market makes competitive behavior—ignoring the responses of other firms—irrational. Furthermore, no court could draft a decree that would force the firms to "ignore" each other in their market decision-making. The only solution, Turner concluded, was structural relief: persistent, poor economic performance in highly concentrated markets should warrant a court decree breaking the firms into smaller units that would give the market a more competitive structure. Turner believed that such an approach would require new legislation.

Turner's critics prefer to emphasize the similarities rather than the differences between cartel and oligopoly behavior.[7] Whether the three firms in the market described above acted in response to an express agreement or simply have read the market's clear signals in the same way should be a mere detail. Under this approach to oligopoly analysis, explicit cartel agreements are referred to as "express collusion," while oligopolistic, interdependent behavior is called "tacit collusion." This term is designed to draw attention to

5. See First Nat'l Bank of Arizona v. Cities Serv. Co., 391 U.S. 253, 88 S.Ct. 1575 (1968); Theatre Enterprises, Inc. v. Paramount Film Distributing Corp., 346 U.S. 537, 74 S.Ct. 257 (1954).

6. Turner, The Definition of Agreement Under the Sherman Act: Conscious Parallelism and Refusals to Deal, 75 Harv.L.Rev. 655 (1962).

7. Posner, Oligopoly and the Antitrust Laws: A Suggested Approach, 21 Stan.L.Rev. 1562 (1969). A critique of both Turner's and Posner's proposal is summarized in Posner, Oligopolistic Pricing Suits, the Sherman Act, and Economic Welfare, 28 Stan.L.Rev. 903 (1976); and Markovits, A Response to Professor Posner, 28 Stan.L.Rev. 919 (1976).

the fact that there is a certain "meeting of minds" of competitors in oligopolistic markets, even though the firms do not formally communicate with each other.

The tacit collusion thesis has produced some significant rewards.[8] First, it has aided analysis and diagnosis of bad economic performance in concentrated markets; in general, the same economic conditions that make a market conducive to explicit cartelization also facilitate tacit collusion. Second, the analysis has provided some insights into how the antitrust laws should deal with the general problem of collusion. The strongest protagonists of a theory of tacit collusion would use the law to go directly after the conditions facilitating monopoly pricing in concentrated markets, without spending much judicial time inquiring whether there was really an "agreement" among competitors.

Economic analysis of concentrated markets has produced two broad conclusions about tacit collusion: 1) it does not enable firms to achieve monopoly profit-maximization as efficiently as explicit collusion or single-firm monopolization; 2) nevertheless, price and output tend to be noncompetitive in highly concentrated markets. The degree to which market price exceeds the competitive price is substantially a function of the market's structure.[9]

Tacit collusion requires not only that a market be highly concentrated on the selling side, but also that it be rather diffuse on the buying side. If the market contains a small number of large and knowledgeable firms on the buying side, they will be able to force the sellers to bid against each other and offer concessions—particularly if the terms of individual sales are kept secret. Likewise, tacit collusion just as much as express price fixing can be frustrated by easy entry or output increases from fringe firms. The lower the number of fringe firms on the "edge" of the market, and the more difficult and time-consuming entry is, the greater will be the returns from tacit collusion.

Tacit collusion is less successful if the firms in the market are not equally efficient or produce distinguishable products. In these ways tacit and express collusion are quite similar. In addition, however, as the number of firms in a market increases, or if one of the above impediments to collusion exists, tacit collusion becomes ineffectual more quickly than express collusion. This is so because tacit collusion relies on more primitive forms of communication, such as price or output signaling by means of public announcements. Although

8. See Hay, Oligopoly, Shared Monopoly, and Antitrust Law, 67 Cornell L. Rev. 439 (1982).

9. For a summary of the theories and the evidence, see H. J. Goldschmid, H. M. Mann, J. F. Weston, Industrial Concentration: The New Learning (1974); F. M. Scherer, Industrial Market Structure and Economic Performance 81–150 (2d ed. 1980). The Herfindahl-Hirschman Index of market concentration can be used to estimate the likelihood of collusion in some markets. The Index is discussed in § 11.4 below.

such signaling can generally enable firms to reach a tacit meeting of minds about price and output, it is less likely to produce detailed agreements covering many variables.

Thus fifteen firms might conceivably manage an explicit cartel. Oligopoly pricing in a market containing fifteen firms is implausible, however, unless one or two firms were extremely large and the others very small. Even a market containing five or six firms will find tacit collusion very difficult if there are significant disparities in firm size or efficiency, a substantial amount of product differentiation or customizing, or if most transactions are confidential. For this reason firms in oligopoly markets often develop certain "facilitating devices" that make tacit collusion easier. For example, if all firms by express or tacit agreement produce uniform products, offer similar terms or conditions of sale, and make all transactions public, they can make the market more conducive to tacit collusion. If the facilitating device results from an express agreement it may receive rule of reason treatment under the antitrust laws, because it does not explicitly affect price. For example, an agreement that all firms will produce "standardized" products may appear to be efficiency creating if it lowers customer search costs. Further, the facilitating devices themselves often result from tacit agreement. The firms never formally communicate with each other but simply reach a shared perception about how they can operate to maximize joint monopoly profits.

One of the most controversial questions in antitrust policy is how courts and enforcers should deal with the problem of poor economic performance in concentrated markets when there is no evidence of express collusion. The Turner proposal favoring structural relief [10]— judicially mandated dissolution of the firms in the market—was predicated on the premise that monopoly pricing was inevitable in oligopoly markets. The poor performance was perfectly rational, profit-maximizing behavior dictated by the environment in which the oligopoly firm found itself. Marginal cost pricing, on the other hand, was irrational.

For example, consider the plight of Ford Motor Company contemplating a price decrease in a market dominated by Ford, General Motors, and Chrysler. A firm considers a price reduction not because it is a charitable organization, but because it believes the price reduction will yield higher demand and larger profits. However, a Ford vice president would respond to any proposed reduction by saying, "If we cut prices, General Motors and Chrysler will have to match us. We will end up with less money per car and our output will probably not be much higher than it is now." For Turner such a response was unavoidable given the structure of the industry. The only remedy was to change the structure.

10. Note 6 above.

Even if courts could administer the restructuring of an entire industry, however, it is by no means clear that such restructuring would be in the best interest of consumers. Absent unusual deterrents to competitive entry, markets are generally concentrated because operation at minimum optimal scale (MOS) requires a firm with a relatively large share of the market.[11] For example, if MOS in the widget industry requires an output level equal to 30% of market demand at the competitive price, the market in equilibrium is likely to have three or fewer firms. Smaller firms would either combine by merger, increase their own market share by driving other firms out of business, or else go out of business themselves.

Furthermore, most economists are not particularly confident about their ability to measure MOS, except perhaps by a rule of survival: inefficiently small firms must either grow or die.[12] It is impossible to sit back and rationalize MOS of, say, an automobile producer. Production economies alone might be such that a plant with 5% of national output could achieve lowest possible cost of production. But the production and distribution of automobiles includes advertising, a retail network, post-sale services, and a host of things that may give a larger firm a cost advantage over small firms.[13] Furthermore, MOS is a function of constantly changing technology and demand. In the 1950's computers filled giant warehouses and cost millions of dollars to produce. As a result production required enormous plants and market demand was relatively small. Minimum optimal scale under such circumstances may have been 30% to 40% of market demand, and the market would have room for only two or three firms. Today, a computer of the same capacity might be the size of a suitcase and cost less than $2000. The result is that smaller firms can manufacture them and the total market is hundreds of times larger. Today a firm might achieve MOS with a market share of 2%–3%, and the market could have room for 30 or 40 efficient firms. Over American economic history such changes in technology and market demand have undoubtedly contributed far more than the antitrust laws to the destruction of monopolies.

The problem of scale economies and concentrated markets leaves the antitrust policy maker in a quandary. An oligopoly is an oligopoly, whether or not the high concentration results from economies of scale. In fact, an oligopoly market in which MOS is very high is likely to perform more poorly than an oligopoly in which MOS is low. The firms in the latter oligopoly have to worry about new entry. When they measure price and output they must consider not only

11. See § 1.4 above.

12. For a somewhat inconclusive attempt to do this, see G. Stigler, The Organization of Industry 71–89 (1983).

13. See Y. Brozen, Concentration, Mergers and Public Policy 56–127 (1983); J. McGee, "Efficiency and Economies of Size," in Goldschmid, Mann & Weston, note 9 above, at 55–97. For one attempt to determine the minimum optimal plant size in several American industries see F. Scherer, A. Beckenstein, E. Kaufer, & R. Murphy, The Economics of Multiplant Operations (1975).

how the other firms in the market will respond, but also the possibility that new equally efficient firms will enter if the price rises too much. On the other hand, if there are three firms in a market in which MOS exceeds a 30% market share, the firms have less reason to fear new entry. Any new entrant whose market share is less than 30% will have a cost disadvantage. The greater that disadvantage, the more room there will be for supracompetitive pricing by the firms already in the market.

It is difficult even for academic economists to predict the consequences of severe structural change in any industry. Break-up of oligopoly firms will certainly yield an industry with more firms, and they will likely price their output closer to their costs—but their costs could be substantially higher. *Ex ante*, it may be difficult to say whether the structural change will yield a price increase or a price decrease.[14] Once we include the large administrative costs of predicting when such relief would be appropriate, and the costs of administering such relief, it is far from clear that the result of structural reorganization of oligopoly industries will be efficient.

In fact, a great deal of economic analysis suggests that the social costs of tacit collusion are small compared to the costs of denying firms the chance to achieve their most efficient rate of output.[15] If that is the case consumers may be best off if firms are permitted to attain minimum optimal scale, even at the expense of some high concentration, but the antitrust laws are used to make both express and tacit collusion as difficult and expensive as possible. This means that the antitrust enforcer must first be able to identify those markets in which express or tacit collusion is likely. Secondly, he must be able to discern the economic evidence that such collusion is actually forcing prices above the competitive level.

Occasionally the Supreme Court has condemned practices as collusive without good evidence of explicit collusion. For example, in

---

14. However, industry performance may provide some hints as to the significance of both scale economies and collusion in concentrated industries. Consider highly concentrated industries that contain a few giant firms and some tiny fringe firms. If both the giant firms and the fringe firms earn supranormal profits, that would indicate that economies of scale are not substantial and that collusion is occurring. On the other hand, if the large firms are earning supracompetitive profits while the fringe firms are earning only competitive returns, that suggests that economies of scale account for the concentration, and that there is some collusion among the larger firms. Several recent studies show that in concentrated industries very large firms consistently show higher profits than very small firms. This suggests that such industries are concentrated because of economies of scale. Breaking the firms up would probably produce higher prices, lower profits, or both. Weiss, The Structure-Conduct-Performance Paradigm and Antitrust, 127 U.Pa.L.Rev. 1104, 1115–19 (1979); Carter, Collusion, Efficiency and Antitrust, 21 J.L. & Econ. 435 (1978); Demsetz, Industry Structure, Market Rivalry, and Public Policy, 16 J.L. & Econ. 1 (1973).

15. See Peltzman, The Gains and Losses from Industrial Concentration, 20 J.L. & Econ. 229 (1977); J. McGee, In Defense of Industrial Concentration (1971).

Interstate Circuit, Inc. v. U.S.,[16] the defendants were a group of eight distributors and several exhibitors of motion pictures. The distributors controlled about 75% of "first-class feature films exhibited in the United States." One of the largest exhibitors sent a letter to the eight distributors suggesting that each insert two clauses in future exhibition contracts with theatres: 1) a clause requiring the theatre to charge at least 40¢ admission for first-run films, and 25¢ admission for subsequent-run films; 2) a clause prohibiting the theatres from exhibiting first-run films with other films as double features. Subsequently the eight distributors incorporated these clauses into most of their contracts. There was no evidence, other than the fact that all eight had received the letter, that the distributors had agreed among themselves.

It is easy to see why an exhibitor would want such clauses in its contracts and those of other exhibitors: the "resale price maintenance" clause effectively prevented the theatres served by these distributors from price competition with each other. Likewise, the clause restricting double features prevented the theatres from competing by increasing the amount of entertainment they would provide at the maintained price.

If each of these restrictions had been imposed unilaterally by a distributor on an exhibitor, the restrictions would probably have been legal. They were not illegal vertical price maintenance because the films were not sold to the exhibitors, but merely licensed to them. The Supreme Court had not yet dealt with vertically imposed non-price restraints, so the status of the clause against double features was uncertain.

The use of the clauses was clearly illegal, however, if the eight distributors had agreed among themselves to place them in every exhibitor's license agreements. In that case there would have been an agreement among competitors which effectively reduced output— fewer people would have attended movies because the price was higher, and those who did attend would have seen fewer movies for their admission price.

Finally, if the eight distributors were competitors it would have been irrational for one of them acting alone to impose the restrictions. A theatre that could make more money by showing double features or charging a lower admission price would simply have licensed its films from a different distributor.[17]

---

16. 306 U.S. 208, 59 S.Ct. 467 (1939).

17. Thus the Court found no liability in a situation in which all distributors followed the same policy (issuing exclusive first runs only to larger downtown theatres, and not smaller suburban theatres), but each firm acting in its own interest plausibly would have followed the policy, even if the other firms in the market did not. Theatre Enterprises, Inc. v. Paramount Film Distrib. Corp., 346 U.S. 537, 74 S.Ct. 257 (1954); see also, Proctor v. State Farm Mutual Ins. Co., 675 F.2d 308 (D.C.Cir.), cert. denied, 459 U.S. 839, 103 S.Ct. 86 (1982).

The Supreme Court held that the offer given to the eight distributors, plus their nearly unanimous acceptance of it, was sufficient evidence from which the district court could infer the existence of an agreement among them. As the Court noted:

> Each [distributor] was aware that all were in active competition and that without substantially unanimous action with respect to the restrictions * * * there was risk of a substantial loss of the business and good will of the * * * exhibitors, but that with it there was the prospect of increased profits.[18]

In other words, each distributor's apparently unilateral decision to impose resale price and double feature restrictions was irrational given the presumption of competition: a theatre that did not wish to be bound by the restrictions would have sought out a different distributor. However, the Court characterized the case not as using the antitrust laws to reach tacit collusion, but as using circumstantial evidence to infer the existence of express collusion. There was an explicit "offer," even though there was no explicit "acceptance." [19]

Factors such as high concentration on the seller's side and diffusion on the buyer's side, significant economies of scale, a standardized product and publicly announced prices and terms, indicate whether a particular market is conducive to express or tacit collusion.[20] Some additional factors can help a law enforcer determine the degree

---

18. 306 U.S. at 222, 59 S.Ct. at 472.

19. However, in a pregnant passage the Court concluded:

> While the District Court's finding of an agreement of the distributors among themselves is supported by the evidence, we think that in the circumstances of this case such agreement * * * was not a prerequisite to an unlawful conspiracy. It was enough that, knowing that concerted action was contemplated and invited, the distributors gave their adherence to the scheme and participated in it.

306 U.S. at 226, 59 S.Ct. at 474.

The closest the Supreme Court has come to developing a theory of tacit collusion is American Tobacco Co. v. U.S., 328 U.S. 781, 66 S.Ct. 1125 (1946), in which it condemned sudden, simultaneous, and fairly radical price movements among three major manufacturers of tobacco products who collectively controlled 90% of the market, under both §§ 1 & 2 of the Sherman Act. Based on the evidence of the price movements, the jury found that a conspiracy existed and the Court concluded that the "record of price changes is circumstantial evidence of the existence of a con-

spiracy * * *." In a particularly ambiguous statement the Court concluded that:

> No formal agreement is necessary to constitute an unlawful conspiracy. Often crimes are a matter of inference deduced from the acts of the person accused and done in pursuance of a criminal purpose. Where the conspiracy is proved, as here, from the evidence of the action taken in concert by the parties to it, it is all the more convincing proof of an intent to exercise the power of exclusion acquired through that conspiracy. The essential combination or conspiracy in violation of the Sherman Act may be found in a course of dealings or other circumstances as well as in any exchange of words. Where the circumstances are such as to warrant a jury in finding that the conspirators had a unity of purpose or a common design and understanding, or a meeting of minds in an unlawful arrangement, the conclusion that a conspiracy is established is justified. 328 U.S. at 809–10, 66 S.Ct. at 1139.

20. See R. Posner, Antitrust Law: An Economic Perspective 39–77 (1976).

to which such collusion is actually occurring. These include: 1) stable market shares; 2) a rigid price structure that seems unresponsive to changes in demand; 3) industry-wide use of certain "facilitating devices" that make tacit collusion easier. Important among these devices are exchanges of price or output information among competitors, standardization of products or terms of sale, and market-wide vertical integration or resale price maintenance. These facilitating devices are especially suspect if they are the product of explicit agreement among the competing firms, or if they result in systematic, market-wide price discrimination. Persistent price discrimination is suspect even if there is no evidence of an explicit agreement.

Both stable market shares and prices that fail to fluctuate with demand are good indicators that a market is not performing competitively. In a competitive multi-firm market the relative positions of individual firms will usually change. The market shares of the most efficient firms are likely to grow, while those of the least efficient firms will become smaller. Prices will generally decline in times of falling demand, as firms try to clear inventories and cut losses. In a cartelized market, however, these things will happen far more slowly. As market demand declines the monopoly profit-maximizing price will decline, but it will not decline as fast. Furthermore, in a cartel it will not decline at all until the cartel members decide to lower it—which they generally will do only in response to widespread cheating or defection, a sure sign that the market as a whole is deteriorating.

Firms may agree among themselves, either explicitly or tacitly, to engage in certain practices that will make collusion easier. One of the most obvious of these is exchanges of price information. Nothing makes monitoring of market prices easier than an agreement that every firm will provide complete disclosure of all sales prices. Like many nonprice agreements that can facilitate collusion, however, information exchanges can also make a market perform more competitively. Their relative merits are discussed in the following section.

Agreements among competitors to standardize products or terms of sale fall into the same ambiguous category. Such standardization can substantially reduce customer information costs and make the market operate more efficiently; if "number two plywood" or "grade A eggs" means exactly the same thing to all sellers and buyers in a market, customers will be able to determine what they are buying far more easily and the market will perform more efficiently. However, in a concentrated industry, product standardization can facilitate express or tacit collusion because it enables each firm more effectively to monitor the pricing of another firm.[21]

---

21. Standardization agreements can sometimes be input restriction agreements. If the firms have monopsony power in some product that they buy, an agreement to "standardize" the product may be no more than an explicit agreement to fix the purchase price. For example, see National Macaroni Manu-

Courts have seldom condemned simple product standardization by agreement among competitors.[22] However, they have been very strict about any agreed standardization of price or other transaction terms. For example, in Sugar Institute, Inc. v. U.S.[23] the Supreme Court condemned a trade association rule prohibiting its members from giving secret discounts or price concessions. The industry was highly concentrated, and the rule probably permitted sugar manufacturers to monitor each other's prices.[24]

More recently, in Catalano, Inc. v. Target Sales, Inc.[25] the Supreme Court condemned an agreement among beer wholesalers to eliminate a short term trade credit that many of them had formerly given to retailers. Under the agreement the wholesalers would sell only if the buyer paid before or at delivery. The effect of the agreement was to standardize the price terms and make a firm's sale prices easier to monitor. For example, a price of $6.00 per case, payable 180 days after delivery is lower than a price of $6.00 per case payable within 30 days of delivery. The Supreme Court treated the agreement as little more than a variant of price fixing and condemned it under the *per se* rule.

Industry-wide vertical integration or resale price maintenance can also facilitate cartel behavior. As the discussion in chapters seven and nine indicate, vertical integration and resale price maintenance generally benefit consumers. Occasionally, however, such vertical practices can facilitate collusion at the manufacturing level by enabling firms to monitor each other's final output prices. If manufacturers deal with large distributors, their sales are likely to be infrequent, covering large amounts of merchandise, and having indi-

facturers v. FTC, 65 F.T.C. 583 (1964), affirmed, 345 F.2d 421 (7th Cir. 1965), condemning an agreement among macaroni manufacturers to "standardize" the contents of macaroni products at 50% semolina and 50% farina. Since the macaroni producers used most of the nation's semolina, they were in a position to depress its price by reducing the proportion of semolina in their products. However, an agreement among bolt manufacturers to standardize a metal alloy for bolts at 50% steel could not plausibly be calculated to depress the market price of steel, for the steel used in bolts is only a tiny part of the steel market.

22. See L. Sullivan, Handbook of the Law of Antitrust 275–76 (1977).

23. 297 U.S. 553, 56 S.Ct. 629 (1936).

24. See Fly, Observations on the Antitrust Laws, Economic Theory and the Sugar Institute Decisions: I, 45 Yale L.J. 1339 (1939).

25. 446 U.S. 643, 100 S.Ct. 1925 (1980), on remand, 625 F.2d 331 (9th Cir. 1980), rehearing denied 448 U.S. 911, 101 S.Ct. 26 (1980). "Relative value scales" (RVSs) can also facilitate tacit collusion. An RVS is a published list of the *relative* values, or time consumed, by individual services delivered by doctors, dentists, auto mechanics, etc. By using such a published book competing professionals can arrive at substantial price uniformity simply by matching each other's hourly fees. On the other hand, the RVS may simply be a form of information exchange designed to tell a professional whether the amount of time and attention she devotes to a certain procedure is in line with that of others in her field. See U.S. v. Amer. Soc. of Anesthesiologists, 473 F.Supp. 147 (S.D.N.Y. 1979); Eisenberg, Information Exchange Among Competitors: the Issue of Relative Value Scales for Physicians' Services, 23 J.L. & Econ. 441 (1980).

vidually and privately negotiated terms. In such cases both express and tacit collusion will be difficult to maintain. However, if all sales are small, with publicly announced prices and terms, then price cutting will be detected far more quickly.[26]

Among the most useful indicators of collusion in a market is price discrimination. Price discrimination occurs whenever a seller has two different rates of return on different sales of the same product.[27] Assuming that the lower price sale is competitive, the higher price sale must give the seller some monopoly profits. Persistent price discrimination is inconsistent with competition: customers asked to pay the discriminatorily high price will seek out a different seller, and in a competitive market there will always be a seller willing to make the sale at marginal cost. The existence of persistent price discrimination is therefore evidence that the market is not performing competitively, because of monopoly or collusion, whether express or tacit.

Among the most revealing collusion cases involving price discrimination are the delivered pricing cases, particularly those involving basing point pricing. Delivered pricing schemes have been common in industries in which transportation costs are high in proportion to the value of the commodity sold. Such schemes involve a certain amount of price discrimination; as a result, their existence alone may be enough to create an inference of express or tacit collusion. Like information exchanges, agreements to standardize products and terms, or vertical integration, delivered pricing schemes can enable firms to monitor each other's prices and respond to changes more effectively.

Suppose that a single firm sells to three customers located 10, 100 and 400 miles away from the seller. All three buyers place the same value on the product, $100, and the seller sells the product to each of them at that price, which includes delivery. If delivery costs are proportional to distance and the sale to the most remote buyer is profitable, the sales to the closer buyers will give the seller a monopoly profit. In this case the seller clearly is engaging in price discrimination.

The fact that such a delivered pricing scheme could exist suggests that the market is not competitive. In a perfectly competitive market the two buyers who were 10 and 100 miles from the seller would have found a seller willing to charge a lower delivered price. Competition tends to drive prices to actual costs and favors the "best placed" or closest seller to any particular buyer, particularly if transportation costs are substantial in relation to the value of the product.

---

26. Likewise, vertical integration by price or territorial restrictions may facilitate cartelization at the *retail* level. See § 9.2 below.

27. See chap. thirteen below.

A cartel will often want to eliminate this "placement" competition. If price fixers merely set a price, to which actual freight costs are added, the firms may continue to compete by establishing a proliferation of "shipping points" close to customers. The firms can then cheat on the cartel by billing a lower freight rate from one of these shipping points, even though the shipment actually originated somewhere else. Further, demand in the industry may shift geographically from one period to the next, and the current sales of individual sellers in a competitive market will reflect these cycles. Most cartels, however, would prefer that market shares of their members be relatively stable from one period to the next.[28]

Finally, widely varying freight costs make policing of the cartel very difficult. If every member of a cartel adds actual freight costs to the cartel price in order to produce a delivered price, final output prices will vary considerably from one transaction to the next. It would be very difficult for one firm to monitor the prices of other firms in the cartel.

In order to solve all these problems many cartels have not only fixed the price of the commodity itself, but they have also "fixed" the freight rates. One of the most effective mechanisms for eliminating all placement competition and producing uniform delivered prices across the entire cartel is basing point pricing. In basing point pricing systems the sellers identify some central point as the "basing point." All quoted prices then add in freight charges measured from the basing point to the buyer's delivery point, even though the product was in fact shipped from somewhere else. For example, under the "Pittsburgh Plus" formula once used in the steel industry, steel mills located across the northeastern and north central United States billed all customers for freight computed from Pittsburgh to the delivery destination.[29] In such a case if the price of the steel were fixed, the buyer would have received identical bids for delivered steel. Likewise, the basing point system could facilitate collusion, for each firm would find it fairly easy to track the actual price of steel in the market.

Basing point pricing systems can increase the social costs of the cartel. As a general rule even the monopolist or cartel has an

---

28. Stable market shares can increase the cartel's overall profitability by permitting individual members to operate with smaller plants. For example, a firm that sells 6,000 units per year will sell 12,000 in a two year period. A firm that sells 10,000 units one year and 2,000 units the next also sells 12,000 units in a two year period. However the first firm needs to carry enough capacity to produce 6,000 units per year. The second must carry enough capacity to produce 10,000 units per year and per-haps operate at far less than the optimal rate of output during the second year. The firm whose output is constant from one year to the next is likely to have lower costs.

29. See United States Steel, 8 F.T.C. 1 (1924); FTC v. Cement Institute, 333 U.S. 683, 68 S.Ct. 793 (1948). For a more detailed economic analysis of basing point pricing see G. Stigler, The Organization of Industry 147–164 (1983).

incentive to reduce costs: the sellers will be able to keep more profits for themselves. Basing point pricing, however, can destroy any incentive for either buyer or seller to reduce transportation costs. If buyers 10 miles and 500 miles from a seller use a basing point formula they will add in the same freight charges, even though the charges incurred by the closer seller are far lower. As a result the buyer has no cost incentive to select the closer seller.

Courts have consistently condemned basing point pricing under § 5 of the Federal Trade Commission Act, when the evidence suggested an agreement among competitors to engage in basing point pricing.[30] More controversial, however, has been judicial treatment of industry-wide basing point pricing when there is no evidence that the sellers agreed to engage in the practice. In Triangle Conduit and Cable Co. v. FTC[31] the Court upheld the FTC's condemnation of market-wide basing point pricing on two different theories: first, that the firms had agreed with each other to engage in basing point pricing; second, that the mere "concurrent use of a formula" in making delivered price bids, with the knowledge that other firms did the same thing, violated § 5 of the FTC Act. The Court affirmed the FTC's finding of a conspiracy, but also approved the second theory, noting that even absent express agreement,

> each conduit seller knows that each of the other sellers is using the basing point formula; each knows that by using it he will be able to quote identical delivered prices and thus present a condition of matched prices under which purchasers are isolated and deprived of choice among sellers so far as price advantage is concerned * * *. [W]e cannot say that the Commission was wrong in concluding that the individual use of the basing point method as here used does constitute an unfair method of competition.

More recently, however, in Boise Cascade Corp. v. FTC[32] the Ninth Circuit called the *Triangle Conduit* decision into question, and refused to condemn industry-wide basing point pricing when there was no evidence of an express conspiracy. The Court concluded that § 5 of the Federal Trade Commission Act requires the Commission to show *either* an "overt agreement" among the firms to engage in basing point pricing or else that the practice "actually had the effect

30. FTC v. Cement Institute, 333 U.S. 683, 68 S.Ct. 793 (1948), condemned basing point pricing under § 5 of the FTC Act. There was no direct evidence of explicit agreement among the firms; however, firms in the industry were notorious for submitting identical competitive bids for projects—in one case 11 bidders all quoted a price of $3.286854. The Court held that the Commission could infer a conspiracy, whether "express or implied," from these data. Basing point pricing has also been condemned as illegal price discrimination under the Robinson-Patman Act. Corn Prod. Ref. Co. v. FTC, 324 U.S. 726, 65 S.Ct. 961 (1945).

31. 168 F.2d 175 (7th Cir. 1948), affirmed sub nom. Clayton Mark & Co. v. FTC, 336 U.S. 956, 69 S.Ct. 888 (1949). Quotation at 181.

32. 637 F.2d 573 (9th Cir. 1980).

of fixing or stabilizing prices." The Fifth Circuit condemned the same practice under § 1 of the Sherman Act, however, by affirming a jury verdict that the practice did have an effect on prices and that the plaintiffs had been injured as a result. There was also evidence from which the jury could have inferred an explicit agreement.[33]

There is some merit to the Ninth Circuit's requirement that, absent sufficient evidence of a horizontal conspiracy, the plaintiff must show that basing point pricing had an anticompetitive effect. Although basing point pricing is a form of price discrimination, and although price discrimination is inconsistent with perfect competition, in the real world competition is never perfect. Many sellers, even in multi-seller markets, have substantial market power over certain classes of customers. In such markets price discrimination some-times can increase competition. This is particularly true of markets in which sellers are dispersed and freight costs are high in relation to the value of the product. In that case a seller may have a great deal of market power over buyers that are near to it but far away from any other seller. At some distance away, however—midway between the firm and a competitor—there will be other buyers who have a choice between two firms that could sell the product at the same delivered price. If a firm wants to make sales at this fringe of its own dominant territory, it will have to compete for them. If it competes by lowering its sale price, however, it must lower the price to all customers, even to those "captive" customers which are nearby and from whom it would otherwise obtain monopoly profits.

Instead, the firm would like to find some mechanism for price discriminating: for selling to nearby "captive" purchasers at a monopoly price but to more remote purchasers at a more competitive price. The seller can do this by establishing a basing point in the direction of the firms on the fringe of the market whose business it would like to obtain. It will bid for sales to those firms, not by lowering its price, but by absorbing part of the freight costs.

For example, firms A and B in Figure Two manufacture cement, in which transportation costs are high. They are located 100 miles apart. Each firm has a natural advantage with respect to buyers located within a 40 mile (solid) circle from its plant. That is, before B could make sales in A's circle, B's delivered price would have to be less than B's marginal costs. However, buyers located in the area between the two solid circles, such as X, are roughly equidistant from A and B. If A wants to obtain X's trade, A will have to compete with B. One way A can compete is by lowering the price of cement. In that case, however, A will have to lower the price to all buyers and A will lose the monopoly profits from customers within his own circle. The alternative is for A to engage in multiple basing point pricing. A

33. In re Plywood Antitrust Litigation, 655 F.2d 627, 634 (5th Cir. 1981), cert. dismissed, ___ U.S. ___, 103 S.Ct. 3100 (1983).

sets up a basing point, A'. If the buyer is located within A's solid circle, A can keep the buyer's trade by charging actual freight costs from its plant. A can effectively give X a lower price, however, by billing X for freight from point A', even though the cement was probably shipped from point A.[34] In the absence of explicit agreement among competitors, therefore, a court must make some kind of determination whether a basing point pricing scheme is competitive or collusive.

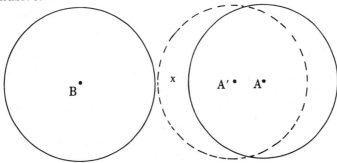

FIGURE TWO

In general, the "contract, combination or conspiracy" requirement has effectively prevented courts from using § 1 of the Sherman Act to reach poor performance in concentrated markets without some evidence of express collusion. Recently the Federal Trade Commission has tried to take advantage of the broader language of § 5 of the FTC Act, which condemns "unfair methods of competition," to attack apparent tacit collusion. So far, however, the Commission's efforts have met little success.

In Ethyl Corp.[35] the FTC relied on § 5 to condemn several sales practices of the four firms that manufacture gasoline antiknock compounds. The practices, all undertaken uniformly but without apparent agreement among the four firms, included 1) a policy of announcing price changes 30 days in advance; 2) "most favored nation" clauses in sales contracts, which promised that the buyer would receive the full benefit of any subsequent price reduction for a certain specified period; and 3) uniform delivered prices.

The Commission placed great emphasis on the fact that FTCA § 5, unlike § 1 of the Sherman Act, does not require proof of agreement among the firms. If a practice both affects competition adversely

---

34. See Haddock, Basing-Point Pricing: Competitive vs. Collusive Theories, 72 Amer.Econ.Rev. 289 (1982); Carlton, A Reexamination of Delivered Pricing Systems, 22 J.L. & Econ. 51 (1983); De-Canio, Delivered Pricing and Multiple Basing Point Equilibria, 99 Q.J.Econ. 329 (1984). However, the evidence in the *Plywood* cases, Id., seems more consistent with collusive rather than competitive use of basing points. For exam-

ple, the defendants in the *Plywood* cases all used exactly the same set of multiple basing points. If the basing points were created unilaterally by firms to enable them to compete at the fringes of their markets, different firms would probably establish different basing points.

35. 101 FTC 425 (1983), reversed sub nom. E.I. du Pont de Nemours & Co. v. FTC, 729 F.2d 128 (2d Cir. 1984).

and violates the "basic legislative goals of the Sherman Act," then it could be reached under § 5 even though it might fall outside the Sherman Act. The Commission evaluated the market and found all the indicators of tacit collusion: very high concentration and firms with roughly equal costs; high entry barriers compounded by extensive government regulations; inelastic demand; a generally homogenous and undifferentiated product; and finally, a net rate of return 50% higher than the rate earned by most producers of chemicals.

In such a market any of the alleged practices could have facilitated tacit collusion. The policy of announcing price changes 30 days in advance would enable firms to monitor and respond to the output decisions of the other firms. In this case, two smaller firms in the market generally followed the price leadership of the two larger firms.

"Most favored nation" or price protection clauses are somewhat more ambiguous. Buyers may think that such clauses protect them from subsequent price reductions that might be given to other firms. If A buys today at a price of $50, and tomorrow the seller sells to B at a price of $45, A will be entitled to a refund of $5. In fact, however, most favored nation clauses are often a sign not of hard customer bargaining but of seller collusion. The effect of such clauses is to make discriminatory price reductions very expensive and easy to detect, and to give the cartel a new set of policemen: customers. If the seller attempts to cheat by giving B a $5 reduction in price, A will demand similar treatment under his price protection clause.[36] In the *Ethyl* case, the fact that most sales contracts contained the price protection clauses suggests collusion and not individual customer bargaining. If the clauses really were individually negotiated they would probably appear in some sales contracts (most likely the larger ones) and not others.

In any case, the Second Circuit was not impressed by any of the Commission's theories of tacit collusion. The court reversed, expressly refusing to hold that § 5 could be "violated by non-collusive, non-predatory and independent conduct of a non-artificial nature," even when the conduct *results* in a substantial lessening of competition. Rather, the Commission would have to show either "1) evidence of anticompetitive intent or purpose on the part of the producer charged, or (2) the absence of an independent legitimate business reason for its conduct." [37] The court opined that oligopoly is a market "condition," not a "method" of avoiding competition. This characterization would appear to be a reference to Professor Turner's observation that price leadership is inherent in oligopoly, and marginal cost pricing would be irrational.[38]

36. See Hay, Oligopoly, Shared Monopoly, and Antitrust Law, 67 Cornell L. Rev. 439, 455 (1982).

37. *du Pont*, note 35 above, 729 F.2d at 139.

38. See note 6 above. The court did note one thing that the Commission failed to account for adequately. The buyers in the additive market were the "large, aggressive and sophisticated"

The court did not rule out any possibility that § 5 could be used in the future to pursue facilitating devices in oligopoly markets. However, it held that the FTC "owes a duty to define the conditions under which conduct claimed to facilitate price uniformity would be unfair," so that firms would be able to predict what they could legally do and what they could not.

A troublesome part of the Second Circuit's reversal is that it fails to consider the limited remedies available to the FTC, which make the social cost of overdeterrence in FTC actions smaller than it would be in cases brought by the Justice Department or private plaintiffs under the Sherman Act. The FTC could not fine or imprison the defendants' officers or make them pay damages. It merely issued a prospective cease and desist order forbidding the defendants from communicating price changes in advance or using delivered pricing, and forbidding the largest two defendants from using price protection clauses.

The fact that FTC remedies are both prospective and limited to injunctive relief justifies somewhat broader standards of liability under the FTC Act than under the Sherman Act. In this particular case, even if the FTC were wrong and the practices at issue were not being used to facilitate tacit collusion, the social cost of enjoining the practices would not be high, for there was no convincing evidence that the practices were efficiency creating either. In a concentrated market, easily conducive to collusion, a little overdeterrence in cases involving ambiguous practices can be a good thing, particularly if the practices have little apparent social value.[39]

An FTC proceeding against the manufacturers of ready-to-eat breakfast cereals fared even less well than the *Ethyl* case.[40] The allegations were that the four national manufacturers of breakfast cereal violated § 5 of the FTC Act by agreeing, either implicitly or explicitly, to monopolize the market. Since there was no worthwhile evidence of conspiracy, the action proceeded on a theory that the FTC characterized initially not as tacit collusion, but as "shared monopoly." This oxymoron has been used to suggest that oligopoly firms might tacitly collude not only in maintaining supracompetitive prices, but also in excluding other firms from the market. For example, the FTC alleged that the cereal manufacturers simultaneously avoided

major oil companies. If profits in the antiknock compound market were high, "nothing would prevent them from integrating backwards into the antiknock industry," thereby transferring these monopoly profits to themselves. 729 F.2d at 131. See § 7.2 below. The fact that they had not integrated backward suggests either that they could not produce the compound at minimum efficient scale, or else that the ethyl market was not performing as anticompetitively as the Commission suggested.

There is an alternative explanation for the oil companies' failure to integrate vertically, however. For environmental reasons, lead antiknock compounds were being phased out; as a result, the industry at issue had a short life expectancy, perhaps not justifying the costs of vertical integration. See 729 F.2d at 131.

39. For the relationship between market concentration and the social cost of overdeterrence, see § 6.4 below.

40. Kellogg Co., 99 F.T.C. 8 (1982).

competition with each other and made entry of new firms more difficult by engaging in excessive product differentiation. Under the theory the firms "made it extremely difficult for new firms to enter, since an entrant would have to offer several brands to achieve minimal scale economies." The Commission noted, however, that consumer demand appeared to support the multiplicity of offerings.

Such product differentiation is probably as consistent with competition as it is with the lack of it. To be sure, the proliferation of cereal offerings gives each manufacturer mini-monopolies in its own products, with their distinctive trademarked names. (Only Kellogg's, for example, manufactures Rice Krispies). As a result each manufacturer probably has at least a small amount of market power. On the other hand, product proliferation vastly complicates and frustrates the processes of tacit collusion—of arriving at consensus about price, output, and quality. In short, product proliferation makes a weak case for tacit collusion. While it may have been exclusionary, it is hard to see how it could have enabled the incumbent firms to earn substantial monopoly profits.

 WESTLAW REFERENCES

digest("sherman act" /p combination conspir*** contract /p agree!)

oligopol! "sherman act" /s express tacit +s agree! collusion

oligopol! "sherman act" /p facilitat*** public similar! standard! uniform*** /5 device product sale term

oligopol! "sherman act" /p court order*** remedy /5 restructur*** structur***

digest("sherman act" /p "price discrimination" %" robinson)

"federal trade" "sherman act" /p base basing +l point

§ 4.3 Joint Ventures and Market Facilitating Agreements

Agreements among competitors are not necessarily monopolistic or harmful to consumers, although the legal presumption against them is strong. Some agreements can enable a group of firms to carry on an activity at a more efficient scale, to reduce information or transaction costs, or eliminate free rider problems.

The widespread application of the *per se* rule to agreements among competitors has often blinded courts to some of these economies. For example, it is not generally a defense to a price fixing charge that the cartel members did not hold enough market power to reduce output profitably. If an urban market contains 50 similar grocers, and three of them jointly run a newspaper advertisement quoting retail prices, the arrangement would reduce advertising costs for each of the three. Furthermore, three grocers out of 50 could not plausibly fix prices—customers would respond to their price increase by buying from the other 47. In such a case the inference that the arrangement creates efficiency is very strong, while the inference of price fixing is very weak. Nevertheless, a court might hold that the *per se* rule prevents it from considering both the argument that the defendants had no market power and that their agreement produced cost reductions that would benefit consumers.[1]

Such agreements among competitors are commonly referred to as "joint ventures." A joint venture is any association of two or more firms for carrying on some activity that each firm might otherwise perform alone. Some joint ventures require the parties to agree about price or output, although many do not. Likewise, the participants in some joint ventures are competitors, while in others they are firms at different levels in a distribution chain, firms producing related products, or the same product in different geographic markets. As a result, to characterize something as a "joint venture" is to say nothing about its effect on competition or its legality under the antitrust laws. When joint ventures are condemned, it is either because they are thought to eliminate competition between the parties to the venture, or else because the joint venture allegedly excludes nonmember firms from access to a certain market.[2]

Firms enter into joint ventures for many reasons. If they are competitors or potential competitors one reason that cannot be overlooked is price fixing. But price fixing, output restriction or monopoly-creating market division explain only a small percentage of joint venture agreements. Most are created to enable the participants to achieve certain economies, either by allowing them to do something at a lower cost, or else by permitting them to do something for themselves that they would otherwise purchase on the marketplace or do without. The benefits of such cost savings will eventually accrue to consumers.

A joint venture of competitors reached the Supreme Court in the very first antitrust case the Court decided on the merits, U.S. v. Trans-Missouri Freight Ass'n.[3] The Association was a consortium of eighteen railroad companies that entered into a joint running agreement. Under the agreement the members coordinated schedules, transfer of cargo, and freight rates. Both the trial court and the federal court of appeals upheld the arrangement. As the circuit court observed,

> The fact that the business of railway companies is irretrievably interwoven, that they interchange cars and traffic, that they act as agents for each other in the delivery and receipt of freight and in paying and collecting freight charges, and that commodities received for transportation generally pass through the hands of several carriers, renders it of vital importance to the public that uniform rules and regulations governing railway traffic should be

§ 4.3

1. See Mt. Vernon Sundat Inc. v. Nissan Motor Corp., 1976–1 Trade Cases ¶ 60,842 (E.D.Va.1975).

2. See §§ 10.2–10.3 below.

3. 166 U.S. 290, 17 S.Ct. 540 (1897).

framed by those who have a practical acquaintance with the subject * * *.[4]

In the 1890's most railroads were small, located entirely within a single state. The Supreme Court had held that states had no power to regulate interstate railway traffic,[5] and it had substantially denied such regulatory power to the Interstate Commerce Commission.[6] Railroads are generally thought to be natural monopolies, however, and they perform poorly under unregulated competition. The circuit court noted that a package shipped several hundred miles would probably be handled by several different railroads. Absent rulemaking by a government agency, the railroads needed an agreement among themselves concerning how such packages or cars should be transferred from one line to the next. Such transfers would naturally be facilitated by coordinated scheduling. Importantly, the freight bill had to be collected either by the railroad that started the package on its route, or else by the railroad that delivered it to its final destination. The money must then be divided up among the participating railroads according to some formula—perhaps in proportion to the number of miles that each line carried the package.

The railroad industry may be unique, but the joint venture at issue in the *Trans-Missouri* case shares two common elements with many such agreements. First, it permitted the participants to operate more efficiently by eliminating much of the chaos that would exist in a market full of small, unregulated railroads. Second, the Association gave the member railroads the power to agree about freight rates.

The most traditional justification for joint ventures is that they can enable two or more firms working together to perform an activity at minimum optimal scale (MOS), while a single firm acting alone could not.[7] For example, suppose that three firms use a particular, specialized metal alloy in the production of certain parts. Efficient production of the alloy requires a plant capable of producing 100,000 tons per year, but the three firms each require only 40,000 tons per year in their production processes. If the three firms together build the plant they will be able to maintain output at an efficient rate. In this case the three firms need not be competitors in the market in which they sell, although they must all be consumers of the same alloy. If the alloy is specialized, however the three firms will likely be competitors in the output market as well.

4. U.S. v. Trans-Missouri Freight Ass'n., 58 F. 58, 79–80 (8th Cir. 1893), reversed, 166 U.S. 290, 17 S.Ct. 540 (1897).

5. Wabash, St. Louis & Pac. Rwy. Co. v. Illinois, 118 U.S. 557, 7 S.Ct. 4 (1886).

6. Cincinnati, New Orleans & Tex. Pac. Rwy. Co. v. I.C.C., 162 U.S. 184, 16 S.Ct. 700 (1896). The Interstate Commerce Commission evidently approved of the joint running agreement at issue in the *Trans-Missouri* case. See 12 ICC Ann.Rep. 10–16 (1898); Hovenkamp, The Economics of Legal History, 67 Minn.L.Rev. 645, 690 (1983).

7. For further discussion of economies of scale and MOS, see § 1.4 above.

This joint venture can save the participating firms (and eventually their customers) a great deal. First of all, the joint venture permits them to produce the alloy at an efficient scale. Second, it enables them to avoid the costs of using the market, and those costs can be rather high, particularly if alternative producers have substantial market power, or if the alloy is specialized and must be made according to individualized specifications, necessitating expensive negotiations with an independent supplier.[8]

Joint ventures can also reduce a firm's marketing costs, or enable it to take advantage of new marketing opportunities. Suppose that three growers of California kiwi berries want to introduce their relatively unfamiliar product to New York. None of the three has output large enough to justify paying a full-time sales agent, but the three operating together could send an agent, each paying one third of the cost. If the product is fungible—that is, if customers cannot distinguish A's kiwi berries from B's kiwi berries—the agent will probably have to charge the same price for all berries of a certain grade or size.[9] In short, the use of the joint selling agency for fungible products may require a certain amount of "price fixing." However, that information alone does not suggest that the growers are reducing output or charging a supracompetitive price for their product. It merely suggests that a common price may be a necessary element of some market facilitating joint ventures.

The Supreme Court approved such a joint sales agency agreement in Appalachian Coals, Inc. v. U.S.[10] The defendants were 137 coal producers who created an exclusive joint selling agency which classified the coal, marketed it, and distributed the proceeds to the participants. Since coal is fungible, the agent had to sell all coal of a certain grade and size at the same price. The Court's decision upholding the agency agreement has been criticized, and has been cast aside by some commentators as a relic of the New Deal's distrust of competition and the antitrust laws. At the very least, however, the decision deserves further study, particularly in light of modern rules for measuring market power.[11] The defendants collectively controlled about 12% of coal production east of the Mississippi River, or about 55% of relevant production in the greater Appalachian region, which was not the region in which the coal was marketed. The market contained a great deal of excess capacity, however, and even these figures seriously overstate the agency's market power.

---

8. See § 7.2 below.

9. If the product of the three farmers was perfectly fungible but the agent charged different prices for the output of the three farmers, buyers would buy all the lowest priced berries first, then all the next lowest, and finally the highest. If the product were not fungible but brand specific, such as televisions, automobiles, or personal computers, then the three producers could each set their own price and customers buying through the agent could compare the merits of each brand, including price.

10. 288 U.S. 344, 53 S.Ct. 471 (1933).

11. See chap. three above.

Joint ventures among competitors can also solve a number of "free rider" problems. A free rider is a firm who takes free advantage of a service or product that is valued by customers but provided by a different firm. If free riding is widespread the valued service or product is likely to disappear.[12]

Research and development (R & D) and advertising are two areas in which free rider problems are significant. For example, many of the results of expensive R & D cannot be patented or, even if patented, cannot effectively be excluded from appropriation by others. If one firm spends vast sums in R & D, a competing firm might be able to reap the benefits without having to pay the high costs. A firm in competition, facing the likelihood that a particular research project will cost a substantial amount but will benefit all firms in the market, will simply forego the project. It cannot afford to subsidize its competitors. A research joint venture will benefit all the firms in the market, however, and force all to share in the costs. Such joint ventures are relatively common in certain industries.[13]

The same arguments generally apply to advertising. If a Sylvania television dealer advertises the qualities of Sylvania televisions, potential television customers will attribute the information only to Sylvanias. The advertising is not likely to benefit dealers in Sonys or Zeniths; on the contrary, it is calculated to attract to the Sylvania dealer customers that might otherwise go to a competitor. However,

---

12. Free riding is discussed more fully in chap. nine.

13. See Kitch, The Law & Economics of Rights in Valuable Information, 9 J. Leg.Stud. 683 (1980). In 1980 the Department of Justice issued guidelines for firms undertaking research joint ventures. Antitrust Guide Concerning Research Joint Ventures, No. 992 Antitrust & Trade Reg. Rptr. 1 (spec. supp., Dec. 4, 1980). The Guidelines noted that the Justice Department has never challenged a "pure" research joint venture that did not impose ancillary restraints on competition. The DOJ identified as ancillary restraints that might warrant challenge: agreements not to produce or market individually any product developed from the joint research; market division with respect to any such manufacturing; agreements not to do competing research independently of the joint venture; agreements to share information not closely related to the purpose of the research joint venture; limitations on access to the venture by other firms. See generally Brodley, Joint Ventures and Antitrust Policy, 95 Harv.L.Rev. 1523 (1982). Research joint ventures have seldom been condemned under the antitrust laws. But see Berkey Photo, Inc. v. Eastman Kodak Co., 603 F.2d 263, 299–304 (2d Cir. 1979), cert. denied, 444 U.S. 1093, 100 S.Ct. 1061 (1980). Kodak, Sylvania and General Electric formed a research joint venture to develop the "Magicube," a flash attachment for cameras. The activity was condemned not for the research, but for the firms' agreement not to disclose the results of their efforts to outsiders.

At the time of this writing both houses of Congress have passed statutes to protect research and development joint ventures from certain forms of antitrust liability. Although the bills of the House and the Senate are different, they generally require parties about to undertake an R & D joint venture to apply to the Justice Department for a certificate that describes the venture. If they should be found liable under the antitrust laws for activity within the scope of the certificate, the remedy will be limited to an injunction or single damages. Under the House version, attorneys' fees will be awarded to the "substantially prevailing party," whether plaintiff or defendant.

if products are fungible advertising will benefit all local producers of the product, whether or not they paid for the advertising.   For example, if Farmer Brown advertises the merits of Farmer Brown's Potatoes, she might be horrified to discover that many customers think potatoes are potatoes.   Farmer Brown's advertisement may increase the number of sales of potatoes, but those sales will be distributed over all producers of potatoes in the advertising market.

In a competitive market Farmer Brown cannot afford to pay for advertising that benefits all local producers of potatoes.   She will not advertise at all, even though the effect of the advertising would be to give consumers better information.   However, the farmers collectively could increase their joint welfare, as well as that of consumers, if they organized a potato growers association, and each paid a proportionate share of the costs of the advertising.   In that case both the benefit and the cost would be shared by all growers.

Alternatively, if the advertising market could be divided, the firms could agree that each would advertise and offer its product in a single geographic area.   The Supreme Court, however, has been intolerant of horizontal agreements to use territorial division to overcome free rider problems.   In the leading case, U.S. v. Topco Associates, Inc.,[14] the Court condemned an arrangement involving about 25 small grocery chains.   Under the agreement the stores marketed their products separately and did not set or advertise prices jointly or pool earnings.   The association created by the agreement bought grocery items in large quantities and redistributed them to members.   Its most distinctive contribution was the "Topco" label that appeared on many of its grocery products, and which had acquired large consumer appeal.   Under the agreement each member promised to sell Topco brand merchandise only in its own assigned marketing territory.   The member was free to open stores in another territory, but these stores could not display or sell the Topco brand. Thus each member had an exclusive area in which it could market Topco brand products.

The government challenged the market division scheme as a cartel, claiming that it operated "to prohibit competition in Topco-brand products among grocery chains engaged in retail operations." The record revealed, however, that each member's share of the grocery market within its assigned territory averaged about 6%. Further, entry into the retail grocery business was quite easy.   The market division in the *Topco* case could not plausibly have turned the defendants into monopolists.

Why would a group of grocery chains divide territories if they could not earn monopoly profits as a result?   The answer in *Topco*

14.   405 U.S. 596, 92 S.Ct. 1126 (1972).
See also U.S. v. Sealy, Inc., 388 U.S. 350,
87 S.Ct. 1847 (1967).

was relatively clear: the defendants wanted to compete more effectively against larger grocery chains. A nationally recognized "Topco" brand could be created only by advertising. If two or more competing chains sold Topco brands in the same market area, however, all chains would benefit from the brand advertising of one. As a result none of the stores would advertise. The territorial division scheme gave each member the exclusive right to sell the Topco brand in a territory, and thus the incentive to advertise the brand there. As the Supreme Court would recognize five years later in a vertical restraint case,[15] the territorial division arguably lessened "intrabrand" competition—that is, competition among different stores selling Topco products. However, it increased "interbrand" competition—competition between stores selling Topco brand products and those selling other brands of the same products. The territorial division scheme enabled the consortium of small chain stores to compete more effectively with the large chain groceries that could afford to produce and advertise their own exclusive labels.

Among the most controversial joint ventures or market facilitating agreements are competitor exchanges of price information. The nature and extent of price information available to buyers and sellers varies considerably from one market to another. For example, current prices of every stock listed by the major stock exchanges are printed in daily newspapers. However, in markets for rare works of art prices are often kept secret from everyone except the parties to the transaction.

Among the least efficient of markets is one in which neither buyer nor seller knows the prevailing market price. The seller probably knows his costs; the buyer probably knows the largest amount she is willing to pay. In such a market the seller can never be sure that he is asking the most the buyer will pay, and the customer can never be sure that she is paying the least the seller will take. The seller will probably begin negotiations by asking an inflated price, and the buyer is sure to respond by making a counteroffer. Each party has an incentive to negotiate as long as he perceives that the other party's position is "soft"—that further negotiations will yield a change in the price. It is not uncommon for the sale of a unique, expensive piece of property, such as a mansion or rare painting, to be negotiated for weeks or even months before the sale is made. It is also common that, after a substantial investment in negotiation, the parties finally decide that they cannot agree on a price.

At the other extreme is a market with a large number of buyers and sellers with full knowledge about current prices. In such a

15. Continental T.V., Inc. v. GTE Sylvania, Inc., 433 U.S. 36, 97 S.Ct. 2549 (1977), on remand, 461 F.Supp. 1046 (1978), judgment affirmed 694 F.2d 1132 (9th Cir. 1982). See chap. nine below.

Some speculate that *Sylvania* overruled *Topco*. See Posner, The Next Step in the Antitrust Treatment of Restricted Distribution: Per Se Legality, 48 U.Chi. L.Rev. 6, 25 (1981).

market price negotiations are virtually nonexistent. Every seller knows that if he asks more than the prevailing price the buyer will not even bother with a counteroffer, but will go to a competitor. Every buyer knows that the price is competitive and that each seller can clear the market at the current price. Transactions will take place at the published market price and someone unwilling to pay that price will never enter the market.

The two extremes are easy to characterize: markets in which information is very bad function poorly; markets in which information is perfect on all sides function well. Unfortunately, there is not a smooth continuum in between. It does not follow that the more information that exists, the more efficiently and competitively the market will perform. In fact sometimes exchanges of price information among competing sellers can facilitate collusion.

The Supreme Court's approach to competitor exchange of price information was first developed in two cases decided during the 1920's, involving trade associations in the hardwood industry. In American Column & Lumber Co. v. U.S.[16] the Supreme Court condemned a price information exchange program under which each member manufacturer furnished the trade association with detailed reports showing the price of each sale and the purchaser's name, the member's rate of production and inventory on hand, plus an estimate of future production. This information was organized around uniform classifications of hardwood sizes and types adopted by the association. The association was clearly concerned about "overproduction," and the members occasionally met to discuss problems that would occur if people did not hold back on output. These discussions convinced the court that the information exchange was really a plan to reduce output and raise prices.

However, the association contained 365 producers who collectively controlled only one-third of American hardwood production. Even assuming an explicit price fixing agreement, it is difficult to see how a cartel with that many members, and controlling only one-third of the market could have a substantial effect on prices.[17]

If collusion was not the motive why did the hardwood producers exchange such detailed information? Justice Brandeis's dissent suggested some reasons: the hardwood manufacturers were small, generally isolated, located in the forests that provided their essential material. No public agency gathered data about production in the industry,[18] and the isolated producers knew very little about market conditions. Furthermore, many of the direct purchasers were very

16. 257 U.S. 377, 42 S.Ct. 114 (1921).

17. See R. Posner, Antitrust Law: An Economic Perspective 135–44 (1976).

18. Justice Brandeis's dissent noted, however, that all information gathered by the defendants was public and open to everyone, and copies of all reports were filed with the Department of Justice and the Federal Trade Commission. 257 U.S. at 414–15, 42 S.Ct. at 122.

large and presumably had good information about their demand. The result in such a situation could be overproduction, particularly if the marginal cost of producing wood from established trees is very low, but the cost of replacing the wood—planting an oak tree and cultivating it for fifty years—is high. For a producer with sunk costs in an established hardwood forest, overproduction would drive prices to a level sufficient to cover the cost of cutting, sawing and planing the lumber, but insufficient to replace the trees.

Four years later, in Maple Flooring Mfrs' Ass'n. v. U.S.[19] the Court approved a program for the exchange of price information among the producers of hardwood flooring, again undertaken through a trade association. The Court distinguished *American Column* by emphasizing that the flooring manufacturers did not give the names of customers and that they reported only completed, past transactions instead of current prices. Why these differences made cartelization less likely the Court did not explain. The Court all but overlooked other facts that distinguished *Maple Flooring*: this time there were only 22 producers instead of 365, and they collectively controlled 70% of the market.

Once again the Court may have come to the wrong conclusion. The items that it stressed were relatively inconsequential: average figures will do as well as specific individual prices for establishing a cartel price, and the names of buyers are not essential. Most likely the Association distributed the information as it did because it had been organized about the time of the Supreme Court's *American Column* decision. It tailored its information exchanges around the language of that opinion.[20]

One incriminating part of the case against the Maple Flooring Association was evidence that the members disseminated a book giving freight rates from Cadillac, Michigan, to various delivery points in the United States.[21] The defendants may have been engaging in basing point pricing.[22] However, the Supreme Court noted that most of the mills were located in northern Michigan and Wisconsin, relatively close to Cadillac, and that for most mills the differences between actual freight costs and costs from Cadillac were trivial. Furthermore, computation of actual freight rates was time consuming, and it was important to the sellers to be able to quote promptly a delivered price. As a result the dissemination of the freight rate book was at best only ambiguous evidence of collusion.

More recently, the Supreme Court has come to regard information exchanges in concentrated markets as more suspect than those in

---

19. 268 U.S. 563, 45 S.Ct. 578 (1925).

20. See R. Posner, note 17 above, at 142.

21. 268 U.S. at 570–72, 45 S.Ct. at 580–581.

22. See § 4.2 above.

diffuse markets.[23] In U.S. v. Container Corp. of America [24] the Court acknowledged that information exchanges are likely to be harmless in competitive markets. However, if concentration is high the exchange is more likely to affect price, and any interference "with the setting of price by free market forces" is illegal. The Court concluded that the information exchange in this case caused prices to "stabilize * * *, though at a downward level." The practical effect of the exchanges was that a prospective seller who knew a competitor's price would try to match it. However, these observations are as consistent with healthy competition in a properly informed market as they are with collusion. Given the tenuousness of any empirical conclusion about the reason for changes in price, the Court would have done well to avoid a rule that required a trial court to determine how a particular information exchange program affected the market price.

Under the rule of reason applied in *Container*, if the market in which the price information exchange occurred is concentrated, if the product is fungible so that price is the predominant element in competition, and if demand at the competitive price is inelastic, the exchange is virtually certain to be condemned, particularly if the court finds *any* relationship, downward or upward, between the information exchange and the market price.[25]

One problem with the rule developed in the *Container* case is that *every* exchange of price information has some effect on price, or else the exchange is of no value. One effect of a published price of $200 for IBM stock is that there will be fewer uninformed buyers paying $2000 for shares, or uninformed sellers parting with their shares for $2.00. All market prices fluctuate, but those in which information is readily available tend to fluctuate within a narrower range than those in which information is scarce.[26]

23. For an argument that information exchanges are generally harmless even in concentrated markets, see Posner, Information and Antitrust: Reflections on the *Gypsum* and *Engineers* Decisions, 67 Geo.L.J. 1187 (1979).

24. 393 U.S. 333, 89 S.Ct. 510 (1969).

25. 393 U.S. at 337, 89 S.Ct. at 512. The Supreme Court did not clearly characterize *Container* as a rule of reason decision until U.S. v. Citizens & Southern Nat. Bank, 422 U.S. 86, 113, 95 S.Ct. 2099, 2115 (1975); see also U.S. v. United States Gypsum Co., 438 U.S. 422, 440 n.16, 98 S.Ct. 2864, 2875 (1978), appeal after remand, 600 F.2d 414 (3d Cir. 1979), cert. denied, 444 U.S. 884, 100 S.Ct. 175 (1979), where the court added that exchanges of current (as opposed to past) price information have "the great-

est potential for generating anti-competitive effects and although not *per se* unlawful have consistently been held to violate the Sherman Act."

Although the Supreme Court did not know it in 1969, the *Container* defendants were probably engaged in explicit price fixing. In 1978 many of the same defendants were indicted for price fixing during the period 1960–1974. After that followed one of the largest private antitrust damages actions in antitrust history. See In re Corrugated Container Antitrust Litigation, 643 F.2d 195 (5th Cir. 1981), rehearing denied, 655 F.2d 1131 (5th Cir. 1981), appeal after remand, 659 F.2d 1322 (5th Cir. 1981), cert. denied, 456 U.S. 998, 102 S.Ct. 2283 (1982).

26. See G. Stigler, The Organization of Industry 171–190 (1983).

The Court's analysis of structural issues, however, made sense. As a basic premise, in the absence of other evidence of express collusion, an exchange of price information in an unconcentrated market, such as the market in *American Column*, should be legal. In such a case the likelihood that the information reduces negotiation costs and facilitates transactions at a level close to the competitive price is high, while the likelihood of collusion is very low.

A concentrated market invites more caution. First, tacit collusion is more likely. Second, in a concentrated market it is less likely that there will be sellers like those in *American Column* who have very poor knowledge of market conditions. As a result, the social loss caused by condemnation of a harmless information exchange is likely to be small. Finally, except in extreme cases courts are incapable of determining how a particular information exchange affects price. The determination of price is a function of countless variables, and no court can realistically account for all of them. The rule announced in *Container* will probably result in some overdeterrence—it is more likely to condemn beneficial exchanges than to approve harmful exchanges. However, in a concentrated market the social costs of any overdeterrence are likely to be low.

Certain joint ventures of competitors are valuable because they reduce transaction costs so substantially that they virtually create a new market for the product. Justice Brandeis characterized the agreement in Chicago Board of Trade v. U.S. [27] this way. At issue was the "call" rule adopted by the Board, which was the world's leading market for grain. During regular trading sessions from 9:30 a.m. to 1:15 p.m. the Board operated as one of the most perfect markets in the real world: hundreds of buyers and sellers of grain met on the floor and made transactions by public bids. Current price information was made available to both buyers and sellers, as fast as it could be displayed on the chalk boards. Under the "call" rule Board members were permitted to trade after the close of the regular session only at the session's closing price. For example, if wheat closed at $1.00 per bushel at the end of the regular Wednesday session, all transactions by Board members after closing until the opening of the Thursday session had to be made at that price. A new price would be established competitively when the Thursday session opened.

In challenging the call rule the government made no attempt to show that it generated an output restriction or enabled the Board members to increase price. They argued simply that the rule "fixed" prices and was therefore illegal. In rejecting that proposition Justice Brandeis noted that the call rule "created" a public market for grain scheduled to arrive. The market, after all, is not where the transaction is consummated but where the price is determined. Under the

27. 246 U.S. 231, 38 S.Ct. 242 (1918).

"call" rule all price determination was made under the most public and competitive of circumstances, with no buyer or seller in a position to take advantage of another party's ignorance. Finding no plausible way that the rule could disguise price fixing, the Court unanimously ordered the complaint dismissed.

Although the Court may have overlooked some important facts,[28] the rationale was obvious enough: markets are often created by sellers. A competitive market usually requires multiple sellers; as a result, the creation of a market may involve a certain amount of joint activity. Some of the most successful and competitive of markets, such as the Board of Trade, the stock exchanges, and many farmers' cooperatives, are created by joint venture of competing firms. One result of such joint activity can be a substantial reduction in transaction costs.

Such markets may themselves be natural monopolies. Often a consumer's highest cost of using a market is search costs. The reasonable consumer will search for the best bargain until the marginal cost of one additional inquiry exceeds its expected marginal utility.[29] As a result, the lower the search costs relative to the value of the product, the more searching the consumer will do before he purchases, and the more likely he will obtain a competitive price. Search costs would be very low if all sellers were gathered together at one place and time so that the consumer could (almost) costlessly survey their offerings. If consumer search costs were zero then we would expect the market price to be uniform—no consumer would buy from any seller who charged more than other sellers. However, when consumer search costs are relatively high there will be wider variations in the market price. The market in *Chicago Board of Trade* forced all transactions into an environment in which consumer search costs were very low.

A dramatic example of a market facilitating agreement was the blanket licensing arrangement at issue in Broadcast Music, Inc. v.

---

28. Brokers on the Board had fixed commission rates which were added to the transaction price. As a result there was no price competition among brokers for sales made during the regular session. A broker might be tempted to "cheat" on post-session sales, however, and steal customers away from another broker. He would do this, not by shaving his commission, which would violate exchange rules, but by shaving the market price. For example, suppose a broker could buy wheat at $1.00 and had a buyer willing to pay $1.05, but the fixed commission rate was 10¢. The broker could make the sale by paying $1.00 for wheat, reselling it at 95¢, and adding in the 10¢ commission. The "call" rule re-

quired the broker to resell the wheat at $1.00. Together, the fixed commission rate plus the call rule effectively prevented brokers from price competing in post-session trades. Whether this fact should have changed the Court's decision is unclear. Price competition among brokers in post-session trades would have moved sales out of the regular session and into the post-session, perhaps undermining the open market. See generally Zerbe, The Chicago Board of Trade Case, 1918, 5 Research in L. & Econ. 17 (1983).

29. See G. Stigler, The Theory of Price 2 (3d ed. 1966).

Columbia Broadcasting System, Inc. (BMI).[30] BMI was an association made up of thousands of composers, publishers and others who owned the performance rights to musical compositions. The performance right gives its holder the exclusive right to perform a composition or license the right of performance to others. The market for such performance rights is vast: tens of thousands of radio stations, television stations, movie producers, and high school glee clubs may need to purchase a performance right before they can perform a musical composition publicly for profit. A substantial problem with such property rights in intellectual property is theft: if someone 1000 miles away performs a song to which you have the exclusive right, you will not notice that any of it is missing; nevertheless you have been robbed.[31]

BMI sold "blanket licenses," which permitted the licensee to perform everything in BMI's library. The library consisted of performance rights to compositions owned by its members. The licensees paid a charge that varied with their revenues. The performance right holder received income that varied with the amount that his compositions were used. BMI also enforced its members' rights by the relatively inexpensive process of listening for the broadcasting of anything in its library by someone who had not purchased a blanket license.

The blanket license arrangement saved untold millions of dollars in transactions costs. Few radio stations could afford to negotiate individually for the right to perform every piece of music they played on the air. If they did, advertising costs would soar and the amount of music played would drop. In fact, if the market had operated on an individual contract per performance basis, the costs of the transactions would often have dwarfed the price of the performance right itself. Furthermore, the "shelf life" of many popular songs is rather short. The performance right might become worthless while the station was negotiating for the right to play it. The single blanket license, however, substituted for thousands of individual transactions and gave licensees immediate access to anything in BMI's library.

BMI differs from *Board of Trade* in one important way: the blanket licensing agreement fundamentally altered the price structure of the market. The "product" that would exist in an uncontrolled market—the right to a single performance of a single composition—all but disappeared, and its price disappeared at the same time. The blanket licensing arrangement certainly seemed to run afoul of the Supreme Court's conclusion that agreements among competitors that tamper with a market's price structure are illegal *per se*.[32] In addition, the agreement completely eliminated price competition among artists. Once a radio station had purchased its blanket license

30. 441 U.S. 1, 99 S.Ct. 1551 (1979).

31. See Kitch, note 13 above.

32. See U.S. v. Socony-Vacuum Oil Co., 310 U.S. 150, 223–224, 60 S.Ct. 811, 844 (1940).

it could perform any composition by any artist in the BMI library at no additional cost.

Furthermore, the blanket licensing agreement was price discriminatory. The price of the blanket license varied with the buyer's revenues; however, this formula bore no relationship to the cost that the blanket licenses imposed on either BMI or the performance right holders. They simply made more money from large purchasers than they did from small ones. This kind of persistent price discrimination can exist only if the seller (or group of sellers) has a significant amount of market power.[33]

All this evidence of price fixing and monopoly power notwithstanding, the Court refused to apply the *per se* rule to blanket licensing. The efficiency-creating potential of the arrangement was too obvious. Moreover, the licenses that the performance right owners conferred on BMI were non-exclusive: any owner could continue to sell the right to perform a single composition or group of compositions on an individual transaction basis. The fact that the blanket licensing arrangement could co-exist with a market in which thousands of individual performance right holders were free to negotiate individual transactions (but few did), suggests that buyers obtained a lower price through blanket licensing than they would have through individual transactions.[34]

The *BMI* case may be regarded as *sui generis.* The product that the defendants sold and the nature of their property rights in it were different than the commodities involved in most cartel cases. Perhaps more importantly, it is far from clear that *BMI* involved price fixing by "competitors." To say that the thousands of owners of performance rights were competitors implies that "Heartbreak Hotel" and the "Moonlight Sonata" are fungible—that radio listeners are indifferent to whether they are hearing one or the other. If "Heartbreak Hotel" and the "Moonlight Sonata" occupy distinct markets, however, then the owner of the exclusive right to perform one of them is a monopolist.[35] Perhaps the blanket licensing arrange-

---

33. See chapter thirteen below.

34. See also Buffalo Broadcasting Co., Inc. v. American Soc. of Composers, ___ F.2d ___ (2d Cir. 1984), in which the circuit court reversed the lower court and upheld the legality of blanket licensing arrangements imposed on local television stations not affiliated with any network. The court rejected the argument that blanket licensing imposed on independent stations was more anticompetitive than blanket licensing imposed on large networks, because the independents would have a far more difficult time negotiating individual licenses. The second circuit did not reject the

argument in principle, but held that it had not been established in this case.

35. The district court in *Buffalo Broadcasting*, id., found that a very small percentage of composers obtained a very large percentage of the blanket license revenues, which were paid in proportion to the number of times a composition was played by a licensee. In 1979 less than .8% of the composers received 75% of all television royalties. 546 F.Supp. at 284. If compositions were fungible the royalties would end up being about evenly distributed among performance right owners.

ment should more accurately be characterized as an association of monopolists than an agreement among competitors.

The economics of the market for musical compositions suggests that the owner of the exclusive right to perform a particular composition may have substantial market power. Virtually all the costs of producing a musical composition are fixed. Once it has been recorded or printed, the costs of licensing it to someone are virtually zero, disregarding transaction costs. In a competitive market, in which price is driven to marginal cost, individual composers would license their compositions for a net price near zero. In that case, of course, the market price would not cover the total costs and many composers—at least those who made their living from composing—would exit the market.

In fact, however, a radio station might be quite willing to pay far more than marginal cost to perform a popular piece of music, even though it could obtain another piece of music more cheaply (or even free). Radio listeners, and therefore radio stations, do distinguish one composition from another, often with a great deal of enthusiasm. As a result the holder of the exclusive right to perform a particular, successful composition faces a downward sloping demand curve. The aggregation of all these little monopolists into BMI's library may have given BMI no more market power than its individual, more successful artists had alone.[36]

 WESTLAW REFERENCES

"joint venture" /70 efficien! "market power" "per se rule" (price /2 fix ***)

co-operative joint trade +1 association venture /p divide* division split /5 territor!

co-operative joint trade +1 association venture /p price /5 exchange information

265k12(18) +p rule /2 "per se" reason

§ 4.4 Characterization and Evaluation: The Per Se Rule and the Rule of Reason

Consider the following statements, all from the Supreme Court:

The true test of legality is whether the restraint imposed is such as merely regulates and perhaps thereby promotes competition or whether it is such as may suppress or even destroy competition. To determine that question the court must ordinarily consider the facts peculiar to the business to which the restraint is applied; its condition before and after the restraint was imposed; the nature of the restraint and its effect, actual or probable.

---

36. For example, if a monopoly manufacturer of toasters and a monopoly manufacturer of televisions were to merge, the post-merger firm would not likely have increased market power. The new firm might find that the profit-maximizing price and output for televisions and toasters were exactly the same as they had been before the merger.

Justice Brandeis, in Board of Trade of City of Chicago v. U.S., 246 U.S. 231, 238, 38 S.Ct. 242, 244 (1918).

> Under the Sherman Act a combination formed for the purpose and with the effect of raising, depressing, fixing, pegging, or stabilizing the price of a commodity　*　*　*　is illegal *per se.*

Justice Douglas, in U.S. v. Socony-Vacuum Oil Co., 310 U.S. 150, 223, 60 S.Ct. 811, 844 (1940).

> Whether or not we would decide this case the same way under the rule of reason used by the District Court is irrelevant.

Justice Marshall, in U.S. v. Topco Associates Inc., 405 U.S. 596, 609, 92 S.Ct. 1126, 1134 (1972).

> [P]er se rules　*　*　*　are　*　*　*　directed to the protection of the public welfare; they are complementary to, and in no way inconsistent with, the rule of reason.

Chief Justice Berger, dissenting, in U.S. v. Topco Associates, 405 U.S. at 621, 92 S.Ct. at 1140.

> Contrary to its name, the Rule [of Reason] does not open the field of antitrust inquiry to any argument in favor of a challenged restraint that may fall within the realm of reason. Instead, it focuses directly on the challenged restraint's impact on competitive conditions.
>
> * * *
>
> There are　*　*　*　two complementary categories of antitrust analysis. In the first category are agreements whose nature and necessary effect are so plainly anticompetitive that no elaborate study of the industry is needed to establish their illegality—they are "illegal per se;" in the second category are agreements whose competitive effect can only be evaluated by analyzing the facts peculiar to the business, the history of the restraint, and the reasons why it was imposed. In either event, the purpose of the analysis is to form a judgment about the competitive significance of the restraint; it is not to decide whether a policy favoring competition is in the public interest, or in the interest of the members of an industry.

J. Stevens, in National Society of Professional Engineers v. U.S., 435 U.S. 679, 688–692, 98 S.Ct. 1355, 1363–65 (1978).

> [The] *per se* rule is a valid and useful tool of antitrust policy and enforcement. And agreements among competitors to fix prices on their individual goods or services are among those concerted activities that the Court has held to be within the *per se* category. But easy labels do not always supply ready answers.
>
> * * *
>
> [The defendants] have joined together into an organization that sets its price for the blanket license it sells. But this is not a

question simply of determining whether two or more potential competitors have literally "fixed" a "price." As generally used in the antitrust field, "price fixing" is a shorthand way of describing certain categories of business behavior to which the *per se* rule has been held applicable. [However, when] two partners set the price of their goods or services they are literally "price fixing," but they are not *per se* in violation of the Sherman Act. * * * Thus, it is necessary to characterize the challenged conduct as falling within or without that category of behavior to which we apply the label *"per se* price fixing." That will often, but not always, be a simple matter.

J. White, in Broadcast Music, Inc. v. CBS, Inc., 441 U.S. 1, 8–9, 99 S.Ct. 1551, 1556–57 (1979).

The costs of judging business practices under the rule of reason * * * have been reduced by the recognition of *per se* rules. Once experience with a particular kind of restraint enables the Court to predict with confidence that the rule of reason will condemn it, it has applied a conclusive presumption that the restraint is unreasonable.

J. Stevens, in Arizona v. Maricopa Cty. Med. Society, 457 U.S. 332, 343–44, 102 S.Ct. 2466, 2473 (1982).

Courts and commentators often say that most practices analyzed as antitrust violations are considered under a "rule of reason," while the *per se* rule applies only to a limited number—perhaps price fixing, horizontal territorial or customer division, concerted refusals to deal, resale price maintenance and some tying arrangements.

In fact, all legal analysis operates under *per se* rules.[1] The *per se* rule says simply that once we know a certain amount about a practice we can condemn it without further inquiry. The difference between a *"per se"* and a "rule of reason" standard lies in how much we need to know before we can make that decision. A rational decision maker will collect information, beginning with that which is most relevant and easiest to gather, until he reaches a point at which the marginal cost of acquiring an additional item exceeds its expected marginal return. In this case the "marginal return" is the increased accuracy of the final decision. If the cost of obtaining a piece of information is very high, and the chance is small that it will make the final decision more accurate than a decision based on information already obtained, then the rational decision maker will not seek the additional information.[2] Even in a so-called rule of reason case, however, the parties

§ 4.4

1. See Posner, The Rule of Reason and the Economic Approach: Reflections on the *Sylvania* Decision, 45 U. Chi.L.Rev. 1, 14–15 (1977); See the debate between professors Easterbrook and Markovits. Easterbrook, The Limits of Antitrust, 63 Tex.L.Rev. (1984); Markovits, The Limits to Simplifying Antitrust: A Reply to Professor Easterbrook, 63 Tex.L.Rev. (1984).

2. See Justice Stevens' statement in the *Maricopa County* case, above.

will not produce *all* the marginally relevant information. They will produce sufficient information to satisfy some judicially created presumptions—for example, that a defendant with 90% of a market has monopoly power, or that a merger between the two largest firms in a concentrated market is anticompetitive.

Justice Marshall was wrong in *Topco* when he said it was "irrelevant" whether a *per se* case would come out the same way under the rule of reason. Given some final, accurate decision, O, the *per se* rule rests on a judicial judgment that the court can approximate O quite accurately once it knows a few specific things. Further, learning more things is likely to be very expensive and unlikely to bring the court substantially closer to O. The *per se* rule manifestly does not rest on a judgment that the two antitrust rules are calculated *ex ante* to yield different decisions.

The *per se* rule, incidentally, is a two-edged sword. Granted that a small number of practices are classified as *per se* illegal under the antitrust laws, a giant host are *per se* legal. For example, a record alleging illegal monopolization but showing that the defendant controls only 25% of its market will probably be dismissed on the pleadings.[3] Even though monopolization is a "rule of reason" offense, once it has been determined that a firm's market share is small, further inquiry into whether the defendant monopolized the market is not likely to yield a different decision.

The *per se* rule is an *empirical* rule. To be sure, the legal jargon sometimes requires a judge to hold certain conduct illegal *per se* as a "matter of law" rather than fact. But the judge arrives at that conclusion only because courts have had sufficient experience with a certain kind of practice that they can comfortably pigeon-hole it into the *per se* box.

Like all empirical rules the *per se* rule is not based on logical necessity but on accumulated observation. Its applications are subject to continual testing, falsification, and modification. Even Newton's laws of motion did not go unchallenged forever. Furthermore, when judges attempt to clarify the *per se* rule, the clarifications are subject to the same limitations. In U.S. v. Socony-Vacuum Oil Co.,[4] the Supreme Court was faced with a public (not surreptitious) agreement among oil and gasoline producers to "allocate" the supply of gasoline. Prices were not fixed, but under the allocation agreement each major oil producer was assigned to independent oil producers who had no marketing outlets. The major producers agreed to buy up the independent producers' output, and in the process each major producer had an opportunity to reduce its own production. As a result, total output in the market may have

---

3. See Dimmitt Agri Indus., Inc. v. CPC Int'l., Inc., 679 F.2d 516 (5th Cir. 1982), cert. denied, 460 U.S. 1082, 103 S.Ct. 1770 (1983).

4. 310 U.S. 150, 60 S.Ct. 811 (1940).

decreased. Prices did move up somewhat, but that change could have been attributed to factors other than the alleged conspiracy.

Whether these practices fell under the *per se* rule against "price fixing" troubled Justice Douglas only as long as it took him to "clarify" the *per se* rule adopted in earlier, more explicit price fixing cases such as U.S. v. Trenton Potteries Co.[5] "Any combination which tampers with price structures is engaged in unlawful activity," he concluded, whether or not the practice fit the pre-*Socony* meaning of "price fixing."

But wasn't Justice Douglas clearly wrong as well? The combination in *Chicago Board of Trade* [6] clearly "tampered" with the price at which wheat could be sold by a Board member outside the regular trading session. The combination at issue sixty years later in *Broadcast Music* [7] "tampered" with the price structure so much that nothing approximating an "unrestrained" market continued to exist. The Supreme Court refused to apply the *per se* rule in either case.

Because *per se* rules are empirical judgments, their fate is to go through a continual evolutionary process. In 1918 the "price fixing agreement" at issue in *Chicago Board of Trade* was sufficiently novel that the Court was forced to distinguish it from earlier cartel cases. Likewise, the blanket licensing agreement in *Broadcast Music* presented the Court with a very Pickwickian sort of price fixing.

The most difficult aspect of the jurisprudence of the *per se* rule is determining when it should be followed. Sometimes this is called the problem of "characterization." Once a court has properly characterized a practice as price fixing, it is *per se* illegal. However, determining *when* a practice should be so characterized can be very difficult, and may involve a fair amount of sophisticated economic inquiry. In *Chicago Board of Trade* and *Broadcast Music* the Court was willing to consider arguments that practices conceded to "fix" prices were not "price fixing" and did not warrant *per se* treatment. On the other hand, *Socony-Vacuum* and, more recently, National Society of Professional Engineers v. U.S.[8] involved arrangements that less obviously "fixed" prices; nevertheless, the Court characterized the arrangements as "price fixing" and applied the *per se* rule.

Consider the arguments offered by the defendants in these cases. In *Socony* the defendants argued that overproduction of oil had led to a glut on the market which was driving prices so low that producers would go bankrupt but for an agreement among themselves to allocate production. In *Engineers* a professional associa-

---

5. 273 U.S. 392, 47 S.Ct. 377 (1927).

6. Chicago Board of Trade v. U.S., 246 U.S. 231, 38 S.Ct. 242 (1918). See § 4.3 above.

7. Broadcast Music, Inc. v. Columbia Broadcasting, 441 U.S. 1, 99 S.Ct. 1551 (1979), on remand, 607 F.2d 543 (2d Cir. 1979), cert. denied, 450 U.S. 970, 101 S.Ct. 1491 (1981), rehearing denied, 450 U.S. 1050, 101 S.Ct. 1772 (1981). See § 4.3 above.

8. 435 U.S. 679, 98 S.Ct. 1355 (1978).

tion of engineers defended a canon that prohibited members from bidding competitively for jobs. The defense was that unrestrained competitive bidding would motivate engineers to cut corners in an effort to produce the lowest bid. As a result they might produce unsafe projects that would injure the public. The Court responded that "the Rule of Reason does not support a defense based on the assumption that competition itself is unreasonable."[9]

The Court's response is ambiguous, because over the years "competition" has been used in antitrust cases to mean several different things.[10] However, Congress passed the antitrust laws in order to give courts a basic presumption that "competition" is the preferred state of affairs in any market. Courts are entitled to presume the contrary only when Congress or another appropriate sovereign has passed a law regulating price or entry into some market. When no such law has been passed, the courts simply are not entitled to listen to a plea that "competition" is not working well in a market and needs a hand from the participants.

Within this paradigm "competition" solves the problem of excess capacity in the same way that nature solves the problem of excess population—by starvation and death. That takes care of the argument in *Socony-Vacuum*. The argument raised by *Engineers* is only a little more difficult: "competition" evidently refers to a state of affairs in which consumers are presumed to know what they want and what they are willing to pay for. The engineer who produces a well-publicized defective product once is not likely to do it twice. Within the competition model that alone should create sufficient incentive not to cut corners.

As the Supreme Court suggested in *Engineers*, an agreement among competitors that arguably affects price will not be saved from the *per se* rule by an argument that "competition" is bad for a particular industry. This is talking in circles, however, unless "competition" has a meaning. The Supreme Court seems to be tending in this direction: "competition" is that state of affairs in which output is maximized and price is minimized. Agreements among competitors likely to affect price are presumed illegal without further inquiry into the market conditions or the nature of the restraint. The presumption can be defeated and the defendant permitted to offer further evidence under the rule of reason only if it can provide a plausible argument that the agreement actually results in lower prices and higher output. Impermissible under *per se* analysis is the defendant's offer to defeat the presumption by showing that low prices or high output are not in the best interest of consumers in this particu-

---

9. Id. at 697, 98 S.Ct. at 1368 (1978).

10. See Hovenkamp, Book Review, 33 Hastings L.J. 755, 762 (1982).

lar case. That determination must be reserved to the appropriate legislative authority.

Within this model the Court was forced to listen to the defendant's answering argument in *BMI*. Blanket licensing did involve an agreement among competitors affecting price. However, the defendants produced a plausible argument that the agreement resulted in substantially larger output and lower prices. On the other hand, the argument in *Engineers* that "excessive" price competition would force engineers to cut corners was impermissible, for it was an argument that the public had an interest in higher bid prices. That argument may or may not be sound, but it must be settled by legislation.

Nevertheless, as stated the principle is deceptively simple. It is easy to say that an agreement whose efficiency effects arguably outweigh its anticompetitive effects ought to receive rule of reason treatment. Courts are not capable of measuring either efficiency or power over price with anything approaching scientific accuracy, however. Most such judicial measurements are simply hunches, based on several presumptions about the nature and effects of certain practices.

Suppose the only three grocers in a rural community place a joint advertisement in a newspaper, advertising tomatoes at 69¢ per pound. The nearest grocer not a party to this agreement is 50 miles away. When a grocery customer sues the three stores for price fixing they offer to show that the cost of the newspaper advertisement was $150. By advertising jointly, at a cost of $50 each, the stores were able to save $100 apiece on advertising costs. These costs were passed along to consumers in the form of lower prices.

On its face the grocers' argument is plausible, and it is an argument that the agreement yields higher output and lower prices. But should a court listen to the grocers' evidence? Probably not. First, the stores obviously agreed about a price before they ran the advertisement. Second, they appear to control 100% of a relevant market, so presumptively they had the power to charge a monopoly price. Conceding that the advertisement lowered each store's costs by $100.00, we might want to say that the relevant question is whether the cost reduction was large enough to offset any price increase that might result from the grocer's exercise of monopoly power.

However, no court is capable of answering that question, unless it blunders into some terribly revealing documents. Furthermore, the court will have to make an important policy judgment: what if the defendants actually did set a higher price for tomatoes, but the advertising costs saved them $100 each? As a result the efficiency gain may have outweighed the monopoly deadweight loss, but the entire efficiency gain accrued to the price fixers.

In this case the court has no choice but to apply the *per se* rule against price fixing. Further inquiry into the relevant factors—the stores' marginal costs, the market elasticity of demand for tomatoes, and the ease and rapidity with which additional tomato retailers could supply the market—would cost a great deal and the information would be so ambiguous that the court would not likely be able to make a better decision. The risk that the agreement will produce anticompetitive consequences is substantial, and the extent of compensating efficiencies is very difficult to measure. The court is better off guessing now than it would be spending vast amounts of time and money and guessing later.

However, evaluation of a case like U.S. v. Topco Associates, Inc.,[11] is easier, and analysis of the market and the effects of the restraint more likely to yield an informed decision. Once again there is an agreement among competitors that arguably increases output by enabling Topco members to compete better with larger grocery chains. This time the agreement enables the defendants to avoid "free rider" problems. No court can quantify the welfare benefits created by the agreement, but in this case the low market shares of the individual members—about 6% each in their respective territories—indicates that there is *nothing* to put in the other side of the scale. The inference that the agreement makes Topco brand sellers more efficient is strong; there is no offsetting inference that the agreement gives them the power to reduce output and raise price.

The *Broadcast Music* case is more difficult, because the defendants collectively controlled a large share of the relevant market. As a result they could have used the blanket licensing arrangement to reduce output and raise prices. In the *BMI* case, however, the inference that the efficiency effects of the arrangement outweighed any anticompetitive consequences was supported by two things. First, the transactional efficiencies achieved by blanket licensing were truly extraordinary: many radio stations would have been unable to function if they had to purchase all their performance rights one at a time.[12] Further, this efficiency was present and manifest, not merely plausible. Even the plaintiff did not want to abolish blanket licensing; it merely wanted the defendants to subdivide the blanket licenses into categories.

Second, and very important, the individual transaction market remained as an alternative. The rights that individual artists conferred on BMI were nonexclusive, and the artists were too numerous to make hidden price fixing plausible. As a result, the "unrestrained" market always remained available as an alternative, competing, so to speak, with blanket licensing. If blanket licensing really

11. 405 U.S. 596, 92 S.Ct. 1126 (1972).   **12.** See § 4.3 above.
See § 4.3 above.

did result in reduced output and higher costs to buyers, the buyers would have gone directly to the artists.

Having been offered these arguments the Court was in a position to conclude that the cost of evaluating the additional information upon which the arguments were predicated was relatively low. The chance that the information, once evaluated, would affect the decision was rather high. As a result, evaluation of the information—application of the rule of reason—was in order.

In Arizona v. Maricopa County Medical Society,[13] the Supreme Court applied the *per se* rule to an agreement among physicians to set the *maximum* fee they would charge for services. The 1750 doctors involved represented about 70% of the medical practitioners in Maricopa County. If Maricopa County was a relevant geographic market the participants in the agreement arguably had significant market power.

The maximum fee agreement in *Maricopa* was ostensibly designed to contain medical costs. The third party health insurance programs that most Americans use to finance health coverage yield little face-to-face accountability for prices. The doctor's fee, or most of it, is paid directly by the health insurer. The fee shows up, of course, in health insurance premiums—but these are either paid by the patient at a different time or paid substantially by the patient's employer. The lack of accountability in the system may help to contribute to rapidly increasing health care costs.

Under the Maricopa Plan a group of doctors agreed not to charge more than a certain price for specified services. Insurance companies in return agreed to pay the full cost of these services if they were provided by a participating doctor.[14] The list of participating doctors was made available to consumers. As a result, purchasers of medical services had information readily available about the price of medical services and an incentive—total coverage—to seek out a doctor who agreed to be bound by the maximum fees. If this argument were sound, the result of the Plan was lower consumer prices.[15] On the other side of the scale was the argument that "maximum" price fixing is really nothing more than disguised minimum price fixing, since most participating doctors charged the full maximum price.

13. 457 U.S. 332, 102 S.Ct. 2466 (1982).

14. Under most private insurance plans the patient must produce some form of "copayment" at the time the services are delivered. The copayment may reflect the difference between the doctor's actual fee and maximum policy coverage, or it may simply be a percent-

age of the total fee, or a combination of the two.

15. See Easterbrook, Maximum Price Fixing, 48 U.Chi.L.Rev. 886 (1981); Leffler, Arizona v. Maricopa County Medical Society: Maximum-Price Agreements in Markets with Insured Buyers, 2 Sup.Ct.Econ.Rev. 187 (1984).

Maricopa presents a particularly difficult problem of characterization. No court could balance the savings from reduced consumer information costs against the monopoly loss that might have accrued from doctor price fixing. However, some unique aspects of the case suggest that the court applied the *per se* rule too quickly. For example, if the "maximum" price fixing agreement was really a disguised minimum price fixing agreement why did the insurance companies agree to participate? The doctors and the health insurers stand in a *vertical* relationship. As a general rule an insurer is made worse off by a price increase that increases the amount of its insured risk. Just as automobile insurance companies are better off in a world of safe drivers and cheap auto body repair shops, health insurers are better off in a world of healthy people and inexpensive doctors.[16]

Because it applied the *per se* rule the Court failed to analyze some additional evidence mentioned in its opinion. For example, it noted that 85%–95% of all physicians in Maricopa County charged rates "at or above" those stipulated in the defendants' program. Since the program involved about 70% of the physicians in the county, this suggests that at least half and perhaps all of the nonparticipating physicians were charging as much as or more than the participants. It would have been worthwhile for a court to compare the rates charged by the participants with those charged by nonparticipants. Rule of reason analysis would have permitted the comparison. If the participants had been engaged in ordinary price fixing and charging their profit-maximizing prices, equally efficient nonparticipating physicians would have maximized their own profits by billing at or slightly less than the cartel price: they could then have obtained all the customers they wanted. However, if all nonparticipating physicians charged *more* than the fees charged by the participating physicians, then either the cartel had made some extraordinary miscalculations about its profit-maximizing prices, or—more likely—the nonparticipating doctors were the true monopolists, taking advantage of high consumer search costs in health care.[17] In short, evidence that nonparticipating doctors charged more than participants would have suggested that the agreement was doing exactly what the defendants argued it was doing: reducing health care costs.

Finally, as Justice Powell noted in his dissent, doctors were free to join or leave the Plan at will, and participating doctors were free to deal with patients outside the Plan on any basis they pleased. These facts are absolutely inconsistent with the economics of cartelization:

---

16. This is simply a variation of the vertical integration argument presented below in § 10.1. In the *Maricopa* case two of the employers were self-insurers: the State of Arizona, and Motorola Corp. A self-insurer stands to gain from an action that reduces the amount of expected claims against it.

17. The only alternative explanation—certainly implausible—is that all nonparticipating physicians had higher costs than all participating physicians.

no cartel could restrict its output and raise price if it permitted its members freely to come and go, or to make unlimited "non-cartel" sales.   On balance, the Supreme Court applied the wrong rule.[18]

 WESTLAW REFERENCES

"per se rule"   /s   (customer geograph! horizontal territor***   /4
    division) "price fix***" (refus**   /2   deal) tying

"per se rule"   /p   "rule of reason"   /p   characteriz! compare*
    compari*** differ!

"per se rule"   /s   competiton

---

18.   In National Collegiate Athletic Ass'n (NCAA) v. Board of Regents of the Univ. of Oklahoma, ___ U.S. ___, 104 S.Ct. 2948 (1984), the Supreme Court condemned an agreement among NCAA football colleges to restrict the number of times that each team's football games could be televised.   The Court of Appeals had held that the NCAA television restriction was illegal per se as an agreement among competitors in the market for televised college football which restricted output in that market. The Court of Appeals rejected the NCAA's defense that the arrangement actually promoted competition in a different market—the market for live attendance at football games.   Incidentally, *all* output restrictions in one market tend to increase the demand in markets for substitute products.   For example, price fixing in the beef industry will drive up the price of pork and lamb. The Circuit Court's rejection of the NCAA's defense made good economic sense.

The Supreme Court affirmed the lower court's judgment, but held that the conduct at issue must be evaluated under the rule of reason.   The NCAA is a special "network" industry in which "horizontal restraints on competition are essential if the product [football games] is to be available at all."   104 S.Ct. at 2961.   As the Court noted, NCAA foot-

ball teams simply cannot produce their product without agreeing with each other about certain things, such as a playing schedule, the size and shape of the football field and the rules of the game, and on rules determining player eligibility.

Some of these agreements clearly have an effect on "output."   For example, the teams must agree with one another whether there should be ten games or twenty games in a football season.   Other agreements, such as one concerning the size of the playing field, may have little or no effect on output. The Supreme Court effectively held that since the delivery of the product at issue *forced* the NCAA members to agree about certain things, and since some of these things necessarily affected output, all agreements among the teams should be subject to the rule of reason.

The Court then went on to condemn the television restriction under the rule of reason.   Faced with substantial evidence that the agreement made televised NCAA football less available, that some schools wanted to televise more football games than the rule permitted, and that no plausible procompetitive justifications for the rule had been offered, the rule was anticompetitive under the rule of reason.

CHAPTER 5

SINGLE–FIRM MONOPOLIZATION

Table of Sections

§ 5.1 The Monopolization Offense

Section 2 of the Sherman Act, 15 U.S.C.A. § 2, condemns "every person who shall monopolize * * *." Today "monopolization" refers to a number of activities that may be illegal when performed by the dominant firm in a relevant market.

The law of monopolization is concerned with what Louis D. Brandeis once called "The Curse of Bigness."[1] Today even more than in Brandeis's time, Americans are dominated by giant corporations.[2] But big business and Americans always have had a love-hate relationship. Big corporations employ more Americans and pay them higher salaries than small businesses do. They do most of our research and development, introduce most of our new products, defend us, entertain and inform us, and pay most of our taxes. In spite of these bounties Americans have always mistrusted big business. We have written and read about the "organization man" who has ceded his freedom and identity to his employer.[3] We believe that big business homogenizes us, over-standardizes us, and—worst of

---

§ 5.1

1. L. Brandeis, The Curse of Bigness (1934).

2. However, some writers dispute the common assertion that industrial concentration in America has risen throughout the last half century. See Y. Brozen, Concentration, Mergers, and Public Policy 119–55 (1982).

3. W. H. Whyte, Jr., The Organization Man (1956).

all—makes us pay high prices for shoddy products or poor service. Antitrust is properly concerned only with the last of these sins.

In United States v. Grinnell Corp.[4] the Supreme Court defined illegal monopolization to include two elements: "(1) the possession of monopoly power in the relevant market and (2) the willful acquisition or maintenance of that power as distinguished from growth or development as a consequence of a superior product, business acumen, or historic accident." Both of these elements must be established before the defendant is guilty of monopolization.

During the first half of the twentieth century the judicial definition of the monopolization offense went through a great deal of flux. Courts generally agreed that the offense required a showing of the defendant's substantial market power. In the earliest cases, however, the defendant's market power was obvious, and courts spent little time discussing it.[5] Today the market power requirement is clearly established, although courts still have difficulty measuring market power and are not entirely clear about how much market power a defendant must have to be guilty of illegal monopolization.

Over the years courts have had broad disagreements about the offense's bad conduct requirements. In U.S. v. United Shoe Machinery Corp.[6] Judge Wyzanski examined the monopolization case law and found three approaches to the monopolization offense. Before Judge Learned Hand's famous decision in *Alcoa* [7] the prevailing view was that "[a]n enterprise has monopolized * * * if it has acquired or maintained a power to exclude others as a result of using an unreasonable 'restraint of trade' in violation of § 1 of the Sherman Act." [8] This definition implied that a firm could not violate § 2 unless it also violated § 1. However, already in the 1911 *American Tobacco* case, Chief Justice White suggested that conduct that would violate § 1 of the Sherman Act when performed by agreement with another firm, would violate § 2 when performed unilaterally by a firm with monopoly power, or perhaps with the intent to monopolize.[9]

Next Judge Wyzanski described a "more inclusive approach" that Justice Douglas had developed in U.S. v. Griffith.[10] Under that rule a firm monopolizes illegally when "it (a) has the power to exclude competition, and (b) has exercised it, or has the power to exercise it." Judge Wyzanski interpreted this to mean at the very least that "it is a violation of § 2 for one having effective control of the market to

4. 384 U.S. 563, 570–71, 86 S.Ct. 1698, 1704 (1966).

5. For example, Standard Oil Co. of N.J. v. U.S. 221 U.S. 1, 31 S.Ct. 502 (1911); U.S. v. American Tobacco Co., 221 U.S. 106, 31 S.Ct. 632 (1911).

6. 110 F.Supp. 295 (D.Mass.1953), affirmed per curiam, 347 U.S. 521, 74 S.Ct. 699 (1954).

7. U.S. v. Alum. Co. of America, 148 F.2d 416 (2d Cir. 1945).

8. 110 F.Supp. at 342.

9. *American Tobacco*, 221 U.S. at 181–184, 31 S.Ct. at 648–650.

10. 334 U.S. 100, 107, 68 S.Ct. 941, 945 (1948).

use, or plan to use, any exclusionary practice, even though it is not a technical restraint of trade" in violation of § 1.

Finally, the third and broadest approach came from Judge Hand in the *Alcoa* case, although Justice Douglas endorsed it in *Griffith* as well. Under this approach "one who has acquired an overwhelming share of the market 'monopolizes' whenever he does business * * * apparently even if there is no showing that his business involves any exclusionary practices." Judge Hand had softened this rule, however. A defendant could escape liability by showing that it had acquired its monopoly exclusively by its own

> superior skill, superior products, natural advantages, (including accessibility to raw materials or markets), economic or technological efficiency, (including scientific research), low margins of profit maintained permanently and without discrimination, or [legally used patents].[11]

Today courts clearly have reached beyond Judge Wyzanski's first, most narrow definition of illegal monopolization. Although violation of § 1 of the Sherman Act by a monopolist is often sufficient to establish illegal monopolization, it is not necessary; firms innocent of § 1 violations have frequently been condemned under § 2.

However, there is little precedent for Judge Wyzanski's third, most expansive rule: that a firm with monopoly power violates the Sherman Act whenever it "does business." Over the years legal scholars and several members of Congress have recommended at least a limited law against so-called "no fault" monopolization, but those debates remain academic. The merits of such proposals are addressed in § 5.3.

Today the prevailing legal rule closely resembles Judge Wyzanski's second proposal: illegal monopolization requires a showing that the defendant (a) has "monopoly power", which is substantial market power; and (b) has "exercised" that power.

What it means to "exercise" monopoly power is ambiguous. The sale of products at a monopoly price is certainly an "exercise" of monopoly power—however, courts have consistently held that even the monopolist may legally sell its product at its profit-maximizing price and reduce output to a level capable of clearing the market at that price.[12] Judge Wyzanski wisely defined the "exercise" of mo-

---

11. *United Shoe Machinery*, 110 F.Supp. at 342.

12. See Berkey Photo, Inc. v. Eastman Kodak Co., 603 F.2d 263, 275 (2d Cir. 1979), cert. denied 444 U.S. 1093, 100 S.Ct. 1061 (1980):

> The mere possession of monopoly power does not *ipso facto* condemn a market participant. But, to avoid the proscriptions of § 2, the firm must refrain at all times from conduct directed at smothering competition. This doctrine has two branches. Unlawfully acquired power remains anathema even when kept dormant. And it is not less true that a firm with a legitimately achieved monopoly may not wield the resulting power to tighten its hold on the market.

nopoly power as an "exclusionary" practice—that is, a practice that deters potential rivals from entering the monopolist's market, or existing rivals from increasing their output in response to the monopolist's price increase. The monopolist's sale of its product at a monopolistic price is not an "exclusionary" practice. Far from it, monopoly profits attract investors and new entry into the market, and the resulting increased output drives the price back to the competitive level. The monopolist, however, would prefer that these investors place their money somewhere else. "Exclusionary practices" are acts by the monopolist designed to discourage potential competitors from entering the field, or to prevent competitors from increasing output.

Even here, however, some qualification is in order. Not all exclusionary practices merit condemnation. Many of them make consumers better off: for example, research and development, or the production of a better product at a lower price. To say that illegal monopolization consists of monopoly power plus *any* exclusionary practice would cut far too broadly. A great deal of case law has been concerned with distinguishing the monopolist's "exclusionary" practices worthy of condemnation from those practices which, although exclusionary, should be tolerated or even encouraged.

 WESTLAW REFERENCES
synopsis,digest(monopoly /p exclusionary exercise use /6 power)
265k12(1.3)
di monopoly

§ 5.2 Monopoly Power and Illegal Monopolization

Chapter three above defines market power and describes how courts attempt to measure it. "Monopoly power," the requirement assessed for illegal monopolization, is a large amount of market power.

If the law of monopolization were directed exclusively at the "curse of bigness," or at vast private concentrations of wealth or political power, then the market power requirement assessed by the courts would be inappropriate to the offense of monopolization. Chrysler Corp., for example, is among the largest manufacturing corporations in the United States, but no court would hold Chrysler capable of monopolizing the market for American passenger cars. Its output is dwarfed by that of General Motors and Ford Motor Co. On the other hand, the owner of the only movie theatre in Ozona, Texas, may well be guilty of illegal monopolization, even though his company is tiny by American corporate standards, and his theatre only one-fourth the size of movie theatres in New York or Chicago.

The notion that the antitrust laws should be used to stop giant accumulations of wealth or influence is directed at absolute size. The law of monopolization is directed at relative size in relation to some market. The Ozona movie theatre may occupy 100% of the market for movie patronage in Ozona. Perhaps you have never heard of the Sanborn Map Company, which designs maps for fire insurors—but the Sanborn Map Co. occupies about 80% of the nationwide market for such maps. If a competitor attempted to enter the field and Sanborn excluded it by improper means, Sanborn easily might be guilty of illegal monopolization.[1]

The monopoly power requirement in monopolization cases helps courts to characterize a firm's conduct and predict its consequences. Much of the "exclusionary" conduct at issue in litigated monopolization cases is ambiguous when considered alone. For example, in a competitive market a refusal to deal, a sudden price reduction, a policy of leasing and not selling a product, or of keeping research secret are absolutely consistent with competition on the merits.

If the firm already has significant market power, however, courts have found these practices to be more threatening to the competitive process and likely to result in reduced output and higher prices. In general, the more market power a firm has, the more damaging its exclusionary practices might be. For this reason some commentators have suggested a "sliding scale" relationship between the amount of a defendant's monopoly power and the bad conduct requirements. If the defendant has enormous monopoly power, relatively trivial conduct may be condemned as anticompetitive. If the defendant's market power is smaller, however, the amount of bad conduct should be proportionately larger.

Courts generally have not adopted such a sliding scale approach to monopolization cases. The whole notion of a "sliding scale" implies that courts are able to measure market power or the effect of alleged exclusionary practices much more accurately than they really can.[2] Rather, courts have developed a compromise. If the evidence suggests a high degree of monopoly power, then the courts have identified a certain set of practices that will condemn the defendant of illegal monopolization. If the evidence suggests a substantially smaller amount of market power, then courts have used the law of attempt to monopolize, which carries stricter and more explicit conduct requirements.

Before a firm can be guilty of illegal monopolization it must be the dominant firm in the relevant market. Courts usually rely on market share data to determine whether the plaintiff has enough market power to be guilty of illegal monopolization. They fairly consistently hold that a 90% market share is enough to support the necessary inference of market power. Several courts have found a

§ 5.2

1. See Y. Brozen, Concentration, Mergers, and Public Policy 227 (1982).

2. See 3 P. Areeda & D. Turner, Antitrust Law ¶¶ 814, 815 (1978).

market share on the order of 75% to be sufficient,[3] but if the share is lower than 70% courts become much more reluctant to find monopoly power.[4] Some courts hold as a matter of law that a share of less than 50% is insufficient, even if the defendant clearly had the power to raise its price by reducing output.[5]

 WESTLAW REFERENCES
"market power" /45 high** illegal! "market share" "sliding scale"

§ 5.3 Conduct Requirements—Is Bad Conduct Necessary?

Judge Wyzanski's third, most expansive definition of illegal monopolization was that a firm with sufficient monopoly power monopolizes whenever it "does business." No court has ever explicitly adopted such a rule, although a few have inadvertently come close.[1] Today illegal monopolization still requires monopoly power *plus* some form of anticompetitive conduct—and the sale of output at a monopoly price is itself not sufficient to brand someone an illegal monopolist.

Over the years, however, both Congress and antitrust scholars have proposed a variety of "no fault" monopoly statutes that would condemn a firm with persistent, substantial market power without evidence of impermissible exclusionary conduct.[2] The idea is worth

3. See United States v. Paramount Pictures, Inc., 334 U.S. 131, 68 S.Ct. 915 (1948) (suggesting that 70% is sufficient); Greyhound Computer Corp. v. IBM Corp., 559 F.2d 488, 496 (9th Cir. 1977), cert. denied, 434 U.S. 1040, 98 S.Ct. 782 (1978).

4. See Moore v. Jas. H. Matthews & Co., 473 F.2d 328, 332 (9th Cir. 1973), appeal after remand, 550 F.2d 1207 (9th Cir. 1977), concluding that a market share of 65%–70% raised a fact question about the defendant's market power; and see Note, The Development of the Sherman Act Section 2 Market Share Test and Its Inapplicability to Dynamic Markets, 49 So.Calif.L.Rev. 154 (1975). Areeda & Turner would presume sufficient market power if the defendant has had at least 75% of the market for 5 or more years. 3 P. Areeda & D. Turner, note 2 above, at ¶ 803.

5. See Dimmitt Agri Indus., Inc., v. CPC Int'l Inc., 679 F.2d 516 (5th Cir. 1982), cert. denied, 460 U.S. 1082, 103 S.Ct. 1770 (1983). But see Broadway Delivery Corp. v. United Parcel Service of Amer., Inc., 651 F.2d 122 (2d Cir. 1981), cert. denied, 454 U.S. 968, 102 S.Ct. 512 (1981), suggesting that 50% is "rarely" sufficient, but holding that the jury may nevertheless consider the issue of monopoly power even if the defendant's market share is established to be less than 50%.

§ 5.3

1. For example, in U.S. v. Alum. Co. of America, 148 F.2d 416, 431 (2d Cir. 1945) Judge Hand suggested that mere expansion of capacity by a dominant firm could constitute illegal monopolization. See also Judge Wyzanski's invitation to the Supreme Court in *Grinnell* to decide that "where one or more persons * * * had acquired so clear a dominance in a market as to have the power to exclude competition therefrom, there was a *rebuttable* presumption that such power had been criminally acquired and was * * * punishable under § 2." The Supreme Court responded with a rule that where a "consciously acquired" monopoly is shown, "the burden is on the defendant to show that [its] dominance is due to skill, acumen, and the like." U.S. v. Grinnell Corp., 236 F. Supp. 244, 248 (D.R.I. 1964), affirmed except as to decree, 384 U.S. 563, 577, n.7, 86 S.Ct. 1698, at 1707 (1966).

2. The proposals are discussed in Note, The "No-Conduct" Approach to Monopoly Power and its Application to Oligopoly, 15 Valparaiso U.L.Rev. 529

brief discussion because it helps illustrate the ambiguity of conduct requirements in monopolization cases.

The framers of the Sherman Act did not intend to condemn someone "who merely by superior skill and intelligence * * * got the whole business because nobody could do it as well as he could * * *." [3] Such "monopolization" and the monopoly profits that may result are essential to economic development. Firms innovate because they expect their successes to produce economic returns. Eventually the high profits will attract other producers into the market. Collectively these producers will increase output and prices will be driven to the competitive level. A rule that condemned all prices higher than, say, average cost could stop innovation dead. The continual creation of monopoly, and its eventual correction by competitive entry is part of a never-ending process that explains most of the technical achievements of modern industry in market economies.

There are other reasons for not condemning mere monopoly. Many markets are large enough to support only one or two firms efficiently. In a natural monopoly market a single incumbent would have lower costs than two or more equally efficient incumbents. Some natural monopoly markets are recognized as such and price regulated by the State. The majority, however, are not.[4]

Courts are generally unable to identify natural monopoly markets except in relatively obvious cases. The court would have to decide whether two or more firms operating in the market could reach minimum optimal scale (MOS) of output. However, even economists can do little more than guess the minimum efficient level of output for a particular firm. The most reliable way of measuring MOS is to watch markets for long periods of time and measure the size of the successful firms.[5] The fact that for many years Ozona, Texas, contained only one movie theatre may indicate that Ozona is big enough to support only one theatre. To condemn the theatre's owner of monopolization on the basis of large market share alone might well result in Ozona's not having any theatre at all.

Most advocates of no fault monopolization rules rely on the fact that exclusionary conduct is often difficult to discover and, when discovered, difficult to interpret. We expect persistent, long-term monopoly profits to invite entry. When entry has not occurred, perhaps we should infer the existence of exclusionary practices even though we do not have convincing evidence of them. Such a rule is

(1981); Dougherty, Elimination of the Conduct Requirement in Government Monopolization Cases, 48 A.B.A. Antitrust L.J. 869 (1979).

3. 21 Cong.Rec. 3151–52 (1890).

4. See § 1.5 above. For a monopolization case in a market that was probably a natural monopoly, see Union Lead-

er Corp. v. Newspapers of New England, Inc., 284 F.2d 582 (1st Cir. 1960), cert. denied, 365 U.S. 833, 81 S.Ct. 747 (1961); see also, Hovenkamp, Vertical Integration by the Newspaper Monopolist, 69 Iowa L.Rev. 451 (1984).

5. See § 1.4 above.

not so much a "no fault" monopolization doctrine as a rule that fault can be inferred from the existence of persistent monopoly power and profits.

Professors Areeda and Turner believe that a legal rule against "mere monopoly" should be adopted for those monopolies that are both "substantial" and "persistent," and where competitive entry is not otherwise restricted by means outside of the monopolist's control. Areeda & Turner would generally require evidence of "substantial market power that has persisted 10 years or more" before intervention would be appropriate.[6] They would never permit intervention where the monopoly power has persisted less than five years, and they would permit intervention against a monopoly between 5 and 10 years old only "on a convincing showing of likely persistency * * *." Finally, Areeda & Turner would permit attacks on monopoly without fault only in equitable proceedings brought by the government and normally seeking divestiture.[7]

The Areeda & Turner proposal presumes an extraordinary ability on the part of courts to measure relevant efficiencies in litigation. If the MOS firm in a certain market must be large enough to satisfy the entire market demand at a price equal to marginal cost—that is, if the market is a natural monopoly—then persistent monopoly can be easily explained: no new entrant will be able to match the incumbent's costs. A rule that permits a court to break up a monopoly without evidence of inefficient, exclusionary conduct greatly increases the risk that the defendant merely has the advantage of economies of scale that are not easily available to a new entrant.[8] In such cases the efficiency losses that result from divestiture could far outweigh any efficiency gains that might result from the competition of incumbents.[9]

 WESTLAW REFERENCES
monopoly /12 (areeda +3 turner) infer! no-fault

§ 5.4 Conduct Requirements—Monopolization and the Rule of Reason

The law of monopolization requires a showing that the defendant has monopoly power and has engaged in impermissible "exclusion-

---

6. 3 P. Areeda & D. Turner, Antitrust Law ¶ 623d (1978).

7. This limitation may be inherent in the "antitrust injury" requirement, which applies to private plaintiffs seeking damages, at least if they are competitors of the defendant. See § 14.5 below.

8. For some of the problems of measuring scale economies see McGee, Effi-

ciency and Economies of Size, in Goldschmid, Mann & Weston, eds., Industrial Concentration: the New Learning 55–96 (1974).

9. Furthermore, even a natural monopolist can face substantial competition—not from incumbents, but from potential entrants. See § 1.5 above.

ary" practices with the design or effect of protecting its monopoly power from erosion by competitive entry. The rule of reason was originally formulated by the Supreme Court in a monopoly case as a means of distinguishing permissible from impermissible exclusionary practices.[1]

The meaning and proper contours of the rule of reason in monopolization cases are nevertheless ambiguous. Most recent Supreme Court analysis of the rule of reason appears not in monopolization cases but in cases involving agreements among competitors. These are discussed in § 4.4 above.

In antitrust litigation most practices are considered to be analyzed under a rule of reason. A *per se* rule is generally appropriate only after judges have had long experience with a certain practice, and have concluded that the practice produces many pernicious results and almost no beneficial ones. Some forms of unilateral conduct by dominant firms might fall into the *per se* category—for example, if the sole incumbent in a market dynamites the newly constructed plant of a prospective entrant. However, such cases seldom end up as monopolization cases.

Litigated monopolization cases generally involve more ambiguous conduct. For example, efficiency itself is an "exclusionary" practice. If a firm continually innovates, expands its output and reduces its price one likely result will be its perpetuation of a large market share. Should expansion of capacity ever be the basis for illegal monopolization? Judge Hand thought so in the *Alcoa* case.[2] In 1980, in the *duPont* (Titanium Dioxide) case, however, the Federal Trade Commission disagreed.[3]

No court has articulated a general theory of what the rule of reason in monopolization cases is, or how it should function. Justice Brandeis's simple conclusion in *Chicago Board of Trade* that practices which "promote" competition should be approved,[4] while practices that "destroy" competition should be condemned, is not very helpful.

The scope of the rule of reason can vary considerably with changes in antitrust ideology. If the goal of the antitrust laws is to

§ 5.4

1. Standard Oil Co. of N.J. v. U.S., 221 U.S. 1, 31 S.Ct. 502 (1911).

2. U.S. v. Alum. Co. of America, 148 F.2d 416, 431 (2d Cir. 1945):

It was not inevitable that [the defendant] should always anticipate increases in * * * demand * * * and be prepared to supply them. Nothing compelled it to keep doubling and redoubling its capacity before others entered the field. It insists that it never excluded competitors; but we can think of no more effective exclusion than progressively to embrace each new opportunity as it opened, and to face every newcomer with new capacity already geared into a great organization, having the advantage of experience, trade connections and the elite of personnel.

3. E. I. du Pont de Nemours & Co., 96 F.T.C. 650 (1980).

4. Board of Trade v. U.S., 246 U.S. 231, 238, 38 S.Ct. 242, 244 (1918).

prohibit bigness or to facilitate ease of entry for small business, for example, then expansion of capacity might be considered an unjustifiable exclusionary practice, as Judge Hand considered it to be in *Alcoa*. However if the goal of the antitrust laws is the maximization of consumer welfare, and if consumers are benefited by low prices, then expansion of capacity should generally not be illegal, because increased output results in lower prices. One important difference between the *Alcoa* case in 1945 and the *du Pont* case in 1980 is that the prevailing ideology had changed.

Assuming that economic efficiency or consumer welfare is the principal goal of antitrust, the rule of reason still presents some important problems of analysis and interpretation. For example, vertical integration is often efficient—it enables a firm to reduce its costs, whether or not the firm is a monopolist. Nevertheless, several courts have held that vertical integration by a monopolist can be illegal monopolization because it gives the monopolist a second monopoly in a market in which it did not have a monopoly before, or because it raises barriers to entry in the primary market (the one in which the monopolist already has a monopoly). Should vertical integration by a monopolist be condemned because it extends or entrenches the monopolist's position, or should it be tolerated or encouraged because it reduces the monopolist's costs and as a result reduces its profit-maximizing price?

The question is difficult only if we assume that vertical integration by the monopolist does both of these things at the same time. Economists of the Chicago School generally believe that substantial efficiencies can result from vertical integration, and they regard the threat of increased barriers to entry as trivial. Vertical integration raises a barrier to entry only if the integrated firm is more efficient than unintegrated competitors.[5] Further, they point out that a monopolist of any single link in a distribution chain can obtain all available monopoly profits from the manufacture and distribution of a product. Thus a monopolist cannot reasonably enlarge its monopoly profits by vertically integrating and extending its monopoly into a second level. Chicago school analysts therefore conclude that vertical integration by a monopolist is just as efficient as vertical integration by a competitor, and presents no significant anticompetitive dangers. It should be legal under the rule of reason.

Others disagree, however. They argue that although a monopolist may not be able to prevent entry by vertical integration, it can often delay entry.[6] Time is money for the monopolist earning monopoly profits. Further, even if vertical integration deters only less

5. For example, see R. Bork, The Antitrust Paradox: A Policy at War With Itself 241–42 (1978).

6. See Wentz, Mobility Factors in Antitrust Cases: Assessing Market Power in Light of Conditions Affecting Entry and Fringe Expansion, 80 Mich.L. Rev. 1545 (1982).

efficient rivals the result might harm consumers. Entry by less efficient firms can be procompetitive. Suppose a monopolist has costs of $1.00 but a short-run profit-maximizing price of $1.50.[7] Now two or three competitors enter the field, each of whom has costs ranging from $1.05 to $1.10. The market price is likely to go down (to same price approaching $1.10), output is likely to go up, and consumers will probably be better off.[8]

Today there is no generalized judicial theory of anticompetitive exclusionary practices, although there is a consensus that a few outrageous practices are anticompetitive. Since the late 1970's, however, circuit courts have been critical in their scrutiny of allegations that a particular, ambiguous exclusionary practice is anticompetitive. The list of such practices appears to be growing shorter, and plaintiffs have not been notably successful in these recent cases.[9]

 WESTLAW REFERENCES
monopoly /16 "rule of reason"

§ 5.5   Conduct Requirements—Intent

The case law of monopolization contains categorical statements that subjective intent is not an element of illegal monopolization, and categorical statements that it is. In *Alcoa* Judge Hand purported to "disregard any question of 'intent,'" concluding that "no monopolist monopolizes unconscious of what he is doing."[1] In *Grinnell*, however, the Supreme Court defined the offense of monopolization to include "the willful acquisition or maintenance of [monopoly] power * * *."[2]

Historically the intent requirement in monopolization cases has followed the formula of the criminal law. In *attempt* cases, the law may require a specific intent to achieve the prohibited result. There is strong precedent that the law of attempt to monopolize requires a showing of specific intent.[3] In the case of the completed offense, however, courts often either dispense with an intent requirement, or

---

7. The short-run profit-maximizing price is the price a monopolist would probably charge if it were completely unconcerned about new entry. The short-run profit-maximizing price is determined by the intersection of the monopolists' marginal cost and marginal revenue curves. If the monopolist were concerned about new entrants it would likely charge a lower, long-run profit-maximizing, or entry deterring, price. See § 1.2 above.

8. See Note, Standing at the Fringe: Antitrust Damages and the Fringe Producer, 35 Stan.L.Rev. 763, 771–73 (1983).

9. See § 5.6 below. For fuller discussion of recent cases see Sullivan, Monopolization: Corporate Strategy, the IBM Cases, and the Transformation of the Law, 60 Tex.L.Rev. 587 (1982).

§ 5.5

1. U.S. v. Alum. Co. of America, 148 F.2d 416, 431–32 (2d Cir. 1945).

2. U.S. v. Grinnell Corp., 384 U.S. 563, 570–71, 86 S.Ct. 1698, 1704 (1966).

3. See § 6.2 below.

else infer intent from evidence of monopoly power plus exclusionary practices.

Evidence of intent comes in two kinds, objective and subjective. Objective evidence of intent is evidence inferred from the defendant's conduct. Subjective evidence of intent is evidence such as statements that indicate that the defendant consciously had a certain end in mind. To require subjective evidence of intent in monopolization cases vastly complicates discovery, and protects those companies who carefully and systematically destroy any paper trail of monopolistic purpose. The result is a great deal of arbitrariness.

Most courts have at least tacitly agreed with Justice Hand that, since no monopolist is unconscious of what he is doing, clear evidence of an impermissible exclusionary practice by a firm with monopoly power is the only proof of intent required. That is virtually the same thing as saying that the law of monopolization does not contain a separate intent requirement.

 WESTLAW REFERENCES

synopsis,headnote(monopoly (attempt** /3 monopol!) /s inten!)

§ 5.6   Conduct Requirements—Illustrative Exclusionary Practices

Since the Sherman Act was passed many practices have been condemned as illegal monopolization if the firm that carried them out had sufficient market power. These include:

espionage or sabotage

mergers

reduction of output

expansion of capacity or output

price discrimination

vertical integration

tying arrangements

refusals to deal

supply or price "squeezes"

predatory or "manipulative" research and development

failure to predisclose research and development

patent abuses, including fraud, patent "accumulation," and refusal to license

predatory pricing

vexatious, repetitive litigation or administrative claims

Predatory pricing and a few other practices are dealt with in chapter six on attempt to monopolize. Any practice that will support a charge of attempt will also support a charge of illegal monopolization, provided that the defendant has monopoly power.

The first wave of monopolization cases to reach the Supreme Court involved defendants who had reached a monopoly position by merger, allegedly by weakening their rivals and then buying them out. A merger is not an "exclusionary" practice, however. The knowledge that a prospective entrant might be bought up would encourage it to enter a market. A merger or acquisition could "exclude" or discourage someone from entering a market only if the merger created a new firm that had lower costs and was harder to compete with than the two firms had been before the merger. However, a merger *can* create a firm with monopoly power, and this firm could then reduce output and raise prices. Further, it would be tempted to engage in exclusionary practices in order to entrench its position. Courts have consistently held that mergers to monopoly ought to be condemned under the Sherman Act.[1]

Several early monopolization cases involved allegations that a dominant firm bought its rivals' plants and shut them down in order to keep market output low. Such a tactic also seems calculated to invite new entry rather than deter it. Any new entrant would be able to use the dominant firm's monopoly price as an umbrella that would permit it to price monopolistically as well. Further, it would have a profitable means of bailing out of the market: it could sell its plant or its output to the dominant firm.[2] Today § 7 of the Clayton Act condemns most horizontal mergers involving firms with sufficient market power to be found guilty of illegal monopolization.[3] As a result Sherman Act treatment of mergers to monopoly is all but superfluous.

In *Alcoa* Judge Hand held that the defendant's continual expansion of capacity to meet anticipated market demand was "exclusionary" because it denied potential competitors a fair share of the market.[4] Expansion of capacity will exclude an equally efficient rival, however, only if the monopolist increases output to the point that it must sell at marginal cost. That is, if a firm builds a plant so large that it can service all the output demanded at a competitive price, there will be no economic profits to attract equally efficient

§ 5.6

1. Northern Securities Co. v. U.S. 193 U.S. 197, 24 S.Ct. 436 (1904); Standard Oil Co. of N.J. v. U.S., 221 U.S. 1, 31 S.Ct. 502 (1911); U.S. v. First Nat'l Bank & Trust Co. of Lexington, 376 U.S. 665, 84 S.Ct. 1033 (1964).

2. See U.S. v. American Can Co., 230 F. 859 (D.Md.1916), *appeal dismissed*, 256 U.S. 706, 41 S.Ct. 624 (1921). The district court found that the defendant had acquired its rivals by buying them at inflated prices. It then became short of capital and raised the price of cans dramatically. The result was a flood of new entry. The defendant's prices were put up to a point which made it apparently profitable for outsiders to start making cans with any antiquated or crude machinery they could find in old lumber rooms * * * or even to resume can making by hand * * *.

In order to keep the price up, the defendant found it necessary to buy "some millions of cans" from these new rivals. 230 F. at 879–880.

3. See § 11.1 below.

4. U.S. v. Alum. Co. of America, 148 F.2d 416, 431 (2d Cir. 1945). See § 5.4 above.

competitors into the market. If the monopolist produces less than that, however, the monopoly profits will attract any rival capable of producing at the same costs. Thus expansion of capacity is exclusionary only at the expense of the monopolist's monopoly profits, which are lost when output is increased to the competitive level.[5]

Likewise, courts have considered price discrimination by the monopolist to be an exclusionary practice warranting condemnation. In U.S. v. United Shoe Machinery Co., for example, Judge Wyzanski condemned the defendant for obtaining a high rate of return from leases of machines in which it had no competitors, and a much lower rate of return from leases of machines in which competition was greater.[6]

Persistent price discrimination is evidence that a seller has market power.[7] But is price discrimination itself an exclusionary practice? Suppose that a monopolist has costs of $1.00 per widget. It identifies two sets of customers who have different elasticities of demand for the monopolized product and therefore are willing to pay different prices. It sells to one set of customers at $1.00 per widget (a competitive but nevertheless profitable price), and to the other set of customers at $1.50 per widget. Now it is suddenly forbidden (perhaps by a court decision) from price discriminating. The firm will either sell to both sets of customers at $1.00, or else it will sell only to the high preference customers at a price of $1.50. Which price maximizes the seller's profits will vary from one situation to another.

Clearly, if the monopolist's non-discriminatory profit-maximizing price is $1.00, its earlier price discrimination was not "exclusionary." On the contrary, the sales at a price of $1.50 to the high preference purchasers would attract new competitors into at least that part of the market. However, if the monopolist's non-discriminatory profit-maximizing price is $1.50, then its price discrimination was exclusionary. If forbidden to price discriminate the monopolist would charge $1.50 for all units, and those customers willing to pay only $1.00 would not be served. They would be available for any new entrant who was willing to serve them at a price of $1.00. By price discriminating, however, the monopolist made the sales to the low preference customers, and competitors were less likely to enter that market.

However, the price discrimination in the above example is exclusionary because it *increases* the monopolist's total output. Price discrimination in the real world sometimes results in larger output than non-discriminatory pricing, and sometimes it does not. When the price discrimination results in a larger output, then the practice

5. An exception to this rule is strategic construction of excess capacity, discussed below in § 6.9.

6. 110 F.Supp. 295, 340, 341 (D.Mass. 1953), affirmed per curiam, 347 U.S. 521, 74 S.Ct. 699 (1954).

7. See § 3.7 above.

also has the effect of excluding competitors. When it does not result in a larger output, however, it excludes no one. On the contrary, the higher profits that accrue from price discrimination will invite new entry. In general, price discrimination "excludes" in the same way that expansion of capacity excludes. Whenever a firm increases its output it must reach marginal customers, by making some or all sales at a lower price. The result tends to exclude potential entrants who would have entered at the higher price but not at the lower one.

Private plaintiffs (and occasionally the government) have frequently alleged that vertical integration by a monopolist is an exclusionary practice warranting § 2 treatment. A common result of vertical integration is that the integrated firm begins to deal only with its newly-acquired suppliers or outlets, and refuses to deal any longer with independent firms. If the monopolist's vertical integration is by merger, exclusive dealing contract, or some form of tying arrangement, an issue will be raised under the Clayton Act, although such practices may constitute illegal monopolization as well. These are analyzed in chapters seven and eight.

The monopolist's vertical integration by new entry, as well as refusals to deal by vertically integrated monopolists, have been condemned as illegal monopolization. In Eastman Kodak Co. of New York v. Southern Photo Materials Co.[8] the defendant manufactured camera film and photographic supplies and also owned several local distributorships of these supplies. The plaintiff was an independent local distributor. In the past the defendant had supplied all distributors of photographic supplies, but in 1910 it began to supply only its own distributorships in the plaintiff's area, and refused to sell to the plaintiff. The Supreme Court affirmed a jury verdict that the refusal to deal was an illegal attempt by the defendant to use its monopoly in the manufacture of photographic supplies to leverage a second monopoly in distribution and resale.

The price or supply "squeeze" is a variation of the refusal to deal. Suppose that a monopolist at the manufacturing level owns some of its retail outlets and also sells its product to independent retailers. The independent retailers have a difficult time competing with the retailers owned by the monopolist, however. They allege that the monopolist always favors its own outlets in times of short supply and sometimes refuses to sell to independents altogether. Further, the monopolist either charges the independents a higher price for the product than it charges its own dealers, or else the outlets owned by the monopolist resell the product at a price that the independents are unable to match. The first of these practices is sometimes referred to as a "supply squeeze," and the second as a "price squeeze". In

8. 273 U.S. 359, 47 S.Ct. 400 (1927); See also Mt. Lebanon Motors, Inc. v. Chrysler Corp., 283 F.Supp. 453 (W.D. Pa.1968), affirmed per curiam, 417 F.2d 622 (3d Cir. 1969); and see Heatransfer Corp. v. Volkswagenwerk, A.G., 553 F.2d 964 (5th Cir. 1977), cert. denied, 434 U.S. 1087, 98 S.Ct. 1282 (1978).

principle they are identical: the integrated monopolist allegedly "manipulates" the market in order to injure the unintegrated rivals. The independent retailers are squeezed both by short supply and by their own high costs relative to those of the monopoly-owned outlets.[9]

Most price and supply "squeezes" result because vertically integrated firms have lower costs than do independent firms who must rely on the market. The monopolist who reduces its costs by vertical integration will sell to the consumer at a lower price,[10] and independent dealers will be unable to compete. Any "squeeze" that results from the monopolist's reduced costs should not be an antitrust problem.

But this analysis presents one problem: although vertical integration can create substantial efficiencies, these efficiencies are almost impossible to measure. Further, an overdeterrent rule (for example, refusals to deal by monopolists are illegal *per se*) is bound to cause injury to consumers in the form of higher prices. As a result courts must have some reliable mechanism for distinguishing efficient refusals to deal or "squeezes" from harmful ones. When might a refusal to deal or squeeze be harmful? Three explanations have been offered. One is the traditional theory that the monopolist is trying to turn one monopoly into two. However, a monopolist at any single level of a distribution chain can recover all monopoly profits available in that chain. As a result a monopolist of two successive links will not make more monopoly profits than a monopolist of only one.[11]

The two remaining explanations are that vertical integration by the monopolist raises barriers to entry or facilitates price discrimination. Vertical integration by the monopolist allegedly creates a barrier to entry in the monopolist's market because any prospective entrant must come in at two levels instead of one. For example, if a monopolist aluminum manufacturer did all its own fabricating there would be no independent market for fabricators. Anyone who wanted to enter aluminum manufacturing might also have to enter aluminum fabricating.

There are two economic objections to this rationale for condemning vertical integration by the monopolist. First, vertical integration by the monopolist will force a new entrant to integrate as well only if the vertical integration lowers the monopolist's costs. Suppose that the cost of manufacturing aluminum to the independent manufacturer is 10¢ per unit, and the cost of fabricating to the independent

9. In *Alcoa* Judge Hand discussed the supply and price squeeze at some length. Alcoa allegedly used the squeeze against independent fabricators of its ingot. U.S. v. Aluminum Co. of America, 148 F.2d 416, 436–38 (2d Cir. 1945).

For an interesting variation on the supply squeeze in a monopolization case, see Aspen Highlands Skiing Corp. v. Aspen Skiing Co., 738 F.2d 1509 (10th Cir. 1984), in which the defendant was found guilty of monopolizing the market for local ski lift tickets.

10. See § 7.2 below.

11. See the discussion of the economics of vertical integration in § 7.2 below.

fabricator is 5¢ per unit. If the monopolist can reduce the total cost to 14¢ per unit by doing its own fabricating, then a new entrant will have to do the same thing or else be at a cost disadvantage. However, if the vertical integration produces no cost savings, then the market can continue to accommodate independent manufacturers and independent fabricators. If the vertical integration is *in*efficient—that is, if the integrated firm has costs higher than 15¢ per unit—independent firms will actually be encouraged to come into the market, for they will have the cost advantage. The example simply illustrates that many so-called "barriers to entry" are nothing more than the efficiency of the firms already in the market. Few things deter entry more effectively than an efficient firm, whose low costs will be difficult to match.

The second objection to the entry barrier theory of vertical integration by the monopolist is that the theory does not explain why vertical integration is a "barrier" in any useful sense. To be sure, two-level entry may require a firm to raise more capital than one-level entry requires. But if profits can be made in the market, the capital will generally follow. About the only times vertical integration by the monopolist can create real barriers to entry are when the monopolist buys up all sources of supply of a scarce natural resource or integrates into an area in which entry is restricted by the government and acquires all the available licenses.[12]

Vertical integration by the monopolist may also facilitate price discrimination. Suppose a monopolist manufactures widgets which are retailed in two kinds of stores, boutiques and discount stores. The stores serve different groups of customers who are willing to pay different prices for widgets. The monopolist believes it could wholesale widgets to the boutiques for $4.00 and to the discount stores for $3.00.

However, the monopolist's attempt to price discriminate between the boutiques and discount stores would be frustrated by two things: 1) arbitrage: the discount stores would resell to the boutiques at a price of $3.50, and deprive the seller of its monopoly profits; 2) the boutique owners would file a secondary-line Robinson-Patman action against the monopolist.

The monopolist can avoid both problems by acquiring its own set of either boutiques or department stores. If it owned its own boutiques, for example, it could sell to the boutiques' retail customers directly at a higher price. On the wholesale market it would sell only to discount stores at the lower price. It could achieve the same result by buying or building its own discount stores. In any case, the

---

12. See § 7.3 below, and see the discussion of the 1984 DOJ Merger Guidelines, noting that vertical integration might create inefficient entry barriers when plants at the two levels achieve minimum efficient scale at widely different outputs. In this case vertical integration could deprive a newcomer of the opportunity to achieve MOS, and it would face higher costs.

same argument applies to price discrimination by vertical integration that applies to other forms of price discrimination: it is not "exclusionary." The higher price charged to customers of the boutiques will, if anything, encourage new entry into the boutique business.

Vertical integration is a commonly alleged exclusionary practice in monopolization cases, largely because it creates an immediate set of victims who are not injured by anything as subtle as a monopoly overcharge—namely, terminated dealers and retailers.[13] In Paschall v. Kansas City Star Co.[14] a sharply divided Eighth Circuit held that a daily newspaper did not violate § 2 of the Sherman Act by terminating all its independent delivery agents and shifting to self-distribution. The defendant occupied 100% of the market for daily newspapers, so its refusal to deal with independent carriers effectively destroyed the secondary market. However, the court could find no injury to competition. It noted that vertical integration by a monopolist could have three anticompetitive effects: it might 1) facilitate price discrimination; 2) increase barriers to entry in the primary market; 3) enable a rate-regulated monopolist to evade the regulated price.

The third effect was dismissed as inapplicable. Likewise, the court discounted the entry barriers argument: the absence of independent carriers would not likely deter a second daily newspaper from entering the market, particularly since independent carriers routinely carried periodicals for more than one supplier.

The court believed that the *Kansas City Star* did not integrate vertically in order to price discriminate, because after integration it charged a uniform price to all newspaper subscribers. Before, independent carriers had set their own prices, which varied considerably from route to route. The court appears to have confused price discrimination with price difference, however. Some routes were more costly to serve than others—for example, a sparsely populated rural route likely cost more per newspaper in time and gasoline than a dense apartment route. The different prices charged by the independent carriers probably reflected these cost differences. By switching to a uniform delivery price the *Star* was almost certainly increasing the amount of price discrimination; however, the effect was probably to increase the *Star's* circulation. Had it charged rural customers a rate that reflected fully the cost of serving them, it would have had fewer subscribers in rural markets. This conclusion must be read in light of the fact that a daily newspaper makes only a small percentage of its revenue from subscriptions. Most of its income comes from advertising, and advertising rates vary with

---

13. The law of monopolization and the law of vertical nonprice restraints are converging on this point. Many circuits now hold that a unilateral dealer termination is lawful unless the defendant has substantial market power. See § 9.4 below.

14. 727 F.2d 692 (8th Cir. 1984), *en banc*, cert denied, ___ U.S. ___, ___ S.Ct. ___ (1984).

circulation. Although the *Star* was a "monopoly" daily newspaper, it was almost certainly not in a position to increase profits by reducing its circulation.

Furthermore, both the *Star* and its independent carriers were monopolists. The carriers had been given exclusive territories, probably because such territories are natural monopolies. The result was a classic bilateral monopoly, in which the second level monopolist could maximize its profits by reducing output at the expense of the first level monopolist. By eliminating the second level monopoly the *Star* could reduce its own costs, increase its circulation and in the process increase its advertising revenues. Nothing in the case suggested that the termination would enable the *Star* to make more money by reducing its output of newspapers.[15]

Many recent private plaintiff cases allege that the defendant was a monopolist and that it "manipulated" the market or the product in such a way as to prevent the plaintiff from competing. These manipulatory practices have included tying arrangements, predatory pricing, "predatory" research and development, or failure to predisclose certain technical or design innovations.

Courts have generally presumed that an attempt by a monopolist to use a tie-in or similar arrangement to extend its monopoly power into a second market is illegal. Suppose, for example, that a monopolist in the film market includes processing in the sale price of its film, and refuses to sell film without the processing. In 1954 the Eastman Kodak Co. agreed in a consent decree not to engage in mandatory package pricing of this sort.[16] The government's theory was that Kodak was attempting to use its monopoly in one market (film) to obtain a second monopoly in another market (processing). Alternatively, the film-processing tie could be seen as raising barriers to entry in the markets for both film and processing. Once Kodak had succeeded in monopolizing both markets, no one could enter at either level without entering both levels simultaneously.[17] Today many commentators and some courts are sceptical about such claims. They note that if monopoly profits are available in any market, the absolute cost of capital will not deter entry or even delay it significantly.[18] Nevertheless, the entry barrier theory in the *Kodak* case makes sense if economies of scale are far more substantial at one level than they are at the other. For example, if a small, local firm can

---

15. Bilateral monopoly is discussed in § 7.2 below. For a situation in which a newspaper unsuccessfully attempted to maintain maximum resale prices in order to avoid bilateral monopoly, see Albrecht v. Herald Co., 390 U.S. 145, 88 S.Ct. 869 (1968), discussed in § 9.3 below. See generally Hovenkamp, Vertical Integration by the Newspaper Monopolist, 69 Iowa L.Rev. 451 (1984).

16. U.S. v. Eastman Kodak Co., Civ. #6450 (W.D.N.Y. Dec. 21, 1954).

17. See J. Bain, Barriers to New Competition 1–41 (1956).

18. See R. Bork, The Antitrust Paradox: A Policy at War With Itself 310–29 (1978); Demsetz, Barriers to Entry, 72 Amer.Econ.Rev. 47 (1982).

efficiently process film but only a large national firm with a significant share of the market can manufacture film, Kodak's film-processing tie would effectively retard entry into the processing market.[19]

A somewhat different tie-in monopolization claim is the kind raised in California Computer Products Co. v. IBM Corp.[20] The defendant manufactured central processing computer units and various "peripherals" such as memories, monitors, and printers. The plaintiff manufactured only disk drives, a type of memory device. The defendant introduced a new line of computers in which the memory units and central processing units were assembled in the same box and sold as a single product. The defendant was generally able to show that the new units performed faster and less expensively than their predecessors. However, the plaintiffs characterized the new line of computers as "technological manipulation" designed only to eliminate the independent market for separate memory units. The court refused to condemn such innovation.

Should the development of a new product which reduces or eliminates the market for some existing product manufactured by a competitor ever be illegal monopolization?[21] Two possibilities come to mind: 1) if it is undisputed that the new product is not superior to the old product, but is perhaps even inferior; 2) if there is clear evidence that the defendant's intent in developing the new product was to destroy the independent market for the competitor's product.

Neither situation merits condemnation. First, whether a new product is "superior" or "inferior" to an old product is entirely a matter of consumer preference, not of judicial decision.[22] If IBM's new computer system with the built-in memory was inferior to the old system in the eyes of consumers, they would refuse to buy the new system.

The question of bad intent is even clearer: every inventor "intends" his invention to injure the competing products of close competitors, for that is the only way his own invention is likely to find a market. Suppose that Henry Ford knew absolutely that production of the Model T would destroy a carriage maker across the street. Should its development be illegal? Suppose that Henry Ford developed the Model T for no other reason than to ruin the business of the carriage maker, whom he disliked intensely? There is simply no way

19. See note 12 above.

20. 613 F.2d 727 (9th Cir. 1979).

21. The Ninth Circuit thought not. See Id. at 744:

IBM, assuming it was a monopolist, had the right to redesign its products to make them more attractive to buyers—whether by reason of lower manufacturing cost and price or improved performance. It was under no duty to help Cal Comp or other peripheral equipment manufacturers survive or expand. * * * The reasonableness of IBM's conduct in this regard did not present a jury issue.

22. See Automatic Radio Mfr. Co. v. Ford Motor Co., 272 F.Supp. 744 (D.Mass.1967), affirmed, 390 F.2d 113 (1st Cir. 1968), cert. denied, 391 U.S. 914, 88 S.Ct. 1807 (1968), where the innovation may have been an aesthetic improvement, but not a technical one.

to distinguish between "legitimate" and "illegitimate" manifestations of intent. Intent is merged into the completed result, in this case a new product the sale of which injures or destroys certain competitors. No reasonable basis exists for concluding that the development of a new product or group of products, without more, is illegal monopolization. Such a rule would certainly do far more harm to the innovative processes in a market economy than it would promote competitive efficiency.[23]

Somewhat different is the claim that a monopolist's failure to predisclose information about a new product is anticompetitive. Suppose that a manufacturer of cameras secretly develops a revolutionary new camera that is cheaper and performs better than anything currently on the market. The camera uses a new type of film which cannot be patented. On January 1 the monopolist introduces the new camera to the public; furthermore, it has already manufactured vast stocks of the new film and can offer camera and film together. Within six months competing film manufacturers will be able to copy the film and bring it to the market themselves. During that six month interval, however, the camera monopolist will enjoy not only the monopoly profits in its new camera, but also will be the only provider of the new film.[24]

Competing film manufacturers are undoubtedly injured by this failure to predisclose. They would have been better off if they also could have had film on the market the day the new camera was introduced. Is competition injured? The camera monopolist can make all available monopoly profits by selling the camera at its profit-maximizing price. It will then have to charge a competitive price for the film anyway. In this case, however, the camera monopolist likely will use its temporary film "monopoly" to price discriminate. The professional photographer who shoots 20 rolls of film per day may value the new camera much more highly than the casual amateur who shoots 3 rolls per year. By transferring part of the available monopoly profits from the camera to the film the camera monopolist will be able to obtain a higher overall rate of return from the professional buyer than from the amateur. Eventually, of course, new entry into the film market will drive the price of film to the competitive level and then the camera monopolist will not be able to price discriminate in this way.[25]

23. For a contrary view see Ordover & Willig, An Economic Definition of Predation: Pricing and Product Innovation, 91 Yale L.J. 8 (1981). For a response, see Sidak, Debunking Predatory Innovation, 83 Col.L.Rev. 1121 (1983).

24. See Foremost Pro Color, Inc. v. Eastman Kodak Co., 703 F.2d 534 (9th Cir. 1983), cert. denied, __ U.S. __, 104 S.Ct. 1315 (1984); Berkey Photo, Inc. v. Eastman Kodak Co., 603 F.2d 263 (2d Cir. 1979), cert. denied, 444 U.S. 1093, 100 S.Ct. 1061 (1980).

25. In this case the failure to predisclose operates in the same way as a variable proportion tying arrangement. See § 8.8 below. Price discrimination is less likely in a case like Automatic Radio, note 22 above, where one product was an automobile and the other product a car radio. Most purchasers of one car will buy only one car radio.

The monopolist's refusal to predisclose may facilitate price discrimination, but once again, the discrimination is not necessarily harmful to society. In this case the price discrimination arrangement probably permitted the monopolist to sell more cameras than it would have otherwise. That will generally benefit consumers, and in the long run it may even mean a larger market for the competing film manufacturers.

Many monopolists have also been condemned for forms of patent "abuse." A patent itself implies a right (Constitutionally protected) to be a monopolist. Nevertheless, courts have often found patent monopolists guilty of exclusionary practices, particularly if they have tied some unpatented article to the patented one, if they have accumulated patents in order to make entry into the monopolized market difficult, or in some situations if they have refused to license the patent to others. In addition, obtaining a patent monopoly by fraud can be illegal monopolization under § 2 of the Sherman Act.[26]

One word of caution in such cases. The "monopoly" legally protected by a patent is not the same thing as the "monopoly" or monopoly power which is a predicate for illegal monopolization. A patent monopoly is the exclusive right to a certain article or process described in the patent application. Even a patented product, however, may compete intensely with similar products which are either unpatented or covered by different patents. As a result, a single patent seldom defines the scope of a relevant market for antitrust purposes. For example, in Diamond Int'l Corp. v. Walterhoefer [27] the Court found that a patented egg carton competed with other egg cartons, which therefore had to be grouped into the relevant market. As a result the patent holder's market share was only 51%.

Courts have often found it illegal for the owner of a patent in one product (such as copying machines) to "monopolize" a second product (such as paper) by requiring all purchasers or lessees of its copying machines to purchase its paper as well. The merits of such arguments are discussed in chapter eight on tying arrangements.

Courts have also condemned patent monopolists for perpetuating their monopoly by continually accumulating or acquiring new patents covering the same process or related processes. Suppose that firm A owns the patents and exclusive right to manufacture a sophisticated machine. A's research laboratory continually improves the machine in various ways, and each significant new improvement is patented. The result may be that the machine will never completely enter the public domain. By the time the patent on any particular component

26. Walker Process Equip., Inc. v. Food Machinery & Chemical Corp., 382 U.S. 172, 86 S.Ct. 347 (1965).

27. 289 F.Supp. 550 (D.Md.1968); see Adelman, The Relevant Market Paradox—Attempted and Completed Patent Fraud Monopolization, 38 Ohio St.L.J. 289 (1977), for a contrary position.

expires it will be obsolete and will have been replaced with a new patented component.

The continuing development and actual use of new patented devices should ordinarily not be treated as an illegal exclusionary practice. The disincentive created to research and development would far outweigh any injury to the competitive process that might result. In high technology fields such as computers, for example, the commercial life expectancy of some components is more like 17 months than 17 years. In any field where technology changes at a rapid rate research and development is likely to render components or processes obsolete long before their patents expire.[28]

A more difficult question arises when the monopolist buys up related patents and refuses to use them or license them to others. Suppose that Firm A has developed patented process X, and uses it to manufacture widgets. Under both the patent and antitrust laws A may use process X exclusively; he does not need to license the process to any competitor.[29] Now, however, an inventor develops process Y, which will manufacture widgets at about the same price as process X. The inventor does not want to manufacture widgets herself, but proposes instead to license the process to anyone who wants it. Firm A then pays the inventor a high price for the exclusive right to use process Y. However, firm A never employs process Y. It continues to manufacture widgets using process X, and continues to have a monopoly in the widget market.

In this case the chance of injury to competition is more substantial. Firm A has its monopoly profits in widgets to protect. Any new entrant into the widget market, using process Y, will face competition from A as well as from other possible licensees of process Y. As a result firm A may be willing to pay more for the exclusive right to use (or in this case to prevent the use of) process Y than any potential competitor would. The accumulation and non-use of patents should therefore be an antitrust concern.[30]

---

28. See Automatic Radio Mfg. Co. v. Hazeltine Research, Inc., 339 U.S. 827, 834, 70 S.Ct. 894, 898 (1950): "The mere accumulation of patents, no matter how many, is not in and of itself illegal." And see, SCM Corp. v. Xerox Corp., 645 F.2d 1195 (2d Cir. 1981), cert. denied 455 U.S. 1016, 102 S.Ct. 1708 (1982), rehearing denied, 456 U.S. 985, 102 S.Ct. 2260 (1982).

29. In the SCM case, Id., the district court held that creating antitrust liability "for a monopolist's unilateral refusal to license patents" would pose "a threat to the progress of science and the useful arts not warranted by a reasonable accommodation of the patent and antitrust laws." 463 F.Supp. at 1014.

30. For a contrary view, see 3 P. Areeda & D. Turner, Antitrust Law ¶ 706c (1978). Some courts have approached the problem by forcing the patent holder to license the unused patent. Foster v. American Machine & Foundry Co., 492 F.2d 1317 (2d Cir. 1974), cert. denied, 419 U.S. 833, 95 S.Ct. 58 (1974), rehearing denied 419 U.S. 1061, 95 S.Ct. 648 (1974). The prevailing case law, however, is that mere nonuse of a patent is not an antitrust violation. See Continental Paper Bag Co. v. Eastern Paper Bag Co., 210 U.S. 405, 28 S.Ct. 748 (1908). A good discussion of these issues is contained in Kaplow, The Patent-Antitrust Intersection: A Reappraisal, 97 Harv.L.Rev. 1813 (1984).

Finally, courts have often found that an incumbent firm's vexatious litigation or appeals to an administrative agency can be an illegal exclusionary practice. Although firms have a First Amendment right to petition the government for redress of their grievances,[31] this right does not extend to "baseless and repetitive" claims filed against a rival or prospective entrant for the purpose of excluding the rival from operating in a certain market.[32]

Such claims are best characterized as mechanisms for raising a rival's costs disproportionately to those of the incumbent.[33] Assume that litigation costs the same amount for both parties—perhaps $100,000 per year. The established incumbent who files the action has an output of 100,000 units per year, while the recent entrant who is the defendant has an output of 10,000 units per year. In this case the litigation costs the established firm $1.00 per unit, and the new entrant $10.00 per unit. If the new entrant has not yet begun to produce, the costs will be felt even more strongly. The costs of litigation in this instance must be considered as fixed costs—that is, they do not vary with the output of either firm. The difference between $1.00 in additional costs per unit and $10.00 in additional costs could easily be the difference between profit and loss selling.

When unfounded litigation or administrative action is undertaken by the dominant firm for no other reasonable purpose than raising a rival's costs disproportionately, it should be condemned as illegal monopolization.

WESTLAW REFERENCES

monopol! /p conglomerate horizontal vertical /8 merg***

monopol! /p (expan*i** /4 capacity) (pric*** /4 discriminat***) % robinson

monopol! /s (price supply +1 squeeze) (refus*** /4 deal negotiat***) "vertical integration"

monopol! /p (predatory /4 pric*** "research and development") (predisclos*** /s innovation)

headnote(monopol! /s tied tying)

digest(monopol! /p patent /s abus*** accumulat*** licens*** tied tying)

monopol! /p administrative appeal law-suit litigation /s baseless repetitive unfounded vex!

265k12(15)

265k17(2.5)

---

31. Eastern R.R. Presidents Conference v. Noerr Motor Freight Co., 365 U.S. 127, 81 S.Ct. 523 (1961).

32. Calif. Motor Transport Co. v. Trucking Unlimited, 404 U.S. 508, 513, 92 S.Ct. 609, 613 (1972). Some courts hold that if the litigation or other claims are clearly baseless they need not be "repetitive." See Clipper Express v. Rocky Mt. Motor Tariff Bureau, Inc., 690 F.2d 1240 (9th Cir. 1982), cert. denied, 459 U.S. 1127, 103 S.Ct. 1234 (1983).

33. See Salop & Scheffman, Raising Rivals' Costs, 73 Amer.Econ.Rev. 267 (1983).

CHAPTER 6

ATTEMPT TO MONOPOLIZE AND PREDATORY PRICING

Table of Sections

§ 6.1   Introduction: The Attempt Offense

The offense of attempt to monopolize is one of the most complex of federal antitrust violations. Although the offense is well established and often alleged, one prominent commentator has characterized the need for a distinct attempt offense as "debatable."[1] Doubts come from two sides. On the one hand, many acts alleged to be illegal attempts may also be illegal monopolization or violations of another antitrust law. In such cases a separate "attempt" offense is superfluous. On the other hand, expansive use of the attempt offense to reach conduct not condemned by the other antitrust laws may do more harm than good to the competitive market. If attempt analysis focuses too heavily on unfair conduct and too little on

§ 6.1

1. 3 P. Areeda & D. Turner, Antitrust Law ¶ 820 (1978).

159

market power the offense can operate to protect inefficient businesses from their more efficient competitors.[2]

§ 2 of the Sherman Act, 15 U.S.C.A. § 2, condemns every "person who shall monopolize or attempt to monopolize * * *." Congress clearly recognized a distinct attempt offense, and the offense itself is statutory. At common law the attempt to commit a crime could be illegal even though the language of the relevant criminal statute condemned only the completed act. One of the great architects of the modern American common law, Justice Oliver Wendell Holmes, Jr.,[3] read the common law formulation of attempt into the Sherman Act in 1905. In Swift & Co. v. U.S. the defendants were accused of attempting "to obtain a monopoly of the supply and distribution of fresh meats throughout the United States * * *."[4] Their defense was that the indictment failed to allege specific acts that were themselves illegal. To this Justice Holmes responded:

> It is suggested that the several acts charged are lawful and that intent can make no difference. But they are bound together as the parts of a single plan. The plan may make the parts unlawful. * * * Where acts are not sufficient in themselves to produce a result which the law seeks to prevent,—for instance, the monopoly—but require further acts in addition to the mere forces of nature to bring that result to pass, an intent to bring it to pass is necessary in order to produce a dangerous probability that it will happen. * * * But when that intent and the consequent dangerous probability exist, this statute, like many others and like the common law in some cases, directs itself against that dangerous probability as well as against the completed result.[5]

The three elements of the attempt offense today are taken directly from Holmes's formulation in the *Swift* case. The plaintiff must establish the defendant's: 1) specific intent to control prices or destroy competition in some part of commerce; 2) predatory or anticompetitive conduct directed to accomplishing the unlawful purpose; and 3) a dangerous probability of success.[6]

---

2. See generally, Cooper, Attempts and Monopolization: A Mildly Expansionary Answer to the Prophylactic Riddle of Section Two, 72 Mich.L.Rev. 375 (1974).

3. See O.W. Holmes, The Common Law 65 (1881).

4. 196 U.S. 375, 393, 25 S.Ct. 276, 278 (1905).

5. Id. at 396, 25 S.Ct. at 279. See also American Tobacco Co. v. U.S., 328 U.S. 781, 785, 66 S.Ct. 1125, 1127 (1946), which defined attempt to monopolize as the "employment of methods, means and practices which would, if successful, accomplish monopolization, and which, though falling short, nevertheless approach so close as to create a dangerous probability of it * * *."

6. See William Inglis v. ITT Continental Baking Co., 668 F.2d 1014, 1027 (9th Cir. 1981), cert. denied, 459 U.S. 825, 103 S.Ct. 57–8 (1982). This three-part test is sometimes called the "classic" formulation of the attempt offense. See 3 P. Areeda & D. Turner, Antitrust Law ¶ 820 (1978).

Today circuit courts are in vague agreement that the offense includes these three elements.[7] When they interpret the elements, however, all agreement stops. The circuits are deeply divided over a host of issues. The discussion that follows will address the element of specific intent first, then dangerous probability of success, and finally the bad conduct requirements.

 WESTLAW REFERENCES
headnote(sherman /s 15 +5 2 /s attempt** /s monopol!)

§ 6.2 Specific Intent

Subjective intent is the bugbear of antitrust litigation. Courts need evidence of intent in order to evaluate the purpose and likely effects of certain business conduct. At the same time, the essence of competition is the intent to triumph over one's rivals. One of the most perplexing problems in antitrust policy is discerning between illegitimate and legitimate intent. Nevertheless, specific intent is an established element of the attempt offense, approved by the Supreme Court.[1]

No one has ever developed a general rule for identifying illegitimate subjective intent. To be sure, at the extremes evidence of intent can be more-or-less conclusive. Evidence that a firm planned to dynamite its competitor's plant shows illegitimate specific intent. On the other hand, evidence that a firm planned to produce a better product that could be sold at a lower price almost certainly reveals legitimate intent, even though the purpose and clear result may be to injure rivals.

In between are a host of phenomena that must be characterized as ambiguous: evidence that a firm dropped its price, knowing that a less efficient rival would go out of business;[2] that a firm initiated unsuccessful litigation, knowing the effect would be to delay or prevent a competitor's entry into a market;[3] that a firm knew that

---

7. Some courts add a fourth requirement of "antitrust injury." See California Computer Products, Inc. v. IBM Corp., 613 F.2d 727, 736 (9th Cir. 1979). The antitrust injury requirement is not part of the substantive law of attempt to monopolize, however, but rather a requirement that private plaintiffs must generally meet in antitrust cases, at least under the rule of reason. See § 14.5 below.

§ 6.2

1. See Times-Picayune Pub. Co. v. U.S., 345 U.S. 594, 626, 73 S.Ct. 872, 890 (1953): "While the completed offense of monopolization under § 2 demands only a general intent to do the act, 'for no

monopolist monopolizes unconscious of what he is doing,' a specific intent to destroy competition or build monopoly is essential to guilt for the mere attempt * * *." See also, U.S. v. Aluminum Co. of America, 148 F.2d 416, 432 (2d Cir. 1945), in which Judge Hand held that the attempt offense required "specific intent," which was "an intent which goes beyond the mere intent to do the act."

2. See the discussion of predatory pricing below in §§ 6.7–6.12.

3. See Otter Tail Power Co. v. U.S., 410 U.S. 366, 93 S.Ct. 1022 (1973), rehearing denied, 411 U.S. 910, 93 S.Ct. 1523 (1973), on remand, 360 F.Supp. 451

its failure to predisclose a product innovation would injure competitors in a complimentary product.[4]

Further, business firms are not monoliths: thinking and decision-making are the product of many minds. Memoranda are written by careless people, and they often contain puffing about competitive prowess that far exceeds a firm's actual planning and policy. The unexpurgated paperwork of every large corporation probably includes memoranda that could appear incriminating to a jury, because they manifest an intent to defeat, abuse or even destroy rivals.[5] Some firms do a better job than others of systematically destroying or suppressing such evidence—but there is no positive correlation between the firms that are good at suppressing suspicious memoranda and the firms that are innocent of antitrust violations. The well-publicized years-long discovery search through corporate documents for evidence of specific intent is a turkey shoot.

An overinclusive rule that finds specific anticompetitive intent readily and relies on it heavily may frequently end up condemning competition on the merits. The result will be higher prices for consumers. This is particularly true when the attempt allegation is predatory pricing. An overinclusive rule can actually force some firms to sell at prices higher than their costs in order to avoid antitrust liability. However, an underinclusive rule may result in the creation of a certain amount of market power, and in the injury to competitors who would not have been injured in a competitive market.

The problem goes deeper than mere determination of subjective intent, however. Intent, once determined, must be evaluated. Most courts agree that mere intent to do better than or to vanquish one's rivals is insufficient to warrant condemnation. Intent of the following kinds, however, has been found sufficient: 1) intent to achieve monopoly power, or to acquire sufficient power to control price;[6] 2) intent to exclude competition;[7] or 3) intent to perform the specific act fulfilling the conduct requirement of the attempt offense.

(1973), judgment affirmed, 417 U.S. 901, 94 S.Ct. 2594 (1974). See § 5.6 above.

4.   See Berkey Photo, Inc. v. Eastman Kodak Co., 603 F.2d 263 (2d Cir. 1979), cert. denied, 444 U.S. 1093, 100 S.Ct. 1061 (1980). See § 5.6 above.

5.   See R. Posner, Antitrust Law: An Economic Perspective 189–90 (1976).

6.   See Photovest Corp. v. Fotomat Corp., 606 F.2d 704, 711 (7th Cir. 1979), cert. denied, 445 U.S. 917, 100 S.Ct. 1278 (1980); FLM Collision Parts, Inc. v. Ford Motor Co., 543 F.2d 1019, 1030 (2d Cir. 1976), cert. denied, 429 U.S. 1097, 97 S.Ct. 1116 (1977).

7.   See U.S. v. Empire Gas Corp., 537 F.2d 296, 302 (8th Cir. 1976), cert. denied, 429 U.S. 1122, 97 S.Ct. 1158 (1977); but see, Blair Foods, Inc. v. Ranchers Cotton Oil, 610 F.2d 665, 670 (9th Cir. 1980): "The mere intention * * * to exclude competition * * * is insufficient to establish specific intent to monopolize by some illegal means. * * * To conclude otherwise would contravene the very essence of a competitive marketplace which is to prevail against all competitors." See also, Buffalo Courier Express, Inc. v. Buffalo Evening News, Inc., 601 F.2d 48, 54 (2d Cir. 1979).

None of these statements adequately distinguishes harmful from competitive intent. Intent to "exclude" is consistent with both efficient practices (research and development) and inefficient ones (predatory pricing). The last alternative—intent to engage in the specific act that satisfies the conduct requirement of the attempt offense—is inadvertently used by courts which hold that the requisite intent can be inferred from the conduct itself. This standard can become dangerously overdeterrent bootstrapping unless courts put strict limits on the kind of conduct that satisfies the requirement, and insist upon a meaningful showing of dangerous probability that the conduct would have yielded a monopoly. If these restrictions are followed, however, the intent requirement becomes superfluous.

Today many economists and some legal commentators believe that subjective intent should either be irrelevant, or else should be used only to help a court characterize ambiguous conduct. Economists would prefer to analyze the structure of a market, and determine both whether the danger of monopoly is real and whether certain conduct was reasonably calculated to create a monopoly. Judges are less sanguine about their ability to evaluate conduct against the background of a particular market structure. They are particularly sceptical when the analysis requires a fair amount of economic sophistication. Predatory pricing is one example. A decade ago judges focused as much on the defendant's subjective intent as on its performance in the market in determining whether a certain price was predatory.[8]

One effect of economic thinking on attempt jurisprudence has been to restore the specific intent element to its historical position in common law attempt analysis. Historically, the specific intent requirement was designed "to confine the reach of an attempt claim * * *."[9] The specific intent requirement acted as a limiting device to help a court decide whether conduct that met the other requirements for an attempt offense should nevertheless be held lawful because the defendant had no evil design. In the 1950's and 1960's the specific intent element in attempt cases often performed an expansionary rather than limiting role. In some cases evidence of bad intentions created a presumption of illegal attempt, and could be used to condemn conduct which itself was not clearly calculated to create a monopoly.[10]

8. For example, Foremost Int'l Tours, Inc. v. Qantas Airways, Ltd., 379 F.Supp. 88, 97–98 (D. Hawaii 1974), affirmed, 525 F.2d 281 (9th Cir. 1975), cert. denied, 429 U.S. 816, 97 S.Ct. 57 (1976).

9. William Inglis & Sons Baking Co., Inc. v. ITT Continental Baking Co., 668 F.2d 1014, 1027 (9th Cir. 1981), cert. denied, 459 U.S. 825, 103 S.Ct. 57–8 (1982).

10. See Union Leader Corp. v. Newspapers of New England, Inc., 180 F.Supp. 125, 140 (D. Mass. 1959), modified, 284 F.2d 582 (1st Cir. 1960), cert. denied, 365 U.S. 833, 81 S.Ct. 747 (1961), where Judge Wyzanski described an attempt offense as prohibiting "a person (a) who has an intent to exclude competition (b) from using not merely technical restraints of trade, but even predatory practices, unfair methods of competition,

Currently the trend is for courts to use the intent requirement as a liability-restricting rather than liability-expanding device. Some courts use specific intent as an aid in characterizing ambiguous conduct. If the conduct is sufficiently close to the line that it could go either way, knowledge of specific intent or its absence can help the court decide whether to condemn it. The Ninth Circuit and others, for example, have taken this approach in predatory pricing cases, where the conduct is almost always ambiguous.[11] In such cases of ambiguous conduct, specific intent generally becomes an additional requirement that the plaintiff must establish. However, if conduct considered alone clearly offers "the basis for a substantial claim of restraint of trade,"[12] most courts are far more willing to dispense with a separate showing of specific intent. They either ignore the intent requirement or else hold that the particular conduct alleged is sufficiently clear that evil intent can be inferred.[13]

 WESTLAW REFERENCES

attempt** /p inten! /p anti-competiti** predatory /4 conduct pric***

attempt** /p inten! /p market monopoly pric*** /4 control power

attempt** /p inten! /p destroy*** exclud*** /4 competit***

attempt** /p specific subjective +1 intent! /p ambigu***

265k12(1.6)

§ 6.3 "Dangerous Probability of Success"

Often the circumstances surrounding an alleged attempt to monopolize indicate clearly the potential harm to competition. If there are only two firms in a relevant market and one dynamites the other's plant the danger to competition is clear. In most cases, however, the danger is difficult to evaluate. The purpose of the "dangerous probability" requirement is to avoid overdeterrence in situations when the defendant's conduct is difficult to assess or the market in which the conduct occurred is not clearly conducive to monopoly.

The "dangerous probability" requirement has been controversial. A few courts have concluded that the element is not essential to an attempt offense.[1] More often, however, the controversy over the

---

or business patterns not honestly industrial—in short, what may loosely be called unfair means." See also, Lessig v. Tidewater Oil Co., 327 F.2d 459 (9th Cir. 1964), cert. denied, 377 U.S. 993, 84 S.Ct. 1920 (1964).

11. See § 6.11 below.

12. See *Inglis*, note 9 above, at 1028.

13. Id. See Hawk, Attempts to Monopolize—Specific Intent As Antitrust's

Ghost in the Machine, 58 Cornell L.Rev. 1121, 1170–75 (1973).

§ 6.3

1. See, Lessig v. Tidewater Oil Co., 327 F.2d 459, 474 (9th Cir. 1964), cert. denied, 377 U.S. 993, 84 S.Ct. 1920 (1964):

"We reject the premise that probability of actual monopolization is an essential element of proof of attempt to

"dangerous probability" requirement has centered on three issues: 1) Whether conduct not clearly creating a dangerous probability of monopolization should nevertheless be condemned under § 2; 2) whether establishment of a "dangerous probability" requires determination of some relevant market in which monopolization might have occurred; 3) whether dangerous probability can be established without a showing that the defendant already has a certain amount of market power. These problems are taken up in this and the following two sections.

The first question—whether conduct not satisfying the dangerous probability requirement can nevertheless be an illegal attempt—arises most often when the conduct violates a different antitrust law. For example, tying arrangements, mergers and certain refusals to deal have all been treated as illegal attempts.[2] In such cases the violation of § 2 is inconsequential, however: a plaintiff's remedy is usually not greater when the same activity violates two statutes instead of one.

More important is whether conduct that does not violate another antitrust statute should be condemned as an attempt when there is little danger of monopoly. Some anticompetitive conduct can injure competitors even though no dangerous probability of monopoly exists. Predatory pricing is an example. Suppose that a firm drops its price far below cost intending to drive its rival out of business. However, the aspiring monopolist has grossly miscalculated its chances of success: it has underestimated the financial strength of its rival, overestimated its own financial strength, and greatly underestimated the cost of a prolonged period of below cost sales. After a year of predation it gives up and raises its price to the competitive level. Meanwhile the intended victim, while still in business, has suffered substantial losses as well. No consumers have been injured however, and there will never be a period in which output is reduced and prices raised as a result of monopolization. Should the injured competitor have a cause of action under the antitrust laws?

---

monopolize. Of course, such a probability may be relevant circumstantial evidence of intent, but the specific intent itself is the only evidence of dangerous probability the statute requires—perhaps on the not unreasonable assumption that the actor is better able than others to judge the practical possibility of achieving his illegal objective."

However, recent Ninth Circuit decisions appear to have abandoned the *Lessig* doctrine. They now require at least some kind of proof of dangerous probability of success. See William Inglis & Sons Baking Co., Inc. v. ITT Continental Baking Co., 668 F.2d 1014, 1029–

30 (9th Cir. 1981), cert. denied, 459 U.S. 825, 103 S.Ct. 57–8 (1982).

2. See Kearney & Trecker Corp. v. Giddings & Lewis, Inc., 452 F.2d 579, 598 (7th Cir. 1971), cert. denied, 405 U.S. 1066, 92 S.Ct. 1500 (1972) (tying arrangement); Knutson v. Daily Review, Inc., 548 F.2d 795 (9th Cir. 1976), cert. denied, 433 U.S. 910, 97 S.Ct. 2977 (1977), on remand, 468 F.Supp. 226 (1979), judgment affirmed, 664 F.2d 1120 (9th Cir. 1981) (acquisition of competitors); Lessig, note 1 above, (refusal to deal); see also, Eastman Kodak Co. of New York v. Southern Photo Materials Co., 273 U.S. 359, 47 S.Ct. 400 (1927) (refusal to deal).

The answer must be no.[3] In this case the simplicity of the facts presented belies the great complexity of an offense like predatory pricing. Perhaps no antitrust offense is more difficult to measure. The risk of condemning competitive behavior is substantial, and one way of reducing the risk of overdeterrence is to condemn conduct only when the market structure itself suggests that monopoly is a real possibility.

Some market situations are conducive to monopolization, while others are not. When monopolization is unlikely any antitrust rule that condemns ambiguous conduct will end up condemning competition on the merits more than it condemns predatory activity. The offense of attempt "to monopolize" must be defined so as to condemn actions reasonably calculated to create a monopoly. Otherwise the offense becomes a general fair practices statute—and legal enforcement of fair practices is often bad for competition.

 WESTLAW REFERENCES
attempt** /s monopol! /p "dangerous probability of success"

§ 6.4 "Dangerous Probability:" The Costs of Miscalculation

Reliable evidence of specific intent can be difficult to find and inconclusive when it is found. Conduct can be equally ambiguous. Often the simplest way to assess the danger a defendant's conduct poses is to examine the market in which the alleged attempt occurred. If the defendant's conduct is ambiguous, arguably consistent with both monopolization and competition on the merits, examination of the market will help a court determine whether a dangerous probability of monopoly existed. If the answer is no, the court need study the conduct no further.

More importantly, recognizing that characterization of ambiguous conduct is imprecise, examination of the market's proclivity to monopolization will reduce the rate and costs of error. The possibility for error is two-fold. First, a legal rule that is too harsh on defendants will tend toward overinclusiveness or overdeterrence: that is, it may recognize all (or most) true instances of conduct likely to cause monopoly, but it will sometimes condemn competition on the merits as well. Secondly, a legal rule that is too harsh on plaintiffs will tend toward underinclusiveness or underdeterrence: it may recognize most instances when monopolization is unlikely, but in the process may overlook some instances when monopoly is a real threat.[1]

3. For a contrary view, see Williamson, Antitrust Enforcement: Where it's Been, Where it's Going, 27 St. Louis Univ.L.J. 289, 312 (1983).

§ 6.4

1. See Joskow & Klevorick, A Framework for Analyzing Predatory Pricing Policy, 89 Yale L.J. 213, 222–39 (1979).

Both kinds of errors can impose substantial economic costs on society. Overinclusive rules are inefficient when they brand efficiency as monopolistic. The result is that firms charge higher prices than necessary in order to avoid legal liability, and they refrain from doing things that benefit consumers but that may harm competitors. Furthermore, to the extent that the more efficient firms refrain from exploiting their efficiencies to the full extent, the market becomes attractive to other, less efficient firms. The result in a market that is already competitive will be higher costs.

Underinclusive rules are also inefficient. A rule that fails to recognize incipient monopolization will permit the growth of some monopolies. Both the monopolist's reduced output and its effort to maintain its monopoly position will be socially costly.[2]

A perfect legal rule would avoid both overdeterrence and underdeterrence. Unfortunately, when conduct is ambiguous, such as predatory pricing, the legal rule is necessarily an oversimplification of reality. For example, no comprehensible legal rule can weigh all the relevant variables in a predatory pricing case. Recognizing then that the rule will sometimes miss the mark, courts must nevertheless strive to minimize the costs of such errors.

When a market is already highly concentrated and has a dominant firm with substantial market power, then the cost of overdeterrence is relatively low, while the cost of underdeterrence is high. The effect of overdeterrence in such a market may be to force the monopolist to create a safe harbor for itself by pricing at above its marginal cost, or by avoiding aggressive developmental or marketing techniques that are ambiguous but might be characterized as exclusionary. However, the market power of such a firm would encourage it to price at above marginal cost anyway. Furthermore, an overdeterrent attempt rule in such a market would tend to protect new entrants—both those that are equally efficient with the dominant firm and those that may be somewhat less efficient. Even a market with one dominant, efficient firm and two or three less efficient ones likely will have higher total output and lower prices than a market containing only the larger firm.[3] The general effect of such protection will be to erode the dominant firm's status. Eventually competition will drive prices, output and innovation to the competitive level. When that happens the less efficient firms will either reform or leave the market.

However, in competitive markets the cost of overdeterrence is high, and of underdeterrence quite low. Predatory conduct is much

2. See § 1.3 above.

3. See note, Standing at the Fringe: Antitrust Damages and the Fringe Producer, 35 Stan.L.Rev. 763, 769–73 (1983), showing that the presence of fringe firms will not necessarily increase the cartel's or monopolist's output, but will reduce their profit-maximizing price. Furthermore, when the fringe output is included, total output in the market will be higher as well.

more expensive in competitive markets, where the expected benefits must be discounted by the decreased likelihood of success. This is particularly true, as we shall see, of predatory pricing. In a competitive market an aspiring monopolist has a relatively small percentage of the market, and it shares the market with many other firms. As a result, even if it succeeds in driving one firm out of business, it will be unable to reap monopoly profits afterwards. An underdeterrent rule in a competitive market will seldom create a monopoly. On the other hand, an overdeterrent rule may force firms to avoid hard competition, even though the market is conducive to competition. In competitive markets the best attempt rule is no rule at all.

 WESTLAW REFERENCES
attempt** /p "dangerous probability of success" /s market possib!

§ 6.5　"Dangerous Probability" and Market Power

Courts have expressed concern that the attempt offense can be used anticompetitively to condemn "unfair" business conduct when there is little likelihood of monopoly.[1] For some courts this means that the plaintiff in an attempt case must show that the defendant has a certain amount of market power.[2] Others have rejected the requirement, arguing that it virtually destroys the distinction between the offense of attempt and completed monopolization.[3] Most courts, however, require a plaintiff to establish a dangerous probability that the defendant could have monopolized some identifiable market.[4] This market generally need not be defined as precisely as it must be in monopolization cases. Further, a substantially lower

---

§ 6.5

1. For example, see Redwing Carriers v. McKenzie Tank Lines, 443 F.Supp. 639, 642–43 (N.D. Fla. 1977), affirmed per curiam, 594 F.2d 114 (5th Cir. 1979): the antitrust laws were "never designed to create a federal remedy for unfair competition. * * * [They were] not concerned, as are the states' laws of unfair competition, with morality."

2. Because courts generally use market share as a proxy for market power, most of the judicial analysis has focused on market share. See Coleman Motor Co. v. Chrysler Corp., 525 F.2d 1338 (3d Cir. 1975); Yoder Bros. v. California-Florida Plant Corp., 537 F.2d 1347 (5th Cir. 1976), cert. denied, 429 U.S. 1094, 97 S.Ct. 1108 (1977). The circuits are in wide disarray on the market share requirements that will support the offense. See Note, Attempt to Monopolize Under the Sherman Act: Defendant's

Market Power as a Requisite to a Prima Facie Case, 73 Col.L.Rev. 1451, 1473–75 (1973); 3 P. Areeda & D. Turner, Antitrust Law ¶ 835c (1978).

3. Lessig v. Tidewater Oil Co., 327 F.2d 459, 474–78 (9th Cir. 1964), cert. denied, 377 U.S. 993, 84 S.Ct. 1920 (1964).

4. See Walker Process Equip., Inc. v. Food Machinery & Chem. Corp., 382 U.S. 172, 177, 86 S.Ct. 347, 350 (1965): "To establish monopolization or attempt to monopolize * * * it would then be necessary to appraise the exclusionary power of the illegal * * * claim in terms of the relevant market for the product involved. Without a definition of that market there is no way to measure * * * ability to lessen or destroy competition." See also Transource Intern. v. Trinity Indus., Inc., 725 F.2d 274 (5th Cir. 1984).

market share will support an attempt case than a monopolization case.

Courts that have tried to produce a generalized formula for market power in attempt cases probably have been wasting their time. The market power requirements in attempt cases vary with the conduct alleged to be an attempt. A firm that seeks to create a monopoly by dynamiting its competitor's plants does not need market power—only a saboteur and a match. The same thing generally applies to other kinds of conduct that have been held to be an attempt to monopolize, such as bad faith litigation or patent fraud. However, in Lorain Journal Co. v. United States [5] the defendant was accused of refusing to sell newspaper advertising to any purchaser who also purchased advertising on a nearby radio station. Lorain Journal's scheme would not have been successful if it had no market power. First of all, if there were competing daily newspapers in the relevant area, anyone who wanted to advertise in both a newspaper and the radio station would have purchased its newspaper advertising from a newspaper that did not assess the restriction. Second, assuming that Lorain Journal did not compensate advertisers for their agreement not to purchase radio advertising, the Journal's restriction amounted to a price increase—a sign that the defendant had some market power.

Thus it is impossible to generalize: some attempts to monopolize require the defendant to have substantial market power, while others do not. Further, the success of a particular attempt scheme sometimes depends not on the defendant's market power, but on its relatively large market share. Predatory pricing is such an offense: the act of predatory pricing does not require a defendant to have the ability to sell its output at a price higher than marginal cost. On the contrary, the offense itself involves selling at a price often lower than short-run marginal cost. However, predatory pricing is prohibitively expensive and unlikely to yield a monopoly unless the predator has a fairly large market share to begin with.[6]

In all cases it is important to remember that the attempt offense is designed to reach conduct likely to create a monopoly. In the debate over the market power requirements in attempt cases some courts seem to have lost sight of this. A few courts have assessed what appears to be a universal market power requirement. Others have dispensed with the requirement and in the process have permitted plaintiffs to prove an attempt without showing a dangerous probability of success. The attempt offense was not designed to condemn the exercise of present market power. Nor was it designed, however, to condemn conduct unlikely to give the defendant a monopoly. At the very least a plaintiff should be required to identify some

5.　342 U.S. 143, 72 S.Ct. 181 (1951).

6.　See § 6.10 below.

market in which the defendant's activities, if allowed to run their course, plausibly would have generated a monopoly.[7]

 WESTLAW REFERENCES

attempt** /p "dangerous probability of success" /21 "market power"

§ 6.6 Conduct Requirements

Courts have identified a diverse host of completed and uncompleted[1] acts as satisfying the conduct requirements of the attempt to monopolize offense.

Any principled rule for determining the kinds of conduct that will support an attempt offense must recognize the following limitations: 1) the conduct, or planned or threatened conduct, must be capable of giving the defendant monopoly power; 2) conduct that is legal for someone who is already a monopolist cannot be illegal for someone who is not a monopolist; 3) sometimes socially beneficial conduct can create substantial market power.

A plaintiff cannot make out an attempt offense if the alleged conduct could not have given the defendant a monopoly. This may be the primary distinction between the offense of attempt to monopolize and the law of so-called business torts or unfair practices. False advertising, misrepresentation, certain refusals to deal, fraudulent inducement, and various dirty tricks may be illegal under the law of many states. They are not attempts to monopolize, however, unless there is measurable likelihood that they will give the actor market power.[2]

To be sure, it is often appropriate to analyze such conduct by determining whether there was a "dangerous probability of success" that it would yield monopoly power. However, determining "dangerous probability" may require a court to make an expensive economic analysis of the market in which the alleged illegal conduct took place. Often one can infer from the conduct itself that monopoly power was not a likely result. A mere claim of false advertising or refusal to deal unaccompanied by allegations that the market is already noncompetitive, for example, should be dismissed on its face.

Any act that is legal for a monopolist in the market in which it has monopoly power should be legal for a nonmonopolist: the conduct requirements for attempt should be, if anything, stricter than the

---

7. Professors Areeda & Turner recognize some *"per se"* conduct for which a plaintiff could show a dangerous probability of success without proof of power: patent fraud, reckless patent infringement, and (with some qualifications) predatory pricing. 3 P. Areeda & D. Turner, Antitrust Law ¶ 836 (1978).

§ 6.6

1. For the problem of unconsummated conduct, see 3 P. Areeda & D. Turner ¶ 826 (1978).

2. See George R. Whitten, Jr. v. Paddock Pool Bldrs., 508 F.2d 547 (1st Cir. 1974), cert. denied, 421 U.S. 1004, 95 S.Ct. 2407 (1975).

requirements for illegal monopolization.[3] Price discrimination,[4] failure to predisclose new technology,[5] aggressive research and development,[6] expansion of capacity,[7] acquisition of or refusal to license patents,[8] and some dealer terminations and exclusive dealing contracts[9] may be legal when they are performed by a monopolist. They are necessarily legal when they are performed by a nonmonopolist.

Finally, some conduct that might be illegal for the monopolist should not be the basis for an attempt offense. This is particularly true of practices that can create efficiency and which may give a firm market power. Research and development is one example of such a practice. Vertical integration is another. There is questionable but nevertheless well established case authority that vertical integration by a monopolist can be illegal, particularly when it results in the termination of dealers or firms at a different distributional level than the one in which the defendant has a monopoly, or when it effectively gives the defendant a monopoly in two markets instead of one. The reasonableness of such claims is discussed in § 5.6 above.

Firms integrate vertically in order to reduce costs. One result of such cost reduction, however, is that the integrated firm may acquire the ability to price its output above its new marginal cost or to steal part of the market away from competitors. This procurement of a "competitive advantage" has occasionally been characterized by courts as an illegal attempt to monopolize the primary market.[10]

Condemning such efficiency creating practices would undermine the entire competitive process, however. The nature of competition is to encourage competing firms to increase their own efficiency, necessarily at the expense of competitors. Any principled, consumer-welfare oriented theory of attempt must condemn only inefficient, socially injurious conduct.

3. Transamerica Computer Co. v. IBM Corp., 698 F.2d 1377, 1382 (9th Cir. 1983), cert. denied __ U.S. __, 104 S. Ct. 370 (1983).

4. See Pacific Eng'r & Prod. Co. v. Kerr-McGee Corp., 551 F.2d 790 (10th Cir. 1977), cert. denied 434 U.S. 879, 98 S.Ct. 234 (1977), rehearing denied, 434 U.S. 977, 98 S.Ct. 543 (1977). But see, United States v. United Shoe Machinery Corp., 110 F.Supp. 295, 297 (D.Mass. 1953) affirmed, 347 U.S. 521, 74 S.Ct. 699 (1954), where Judge Wyzanski included price discrimination among the exclusionary practices that made the defendant an illegal monopolist.

5. Berkey Photo, Inc. v. Eastman Kodak Co., 603 F.2d 263 (2d Cir. 1979), cert. denied 444 U.S. 1093, 100 S.Ct. 1061 (1980).

6. Cal. Computer Products v. IBM Corp., 613 F.2d 727, 744 (9th Cir. 1979).

7. E.I. du Pont de Nemours & Co., 96 F.T.C. 650 (1980).

8. See SCM Corp. v. Xerox Corp., 645 F.2d 1195 (2d Cir. 1981) cert. denied, 455 U.S. 1016, 102 S.Ct. 1708 (1982), rehearing denied, 456 U.S. 985, 102 S.Ct. 2260 (1982).

9. Paschall v. Kansas City Star Co., 727 F.2d 692 (8th Cir. 1984), en banc, cert. denied, __ U.S. __, __ S.Ct. __ (1984). See generally 3 P. Areeda & D. Turner, Antitrust Law ¶¶ 723-732 (1978).

10. Industrial Building Materials v. Interchemical Corp., 437 F.2d 1336 (9th Cir. 1970).

WESTLAW REFERENCES
attempt** /p conduct /s market monopoly +1 position power

§ 6.7 Conduct: Predatory Pricing

"Predatory pricing" refers to a firm's efforts to acquire or preserve monopoly power by underselling its rivals. In its most orthodox form, predatory pricing refers to driving rivals out of business by selling at a price below cost. Today predatory pricing is analyzed under the antitrust laws as illegal monopolization or attempt to monopolize under § 2 of the Sherman Act, or sometimes as a violation of § 2 of the Clayton Act, as amended by the Robinson-Patman Act.

Courts once believed that predatory pricing was easy for a well-financed firm to accomplish, and that it was a common means by which monopolies came into existence.[1] In the last generation, however, many economists and antitrust analysts have concluded otherwise: predatory pricing is in fact very expensive, often likely to fail, and not plausible in the vast majority of markets in which it has been alleged to occur.[2] Today some respected legal scholars believe that predatory pricing in any market is irrational and virtually never happens.[3]

The legal tests for predatory pricing have changed with judicial attitudes about how frequently it occurs. When courts believed that predatory pricing was common plaintiffs could sometimes establish it by showing that the defendant firm was large, the victim small, and that prices in the predated area went down.[4] Today, however, increased scepticism about the frequency of predatory pricing has led courts to develop much stricter tests for identifying it. Since 1975 when the Areeda-Turner test for predatory pricing was introduced,[5] only a small number of plaintiffs have prevailed in predatory pricing actions.[6] No circuit has held, however, that pricing at below cost is *per se* legal. The Supreme Court has not considered a predatory pricing case since the Areeda-Turner test was first developed.

§ 6.7

1. For example, in the early twentieth century it commonly was believed that the Standard Oil monopoly was created this way. See McGee, Predatory Price Cutting: the Standard Oil (N.J.) Case, 1 J. L. & Econ. 137 (1958).

2. See R. Posner, Antitrust Law: An Economic Perspective 184–192 (1976).

3. For example, see R. Bork, The Antitrust Paradox: A Policy at War With Itself 144–55 (1978); Easterbrook, Predatory Strategies and Counterstrategies, 48 Univ.Chi.L.Rev. 263 (1981).

4. See Utah Pie Co. v. Continental Baking Co., 386 U.S. 685, 87 S.Ct. 1326 (1967).

5. Areeda & Turner, Predatory Pricing and Related Practices Under Section 2 of the Sherman Act, 88 Harv.L.Rev. 697 (1975). See § 6.8 below.

6. But there have been some. See D & S Redi-Mix v. Sierra Redi-Mix and Contracting Co., 692 F.2d 1245 (9th Cir. 1982); and see Sunshine Books, Ltd. v. Temple Univ., 697 F.2d 90 (3d Cir. 1982).

Few antitrust allegations are more sensitive or difficult for courts to measure than predatory pricing. Low prices are a principle if not the primary goal of the antitrust laws. In a predatory pricing case, however, a judge must consider a charge that a price violates the antitrust laws because it is too low. Further, the relationship between any firm's prices and its costs is ambiguous and difficult to compute. If the judge uses an overdeterrent rule the result will be inefficiently high prices. This in turn will permit less efficient firms to stay in the market. Small wonder that some commentators argue that courts should dismiss all predatory pricing complaints, at least when the plaintiff and the defendant are competitors.[7]

Predatory pricing is not condemned, however, because it results in current lower prices. It is condemned because, if successful, it will eventually result in reduced output and higher prices. A price is predatory if it is reasonably calculated to drive rivals from the market today or else discipline them so that the predator can enjoy profitable monopoly pricing in the future.

In order for such a scheme to be successful, several things must be true. First, the victims must be sufficiently weak or have sufficiently high costs that the predator can drive them from business or make them obey. Second, the market must be structured in such a way that the predator can predict a profitable period of monopoly pricing. Third, the discounted present value of the future period of monopoly pricing must be greater than the present losses that the predator will incur during the predatory period. The following sections analyze these requirements and describe some of the difficulties that courts recently have encountered in evaluating predatory pricing claims.

 WESTLAW REFERENCES
attemp** /s anti-competiti** predatory /4 conduct pric***

§ 6.8   When Is a Price Predatory? The Areeda-Turner Test

Competition drives prices to marginal cost.[1] When a firm considers whether to produce one additional unit, it weighs the added revenues the additional sale will generate against the added costs of production and sale. Two things are generally true of competitive markets: 1) prices will tend toward marginal costs, although in some real world markets they may stabilize at a point somewhat higher than marginal cost; 2) dropping a price below short-run marginal cost is not a reasonable way for a firm to increase profits—unless the increase is the present value of future monopoly pricing.

---

7. However, Easterbrook, note 3 above, at 331–33, would permit suits by consumers forced to pay a higher price after the predation was successful.

§ 6.8

1. See E. Mansfield, Microeconomics: Theory & Applications 252–257 (4th ed. 1982); and see § 1.1 above.

Marginal cost pricing is consistent with competition on the merits; prices lower than marginal cost are not. In an influential law review article published in 1975 Professors Areeda and Turner argued that a price lower than reasonably anticipated short-run marginal cost is predatory, while a price higher than reasonably anticipated short-run marginal cost is nonpredatory.[2] Few courts or commentators take issue with the first conclusion, but several have criticized the second.

Areeda and Turner argued, however, that use of short-run marginal cost as a benchmark for predation is impractical because marginal cost is extraordinarily difficult to compute. The primary value of marginal cost to economists is conceptual. The question it asks— given any level of production, what will be the additional costs incurred in producing one more unit of output—is virtually unanswerable when one studies a firm's history over perhaps two years and inquires as to its marginal costs during that period. Economists laboring under the best of academic conditions find marginal cost difficult to compute. It almost certainly cannot be computed in litigation when the relevant question is whether over some past, extended period of time a seller's prices were lower than its marginal costs, unless the disparity between the two is very large.

Therefore Areeda and Turner proposed a surrogate: average variable cost (AVC).[3] A firm's total production costs can be divided into two kinds, fixed and variable. A fixed cost is one that does not change with variations in output over a given time period; a variable cost is one that does. For example, over a one-year period the capital cost of the plant itself is a fixed cost: it will have to be paid whether or not the firm produces, and the amount of the payment will not change as output varies. However, most labor costs, the costs of basic raw material or ingredients, and utility costs are generally variable. A bakery that increases its bread production by 100 loaves per day for three weeks likely will not enlarge its plant. However it will spend more money on flour, salt, electricity and labor.

Although marginal cost is virtually impossible to compute in litigation, AVC is not—at least theoretically. One must identify

2. Areeda & Turner, Predatory Pricing and Related Practices Under Section 2 of the Sherman Act, 88 Harv.L.Rev. 697 (1975). The current formulation of the Areeda-Turner test is contained in 3 P. Areeda & D. Turner, Antitrust Law ¶¶ 710–22 (1978). All references here are to the latter. "Short-run" marginal cost is the appropriate standard because the evaluation of a firm's pricing behavior must be based on its existing plant and durable equipment, not on the most efficient possible plant and equipment. Long-run marginal cost, just as long-run average cost, measures a firm's costs when it is in a position to choose plant

size as well as rate of output. See § 1.4 above.

3. Id. at ¶ 715d. AVC is discussed more fully in § 1.1 above.

One place where neither the marginal cost nor the AVC rule for predatory pricing will work is in markets for intellectual property—licensing of films, performance rights, computer software, etc. In many such cases short-run marginal cost or AVC is very close to zero. A rule that permitted the licensor of, say, performance rights to cut price to AVC would be a virtual nonliability rule.

which costs are variable, add them up, and divide by the number of units produced. The Areeda-Turner test holds that a price above AVC is presumed to be lawful. A price below AVC, if other prerequisites are met, is conclusively presumed to be illegal.[4]

Distinguishing fixed from variable costs can itself be difficult. The categories change from one industry to another and they vary depending on the time period being considered. Further, accountants are not in complete agreement about how certain costs, such as advertising, whose effects can last a long time, ought to be calculated. Distinguishing fixed from variable costs in litigation can add serious complexities to a fact finder's already difficult task. Areeda and Turner therefore proposed a "more categorical" laundry list of costs that should always be considered fixed. These include interest on debt, all taxes that do not vary with output, such as property taxes, and depreciation on the plant. Under the Areeda-Turner test all other costs are considered as part of marginal costs, or as part of AVC when it is used as a surrogate.[5]

 WESTLAW REFERENCES
arreda /p anti-competiti** predatory /4 conduct pric***

§ 6.9　Predatory Pricing: Criticism of the Areeda-Turner Test

Courts were initially enthusiastic about the Areeda-Turner test, and many circuits adopted it with little qualification.[1] Academics were more critical, and a lively scholarly debate developed about the proper legal standards for predatory pricing.[2] Eventually this debate influenced courts as well, and many circuits that initially embraced the Areeda-Turner test had second thoughts.

The Areeda-Turner test has been subjected to two criticisms: 1) Even assuming marginal cost is the proper benchmark for predation, AVC is often a poor surrogate; 2) short-run marginal cost is not an appropriate benchmark for identifying predation: although few prices below short-run marginal cost are nonpredatory, a price higher than short-run marginal cost can also be "predatory."

4. Id. at ¶ 711d. A price above average total cost (the sum of fixed and variable costs divided by the number of units of output) is *per se* legal under the Areeda-Turner test.

5. Id. at ¶ 715c.

§ 6.9

1. For example, Janich Bros., Inc. v. Amer. Distilling Co., 570 F.2d 848, 858 (9th Cir. 1977), cert. denied, 439 U.S. 829, 99 S.Ct. 103 (1979); Pacific Eng'r. & Prod. Co. v. Kerr-McGee Corp., 551 F.2d 790, 797 (10th Cir. 1977), cert. denied,

434 U.S. 879, 98 S.Ct. 234 (1977), rehearing denied, 434 U.S. 977, 98 S.Ct. 543 (1977); Inter. Air Indus., Inc. v. American Excelsior Co., 517 F.2d 714, 724 (5th Cir. 1975), cert. denied, 424 U.S. 943, 96 S.Ct. 1411 (1976).

2. The debate is summarized in Hurwitz & Kovacic, Judicial Analysis of Predation: the Emerging Trends, 35 Vand. L.Rev. 63 (1982); Brodley & Hay, Predatory Pricing: Competing Economic Theories and the Evolution of Legal Standards, 66 Cornell L.Rev. 738 (1981).

Figure One illustrates some of the problems of the AVC test. The figure shows the cost functions of a plant of roughly optimal size. Its competitive rate of output is Q_c, which is at the intersection of the demand curve and the firm's marginal cost curve.[3] At this rate of output and with a market price of P_c the firm is earning enough to cover its average total costs (AC), and more than AVC.

At the competitive rate of output marginal costs are higher than AVC. More importantly, the two are diverging: if the firm increases its output marginal costs and AVC will be even further apart. Under the Areeda-Turner rule, however, the firm legally would be able to increase its output all the way to Q_p and drop its price to P_p. At levels of output higher than optimum capacity (where predation often occurs) marginal cost and AVC tend to diverge, with marginal cost higher than AVC. The result is that the Areeda-Turner test can give the predator considerable room for maneuvering. In fact, under the Areeda-Turner rule a firm could compute its AVC and legally sell at a price one cent higher, all the while imposing significant losses on its victim. Areeda and Turner have attempted to correct this problem by requiring that a predator "relying on a defense that price was not less than average variable cost should be required to offer proof that his marginal cost * * * did not significantly exceed average variable cost."[4] This solution, however, may discard the baby with the bath water: it once again requires one of the parties (this time the defendant) to produce information about its marginal costs during the relevant time period.

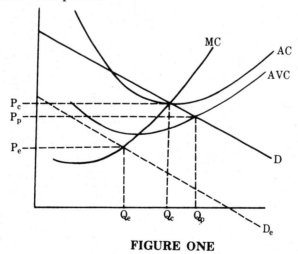

FIGURE ONE

Precisely the opposite happens in a sick industry, plagued with excess capacity. As § 6.10 below shows, an industry with substantial excess capacity is not a plausible candidate for predatory pricing

3. The demand curve slopes downward because, although the firm may not have market power, it will make more sales if it lowers its price.

4. 3 P. Areeda & D. Turner, Antitrust Law ¶ 715d (1978).

because the predator cannot reasonably look forward to a period of monopoly pricing. Shifted demand curve D_e in Figure One shows the consequences of excess capacity. Price will drop to P_e and output to Q_e, less than the optimal rate of output for the plant. Marginal cost and AVC also diverge, but this time AVC is higher. Under the Areeda-Turner test a firm pricing its output at marginal cost could nevertheless be guilty of predatory pricing.[5]

In short, the Areeda-Turner test makes predatory pricing easy to "prove" in markets where it is almost certain not to occur, but very difficult to prove in markets that are conducive to predation.

The second criticism of the Areeda-Turner test is both more complex and more substantial, because it goes to the fundamental premise of the test: that short-run marginal cost is the proper benchmark for predation. Virtually everyone agrees that a price below short-run marginal cost is likely to be predatory. Several of Areeda's and Turner's critics have argued, however, that often a price higher than short-run marginal cost can be predatory as well— that is, it can be calculated to exclude an equally efficient rival or to permit the predator to engage in prolonged periods of monopolistic pricing.[6]

The models for such behavior are complex, and only a few generalizations are offered here. Critics have argued that the Areeda-Turner test ignores the possibility of "strategic entry deterrence." Sometimes dominant firms intentionally can create excess capacity and use it to deter potential entrants, without ever lowering their price below marginal cost or even average total cost.

Suppose, for example, that an industry operating at optimal efficiency can produce widgets at $1.00 each. Demand at that price is 1000 per year. The minimum optimal scale (MOS) for a widget plant is 250 widgets per year, but a plant will not suffer from diseconomies of large size until it reaches an output level in excess of 1000 widgets per year. That is, the most efficient plant sizes occur in an output range of 250 to 1000+ widgets per year. Such a market has room for three or four MOS firms. However, an efficient firm

---

5. In the short-run a firm would ordinarily cease production if the price dropped to a level below its average variable costs—that is, it could then minimize losses by producing nothing at all. However, the firm must consider the cost of ceasing production and restarting it. If it intends to stay in business and wants to retain certain customers or contracts, short periods of producing at a price lower than AVC may be more profitable than ceasing production. In any case, prolonged periods of pricing below AVC are not likely to occur in an industry with excess capacity. See Joskow & Klevorick, A Framework for Analyzing Predatory Pricing Policy, 89 Yale L.J. 213, 251 n. 77 (1979).

6. See Scherer, Predatory Pricing and the Sherman Act: A Comment, 89 Harv.L.Rev. 869 (1976); Williamson, Predatory Pricing: A Strategic and Welfare Analysis, 87 Yale L.J. 284 (1977); W. Sharkey, The Theory of Natural Monopoly 159–164 (1982).

could be constructed that could satisfy the entire market. Several industries probably have structural characteristics similar to this.[7]

A single dominant firm that built a plant capable of producing 1000 widgets per year could effectively deter future competitors. Having built a 1000-widget plant, the dominant firm could actually produce widgets at a rate of perhaps 700 per year and sell them at a monopoly price of $1.50. Any time a prospective entrant appeared, however, the dominant firm could increase its output to 900 widgets per year and drop its price to slightly more than $1.00. The new entrant would have to be satisfied with the "residual" demand—that is, the demand for widgets at a profitable price which is not being filled by the incumbent. If this demand is not sufficient to enable the new entrant to achieve MOS, the new entrant will face higher costs than the incumbent and will not be able profitably to satisfy the residual market (which is composed mostly of marginal buyers unwilling to pay the slightly supracompetitive price charged by the incumbent, but presumably willing to pay $1.00). The aspiring new entrant, assessing the prospect of a prolonged period of losses, will invest its money elsewhere. The incumbent will once again reduce output and resume pricing at the monopoly level. At no time will it have lowered its price below its own marginal cost or its average total cost.[8]

In this way the excess capacity of the dominant firm can always stand ready as a weapon in its hands: prospective entrants know that the incumbent can easily increase output and reduce price in response to any attempt at entry or output expansion.

Scholars have suggested a number of legal approaches to the problem of strategic entry deterrence, or so-called "limit pricing." For example, Oliver Williamson proposed a rule that would make it illegal for a dominant firm to increase its output in response to entry by a competitor.[9] William Baumol suggested that if a competing firm is driven from business by a dominant firm's price reduction, the dominant firm should be prohibited from increasing its price for several years thereafter.[10] Finally, Paul Joskow and Alvin Klevorick proposed a more complex test that includes elements of the Areeda-Turner AVC test: 1) a price below AVC is predatory; 2) a price between AVC and average total cost is presumed predatory, but the defendant can rebut by showing that it has excess capacity that was not caused by its own exclusionary policy; 3) a price increase following a price reduction within two years is presumptive evidence of

7. See F.M. Scherer, Industrial Market Structure and Economic Performance 91–118 (2d ed. 1980).

8. The illustration is a simplification of the strategy developed in Williamson, note 6 above, at 292–301.

9. Id. at 331–337.

10. Baumol, Quasi-Permanence of Price Reductions: A Policy for Prevention of Predatory Pricing, 89 Yale L.J. 1, 5 (1979).

predation, even if the lower price was above average total cost.[11] So far no court has adopted any of these proposed alternative tests. Although courts have occasionally noted in dicta that strategic entry deterrence or "limit pricing" could violate § 2 of the Sherman Act,[12] no court has found a violation under such circumstances.

 WESTLAW REFERENCES

anti-competiti** predatory /4   conduct pric*** /p "average variable"
     marginal +4 cost
anti-competiti** predatory /4   conduct pric*** /p (capacity /2
     excess***) (deter deterr! /2   entrance entry) "limit pricing"

§ 6.10   Structural Issues: When Is Predatory Pricing Plausible?

The above discussion dealt only with how to identify a *price* as predatory. Even if it were legal, predatory pricing is risky and expensive and is plausible only in markets conducive to monopolization. Often a court can evaluate the market much more easily than it can determine whether a defendant's particular price level was predatory. In general, before a claim of predatory pricing is plausible, two things must be true: 1) the market must be susceptible of monopolization; 2) the defendant must be a dominant firm within that market. Virtually all the proposed predatory pricing tests discussed in the preceding section apply only to dominant firms. For example, Areeda and Turner apply their influential test "to a monopolist's general (non-discriminatory) pricing in the market in which he has monopoly power." [1]

Suppose that a market contains five firms of the following size: A has 30% of the market, B, C & D each have 20%, and E has 10% of the market. B attempts predatory pricing and drops its price from a competitive level of $1.00 to a predatory level of 80¢.

If the market has an average elasticity of demand of 1, the 20% price reduction will cause a 20% general increase in market demand.

---

11. Joskow & Klevorick, note 5 above at 255.

12. For example, see Cal. Computer Products v. IBM Corp., 613 F.2d 727, 743 (9th Cir. 1979): "* * * limit pricing by a monopolist might, on a record which presented the issue, be held an impermissible predatory practice. * * * And we do not foreclose the possibility that a monopolist who reduces prices to some point above marginal or average variable costs might still be held to have engaged in a predatory act because of other aspects of its conduct." Likewise in Transamerica Computer Corp. v. IBM, 698 F.2d 1377, 1388 (9th Cir. 1983), cert. denied, ___ U.S. ___, 104 S.Ct. 370 (1983), the Ninth Circuit held that a price above average total cost created a presumption of legality that could be defeated by clear and convincing evidence of predatory design. The First and Sixth Circuits expressly disagree and hold prices above average total cost to be legal. Barry Wright Corp. v. ITT Grinnell Corp., 724 F.2d 227, 231–34 (1st Cir. 1983); Arthur S. Langenderfer, Inc. v. S.E. Johnson Co., 729 F.2d 1050 (6th Cir. 1984). The economics of limit pricing is discussed in See & Gunther, Limit Pricing and Predation in the Antitrust Laws: Economic and Legal Aspects, 35 Ala.L.Rev. 211 (1984).

§ 6.10

1. 3 P. Areeda & D. Turner, Antitrust Law ¶ 711d (1978).

The predator will have to pick up all these sales. Assuming that the total market demand before predation was 1000 units per year, and that B's output had been 200 units, B will now have to increase its output to 400 units just to take care of new customers who have entered the market: B has doubled its output without stealing a single customer from a competitor!

If B triples its output to 600 units, it will presumably steal 200 sales from competitors. These will not come from any single firm, however, but from each of the other firms in proportion to their market share. In this case each firm will lose about 25% of its business. Now the predator has increased its output threefold—accruing 20¢ in losses on each sale—and has caused a mere 25% loss of sales to its competitors.

Suppose that one firm is so weak that B actually manages to drive it from the market. If firm C leaves the market, its market share will be divided among each of the four surviving firms in proportion to their market shares, with perhaps a somewhat larger percentage going to the predator because of its large current output. At most, however, firm B can expect to end up with a market share on the order of 30%—hardly enough to engage in prolonged monopoly pricing.

Worse yet, what will become of victim C's plant? More often than not, when a firm goes out of business its plant passes into the hands of a successor.[2] Further, the successor will probably buy the bankrupt firm's plant at a bargain price and as a result will have lower fixed costs than its predecessor. Firm B's predation could well end up giving B a stronger rival than it had before.

If a predator has a 90% market share and its only rival 10%, however, the picture is considerably different. In that case a 10% price reduction in a market with demand elasticity of 1 would require a 10% output increase to take care of new customers. A 20% output increase would virtually wipe out the smaller rival. Once the rival was eliminated no one would be left to restrain the predator's ability to raise prices. In short, a market with two competitors, one of which is very large, is far more conducive to predatory pricing than a market with several relatively small competitors. Predatory pricing is simply implausible in the competitive market. In such situations a court would do well to dismiss a predatory pricing complaint without analyzing the relationship between the defendant's prices and its costs.[3] One way courts could achieve this is by characterizing predatory pricing as monopolization, requiring a showing of a large market share, rather than as an attempt to monopolize.

2. Unless the market contains a large amount of excess capacity.

3. For further elaboration, see Hovenkamp & Silver-Westrick, Predatory Pricing and the Ninth Circuit, 1983 Arizona St.L.J. 443, 460–64.

When a court evaluates a predatory pricing claim it should consider two additional structural features of the relevant market: barriers to entry and excess capacity.

Barriers to Entry

The rationale for predatory pricing is the sustaining of losses today that will give a firm monopoly profits in the future. The monopoly profits will never materialize, however, if the market is flooded with new entrants as soon as the successful predator attempts to raise its price. Predatory pricing will be profitable only if the market contains significant barriers to new entry.

To say that rational predatory pricing requires a market containing barriers to entry is one thing. To define relevant entry barriers is quite another, however. Over the years economists and antitrust scholars have identified a host of "barriers to entry"—including government regulation, economies of scale or other forms of efficiency, high capital costs, "human" capital requirements, the need for scarce natural resources, and advertising.[4] The ambiguity of this list is troublesome: not everything that has been called a "barrier to entry" is socially bad, and some, such as economies of scale, are good. Society is generally better off when firms operate at their most efficient size, even though such operation will deter any potential entrant that cannot achieve MOS. Today, for example, it is likely not illegal monopolization for a firm with market power to build a plant of optimal size, although the effect will be to deter entry by smaller firms.[5]

In short, "barriers to entry" is a slippery concept: things that might be evil barriers for one purpose are good for another. It would be bad antitrust policy to forbid firms from erecting "barriers to entry" when efficiency itself is such a barrier. A consumer-oriented theory of entry barriers ought to distinguish purported barriers that are a product of efficiency from those that are not.[6]

Nevertheless, as the preceding section suggests, economies of scale plus the strategic development of excess capacity can effectively deter entry and permit supracompetitive pricing. For purposes of analyzing predatory pricing the following definition of barriers to entry is helpful: a barrier to entry is something that makes "entry unprofitable while permitting established firms to set prices above marginal cost, and to persistently earn monopoly returns."[7] Under

4. See generally J. Bain, Barriers to New Competition (1956); F.M. Scherer, Industrial Market Structure and Economic Performance 275–280 (2d ed. 1980).

5. E.I. duPont de Nemours & Co., 96 F.T.C. 650 (1980).

6. See R. Bork, The Antitrust Paradox: A Policy at War With Itself 310–

329 (1978); Wentz, Mobility Factors in Antitrust Cases: Assessing Market Power in Light of Conditions Affecting Entry and Fringe Expansion, 80 Mich. L. Rev. 1545 (1982).

7. J.M. Ferguson, Advertising and Competition: Theory, Measurement, Fact 10 (1974).

this definition economies of scale *can* be a barrier to entry. In predatory pricing cases, the purpose of the analysis is not to determine generally whether economies of scale are a good thing (presumably they are) but to discern whether they can be abused. Clearly they can be.

For this reason much analysis attacking the traditional concept of barriers to entry misses the point. The relevant question for evaluating strategic price and output behavior is not whether a purported "barrier to entry" is inefficient in the abstract, but whether it is being used for an inefficient purpose. Efficiency-creating entry barriers—particularly those that are a function of scale economies—can be used to enable a dominant firm to reap monopoly profits.

If a market contains sufficient barriers to new entry to make predatory pricing plausible, it should therefore not be a defense that the barriers are a function of the superior efficiency of the incumbent, particularly if the barriers are a function of scale economies. However, the existence of *some* kind of entry barriers ought to be a prerequisite for any predatory pricing claim. Predatory pricing will not be successful in markets in which potential entrants can respond quickly and easily to any attempted price increase.

Excess Capacity

Excess capacity is the capacity of the firms in a market to produce more than the market demands at a competitive price. Excess capacity is generally inefficient unless the market is volatile and subject to indefinite but dramatic spurts in demand.

Excess capacity can exist for a number of reasons, and can be distributed in a corresponding number of ways. Excess capacity sometimes exists because the industry itself is in decline. The invention of the electronic calculator, for example, created excess capacity in the market for slide rules. In such cases excess capacity is ordinarily distributed among the firms in the market in rough proportion to their market shares.

Excess capacity can also exist because a new entrant has appeared, and its additional plant creates more productive capacity than the market is able to absorb in a short period of time. In this case the new entrant is likely to have more excess capacity than the incumbents, whose markets are already established.

Finally, as the preceding section indicates, excess capacity can be part of the entry deterrence strategy of a dominant firm. The dominant firm can hold its excess capacity, plus the threat of future output increases, over the heads of smaller firms thinking about enlarging output or entering the market. In this case the dominant firm is likely to have more excess capacity than its competitors.

Excess capacity can distort analysis of predatory pricing in several ways. First, it can affect the definition of which costs are fixed and which are variable. As the discussion above noted, a variable cost is a cost that varies with changes in output as measured over some given period. A fixed cost is one that does not respond to changes in output. Because of measurement difficulties, the Areeda-Turner test for predatory pricing uses a pre-established "laundry list" of fixed and variable costs.[8] Some courts have rejected this approach, however, as too arbitrary. They hold that the pricing period alleged to be predatory ought to be used to determine variable costs. For example, the Ninth Circuit's definition of variable costs in predatory pricing cases is "those expenses that increased as a result of the output expansion attributable to the price reduction" alleged to be predatory.[9]

If a firm is already operating at full capacity, any enlargement of output may require additional capacity, which would then have to be considered a variable cost. However, a firm that operates at far less than full capacity may be able to increase output substantially at relatively low cost. For example, in the *Inglis* case the district court determined that the defendant's excess capacity was so large that the ovens could accommodate more bread at no additional cost, that delivery trucks were running half empty, and that wages were being paid to people who were working only part of the time. The court concluded that the only variable costs that the firm would incur in increasing its output of bread were "ingredients, wrappers, fuel and commission."[10]

The effect of excess capacity in the hands of the defendant can therefore reduce the number of costs considered variable and increase the proportionate amount of costs considered fixed. The result is to make it more difficult for the plaintiff to prove predatory pricing under the Areeda-Turner test.

Whether such a result is good depends on the reasons for the excess capacity in the market. If the excess capacity is the result of a sick industry, the effect is good. Competition in a declining industry drives prices below average total costs, because the capacity far exceeds the demand in the market, but the capacity must be paid for. Eventually the firms in the market will either retire some of their plants as they wear out, or else exit the market. Sales at below average total cost in such a sick industry do not represent predatory pricing, but rather the market's natural correcting processes.

However, if the excess capacity is a result of the dominant firm's strategic entry deterrence scheme, the lowered estimate of AVC plays precisely into the firm's hands. In such a situation the excess

8. See § 6.8 above.

9. William Inglis & Sons Baking Co. v. ITT Continental Baking Co., Inc., 668 F.2d 1014, 1037 (9th Cir. 1981), cert. denied, 459 U.S. 825, 103 S.Ct. 57–8 (1982).

10. Id. 461 F.Supp. 410, 418 (N.D. Cal. 1978), judgment affirmed in part, reversed in part, 668 F.2d 1014 (9th Cir. 1981), cert. denied, 459 U.S. 825, 103 S.Ct. 57 (1982).

capacity was designed by the defendant to enable it to deter prospective entry without reducing its price below AVC. Any rule that defines variable costs as those costs a defendant incurs as part of an allegedly predatory output expansion gives the firm even more room for strategic maneuvering. If the defendant's excess capacity was strategically planned the court would be better off to use Areeda's and Turner's laundry list of fixed and variable costs.

Finally, excess capacity held by a firm's competitors can frustrate any predatory pricing scheme. The success of predatory pricing depends on the predator's ability eventually to reduce output and charge a monopoly price. If competitors have excess capacity, however, they will be able to respond quickly to the predator's output reduction with an offsetting output increase, and the predator's monopoly profits will never be realized. The best way to account for this fact is to include the excess capacity of competing firms in the relevant market.[11] The result will be to give the defendant a lower market share. If it is too low—perhaps less than 40%[12]—the claim should be dismissed without inquiry into the defendant's prices.

 WESTLAW REFERENCES

anti-competiti** predatory /4 conduct pric*** /p dominant leading
    preeminent monopoly /2 company corporation firm

(a) Barriers to Entry

anti-competiti** predatory /4 conduct pric*** /p bar barrier deter
    deterr! /3 entrance entry

(b) Excess Capacity

anti-competiti** predatory /4 conduct pric*** /p capacity /3
    excess*** extra redundant surplus

§ 6.11 The Areeda-Turner Test in the Courts

Courts initially embraced the Areeda-Turner test with enthusiasm.[1] Eventually, however, the excitement waned and courts began to create various exceptions and qualifications to the test. No court has completely rejected every aspect of the test, however, and the basic Areeda-Turner AVC paradigm continues to influence every circuit that has considered a predatory pricing case since 1975.

The original promise of the Areeda-Turner average variable cost test lay in its simplicity. AVC seemed much easier to calculate than marginal cost, and the test itself greatly simplified judicial analysis of

---

11. As a general rule measurement of market share includes the total capacity of competing firms. See § 3.4 above.

12. In Zoslaw v. MCA Distrib. Corp., 693 F.2d 870, 888 (9th Cir. 1982), cert. denied, 460 U.S. 1085, 103 S.Ct. 1777 (1983), on remand ___ F.Supp. ___ (N.D.Cal1984), the court dismissed a predatory pricing claim without inquiring into price, because the record demonstrated that the defendant's market share was only 10%. For a fuller discussion of the problem of excess capacity in predatory pricing cases, see Hovenkamp & Silver-Westrick, note 3 above at 459–60.

§ 6.11

1. See § 6.9 above.

the structural features of the markets in which predatory pricing occurred. Much of the subsequent disaffection with the test has resulted from two phenomena: 1) the AVC test is more difficult to apply than its proponents suggested; and 2) sometimes the test fails to consider all relevant variables.

The Areeda-Turner test *sounds* simple: a price lower than AVC is illegal, and the court can refer to a "laundry list" describing which costs should be considered fixed and which variable. An accountant should be able under this formulation to give rather easy testimony about the relationship between a defendant's prices and its costs.

As some courts discovered, however, computing variable costs was not always as easy as first appeared.[2] Second, the presumption that the average variable cost surrogate should be used only when AVC is relatively close to marginal cost was unworkable. Third, the proposed "laundry list" of fixed and variable costs did not account for the wide variety of industries in which predatory pricing might occur—concrete and college textbooks, bakery bread, industrial chemicals, price-competitive and price-regulated industries. Fourth, the test seemed unable to take strategic long-term behavior into account—particularly because it disavowed any attempt to measure the defendant's subjective intent. Finally, the test was an absolute paradise for defendants, and virtually none lost a case.[3]

No attempt is made here to describe the various directions that each circuit has taken in interpreting the Areeda-Turner test. In general, however, the courts have been uncomfortable with Areeda's and Turner's refusal to consider the defendant's intent. They have responded by "softening" the rule. The Ninth Circuit, for example, now holds that a price below AVC creates a rebuttable presumption of predation.[4] A price above AVC but below average total cost creates a rebuttable presumption of nonpredation.[5] A price above average total cost is not conclusively legal, as it would be under the Areeda-Turner formulation, but creates a presumption of legality that can be defeated only by clear and convincing evidence.[6] The

2. For some of the difficulties, see Weber v. Wynne, 431 F.Supp. 1048, 1059 (D.N.J.1977); William Inglis & Sons Baking Co. v. ITT Continental Baking Co., 461 F.Supp. 410, 418 (N.D.Cal.1978), judgment affirmed in part, reversed in part, 668 F.2d 1014 (9th Cir. 1981), cert. denied, 459 U.S. 825, 103 S.Ct. 57–8 (1982).

3. This, of course, is consistent with Areeda's and Turner's premise that bona fide predatory pricing occurs only rarely. See Brodley & Hay, Predatory Pricing: Competing Economic Theories and the Evolution of Legal Standards, 66 Cornell L.Rev. 738, 768–89 (1981). In 1982 a plaintiff finally won a case with a jury finding of pricing lower than AVC. D & S Redi-Mix v. Sierra Redi-Mix and Contracting Co., 692 F.2d 1245, 1248 (9th Cir. 1982).

4. William Inglis & Sons Baking Co. v. ITT Continental Baking Co., Inc., 668 F.2d 1014, 1036 (9th Cir. 1981), cert. denied, 459 U.S. 825, 103 S.Ct. 57–8 (1982).

5. Id. at 1035–36.

6. Transamerica Computer Co. v. IBM Corp., 698 F.2d 1377, 1388 (9th Cir. 1983), cert. denied, ___ U.S. ___, 104 S.Ct. 370 (1983). The First and Sixth Circuits agree with Areeda and Turner that a price above average total cost

court will consider evidence of predatory intent and market structure
in determining whether any one of these presumptions can be defeated. Other circuits have also expressed their willingness to soften the
hard presumptions of the Areeda-Turner test.[7]

Courts have generally done a remarkable job of analyzing price
evidence in predatory pricing cases. They have not done as well with
issues of market structure. This is both ironic and unfortunate,
because often analysis of structural issues would take the court to a
much easier and more certain decision than analysis of the complexities of the AVC test. For example, in the *Inglis* case the court paid
scant attention to the fact that the bakery market contained several
competitors, and the defendant was only the second largest. Second,
the industry had a large amount of excess capacity. Computation of
the defendant's market share including the excess capacity of competitors indicates that the defendant had approximately 8% of the
market. Third, barriers to entry were quite low, and at least one new
firm entered the market even as the alleged predation was occurring.[8] The defendant could not reasonably have expected a future
period of monopolistic pricing in such a market. The court would
have done better to dismiss the complaint without considering the
price evidence.

 WESTLAW REFERENCES

anti-competiti** predatory /4 conduct pric*** /p areeda /p inten!
(market +1 structure)

§ 6.12   Predatory Pricing and the Robinson-Patman Act

Predatory pricing can also violate § 2 of the Clayton Act, which
was amended in 1936 by the Robinson-Patman Act. The Act forbids
sales of the same product at two different prices under certain
conditions. Robinson-Patman lawsuits brought by competitors alleg-

should be legal. Barry Wright Corp. v.
ITT Grinnell Corp., 724 F.2d 227, 231–34
(1st Cir. 1983); Arthur S. Langenderfer,
Inc. v. S.E. Johnson Co., 729 F.2d 1050
(6th Cir. 1984).

7. For example, D.E. Rogers Assoc.,
Inc. v. Gardner-Denver Co., 718 F.2d
1431, 1437 (6th Cir. 1983), cert. denied
___ U.S. ___, 104 S.Ct. 3513 (1984); Ad-
justers Replace-A-Car, Inc. v. Agency
Rent-A-Car, Inc., 735 F.2d 884, 890–91
(5th Cir. 1984).

8. Even the plaintiff's plant was sold
to a competitor who remained in business after the plaintiff went bankrupt.
For an analysis of the market in the
Inglis case, see, Hovenkamp & Silver-

Westrick, Predatory Pricing and the
Ninth Circuit, 1983 Arizona State L.J.
443, 464–67. The Federal Trade Commission has generally done a much better job than the courts of analyzing market structure *first* to determine whether
predatory pricing was plausible in the
market at issue, before getting to much
more difficult and ambiguous price data.
See In re ITT, ___ FTC ___ (1984), which
involved predatory pricing in the same
wholesale bakery market at issue in the
Inglis case. The FTC dismissed the
complaint, largely on the basis of ITT
Continental's lack of a dominant position
in the market. See also In re General
Foods Corp., ___ FTC ___ (1984).

ing price predation are known as "primary-line" Robinson-Patman cases.[1]

The framers of the Clayton Act adhered to the "recoupment" theory of predatory pricing. They realized that extended periods of loss selling made predation costly. They concluded that a predator "must of necessity recoup its losses in the particular communities or sections where [its] commodities are sold below cost or without a fair profit by raising the price of this same class of commodities above their fair market value in other sections or communities   *   *   *."[2]

In the framers' view of the world most predators were large firms that operated in several different geographic markets. Their victims were small firms that operated in only one. Under the recoupment theory a predator could "subsidize" its below-cost sales in one market by raising its price in a different market. Predation would thereby be cost-free.

The most obvious criticism of the recoupment theory is that a reasonable profit-maximizing firm would *already* be charging its profit-maximizing price in each market in which it operated. In that case a price increase in any market would produce less, not more revenue.[3]

The Robinson-Patman Act, however, may prevent a large firm from charging its profit-maximizing price in each market individually. The Act makes it illegal to sell products of like grade or quality at different prices. Assume, for example, that A sells in markets #1, #2, and #3. It has monopoly power in #1 and #2, but is in competition in #3. The profit-maximizing monopoly price in #1 and #2 considered separately would be $1.00. The market price in market #3, however, is 90¢.

The Robinson-Patman Act may require A to make a hard choice. It can sell in all three markets at 90¢, in which case it will make sales in all three markets but lose its monopoly profits in markets #1 and #2. Otherwise it can sell in all three markets at $1.00, retaining the monopoly profits in #1 and #2, but losing most or perhaps all its sales in market #3. The first choice certainly may be more profitable, particularly if market #3 is large. In that case the Robinson-Patman Act has increased competition. A may find it more profita-

---

§ 6.12

1. 15 U.S.C.A. § 13(a): "It shall be unlawful for any person   *   *   *   to discriminate in price between different purchasers of commodities of like grade and quality   *   *   *   where the effect of such discrimination may be substantially to lessen competition or tend to create a monopoly   *   *   *." For further discussion of price discrimination and the Robinson-Patman Act, see chapter thirteen below.

2. Senate Report No. 698, 63d Cong., 2d Sess. 3 (1914). The "recoupment" theory of predatory pricing is at least a generation older than the Clayton Act. See Stimson, Trusts, 1 Harv.L.Rev. 132, 134 (1887).

3. For a critique of the recoupment theory see R. Bork, The Antitrust Paradox: A Policy at War With Itself 383–91 (1978).

ble, however, to keep its monopoly returns in #1 and #2, and give up market #3. In that case the Robinson-Patman Act will actually diminish competition.

Assume A decides to drop its price in market #3 to 80¢ and drive its rivals there out of business, so that it can have a monopoly in all three markets. Again it has two choices. First it can drop the price in market #3 to 80¢ and raise the price in markets #1 and #2 to their profit-maximizing level, $1.00. Then A would be violating the Robinson-Patman Act. Alternatively, A could drop its price in all three markets to 80¢. In that case A would not be violating the Robinson-Patman Act.

In short, the Robinson-Patman Act can make predatory pricing much more expensive for a seller who operates in many markets but wants to predate only in one. It must lower its price in all markets simultaneously. Further, predatory pricing is difficult to identify: it requires a sophisticated knowledge of cost figures that are generally in the exclusive control of the predator and may not become available until after an action has been filed. Price differences, however, are easily detectable: if A sells its output at 80¢ in market #3 and at $1.00 in markets #1 and #2, competitors will know almost immediately.[4]

Unfortunately, analysis of the effect of the Robinson-Patman Act is not quite this simple. Although the Act may make predatory pricing either more expensive or harder to conceal, it also makes competitive pricing more expensive, for precisely the same reason.

Assume A has had a monopoly in markets #1, #2, and #3 for some time and has charged a monopoly price of $1.00 in each market. Now B enters market #3 and begins price-cutting to a competitive price of 90¢. The Robinson-Patman Act may put A to the difficult choice of dropping its price to 90¢ in *all three markets* in order to compete with B in market #3, or else simply closing its outlets in #3, effectively conceding a monopoly to B. The latter option may be more attractive, particularly if market #3 is relatively small.

A statute preventing differential pricing is just as likely to prohibit competitive pricing as predatory pricing. Which of the two it does more often depends on which occurs more often. At the time the Robinson-Patman Act was passed many people thought that predatory pricing was inexpensive, easy to accomplish and relatively common. Today we are much more inclined to think it is rare. If that is true, then the Robinson-Patman Act may condemn competition on the merits much more often than it reaches price predation.

For example, in Utah Pie Co. v. Continental Baking Co.,[5] the defendants were three, independently-acting sellers of frozen pies,

4. See Hovenkamp, Judicial Reconstruction of the Robinson-Patman Act: Predatory Differential Pricing, 17 U.C. Davis L.Rev. 309 (1983).

5. 386 U.S. 685, 87 S.Ct. 1326 (1967).

each of whom had less than 20% of the relevant market.[6] The plaintiff's market share was about 50%. The evidence showed a period of intense competition in which prices went down, although the plaintiff continued to show a profit throughout the complaint period.[7] The defendants actively competed for customers, not only with the plaintiff, but also with each other.[8] The defendants' violation was to sell pies in the Salt Lake City market at a lower price than they were selling them in other cities. The Court never explained what would have happened if the three defendants had driven the plaintiff out of business: they still would have been in competition with each other. Further, the court did not discuss the relationship between the defendants' prices and their costs, except to observe that some prices were "below cost." [9] In *Utah Pie* the Supreme Court almost certainly used the Robinson-Patman Act to condemn hard competition rather than predation. The result was to protect the plaintiff's monopoly position and force consumers to pay a higher price.[10]

One way to avoid the anticompetitive trap of *Utah Pie* is to interpret the Robinson-Patman Act to condemn differential pricing when it is predatory but tolerate or even encourage it when it is competitive. But how does a court tell the difference? By determining if the sales in the low-price market were made below cost and with the reasonable expectation that they would dispatch or discipline competitors in that market so that the predator could charge monopoly profits in the future.

This is precisely the determination that courts make in cases alleging predatory pricing under § 2 of the Sherman Act. The presence or absence of sales at a different price in a different geographic market is *absolutely irrelevant* to determining whether a seller is engaging in predatory pricing in a particular market. Although a law against differential pricing makes both predation and competition in a single market more expensive for a firm that sells in other markets as well, the presence of differential pricing does not help determine whether a low price sale in a particular market is predatory or competitive. In order to know that we need to determine the relationship between the seller's prices and costs in the market in which predation is alleged, just as we would in a Sherman Act predatory pricing case.

6. The relevant market was frozen dessert pies in Salt Lake City, Utah.

7. At the beginning of the complaint period the market share of plaintiff Utah Pie was 66.5%. The market shares of the defendants were: Carnation, 10.3%; Continental, 1.3%; Pet, 16.4%. By the end of the complaint period the plaintiff's share had dropped to 45.3%, but it was still making a profit. Pet's share had risen to 29.4%. 386 U.S. at 692, n. 7, 87 S.Ct. at 1330.

8. Id. at 695, 87 S.Ct. at 1332.

9. Id. at 703 n. 14, 87 S.Ct. at 1336.

10. See Bowman, Restraint of Trade by the Supreme Court: the *Utah Pie* Case, 77 Yale L.J. 70 (1967); Elzinga & Hogarty, *Utah Pie* and the Consequences of Robinson-Patman, 21 J.L. & Econ. 427 (1978).

Operating from this premise, several federal courts have now imported the Areeda-Turner test, or their own variation of it, into primary-line Robinson-Patman Act cases as well. In these circuits a plaintiff must show not merely that the defendant made sales at two different prices in two different areas. The plaintiff must also show that the price in the low-price (predatory) market was lower than the defendant's average variable cost. The result is to make the Robinson-Patman Act all but superfluous in predatory pricing cases: a plaintiff must prove a nearly complete Sherman Act attempt case, but must make the additional, irrelevant showing that the defendant was selling the same product at a higher price in a different geographic market. The result has been that the Robinson-Patman Act has not brought success to many predatory pricing plaintiffs.[11]

 WESTLAW REFERENCES

anti-competiti** predatory /4 conduct pric*** /p differ! several /3 market pric***

anti-competiti** predatory /4 conduct pric*** /p clayton recoup! % robinson-patman

anti-competiti** predatory /4 conduct pric*** /p primary-line robinson-patman

---

11. See, D.E. Rogers Assoc., Inc. v. Gardner-Denver Co., 718 F.2d 1431, 1439 (6th Cir. 1983), cert. denied ___ U.S. ___, 104 S.Ct. 3513 (1984); O. Hommel Co. v. Ferro Corp., 659 F.2d 340, 348–350 (3d Cir. 1981), cert. denied, 455 U.S. 1017, 102 S.Ct. 1711 (1982), rehearing denied, 456 U.S. 965, 102 S.Ct. 2047 (1982); William Inglis & Sons Baking Co. v. ITT Continental Baking Co., 668 F.2d 1014, 1039–42 (9th Cir. 1981), cert. denied, 459 U.S 825, 103 S.Ct. 57–8 (1982); Pacific Engineering & Prod. Co. v. Kerr-McGee Corp., 551 F.2d 790, 798 (10th Cir. 1977), cert. denied, 434 U.S. 879, 98 S.Ct. 234 (1977), rehearing denied, 434 U.S. 977, 98 S.Ct. 543 (1977); International Air Industries, Inc. v. American Excelsior Co., 517 F.2d 714, 720 n. 10 (5th Cir. 1975), cert. denied, 424 U.S. 943, 96 S.Ct. 1411 (1976).

CHAPTER 7

VERTICAL INTEGRATION AND VERTICAL MERGERS

Table of Sections

§ 7.1 Introduction

A firm is vertically integrated whenever it performs for itself some function that could otherwise be purchased on the market.[1] A lawyer who washes her own office windows and a pizza parlor that makes its own deliveries are both vertically integrated firms. The examples should illustrate that all firms are vertically integrated to some degree. A rule that prohibited firms from providing for themselves anything that could be procured on the market would impose unimaginable costs on society.

A firm can integrate vertically in three different ways. First, and most commonly, it can enter a new market on its own. The pizza parlor that purchases its own delivery van, or the lawyer who begins washing her own windows in order to cut operating costs, has integrated vertically by new entry.

Second, a firm can integrate vertically by acquiring another firm that is already operating in the secondary market. A lawyer who wanted to wash her own windows would be unlikely to acquire a window washing firm. However, a gasoline refiner might often

---

§ 7.1

1. The economic and legal literature on vertical integration is particularly rich. Good discussions can be found in F.M. Scherer, Industrial Market Structure and Economic Performance (2d ed.

1980); R. Bork, The Antitrust Paradox: A Policy at War With Itself 225–245 (1978); O. Williamson, Markets and Hierarchies: Analysis and Antitrust Implications (1975); G. Stigler, The Organization of Industry (1983 ed.).

acquire its own distributors or retail stations; a manufacturer might acquire its own retail outlets; or an electric utility might acquire its own coal or oil production company and its reserves.

Third, a firm might enter into a long-term contract with another firm under which the two firms coordinate certain aspects of their behavior. Although such long-term contracts are market exchanges, they can eliminate many of the uncertainties and risks that accompany frequent uses of the market.

All three forms of vertical integration have been condemned under the antitrust laws, under a variety of theories. Vertical integration by new entry generally raises antitrust issues only when the integrating firm is a monopolist. It is analyzed under § 2 of the Sherman Act.[2] Vertical acquisitions are analyzed as mergers, most often under § 7 of the Clayton Act. Vertical integration by long-term contract is often condemned under § 1 of the Sherman Act if it is found to involve resale price maintenance or some other agreement in restraint of trade.[3] Vertical integration by contract can also be condemned as illegal tying or exclusive dealing under § 3 of the Clayton Act or § 1 of the Sherman Act.[4]

A firm can integrate vertically in two different directions. If a firm integrates into a market from which it would otherwise obtain some needed raw material or service (such as the utility that purchases a coal production company or the lawyer who washes her own windows), the integration is said to be "backward." If a firm integrates in the direction of the end-use consumer (such as the oil refiner that acquires its own retail stations) the integration is said to be "forward."

 WESTLAW REFERENCES
vertical** /2 integrat*** /p "new entry" (acqui! /7 firm company business) "long-term contract"

§ 7.2 The Economics of Vertical Integration

Most vertical integration results from a firm's desire to reduce its costs. The lawyer washes her own windows because she "cannot afford" to have them done by an outside firm. More often than not, the same motivation impels the manufacturer to build or acquire its own retail stores, or the grocery chain to operate its own dairies or farms. Often little formal economic analysis goes into these decisions. A firm simply becomes dissatisfied with the way someone else is providing a service and believes it can perform the service better or more cheaply itself.

2. See § 5.6 above.   4. See chapter eight below.

3. See chapter nine below.

Some cost savings from vertical integration are a result of technological economies. The classic example is the steel mill combined with a rolling mill. The steel mill produces steel in the form of ingots. The rolling mill presses very hot steel ingots into various shapes used in fabricating steel structures. If the steel mill sold the ingots on the open market they would have to be transported and reheated—two processes which are very expensive in proportion to the value of the steel. On the other hand, the steel mill that operates its own rolling mill can produce ingots as they are needed and roll them in the same plant while they are still hot. Thus, although steel mills and rolling mills are both large industries producing distinct products, most steel mills own and operate their own rolling mills.

Such economies in technology generally cannot be achieved by vertical merger, because they require new construction of fully integrated plants. However, this does not mean that vertical mergers contain little potential for producing efficiencies. Technological efficiencies are only a small proportion of the economies that can be achieved by vertical integration. Far more substantial are "transactional" efficiencies—economies that a firm achieves by avoiding the costs of using the marketplace.[1] In fact, there is no *technological* reason why the steel mill and the rolling mill could not be separate firms located in the same building and having a contractual relationship with each other. Such a relationship would be impractical for other reasons, however: two firms would be forced to deal with each other exclusively even though they likely would have inconsistent goals (each wants to maximize its own profits, and the two may have different profit-maximizing rates of output). The costs of writing a contract that would satisfy both firms and cover every contingency would be prohibitive.[2]

Use of the market can be expensive. Negotiating costs money. Dealing with other persons involves risk, and the less information one firm has about the other, the greater the risk. The two parties to a bargain almost always have different incentives. Suppose a manufacturer of aircraft agrees to buy its aircraft radios from another

§ 7.2

1. The classic statement of this theory is Coase, The Nature of the Firm, 4 Economica (n.s.) 386 (1937).

2. O. Williamson, Markets and Hierarchies: Analysis and Antitrust Implications 83–84 (1975). In this case the contracting costs would be even higher because the two firms are in a "bilateral monopoly"—that is, a monopolist and a monopsonist forced to deal with each other. The technological efficiencies created by the presence of the steel mill and rolling mill in the same building give each of the two a cost advantage over competitors. For example, the steel mill might be able to supply the rolling mill in the same building with hot steel at a cost of $1.00 per unit. However, it would cost $1.50 for the rolling mill to purchase steel from the second closest steel mill and then transport and reheat it. Knowing this, the steel mill has a "captive" purchaser in the in-house rolling mill. It will not be content to charge $1.00 when it knows that it can charge any price up to $1.49. However, the rolling mill will be a monopsony buyer for the same reason. The result will be a great deal of wasteful negotiating. See G. Stigler, The Theory of Price 207–208 (3d ed. 1966).

firm. Once the contract price has been established, the aircraft manufacturer wants the best radio it can get for the price, for that will increase the satisfaction of its aircraft customers at no additional costs to itself. The radio producer, on the other hand, wants to produce as inexpensively as possible a radio that satisfies the specifications in the purchase agreement. The firms might try to outline in detail all the specifications of the radio. Many such contracts contain detailed specifications. However, such a contract may be negotiated several years before the radios are delivered. The aircraft itself is a developing and changing product, subject to new technology and unforeseen economic constraints. If the contract were drafted to anticipate every possible change, the contract negotiations would be prohibitively expensive. Sooner or later the radio manufacturer will have some discretion—perhaps in whether to use a more expensive component that clearly meets the specifications in the contract, or a cheaper component that is marginal. The radio manufacturer is likely to use the cheaper component if he predicts that it will meet the standard. If he miscalculates, or if the standard is ambiguous, there may be a dispute and perhaps costly litigation.

These problems multiply when the final cost of a product is uncertain, as is frequently the case in construction projects, and with projects that need future research and development. If the aircraft manufacturer is not purchasing a radio "off the shelf" but is having a new type of radio designed, neither the aircraft producer nor the radio producer knows its final cost. If the aircraft manufacturer insists on a "firm" bid—i.e., if the radio manufacturer is asked to bear the risk of the uncertain final cost—the radio manufacturer will calculate the risk into his bid price. That risk premium may be very high.

The alternative is for the aircraft manufacturer to bear the risk. This can generally be done in two ways. First, the parties can enter a "cost-plus" contract, under which the radio manufacturer develops the radio and adds a specified mark-up to its costs. In that case, however, the radio manufacturer loses all incentive to reduce costs. In fact, the higher his costs, the higher his percentage mark-up will be.

The second alternative is for the radio manufacturer to submit an estimated bid that can be adjusted in the future for "overruns," or unanticipated cost increases. The United States Government, particularly the Department of Defense often purchases equipment under such contracts. Similar problems obtain here, however. First, all the information about costs originates with the seller, and the buyer often cannot be sure that the seller is spending the money efficiently. Second, the transaction costs of accounting for and justifying cost overruns with respect to each component in a complex product can be very high, perhaps more than the cost of the components themselves.

The final and cheapest alternative may be for the aircraft manufacturer to produce its own aircraft radios. To be sure, this is not always feasible. If minimum optimal scale (MOS) of a radio plant is 1000 units per year, but the aircraft manufacturer produces only 40 aircraft per year, its production costs per radio might far exceed the uncertainty and transaction costs described above. Whether a particular instance of vertical integration will reduce a firm's costs is an empirical question—sometimes it will, and other times it will not, depending on the structure of the relevant markets and the technology involved in the manufacturing process. Since technology changes through time, incentives for vertical integration change as well.

When a firm supplies a certain product or service for itself, the "price" it pays equals the cost of producing the product or service. As a result, *if* a firm can produce the product or service as cheaply as existing independent producers can, then any imperfection in the market for that product or service will make it more expensive to buy than to produce. All markets contain some imperfections, and two of these are particularly important in considering vertical integration. First, a firm almost always has better information about itself than it does about other firms. Lack of information about an outside supplier or outlet increases a firm's risks, and therefore its costs. Firms transacting business in the market are inclined to overstate both their capacity and their financial stability. Often the true information is easy to disguise. On the other side, the firm negotiating a contract may often be asked to produce information that it would prefer to keep confidential. Vertical integration enables a firm substantially to solve both these problems of information "impactedness" and confidentiality.

Second is the problem of another firm's market power. One firm is likely to have little information about the relationship between another firm's prices and its costs. This is particularly true if the other firm produces a variety of products. In that case a high published rate of return may come from a different product than the one being purchased. Conversely, the seller's low rate of return may suggest that the buyer is obtaining a product at a competitive price, but it may also indicate that the selling firm is suffering losses in a different product. Every firm would like other firms in its distribution chain to charge the lowest possible price—but often a firm simply cannot be sure that this is really the case. Whenever vertical integration eliminates transactions with a monopolist, however, the result will be higher profits for the integrating firm *and* lower prices for consumers, provided that the integrating firm can produce the product or service as efficiently as the monopolist did. A firm that suspects it is paying monopoly prices for a particular product or service will be highly motivated to provide that product or service for itself.

Vertical integration has been perceived as particularly pernicious when the integrating firm is a monopolist. However, the above rule holds true even for the monopolist: the monopolist that can eliminate another monopolist from its distribution chain will make more profits and will have a lower profit-maximizing price.

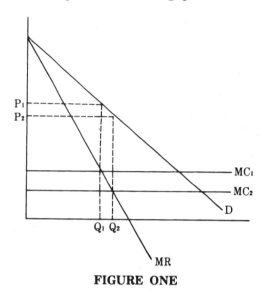

FIGURE ONE

Figures One and Two illustrate the consequences of upstream and downstream vertical integration by a firm with substantial market power. Figure One shows what will happen if a monopolist which has been purchasing some input from another monopolist begins to produce the input itself at a competitive price. The MC_1 curve represents the firm's marginal costs when it was paying a monopoly price, while the lower MC_2 curve represents its marginal costs after it provides the input for itself. The monopolist's profit-maximizing output and price, you will recall, are determined by the intersection of its marginal cost and marginal revenue (MR) curves. As the monopolist's marginal costs move downward from MC_1 to MC_2 that intersection moves downward and to the right. As a result of the cost reduction the monopolist will increase its output from Q_1 to Q_2 and lower its price from P_1 to P_2.

Figure Two, which illustrates the consequences of downstream vertical integration by the monopolist, is more complex. Suppose that a monopoly manufacturer distributes its product through a retailer who is also a monopolist. The manufacturer's profit-maximizing price and output in Figure Two are P_2 and Q_2, determined by the intersection of the manufacturer's MC and MR curves. Since P_2 is the final retail price, where demand for the product is determined, the manufacturer sells the product to the retailer at price P_3. The vertical distance from P_3 to P_2 is the retailer's costs. If the retailer behaved competitively, it would purchase at the wholesale price of P_3

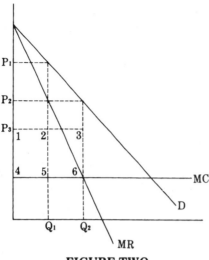

FIGURE TWO

and resell at price P_2, which would maximize the manufacturer's profits.

However, if the retailer is also a monopolist it will determine its own profit-maximizing price by equating its own marginal cost and marginal revenue. In this case the retailer's marginal costs are P_2 (the sum of the wholesale price plus its operating costs). Since the retail price determines demand, the retailer faces the same marginal revenue curve as the manufacturer. The retailer will maximize its profits by raising price to P_1 and reducing output to Q_1, making both the manufacturer and the retail customers worse off. The manufacturer's economic profits are reduced from rectangle 1–3–6–4 to rectangle 1–2–5–4. Costumers are forced to pay P_1 for the product, rather than P_2.

By building (or buying) its own retail outlets, however, the manufacturer will be able to maximize its own profits, which it will do when output is Q_2 and price is P_2. Both the manufacturer and consumers will be better off.

The economic effects of eliminating a monopolist from a distribution chain are the same whether the vertical integration occurs by new entry or by merger. A law firm might eliminate the monopoly payout to a monopoly window washer simply by washing its own windows. Likewise, a shoe manufacturer might respond to price increases by a monopoly shoe store by opening its own shoe store in that area. An electric utility that buys its coal and suspects that the coal producers are engaged in price fixing, however, might respond by acquiring an existing coal producer.

Some markets are more conducive to vertical integration by merger rather than by new entry. Vertical integration by new entry increases the capacity of the level into which the integration occurs. If a city has three movie theatres and a major film producer vertically integrates into the theater market by building a new theatre, the city will have four. If the industry already has excess capacity, vertical integration by merger (in this case by acquisition of an existing theatre) can be more efficient.

Sometimes vertical integration by contract is used by firms to control monopoly pricing by other firms in the distribution chain. For example, in Albrecht v. Herald Co.[3] The Supreme Court used the *per se* rule to condemn a maximum resale price maintenance agreement between a newspaper and its route carriers. Today most commentators believe that the case was wrongly decided. The route carriers were monopolists who could maximize their profits by reducing output and charging a higher price for delivering newspapers. The result, of course, was lower circulation and lower profits for the newspaper, as well as higher prices to the consumer. A firm forbidden by the antitrust laws to protect itself from monopoly pricing will likely choose the second-best alternative—perhaps outright termination of the independent carriers and their replacement by employees of the newspaper.[4]

Vertical integration can facilitate other efficiency savings that have nothing to do with the elimination of market power in the distribution chain. For example, integration is important to a firm that has a strong interest in the way its product is distributed. A refiner of gasoline might increase sales by assuring retail customers that the quality of its product and of the service given by retailers is uniformly high across the country. The refiner can make such an assurance, however, only if it has substantial control over the gasoline retailers themselves. One way the refiner can obtain such control is by building and operating its own retail stations. Another very common way is by means of elaborate franchise contracts that permit the retailers to retain their identity as separate firms while being substantially controlled by their larger supplier. Much of the law of tying arrangements and exclusive dealing is concerned with such vertical integration by contract.[5]

Firms frequently integrate vertically to avoid the consequences of governmental restrictions in a certain market. For example, electricians and accountants are often subject to expensive educational and licensing requirements. Professional electricians and accountants who hire out their services naturally pass these costs to their customers in the form of higher hourly rates. Often, however, the requirements do not apply to full-time employees. A firm that is large enough to maintain its own full-time electrician or accountant may save substantially.

3. 390 U.S. 145, 88 S.Ct. 869 (1968).

4. See Paschall v. Kansas City Star Co., 727 F.2d 692 (8th Cir. 1984 *en banc*), cert. denied, — S.Ct. — (1984);

Hovenkamp, Vertical Integration by the Newspaper Monopolist, 69 Iowa L.Rev. 451 (1984).

5. See Chap. eight below.

In most of the instances described above vertical integration enlarged a firm's profits but also benefitted the consumer. Sometimes the value of vertical integration to the consumer is not so clear, however, and some instances of vertical integration may be anticompetitive. If this were not the case there would be no need for antitrust laws against vertical practices.[6]

Increased market power is *not* a likely consequence of vertical integration. The monopolist of a single distribution level can generally obtain all the available monopoly profits in that distribution chain. For example, a monopoly manufacturer of bicycles generally could not increase its monopoly profits by becoming a distributor or retailer of bicycles as well. The profit-maximizing price of bicycles is determined on the demand side by the amount that final consumers of bicycles are willing to pay. If the total cost of manufacturing a bicycle and distributing it to a cyclist is $70.00, but the profit-maximizing price is $90.00, the $20.00 in monopoly profits could be claimed by any single monopolist in the distribution chain, provided that the other links in the chain are competitive. If the monopoly manufacturer is already obtaining $20.00 in monopoly profits from sales to distributors, it will not be able to make more monopoly profits by acquiring its own distributor.

The above rule has an important exception, however. A firm with market power can sometimes increase its profits by practicing price discrimination, and vertical integration can facilitate price discrimination.

Suppose that a monopoly manufacturer of Polish sausages discovers that it has two different groups of customers with different demands for sausages. One group purchases the sausages in grocery stores for home consumption. The profit-maximizing price for that group of customers is 25¢ per sausage. The other group of customers buys the Polish sausages from concessionaires at public events such as baseball games. The profit-maximizing price for them is $1.00 per sausage.

If the firm must charge the same price to all buyers, its profit-maximizing price will depend on the circumstances. At one extreme it might charge 25¢ to all customers and make sales in both concessions and grocery stores. However, it might also charge $1.00 per sausage, in which case it will make higher profits from concession sales but lose most grocery store sales. Alternatively, it might find a profit-maximizing price somewhere between 25¢ and $1.00. Where

---

6. For an argument that the preferred rule for most vertical practices should be legality, see Posner, The Next Step in the Antitrust Treatment of Restricted Distribution: Per Se Legality, 48 U.Chi.L.Rev. 6 (1981); Easterbrook, Vertical Arrangements and the Rule of Reason, 53 Antitrust L.J. 135 (1984). For an argument that all vertical mergers should be legal, see R. Bork, The Antitrust Paradox: A Policy At War With Itself 226 (1978).

that price lies depends on the marginal cost of the sausages and the relative size of the two groups of customers.

The firm might make substantially more money by price discriminating—by selling sausages for 25¢ each in grocery stores and for $1.00 each through concessionaires. Any attempt to price discriminate raises two problems, however. First is the Robinson-Patman Act, which might prevent the firm from selling the same product to two classes of buyers at two different prices.[7]

The second problem is arbitrage. If grocers were sold sausages for 25¢ each (less their mark-up), but concessionaires were charged $1.00 each (less their mark-up), the concessionaires would have a simple solution. They would go to grocery stores and fill their shopping carts with 25¢ Polish sausages. The sausage maker would end up making all his sales to grocery stores at the lower price.

The solution for the Polish sausage maker is to enter the concessions business itself, either by new entry or else by acquiring an existing concessionaire. Then the manufacturer will be able to retail its sausages directly to baseball fans at $1.00 each, while continuing to make 25¢ sales to grocery stores.

Vertical integration is a very common way by which firms price discriminate.[8] Whether vertical integration to achieve price discrimination should be condemned under the antitrust laws is a difficult question. On the one hand, price discrimination often results in higher output than a monopolist's nondiscriminatory pricing. For example, if the Polish sausage maker were forced to sell all sausages at the same price, it might decide to charge $1.00 and make only the concession sales. In that case many grocers and their customers would be impoverished. On the other hand, any imperfect price discrimination scheme produces a certain amount of inefficiency, both from less-than-competitive output and from the costs of operating the price discrimination scheme itself.[9]

Other alleged injuries from vertical integration come not from vertical integration *per se*, but from the self-dealing that results from vertical integration. If a manufacturer of shoes acquires a chain of shoe stores it may sell its manufactured shoes only through its own stores, and the stores may cease buying shoes from other manufacturers. Before complete exclusivity would occur on both sides, however, the manufacturer's output and the shoe stores' demand

7. Price discrimination and the Robinson-Patman Act are discussed more fully below in chapter thirteen.

8. George Stigler notes, for example, that Alcoa integrated into the aluminum cable business so that it could compete with copper cable, which drove the price of aluminum cable to less than the price of aluminum ingot sold in other markets. G. Stigler, The Organization of Industry 138 (1983 ed.). Price discrimina-

tion may also explain why Brown Shoe Company, which manufactured medium priced shoes, acquired the stores of Kinney, which specialized in lower priced shoes. If the lower priced shoes sold for more than Brown's costs, Brown would be able to label them Kinney's and sell them at a lower price. See Brown Shoe Co. v. U.S., 370 U.S. 294, 326, 82 S.Ct. 1502, 1524 (1962).

9. See § 13.5 below.

must be roughly the same. If the manufacturer is large, it likely will continue to make some sales to other shoe stores as well. Ordinarily, however, if vertical integration produces lower costs, we would expect the integrated firm to take advantage of these economies by self-dealing up to its fullest available capacity.

On the other hand, if vertical integration yields no economies, self-dealing yields no advantages. In the *duPont* (GM) case, for example, the record revealed that General Motors bought fabrics and finishes from the lowest bidder, and that the lowest bidder was not always duPont, even though duPont had a large ownership interest in General Motors and influenced its decisions.[10] The reason for this is clear. A profit-maximizing firm will purchase from its lowest-cost source of supply. If vertical integration yields measurable transaction savings, the lowest cost source of supply is likely to be the parent or controlled firm. If vertical integration yields no such savings, however, it may not be. In that case the firm would lose money by dealing with its own subsidiary when it could buy more cheaply somewhere else.

In condemning specific instances of vertical integration, particularly by merger, courts have generally relied on two arguments. Both contain serious economic weaknesses and apply in a much narrower range of circumstances than courts have in fact applied them. One of these arguments is that vertical integration "forecloses" competitors from access to markets; the other is that vertical integration increases barriers to entry. The merits of these arguments are discussed in the following section on the case law of vertical mergers.

There may be other economic objections to certain uses of vertical integration. Price-regulated firms have been known to integrate vertically in order to cheat on a regulatory statute. For example, a price-regulated electric utility might acquire its own coal producer and sell coal to itself at an inflated price. If it is clever it will be able to convince the regulatory agency that the higher costs merit an increase in the regulated price. Whenever a price regulated natural monopoly integrates vertically with an input or output that is competitive, the regulated firm has an opportunity to hide profits in the competitive product. The solution is to condemn the acquisition, or else to make sure that the regulatory agency scrutinizes carefully all markets in which the price regulated firm operates.[11]

10. See U.S. v. E.I. duPont de Nemours & Co., 353 U.S. 586, 629–633, 77 S.Ct. 872, 896–98 (1957) (J. Burton, dissenting). Because of the absence of consistent self-dealing, at least one economist sees the *duPont* (GM) cases as having no economic consequences whatsoever, except for breaking up "a corporate arrangement that makes many of us uneasy." See D. Dewey, The New Learning: One Man's View, in H. Goldschmid, H. Mann, & J. Weston, Industrial Concentration: The New Learning 12–13 (1974).

11. See Williamson, Markets and Hierarchies 114. The use of tying arrangements to avoid regulated pricing is discussed below in § 8.6.

The converse of the above theory is that a price-regulated utility might integrate vertically into a competitive market and "cross-subsidize" the competitive subsidiary with revenues obtained in the regulated area. The danger of cross-subsidization was one of the principal justifications for the divestiture of American Telephone & Telegraph's local telephone exchanges from its long distance lines. Because of changes in technology long distance lines have become competitive, while local telephone services continue to be regulated natural monopolies. If AT&T operated both, it could drain funds off from the price regulated local exchanges and use them to engage in subsidized, below-cost pricing in the long distance lines. The effect would be to deter independent competitors in the otherwise competitive long distance market. Before such a strategy would be profitable the competitive market would have to be conducive to predatory pricing—for example, entry barriers would have to be high so that the predator could count on a future period of monopoly returns.[12]

Finally, vertical integration can be used by a cartel to discourage cheating by its members. Suppose that the market for televisions contains six firms who are fixing prices. As long as the firms deal with large distributors they will make sales in large quantities at terms which are individually negotiated. Furthermore, the wholesale prices will not normally be made public. This combination of large sales and secret, negotiated contracts will invite members of the cartel to cheat by means of secret rebates, reciprocity or other kinds of price concessions to the larger buyers.

If all the cartel members agree to sell exclusively through their own retail stores, however, cheating becomes much more difficult. As a general rule concessions and special deals to retail customers must be advertised publicly. Furthermore, most retail customers purchase only one television at a time, so there is little incentive to offer a concession that violates the terms of the cartel.[13]

 WESTLAW REFERENCES
vertical** /2 integrat*** /s cost saving cheap**
vertical** /2 integrat*** /s discriminat***

§ 7.3 Vertical Mergers and Antitrust Law

In spite of their extraordinary potential for creating efficiency and their rather limited threat of economic harm, vertical mergers have not fared well under the antitrust laws. Most of the law of vertical

12. See chapter six above, and see U.S. v. Amer. Tel. & Tel., 552 F.Supp. 131 (D.D.C.1982), affirmed sub nom Maryland v. U.S., 460 U.S. 1001, 103 S.Ct. 1240 (1983). A charge of cross-subsidization was made and rejected in MCI Commun. v. AT&T, 708 F.2d 1081, 1123–25 (7th Cir. 1983), cert. denied, ___ U.S. ___, 104 S.Ct. 234 (1983). See L. Johnson, Competition and Cross-Subsidization in the Telephone Industry 42–49 (1982).

13. See §§ 4.1–4.2 above.

mergers was written at a time when protection of small businesses rather than encouragement of efficiency was the underlying antitrust policy.[1] Efficiency-creating vertical mergers invariably injure smaller, unintegrated rivals.

This concern with small business welfare appeared in the earliest vertical acquisition cases. However, early opinions also drew from the common law of trade restraints, which placed heavy reliance on the defendant's intent. For example, in the 1911 *American Tobacco Co.* case the Supreme Court found that "the conclusion of wrongful purpose and illegal combination is overwhelmingly established" by the defendants' "gradual absorption of control over all the elements essential to the successful manufacture of tobacco products, and placing such control in the hands of seemingly independent corporations serving as perpetual barriers to the entry of others into the tobacco trade." [2]

This emphasis on evil intent prevailed for forty years. In U.S. v. Yellow Cab Co., the Supreme Court held that a manufacturer of taxicabs (Checker) violated § 1 of the Sherman Act by acquiring cab operating companies in several large American cities, if it intended by the acquisition to suppress competition in the taxi operating market.[3] The Court found that as a result of the acquisition the operating companies might be forced to purchase their taxicabs exclusively from Checker, and other manufacturers of cabs would be excluded from competing for their business. The alleged result was that the cab companies "must pay more for cabs than they would otherwise pay, their other expenditures are increased unnecessarily, and the public is charged high rates for the transportation services rendered."

The Court's analysis is perplexing. No vice president has yet figured out how a vertically integrated firm can become rich by selling to itself at an inflated price. More likely, the cab companies (which already had monopolies in the individual cities) were buying taxicabs in a competitive market but charging monopoly prices to taxicab riders. By acquiring the companies, Checker was able to transfer these monopoly returns to itself. Alternatively, if the taxi-

§ 7.3

1. For example, Brown Shoe Co. v. U.S., 370 U.S. 294, 82 S.Ct. 1502 (1962), which condemned a vertical merger because it permitted the post-merger defendant to undersell its unintegrated rivals.

2. U.S. v. American Tobacco Co., 221 U.S. 106, 182–83, 31 S.Ct. 632, 649 (1911). The *American Tobacco* trust included horizontal and conglomerate, as well as vertical acquisitions.

3. 332 U.S. 218, 67 S.Ct. 1560 (1947). The Court later affirmed a lower court finding that there was no such intent. U.S. v. Yellow Cab Co., 338 U.S. 338, 70 S.Ct. 177 (1949). See also U.S. v. Paramount Pictures, 334 U.S. 131, 174, 68 S.Ct. 915, 937 (1948), holding that a vertical merger "runs afoul of the Sherman Act if it was a calculated scheme to gain control over an appreciable segment of the market and to restrain or suppress competition, rather than an expansion to meet legitimate business needs * * *."

cab fares were price-regulated (as most taxi fares are today), then Checker could charge supracompetitive prices to its own operating companies, and the increased costs could be shown to the regulatory agency as justification for a fare increase.

In any case, the Court's alternative argument against the merger became more prominent in the case law—namely, that Checker's acquisition of the operating companies excluded other cab manufacturer's "from that part of the market represented by the cab companies under [its] control * * *" For many years vertical mergers were condemned under this "foreclosure" theory.

Foreclosure occurs when vertical integration by one firm denies another firm access to the market. Both vertical integration by new entry and vertical integration by merger can foreclose competitors. For example, if the only newspaper in a city terminates its contracts with independent carriers and switches to self-delivery the result will be foreclosure of the independent carriers. They no longer have a newspaper to deliver.[4]

Foreclosure generally occurs only if one of the integrating firms is a monopolist. Suppose that eight firms manufacture typewriters and fifty firms retail them. If a manufacturer acquires one retailer, the manufacturer likely will begin selling its typewriters through this retailer. This will force some realignment of buyers and sellers— firms that formerly dealt with one of the merging firms may have to find each other and enter new contracts. No one will be foreclosed, however.

After 1950 the Supreme Court condemned vertical mergers under the foreclosure theory, even when both merging levels were competitive.[5] In 1950 § 7 of the Clayton Act was amended, in part to clarify that the statute applied to vertical as well as horizontal mergers.[6] More importantly, the legislative history of amended § 7 reveals that Congress wanted stronger merger standards that would condemn acquisitions in their "incipiency," before they had a chance to work their full evil.

The Supreme Court's first big vertical merger case after § 7 was amended was U.S. v. E.I. duPont de Nemours & Co.[7] The action had

4. See Paschall v. Kansas City Star Co., 727 F.2d 692 (8th Cir. 1984), *en banc*, cert. denied —— S.Ct. —— (1984).

5. In 1948, however, the Supreme Court refused to condemn a vertical merger under the foreclosure theory when the vertical acquisition left several alternative buyers and sellers in the market. U.S. v. Columbia Steel Co., 334 U.S. 495, 507–510, 68 S.Ct. 1107, 1114–1115 (1948).

6. Before its 1950 amendments § 7 applied only to mergers that might less-

en competition "between" the acquiring and acquired firms. A vertical merger involves firms that were not competitors before the merger. The legislative history of the 1950 Celler-Kefauver Amendments to § 7 is discussed in 4 P. Areeda & D. Turner, Antitrust Law ¶¶ 902–903 (1980); and in Brown Shoe Co. v. United States, 370 U.S. 294, 315–23, 82 S.Ct. 1502, 1518–23 (1962).

7. 353 U.S. 586, 77 S.Ct. 872 (1957).

been filed in 1949 under original § 7, and the amendments did not apply to acquisitions that occurred before 1950. Nevertheless, the Court applied the "policy" of the Amendments. It found a violation in duPont's 1917–19 acquisitions of a 23% stock interest in General Motors Co. DuPont was a manufacturer of finishes and fabrics for automobiles. General Motors, a manufacturer of automobiles, purchased such finishes and fabrics for its manufactured cars.

The Court held that the market should be evaluated as of the time of the trial, not the time of the acquisition. In the 1950's General Motors manufactured about 50% of the nation's automobiles, and duPont supplied roughly 67% of GM's requirements for finishes. This suggests foreclosure of the finishes market on the order of 30%, provided that the relevant market was correctly defined as finishes for automobiles.[8] That is, 30% of automobile finishes were no longer sold on the open market, but passed from a supplier to a consumer which it substantially controlled.

The Court went much further in the first vertical merger decision under amended § 7. In Brown Shoe Co. v. U.S.[9] it condemned a shoe manufacturer's acquisition of a shoe retailer when the manufacturer's market share was about 5% and the retailer's market share in the same market was about 1%. In justifying its condemnation on the basis of such small market shares the Court cited a " 'definite trend' among shoe manufacturers to acquire retail outlets," followed by a " 'definite trend' for the parent-manufacturers to supply an ever increasing percentage of the retail outlets' needs, thereby foreclosing other manufacturers from effectively competing for retail accounts." The "necessary corollary" of these trends, concluded the Court, was "the foreclosure of independent manufacturers from markets otherwise open to them." The result was that other shoe manufacturers and retailers were forced to integrate vertically as well.

What did the Court mean by foreclosure "forcing" vertical integration in a market as atomized as the shoe industry? Clearly it could not mean that independent shoe retailers were unable to find independent manufacturers willing to sell them shoes. In 1963 less than 10% of American shoes were distributed through manufacturer-owned or -operated stores.[10] The real cause of the "foreclosure" was the efficiency of the vertically integrated firms. By vertically integrating, firms were able to reduce their costs. Competition among vertically integrated firms drove prices below the costs of the unintegrated firms. They were forced to integrate not because outlets or sources of supply were unavailable, but because only

8. The market was probably defined too narrowly. Virtually all the "automobile finishes and fabrics" identified by the court were purchased by a wide variety of manufacturers, including clothing, furniture and luggage manufacturers. See Markham, The DuPont-General Motors Decision, 43 Va.L.Rev. 881, 887 (1957).

9. 370 U.S. 294, 82 S.Ct. 1502 (1962).

10. See Peterman, The *Brown Shoe* Case, 18 J.L. & Econ. 81, 117 (1975).

vertical integration would enable them to compete with integrated firms.

Suppose that an independent shoe manufacturer has total production and wholesaling costs of $20.00 per pair. The independent shoe store, which buys them at wholesale and retails them to consumers, has additional costs of $10.00. If vertical integration reduces the combined costs to $28.00 the result will be a trend in the industry toward vertical integration—initially because of the extra $2.00 in profits; later, when competition among integrated firms drives the price to $28.00, because integration is essential to survival. If the vertical integration achieves no cost savings, however, then there will be no trend and independent firms at each level will continue to earn profits as before.

A related argument against vertical mergers is that they enhance the merging firm's market power by making entry into the industry more costly or more difficult. If incumbents are vertically integrated a prospective entrant may have to enter at two levels instead of one. The Supreme Court relied on this "barriers to entry" argument in Ford Motor Co. v. U.S.,[11] when it condemned Ford's acquisition of Autolite, a spark plug manufacturer.

The barriers to entry argument against vertical integration generally fares no better than the foreclosure argument. If vertical integration is efficient—if two processes that formerly cost $30 can be performed for $28.00 by a vertically integrated firm—then vertical integration is a "barrier to entry." *All* efficient practices are barriers to entry, because any new entrant must match the efficiency. However, vertical integration in a competitive market which produces no cost savings will not produce a barrier to entry either. If the vertically integrated firm still faces $30.00 in costs, as do its pairs of unintegrated rivals, then entry at each separate level will be as profitable as before.

The barriers to entry argument may have some force, however, when one of the integrating firms is a monopolist. If the world's only aluminum producer acquires an aluminum fabricator and refuses to sell to independent fabricators, the result will be complete foreclosure for existing fabricators and a substantial entry barrier for potential fabricators—neither will be able to obtain aluminum. There will also be a barrier to entry into the aluminum manufacturing industry: once all independent fabricators have disappeared, anyone who wants to enter the aluminum manufacturing industry will have to enter the fabricating industry at the same time.

Suppose that vertical integration by a monopolist can injure firms at the secondary level. For example, the aluminum monopolist's acquisition of a fabricator may destroy the business of rival

---

11. 405 U.S. 562, 92 S.Ct. 1142 (1972). For the same theory see the quotation from *American Tobacco* (1911) at note 2 above.

fabricators. Does it follow that consumers have been injured? It does not, for two reasons. First, all the available efficiencies that can result from vertical integration may accrue to the monopolist as much as the competitor. Vertical integration by the monopolist may reduce its costs, and when its costs go down its profit-maximizing price will go down.[12] Second, assuming that the aluminum monopolist was charging its profit-maximizing price for raw aluminum, it will not be able to obtain higher monopoly profits by creating a second monopoly in the fabricating market (although it may be able to price discriminate).[13] In fact, if the independent fabricators had any market power at all, the newly-integrated monopolist's profit-maximizing price for fabricated aluminum will be lower than was the final output price of the independent firms before integration occurred. Although the monopolist's acquisition may injure independent fabricators, it is more likely to result in lower prices than higher ones. Any antitrust policy concerned exclusively with consumer welfare generally should permit such acquisitions.

Vertical integration by the monopolist may sometimes preserve its monopoly position for a longer time. This will injure consumers even though it does not increase the monopolist's short-run profit-maximizing price. A monopoly that lasts ten years is more damaging to the economy than a monopoly that lasts two years, although both reduce annual output by the same amount.[14]

The mere fact that it is more expensive for a potential rival to enter two markets instead of one, however, will not be sufficient to delay competitive entry significantly. The market for capital is quite competitive, and investors uniformly look for the highest rates of return. Money will flow toward a $10,000,000 project promising high profits more quickly than it will flow to a $10,000 project whose expected rate of return is low.

Vertical integration by the monopolist can effectively delay competitive entry when the monopolist integrates into a market containing *independent* entry barriers—that is, entry barriers which have nothing to do with the integration itself. Suppose, for example, that the aluminum monopolist fears competitive entry. Aluminum requires bauxite for its production, however, and the world contains only two known bauxite fields—Field A and Field B. The aluminum monopolist already owns Field A. By acquiring Field B and refusing to sell bauxite to any competitor, the aluminum monopolist could delay competitive entry into aluminum production indefinitely. This might not give the aluminum producer any immediate power to

12. See § 7.2 above.

13. Id.

14. See Wentz, Mobility Factors in Antitrust Cases: Assessing Market Power in Light of Conditions Affecting Entry and Fringe Expansion, 80 Mich.L. Rev. 1545 (1982).

reduce output further.[15] It would, however, increase the time over which it could expect to earn monopoly profits.

The barriers to entry in such cases may be the result of legal restrictions. Returning to the *Yellow Cab* case, suppose that Checker was a monopolist in the manufacture of taxicabs but feared competitive entry by other automobile manufacturers. Suppose further that each of America's large cities licensed a legal maximum number of taxicabs and that all cities had reached the maximum. By acquiring the operating companies, Checker can effectively foreclose entry into those cities by competing manufacturers of taxicabs. Independent cab companies, even if they had a monopoly in their respective cities, would buy their cabs from the lowest bidder. By acquiring the cab companies, however, Checker perhaps did exactly what the court suggested—transferred cabs to its operating company subsidiaries at a supracompetitive price, which was reflected in the meter price paid by taxicab passengers.

The Supreme Court has not decided a vertical merger case since *Ford Motor* in 1972. During that time some circuit courts have displayed increasing resistance to the foreclosure and entry barrier theories. For example, in Fruehauf Corp. v. FTC [16] the Second Circuit refused to enforce an FTC ruling condemning a vertical merger under § 7 and ordering divestiture. Fruehauf, the largest manufacturer of truck trailers in the United States, with about 25% of that market, acquired Kelsey-Hayes, which controlled about 15% of the market for heavy duty truck and trailer wheels. The FTC alleged that the acquisition foreclosed about 6% of the market for heavy duty wheels. However, the court was

> unwilling to assume that any vertical foreclosure lessens competition. Absent very high market concentration or some other factor threatening a tangible anticompetitive effect, a vertical merger may simply realign sales patterns, for insofar as the merger forecloses some of the market from the merging firms' competitors, it may simply free up that much of the market * * * for new transactions * * *.

The Court then went on to require some showing of an anticompetitive effect, in addition to the mere fact of foreclosure. The FTC alleged one anticompetitive effect: that in times of shortage Fruehauf would deny wheels to its competitors in the trailer market. The Court found no evidence that this would happen. It tentatively agreed with the FTC's finding that barriers to entry into the wheel market were high, based on evidence that entry required a minimum investment of $10–$20 million, and that MOS for a new plant would

---

15. If the aluminum manufacturer had been charging an entry deterring price before its acquisition of the second bauxite field, however, it might reduce output and raise price after the acquisition. See § 6.9 above.

16. 603 F.2d 345 (2d Cir. 1979). Quotation at 352 n. 9.

be about 9% of the market. However, the Court found no evidence that these barriers would require any new entrant to come into the market at both levels, or would make entry at a single level more difficult.

Fruehauf is difficult to harmonize with the Supreme Court's decision in *Brown Shoe*. Other circuits have adhered more closely to the older standards. For example, in Ash Grove Cement Co. v. FTC [17] the Ninth Circuit enforced an FTC order condemning a cement manufacturer's acquisition of two companies that used the cement to manufacture ready-mix concrete for delivery to construction sites. The acquiring company controlled about 15% of the relevant market in raw cement. The larger acquired company purchased about 10% of the relevant market in cement, while the smaller company purchased about 3%.

The *Ash Grove Cement* case can be distinguished from *Fruehauf*. Most importantly, the foreclosure percentages in the cement case were higher. Under the foreclosure theory as it was accepted in the 1970's, a foreclosure of 5%–6% in the acquiring firm's market was marginal, but foreclosure of 15% was generally considered illegal. Furthermore, in *Ash Grove Cement* the administrative law judge had found that entry into the ready-mix market alone was "virtually impossible" in view of the extent of vertical integration already apparent in the industry.[18] The ALJ's fact-findings suggested, however, that entry was difficult because the vertically integrated companies could undersell their unintegrated rivals.

At the present time the case law of vertical mergers is inconsistent and in rapid flux. Some circuits continue to accept the orthodox foreclosure and entry barrier theories developed by the Supreme Court. Others have qualified them substantially. The 1984 Justice Department Merger Guidelines, discussed in the following section, are likely to exacerbate the differences among the circuits, for they abandon the foreclosure theory altogether and place rigorous limits on the barriers to entry theory.

---

17. 577 F.2d 1368 (9th Cir. 1978), cert. denied, 439 U.S. 982, 99 S.Ct. 571 (1978), affirming 85 F.T.C. 1129 (1974). See also, Heatransfer Corp. v. Volkswagenwerk, A.G., 553 F.2d 964 (5th Cir. 1977), cert. denied 434 U.S. 1087, 98 S.Ct. 1282 (1978), where the Court condemned an automobile manufacturer's acquisition of a manufacturer of automobile air conditioners. A finding of very high foreclosure was guaranteed by the court's conclusion that the relevant market was "Volkswagen air conditioners," and not automobile air conditioners. This effectively made the defendant a monopsonist.

18. 85 F.T.C. at 1150. A third distinction, generally absent from the *Ash Grove Cement* opinion, is that there is a long history of price fixing in the cement manufacturing industry, and vertical integration was an important mechanism by which cartel members could police the cartel's output prices. See McBride, Spatial Competition and Vertical Integration: Cement and Concrete Revisited, 73 Amer.Econ.Rev. 1011 (1983); Peck & McGowan, Vertical Integration in Cement: A Critical Examination of the FTC Staff Report, 12 Antitrust Bull. 505 (1967).

WESTLAW REFERENCES
di vertical merger
"vertical merger" /p foreclosure

§ 7.4 Vertical Mergers and the 1984 DOJ Merger Guidelines

In 1984 the Antitrust Division of the U.S. Department of Justice (DOJ) issued revised Guidelines describing its standards for approving mergers.[1] The Guidelines are described more fully in §§ 11.4–11.5 below.

The position of the DOJ on vertical mergers is revisionist, reflecting in large part the DOJ's view that few vertical mergers pose a danger to competition. The Guidelines abandon the traditional three-part division of mergers into horizontal, vertical and conglomerate, and substitute instead two broad categories: horizontal and non-horizontal. The latter category includes what have traditionally been called vertical and conglomerate mergers. The new division is odd in at least one respect: conglomerate mergers are generally analyzed under the potential competition doctrine, which is concerned with competition *between* the merging firms. As a general rule potential competition mergers are more similar to horizontal mergers than to vertical mergers. Horizontal mergers involve firms for whose output the cross-elasticity of demand is very high, while potential competition mergers involve firms for which the cross-elasticity of supply is high. The line between "actual" competition, the concern of horizontal mergers, and "potential" competition, the concern of conglomerate mergers, is often fuzzy.[2]

According to the 1984 Guidelines the DOJ perceives three possible dangers to competition from vertical mergers: increased barriers to entry, facilitation of collusion, and avoidance of rate regulation. The DOJ appears to have abandoned the foreclosure theory.

Increased Barriers to Entry

The Guidelines state that three conditions are generally necessary (but not sufficient) for vertical mergers to raise anticompetitive entry barrier problems. First, vertical integration in the market must be so extensive that entrants must enter both markets simultaneously. The DOJ is "unlikely" to challenge a merger on the entry barrier theory if the market contains enough unintegrated firms that a new, unintegrated entrant could find its essential outlets or sources of supply. As a rule of thumb, the DOJ suggests that there must be sufficient unintegrated capacity at one level to service two minimum efficient scale plants at the other level involved in the merger.

§ 7.4

1. 49 Fed.Reg. 26,823 (1984). The earlier 1968 DOJ Guidelines relied heavily on the foreclosure and entry barrier theories for vertical mergers. See 1 Trade Reg.Rep. (CCH) ¶ 4430 (1968).

2. See § 11.7 below.

The mere need for two-level entry is not sufficient to brand the merger anticompetitive, however. Second, the need for two-level entry must be shown to be a significant deterrent to new entry. If two-level entry into the market is so easy that existing competitors could not succeed in raising price for any significant period of time, the DOJ will probably not challenge the merger under the barriers to entry theory. The DOJ rejects any notion that the increased capital demands of two-level entry, standing alone, are a sufficient barrier. It acknowledges, however, that two-level entry by firms that are inexperienced at one level may increase the risk, and therefore the cost of capital. In this case the DOJ will treat the increased cost of capital as a barrier to entry.[3]

Third, the DOJ notes that economies of scale may constitute an entry barrier warranting challenge if the capacity of minimum efficient scale plants differs significantly at the two levels. Suppose that a widget manufacturer has 80% of the widget market. Widgets are an essential ingredient for the manufacture of gidgets. The minimum optimal scale (MOS) of a widget plant, however, is 70% of the market, while MOS for the gidget makers is not more than 2%–3% of the market. Now the widget manufacturer begins acquiring its own gidget plants and selling only to them. If the number of uncommitted widgets available on the market declines substantially, any new entrant into the gidget market must either build a huge widget plant and look for a market for its excess widgets, or else build an inefficiently small widget plant and operate with higher costs. The DOJ notes that there would be no problem if a "significant outside market exists at the secondary level"—in this case, the market for widgets.[4]

Finally, the DOJ notes that barriers to entry have no effect on competitive markets—a market containing 100 perfect competitors will perform competitively in spite of insurmountable barriers against a potential 101st entrant. As a result the DOJ is unlikely to challenge mergers on a barrier to entry theory unless overall concentration in one market is above 1800 as measured by the Herfindahl-Hirschman Index (HHI).[5]

---

3. 49 Fed.Reg. at 26,835–36. See Williamson, Vertical Merger Guidelines: Interpreting the 1982 Reforms, 71 Calif.L.Rev. 604, 606 (1983). Professor Williamson's article is a critique of an earlier version of the DOJ Guidelines published in 1982. The treatment of vertical mergers in the 1982 and 1984 Guidelines is almost identical.

4. This theory was first suggested by Areeda and Turner in 1980, who noted that no reported cases have relied on it. 4 P. Areeda & D. Turner, Antitrust Law ¶ 1008 (1980).

5. The Herfindahl-Hirschman Index (HHI) is discussed more fully below in § 11.4. Briefly, the HHI is the sum of the squares of the market shares of all firms operating in the relevant market. A typical market with an HHI of 1800 would have one firm with a market share of 30%, one with 20%, and five firms with market shares of 10% each. $(30^2 + 20^2 + 10^2 + 10^2 + 10^2 + 10^2 + 10^2 = 1800)$. A market with four 20% firms and two 10% firms also has an HHI of 1800.

Vertical Mergers that Facilitate Collusion

The DOJ may also challenge vertical mergers that increase the likelihood of collusion. The theory is discussed in § 7.2 above. The risk of collusion may be greater when manufacturers or distributers systematically acquire their own retail outlets. If the manufacturers or distributors are engaged in price fixing, they will find it easier to detect cheating by cartel members at the retail level, where prices and terms are generally made public. Vertical mergers are not likely to facilitate collusion, however, unless the manufacturer or distributor market is itself conducive to collusion. As a general rule, therefore, the DOJ will not challenge such mergers unless the HHI in the upstream market exceeds 1800.

The DOJ also notes that a vertical merger might facilitate collusion if it eliminates a large, particularly disruptive buyer which in the past had effectively forced sellers to compete with each other.[6] Once again, the disruptive buyer theory applies only when the upstream market is itself conducive to collusion. The DOJ is not likely to challenge a merger on this ground unless the upstream market's HHI exceeds 1800.

Avoidance of Rate Regulation

Finally, the DOJ notes that vertical mergers may enable price-regulated utilities to circumvent rate regulation by inflating the costs of internal transactions with the unregulated subsidiary.[7] This could be particularly problematic, the DOJ notes, if there is no independent market for the unregulated product or service, for the regulatory agency will have no basis for comparing prices. On the other hand, vertical integration by price-regulated firms can generate the same efficiencies that are available to competitive firms. Therefore the DOJ will challenge such mergers only if they produce "substantial opportunities for such abuses."

The overwhelming impression created by the DOJ vertical merger Guidelines is that the DOJ does not intend to waste much time chasing vertical mergers. The "theories" to which it gives the most attention are really nontheories, never used by courts before and sometimes not even well developed in academic literature. Established judicial theories of vertical mergers are all but forgotten. A sceptical reader might think that the DOJ developed these "Guidelines" only to make people think that it still intends to scrutinize vertical mergers. In fact, most of the factual predicates for the new

6. 49 Fed.Reg. at 26,836. This theory was suggested by Areeda & Turner in 1980. 4 P. Areeda & D. Turner, Antitrust Law ¶ 1006 (1980). The authors cite no cases condemning vertical mergers under this theory, although they do note an "obscure passage" that may refer to it in an FTC decision: Union Carbide Corp., 59 F.T.C. 614 (1961).

7. 49 Fed.Reg. at 26,836. Tying arrangements can be used by price-regulated firms for a similar purpose. See § 8.6 below.

theories are so implausible that they will seldom or never occur.[8]
This is consistent with the position that vertical mergers seldom
injure competition.

 WESTLAW REFERENCES

"vertical merger" /p "department of justice" d.o.j. /p guideline

---

8. For criticism of the 1982 version
of the Guidelines, see Schwartz, The
New Merger Guidelines: Guide to Governmental Discretion and Private Counseling or Propaganda for Revision of the
Antitrust Laws? 71 Calif.L.Rev. 575,
590–94 (1983); Ordover & Willig, The
1982 DOJ Merger Guidelines: An Economic Assessment, 71 Calif.L.Rev. 535,
571–73 (1983).

CHAPTER 8

TIE–INS, RECIPROCITY, EXCLUSIVE DEALING AND THE FRANCHISE CONTRACT

Table of Sections

§ 8.1 Introduction: The Judicial Test for Tie-ins

A tie-in or tying arrangement is a sale or lease of one product on the condition that the buyer take a second product as well. Tie-ins may be illegal under § 1 of the Sherman Act or § 3 of the Clayton Act.[1]

The courts have developed an easily articulated test for tying arrangements, although the test varies from one circuit court to

---

§ 8.1

1. 15 U.S.C.A. § 14: "It shall be unlawful for any person * * * to lease or make a sale or contract for sale of goods * * * on the condition, agreement or understanding that the lessee or purchaser thereof shall not use or deal in the goods * * * of a competitor * * * of the lessor or seller, where the effect * * * may be to substantially lessen competition or tend to create a monopoly in any line of commerce."

another. Some courts analyze tie-ins under a five-part test, others under a four-part test, and still others under a three-part test. In operation the tests are roughly similar, and the three-part test combines elements that are separated in the tests of other circuits. For purpose of analysis we use the five-part test that is now the law of the Second Circuit:[2] 1) There must be separate tying and tied products; 2) there must be "evidence of actual coercion by the seller that in fact forced the buyer to accept the tied product * * *"; 3) the seller must possess "sufficient economic power in the tying product market to coerce purchaser acceptance of the tied product * * *"; 4) there must be "anticompetitive effects in the tied market * * *"; and, 5) there must be "involvement of a 'not insubstantial' amount of interstate commerce in the tied product market * * *."

Although the Supreme Court has approved several elements of this test, it has never articulated a universal test of its own.[3] The circuit courts have assembled their tests from various statements contained in different Supreme Court opinions. The circuits are virtually unanimous in requiring elements 1, 3 and 5 of the test set forth above. Further, if the "coercion" requirement in element 2 means only that the seller must put pressure on a buyer to take a tied product as well as the tying product, courts agree that the plaintiff must show number 2 as well.

The fourth element, "anticompetitive effects," is the most ambiguous, with some courts using it as a synonym for coercion, some as a synonym for antitrust injury, and some not assessing it at all.

 WESTLAW REFERENCES

digest(tie tying /p (anticompetitive /3 effect) coercion injury)

---

2. Yentsch v. Texaco, Inc., 630 F.2d 46, 56–57 (2d Cir. 1980). The Fifth Circuit uses a four element test. Bob Maxfield, Inc. v. American Motors Corp., 637 F.2d 1033, 1037 (5th Cir. 1981), cert. denied, 454 U.S. 860, 102 S.Ct. 315 (1981). The most frequently cited test comes from the Ninth Circuit, and has three elements:

> *First,* * * * the scheme in question involves two distinct items and provides that one (the tying product) may not be obtained unless the other (the tied product) is also purchased. * * * *Second,* * * * the tying product possesses sufficient economic power appreciably to restrain competition in the tied product market. * * * *Third,* * * * a "not insubstantial" amount of commerce is affected by the arrangement.

Siegel v. Chicken Delight, Inc., 448 F.2d 43, 47 (9th Cir. 1971), cert. denied, 405 U.S. 955, 92 S.Ct. 1172 (1972); Digidyne Corp. v. Data General Corp., 734 F.2d 1336 (9th Cir. 1984).

3. But see Justice O'Connor's concurring opinion in Jefferson Parish Hosp. Dist. No. 2 v. Hyde, ___ U.S. ___, 104 S.Ct. 1551, 1573 (1984), noting that under the rule of reason an illegal tie must meet three "threshold" conditions— "market power in the tying product, a substantial threat of market power in the tied product, and a coherent economic basis for treating the products as distinct * * *." In addition, there must be some kind of exclusionary or anticompetitive effect in the tied product market.

§ 8.2　Tying Arrangements and Consumer Welfare

Virtually every product or service sold can be divided into components or parts. A coat can be sold without its buttons, a desk without its drawers and a jar of pickles can probably be sold without its lid. The market would come to a standstill, however, if the antitrust laws gave every customer a legal right to atomize his purchases as much as he chose.

Why then a law of tying arrangements? Quite simply, some forced package sales have been perceived by both Congress and the courts as anticompetitive or injurious to the seller's competitors or customers. The law of tie-ins is concerned with segregating this group of forced combined sales from others that the law should tolerate or even encourage.

An antitrust policy maker might take a number of approaches to this problem. One would be to adopt a rule that maximized consumer welfare in the short run. Such a rule might permit any consumer to subdivide any purchase to any extent. A store selling a coat would be required to snip off a single button for any customer who wanted to buy it. Such a rule would impose enormous costs on sellers, and consumers would end up paying higher prices for products. Looking at any range of transactions larger than the shortest run possible (a single purchase by a single consumer) such a rule clearly would not be in the best interest of consumers as a group.

This analysis raises an important issue, however. A legal policy designed to maximize the welfare of consumers will not necessarily make every single consumer better off in every situation.[1] Consider Captain Ahab, for example, who would greatly prefer to buy a single right shoe rather than a pair. Unfortunately for Ahab, shoe stores sell shoes only in pairs, because the cost of stocking, returns, and record-keeping would soar if they sold individual right shoes and were stuck with the remaining left shoes. These costs would be passed on to consumers, all of whom would pay a higher price for shoes. Although shoe sellers' (nearly) universal policy of selling shoes only in pairs makes most consumers better off, it injures a small number of consumers who would prefer a single shoe.

A law of tying arrangements derived from the consumer welfare principle would try to identify those forced combined sales that make most consumers better off, or that generate consumer gains that outweigh consumer losses. However, it is impossible to measure how all consumers are affected by a particular forced combined sale. Therefore a test must be designed to produce an inference that a particular tying arrangement injures consumers as a group. The

§ 8.2

1. See Hovenkamp, Distributive Justice and the Antitrust Laws, 51 Geo. Wash.L.Rev. 1, 5 (1982).

judicial test described in the preceding section should be evaluated as an attempt to arrive at these necessary inferences.

§ 8.3　Tie-ins, Market Power, and the Per Se Rule

In Times-Picayune Pub. Co. v. United States [1] Justice Clark tried to establish some differences between the law of tie-ins considered under § 1 of the Sherman Act and § 3 of the Clayton Act. Justice Clark believed that the Clayton Act must have broader coverage than the Sherman Act. Otherwise § 3 of the Clayton Act would have been superfluous. [2] The Sherman Act applied only to agreements actually "in restraint of trade," while the Clayton Act reached every agreement the effect of which "may be substantially to lessen competition."

Justice Clark concluded that a plaintiff can have the benefit of a *per se* rule under § 1 of the Sherman Act by showing *both* that the seller had sufficient market power in the tying product to restrain competition in the tied product *and* that the tie-in restrained a substantial volume of competition in the market for the tied product. If the plaintiff could show only one of these, however, the tie-in might still be a violation of § 3 of the Clayton Act under the rule of reason. [3]

Justice Clark's distinction made little sense in either law or economics, and it raised two particularly unfortunate possibilities: 1) that some tie-ins could be found illegal even though the seller had no market power in the tying product market; 2) that if a seller had market power, its tie may be illegal *per se*: that is, evidence about the actual procompetitive or efficiency effects of a particular arrangement would be irrelevant. Fortunately, the circuit courts have generally not followed Justice Clark's prescription and have softened both of these rules.

Justice Clark's distinction suggested that a tying arrangement could be illegal even when the defendant had no market power in the tying product market. However, a seller in competition could not impose an unwanted second product on a buyer unless the seller compensated the buyer for taking the product. Suppose that a market contains 100 sellers of identical wheat, and one seller requires a buyer to purchase a chicken for $2.00 as a condition of taking the

---

§ 8.3

1.　345 U.S. 594, 73 S.Ct. 872 (1953). The alleged tie-in involved "unit pricing": the defendant sold identical advertisements in its morning newspaper and evening newspaper as a package, and refused to sell advertising in either newspaper separately.

2.　There is a better explanation: shortly before the Clayton Act was en-

acted the Supreme Court had suggested that the Sherman Act did not reach tie-ins at all. Henry v. A.B. Dick Co., 224 U.S. 1, 29–30, 32 S.Ct. 364, 372 (1912).

3.　345 U.S. at 608–09, 73 S.Ct. at 880. In Jefferson Parish Hosp. Dist. No. 2 v. Hyde, ___ U.S. ___, 104 S.Ct. 1551, 1569 (1984), four concurring Justices argued that the per se rule for tying arrangements should be abandoned.

wheat. Some purchasers who want a chicken anyway might purchase the "package" from the farmer, if both the wheat and the chicken were competitively priced. Anyone who did not want a chicken, however, would treat the requirement as a $2.00 increase in the price of wheat and buy wheat from a competitor who had no chickens.

Tie-ins that are contrary to consumer welfare are implausible in a competitive market. Competition drives prices to marginal cost, and the forced purchase of an unwanted product will be treated by a purchaser as a price increase. Such an increase is possible only if the seller has some market power. But in such a case would not the monopoly seller be better off merely increasing the price by $2.00 rather than throwing in the chicken?

Today many courts ignore Justice Clark's two-fold standard for tie-ins. Several have adopted a single test under both statutes that resembles Justice Clark's Sherman Act test and requires both market power and a significant amount of commerce in the tied product market. In 1977 the Ninth Circuit concluded that "[t]he practical difference between the two standards has eroded steadily since Justice Clark's attempt to draw a fine line" between the two.[4] Other circuits appear to permit a Clayton Act rule-of-reason analysis in which market power is not a requirement.[5] In no recent case, however, has a court condemned a tie-in when there was an express finding that the defendant had no market power in the tying product.[6]

Courts generally presume market power, however, when the tying product is patented[7] or copyrighted,[8] and some courts give the same presumption when the tying product is trademarked.[9] In most cases

4. Moore v. Jas. H. Matthews & Co., 550 F.2d 1207, 1214 (9th Cir. 1977), appeal after remand 682 F.2d 830 (9th Cir. 1982).

5. For example, see Ware v. Trailer Mart, Inc., 623 F.2d 1150, 1153 (6th Cir. 1980), holding that market power in the tying product is "relevant only if [the plaintiff] intends to prove a *per se* violation of Section 1" of the Sherman Act, but not in a rule of reason case under § 3 of the Clayton Act.

6. For an argument that some tie-ins should be illegal even when the seller has no market power, see Craswell, Tying Requirements in Competitive Markets: the Consumer Protection Issues, 62 Boston Univ.L.Rev. 661 (1982). The argument rests on the proposition that in certain markets, such as health care, consumer search costs are very high. As a result, one seller can coerce acceptance of a tied product even in a multi-

seller market, because the consumer is not in a good position to shop around. The Fifth Circuit relied on this argument to condemn a hospital's requirement that all patients operated on in its facilities use a particular anesthesiologist. The Supreme Court reversed. See the *Jefferson Parish Hospital case*, note 3 above, 686 F.2d at 290, reversed at 104 S.Ct. 1551 (1984).

7. See International Salt Co. v. United States, 332 U.S. 392, 68 S.Ct. 12 (1947), and see *Jefferson Parish Hospital*, note 3 above, 104 S.Ct. 1551, 1560 (1984).

8. U. S. v. Paramount Pictures, Inc., 334 U.S. 131, 158, 68 S.Ct. 915, 929 (1948); Digidyne Corp. v. Data General Corp., 734 F.2d 1336, 1341–42 (9th Cir. 1984).

9. Photovest Corp. v. Fotomat Corp., 606 F.2d 704 (7th Cir. 1979), cert. denied,

courts regard the presumption as rebuttable.[10] Many patents confer absolutely no market power on their owners, and often patented products are not even marketable at their cost of production. Likewise, any group of words or symbols can be copyrighted.

The rule creating a presumption of market power in such cases overlooks the fact that in a world of brand-specific products almost everything except fungibles is protected at least to a certain extent by a patent, copyright or trademark. These are the mechanisms by which consumers distinguish among brands. More often than not the patent or trademark makes a product "distinguishable" but confers little or no measurable market power upon its owner. Automobiles, stereo equipment, home computers, watches, fast food franchises, clothing and canned food are all likely to be patented, trademarked or copyrighted, but all are sold in arguably competitive markets. The economic case for "presuming" sufficient market power to coerce consumer acceptance of an unwanted tied product simply because the tying product is patented, copyrighted, or trademarked is very weak.[11]

A forced package sale by a seller without market power must be efficiency creating or else the seller could not successfully sell its product this way. "Efficiency-creating" means that the gains that accrue to customers who benefit from the combination are greater than the losses that accrue to those who are injured, and that the gains can be realized only if the combination is forced on everyone.

For example, a shoe store does not need market power to force all its customers to buy shoes in pairs. If it sold shoes singly it would face higher costs that would be passed on to customers. These costs would outweigh the benefit to the relatively small number of people who would be better off if they could buy a single shoe. Likewise, stores with no market power force customers to buy coats with their buttons, automobiles with their spare tires and dressed geese with

445 U.S. 917, 100 S.Ct. 1278 (1980); Siegel v. Chicken Delight, Inc., 448 F.2d 43 (9th Cir. 1971), cert. denied, 405 U.S. 955, 92 S.Ct. 1172 (1972). Other circuits reject the presumption for trademarks: Carpa, Inc. v. Ward Foods, Inc., 536 F.2d 39 (5th Cir. 1976), appeal after remand, 567 F.2d 1316 (5th Cir. 1978).

10. However, some cases suggest a *conclusive* presumption of economic power when the tying product is patented. See United States Steel Corp. v. Fortner Enterprises (Fortner II), 429 U.S. 610, 619, 97 S.Ct. 861, 867 (1977); Fortner Enterprises v. United States Steel Corp. (Fortner I), 394 U.S. 495, 505 n. 2, 89 S.Ct. 1252, 1259 n. 2 (1969).

11. See Digidyne Corp. v. Data General Corp., 734 F.2d 1336, 1341–1345 (9th Cir. 1984), in which the Court presumed that the defendant had market power in its computer software because the software was copyrighted. Under that rationale *all* licensors of computer software have market power in their product. An additional problem with the presumption of market power is that the scope of the patent or copyright is frequently different than the scope of a relevant market for antitrust purposes. For example, the *Good Food Cookbook* is copyrighted. However, the relevant market for estimating market power is probably "cook books." Within that market the *Good Food Cookbook* may be an intense competitor. The same analysis generally applies to patents. See § 5.6 above.

their gizzards—even though there are people who would prefer all these "tying" products without their respective "tied" products. Often courts have addressed this efficiency, or consumer welfare, problem by deciding that the two items were in fact a single legal "product."

If a seller is a competitor, its forced combination sale is probably efficient. It does not follow, however, that if the seller has market power its forced combination sale is inefficient. Equally pernicious was Justice Clark's suggestion that if a seller has market power, its tie-in involving a significant amount of interstate commerce is *per se* illegal—that is, illegal without regard to possible procompetitive effects.[12]   Even a monopoly seller of shoes would probably sell them in pairs. It would be efficient for the monopolist to do so, and both the monopolist and its customers are better off when the monopolist has lower costs. Unfortunately, some courts have held that once the accepted test for tie-ins has been met, the court must condemn the tie regardless of any evidence that the tie-in created efficiency.[13]

The *per se* rule, as you may recall, is applied to certain practices after the court understands them sufficiently well to conclude that they are almost always harmful. In that case the risk of overdeterrence is very low; that is, there is little chance that the court will end up condemning a practice that is really efficient. On the other side, the cost of litigating under the rule of reason is very high.

But are tie-ins even arguably within the category of practices, such as price fixing, that are almost always harmful? The Supreme Court concluded that they were in Northern Pacific Rwy. Co. v. U.S.[14] Justice Black wrote:

> Indeed, "tying agreements serve hardly any purpose beyond the suppression of competition * * *." They deny competitors free access to the market for the tied product, not because the party imposing the tying requirements has a better product or a lower price but because of his power or leverage in another market. At the same time buyers are forced to forego their free choice between competing products. For these reasons * * * [t]hey are unreasonable in and of themselves whenever a party has sufficient economic power with respect to the tying product to appreciably restrain free competition in the market for the tied

---

12. The *per se* rule against tie-ins is sometimes called a "soft core" *per se* rule because the plaintiff must define a relevant market and show that the defendant has a certain amount of market power. The rule is criticized in Baker, The Supreme Court and the Per Se Tying Rule: Cutting the Gordian Knot, 66 Va.L.Rev. 1235 (1980).

cert. denied 419 U.S. 1022, 95 S.Ct. 498 (1974) holding that if a seller already has a monopoly in *both* the tying product (regular season football tickets) and the tied product (preseason exhibition tickets), then the action must fail because both products were already monopolized and tying could not monopolize them further.

13. But see Coniglio v. Highwood Svce., Inc., 495 F.2d 1286 (2nd Cir. 1974),

14. 356 U.S. 1, 6, 78 S.Ct. 514, 518, (1958).

product and a "not insubstantial" amount of interstate commerce is affected.

The result of the *Northern Pacific* rule has been that often when the defendant has market power in the tying product the court has condemned its tie-in, even when the forced combined sale was probably in the best interest of consumers.[15]

The Supreme Court has never provided a useful rule for determining *how much* market power the seller must possess before the tying arrangement is illegal. In the *Times-Picayune* case the Supreme Court appeared to require the seller's "dominance" in the tying product market.[16] On the other hand, in the *Northern Pacific Rwy.* case the Court assessed a much weaker requirement that the defendant control a "substantial" amount of the tying product and failed even to define a relevant market.[17] In Fortner Enterprises, Inc. v. U.S. Steel Corp. (Fortner I) the Court not only found it unnecessary to define a relevant market for the tying product, but held that market power in the tying product could be inferred from the fact that the seller had "unique economic advantages over his competitors."[18]

This trend toward dilution of the market power requirement came to an abrupt halt, at least for Sherman Act cases, in Jefferson Parish Hosp. Dist. No. 2 v. Hyde, in which the plaintiff anesthesiologist alleged that the hospital illegally tied the use of its operating rooms to a particular firm of anesthesiologists. The Court found that a market share of 30% in the tying product market was insufficient, because 70% of the market continued to be available to patients who wanted to use a different anesthesiologist than the one employed by the defendant. At the same time, the Court appeared to return to the "market dominance" test of *Times-Picayune*.[19]

The *Jefferson Parish Hospital* case appears calculated to have a large impact on the law of tying arrangements, for the trend in circuit court opinions has been to condemn tying arrangements even when the defendant's market share of any properly defined relevant market for the tying product was very small.[20] If the true market

15. See Hyde v. Jefferson Parish Hosp. Dist. No. 2, 686 F.2d 286, 294 (5th Cir. 1982), reversed, ___ U.S. ___, 104 S.Ct. 1551 (1984). In reversing, however, the Supreme Court concluded that "It is far too late in the history of our antitrust jurisprudence to question the proposition that certain tying arrangements pose an unacceptable risk of stifling competition and therefore are unreasonable 'per se.'" 104 S.Ct. at 1556. Some courts, however, will consider a "business justification" defense, including economic efficiency, even in *per se* cases. See Grappone, Inc. v. Subaru of New England, Inc., 534 F.Supp. 1282, 1290–92 (D.N.H.1982).

16. See *Times-Picayune*, note 1 above, 345 U.S. at 611, 73 S.Ct. at 882.

17. *Northern Pacific Rwy.*, note 14 above, 356 U.S. at 6–8, 78 S.Ct. at 518–19.

18. 394 U.S. 495, 505, 89 S.Ct. 1252, 1259 (1969).

19. Note 15 above. 104 S.Ct. 1551, 1556 (1984).

20. For example, Heatransfer Corp. v. Volkswagenwerk, A.G., 553 F.2d 964 (5th Cir. 1977), cert. denied, 434 U.S. 1087, 98 S.Ct. 1282 (1978).

power test is whether sufficient alternatives were available to buyers in the market, much of that law will fall aside.

That leaves one difficult question: when are tie-ins inefficient or injurious to consumer welfare and why do sellers impose them? Both courts and commentators have suggested several reasons why sellers impose tie-ins: 1) someone with a monopoly in the tying product can use a tie-in to create a second monopoly in the tied product and reap two sets of monopoly profits instead of one; 2) a monopolist can use a tie-in to raise barriers to entry and thereby protect its monopoly status; 3) a tie-in can enable a price-regulated seller to avoid or conceal avoidance of price regulation; 4) tie-ins can facilitate or conceal predatory pricing; 5) tie-ins can permit monopoly sellers to engage in or conceal price discrimination without violating the Robinson-Patman Act; alternatively tie-ins can facilitate nondiscriminatory metering; 6) tie-ins may increase productive or transactional efficiency by improving the quality of a product, lowering its costs, or by facilitating its distribution.

The current judicial test for tying arrangements is not well suited to discriminating among these rationales for tying arrangements. Neither is the test well designed to distinguish between efficiency-creating and efficiency-destroying tie-ins. *If* antitrust policy should encourage efficient practices, however, certain tying arrangements should be legal. They make consumers better off.

 WESTLAW REFERENCES
digest(tie tying   /s   "per se")
digest(tie tying   /p   patent** copyright** trademark**)

§ 8.4   The Leverage Theory: Using Tie-ins to Turn One Monopoly Into Two

The leverage theory is the oldest theory under which tie-ins have been condemned. Under the theory a seller who has a monopoly in one product, which is often patented, uses a tie-in to create a "limited" monopoly in a second product that is essential to the use of the tying product. Suppose that a seller has a patent monopoly in a freezer that preserves ice cream in transit better than any competing technology. The freezer requires carbon dioxide, a common chemical, as a refrigerant. The seller requires all purchasers of its freezer to buy its carbon dioxide as well, and effectively corners the market for the carbon dioxide used in its freezers. In condemning this arrangement Justice Brandeis wrote in 1931 that it permitted

> the patent-owner to "derive its profit, not from the invention on which the law gives it a monopoly, but from the unpatented supplies with which it is used" [and which are] "wholly without the scope of the patent monopoly" * * *. If a monopoly could be so expanded, the owner of a patent for a product might

conceivably monopolize the commerce in a large part of the unpatented materials used in its manufacture. The owner of a patent for a machine might thereby secure a partial monopoly on the unpatented supplies consumed in its operation.[1]

The perceived evils of tie-ins under the leverage theory are twofold. First, by creating two monopolies where there had been only one the seller can make two monopoly profits and force consumers to pay even more for products than if there were only one monopoly. Second, by creating a monopoly in a second product, the monopolist in the tying product can drive other producers of the tied product out of business, or at least foreclose them from part of the market.

Such "leveraging" is not a plausible way to increase monopoly profits. Suppose that seller A has a monopoly in a patented glass jar. Each jar requires one lid, but the lids are not patented and are manufactured by many competitors. A produces jars for $1.00, but she sells them at $1.50, which is her profit-maximizing price. The competitive price of lids is 30¢.

A decides to manufacture lids herself and sell a jar and a lid as a package. What is A's profit-maximizing price for the package? The answer, quite clearly, is $1.80. A's computation of her profit-maximizing price for jars as $1.50 was *predicated* on the fact that lids were sold for 30¢. Since every jar must have a lid, buyers place a certain value on the package. Someone who buys a jar and a lid for $1.80 is generally indifferent whether the price is $1.00 for the jar and 80¢ for the lid, or $1.50 for the jar and 30¢ for a lid. As long as the proportion of jars to lids is constant the purchaser will attribute a price change in either to the price of the entire package. A monopolist of either jars or lids can extract all available monopoly profits from the sale of jars with lids. The jar monopolist cannot make any more monopoly profits by monopolizing the lid market as well.[2]

§ 8.4

1. Carbice Corp. of Amer. v. Amer. Patents Development Corp., 283 U.S. 27, 31–32, 51 S.Ct. 334, 335–36 (1931); See also Fortner Enterprises v. U.S. Steel (Fortner I), 394 U.S. 495, 498–99, 89 S.Ct. 1252, 1256 (1969): "[tying arrangements] deny competitors free access to the market for the tied product, not because the party imposing the tying requirements has a better product or a lower price but because of his power or leverage in another market."; Motion Picture Patents Co. v. Universal Film Mfg. Co., 243 U.S. 502, 37 S.Ct. 416 (1917); International Salt Co. v. U.S., 332 U.S. 392, 68 S.Ct. 12 (1947); IBM Corp. v. U.S., 298 U.S. 131, 56 S.Ct. 701 (1936); and see Jefferson Parish Hosp. Dist. No. 2 v. Hyde, ___ U.S. ___, 104

S.Ct. 1551, 1571 (1984): "Tying may be economically harmful primarily in the rare cases where power in the market for the tying product is used to create additional market power in the market for the tied product." (J. O'Connor, concurring). See generally W. Bowman, Jr., Patent and Antitrust Law—A Legal and Economic Appraisal 100–153 (1973).

2. This analysis assumes that the lids are being sold competitively. Suppose, however, that lids are sold by a monopolist or cartel for 50¢, 20¢ more than the competitive price. Since the profit-maximizing price of a jar-lid package is $1.80, the effect of the monopoly price in lids is to reduce the profit-maximizing price of jars. There are still 50¢ worth of monopoly profits in the market for jars with lids, but only 30¢ of those profits

The leverage theory does not successfully explain how a seller can enlarge its monopoly profits by means of a tie-in. In fact, the jar monopolist is best off when lids are sold at the lowest price, for a lower lid price will increase the profit-maximizing price of the jars. If an efficient lid producer can sell lids for 28¢ the jarmaker will be better off: the profit-maximizing price of jars will rise by 2¢. Conversely, if the jarmaker made lids but was less efficient than its competitors, a tie-in would actually cost it money. Suppose that the jar monopolist makes lids, but because of an obsolete plant or other production inefficiencies its costs are 35¢. Most purchasers refuse to buy lids from the jar monopolist at 35¢ when they can obtain them elsewhere at 30¢. The jar monopolist hits upon a scheme, however: she will force purchasers of her jars to take her lids as well.

The scheme, far from being profitable, will reduce profits by 5¢ on each sale. Since the profit-maximizing price of a jar-with-a-lid remains constant, the jarmaker can force purchasers to take a 35¢ lid instead of a 30¢ lid and maintain her revenues only by reducing the price of jars by 5¢. The additional 5¢ in the lid price is not profit to the monopolist, however, because it is eaten up in the production inefficiencies. If the jar monopolist cannot manufacture lids as efficiently as its competitors it would be better off to get rid of its lid factory and leave the lid market to more efficient producers.

The theory that a monopoly seller can use a tie-in to enlarge monopoly profits has been condemned repeatedly by commentators for three decades.[3] In a few judicial opinions judges have also noted the implausibility of the leverage theory.[4] Even today, however, courts sometimes rely on the leverage theory to condemn a tying arrangement.[5]

 WESTLAW REFERENCES
265k17(2.5) +p leverag***

§ 8.5 Tying Arrangements and Barriers to Entry

Closely related to the leverage theory is the argument that a tying arrangement can raise entry barriers in the market for either the tying or the tied product. For example, suppose a newspaper company publishes both a morning newspaper and an evening newspaper.

accrue to the jarmaker. By manufacturing lids and selling them herself the jar monopolist will be able to transfer this 20¢ in monopoly profits to herself.

3. For example, see Bowman, Tying Arrangements and the Leverage Problem, 67 Yale L.J. 19 (1957); Markovits, Tie-ins, Leverage, and the American Antitrust Laws, 80 Yale L.J. 195 (1970); R. Bork, The Antitrust Paradox: A Policy at War With Itself 365–81 (1978).

4. For example, Hirsh v. Martindale-Hubbell, Inc., 674 F.2d 1343, 1349 n. 19 (9th Cir. 1982), cert. denied ___ U.S. ___, 103 S.Ct. 305 (1982).

5. For example, Sandles v. Ruben, 89 F.R.D. 635 (S.D.Fla.1981); Martino v. McDonald's Sys., 86 F.R.D. 145 (N.D.Ill. 1980).

A second firm attempts to enter the market with an evening newspaper. The incumbent firm responds by engaging in "unit pricing": requiring all purchasers of advertising in its morning paper to buy an identical advertisement in the evening paper. The unit pricing scheme will foreclose the new entrant from advertisers who want to advertise in the morning, because they will be required to place their evening advertising in the incumbent's evening newspaper instead of the competitor's.[1]

Many tying arrangement cases in which the plaintiff and defendant are competitors are brought under a foreclosure theory like this one. In Heatransfer Corp. v. Volkswagenwerk, A.G.,[2] the Fifth Circuit condemned an arrangement under which an automobile manufacturer required its distributors and retail dealers to use their "best efforts" to sell Volkswagen's own air conditioners rather than those of competitors, which included the plaintiff. The Fifth Circuit decided that the plaintiff, which manufactured air conditioners suitable for installation in new Volkswagens, was illegally foreclosed from the market for Volkswagen air conditioners.

The theory that tying arrangements raise barriers to entry is generally susceptible of the same criticisms that can be raised against all "entry barrier" arguments: namely, the fact that something is an entry barrier says nothing about whether it is socially harmful or beneficial.[3] Efficiency itself is a remarkably strong barrier to entry. Suppose the daily newspaper can show that by forcing all advertisers to buy space in both morning and evening newspapers it can print identical advertising sections in the two newspapers and thereby set type once instead of twice. The largest cost of running an advertisement is the cost of setting the type. The cost saving can be realized, however, only if *all* purchasers of advertising advertise in both the morning and evening editions. Unit pricing may permit the incumbent to sell an advertisement in both newspapers together for $7.00, while the potential entrant must charge $5.00 for the evening advertising alone. The "barrier to entry" results from the lower cost of the unit pricing scheme.[4]

If the tie-in is inefficient no barrier to entry will result. Suppose that a monopoly manufacturer of bolts requires customers to purchase one nut with each bolt. Bolts would sell in a competitive market for 25¢, and nuts for 10¢. Because of inefficiencies in

§ 8.5

1. See Kansas City Star Co. v. U.S., 240 F.2d 643 (8th Cir. 1957), cert. denied, 354 U.S. 923, 77 S.Ct. 1381 (1957). See Turner, The Validity of Tying Arrangements Under the Antitrust Laws, 72 Harv.L.Rev. 50, 63 (1958).

2. 553 F.2d 964 (5th Cir. 1977), cert. denied, 434 U.S. 1087, 98 S.Ct. 1282 (1978).

3. See R. Bork, The Antitrust Paradox: A Policy at War With Itself 310–29 (1978); Demsetz, Barriers to Entry, 72 Amer.Econ.Rev. 47 (1982); Schmalensee, Economies of Scale and Barriers to Entry, 89 J.Pol.Econ. 1228 (1981).

4. See Record at 1127–29, Times-Picayune Pub. Co. v. U.S., 345 U.S. 594, 73 S.Ct. 872 (1953). The case is discussed in § 8.9 below.

production, however, the seller must charge 38¢ for the package. No barriers to entry will result. It will still be profitable for an efficient bolt manufacturer to enter the bolt market alone, and for an efficient nut manufacturer to enter the nut market alone. On the other hand, if the bolt monopolist's tie reduces the cost of a bolt-nut package, then a single entrant will have to enter both the bolt market and nut market simultaneously in order to achieve the same efficiencies. Even in this case, however, the mere requirement of two-level entry is not a "barrier" unless economies of scale are substantially different at one level than they are at the other.[5]

The entry barrier argument may have some force when the seller is a statutory monopolist and ties a product which does not have legal monopoly protection. For example, the telephone company, which has a legally protected monopoly in its lines, may require all lessees of its lines to rent a telephone instrument from the telephone company as well. The result will be to create an effective barrier to entry into the market for the tied product. Such a scheme will be profitable to the telephone company if it can use it to "cheat" on its regulated price. Such tying arrangements in price-regulated industries are discussed in the following section.

 WESTLAW REFERENCES
digest(barrier /3 entry)

§ 8.6   Tying Arrangements in Price-Regulated Markets

Many firms are required by law to sell their products or services at a specified price. The price is usually calculated by a public regulatory agency to give the firm a "fair" rate of return on the basis of information provided by the firm itself.[1]

Price-regulated firms generally have stockholders, pay dividends, and seek to maximize their profits. Sometimes they can increase their profits by avoiding the price regulation. If the regulated price is lower than the unregulated profit-maximizing price, as is often the case in public utilities, then the seller may tie an unregulated product or service to the regulated one. If the regulated price is higher than the unregulated profit-maximizing price, as was the case during price regulation of airline fares, then the seller may try to avoid the price regulation by throwing in some additional good or service at less than its market value.

Most litigated tie-in cases in price-regulated industries are of the first sort: the tie-in acts as a "leverage" device to enable the seller to obtain more net profit than the price regulation would permit. For

---

5. The tying arrangement in this case would have the same effect as vertical integration by the monopolist. See § 5.6 above.

§ 8.6

1. See generally S. Breyer, Regulation and its Reform (1982).

example, if the profit-maximizing price of a monthly telephone line subscription is $12.00, but a regulatory authority limits the phone company's price to $8.00, the telephone company might require all lessees of its lines to rent their equipment from the phone company as well, and build a $4.00 monopoly overcharge into the price of the equipment. In this case a version of the leverage theory works: the phone company makes more profits by adding an unregulated monopoly to a regulated monopoly and thereby evading the regulation.[2]

Public utilities are ideal candidates for such tying arrangements. First, most of them are natural monopolies, or are thought to be. Their monopoly status is often protected by statute. Second, most public utilities have very low marginal costs and very low elasticities of demand at a marginal cost price. Most people would be willing to pay considerably more for electricity and telephone service than the marginal cost of providing it. The result is that the profit-maximizing price for a telephone or electricity subscription is often much higher than the regulated price.

Tie-ins in price-regulated monopolies can injure two groups of people: competitors and consumers. Competitors are injured because the tying product is a monopoly and the tie-in effectively turns the tied product into a monopoly as well. If a telephone line monopoly requires all subscribers to lease telephones from itself, then the market for competing sellers of telephones vanishes.[3]

Such tie-ins can also injure consumers, for the reasons outlined above. A few consumers are injured because the tie-in pushes the price of the service above their reservation price and they substitute away. The majority are injured, however, because they continue to buy the service, effectively paying more than the competitive price.

Tie-ins in price-regulated industries are not necessarily inefficient. First of all, marginal cost pricing is inappropriate in many natural monopolies because marginal costs are low in comparison with capital costs. Most regulated industries have legal rates that are substantially higher than short-run marginal cost. However resources are generally used most efficiently when they are priced at marginal cost. Once the telephone system is in place, for example, the marginal cost of serving one subscriber signals properly the resources that will be consumed in serving him. As a result, most utilities engage in various forms of price discrimination: people who will pay no more

2. See Litton Systems, Inc. v. Amer. Tel. & Tel. Co., 700 F.2d 785, 790–91 (2d Cir.1983), cert. denied, ___ U.S. ___, 104 S.Ct. 984 (1983); Cantor v. Detroit Edison Co., 428 U.S. 579, 96 S.Ct. 3110 (1976). See also O. Williamson, Markets and Hierarchies: Analysis and Antitrust Implications 113–15 (1975).

3. See Phonetele, Inc. v. Amer. Tel. & Tel. Co., 664 F.2d 716 (9th Cir. 1981),

cert. denied, 459 U.S. 1145, 103 S.Ct. 785 (1983). For a good discussion of the various tying arrangements, used by the telephone company, which have effectively restricted entry into the otherwise competitive markets for terminal equipment, see Fuhr, Competition in the Terminal Equipment Market after *Carterfone*, 28 Antitrust Bull. 669 (1983).

than marginal cost pay it, but people who place a higher value on the service are charged a higher price.[4] One way to facilitate such price discrimination is through various tying arrangements. For example, some phone companies offer so-called "life-line" service—a single black dial telephone and the right to make ten calls per month—at a very low monthly charge. More exotic service—push buttons, multi-phone installations, answering devices, and call-forwarding services—cost more money, often much more than the additional cost of providing the service. Most such price discrimination is explicitly sanctioned by the regulatory authority.

Tie-ins in price-regulated markets can also result in increased output and arguably better overall use of resources. This often occurs if the regulated price is *higher* than the seller's profit-maximizing price. For example, during the days of price regulation in the airline industry many fares were set so high that empty seats and excessive flights resulted. If a firm found a way to avoid the price regulation—for example, by selling the air ticket at the regulat-ed price but throwing in a rental car at no additional cost—it might actually benefit everyone except competitors: the airline makes an even higher profit, output is increased, and customers effectively pay a lower price.[5] The rental car in this case is the tying product and the airline ticket the tied product: presumably the airline will not give a free rental car to someone who does not purchase an airline ticket.

Upholding the tie-in in such circumstances is tantamount to legal-izing price regulation avoidance.[6] The regulatory authority has es-tablished a fare under a policy given by some sovereign. The regulated firm should not be permitted to avoid the price regulation even if avoidance would be more efficient by free market standards.

 WESTLAW REFERENCES
carterfone

§ 8.7   Tie-ins and Predatory Pricing

Dominant firms generally engage in predatory pricing by lower-ing the price of their product below its marginal cost. They can accomplish the same purpose, however, by maintaining the price but providing an additional product or service at no additional charge or

---

4. Such price discrimination, common in regulated utilities, is called "Ramsey pricing." See Ramsey, A Contribution to the Theory of Taxation, 37 Econ. Journal 47 (Mar., 1927); see also Baumol & Bradford, Optimal Departures from Marginal Cost Pricing, 60 Amer.Econ. Rev. 265 (1970); R. Schmalensee, The Control of Natural Monopolies 39–40 (1979).

5. See Robert's Waikiki U-Drive, Inc. v. Budget Rent-A-Car Sys., 491 F.Supp. 1199 (D. Hawaii 1980), judgment af-firmed, 732 F.2d 1403 (9th Cir. 1984).

6. In the *Robert's* case, Id., 732 F.2d at 1406, the court noted that the Civil Aeronautics Board had found the defen-dant's activity to be improper rate regu-lation avoidance.

at some price less than cost. The price for the resulting combination is predatory under the Areeda-Turner test if it is less than average variable cost.[1] For example, a computer manufacturer might try to drive a competitor out of business by providing software with its computers at no additional charge.[2] In this case, the software is the tying product and the computer is the tied product: the predator will give free software only to someone who also buys its computer.

Such predatory pricing schemes are generally unsuitable for litigation as illegal tie-ins. Competitors are injured by the package only if the net price is predatory, and they have a cause of action for predatory pricing.[3] Consumers are injured not by the attractively priced package but by the monopoly prices that will result after the rival has been driven out of business. They more appropriately have a cause of action for illegal attempt to monopolize.

 WESTLAW REFERENCES
"predatory pricing" /p tie tying

§ 8.8   Tie-ins as Price Discrimination and Metering Devices

Sellers often use tying arrangements to facilitate price discrimination.[1] Courts have discovered this only recently, however[2], and the presence of price discrimination has generally been irrelevant to judicial analysis or determination of legality.

Although price discrimination can be very profitable, it is often difficult for sellers to accomplish for three reasons. First, certain forms of it are illegal under the Robinson-Patman Act,[3] which prevents the sale of the same product at two different prices. Second, in order to price discriminate a seller must identify and segregate different groups of customers for whom the elasticity of demand differs. That is, the seller must be able to distinguish in some

§ 8.7

1. See the discussion of predatory pricing in § 6.8.

2. See Symbolic Control, Inc. v. IBM Corp., 643 F.2d 1339, 1341 (9th Cir. 1980).

3. For example, in *Symbolic Control*, Id., the allegation was predatory pricing, not tying. Furthermore, there was neither allegation nor evidence that IBM had market power in the software, which would have constituted the tying product.

§ 8.8

1. See Bowman, Tying Arrangements and the Leverage Problem, 67 Yale L.J. 19 (1957); Markovits, Tie-ins and Reciprocity: A Functional, Legal and Policy Analysis, 58 Tex.L.Rev. 1363,

1407–10 (1980); Posner, Exclusionary Practices and the Antitrust Laws, 41 U.Chi.L.Rev. 506, 506–15 (1974). Price discrimination is discussed in chapter thirteen below.

2. See United States Steel Corp. v. Fortner Enter., 429 U.S. 610, 616 n.7, 97 S.Ct. 861, 866 n.7 (1977) (Fortner II); Fortner Enter., Inc. v. United States Steel Corp., 394 U.S. 495, 513, 89 S.Ct. 1252, 1264 (1969) (Fortner I) (White, J., dissenting); Hirsh v. Martindale-Hubbell, Inc., 674 F.2d 1343, 1349 (9th Cir. 1982), cert. denied, 459 U.S. 973, 103 S.Ct. 305 (1982); Moore v. Jas. H. Matthews & Co., 550 F.2d 1207, 1213 (9th Cir. 1977), appeal after remand 682 F.2d 830 (9th Cir. 1982).

3. 15 U.S.C.A. § 13. See chap. thirteen.

relatively low-cost way buyers who place a high value on the seller's product from buyers who place a much lower value on it but are still willing to pay a price that is profitable to the seller. Finally, the seller must be able to prevent arbitrage, which occurs when favored purchasers (those charged a lower price) resell the product to disfavored purchasers (those charged a higher price).

A seller can solve all three problems by using a variable proportion tying arrangement, in which different customers use different amounts of the tied product. For example, a seller of patented mimeograph machines might believe that a buyer planning to make 10,000 copies per week will place a higher value on the machine than a buyer intending to make only 1,000 copies per week. The seller sells the machine subject to a condition that all purchasers buy their mimeograph paper from the seller as well.[4] The seller prices the machine at the competitive level or perhaps even lower. However, the seller charges a high price for the paper. If the rate of return on the machine itself is 5% and the rate of return on the paper is 40%, the seller's net rate of return will be much higher from the 10,000 copy per week user than from the 1000 copy user.[5]

The variable proportion tying arrangement does not violate the Robinson-Patman Act, which applies only when the same product is sold to two different buyers at two different prices. Here, all machines are sold at the same price and all paper at the same price. Second, the tie-in makes identification of high demand and low demand customers easy: the variable use by the customers in practice tracks the value they place on the machine. Third, arbitrage will not work because there is no "spread" between the price of either machine or paper to favored and disfavored purchasers.

A seller must generally have market power in order to price discriminate. If the seller is a competitor, disfavored purchasers— those asked to pay a supracompetitive price—will go to a different seller. Many courts analyzing variable proportion tie-ins have wasted their time trying to decide whether the defendant had market power in the tying product.[6] In most variable proportion ties the fact of the tie establishes the defendant's market power.[7]

---

4. See Henry v. A.B. Dick Co., 224 U.S. 1, 32 S.Ct. 364 (1912).

5. Suppose the machine is priced at $1,000 and lasts one fifty-week year. Profits on the machine are $50.00, or $1.00 per week. Paper is priced at 1¢ per sheet, of which 40% is profit. The profits from the 1,000 sheet-per-week user will be $4.00 on paper and $1.00 on the machine, per week. The profits from the 10,000 sheet-per-week user will be $40.00 on paper and $1.00 on the machine, per week. The net rate of return on sales in the first case is about 17%, and in the second about 34%.

6. For example, see Siegel v. Chicken Delight, Inc., 448 F.2d 43 (9th Cir. 1971), cert. denied, 405 U.S. 955, 92 S.Ct. 1172 (1972), where the tie-in was expressly used for purpose of price discrimination, but the court nevertheless based its finding of sufficient market power on the defendant's trademark in the tying product. See § 8.3 above.

7. Not all variable proportion ties are price discrimination devices, however; so any presumption of market power ought to be rebuttable. One exception is when the tie-in is merely a metering device to measure the wear and tear

Should tie-ins designed to achieve price discrimination be illegal? A monopolist may legally charge its nondiscriminatory profit-maximizing price. An antitrust policy based on economic efficiency would condemn such price discrimination only if its social costs are higher than the social cost of the single monopoly price. Some commentators argue that price discrimination is preferable because it results in higher output than nondiscriminatory monopoly pricing.[8] This argument applies only to perfect price discrimination, however—that is, price discrimination in which every buyer pays its reservation price for the product. "Imperfect" price discrimination, which is the only kind that exists in the real world, does not necessarily result in increased output and sometimes the output may be even less than it is under nondiscriminatory monopoly pricing. The effect of imperfect price discrimination on output can be a fairly complex empirical question.

However, a variable proportion tie-in can come as close to perfect price discrimination as any real world arrangement. Often the circumstances of a variable proportion tie-in suggest that it results in larger output than nondiscriminatory monopoly pricing would. In Siegel v. Chicken Delight, Inc., for example, the tying product, a license for the defendant's trademark and the right to use its method of doing business, was given to franchisees at no charge.[9] They paid a supracompetitive price, however, for the tied products: breading, spices, cooking equipment and other things necessary for running a fast-food fried chicken take-out.

Such an arrangement will result in more franchises, and thus larger output, than will result from nondiscriminatory pricing. Once the Chicken Delight trademark and method of doing business have

imposed on the tying product. See the text following note 11. Sometimes variable proportion ties are used for efficiency reasons, such as protection of the seller's or lessor's equipment or goodwill. For example, in International Salt Co. v. United States, 332 U.S. 392, 68 S.Ct. 12 (1947) the defendants argued that the tying of salt to its patented salt injecting machines was designed to ensure that the machines functioned properly: they would break down if used with inferior grades of salt. The Supreme Court rejected the argument and condemned the arrangement. The defendants were probably correct, however, for their contract permitted lessees of the machine to purchase salt from a competitor if the competitor offered equally good salt at a lower price that the defendant would not match. 332 U.S. at 396–97, 68 S.Ct. at 15. Tie-ins work as price discrimination devices only if the seller or lessor charges a monopoly price in the tied product. See

Peterman, The *International Salt* Case, 22 J.L. & Econ. 351 (1979). The efficiency or "goodwill" defense was also raised and rejected in IBM Corp. v. U.S., 298 U.S. 131, 56 S.Ct. 701 (1936), where IBM was accused of tying paper tabulating cards to its patented computation machines.

In most variable proportion tie-in cases the tied product is something readily obtainable on the open market (for example, salt, spices, ice cream, leaseholds, gasoline, tires, or paper cards). A useful legal rule would be that a variable proportion tie-in creates a presumption of market power in the tying product, which can be rebutted by a showing that the defendant sells the tied product at the prevailing market price.

8. See R. Bork, The Antitrust Paradox: A Policy at War With Itself 394–98 (1978).

9. *Chicken Delight*, note 6 above, 448 F.2d at 46–47.

been established, the marginal cost of licensing it to one additional franchisee is extremely low—perhaps zero, except for transaction costs. On the other hand, the franchisor has significant sunk costs invested in developing its name and trademark; furthermore, it is probably a monopolist in those products. The franchisor's nondiscriminatory profit-maximizing price might well be $100,000 in fees per franchise. A franchise that did only enough business to be able to pay $10,000, however, would still be profitable to the franchisor— even $10,000 in franchise fees would exceed the marginal cost of licensing the franchise.

Price discrimination by tie-in is common in franchise agreements.[10] By price discriminating the franchisor takes advantage of the fact that some franchise locations are far more profitable than others— but that almost any location profitable enough to keep the franchisee in business will also be profitable to the franchisor. The result of the variable proportion tie is that the $10,000 franchise, which would not exist at all if the franchisor charged each franchisee its nondiscriminatory profit-maximizing price, can be profitable to both franchisee and franchisor. Consumers will also be better off.[11] Those injured by such a scheme are the very successful franchisees who, because of the price discrimination, are forced to pay more than the franchisor's nondiscriminatory profit-maximizing price.

Not all variable proportion ties are used for price discrimination. The tie may simply be a metering device, designed to measure costs that vary with intensity of use. To use the mimeograph machine and paper as an example, if wear and tear on a lessor's machine varies directly with the number of copies the machine makes, a lessor of the machine can use a tie-in of the paper to meter the costs that the lessee's use imposes on the lessor. There is no price discrimination if the price of the paper is calculated precisely to cover the wear and tear caused by each use.

Finally, some economists have argued that even fixed proportion tie-ins can serve as price discrimination devices. In a fixed proportion tie the ratio between the amount of the tied product and tying product is constant: a single left shoe with a single right shoe, one bolt with one nut, one grave site with one tombstone. Fixed proportion ties are not conducive to price discrimination in the way that

10. For example, Kypta v. McDonald's Corp., 671 F.2d 1282 (11th Cir. 1982), cert. denied, 459 U.S. 857, 103 S.Ct. 127 (1982) (tying the franchise license to a variable-rate rental of the franchise location); Krehl v. Baskin-Robbins Ice Cream Co., 664 F.2d 1348 (9th Cir. 1982) (in which the tied product was ice cream); Bogosian v. Gulf Oil Corp., 561 F.2d 434 (3d Cir. 1977), cert. denied, 434 U.S. 1086, 98 S.Ct. 1280 (1978); Ungar v. Dunkin' Donuts of America, Inc., 531 F.2d 1211 (3d Cir. 1976), cert. denied, 429 U.S. 823, 97 S.Ct. 74 (1976); see generally, Harkins, Tying and the Franchisee, 47 A.B.A. Antitrust L.J. 903 (1978).

11. See generally, Hovenkamp, Tying Arrangements and Class Actions, 36 Vand.L.Rev. 214 (1983). Rubin, The Theory of the Firm and the Structure of the Franchise Contract, 21 J.L. & Econ. 223 (1978).

variable proportion ties are; however, a kind of price discrimination can result when package sales are made to purchasers who place differential values on the components of the package.

The classic example is "block-booking" in the film rental industry. Suppose that television stations A and B want to rent Hollywood films from Q. Q's inventory includes *Casablanca* and *Robinson Crusoe on Mars.* Stations A and B have different audiences, who have somewhat different tastes in films. Station A values *Casablanca* at $7,000 and *Crusoe* at $3,000. Station B values *Casablanca* at $4,000 and *Crusoe* at $6,000. Q wants to maximize its profits.

Q can rent *Casablanca* once at $7,000 to A and *Crusoe* once at $6,000 to B, and its total revenues will be $13,000. Alternatively, Q can lower the price and rent both movies to both stations. It can rent *Casablanca* to both stations at $4,000 each and *Crusoe* to both stations at $3,000 each. In that case its total revenue will be $14,000.

Finally, Q can package, or "block" the two films and offer the package at $10,000. Since A is willing to pay $7,000 for *Casablanca* and $3,000 for *Crusoe*, A will buy the package. Since B is willing to pay $4,000 for *Casablanca* and $6,000 for *Crusoe*, B will also buy. Q's revenues now shoot up to $20,000. Whether or not this is "price discrimination" depends on one's definition. If one looks at the seller's rate of return on each sale there is no discrimination. The seller obtains $20,000 from each sale and presumably the cost of delivering the package to each of the two stations is the same. On the other hand the two stations will assign different values to each film in the package. From their viewpoint Q may be price discriminating. Economists have been content to call this "simulated price discrimination." [12]

 WESTLAW REFERENCES
price /3 discriminat*** /p tie tying

§ 8.9   Tie-Ins and Efficiency: The Two-Product Test

Most forced package sales are the product of simple efficiency. For example, the retail grocery business would come to a standstill if every purchaser were legally entitled to buy one egg instead of a dozen, half a jar of jam without the other half, or dressed geese without their gizzards.

The legal test for tie-ins, however, never explicitly takes efficiency into account. This is unfortunate because a mechanical application of

12. See Stigler, United States v. Loew's, Inc.: A Note on Block-Booking, 1963 Sup.Ct.Rev. 152 (1963); Markovits, Tie-ins, Reciprocity, and the Leverage Theory, 76 Yale L.J. 1397, 1454–58 (1967).

the test can lead a court to condemn an efficient arrangement.[1] However, creative courts have manipulated the judicial test to make it distinguish efficient from inefficient forced combination sales.

First, the test requires the plaintiff to show the defendant's market power in the tying product market. Market power makes an inefficient tie-in plausible: if the seller had no market power, someone who did not want the tied product would buy the tying product from a competitor.

Even a seller with market power can use ties efficiently, however. Therefore courts additionally require that the tie-in combine "separate" tying and tied products. "Separate products" is a legal term of art. Virtually everyone agrees that a pair of shoes is a single product, as is a coat and its buttons or a goose and its gizzard. But how about classified advertising in a morning newspaper and an evening newspaper? In the *Times-Picayune* case [2] the Supreme Court decided that it was legal for a newspaper to require advertisers to buy space in both its morning and evening newspapers simultaneously, because advertising in the two were all part of a single product, "readership."

Justice Clark's identification of access to readers as the single product being sold in *Times-Picayune* confused rather than clarified his analysis. Clark never defined "readership"; however, he was quite impressed by the fact that when the sale of morning and evening advertising was combined into a single transaction most of the costs of running an advertisement—soliciting, billing and, most importantly, setting type—were performed only once instead of twice. The newspaper could lower the cost of advertising by running identical advertising sections in its morning and evening newspapers.[3]

The efficiencies that can be generated by forced combined sales can be broadly grouped into two kinds, transactional, and productive or technological. The sale of shoes only in pairs is a good example of a transactional efficiency. Presumably shoes cannot be manufactured more cheaply in pairs than by the piece. However, they can be distributed and sold far more cheaply in pairs. The vast majority of customers buy shoes in pairs. If a store had to offer a solitary left shoe to the occasional customer who wanted one it would be stuck with the right shoe, and a very long wait until another customer came along who wanted a right shoe of the same size and style. The shoe store would probably return it or order a new mate for it. If the additional costs generated by these extra maneuvers are greater than

---

§ 8.9

1. See § 8.3 above.

2. Times-Picayune Pub. Co. v. U.S., 345 U.S. 594, 613, 73 S.Ct. 872, 883 (1953).

3. Id. See also Fortner Enter., Inc. v. United States Steel Corp., (Fortner I),

394 U.S. 495, 514 n. 9, 89 S.Ct. 1252, 1264 n. 9 (1969), J. White, dissenting, observing that "if the tied and tying products are functionally related, they may reduce costs through economies of joint production and distribution."

half the cost of a pair of shoes, it would be more efficient to force the one-legged purchaser to take a pair, even if he throws the left shoe away. If the purchaser were legally entitled to take a single left shoe at half the price of a pair, however, any added transaction costs would be shared by all other customers. Collectively they would be injured by a greater amount than the one-legged purchaser would be benefitted.

Many franchising arrangements are also methods for improving the efficiency of the franchisor's distribution scheme. Franchises can be divided into two broad categories. In one the franchisor's primary business is the sale of franchises. The *Chicken Delight* case involved such a franchise.[4] The franchisor did not grow or fry chickens or produce any product identifiable as "Chicken Delight" except the trademark and method of doing business itself. In such franchises the chief purpose of any tying arrangement in the franchise contract is price discrimination.

In the second kind of franchise agreement the franchisor is the manufacturer of a product and the franchise is an integral part of the franchisor's distribution scheme.[5] For example, Baskin-Robbins Ice Cream Co. produces not only the Baskin-Robbins trademark. It also produces ice cream, which it distributes through independently owned franchises. In this case the franchise system creates a set of clearly recognizable retail outlets that customers have learned to identify with a certain kind of ice cream. For them "Baskin-Robbins ice cream" is distinctive. The franchise system is an effective substitute for outright manufacturer ownership of its stores.[6] Several courts have held that in such "distribution system" franchises the trademark and the good distributed by the franchise are a single "product," and there is no illegal tie-in.[7]

Forced package sales can also be the result of technological innovation or manufacturing processes that make it cheaper to produce two products together instead of one. The typesetting in the *Times-Picayune* case above is an example of such a technological efficiency, but there are others. For a long time the elements of electronic computers, such as central processing units and disk drives, were manufactured in separate boxes and connected to each

---

4. See Siegel v. Chicken Delight, Inc., discussed in § 8.8 above.

5. There is a third type of franchise in which the *franchisee* actually produces the product, according to detailed specifications provided by the franchisor. Products as diverse as mattresses and soft drinks are manufactured under such arrangements. See U.S. v. Sealy, Inc., 388 U.S. 350, 87 S.Ct. 1847 (1967); Sulmeyer v. Coca Cola Co., 515 F.2d 835 (5th Cir. 1975), cert. denied, 424 U.S. 934, 96 S.Ct. 1148 (1976).

6. Such distribution schemes are sometimes treated as exclusive dealing arrangements. The line between tying arrangements and exclusive dealing is often difficult to locate. See § 8.12 below.

7. Krehl v. Baskin-Robbins Ice Cream Co., 664 F.2d 1348, 1354 (9th Cir. 1982); see McCarthy, Trademark Franchising and Antitrust: the Trouble with Tie-ins, 58 Calif.L.Rev. 1085, 1108 (1970).

other with cables. They could be sold separately, and were often sold by competing sellers. In the 1960's and 1970's IBM Corp. developed new computer technology with more compact circuitry. Many of the peripheral devices were then placed in the same metal box with the data processing unit itself. When IBM combined a data processing unit and a disk drive memory in the same container they necessarily were sold as a unit. The effect was to injure small companies that had been in the business of manufacturing only the peripheral devices, for connection to IBM processing units.[8] In such cases the "tying arrangement" is not imposed contractually, but technologically. As a result some commentators have dubbed these arrangements "physical tie-ins." Courts have been sceptical about condemning such "tie-ins," noting that a rule prohibiting them could deter research and development.[9] No court could possibly balance the social losses that a forced combination sale may impose against potential social gains. It must use short cuts and make inferences. Any demonstrated cost reduction that results from the way an arrangement of items is manufactured or sold should create an inference that the combination is a single product. Such "tie-ins" should be legal, even if the seller is a monopolist.[10]

---

8. See ILC Peripherals Leasing Corp. v. IBM Corp., 448 F.Supp. 228 (N.D. Cal. 1978), decision affirmed, 636 F.2d 1188 (9th Cir. 1980), cert. denied, 452 U.S. 972, 101 S.Ct. 3126 (1981); see also Anderson Foreign Motors v. New England Toyota Distrib., 475 F.Supp. 973 (D. Mass.1979). Many such cases are brought as attempts to monopolize under § 2 of the Sherman Act, 15 U.S.C.A. § 2. Other cases are discussed in Note, An Economic and Legal Analysis of Physical Tie-ins, 89 Yale L.J. 769 (1980).

9. See Foremost Pro Color v. Eastman Kodak Co., 703 F.2d 534 (9th Cir. 1983), cert. denied, ___ U.S. ___, 104 S.Ct. 1315 (1984), refusing to find an illegal tie-in in Kodak's introduction of a new camera and new film. Only the new Kodak film was compatible with the new camera, and the result was that purchasers of the new camera were required to use Kodak's film. However, purchasers of the new camera did not expressly "agree" to buy only Kodak film. The Ninth Circuit held that the law of tie-ins requires a sale of one product only on the contractual condition that the buyer take a second product as well. Further, it held that any rule condemning such "technological ties" could "unjustifiably deter the development and introduction of those new technologies so essential to the contin-

ued progress of our economy." Id. at 542–43.

Such a technological tie-in could be used for price discrimination. For example, if Kodak charged a monopoly price for the film, a serious photographer who used 10 rolls of film per week would be far more profitable to Kodak than a photographer who used only one roll per month.

10. See Jefferson Parish Hosp. Dist. No. 2 v. Hyde, ___ U.S. ___, 104 S.Ct. 1551, 1573 (1984), J. O'Connor, concurring: "When the economic advantages of joint packaging are substantial the package is not appropriately viewed as two products, and that should be the end of the tying inquiry." However, Justice O'Connor went on to conclude that "since anesthesia [the alleged tied product] is a service useful to consumers only when purchased in conjunction with hospital services [the tying product], the arrangement is not properly characterized as a tie between distinct products." Under such a rule all package sales of complimentary products—products that must be consumed together—would be viewed as sales of single products. Justice O'Connor's proposal would effectively wipe out three-fourths of the law of tying arrangements, for most involve complimentary products: for example, IBM v. U.S., 298 U.S. 131, 56 S.Ct. 701

WESTLAW REFERENCES
two-product /5 test /p tie tying

§ 8.10   Coercion

The current judicial test for tying arrangements described in § 8.1 does a poor job of accounting for the economic functions of tying arrangements in sellers' distribution schemes. The test is not well designed to enable a court to determine whether a particular tie-in is socially harmful. Whether it is used for price discrimination, metering, or rate regulation avoidance is all but irrelevant to the formal judicial analysis. At the same time, the test has mired countless courts in analysis of issues that are not central to the economic functions of tie-ins and their potential for injury. For example, some courts have become obsessed with the so-called "individual coercion" doctrine.

The term "coercion" seems innocuous enough. Coercion is at the heart of most exclusionary practices. As the Second Circuit stated most simply, "* * * there can be no illegal tie unless unlawful coercion by the seller influences the buyer's choice."[1] However, the coercion doctrine has become a bugbear in tie-in analysis.[2] "Coercion" has been used by courts in tie-in cases to mean several things: 1) whether purchasers were actually forced to take the tied product as a condition of taking the tying product, or had the option of taking the tying product alone; 2) whether the defendant-seller had market power in the market for the tying product; 3) whether a particular purchaser would have taken the tied product anyway, and therefore was not injured by being "forced" to take it; 4) whether the tie-in foreclosed other options that the customer would have exercised but for the tying arrangement.

The first meaning of "coercion" is more appropriately a question of evidence than of the economic structure of a tying arrangement.

(1936) (computers and computer cards); International Salt Co. v. U.S., 332 U.S. 392, 68 S.Ct. 12 (1947) (salt injecting machines and salt); Siegel v. Chicken Delight, Inc., 448 F.2d 43 (9th Cir. 1971), cert. denied, 405 U.S. 955, 92 S.Ct. 1172 (1972) (a fast-food franchise and various cooking appliances and ingredients).

The most sophisticated judicial discussion of the relationship between economic efficiency and the two-product test for tying arrangements appears in Jack Walters & Sons Corp. v. Morton Bldg., Inc., 737 F.2d 698 (7th Cir. 1984). Judge Posner held that two items should be considered a single product under the law of tying arrangements if there were "rather obvious economies of joint provi-

sion." Id. at 703. The court then held that a manufacturer's prefabricated building kits and its trademark were not separate products.

§ 8.10

1. American Mfs. Mut. Ins. Co. v. Amer. Broadcasting-Paramount Theatres, Inc., 446 F.2d 1131, 1137 (2d Cir. 1971), cert. denied, 404 U.S. 1063, 92 S.Ct. 737 (1972).

2. See Matheson, Class Action Tying Cases: A Framework for Certification Decisions, 76 Northwestern U.L.Rev. 855 (1982); Austin, The Individual Coercion Doctrine in Tie-In Analysis: Confusing and Irrelevant, 65 Calif.L.Rev. 1143 (1977).

If a customer for item A is free to take or refuse item B as he pleases, there is no tie-in and there should be no liability. At the other extreme, if all purchasers of item A must also take item B there is coercion, or "conditioning," in this sense. In the middle are several possibilities. One, which arises often in class actions, concerns transactions that are individually negotiated by class members, some of whom received more pressure from the seller than others to take the tied product, depending on the economic position of each purchaser-class member. In such cases the fact of coercion must be answered on an individual basis, and most courts have properly refused class certification.[3]

Some courts infer coercion, or conditioning, from an explicit contractual provision requiring purchase of the tied product.[4] Other courts have refused to infer coercion if there is no such explicit contractual provision.[5] No basis exists in reason or economics, however, for the Sixth Circuit's broad rule that coercion, or conditioning is not "an element of an illegal tying arrangement" if the contract explicitly provides for the purchase of both tying and tied products. By that reasoning a contract to purchase "one thousand bolts and one thousand nuts" eliminates any need for the plaintiff to prove coercion, in spite of the fact that the plaintiff wanted to buy the nuts and bolts in the same transaction. The evidence in the Sixth Circuit case suggested as much.[6]

Another sort of conditioning occurs when the tie-in appears not as an absolute requirement, but as a discount or other favorable term to a customer who takes two products together. In such cases there is ample "coercion." If product A is $10.00 purchased alone but only $6.00 purchased with product B, coercion exists just as much as if all purchasers of A must also take B.[7]

The second "coercion" question—whether the seller has market power in the tying product market—is a good one: a perfect competitor could not coerce any buyer into taking anything. Although market power is a necessary condition for inefficient coercion, howev-

3. Federal Rule of Civil Procedure 23(b)(3), which governs most class actions in antitrust cases, requires that the "fact" of injury be established by common proof for all class members; otherwise certification is inappropriate. See 7A C. Wright & A. Miller, Federal Practice and Procedure § 1778 (1972); Plekowski v. Ralston Purina Co., 68 F.R.D. 443, 449–51 (M.D.Ga.1975), appeal dismissed, 557 F.2d 1218 (5th Cir. 1977); Matheson Id.; Hovenkamp, Tying Arrangements and Class Actions, 36 Vand.L.Rev. 213 (1983).

4. Bell v. Cherokee Aviation Corp. 660 F.2d 1123, 1131 (6th Cir. 1981); Bogosian v. Gulf Oil Corp., 561 F.2d 434 (3d Cir. 1977), cert. denied, 434 U.S. 1086, 98 S.Ct. 1280 (1978).

5. See Petrolera Caribe, Inc. v. Avis Rental Car Corp., 735 F.2d 636, 638 (1st Cir. 1984); Moore v. Jas. H. Matthews & Co., 550 F.2d 1207, 1212 (9th Cir. 1977), appeal after remand, 682 F.2d 830 (9th Cir. 1982); Response of Carolina, Inc. v. Leasco Response, Inc., 537 F.2d 1307 (5th Cir. 1976).

6. Bell v. Cherokee Aviation Corp., 660 F.2d 1123, 1131 (6th Cir. 1981). See the well-reasoned dissent at pp. 1134–36.

7. United States v. Loew's, Inc., 371 U.S. 38, 50, 83 S.Ct. 97, 104–5 (1962).

er, it is not a sufficient condition. A monopoly shoe seller who sells shoes only in pairs undoubtedly "coerces" the buyer of a right shoe to take a left shoe as well. That sale of shoes in pairs is not illegal for a monopolist, however, just as it is not illegal for a perfect competitor. Unfortunately, some courts have held that the seller's market power in the tying product creates a presumption of coercion.[8] In so doing they overlook the fact that even monopolists (and their customers) can profit from efficiency-creating package sales.

The third and fourth questions are closely related. They look at the tie-in from the buyer's side instead of from the seller's: conceding that the seller imposed the tie, must the buyer show that it was forced to take something it would not have taken anyway? Courts have disagreed about the need for such a showing. The Fifth Circuit explicitly requires it,[9] while the Sixth explicitly rejects the requirement.[10]

The Supreme Court probably put the issue to rest in Jefferson Parish Hosp. Dist. No. 2 v. Hyde, although its analysis is ambiguous.[11] The Court said that tying arrangements warrant condemnation when the seller has sufficient market power "to force a purchaser to do something that he would not do in a competitive market." Furthermore, condemnation would be warranted only if the tie restrains "competition on the merits by forcing purchases that would not otherwise be made." The Court then upheld the hospital-anesthesiologist tie, because there were several other hospitals in the market. As a result, a patient who wanted a different anesthesiologist than the one provided by the defendant could easily seek out an alternative. This analysis appears to require "coercion" under all four meanings listed above.

One thing seems clear: in order to collect damages a plaintiff must prove economic injury. Suppose an auto manufacturer installs heaters in all its cars and refuses to sell a car without a heater. A purchases a car and sues the manufacturer for illegally tying the heater to the car; however, A admits that he would have purchased the installed heater even if he had not been required to do so. A has not been injured, even though the tie-in may be illegal and dozens of other automobile customers may have been injured.

In such cases "coercion" analysis can help a court determine whether a tie-in is really efficient. For example, if 98% of all

---

8. See Tire Sales Corp. v. Cities Serv. Oil Co., 410 F.Supp. 1222, 1227–29 (N.D. Ill.1976), reversed on other grounds 637 F.2d 467 (7th Cir. 1980), cert. denied, 451 U.S. 920, 101 S.Ct. 1999 (1981); Lessig v. Tidewater Oil Co., 327 F.2d 459, 469–70 (9th Cir. 1964), cert. denied, 377 U.S. 993, 84 S.Ct. 1920 (1964).

9. Response of Carolina, Inc. v. Leasco Response, Inc., 537 F.2d 1307, 1327 (5th Cir. 1976); see also, Ungar v. Dunkin' Donuts of America, Inc., 531 F.2d 1211, 1218 (3d Cir. 1976), cert. denied, 429 U.S. 823, 97 S.Ct. 74 (1976).

10. Bell v. Cherokee Aviation Corp., 660 F.2d 1123, 1131 (6th Cir. 1981).

11. ___ U.S. ___, 104 S.Ct. 1551, 1558–59 (1984).

automobile purchasers want factory-installed car heaters while 2% do not, and the transaction costs of special treatment for 2% of the automobiles sold are high, the requirement is probably efficient. The car and the heater are a single "product." In this case a purchaser who would prefer not to have a heater certainly is being "coerced," but his loss is more than offset by the gains that accrue to other customers.

 WESTLAW REFERENCES
coercion /p tie tying

§ 8.11 Reciprocity

Reciprocity, or reciprocal dealing, is the sale or lease of a product on the condition that the seller *purchase* a different product from the buyer. Reciprocity also occurs when a buyer conditions its purchase of one product on the sale of one of its own products to the seller.[1] The spectre of reciprocity has often been raised in merger cases, and the Supreme Court has condemned conglomerate mergers on the theory that they would facilitate reciprocity.[2]

Courts have generally analyzed reciprocity much as they have analyzed tie-ins, under a leverage theory or a foreclosure or barrier to entry theory. For example, in Spartan Grain & Mill Co. v. Ayers, the court held that reciprocity should be judged under the *per se* rule used for tie-ins, because both practices involved "the extension of economic power from one market to another market."[3]

However, the leverage and entry barrier theories of reciprocity are subject to the same criticisms as the corresponding theories of tie-ins. They will not be repeated here.[4] Most firms engage in reciprocity for other reasons, not the least of which is efficiency.

The efficiencies that can be obtained by tie-ins are not as obviously attainable by reciprocity agreements. The products come from different sources and move in the market in opposite directions. Thus there is no opportunity for many of the productive or transactional efficiencies that justify some tying arrangements.

However, reciprocity agreements can be efficient. By merging two sales into a single transaction they can reduce the costs of using the market. Further, they can yield certain efficiencies in distribution. Suppose that Firm A manufactures baseballs and Firm B

§ 8.11

1. See Flinn, Reciprocity and Related Topics Under the Sherman Act, 37 Antitrust L.J. 156 (1968); Hausman, Reciprocal Dealing and the Antitrust Laws, 77 Harv.L.Rev. 873 (1964).

2. FTC v. Consolidated Foods Corp., 380 U.S. 592, 85 S.Ct. 1220 (1965); See

also U.S. v. I.T. & T. Corp., 324 F.Supp. 19 (D.Conn.1970). See § 12.3 below.

3. 581 F.2d 419, 425 (5th Cir. 1978), cert. denied, 444 U.S. 831, 100 S.Ct. 59 (1979). The Ninth Circuit agrees. Betaseed, Inc. v. U and I Inc., 681 F.2d 1203, 1216–17 (9th Cir. 1982).

4. See §§ 8.4–8.5 above.

manufactures baseball bats. Both firms operate retail stores in which baseballs and bats are sold. Firm A and Firm B might save on transportation costs if Firm A can sell a load of baseballs to Firm B, deliver them, and return with a load of bats purchased from Firm B. As a result they might negotiate a contract which conditions A's sale of baseballs on its purchase of bats from B.

Reciprocity may also enable a firm to price discriminate without violating the Robinson-Patman Act. Suppose that a seller has been selling its product at $3.00 and has a chance to make a large profitable sale at $2.70. If the seller made the sale at that price, the disfavored purchasers might have a secondary-line Robinson-Patman action against him.[5] Instead the seller may make the sale at $3.00 but in return buy a product from the customer at a premium price. Likewise, a cartel member can use a reciprocity agreement to "cheat" on the cartel—by selling at the cartel price but agreeing to buy something in return at a supracompetitive price. A similar arrangement will enable a price-regulated firm to cheat on the regulatory statute. Analysis of all these functions of reciprocity agreements is the same as the analysis of tie-ins in the preceding sections.

 WESTLAW REFERENCES
reciproc*** /p leverage foreclosure (barrier /3 entry) "per se"

§ 8.12   Exclusive Dealing

An exclusive dealing arrangement is a contract under which a buyer promises to buy its requirements of one or more products exclusively from a particular seller. Exclusive dealing arrangements have been condemned under § 1 of the Sherman Act and § 3 of the Clayton Act, as well as under § 5 of the FTC Act.[1]

Exclusive dealing arrangements have been disapproved under the same inadequate "foreclosure" theory that courts have applied in vertical merger cases.[2] For example, if independent gasoline retailers agree to buy all their gasoline needs from one refiner and no one else, the stations are "foreclosed" from other gasoline refiners for the duration of their contracts. In Standard Oil Co. of California v. United States (Standard Stations)[3] the Supreme Court found such contracts illegal when they collectively foreclosed 6.8% of the gasoline market to the defendant's competitors and the exclusive dealing arrangements were common in the market. As a result, the actual percentage of independent stations "foreclosed" from the market by *all* refiners was considerably higher.[4]

5. See § 13.6 below.

§ 8.12

1. 15 U.S.C.A. § 45. See FTC v. Brown Shoe Co., 384 U.S. 316, 86 S.Ct. 1501 (1966).

2. See § 7.3 above.

3. 337 U.S. 293, 69 S.Ct. 1051 (1949).

4. Id. at 295, 69 S.Ct. at 1053. Only 1.6% of the retail stations had "split

Did such contracts make the market less competitive? All the arguments against the foreclosure theory presented in chapter seven on vertical integration apply equally to exclusive dealing. The competitive threat, if any, is less in exclusive dealing than in more durable and extensive forms of vertical integration, such as vertical mergers. Unlike mergers, exclusive dealing contracts usually do not govern every aspect of an independent firm's business. Further, exclusive dealing contracts are of limited duration. Every year or five years, depending on the contract term, the supplier must bid anew against competing suppliers.[5]

Justice Frankfurter argued in the *Standard Stations* case that exclusive dealing contracts should be dealt with more leniently than tie-ins. While "[t]ying arrangements serve hardly any purpose beyond the suppression of competition," exclusive dealing arrangements

> may well be of economic advantage to buyers as well as to sellers, and thus indirectly of advantage to the consuming public. In the case of the buyer, they may assure supply, afford protection against rises in price, enable long-term planning on the basis of known costs, and obviate the expense and risk of storage in the quantity necessary for a commodity having a fluctuating demand.[6]

Justice Frankfurter identified precisely the rationale for exclusive dealing contracts in most business situations: not to suppress competition but to make the market perform better in conditions of uncertainty.

However, Justice Frankfurter's distinction between exclusive dealing contracts and tying contracts is elusive. Furthermore, there is no basis for the distinction in the language of § 3 of the Clayton Act. If by contract a retail gasoline dealer is permitted to display the "Standard" emblem and is required to take all its gasoline for resale from Standard Oil Co., should the arrangement be treated as exclusive dealing or as a tie-in? Likewise, if a dealer agrees to purchase all its tires, batteries and other accessories from Standard, as well as all its requirements of gasoline, the accessories appear to be tied to the gasoline and vice-versa. Justice Frankfurter recognized the artificiality of the distinction in the *Standard Stations* case, and had some difficulty deciding whether "exclusive supply provision[s] * * * should perhaps be considered, as a matter of classification,

pumps"—that is, sold gasoline from two or more different refiners.

5. The exclusive dealing contracts in the Standard Stations case were of varying terms. Many, however, were from year-to-year, requiring a 30 day notice by either party for termination. Id. at 296, 69 S.Ct. at 1053. In such cases competitive bidding for the contracts could be substantial, even though a station carried the gasoline of only one supplier at any given time. See U.S. v. El Paso Natural Gas Co., 376 U.S. 651, 84 S.Ct. 1044 (1964), discussed at § 12.4 below.

6. 337 U.S. at 305–6, 69 S.Ct. at 1058.

tying rather than requirements agreements."[7] In most franchise agreements, tie-ins and exclusive dealing arrangements perform the same economic function. Courts have distinguished the two, however, and apply a different test to exclusive dealing, once they have characterized it as such.

The exclusive dealing arrangement stands between the vertical merger and the individual sale as a device for facilitating distribution of a manufacturer's product to the ultimate consumer. Markets are uncertain, some much more uncertain than others.[8] Long-term, flexible contracts can minimize the costs and risks to both parties of dealing with these uncertainties. For example, no retail gasoline dealer knows in advance precisely what its sales will be over some future period. Nor may he have anything approaching reliable information about the status of his suppliers. Some markets are so uncertain that no reasonable investor will build an outlet unless he has advance assurance of a steady source of supply.[9] If summer travel is brisk, the gasoline retailer needs to know that it can obtain enough gasoline, and relying on the spot market for short-notice purchases can be risky and expensive.

The refiner, on the other side, wants a steady outlet for its product. Customers become accustomed to buying a particular brand at a particular location. A customer's ability to know in advance that a particular station carries a brand he prefers makes the customer

---

7. Id. at 305 n. 8, 69 S.Ct. at 1058 n. 8. The chief difference between exclusive dealing and tying, at least in the franchise setting, appears to be that in exclusive dealing the court recognizes no distinct "tying" product. For example, see Justice O'Connor's concurrence in Jefferson Parish Hosp. Dist. No. 2 v. Hyde, 104 S.Ct. 1551, 1575–76 (1984). Once Justice O'Connor decided that hospital services and anesthesiology were the same "product" and could not constitute a tying arrangement, she dealt with the arrangement as an exclusive dealing contract. In fact, however, a "tying" product exists even in exclusive dealing contracts—namely, the right of the retailer to sell the supplier's merchandise and perhaps to display a sign showing itself to be an "authorized dealer." That right is worth more to the high volume seller than to the low volume seller. As a result exclusive dealing is probably used to facilitate price discrimination just as tie-ins. See § 8.8 above. That was almost certainly true in *Standard Stations*. Standard had a great deal invested in public recognition of its name. By entering exclusive dealing contracts with stations, permitting them to display the Standard brand, and

charging a supracompetitive price for its gasoline, Standard was in effect selling its name as well as its gasoline to the retailer; however, it was selling its name at a price that varied with the amount the retailer sold. See Krehl v. Baskin-Robbins Ice Cream Co., 664 F.2d 1348 (9th Cir. 1982), in which the plaintiff-franchisees were permitted to display the defendant's trademark but also required to sell the defendant's ice cream exclusively. The plaintiffs and the court characterized this as a tying arrangement; however the difference between *Baskin-Robbins* and *Standard Stations* is difficult to discern. Another case in which a practice characterized as exclusive dealing was probably used by the defendant to sell the right to be a dealer at discriminatory prices, is Beltone Elect. Corp., 100 F.T.C. 176 (1982).

8. For an excellent discussion of the use of vertical integration to avoid market uncertainties, see O. Williamson, Markets and Hierarchies 82–131 (1975).

9. See Great Lakes Carbon Corp., 82 F.T.C. 1529, 1656 (1973); Robinson v. Magovern, 521 F.Supp. 842, 890–91 (W.D.Pa.1981).

better off. The exclusive dealing arrangement gives both refiners
and ultimate consumers the advantages of outright refiner ownership
of retail stations, but permits the refiner to avoid the high capital
costs of investing in stations. The exclusive dealing contract may
also provide incentives at the retailer level. If the refiner owns its
own stations, the station operator is merely an employee. The
independent dealer is a businessman who usually maximizes his
profits by selling as much as possible of the refiner's gasoline.

Additionally, vertical integration by contract gives both parties to
the agreement an economic interest in productive facilities. The
value of a gasoline refinery, for example, is a function of the stream
of future earnings that the sale of refined gasoline will generate. By
arranging in advance for such a steady stream, the refiner essentially
shares the risk of the investment with the gasoline retailers. In
general, the more specialized the plant, the greater this risk will be.
If the refiner builds without this assurance, retailers can later take
advantage of the refiner's sunk costs and bargain for any price
sufficient to cover the variable costs of refining gasoline.[10] As a
result, the refiner unsure about future demand is likely to build a
smaller refinery than it would if the demand were certain, or else not
build at all. This situation is exacerbated if information in the
market is poor. For example, if I am planning to build a refinery but
I do not know what competing refiners are planning to build, I may
fear there will be excess refining capacity. By guaranteeing my
market now—by long term requirements contracts—I can spread this
risk and reduce my uncertainty.[11]

Finally, from the supplier's viewpoint exclusive dealing or tying
may prevent "interbrand free riding." Free riding is an important
reason why suppliers impose resale price maintenance and other
vertical restraints.[12] The free rider would otherwise take advantage
of the promotional activities undertaken by another dealer of the
same brand. Interbrand free riding occurs when a dealer having an
ongoing supply relationship with one supplier sells a second brand at
the same location and takes advantage of facilities or goodwill
contributed by the supplier of the first brand. For example, when
Standard licenses a new gasoline station it may help the dealer with
financing, acquisition and maintenance of equipment, certain amenities such as "free" road maps, and most importantly, the large
Standard sign at the top of the station. If the dealer were permitted

10. For one likely instance of this see Great Alantic & Pacif. Tea Co. v. F.T.C., 440 U.S. 69, 73, 99 S.Ct. 925, 929 (1979), where A&P was able to obtain a very low bid from Borden milk company, allegedly in violation of the Robinson-Patman Act, because Borden had just built an enormous plant in the area in reliance on A&P's continued business, and feared underutilization if it did not retain A&P's account.

11. See Liebeler, Antitrust Law and the New Federal Trade Commission, 12 Sw.U.L.Rev. 166, 186–196 (1981); Marvel, Exclusive Dealing, 25 J.L. & Econ. 1 (1982).

12. See § 9.2 below.

to pump a second brand of "equally good" discount gasoline—even if it were properly distinguished from the true Standard pumps—neither Standard nor the dealer could segregate all these facilities and amenities supplied by Standard. Invariably, part of Standard's investment would contribute to the sale of a competitor's gasoline. The solution for Standard is to force dealers to sell its gasoline exclusively.

Justice Douglas, always the champion of the small business, recognized many of the economies that exclusive dealing would generate. In his *Standard Stations* dissent, Justice Douglas, who usually opted for expansive antitrust liability, recognized the obvious: if the oil companies could not integrate by exclusive dealing, they would do so by outright ownership:

> The Court * * * [decision] promises to wipe out large segments of independent filling station operators. The method of doing business under requirements contracts at least keeps the independents alive. They survive as small business units. The situation is not ideal from either their point of view or that of the nation. But the alternative which the Court offers is far worse from the point of view of both.
>
> The elimination of these requirements contracts sets the stage for Standard and the other oil companies to build service-station empires of their own.[13]

The statement is one of Justice Douglas' most candid recognitions of the conflict between small business welfare and economic efficiency. If vertical integration gives an oil company a "competitive advantage" but exclusive dealing is unlawful, competition may force the companies to build their own retail stations. Justice Douglas was not willing to make a second admission, however: the "competitive advantage" meant lower prices for consumers.

The district court's opinion in the *Standard Stations* case had created a *per se* rule against requirements contracts if the percentage of the market foreclosed by the agreement exceeded about 7%. Having concluded that the percentage was high enough, the district court refused to consider evidence concerning "the economic merits or demerits of the present system" and whether the number of dealers had increased or decreased since the exclusive dealing contracts had come into existence.[14] In affirming the district court, the Supreme Court appeared to approve this *per se* approach to exclusive dealing contracts.

The Court retreated from that position, however, in Tampa Elect. Co. v. Nashville Coal Co.,[15] decided 12 years later. The most significant part of the *Tampa* decision was its definition of the relevant

---

13. *Standard Stations*, 337 U.S. at 319–320, 69 S.Ct. at 1066–67.

14. Id. at 298, 69 S.Ct. at 1054.

15. 365 U.S. 320, 81 S.Ct. 623 (1961).

market, which reduced effective foreclosure to lower than 1%.[16]   As a result, the Court's discussion of the legal standard to be applied can be considered dicta.   In an ambiguous but potentially powerful statement, the Court concluded that:

> To determine substantiality [of foreclosure] in a given case, it is necessary to weigh the probable effect of the contract on the relevant area of effective competition, taking into account the relative strength of the parties, the proportionate volume of commerce involved in relation to the total volume of commerce * * * and the probable immediate and future effects which pre-emption of that share of the market might have on effective competition therein.[17]

Most circuit courts have followed *Tampa*'s suggested rule of reason approach.   Under that approach a foreclosure on the order of 15% is necessary to avoid judgment for the defendant.   Once foreclosure in that amount is found, the court looks at the factors spelled out in the *Tampa* opinion.   For example, in American Motor Inns, Inc. v. Holiday Inns, Inc.[18] the court held that even though foreclosure was about 15% the district court should have considered "the economic justification for the [exclusive dealing] arrangement." [19]

The effect of the 1984 Justice Department Merger Guidelines on exclusive dealing cases remains to be determined.   The Guidelines apply only to the Department's merger enforcement policy, not to integration by contract.   However, courts traditionally have been more tolerant of vertical integration by contract than they have been of vertical acquisitions.

The 1984 Guidelines are especially lenient toward vertical acquisitions.[20]   The Department is not likely to challenge one unless the market is highly concentrated and foreclosure is on the order of 25%.   In fact, the primary firm must virtually be a monopolist.   If courts follow the substantive tests for vertical mergers proposed by the Guidelines, they should modify the law of exclusive dealing to correspond.

 WESTLAW REFERENCES
265k17(2.1)   +p   "exclusive dealing"

---

16. See § 3.5 above.

17. 365 U.S. at 329, 81 S.Ct. at 629.

18. 521 F.2d 1230 (3d Cir. 1975).

19. However, in Twin City Sportservice, Inc. v. Charles O. Finley & Co., Inc., 676 F.2d 1291 (9th Cir.), cert. denied, 459 U.S. 1009, 103 S.Ct. 364 (1982), the court appears to approve a *per se* rule if the foreclosure exceeds 25% of the relevant market.

20. See Dep't of Justice, Antitrust Division, Merger Guidelines, 49 Fed. Reg. 26,823 (1984).   Application of the guidelines to vertical mergers is discussed in § 7.4 above.

CHAPTER 9

RESTRICTIONS ON DISTRIBUTION

§ 9.1 Introduction

This chapter deals with two broad categories of vertical integration by contract. One is vertical price fixing, or resale price maintenance (RPM), which is manufacturer or supplier regulation of the price at which a product is resold by independent retailers. The second category is best classified as vertical nonprice restraints. The most common of these is vertical territorial division, which is supplier regulation of the location or sales territories of its distributors or retailers. Another important vertical nonprice restraint is the customer restriction, which limits the classes of buyers with whom a distributor or other middleman may deal.

Few areas of antitrust law have provoked more reconsideration of established rules, or more disagreement between courts and commentators, than these two classes of vertical restrictions. Like all practices, they can be governed by three possible legal rules: *per se* illegality, rule of reason analysis, or *per se* legality. Unlike most other practices, however, in this area serious arguments have been made for all three positions.

Equally controversial is the fact that today the two sets of practices are governed by two different legal standards. RPM is *per se* illegal. Vertical territorial division, however, has received rule of reason treatment since 1977. Many critics believe that the two practices contain more similarities than differences, and that there is little justification for the different legal treatment. In fact, it has

247

been argued that to the extent the effect on competition differs, vertical territorial restraints can actually be more anticompetitive than RPM.[1]

However, an ambiguous Congressional mandate exists for making all resale price maintenance illegal. From 1937 until 1975 § 1 of the Sherman Act contained an amendment that permitted states to authorize "fair trade," or resale price maintenance. At one time or another 46 states passed such legislation. The federal "fair trade" enabling statute was repealed [2] because Congress believed that prices were higher in fair trade states than they were in other states.[3]

To be sure, repeal of fair trade is not a clear Congressional preference for a *per se* rule against resale price maintenance. However, it was a clear expression of Congress' general disapproval of resale price maintenance. If òur experience with the rule of reason for nonprice restraints is any guide, a rule of reason for RPM would clearly undermine Congress' intent. Since the rule of reason was adopted for nonprice restraints, the vast majority have been upheld. Virtually all have been upheld when the defendant did not have substantial market power. The Supreme Court has said that by repealing the fair trade statute Congress "expressed its approval of a *per se* analysis of vertical price restrictions." [4]

 WESTLAW REFERENCES
"vertical price fixing" "resale price maintenance" /p "per se"
   (rule /2 reason)
vertical +1 non-price +1 restraint restriction

§ 9.2   The Economics of RPM and Vertical Territorial Restraints

Courts have suggested conflicting reasons why RPM should be illegal. One is that it permits a manufacturer to take advantage of its retailers and deny them the freedom to set a price most advantageous to themselves.[1] Another is that RPM is really a manifestation

§ 9.1

1. Posner, The Next Step in the Antitrust Treatment of Restricted Distribution: Per Se Legality, 48 U.Chi.L.Rev. 6, 9 (1981); R. Bork, The Antitrust Paradox: A Policy At War With Itself 281–82 (1978); see also Justice White's concurring opinion in Continental T.V., Inc. v. GTE Sylvania, Inc.: "It is common ground among the leading advocates of a purely economic approach to the question of distribution restraints that the economic arguments in favor of allowing vertical nonprice restraints generally apply to vertical price restraints as well." 433 U.S. 36, 69, 97 S.Ct. 2549, 2567 (1977), on remand, 461 F.Supp. 1046 (D.

Cal.1978), judgment affirmed, 694 F.2d 1132 (9th Cir. 1982).

2. Consumer Goods Pricing Act, 89 Stat. 801, amending 15 U.S.C.A. §§ 1, 45.

3. See Hearings on S. 408 Before the Subcommittee on Antitrust and Monopoly of the Senate Judiciary Committee, 94th Cong., 1st Sess. 174 (1975).

4. *Continental T.V.*, note 1 above, 433 U.S. at 51 n.18, 97 S.Ct. at 2558 n.18.

§ 9.2

1. Simpson v. Union Oil Co., 377 U.S. 13, 20–21, 84 S.Ct. 1051, 1056–57 (1964);

of price fixing among the retailers, who have involved the manufacturer in the agreement so that it can help police the cartel.[2]

The first argument is specious when applied to minimum resale price maintenance, which is the kind of RPM manufacturers most generally impose on retailers. The argument may apply to maximum resale price maintenance, in which case the manufacturer is generally attempting to prevent a retailer with market power from reducing output and charging a monopoly price at the expense of the manufacturer as well as of consumers.

The retailer's mark-up is the price a manufacturer pays to have its product distributed. Naturally, the manufacturer wants to keep these costs as low as possible. Any firm is best off if other firms in the distribution chain behave as competitively as possible.[3] Any profits that result from a retailer's mark-up accrue to the retailer, not to the manufacturer. Suppose a manufacturer's profit-maximizing price to consumers is $8.00, and the retailers' distribution costs are $1.00. The manufacturer will wholesale the product for $7.00 and the retailers, if they are competitive, will resell it at $8.00. If the manufacturer sells to its retailers for any price less than $7.00 but forces the retailers to charge $8.00, part of the monopoly profits will accrue to the retailers and be lost to the manufacturer. That is hardly "taking advantage" of retailers.

The second argument is that RPM is really carried out at the instigation of the retailers, who are engaged in price fixing. There are good reasons why retailers would want to involve their suppliers in a cartel. The suppliers may be in a better position to monitor the pricing activities of the retailers, since the manufacturers normally deal with each retailer, but the retailers do not normally deal with each other. In addition, if the manufacturers manage to take advantage of the *Colgate*[4] exception, they will be able to enforce RPM legally.

Such retailer cartels are alleged to come in two kinds. If the manufacturers in the market have no market power, then the retailers of any single manufacturer could not raise the price of the manufacturer's product to monopoly levels. Customers would switch to a different brand. For example, if Sylvania makes 5% of the nation's televisions, a cartel of Sylvania retailers could not charge a monopoly price for Sylvania televisions, any more than Sylvania itself could set a monopoly price. Customers would switch to Sony,

U.S. v. A. Schrader's Son, Inc., 252 U.S. 85, 99, 40 S.Ct. 251, 253 (1920).

2. Dr. Miles Medical Co. v. John D. Park & Sons Co., 220 U.S. 373, 407–08, 31 S.Ct. 376, 384–85 (1911). The antinomy between the two arguments is discussed in Posner, Antitrust Policy and the Supreme Court: An Analysis of the Restricted Distribution, Horizontal Merger and Potential Competition Decisions, 75 Col.L.Rev. 282 (1975).

3. See § 7.2 above.

4. See U.S. v. Colgate & Co., 250 U.S. 300, 39 S.Ct. 465 (1919), discussed below in § 9.3.

Magnavox, Zenith or some other brand of television. In this situation the only retail cartel that will work is an "interbrand" cartel—one encompassing enough brands of televisions that the price fixers collectively have market power. Likewise, the RPM agreements facilitating the cartel would have to come from all these manufacturers.

On the other hand, if Sylvania were a television monopolist, itself capable of charging a monopoly price, then the cartel of Sylvania retailers could likewise charge a monopoly price. Such "intrabrand" cartels are plausible only if the supplier to the cartels has substantial market power. In that case the RPM agreements facilitating the cartel need come only from this monopoly manufacturer.[5]

Admittedly, retailers engaged in price fixing would profit greatly if manufacturers policed the cartel for them. However, why would the manufacturers agree to participate? The retailers' cartel will reduce output and therefore the retailers will buy less from the manufacturer. This will force the manufacturer's output below its profit-maximizing level. Even if the manufacturer is a monopolist, a cartel of its independent retailers will charge a price higher than the manufacturer's profit-maximizing price, and reduce output further.[6]

Perhaps the retailers will buy the manufacturers' participation by agreeing to share their monopoly profits. However, the manufacturer can keep *all* the monopoly profits to itself, either by substituting new retailers who behave competitively or else by vertically integrating into retailing. If the manufacturer is a monopolist vertical integration will enable it to retain all the monopoly profits for itself. If the manufacturer is a competitor and the retailers are engaged in an interbrand cartel, vertical integration will enable the manufacturer to raise its own retail prices up to the level charged by the cartel, while retaining all the monopoly profits itself.[7] If all else fails, the manufacturer can report the cartel to the Department of Justice. Considering the fact that manufacturer participation in a retailer cartel is *per se* illegal under the antitrust laws and can yield treble damages or criminal liability, such manufacturer participation is probably rare.

Analogous reasoning can be applied to manufacturer imposed territorial restrictions. Retailers may find it advantageous to engage in *horizontal* territorial division—in fact, division of territories can be an effective form of price fixing. Each retailer can become a

5. See Hovenkamp, Vertical Restrictions and Monopoly Power, 64 Boston Univ.L.Rev. (1984); Liebeler, 1983 Economic Review of Antitrust Developments: The Distinction Between Price and Nonprice Distribution Restrictions, 31 UCLA L.Rev. 384 (1983); Liebeler, Intrabrand "Cartels" under *GTE Sylvania*, 30 UCLA L.Rev. 1 (1982).

6. See Figure Two and accompanying discussion in § 7.2 above.

7. The best possible position for any firm is to be a nonmember of a cartel in a cartelized market. The firm can sell all it can produce at slightly under the cartel's price with no risk of legal liability. See § 4.1 above.

monopolist in its own territory and establish its own profit-maximizing price and rate of output. Thus many of the incentives to cheat on the cartel are removed, and detection of cheating is often easier.[8]

Likewise, the retailers would prefer the territorial restrictions to be imposed from above. The manufacturers are better able to monitor the retailers than the retailers can monitor each other. Further, since 1977 vertical territorial restraints have been analyzed under the rule of reason, while horizontal territorial division is probably illegal *per se*.[9]

Again, however, the theory does not explain why the manufacturers would participate in the scheme. Any monopoly profits earned by the retailers are taken away from the manufacturers. It would be much more profitable for them to sell to additional outlets in the territories, or to open their own outlets.

There is also an empirical reason, derived from the case law, for believing that few vertical price or territorial restrictions are really disguised retailer cartels. As the discussion above noted, a cartel cannot succeed unless its members collectively have substantial market power. RPM and vertical territorial restrictions can be evidence of retailer collusion only if 1) the manufacturer imposing the restriction is a monopolist; or 2) the restriction is used by all (or at least most) of the manufacturers in the market. Either of these phenomena would support the inference that the retailers subject to the restriction collectively have enough market power to engage in price fixing. In the big vertical cases that have come to the Supreme Court, however, the products at issue were generally produced by manufacturers with relatively small market shares, and there was no evidence that other manufacturers of the same product were imposing similar restrictions.[10]

8. See § 4.1 above.

9. U.S. v. Topco Assoc., Inc., 405 U.S. 596, 92 S.Ct. 1126 (1972). See § 4.3 above.

10. For example, in Monsanto Co. v. Spray-Rite Svce. Corp., ___ U.S. ___, 104 S.Ct. 1464 (1984) the defendant's market share in corn herbicides was 15% and in soybean herbicides was 3%. In Continental T.V., Inc. v. GTE Sylvania, Inc., 433 U.S. 36, 97 S.Ct. 2549 (1977), on remand, 461 F.Supp. 1046 (D. Cal. 1978), judgment affirmed, 694 F.2d 1132 (9th Cir. 1982), the defendant's national market share was less than 5% and its market share in the restricted territories involved in the litigation was 2.5% and 15%. In U.S. v. Arnold, Schwinn & Co., 388 U.S. 365, 87 S.Ct. 1856 (1967), defendant's market share ranged from 22.5% to 12.8% during the relevant period. In U.S. v. Sealy, Inc., 388 U.S. 350, 87 S.Ct. 1847 (1967), the aggregate market share of the manufacturers was 20%. In the FTC Magnovox investigation, which yielded a consent decree, Magnavox's market share was found to be about 9%. Magnavox, 78 F.T.C. 1183 (1971). However, there are cases in which the manufacturer's market share was high enough to warrant a finding of monopoly power. For example, U.S. v. General Elec. Co., 272 U.S. 476, 47 S.Ct. 192 (1926), where the market share exceeded 80%. Market power has become an issue in several recent vertical territorial division cases, and some defendants have been found to have substantial market power. See § 9.4 below.

Nevertheless, the possibility of retailer cartels facilitated by RPM or vertical nonprice restraints cannot be ruled out entirely. If it occurs at all, it is when economies of scale at the *retail* level make single-brand distribution impracticable. For example, the monopolist manufacturer of men's lizard belts would probably not find it economical to open its own stores that sell nothing but the belts. The manufacturer must rely on multi-brand, multi-product men's stores or department stores to distribute its product. As a result the manufacturer cannot vertically integrate in order to circumvent a retailer cartel. If all retailers in a particular retail market are members of the cartel, the belt maker may be forced to participate.

Writers have also argued that vertical restrictions may facilitate a cartel at the *manufacturer* rather than the retailer level. This argument is inherently more plausible. As the discussion in § 4.2 above noted, vertical integration can enable a cartel to police its members more carefully. Sales made to wholesalers or distributors are generally large, secret, and individually negotiated. The cartel member has an incentive to cheat by shading price, providing extra services, engaging in reciprocity, or accepting secret rebates. Since the chances of detection increase with the number of such cheating sales, it is important that each sale be large. Retail prices, on the other hand, are generally public, relatively standardized at particular locations, and small. By imposing RPM or territorial restrictions on retailers, a manufacturers' cartel could monitor prices and number of sales at the retail level.

The manufacturers' cartel will work, however, only if its members collectively control enough of the market to wield monopoly power. Furthermore, price or output verification by vertical restrictions will work only if all cartel members use it. As a result the restrictions are evidence of a manufacturers' cartel only if virtually all (or most) manufacturers in the market are using them. In most litigated cases this has not been true.

Most instances of RPM or vertical territorial division cannot be explained on either the retailer cartel or the manufacturer cartel theory. Most manufacturers use such restrictions not to facilitate price fixing, which will reduce output, but to enlarge output by enabling retailers to do a better job of marketing the product. In most cases the manufacturer is attempting to avoid one of the many variations of the "free rider" problem.

Suppose that Chrysler Motor Co. has two auto dealerships in Wichita. Dealer A is stocked with a full inventory of cars (which the dealer carries at its own expense), has a large and expensive showroom, many sales agents who spend a great deal of time displaying cars and giving test drives to prospective purchasers, and an excellent service department that makes many pre-sale and post-sale adjustments to new cars. Dealer B, located across town, rents one room in a warehouse, has no inventory, gives no test rides, has no service department, and does all his negotiating over the telephone.[11]

The point-of-sale services given by Dealer A are expensive, and Dealer A must charge about $500 more than it pays for a new car. Dealer B does quite well, however, with a mark-up of $100. What do you do as a new car buyer? Chances are good that you go to Dealer A's large showroom, look at his cars, test drive one or more, collect a good deal of information, and leave, telling the salesman that you will "think about it." Then you go to Dealer B and place an order for the car you want.

The information you obtained from Dealer A was essential to your decision making—for example, you would not have purchased a Chrysler had you not been permitted to test drive one. You avoided paying for the information you gathered, however, by purchasing from a different dealer who did not supply the information and was able to sell the car at a lower price. You and Dealer B in this case took a "free ride" on the point-of-sale information offered by Dealer A.

Unfortunately, Dealer A does not make money giving test drives; he makes it selling cars. He will not stay in business long if everyone takes advantage of his information system but purchases their cars from Dealer B. Furthermore, if Dealer A goes out of business Chrysler's Wichita sales will decline substantially, because most customers insist on being able to obtain this vital information *somewhere* before they purchase a particular brand of automobile. In order to compete effectively with other automakers Chrysler must have a mechanism for providing potential customers with test drives and other vital information. It cannot easily do that itself. It must rely on its dealers.

Suppose, however, that Chrysler requires its Wichita dealers to charge the same resale price for various models of automobiles—say, $8,000 for a particular model. Now you as customer have no incentive remaining to make your purchase from the cut-rate dealer—he will charge the same price anyway. You will go to the dealer who does the best job of providing the kind of information and customer service that is important to you when you buy a car. The cut-rate dealer will have to clean up his act or lose his business. In fact, with the final output price given, the two dealers will compete with each other, not in price, but in the amount of services they can deliver. Competition between them will drive the level of services up to the point at which their marginal cost equals the maintained price. They will be left with a competitive rate of return, and the auto manufacturer will obtain the amount of services that it has calculated will do the best job of marketing its cars.[12]

---

11. See U.S. v. General Motors, 384 U.S. 127, 86 S.Ct. 1321 (1966).

12. See Telser, Why Should Manufacturers Want Fair Trade? 3 J.L. &

Similar analysis applies to vertical territorial restraints. Instead of establishing a resale price, Chrysler might simply terminate Dealer B (the cut-rate dealer) and give Dealer A the exclusive right to retail new Chryslers in Wichita. Now Chrysler can be assured that its customers will obtain the point-of-sale information and services that they want. Dealer A will have a contract with Chrysler which tells him how much service he must provide, and he no longer has the disincentive of a cut-rate dealer stealing his customers. Further, Dealer A is not a monopolist: he still competes intensively with other automobile retailers in Wichita, and he cannot take a free ride on their services. For example, a customer will not test drive a Ford in order to determine whether she wants to purchase a Chrysler. Nor will the Ford dealer perform warranty maintenance on new Chryslers. The Chrysler dealer who wants to compete with the Ford dealer will do these things for itself. The result is that Chrysler will make more sales in Wichita.

The free rider problem also applies to advertising. If a city contains five dealers in Sony stereo equipment, and one of them advertises that Sony equipment is better than the equipment of other manufacturers, the benefit of the advertising will accrue to all five dealers. No dealer will be willing to pay for the advertising if it is likely to pick up only 20% of the increased purchases that result. There may be alternative solutions to this problem: one is a joint advertising venture among the dealers; another is for the manufacturer itself to pay for the advertising and pass on the costs to the dealers; a third is exclusive territories within which all the benefits of the advertising are likely to accrue to a single dealership.

Under the free rider theory, manufacturer-imposed RPM or territorial restraints are a mechanism for *increasing* output, not reducing it. When Chrysler (who is not a monopolist) imposes RPM or territorial restraints on its dealers, it has predicted that retail customers will value the point-of-sale information and services more than the cost of providing them.

Figure One illustrates the manufacturer's prediction. Demand curve D represents demand for the product without point-of-sale services. Demand curve D′ represents market demand for the product with the point-of-sale services. At any given level of output, D′ yields a higher price than D, because customers are willing to pay

Econ. 86 (1960); Bork, The Rule of Reason and the Per Se Concept: Price Fixing and Market Division (part 2), 75 Yale L.J. 373 (1966); Posner, The Rule of Reason and the Economic Approach: Reflections on The *Sylvania* Decision, 45 U.Chi.L.Rev. 1 (1977).

RPM will minimize free riding, but it may not eliminate all free riding. Dealer B in the example in the text might still free ride on Dealer A's test drive and other point-of-sale information but steal customers by offering large warranties, post-sale maintenance or some other service valued by the buyer. See Pitofsky, In Defense of Discounters: the No-Frills Case for a *Per Se* Rule Against Vertical Price Fixing, 71 Geo. L.J. 1487, 1493 (1983).

more for the product if the services are provided. If the dealers are forced to sell the product at a certain price they will continue to compete, not in price, but in delivery of the services. In Figure One MC is the marginal cost curve of dealers not providing the services. MC' is the higher marginal cost curve of dealers who provide the services. Without RPM dealers would tend not to give the services in order to compete in price. Their price would be P and output would be Q. However, if the manufacturer maintained the resale price at level P' the dealers would compete in services until their marginal costs equaled the maintained price. That would happen when output reached Q'. The difference between Q and Q' is the number of additional sales that the manufacturer would make as a result of RPM. Essentially the same thing would happen if the manufacturer relied on vertical territorial restraints. The dealer would then be competing with the dealers of other brands. Since customers value the services more than the cost of providing them, competition will drive the level of services up to MC' and output 'to Q'.

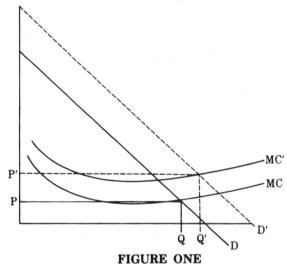

FIGURE ONE

Whether a particular manufacturer chooses resale price mainte- nance or some form of territorial restriction to enhance sales of its product depends on the circumstances. Among the most significant circumstance is the relevant legal rule. Since RPM is illegal *per se* but vertical territorial division obtains a rule of reason,[13] some manufacturers undoubtedly have turned to territorial restrictions.

Additionally, however, some products are more conducive to re- sale price maintenance and others to territorial division. For exam- ple, it would not make much sense for a manufacturer of a nonpre- scription medicine to establish a single store in a large city: convenience and number of outlets is an important element in the marketing of drugs. If the manufacturer wants retailers to provide

13. See § 9.4 below.

a certain level of services, such as point-of-sale information, resale price maintenance would be more sensible.

On the other hand, restrictions on location may be more useful for "big ticket" items that involve rather expensive customer services—major appliances, televisions, or automobiles, for example. First of all, numerous locations are relatively less important with such items. Second, prices are often negotiated individually with customers, at least over a relatively narrow range. Third, price competition with other brand manufacturers may be very intense at the retail level (the more expensive the item, the more sensitive customers are to price), making resale price maintenance too inflexible.

Free riding is a much greater problem in some markets than it is in others. As a result the nature of the product can help a court determine whether a particular restraint was designed to combat free rider problems, or was imposed for another, perhaps anticompetitive reason. Free rider problems are greatest in "brand-specific" products—products in which customers can distinguish brands of the same product and are not indifferent as to which brand they purchase. For example, a prospective automobile customer is likely to need a point-of-sale service such as a test drive in order to help her decide whether to buy a Ford, Chrysler or Toyota. Such point-of-sale services are generally not important in markets for fungible products. As a result, vertical restrictions in the markets for potatoes, lumber, cement, or paper clips should be viewed with greater suspicion.

The explanations for vertical restraints, particularly RPM, in products that appear to require no point-of-sale services have been complex and not particularly enlightening. A simple common-sense explanation is offered here. Most of the commodities that fit into this category and in which RPM has been imposed—candy, blue jeans, men's underwear, pet supplies, and beer—share one characteristic: economies of scale at the retail level demand that they be sold by multi-brand or multi-product retailers. For example, a store would be unlikely to deal exclusively in Levi's brand blue jeans. Jeans are distributed most efficiently if they can be placed in a large number of stores in a single city. In that case demand in each location will be insufficient to sustain the entire store. As a result Levi's are sold in clothing stores which generally offer other brands of blue jeans as well as other types of clothing, or even in department stores that sell a wide array of products.

When Levi Strauss sells its blue jeans through, say, Macy's Department Stores, Levi is effectively purchasing distribution services from Macy's. Importantly, these services are not fungible. Macy's has preferred shelf space in the center of the store, and less satisfactory space hidden in the corners. It hires people to assemble displays, and has considerable discretion about how much expense and effort will go into one particular item's promotion rather than another's.

The amount and quality of shelf space, and the amount that Macy's will spend promoting a particular product in its multi-product store is a function of the anticipated profitability of that particular product. If RPM insulates Macy's from price competition for Levi's and enables it to take a relatively high mark-up, Macy's will respond by providing shelf space and promotion up to the point that the expense and opportunity cost of providing these amenities rise to the maintained price. In short, RPM in Levi's will encourage Macy's to sell Levi's a little harder, necessarily at the expense of other items in Macy's stores. The "point-of-sale" services exist, just as much as they would for home computers or automobiles. However, they are more subtle, buried in the retailer's pre-sale decisions about what combination of sales efforts will maximize its profits.

One final rationale for vertical restrictions, particularly vertical territorial division, cannot be overlooked. The restrictions may be designed to facilitate price discrimination by the manufacturer. Price discrimination occurs when the seller makes higher profits from one set of customers than from another. In order to engage in persistent price discrimination a seller must have a certain amount of market power: assuming the low profit sales are profitable, the high profit sales have at least a certain amount of monopoly profit built in. If the seller had no market power, those customers asked to pay a monopoly price would seek out a different seller.

The two most significant practical barriers to price discrimination are the difficulty of identifying and segregating groups of customers willing to pay different prices, and the difficulty of preventing arbitrage. Arbitrage occurs when favored purchasers (those who pay the lower price) resell the product to disfavored purchasers and frustrate the price discrimination scheme.

Vertically imposed territorial or customer restrictions can enable a manufacturer to solve both these problems. For example, suppose that the manufacturer produces a disinfectant used by both hospitals and restaurants. The hospitals have fewer available substitutes for the disinfectant, and they are willing to pay a higher price than the restaurants. The manufacturer could discriminate in price between the two groups of customers by using two different distributors, giving one the exclusive right to sell to hospitals, and the other the exclusive right to sell to restaurants. Alternatively, the manufacturer could engage in "dual distribution," by selling to the hospitals itself but using an independent distributor for the restaurants. In this case the customer restrictions help the manufacturer segregate the customers and prevent arbitrage, because each class of customers deals with a different seller and has little reason to know that a different group of customers is buying the same product from someone else. Both vertical customer restraints and vertical territorial restraints have probably been used by manufacturers to facilitate price discrimination in this way.[14]

 WESTLAW REFERENCES
"vertical territorial restraint"
"dual distribution"

§ 9.3   Resale Price Maintenance in the Courts: The Per Se Rule and Its Exceptions

In Dr. Miles Medical Co. v. John D. Park & Sons Co.[1] the Supreme Court held that a contract that required a dealer to resell a manufacturer's product at a specified price was unenforceable because it was contrary to the policy of the Sherman Act. The Court could not determine why a manufacturer would want to impose such a requirement upon its dealers. It admitted that "the advantage of established retail prices primarily concerns the dealers," who would receive "enlarged profits" as a result. The injury that the Court perceived was that only "favored" dealers would be able to realize these profits. Presumably there were disfavored dealers who could not obtain a fair share of the market unless they cut the resale price.

On this dubious rationale was born the rule that "vertical price-fixing" or resale price maintenance (RPM) is illegal *per se*. The Court found no theory under which the manufacturer would be benefitted by RPM. Since under the Court's theory the end result was higher retail prices, the only thing that accrued to the manufacturer was reduced output and therefore lower profits.

The basic rule of *Dr. Miles* persists today,[2] although it took later courts to explain that the rule to be applied was *per se*—that is, once an agreement was satisfactorily characterized as RPM no further economic analysis was necessary to establish its illegality.[3] However, within fifteen years following *Dr. Miles* the Court attached two

---

14. Likely examples are Graphic Prods. Distrib., Inc. v. Itek Corp., 717 F.2d 1560 (11th Cir. 1983); Davis Watkins Co. v. Service Merchandise, 686 F.2d 1190 (6th Cir. 1982), cert. denied, ___ U.S. ___, 104 S.Ct. 1718 (1984), both of which involved territorial restrictions. See JBL Enterprises, Inc. v. Jhirmack, Inc., 698 F.2d 1011 (9th Cir. 1983), cert. denied, ___ U.S. ___, 104 S.Ct. 106 (1983), which involved customer restrictions. And see Hovenkamp, note 5 above.

§ 9.3

1. 220 U.S. 373, 400, 31 S.Ct. 376, 381 (1911). One year earlier the defendant in the *Dr. Miles* case had signed a con-

sent decree agreeing not to engage in price fixing of drugs. See Jayne v. Loder, 149 F. 21, 25 (3d Cir. 1906). It is therefore likely that the RPM in *Dr. Miles* was being used to facilitate horizontal collusion. See § 4.1 above, and see Baxter, Vertical Practices—Half Slave, Half Free, 52 A.B.A. Antitrust L.J. 743 (1983).

2. In Monsanto Co. v. Spray-Rite Svce. Corp., ___ U.S. ___, 104 S.Ct. 1464 (1984), the Supreme Court was invited to reconsider the *per se* rule for RPM, but refused to do so.

3. For example, see U.S. v. Parke, Davis and Co., 362 U.S. 29, 47, 80 S.Ct. 503, 513 (1960).

exceptions. In U.S. v. Colgate & Co.[4] it permitted a manufacturer "unilaterally" to refuse to deal with a firm that failed to resell the product at the manufacturer's previously announced resale price. Then, in U.S. v. General Electric Co.,[5] the Court held that the *Dr. Miles* rule does not apply to a consignment agreement in which the retailer is the manufacturer's agent rather than a purchaser and reseller, and title to the merchandise remains with the manufacturer.

Given RPM's great potential to increase efficiency and its relatively small potential for economic harm, the *per se* rule condemning it makes little sense. This suggests that *Colgate* is better law than *Dr. Miles*. The difficulty with the *Colgate* exception, however, is its lack of any coherent policy justification. *Colgate* stands for the troublesome proposition that when a manufacturer simply announces its intention not to deal with price cutters and later refuses to deal with one, Sherman § 1 is not violated because there was no "agreement" between the manufacturer and the price cutting retailer. This is pure formalism.[6]

Courts have generally construed the *Colgate* doctrine narrowly. In order to claim the exception the manufacturer can do no more than announce its intent not to deal with price cutters, and later refuse to deal with a violator. If the manufacturer warns, threatens, or intimidates its retailers in any way, it is likely to fall out of the exception and into the *per se* rule of *Dr. Miles*.[7]

Nevertheless, the *Colgate* doctrine continues to have vitality.[8] In Russell Stover Candies, Inc. v. FTC.[9] the Eighth Circuit reversed a Federal Trade Commission decision that would have emasculated the doctrine. A divided FTC had found that Stover, a large candy

4. 250 U.S. 300, 39 S.Ct. 465 (1919).

5. 272 U.S. 476, 47 S.Ct. 192 (1926).

6. See U.S. v. A. Schrader's, Inc., 264 F. 175, 183 (N.D.Ohio 1919), reversed, 252 U.S. 85, 40 S.Ct. 251 (1920): "Personally, and with all due respect, * * * I can see no real difference * * * between the Dr. Miles Medical Co. case and the Colgate Co. case. * * * The tacit acquiescence of the wholesalers and retailers in the prices thus fixed is the equivalent for all practical purposes of an express agreement * * * ."

The *Colgate* doctrine is probably the unforeseen result of a badly drafted indictment, which neglected to "charge Colgate * * * with selling its products to dealers under agreements which obligated the latter not to resell except at prices fixed by the company." Rather, the indictment alleged 1) that Colgate entered into sales contracts with retailers; 2) that it separately an-nounced an intention not to make such contracts with retailers who sold for less than Colgate's posted retail prices; 3) that it subsequently refused to deal with price cutters, as it announced. In an age overly inclined toward legal formalism, it was quite easy for the Court to separate the sales contract on the one hand from Colgate's apparent "unilateral" refusal to deal on the other.

7. U.S. v. Parke, Davis & Co., 362 U.S. 29, 80 S.Ct. 503 (1960).

8. See Dunn v. Phoenix Newspapers, Inc., 735 F.2d 1184, 1187 (9th Cir. 1984), which applied the *Colgate* exception to an allegation of maximum resale price maintenance in the newspaper carrier market. For a discussion of other cases see Andersen, The Antitrust Consequences of Manufacturer Suggested Retail Prices—The Case for Presumptive Illegality, 54 Wash.L.Rev. 763, 773–776 (1979).

9. 718 F.2d 256 (8th Cir. 1983).

manufacturer, fell out of the *Colgate* exception because its announcements of intent not to deal with price cutters and its subsequent refusals to do so established a "course of dealing" that amounted to an agreement. The Commission concluded that "there is no sound legal distinction between coercion resulting from the threat of * * * terminating a franchise and coercion resulting from a communicated policy of terminating supply * * * to dealers who fail to comply with the manufacturer's pricing policies."

In reversing the FTC's decision, the Eighth Circuit conceded that the *Colgate* doctrine might be formalistic and irrational. Nevertheless, the doctrine had been created by the Supreme Court and no one but the Supreme Court should overrule it. A few months later in the *Monsanto* case,[10] the Supreme Court expressly refused to overrule *Colgate*, holding that it continues to be "of considerable importance that independent action by the manufacturer * * * be distinguished from price-fixing agreements," since only the latter are subject to the *per se* rule. In fact, the Court went so far as to say that an agreement could not be inferred from the fact that a supplier terminated one dealer in response to a second dealer's complaints about the first dealer's price cutting.

The most serious flaw in the *Colgate* doctrine is not that it is formalistic and irrational but that it is inimical to the basic rationale for RPM and other vertical restrictions. Such restrictions are a form of vertical integration which enable a manufacturer to achieve optimal distribution of its product. The restrictions should be approved when their potential for creating efficiency is apparent, and condemned only when there is some potential for economic harm.

Colgate, however, is predicated on the natural right of retailers to be free from manufacturers. In order to claim the exception a manufacturer must not become too involved with its retailers. Vertical integration often necessitates a great deal of cooperation and communication between a manufacturer and the retailers who make up its distribution system. One of the chief advantages that a manufacturer obtains from outright ownership of its own retail outlets is the right to operate the stores and display and price the merchandise as it sees fit. Often the manufacturer is a specialist, while the retailer is a generalist. However, *Colgate* approves RPM only when the level of vertical integration between manufacturer and retailer is very small. The result is that RPM is most available in those situations where it is least valuable—where there is no organized "distribution system" at all.

An important variation of the *per se* rule against RPM and the *Colgate* exception was a rule adopted by several circuit courts that it

---

10. Monsanto Co. v. Spray-Rite Svce. Corp., ___ U.S. ___, 104 S.Ct. 1464, 1470 (1984).

was illegal *per se* for a supplier to terminate a distributor in response to a competing distributor's complaints that the terminated distributor had been cutting prices. In applying the *per se* rule, different courts characterized this conduct in different ways. For example, in Cernuto, Inc. v. United Cabinet Corp.[11] the Third Circuit held that when a supplier terminates a dealer as a result of a competing dealer's complaints "the restraint becomes primarily horizontal in nature in that one [dealer] is seeking to suppress its competition by utilizing the power of a common supplier." In Spray-Rite Service Corp. v. Monsanto Co.[12] the Seventh Circuit agreed that such conduct should fall within the *per se* rule, but it developed two different theories than the "horizontal" theory used in *Cernuto*. One theory was that by acting in response to a distributor's complaint, the supplier and distributor were effectively engaged in a *per se* illegal group boycott of a competitor,[13] the terminated distributor. The second theory developed by the Seventh Circuit was that the termination in response to a competitor's price complaint effectively took any attempt by the supplier to control distributor pricing out of the *Colgate* exception, because the conduct could no longer be described as "unilateral."

The Supreme Court affirmed the Seventh Circuit's finding of liability, but it expressly held that a court could not infer the existence of an RPM agreement "merely from the existence of complaints, or even from the fact that termination came about 'in response to' complaints." Rather, the evidence must show "a conscious commitment to a common scheme designed to achieve an unlawful objective." [14] In this case the evidence was sufficient to support the jury's finding of a "common scheme" to set resale prices. As the court noted, however, most cases involving allegations that a supplier terminated one dealer in response to another dealer's complaints arose in the context of distribution systems that contained nonprice restrictions. As a result the termination may not have been the result of illegal RPM at all, but was really motivated by a dealer's violation of territorial restraints. Any rule that prevented a "manufacturer from acting solely because the information upon which it acts originated as a price complaint would create an irrational dislocation in the market."

Although the Supreme Court clearly came to the correct conclusion, about the relevance of price complaints, the presence or absence or any "agreement" between the supplier and one or more dealers is formalistic and economically irrelevant. Nor was there any basis for

11. 595 F.2d 164 (3d Cir. 1979). See also Bostick Oil Co. v. Michelin Tire Corp., 702 F.2d 1207, 1213–15 (4th Cir. 1983), cert. denied, ___ U.S. ___, 104 S.Ct. 242 (1983).

12. 684 F.2d 1226, 1238 (7th Cir. 1982). The decision was affirmed on

other grounds in *Monsanto*, note 10 above.

13. See § 10.2 below.

14. *Monsanto*, note 10 above, 104 S.Ct. at 1471.

its distinction between price and nonprice restraints. In most cases a supplier imposes either RPM or nonprice restraints in order to combat free riding problems.[15] Furthermore, free riding injures *both* the manufacturer or supplier and the dealers who compete with the free rider. As a result, no inference can be drawn from the fact that a dealer or retailer complained.

Suppose that a manufacturer plagued with dealer free riding imposes vertical territorial division. It gives dealer A Massachusetts as an exclusive territory and dealer B New Hampshire. However, B persists in cheating by making unauthorized sales in Massachusetts. Dealer B can probably make these sales in Massachusetts at a lower price than dealer A charges there, because A bears the burden of promotional and post-sale service expenses in Massachusetts. Further, dealer B is likely to steal customers in dealer A's territory only by underselling A there. That is, customers in A's territory will not be motivated to purchase from a remote dealer unless the dealer gives them a better buy.

Everything about this illustrated distribution practice suggests that it involves "nonprice" restraints; however, a court will likely characterize the restrictions as pertaining to price. For example, when dealer A complains to the supplier that B is violating the restrictions, A will complain about the territorial invasion and the price-cutting simultaneously. Even though the supplier is not concerned with the price that B charges in B's territory, it will discipline B for invading A's territory and cutting prices there.

The evidence in the *Monsanto* case suggested that the defendant has been imposing nonprice rather than price restraints. Spray-Rite had argued that it was terminated because it was a price-cutter and other dealers complained about the price-cutting. Monsanto responded that Spray-Rite was terminated not because it was a price-cutter, but because it "lacked technically trained employees capable of promoting Monsanto products." The posture of this argument invited the jury to decide that Spray-Rite was terminated for *either* a price reason or a nonprice reason, and it chose the former. More appropriately, however, Spray-Rite was a price-cutter *because* it lacked adequately trained employees. It was able to charge less because it took a free ride on information provided by the specialists hired by its competitors. Naturally, however, when competing dealers complained, they complained about the phenomenon that appeared to cause their injury: the price-cutting, not the absence of skilled personnel.[16]

The second exception to the *per se* rule against RPM exempts consignment agreements, in which the manufacturer retains owner-

15. See § 9.2 above.

16. See Hovenkamp, Vertical Restrictions and Monopoly Power, 64 Boston Univ.L.Rev. (1984)

ship of its product and the reseller is merely the manufacturer's agent. The agency exception is less offensive than *Colgate* to the basic theory of vertical integration by contract. Unfortunately, the doctrine has been rather woodenly applied, with a great deal of emphasis on such metaphysical questions as when "title" to goods passes from one person to another.

Theoretically, everything that can be achieved by a consignment agreement can also be achieved by a properly drawn resale contract. Nevertheless, consignment agreements persist in certain situations as an alternative to sale and resale. Two properties make consignment attractive to certain retailers. First, consignment can enable a retailer to obtain inventory without tying up capital or credit. Second, under consignment agreements a manufacturer typically assumes more of the risks of nonsale than under a resale agreement. For example, sometimes highly perishable products such as bread are distributed to small grocers on consignment. Under the agreement the wholesaler baker comes to the store each morning, dropping off fresh loaves and picking up loaves left unsold from the previous day. The grocer pays only for the loaves that were sold. The baker—who likely has a specialized outlet for "day old" bread—can sell the outdated bread more efficiently than the grocer. By this mechanism a great deal of the risk of nonsale is transferred from the retailer to the manufacturer.

Consignment can also permit certain suppliers to reach a market more efficiently, particularly if market demand for the product is highly uncertain. An unknown artist, for example, may give her painting or sculpture to a retail gallery on consignment. The artist and gallery will agree on a retail price, from which the gallery will take its mark-up if the work is sold. If it is not sold within a certain time the artist and gallery may renegotiate the price or the artist may withdraw the work. By this mechanism the gallery avoids investing its capital in a high risk enterprise. The artist, on the other hand, is likely to have more confidence (perhaps unwarranted) in her ability to sell to the public than the gallery does. If the gallery were forced to pay for the painting before resale it would probably demand a much larger discount from the artist's expected resale price than the artist would be willing to accept.

Consignment's usefulness notwithstanding, making consignment agreements an exception to the *per se* rule against RPM presents a problem. Manufacturers who want to maintain prices can easily change the form of their resale contracts to make them look like consignment agreements. If there is to be a meaningful "consignment" exception to *Dr. Miles* it should apply when the economics of a particular distribution system justify a relationship in which the manufacturer bears an unusually high proportion of the risk of nonsale. The real issues in the consignment cases are not when "title" passes, whether there was a "sale", or whether the retailer was the "agent" of the manufacturer. Even the wholesale bakery could sell its bread to the grocer one day and buy it back the following day. The realistic distinction between consignment and resale rests not on the form of the written contract between the parties, but on the division of risk between them.

In Simpson v. Union Oil Co.[17] the Supreme Court applied the *Dr. Miles* rule to a "consignment agreement" between a large refiner and its retail gasoline stations. All risks of loss were on the station operators, who leased their stations from the refiner. The refiner refused to renew the plaintiff's lease because the plaintiff sold gasoline at less than the refiner's stipulated resale price.

In condemning the arrangement Justice Douglas expressly approved a bona fide consignment arrangement under which an owner took a single article to a dealer who would sell the article as the owner's agent. However, when such arrangements are used "to cover a vast gasoline distribution system, fixing prices through many retail outlets," then "the antitrust laws prevent calling the 'consignment' an agency * * *." Union Oil's consignment device was nothing more than a "clever manipulation of words."

The *Simpson* rule did not draw the traditional line between bona fide consignment arrangements and resale agreements. Justice Douglas rested the distinction on whether the producer had a distribution "system" or was simply negotiating a single sale of a single article. For this reason Justice Stewart wrote in dissent that *Simpson* really overruled *General Electric*.[18] *Simpson* effectively held that there was no consignment exception to the *per se* rule for large manufacturers with established distribution networks.

Many courts have agreed. A few years later the very distribution arrangement approved by the Supreme Court in the *General Electric* case was condemned by a district court under the *Simpson* rationale.[19] Other courts have held however, that when there is an actual agent, not part of a "giant" distribution system, a good faith consignment will still be governed by *General Electric*.[20]

17. 377 U.S. 13, 84 S.Ct. 1051 (1964).

18. Id. at 21–22, 84 S.Ct. at 1057. See also L. Sullivan, Handbook of the Law of Antitrust 388–89 (1977).

19. U.S. v. General Electric, 358 F.Supp. 731 (S.D.N.Y.1973); in *Simpson* Justice Douglas had also attempted to distinguish *General Electric* by observing that the lightbulbs there were patented, while the gasoline in *Simpson* was not. In his dissent in *Simpson*, J. Stewart found this distinction to be meaningless. 377 U.S. at 26, 84 S.Ct. at 1060. In any case, the district court in the 1973 *General Electric* case felt free to condemn the lightbulb consignment arrangement, because since the Supreme Court's decision GE's patents had expired. See also, Greene v. Gen. Foods Corp., 517 F.2d 635, 652 (5th Cir. 1975), cert. denied, 424 U.S. 942, 96 S.Ct. 1409 (1976).

20. For example, Mesirow v. Peppridge Farms, Inc., 703 F.2d 339 (9th Cir. 1983), cert. denied, __ U.S. __, 104 S.Ct. 83 (1983); Hardwick v. Nu-Way Oil Co., Inc., 589 F.2d 806, 809 (5th Cir. 1979), rehearing denied, 592 F.2d 1190 (5th Cir. 1979), cert. denied, 444 U.S. 836, 100 S.Ct. 70 (1979); Pogue v. Intern. Indus., Inc., 524 F.2d 342 (6th Cir. 1975). For discussion of the generally

Although the *per se* rule against minimum RPM has some supporters, few people have had good things to say about the decision that *maximum* resale price maintenance is also illegal *per se*. In Albrecht v. Herald Co.[21] the Supreme Court condemned a newspaper's contractual limitation on the maximum price that its carriers could charge their customers.

Few Supreme Court decisions have proved more anticompetitive than *Albrecht*. A manufacturer would establish maximum resale prices for one reason: to prevent retailers from charging a monopoly price, either because they had formed a cartel or because individually they had monopoly power in their respective geographic markets. In *Albrecht* the dealers (newspaper delivery agents) were monopolists: each had an exclusive territory.[22] Even a small monopolist such as a newspaper carrier has the power to reduce output and raise price. One set of victims of this monopolization was newspaper customers, who would either pay a higher price or substitute away. Another victim, however, was the newspaper, which obtained no additional revenues from the higher price but made fewer sales because of the monopoly output reduction.

As a general rule, any action by a supplier to reduce the market power of its dealers makes both the supplier and consumers better off. Output will be higher, prices lower and the supplier will obtain larger profits. This is what the defendant was attempting to do in *Albrecht*.[23] Any antitrust policy that places a high value on efficiency or consumer welfare should approve bona fide maximum RPM agreements.

 WESTLAW REFERENCES
"resale price maintenance" /p "per se"

§ 9.4   Vertical Nonprice Restraints and the Rule of Reason

Vertical nonprice restrictions come in a number of varieties that vary with the nature of the product and its distribution system. A manufacturer might specify the locations of its retail outlets and not deal with anyone who resells the product somewhere else. The manufacturer might restrict the number of retailers with whom it will deal in a particular city, sometimes by giving a particular retailer a contractually-guaranteed exclusive right to sell there. Occasionally

---

inconsistent cases, see A.B.A. Monograph No. 2, Vertical Restrictions Limiting Intrabrand Competition 75 (1977).

21. 390 U.S. 145, 88 S.Ct. 869 (1968). See also Kiefer-Stewart Co. v. Jos. E. Seagram & Sons, Inc., 340 U.S. 211, 71 S.Ct. 259 (1951).

22. The territories were exclusive according to the terms of the carrier con-

tracts, probably because they were natural monopolies. See § 1.5 above; and see Hovenkamp, Vertical Integration by the Newspaper Monopolist, 69 Iowa L. Rev. 451 (1984).

23. See § 7.2 above.

a manufacturer makes this decision after it has established multiple dealerships in a city, and then it must terminate one or more existing dealerships. Many lawsuits alleging illegal territorial restrictions are brought by such terminated dealers.

Territorial restraints are sometimes placed on traveling distributors rather than retailers, with each distributor assigned to an exclusive territory. In addition, sometimes manufacturers assign particular customers by size or type to a distributor, and forbid other distributors from making sales to those customers. The manufacturer may reserve particular territories or customers to itself. A "dual distribution" system is one in which the supplier distributes part of its product through independent resellers and part through its own agents.

The history of Supreme Court analysis of vertical territorial restrictions is shorter but less consistent than its analysis of RPM. In White Motor Co. v. U.S. the Supreme Court refused to condemn a truck manufacturer's vertical territorial restrictions under a *per se* rule.[1] Neither did the Court approve rule of reason analysis, however. Rather, it held that the district court had acted too quickly in fashioning a *per se* rule condemning the practice, and should have waited until after a trial.

In a dissent in *White Motor* Justice Clark noted an important inconsistency in the Court's refusal to condemn vertical territorial restraints under a *per se* rule: *Dr. Miles* had premised its condemnation of RPM on a finding that it eliminated competition among dealers. *Horizontal* territorial division by competitors was clearly illegal *per se* because it eliminated competition among sellers. What sense did it make for the Court to treat vertical price restraints differently from vertical nonprice restraints?

Justice Clark's argument eventually carried the day, at least for a time. In U.S. v. Arnold, Schwinn & Co. the Supreme Court declared illegal *per se* all territorial restrictions imposed by a manufacturer on either a distributor or a retailer.[2] No further economic analysis was necessary to convince the Court that territorial restraints in sales transactions were "so obviously destructive of competition that their mere existence is enough" to warrant condemnation. However, the Court distinguished sales from consignment agreements in which the manufacturer "completely retains ownership and risk of loss."[3]

For the next decade the lower courts thrashed through the same mud left in the wake of the *General Electric* case—of distinguishing between legitimate and illegitimate uses of territorial restrictions

§ 9.4

1. 372 U.S. 253, 83 S.Ct. 696 (1963). The restrictions gave exclusive territories to independent distributors and also reserved certain named customers to the manufacturer.

2. 388 U.S. 365, 87 S.Ct 1856 (1967), overruled by, 433 U.S. 36, 97 S.Ct. 2549 (1977).

3. See § 9.3 above.

that appeared to be contained in consignment or licensing contracts.[4] More importantly, lower courts revolted against the *per se* rule in *Schwinn* because the value of territorial restrictions in certain distribution systems was obvious. *Schwinn* became riddled with exceptions created by the lower courts.[5]

The *Schwinn* era came to an abrupt end in 1977, when it was expressly overruled in Continental T.V., Inc. v. GTE Sylvania, Inc.[6] Sylvania, a struggling television manufacturer with 1% to 2% of the national market sought to improve its market performance by selling exclusively through a small group of carefully selected retailers. Its purpose was to minimize the amount of competition among Sylvania dealers located in the same city, and to enable them to compete better with other brands. Sylvania both limited the number of dealers that could operate in any particular area, and required each dealer to sell its products only from locations specified in its franchise contract. From 1962, when this strategy was implemented, to 1965, Sylvania's share of the television market increased to 5%.

The plaintiff Continental T.V. was a San Francisco retailer who became unhappy when Sylvania licensed an additional dealer in San Francisco. Continental began selling more televisions manufactured by other television makers and opened an unauthorized store in Sacramento. Sylvania responded first by reducing Continental's wholesale credit, and eventually by terminating its franchise.

The Court could have distinguished *Sylvania* from *Schwinn*. For example, Sylvania's market share was much lower than Schwinn's. Such distinctions might justify different outcomes under a rule of reason. However, they could not permit Sylvania to escape from the *per se* rationale developed in the *Schwinn* case. The Supreme Court overruled *Schwinn* and adopted a rule of reason for all nonprice vertical restrictions. The Court suggested that vertical territorial restraints lessened or eliminated *intrabrand* competition—that is, competition among different distributors or retailers of the same manufacturer. For example, under Sylvania's location clause, there would be fewer dealers in Sacramento than if Continental had been permitted to move there. However, Sylvania's increase in market share indicated that vertical restraints could improve *interbrand*

4. For example, Williams & Co., Inc. v. Williams & Co.—East, 542 F.2d 1053 (9th Cir. 1976), cert. denied 433 U.S. 908, 97 S.Ct. 2973 (1977).

5. See Copper Liquor, Inc. v. Adolph Coors Co., 506 F.2d 934, 944 (5th Cir. 1975), rehearing denied, 509 F.2d 758 (5th Cir. 1975), appeal after remand, 624 F.2d 575 (5th Cir. 1980), which followed *Schwinn* but suggested that the *per se* approach was irrational when the defendant's product was perishable or subject to deterioration if not delivered speedily and properly. For analysis of other judicial opinions and scholarly articles criticizing *Schwinn*, see Continental T.V. v. GTE Sylvania Inc., 433 U.S. 36, 47–48, 97 S.Ct. 2549, 2556–57 (1977), on remand, 461 F.Supp. 1046 (D.Cal.1978), judgment affirmed, 694 F.2d 1132 (9th Cir. 1982).

6. Id.

competition—competition among different brands of the same product.

The possibility of substantial procompetitive effects warranted taking nonprice restraints out of the *per se* rule, which applies only when judicial experience with a practice suggests that it is almost always injurious and almost never beneficial to competition. Under the *per se* rule, the Court noted, restraints would be "conclusively presumed to be unreasonable and therefore illegal without elaborate inquiry as to the precise harm they have caused or the business excuse for their use."[7] The possibility that nonprice restraints could improve interbrand competition made such a conclusive presumption inappropriate.

The *Sylvania* rule is easy to formulate. Vertical territorial restraints may lessen competition among the dealers of the manufacturer imposing the restraints. However, they may increase competition among the brands of different manufacturers. The rule of reason requires a court to weigh these two effects against each other and determine whether the net result is competitive or anticompetitive. More commonly, courts say that "a vertical restraint may be reasonable if it is likely to promote interbrand competition without overly restricting intrabrand competition."[8]

However, the rule of reason analysis developed in *Sylvania* leaves two unanswered questions: 1) What does it mean to say that intrabrand competition is "lessened"? 2) How does a court "balance" an increase in interbrand competition against a decrease in intrabrand competition?

The *Sylvania* court's notion of intraband "competition" apparently described a situation in which many sellers of the same brand were wedged into the same market. Its concession in *Sylvania* that "[v]ertical restrictions reduce intrabrand competition" really meant that territorial restrictions can reduce the number of sellers of a particular brand in a particular geographic area. "Intrabrand competition" as the court used it did *not* refer to a situation in which output is maximized and prices are driven toward marginal cost. A manufacturer who has no market power (such as Sylvania) will not be able to create it by the simple device of dividing territories. If it already has market power, it will not be able to enlarge it by territorial division, although it might foolishly transfer some monopoly profits to its dealers.[9]

This much seems inescapable: Sylvania was a struggling television manufacturer with a market share of less than 5%. It could not obtain a higher price for televisions by reducing the number it sold.

7. 433 U.S. at 57, 97 S.Ct. at 2561, quoting from the *White Motor* case.

8. Continental T.V., Inc. v. GTE Sylvania, Inc., 694 F.2d 1132, 1137 (9th Cir. 1982).

9. See § 9.2 above.

The retailers were Sylvania's distributors, and the same rule applies to them. When the manufacturer has no market power, the entire notion that a vertical restriction lessens intrabrand "competition" is empty. To be sure, if the manufacturer miscalculated about the effect of the restriction, the result might be that it would simply sell fewer units—that is apparently what happened in the *Schwinn* case.[10] However, rival manufacturers would immediately make up the difference. Neither Sylvania nor its retailers had the power to lessen competition in any meaningful sense of that word. Today several circuits hold that intraband competition cannot be "lessened" at all unless the manufacturer imposing the restraints has market power.[11]

Even when the manufacturer is a monopolist, however, some explanation must be found for how it can increase its profits by dividing territories. More importantly, will these increased profits come about from reduced output or increased output? The most plausible explanation for vertical territorial restrictions, even when the manufacturer is a monopolist, is control of free rider problems. In that case, however, the restrictions are designed to increase output—not a very good argument that intrabrand competition has been "lessened." [12]

The second problem with *Sylvania's* rule of reason is more ambiguous. Conceding that a vertical restriction might somehow injure intrabrand "competition," can any court really balance the reduced competition in one "market" (Sylvania televisions) against the increased competition in a different market (all televisions)? Efficiency is generally measured as a reduction in marginal cost; market power is measured by the ratio of price to marginal cost. Courts measure both of these things by extremely crude approximations—often little more than hunches guided by a few historically developed presumptions. Even if the *Sylvania* rule of reason could be given a content, no court would be able to use the rule, except perhaps in the clearest of cases.

Some of the difficulties are apparent in the Ninth Circuit's treatment of the *Sylvania* case on remand. The Court dismissed Continental's complaint, after purporting to balance the reduction in intrabrand competition against the increase in interbrand competition.

10. After the territorial restrictions in *Schwinn* were put into effect, the company's market share declined from 22% to 13%, while at least one competitor's sales doubled. 388 U.S. at 368–69, 87 S.Ct at 1861.

11. JBL Enter., Inc. v. Jhirmack Enter., Inc., 698 F.2d 1011, 1017 (9th Cir. 1983), cert. denied, ___ U.S. ___, 104 S.Ct. 106 (1983); Graphic Prod. Distrib., Inc. v. Itek Corp., 717 F.2d 1560, 1568 (11th Cir. 1983); Valley Liquors, Inc. v.

Renfield Importers, Ltd., 678 F.2d 742, 743 (7th Cir. 1982); Muenster Butane, Inc. v. Stewart Co., 651 F.2d 292, 298 (5th Cir. 1980). But see Eiberger v. Sony Corp. of Amer., 622 F.2d 1068 (2d Cir. 1980), where the court condemned a vertical restriction even though the defendant's market share was 12%. See Hovenkamp, Vertical Restrictions and Monopoly Power, 64 Boston Univ.L.Rev. (1984).

12. See § 9.2 above.

As evidence that Sylvania's restraints on intrabrand competition were not substantial, the Court noted that the territorial restrictions were not "airtight"—any time it wanted Sylvania could add a second dealer to a territory. Further, no Sylvania dealer was terminated in response to a complaint about price-cutting from a competing Sylvania dealer, and there was no evidence that "Sylvania adopted its location clause policy to prevent price discounting * * *." The Court concluded that the restraints improved interbrand competition because any retailer who wished to sell televisions could obtain equivalent units from a different manufacturer, because Sylvania did not prevent its dealers from handling televisions manufactured by competitors and did not adopt its territorial restrictions at the request of retailers other than the plaintiff.[13]

This potpourri of factors may say something about the degree of competition in the retail market for televisions—but it is a long way from "balancing" injury to intrabrand competition against benefits to interbrand competition. In fact, the Court overlooked the factors that would seem most relevant—that Sylvania never had a significant share of any market relevant to the case, and that its market share increased after the restraints were put into place. Increases in output or market share are not good evidence that a practice is monopolistic.[14]

Antitrust analysis proceeds by a series of rebuttable presumptions with a conclusive presumption at the end. The burden flops back and forth until one party reaches a presumption that cannot be defeated. The chief difference between the *per se* rule and the rule of reason lies in the number of presumptions. The simplest price fixing case may contain only one presumption, and it is usually conclusive: for example, if the defendants agreed about price they are guilty. The list of presumptions in a merger or monopolization case is likely to be longer. The complex facts presented in a rule of reason case oblige the court to simplify, however, and it simplifies with presumptive rules. For example a merger between dominant firms in a concentrated market is presumptively illegal. A firm whose market share is 90% is presumed to have monopoly power. The rule announced in *Schwinn* was defective because the Court misunderstood the economics of distribution and applied the wrong conclusive presumption. The rule in *Sylvania* was defective because the Court never explained what the appropriate presumptions were, and the lower courts are still struggling to find them.

---

13. Continental T.V., Inc. v. GTE Sylvania, Inc., 694 F.2d 1132, 1137 (9th Cir. 1982).

14. For further criticism of the rule of reason in restricted distribution cases see Posner, The Next Step in the Anti-trust Treatment of Restricted Distribution: Per Se Legality, 48 U.Chi.L.Rev. 6 (1981); Baker, Interconnected Problems of Doctrine and Economics in the Section One Labyrinth: Is *Sylvania* A Way Out? 67 Va.L.Rev. 1457 (1981).

Given the economics of vertical territorial restraints, the best presumptive rule would be that such restraints are legal. To defeat the presumption a plaintiff should show 1) interbrand collusion at either the dealer or manufacturer level; or 2) that the defendant has market power *and* that the restraints are being used to facilitate intrabrand collusion or inefficient price discrimination.[15]

Courts are simply incapable of dealing with the kind of nondescript, open-ended "rule of reason" articulated in *Sylvania*. They are inveterately inclined to fill in with presumptions that will enable them to simplify complex facts. Often these presumptions lead courts astray. Two have been particularly troublesome. One presumption is that when a manufacturer imposes restrictions or disciplines a dealer at the request of a competing dealer, the restriction is really "horizontal" and falls under the *per se* rule. That presumption, which is discussed in the previous section, has probably been laid to rest by the Supreme Court.[16]

The second presumption is that territorial restrictions are inherently suspect, likely to be "horizontal," when the manufacturer is engaged in dual distribution. In a dual distribution system the manufacturer both operates its own dealerships and sells its manufactured product to independent dealers.[17] Many oil companies, for example, operate some company-owned retail stations themselves, while they also enter into franchise agreements with independently owned stations. The contracts with the independent stations may contain various territorial or customer restrictions which sometimes insulate the manufacturer owned outlets from the competition of independents.

In *Sylvania* the Supreme Court suggested in an ambiguous footnote, probably not referring to dual distribution, that some arrangements may present "occasional problems in differentiating vertical restrictions from horizontal restrictions." The latter would clearly be "illegal *per se*." [18] This language has suggested to some courts that they must determine whether restrictions in a dual distribution system are "really" horizontal or vertical.[19]

---

15. Both the market power and the anticompetitive effect must be established. See Cowley v. Braden Indus., 613 F.2d 751 (9th Cir. 1980), cert. denied 446 U.S. 965, 100 S.Ct. 2942 (1980). The Court affirmed a judgment for the defendant, in spite of its 70% market share, because the plaintiff could not establish that the territorial restrictions at issue had any anticompetitive effect.

16. Monsanto Co. v. Spray-Rite Svce. Corp., ___ U.S. ___, 104 S.Ct. 1464 (1984), rehearing denied, ___ U.S. ___, 104 S.Ct. 2378 (1984).

17. See Altschuler, *Sylvania*, Vertical Restraints and Dual Distribution, 25 Antitrust Bull. 1 (1980).

18. 433 U.S. at 58 n. 28, 97 S.Ct. at 2561.

19. Photovest Corp. v. Fotomat Corp., 606 F.2d 704 (7th Cir. 1979), cert. denied, 445 U.S. 917, 100 S.Ct. 1278 (1980); Coleman Motor Co. v. Chrysler Corp., 525 F.2d 1338 (3d Cir. 1975).

However, the same analysis applies to dual distribution systems as to all other systems. A manufacturer who has no market power cannot use dual distribution to create it. Furthermore, there is no theory under which even a monopoly manufacturer can increase its profit-maximizing price by "conspiring" with its wholly-owned retailers, even if the effect is to injure competing, independent retailers. If the manufacturer has market power, any monopoly profits earned at the retailer level could also be earned at the manufacturer level.

Dual distribution networks are even more susceptible to free rider problems than wholly independent networks are. Manufacturer-owned outlets have no incentive to take a free ride, for their profit-and-loss statement is the same as that of their parent. Knowing this, the independent dealers have a strong incentive to free ride: the manufacturer-owned outlet is forced to provide the point-of-sale services and is unlikely to respond to the free rider by cutting services and price itself.

Further, at least one thing suggests that the manufacturer engaged in dual distribution is *not* participating in a retailer cartel: the fact that the manufacturer can and is selling part of its output through its own stores. Any retail cartel would transfer monopoly profits away from the manufacturer and toward the independent retailers. As § 9.2 above noted, the manufacturer's best response to such retailer price fixing is to enter retailing itself and keep the monopoly profits. The manufacturer engaged in dual distribution has already entered. Indeed, the existence of a dual distribution scheme is often evidence that the manufacturer is trying to combat chronic retailer collusion or poor performance by forcing independent retailers to match its prices.

As a general rule the existence of a dual distribution system should be irrelevant to the court's analysis of vertical restrictions. Some recent decisions tend toward this view.[20]

 WESTLAW REFERENCES
rule /2 reason /p vertical +1 price +1 restraint restriction
horizontal /s restriction restraint /p "per se"

---

20. See Copy Data Systems, Inc. v. Toshiba America, Inc., 663 F.2d 405, 411 (2d Cir. 1981), on remand, 582 F.Supp. 231 (D.N.Y.1984); Red Diamond Supply, Inc. v. Liquid Carbonic Corp., 637 F.2d 1001, 1004–05 (5th Cir. 1981), cert. denied, 454 U.S. 827, 102 S.Ct. 119 (1981).

CHAPTER 10

REFUSALS TO DEAL

Table of Sections

§ 10.1 When Is the Refusal to Deal a Distinct Antitrust Offense?

An unregulated firm is generally free to deal or refuse to deal with whomever it pleases. Nevertheless, a great deal of antitrust litigation arises out of refusals to deal, the plaintiff usually claiming either that the defendant refused to deal with it or forced others to refuse to deal, and that competition was injured as a result. The "concerted" refusal to deal—an agreement of two or more persons not to deal with a third—is often characterized as *per se* illegal under the antitrust laws.[1]

In most antitrust litigation involving refusals to deal the refusal itself is not the violation. Most antitrust complaints brought by victims of refusals to deal allege that the defendants were involved in illegal monopolization, tying, price fixing, resale price maintenance or vertical nonprice restraints, or an illegal merger. Other complaints of refusal to deal do not explicitly allege a secondary violation, but the theory of the complaint makes sense only on the premise that the defendant was commiting a secondary violation. If this "supporting" antitrust violation is not apparent, often the plaintiff is unable to offer any explanation why the refusal to deal is anticompetitive.

§ 10.1

1. Klor's, Inc. v. Broadway-Hale Stores, Inc., 359 U.S. 207, 79 S.Ct. 705 (1959).

273

In such cases the refusal to deal might more appropriately be considered a type of antitrust injury than a substantive violation. For example, if a firm engaging in resale price maintenance refuses to sell to a noncomplying retailer, the alleged antitrust violation is the attempt to control resale prices.[2] If the plaintiff's theory of injury is that the defendant refused to sell to it because the plaintiff was a price cutter, then the plaintiff must prove illegal resale price maintenance in order to recover.

The refusal to deal can perform two important functions in antitrust law, however, even when it is not a separate violation. First, it gives a cause of action to a set of plaintiffs who have good knowledge about a market and are highly motivated to bring their action. A high percentage of private antitrust filings come from terminated retailers, distributors, or other franchisees.[3]

Second, the presence or absence of a refusal to deal often helps a court evaluate activities such as joint ventures, that are arguably both efficient and anticompetitive. No court can quantify efficiency and injury to competition and balance one against the other, particularly in close cases. This complicates legal analysis of joint ventures that have a potential to be both anticompetitive and efficient. In many such cases, however, all the efficiencies could be attained without the refusal to deal—that is, although the joint venture might be competitive, an anticompetitive motive best explains the refusal to deal. For example, Appalachian Coals, Inc. v. U.S.[4] involved a joint selling agency created by a group of competing coal producers. The agency almost certainly marketed coal more efficiently than the members did separately. Because coal is fungible, however, the agency charged the same price for all deliveries of a particular grade of coal. Therefore producers had to agree about price. The members were required to sell their coal exclusively through the agency. A member of the venture would have refused to deal with anyone who tried to buy coal from it directly. Even assuming that the sales agency was efficient, there was no reasonable explanation offered why the agreement required exclusivity. One explanation is that the defendants were fixing prices and wanted to prevent members from making noncartel sales.

On the other hand, Broadcast Music, Inc. v. CBS[5] involved a nonexclusive joint sales agency engaged in blanket licensing. Under the blanket licensing agreement any artist was free to sell performance rights either through the blanket license or else separately by

2. For example, Monsanto Co. v. Spray-Rite Svce. Corp., __ U.S. __, 104 S.Ct. 1464 (1984), rehearing denied, __ U.S. __, 104 S.Ct. 2378 (1984).

3. See chapters eight and nine above.

4. 288 U.S. 344, 53 S.Ct. 471 (1933). See § 4.3 above.

5. 441 U.S. 1, 99 S.Ct. 1551 (1979), on remand, 607 F.2d 543 (2d Cir. 1979), cert. denied, 450 U.S. 970, 101 S.Ct. 1491 (1981), rehearing denied, 450 U.S. 1050, 101 S.Ct. 1772 (1981). See § 4.3 above.

an individual per-use transaction. The fact that the members were free to sell outside the joint venture undermines any notion that blanket licensing was an output reduction scheme.

Refusals to deal have been considered separate antitrust violations in two different circumstances: 1) when two or more firms acting in concert deny market access to another firm or force someone else to do so; 2) when the firm refusing to deal is a monopolist and the refusal tends to create a monopoly in a second market. The first of these practices is generally analyzed as a combination in restraint of trade under § 1 of the Sherman Act, the second as illegal monopolization under § 2 of the Sherman Act.

 WESTLAW REFERENCES
refus** /2 deal /p offense

§ 10.2   Exclusionary Practices and Concerted Refusals to Deal: The Per Se Rule

The most common explanation why concerted refusals to deal are anticompetitive is that they create or enhance the market power of the participating firms. In Eastern States Retail Lumber Dealers' Ass'n v. U.S.[1] the Supreme Court decided that, although a firm acting alone may refuse to deal with anyone, an agreement among competitors not to deal with certain persons acts as a clog on the market and hinders competition. *Eastern States* involved an agreement among lumber retailers to identify lumber wholesalers who were dealing directly with consumers. If a wholesaler was found to be retailing directly, the wholesaler's name was put on a "blacklist" and the retailers refused to purchase at wholesale from him.

The lumber retailers might have wanted to force wholesalers to stay out of retailing for two reasons. First, by eliminating one firm in the distribution chain, the wholesalers may have been more efficient retailers than the unintegrated retailers themselves.[2] By refusing to deal with wholesalers engaged in such vertical integration, the independent retailers may have tried to prevent the wholesalers' entry into retail markets. If vertical integration to retailing reduced the lumber wholesalers' costs, however, the boycott by the independent retailers would probably only delay, not prevent, the vertical integration. Some wholesalers would establish retail outlets and retail *all* their lumber through them. Then they would be immune from the boycott.

The second possibility is that the lumber retailers were fixing prices. The retailers' mark-up is the wholesalers' cost of distribution, and the wholesalers would naturally prefer to keep that cost as low

§ 10.2

1. 234 U.S. 600, 34 S.Ct. 951 (1914).

2. See the discussion of vertical integration in § 7.2 above.

as possible. If the retailers were engaged in price fixing the whole-salers would lose volume to the cartel's output reduction, but all the monopoly profits would go to the retailers. The wholesalers might try to protect their own interests by finding retailers who were not members of the cartel or else by retailing the lumber themselves. The concerted refusal to deal may have been a cartel's effort to prevent loss of sales because of competitive entry by the wholesal-ers.[3]

Many concerted refusals assume the general appearance of the *Eastern States* boycott—the refusal either facilitates a different antitrust violation, such as price fixing, or else protects the defen-dants from competitive entry. In fact, if the often repeated rule that concerted refusals are illegal *per se* has any meaning, it must be confined to circumstances when the purpose of the refusal is to enhance the market power of the parties to the agreement. For example, Fashion Originators' Guild of Amer. v. FTC [4] (FOGA) in-volved an agreement among garment designers and manufacturers not to sell their "original creations" to retailers who also purchased garments from "pirates"—manufacturers who allegedly copied the designs of FOGA members and sold the garments at a lower price. As a defense, the FOGA members offered to show that the boycott was reasonable because manufacturers, laborers, retailers and con-sumers needed protection from the pirates. However, the garment designs could not themselves be copyrighted or patented. Two decades earlier, in International News Service v. Associated Press[5], the Supreme Court had decided that Associated Press had a property right in its uncopyrighted news stories and could enjoin a competitor from paraphrasing them. However, in Cheney Bros. v. Doris Silk Corp.[6] Judge Learned Hand decided that the *International News* protection did not extend to clothing design piracy.

The patent and copyright laws encourage innovation by giving a limited legal monopoly to the developer of a new invention, composi-tion or design. The kind of innovation that qualifies for such protection has always been a subject of intensive legislative and judicial regulation. Both Congress and the courts had agreed that clothing designers did not merit such monopoly protection. The

3. A third possibility is that there were large retail buyers who did not require the special services provided by the retailers. The wholesalers could en-large their profits by making these large sales directly to the retail buyers, and eliminating an additional market trans-action, transportation, storage, etc. See also Engine Specialties, Inc. v. Bombar-dier Ltd., 605 F.2d 1 (1st Cir. 1979), on rehearing, 615 F.2d 575 (1st Cir. 1980), cert. denied, 446 U.S. 983, 100 S.Ct. 2964 (1980), rehearing denied, 449 U.S. 893, 101 S.Ct. 259 (1980), where the refusal

to deal was probably part of a horizontal territorial division scheme. For further discussion of vertical integration as a means of cartel avoidance, see § 7.2 above.

4. 312 U.S. 457, 61 S.Ct. 703 (1941).

5. 248 U.S. 215, 39 S.Ct. 68 (1918).

6. 35 F.2d 279 (2d Cir. 1929), cert. denied, 281 U.S. 728, 50 S.Ct. 245 (1930). See Baird, Common Law Intellectual Property and the Legacy of Internation-al News Service v. Assoc. Press, 50 U.Chi.L.Rev. 411 (1983).

members of FOGA were effectively trying to give themselves the monopoly protection that the legislative and judicial branches had denied them. Justice Black concluded that it was not error for the FTC to refuse to consider FOGA's defense that many constituents needed protection from style pirates.[7]

The "piracy" claim makes *FOGA* more difficult to characterize than *Eastern States*. Lack of copyright or patent protection notwithstanding, the members of FOGA had a substantial free rider problem. If one group of manufacturers spends money developing new fashion designs, but another group is entitled to copy the designs at no charge, the result might be that creating original designs will become unprofitable and no one will do it.[8] In that case the Guild was correct and consumers are better off if the free riders can be controlled. Nevertheless, the concerted refusal to deal employed by the defendants has a large potential to cover price fixing. If the free rider problem in this instance is serious enough to have a solution, it should come from Congress.

In Klor's, Inc. v. Broadway-Hale Stores, Inc.[9] the Supreme Court clearly held that a concerted refusal to deal could be a *per se* violation of § 1 of the Sherman Act. The Court held that the plaintiff's mere allegation of a concerted refusal was sufficient to withstand a motion for summary judgment, even though the plaintiff had not alleged any injury to the "public," in the form of reduced output or higher prices.

The facts of *Klor's* are perplexing, and there is some reason to think the Court would reconsider its decision today. Some federal circuit courts have made decisions that are inconsistent, at least in principle, with its holding.[10] The plaintiff was a retailer in kitchen

---

7. 312 U.S. at 468, 61 S.Ct. at 708. Some states have tried to give designs greater protection than is offered by federal law. In Sears, Roebuck & Co. v. Stiffel Co., 376 U.S. 225, 84 S.Ct. 784 (1964), the Supreme Court declared one such attempt to be preempted by federal patent and antitrust law. Even today there is little protection against clothing design piracy. See Comment, Designer Law: Fashioning a Remedy for Design Piracy, 30 U.C.L.A.L.Rev. 861 (1983).

8. For discussion of free rider problems see § 9.2 above. Presumably, however, the members of FOGA had labels, which were trademarked. Although a pirate might be entitled to copy an Yves St. Laurent design, he would not be entitled to copy the Yves St. Laurent label affixed to the article of clothing. Many customers might value the label as much as they value the design itself. This explains the proliferation of "designer" clothing in which the designer's label

appears prominently on the article of clothing itself.

9. 359 U.S. 207, 79 S.Ct. 705 (1959).

10. For example, Valley Liquors, Inc. v. Renfield Importers, Ltd., 678 F.2d 742 (7th Cir. 1982), applying a rule of reason to an allegation of dealer termination in response to complaints from competing dealers. In Monsanto Co. v. Spray-Rite Svce. Corp., ___ U.S. ___, 104 S.Ct. 1464 (1984), rehearing denied, ___ U.S. ___, 104 S.Ct. 2378 (1984), the Supreme Court held that mere evidence that a supplier refused to deal with a distributor as a result of another distributor's complaint was not sufficient to create a jury question about the existence of an agreement in violation of the antitrust laws. In *Klor's* the plaintiff alleged a "wide combination consisting of manufacturers, distributors and a retailer," and the Supreme Court held that the allegation of conspiracy stated a cause of action un-

appliances. One defendant, Broadway-Hale, was a competing, although larger, retailer. The other defendants were major manufacturers and distributors of kitchen appliances. Klor's claimed that Broadway-Hale conspired with these distributors and manufacturers to refuse to supply Klor's with appliances, or else to supply them only at discriminatorily high prices and unfavorable terms.

Assuming that Broadway-Hale had a motive for driving its competitor out of business, why would the major appliance manufacturers participate in such a scheme? The plaintiff alleged that Broadway-Hale used its "monopolistic" buying power to force manufacturer agreement. That allegation is plausible only on the assumption that Broadway-Hale had market power in its local retail market, and Klor's was underselling its monopoly price. However, the large appliance manufacturers would be best off if their retailers were behaving as competitively as possible, and Broadway-Hale's monopoly mark-up would make them worse off.

There is a more plausible explanation: Klor's was a free rider and Broadway-Hale complained to the manufacturers. The manufacturers wanted their retailers to spend substantial resources in displaying and servicing their merchandise, and in providing information to customers. If Broadway-Hale performed these services but Klor's did not, Klor's would be able to charge a lower price. Furthermore, customers would be tempted to take a free ride on Broadway-Hale's services—they might go to Broadway-Hale and obtain all essential information about appliances, but then go to Klor's to make their purchases. A manufacturer might try to solve the problem of free riding either by giving its retailers exclusive territories, or else by resale price maintenance.[11] When *Klor's* was decided, the status of the first practice was undetermined, but the second was *per se* illegal.

Since *Klor's* many courts have said that concerted refusals to deal are *per se* illegal.[12] The rule has become so riddled with exceptions,

der the *per se* rule. However, the Ninth Circuit in *Klor's* had dismissed the complaint because there was "no charge or proof that by any act of defendants the price, quantity, or quality offered the public was affected," nor was there "any intent or purpose to effect a change in, or an influence on, prices quantity, or quality * * *." 255 F.2d at 230. The alleged agreement in *Klor's* should therefore be characterized as a "nonprice" agreement. As the Supreme Court noted in the *Monsanto* case, since the decision in Continental T.V., Inc. v. GTE Sylvania, Inc., 433 U.S. 36, 97 S.Ct. 2549 (1977), on remand, 461 F.Supp. 1046 (1978), judgment affirmed, 694 F.2d 1132 (9th Cir. 1982), the court has made an "important distinction in

distributor-termination cases * * * between concerted action to set prices and concerted action on nonprice restrictions. The former have been per se illegal * * * [while the] latter are judged under the rule of reason." *Monsanto*, 104 S.Ct. at 1469.

11. See § 9.2 above.

12. For example, Malley-Duff & Assoc., Inc. v. Crown Life Ins. Co., 734 F.2d 133 (3d Cir. 1984), which adopted the entire line of reasoning in *Klor's*. The court reversed a district court decision holding that a plaintiff must show that the concerted refusal had an adverse impact on consumers. See Bauer, Per Se Illegality of Concerted Refusals to Deal: A Rule Ripe for Reexamina-

however, that it has lost all meaningful content. There are exceptions for so-called noncommercial boycotts,[13] for certain boycotts
designed to enforce disciplinary rules or safety standards, and for a
broad category of efficiency-creating joint ventures.[14] Unfortunately, there is no easy way to determine whether a particular concerted
refusal qualifies for one of these exceptions. In 1968 the Supreme
Court attempted a somewhat narrower statement of the *per se* rule,
suggesting that under "the Sherman Act, any agreement by a group
of competitors to boycott a particular buyer or group of buyers is
illegal *per se*."[15] The Court did not mean to suggest that all other
concerted refusals should receive the rule of reason. However, some
circuit courts have suggested that the *per se* rule should not generally apply to concerted refusals unless the parties to the refusal are
competitors.[16]

In Berkey Photo, Inc. v. Eastman Kodak Co.[17] the Second Circuit
applied the rule of reason to a concerted refusal that accompanied a
research and development joint venture of noncompetitors. Kodak
and General Electric jointly developed a new line of cameras and a
new flash attachment to accompany them. They also agreed not to
predisclose details of the new technology to competing camera and
flash attachment manufacturers, one of which was the plaintiff. As
a result, Berkey could not quickly enter the market for either the
new camera or the new flash equipment. The court held that a joint
agreement between "a monopolist [Kodak] and a firm in a comple-
mentary market" necessarily qualified for rule of reason treatment,
because the parties to the agreement did not eliminate competition
between themselves. The court went on, however, to find the agreement not to predisclose unreasonable. Kodak's monopoly position
was essential to that determination. As a result the refusal to
predisclose might more appropriately be treated as an exclusionary
practice by a monopolist, rather than a "concerted" refusal to deal.[18]

An antitrust policy based on efficiency would try to condemn
inefficient concerted refusals and approve efficient ones. A court
would apply the *per se* rule if a practice was highly likely to be
inefficient, but the cost of full economic inquiry was very large when

tion, 79 Col. L. Rev. 685 (1979), which
summarizes other decisions and scholarly writings.

13. Missouri v. National Organiza-
tion for Women, Inc., 620 F.2d 1301 (8th
Cir. 1980), cert. denied, 449 U.S. 842, 101
S.Ct. 122 (1980). See Note, *NOW or
Never: Is There Antitrust Liability for
Noncommercial Boycotts*, 80 Col.L.Rev.
1317 (1980).

14. See the following section.

15. FMC v. Svenska Amerika Linien,
390 U.S. 238, 250, 88 S.Ct. 1005, 1012
(1968). The Supreme Court later applied

this rule in St. Paul Fire & Marine Ins.
Co. v. Barry, 438 U.S. 531, 98 S.Ct. 2923
(1978).

16. See Cascade Cabinet Co. v. Western Cabinet and Millwork, Inc., 710 F.2d
1366, 1370–71 (9th Cir. 1983).

17. 603 F.2d 263 (2d Cir. 1979), cert.
denied, 444 U.S. 1093, 100 S.Ct. 1061
(1980).

18. The evidence indicated that the
agreement not to predisclose was initiated by Kodak, and General Electric went
along only reluctantly. 603 F.2d at 300.

balanced against the likelihood that such inquiry would produce a substantially more accurate result.[19] The *Eastern States* boycott was a good candidate for *per se* treatment because the only plausible explanations for the boycott were anticompetitive. The same thing generally holds true of *FOGA*. *Klor's*, on the other hand, was a good candidate for rule of reason treatment because there was at least one alternative explanation consistent with the alleged facts— the defendant manufacturers were trying to control free rider problems.

The courts' general refusal to apply the *per se* rule to concerted refusals by noncompetitors is wise: agreements between firms that do not compete are far less likely to be anticompetitive than agreements of competitors. However, application of the *per se* rule to all concerted refusals by competitors would cut much too broadly. As the following section illustrates, joint ventures of competitors may frequently use refusals to deal efficiently, particularly if the joint venture is involved in rule making or standard setting.

Refusals to deal by joint ventures of competitors may easily become anticompetitive, and they merit close judicial scrutiny. However, their potential for efficiency generally makes the rule of reason appropriate. The best rule is that a "naked" refusal to deal by competitors—that is, a refusal unaccompanied by any integration of business activities—should be illegal *per se*. However, any refusal that accompanies a joint venture or broader integration of activities than the refusal itself should initially receive the rule of reason.[20]

A properly defined *noncommercial* boycott is generally exempt from antitrust liability, even though the boycott is inefficient.[21] The exemption rests on two different theories. One is that the boycotters are protected by Constitutional rights that "trump" the antitrust laws, such as the first amendment or equal protection clause.[22] The other theory, which may preclude litigation of the constitutional issues, is that the Sherman and Clayton Acts were not designed to be applied to noncommercial activities.[23] In cases involving allegedly noncommercial boycotts the question is generally not whether to apply a *per se* rule or a rule of reason, but whether the antitrust laws should be applied at all.

  WESTLAW REFERENCES

(exclusionary /4 practice) (concerted /3 refus** /3 deal) /p "per se"

---

19. On the *per se* rule, see § 4.4 above.

20. The proposal comes from R. Bork, The Antitrust Paradox: A policy at War With Itself 334 (1978).

21. Even a noncommercial boycott may force its targets out of business and may inadvertently create a monopoly.

22. NAACP v. Claiborne Hardware Co., 458 U.S. 886, 102 S.Ct. 3409 (1982), rehearing denied, 459 U.S. 898, 103 S.Ct. 199 (1982). See Sullivan, First Amendment Defenses in Antitrust Litigation, 46 Mis.L.Rev. 517 (1981).

23. Missouri v. National Organization for Women, Inc., 620 F.2d at 1309. See note 13 above.

§ 10.3 Concerted Refusals and Efficiency

Many joint ventures involving refusals to deal are efficient—they enable the participating firms to operate at lower cost. As a result a court considering the legality of a refusal to deal that accompanies a joint venture must ask two questions. First, is the joint venture itself competitive or anticompetitive?[1] Second, if the venture is competitive, what policy is furthered by the refusal to deal? A refusal to deal might injure competition even if it is attached to a joint venture which is, on balance, efficient.

The clearly anticompetitive joint venture presents the simplest case. If the only plausible motive for the joint activity is price fixing or delay of competitive entry, as it was in the *Eastern States Lumber* case discussed in the preceding section, both the joint venture and the refusal to deal are illegal.

At the other extreme is the joint venture whose capacity for efficiency is large and whose danger to competition is very small. Consider a decision by three small firms in an unconcentrated market to undertake jointly a risky, expensive, but potentially profitable project. For any firm acting alone, the risk in proportion to the cost would make the venture unwise. For three working together, however, the investment is far more attractive.[2] A fourth firm in the market is invited to participate but refuses. The project is developed, succeeds, and the new product or process is profitable. Now the fourth firm changes its mind and asks to "buy in." The three participants refuse.

In this example any question about the competitive effects of the joint venture can be answered by looking at one fact: the participants collectively appear to have no market power. Three firms in an unconcentrated market could not likely be reducing output or injuring competition in some other way. They did not combine to fix prices but to reduce their costs.

Given that the venture itself appears to be both harmless and efficient, should the antitrust laws require the three defendants to admit the fourth firm? Once again, the answer is a relatively easy no: the fourth firm is attempting to take a free ride on the participants' willingness to take a risk. If any firm could refuse to participate in a high risk project today, knowing that later when the project has become a success it will have a legal right to enter, the

§ 10.3

1. Joint ventures are discussed in § 4.3 above.

2. This is particularly true of research and development joint ventures. A three-way joint venture to develop a patentable product or process will cost each firm one-third as much as individual development would. However, the process, once developed, can be duplicated by all three firms. Each one will receive as great a benefit as if it had developed the patented product or process alone (ignoring monopoly profits that might be obtained by an individual developer but not by each of three competing developers). See § 4.3 above.

result would be that no firms would join immediately, but all would wait and see.

The problem of evaluation is much more difficult when the overall impact of the joint venture is ambiguous—for example, when the joint venture has the potential to create substantial efficiency but the participants collectively have a great deal of market power. In evaluating the claim of an excluded rival a court might be asked to balance the injury to competition that results from the exclusion, against the inefficiency of a rule that permits all latecomers to join. Courts are not capable of quantifying these two things and measuring them against each other.

The inefficient refusal to deal accompanying an efficient joint venture has often come to the courts. Two Supreme Court decisions are particularly important because the joint ventures at issue clearly created substantial economies—in fact, the joint ventures were natural monopolies that gave the participants significant cost advantages over nonparticipating competitors. In both cases the Supreme Court condemned the accompanying refusal to deal under § 1 of the Sherman Act.

The first case, U.S. v. Terminal R.R. Ass'n. of St. Louis,[3] involved an association of several railroad companies and bridge companies into a giant railroad terminal and transfer system in St. Louis, Missouri, where the Mississippi River and several railroad lines came together. The system greatly facilitated transfers of cargo and coordination of traffic and was obviously efficient; in fact, it was almost certainly a natural monopoly. The system was initiated by six of the railroads, however, and latecomers were admitted to joint ownership only upon a unanimous vote of all existing owners. A nonowner could use the system only by unanimous consent of existing owners.

The Supreme Court held that the efficiency-creating potential of the system, plus the fact that outsider railroads could not effectively compete with it, gave the owners a duty to admit "any existing or future railroad to joint ownership and control of the combined terminal properties, upon such just and reasonable terms as shall place such applying company upon a plane of equality" with the existing owners. Secondly, the terminal operators must make the system available on nondiscriminatory terms to any railroad who wished to use it but elected not to become an owner.[4]

3. 224 U.S. 383, 32 S.Ct. 507 (1912).

4. Id. at 411–12, 32 S.Ct. at 516. The court was in fact applying a set of rules that were frequently applied to monopoly utilities: they must serve all paying customers, and they must serve them on a nondiscriminatory basis. See Hovenkamp, Technology, Politics and Regulated Monopoly: An American Historical Perspective, 62 Tex.L.Rev. 1263 (1984).

In U.S. v. Realty Multi-List, Inc., 629 F.2d 1351 (5th Cir. 1980) the court condemned the restrictive membership rules established by a multiple-listing service for real estate brokers in Columbus, Georgia. Once again, the service was likely a natural monopoly. The cost of

Because the joint venture in *Terminal Railroad* was a natural monopoly, anyone denied access would face higher costs. As a result the member firms might be able to reduce output and charge a monopoly price without worrying about competition.[5] When a natural monopoly market contains a single firm, the State may have to decide whether to permit the natural monopolist to charge a monopoly price, force divestiture even though multiple firms would have higher costs, or impose statutory price regulation.

In the case of a natural monopoly joint venture such as *Terminal Railroad*, however, the court may force competition *within* the joint venture by throwing it open to new entry. If the giant railroad transfer system were operated by a single firm the opportunity for monopoly profits would be substantial. In fact, such systems are generally either publicly owned or price regulated. In the *Terminal Railroad* case, however, the Supreme Court used the Sherman Act to produce an alternative: common ownership and control of the system by a large number of competing railroads. Assuming that the railroads continued to compete with each other, the jointly operated transfer system would be unable to earn monopoly profits.

Perhaps the leading case involving a refusal to deal by a natural monopoly joint venture is Associated Press v. U.S.[6] Associated Press (AP) was a joint venture whose members were about 1,200 newspapers. AP gathered, drafted and disseminated news. Part of the work was done by employees who worked for AP, and part by reporters that AP borrowed from member newspapers. When the AP correspondent gathered news and wrote a news story in, say, Washington, D.C., all member newspapers were entitled to a copy of the story. In effect, AP enabled a single reporter to gather news that would be reported by each of the 1,200 member newspapers.

At issue in *Associated Press* was not the joint venture itself, which was conceded to be very efficient, but rather various by-laws adopted for AP by its members. The members were prohibited from selling news to non-members, and AP took several steps to insure that non-AP newspapers had no access to AP-gathered news until after it was published. AP's board of directors could freely elect new members unless the applicant competed with a newspaper that was already an AP member. In that case, if the competing member objected the new member had to pay a large fee and receive a majority vote of existing AP members. The Supreme Court held that these provisions on their face violated the Sherman Act.

assembling a weekly publication showing all houses for sale in an area is rather large; however, the marginal cost of producing one additional copy of the book is small. Total costs of producing one copy would likely decline continuously as the number of copies produced increased.

5. Since the natural monopolist faces lower costs than any outsider, it might be able to set a price high enough to give itself monopoly returns, but low enough to make entry by smaller firms unprofitable. See § 6.9 above.

6. 326 U.S. 1, 65 S.Ct. 1416 (1945).

Associated Press's organization and its by-laws are relatively easy to understand. Assuming that news stories are fungible—that one reporter's coverage of President Kennedy's inauguration is as good as another's—the creation of news is a natural monopoly. The costs of producing a news story are largely the costs of sending a reporter to the scene to collect the information and write the story. Once the story is finished it can be transmitted to another newspaper for little more than the costs of the wire service. If ten daily newspapers want to gather news from Washington, D.C., the cheapest method would be for the ten newspapers to have a single news staff in Washington, D.C., which would compose the stories and simultaneously send copies to all ten.

Assume that the world contains ten cities and that each city has one or two newspapers. One reporter is sufficient to cover one city's news, and the costs of maintaining one reporter are $100 per week. Absent news sharing, each newspaper would have total news gathering costs of $1,000—$100 for each reporter in each of the ten cities. Suppose that eight of the newspapers agree that the home reporter for each of them will distribute the news to the other seven. Assuming that transmission of the story is costless, each of these eight newspapers will now be able to gather news at a cost of $300 per week: $100 for its own home reporter, who will also supply news to the other seven joint venturers, and $200 in order to maintain reporters in each of the two cities not having a participating newspaper.

Suppose now that a newspaper in city #9 wants to join the news-sharing venture. The existing members will likely agree. News-gathering costs will drop by another $100, for there will be joint venture members in nine cities instead of eight. No newspaper will be injured by the "competition" of the newcomer, for newspapers compete with each other only in their own circulation market. Everyone will be better off if the newspaper in the ninth city is permitted to join.

But what will happen if a *second* newspaper in city #1 wants to join? The members are already being provided with news from city #1, through its first member newspaper. As a result, entry by the second newspaper in city #1 will not lower the costs of the incumbent newspapers—it will not add anything to the efficiency of the organization, assuming that news stories are fungible and that the incumbent newspaper in city #1 is doing its job well. However, entry by the second newspaper in city #1 may injure the first member newspaper in city #1 substantially. Before entry, the first newspaper in city #1 had a $700 cost advantage over the second newspaper in city #1. After the second newspaper's entry the first newspaper will face much stiffer competition. The cost savings produced by membership in the joint venture will accrue not to the member newspaper, but to the newspaper's subscribers or advertisers.

This analysis suggests that although the joint venture in the *Associated Press* case was efficient, the by-laws that permitted competitors to object to new applicants were anticompetitive. Furthermore, AP could maintain all the efficiencies created by the venture without the anticompetitive by-laws. Finally, AP seemed not to be concerned about latecomers wishing to take a free ride on its earlier risk taking, for the organization was willing to admit latecomers who did not compete with existing members. The decision condemning the restrictive by-laws was a good one.

Concerted refusals can also be a mechanism by which firms facilitate standard setting or rule making. Both standard setting and rule making are generally in the best interests of consumers, because they substantially reduce information costs, and therefore consumer search costs.[7] The labels "grade A beef," "number two plywood," or "licensed electrician" all convey information to a consumer about the product or service that he is purchasing.

An inevitable result of any meaningful standard-setting procedure is that some providers will not meet the standard. This becomes an antitrust problem when the persons making and enforcing the standards are competitors of the person who is excluded by them. At the same time, the providers of certain products or services are experts, and often are in a better position than anyone else to evaluate the quality of a competitor's product. For example, a patient would have a difficult time determining whether a particular surgeon is competent, unless perhaps she knows several people who have been under the surgeon's scalpel. The people in the best position to evaluate a particular surgeon's expertise are fellow surgeons familiar with the same area of practice. For this reason most medical institutions have peer review boards, composed largely of doctors, which evaluate the performance of other doctors.

The doctors doing the evaluating are competitors of the doctor being evaluated, however, and they may have anticompetitive motives. They may believe that the surgeon being evaluated is cutting prices, perhaps by eliminating certain pre-surgical services that he regards as optional. Alternatively, the peer review board may believe that the hospital already has "too many" surgeons. Rather than reducing fees to attract more patients to the hospital, they would prefer to reduce the supply. In that case, assuming that the excluded or disciplined doctor can show the proper motive and agreement, the peer review board may have violated § 1 of the Sherman Act.[8]

7. See Carlton & Klamer, The Need For Coordination Among Firms, With Special Reference to Network Industries, 50 U.Chi.L.Rev. 446 (1983).

8. See Crane v. Intermountain Health Care, Inc., 637 F.2d 715 (10th Cir. 1981); Robinson v. Magovern, 521 F.Supp. 842 (W.D.Pa.1981); and see Kissam, Antitrust Law and Professional Behavior, 62 Tex.L.Rev. 1 (1983); Kissam, Government Policy Toward Medical Accreditation and Certification: the Anti-

Standard setting can be just as important in products as it is in professional services, particularly if the product is sophisticated or likely to be dangerous. In some cases public agencies such as the Food and Drug Administration evaluate and approve products. In other cases, however, evaluation is performed by private laboratories, often operated by associations composed of sellers and related firms.[9]

Radiant Burners, Inc. v. People's Gas Light & Coke Co.[10] involved an association of gas heater manufacturers, gas pipeline companies and gas utilities which evaluated products that burned natural gas and placed a "seal of approval" on products it judged to be safe. If a product was judged unsafe the association not only refused its seal of approval, but the utility companies in the association refused to provide gas to a home or business containing the disapproved product. The plaintiff manufacturer claimed that its Radiant Burner had been disapproved by the association, and that the standards used to evaluate the Burner were arbitrary and capricious, largely because the burner was evaluated by the manufacturers of competing gas burners. In a *per curiam* opinion the Supreme Court concluded that the allegations stated a cause of action for a *per se* violation of the Sherman Act, citing Klor's, Inc. v. Broadway-Hale Stores.[11]

The plaintiff's complaint in *Radiant Burner* contained two important allegations, both of which may be necessary to bring the concerted refusal by competitors under the *per se* rule: 1) that the plaintiff's product was not evaluated objectively, but in a capricious way by competitors who had a vested interest in disapproving the product; 2) that the defendants actually forced customers not to buy the disapproved product, or in some way prevented it from entering the market. Courts have been far less clear when one of these elements was present but not the other. They have usually approved the activity when neither was present.

trust Laws and Other Procompetitive Strategies, 1983 Wis.L.Rev. 1.

Similar problems have arisen in professional sports. For example, see Molinas v. National Basketball Assn., 190 F.Supp. 241 (S.D.N.Y.1961) upholding a rule formulated by agreement among professional basketball teams requiring the suspension of a player who placed bets on his own team. The teams in this case were not competitors with the individual player. However, see Blalock v. Ladies Professional Golf Assn, 359 F.Supp. 1260 (N.D.Ga.1973), declaring *per se* unlawful a rule suspending the plaintiff for alleged cheating. The makers and enforcers of the rule were the plaintiff's competitors, and the rule gave them "unfettered, subjective discretion." See Weistart, Player Discipline in Professional Sports: the Antitrust Issues, 18 Wm. & Mary L.Rev. 703 (1977).

9. Today much industry standard setting is done under the guidance of two quasi-public organizations, the American National Standards Institute (ANSI) and the International Organization for Standardization (IOS). See Carlton and Klamer, note 7 above.

10. 364 U.S. 656, 81 S.Ct. 365 (1961).

11. 359 U.S. 207, 79 S.Ct. 705 (1959), discussed in the preceding section. See also American Medical Association v. U.S., 317 U.S. 519, 63 S.Ct. 326 (1942) which stands for the proposition that an accreditation or standard-setting association may not dismiss or discipline a member because she is a price cutter.

For example, in Eliason Corp. v. National Sanitation Foundation [12] the plaintiff, who manufactured commercial refrigerators, accused the defendant testing association of refusing to approve the design of one of its refrigerators. The standards were drawn up by a large group of manufacturers and users of commercial refrigerators. There was no evidence that the testing laboratory itself was "controlled" by competing refrigerator manufacturers, or that the plaintiff's equipment was treated any differently than the equipment of competitors. Furthermore, several other manufacturers had also received disapprovals and were forced to make design changes. Finally, approved products received the testing laboratory's seal of approval. The consequence of disapproval was merely that the seal was withdrawn. The defendants made no effort to force anyone not to purchase a refrigerator not having the seal.

In refusing to apply the *per se* rule the Sixth Circuit held that if the alleged boycott resulted from industry self-regulation or standard making, the plaintiff "must show either that it was barred from obtaining approval of its products on a discriminatory basis from its competitors, or that the conduct as a whole was manifestly unreasonable." Finding no such evidence, the court affirmed dismissal of the complaint.

If the purpose of testing and approval is to provide buyers with needed information, then the forced exclusion of the unapproved product from the market, as was alleged in *Radiant Burners*, is likely to be anticompetitive. The presence or absence of the "seal of approval" will provide the consumer with information about whether a product is safe. Forcing the product off the market is competitive only on the theory that consumers will not be able to respond rationally to the information that the seal (or its absence) provides, perhaps on the assumption that consumers do not know about the seal's existence or meaning.

A case can be made that even a coercive refusal to deal with buyers of an unapproved product is not anticompetitive if the refusal does not originate from the excluded firm's competitors, but from firms in a complimentary market. For example, in *Radiant Burners* the defendant gas utilities might have justified their refusal to provide gas to installations using the Radiant Burner on the grounds that the product could injure the utility companies' lines or increase their insurance risks.[13] Similarly, Bell Telephone Co. for many years

12. 614 F.2d 126 (6th Cir. 1980), cert. denied, 449 U.S. 826, 101 S.Ct. 89 (1980); see also Structural Laminates, Inc. v. Douglas Fir Plywood Assoc., 261 F. Supp. 154 (D.Or.1966), affirmed, 399 F.2d 155 (9th Cir. 1968), cert. denied, 393 U.S. 1024, 89 S.Ct. 636 (1969).

13. The gas companies were not required to justify their refusal because the district court dismissed the complaint for failure to state a claim, and the Seventh Circuit affirmed. Radiant Burners, Inc. v. Peoples Gas, Light & Coke Co., 273 F.2d 196 (7th Cir. 1959).

took the position that use of telephone equipment not manufactured by its Western Electric subsidiary might damage its telephone lines.[14]

The possible reasonableness of such claims notwithstanding, they should generally not be permitted as defenses in a case alleging *concerted* refusal. A gas utility might reasonably decide that a particular gas heater is so dangerous that it should not be connected to the utility's lines. However, individual utilities have access to all the information they need to make such decisions. Furthermore, each firm would make the decision in its own self-interest.[15] If the decision is justifiable, each utility would make it unilaterally, without any need for an agreement.

Finally, a requirement that the standards by which a product is evaluated be reasonable and applied in a nondiscriminatory way is important if a court is to assess motive. To be sure, the protection offered by such a legal requirement is not perfect. Often, however, it is the only means by which an outsider can assess the true purpose of what purports to be a disciplinary act.

For example, in Silver v. New York Stock Exchange (NYSE)[16] a stockbroker complained that the Exchange members denied him access to the private telephone connections necessary to monitor and execute stock transactions on the exchange. Without such lines a stockbroker is generally unable to carry on its business. The NYSE refused to provide any explanation why Silver's communication was cut off, telling him only that "it was the policy of the Exchange not to disclose the reasons for such action." When Silver charged the Exchange members with violating the Sherman Act, they answered that under the Securities Exchange Act of 1934 the members were authorized to pass and enforce their own rules and regulations governing broker activity. As a result the termination was exempt from antitrust scrutiny.

The Supreme Court did not deny that the Securities Exchange Act gave members the authority to make and enforce their own business rules. However, "nothing built into the regulatory scheme * * * performs the antitrust function of insuring that an exchange will not in some cases apply its rules so as to do injury to competition which cannot be justified as furthering legitimate self-regulative ends." At the time *Silver* was decided brokerage commissions on the NYSE were fixed. The purpose of fixed commissions was arguably to force brokers to provide the optimal number of customer services. However, the members may have reached an "understanding" about the number of services they would give. A disruptive broker who provided more services could do substantial damage to such a service

14. See Use of the Carterfone Device in Message Toll Telephone Service, 13 F.C.C.2d 420, 424 (1968).

15. I.e., there are no free rider problems. Each firm would bear the cost of its own decision, and no firm could profit by permitting installation of defective heaters in its lines while other firms refused.

16. 373 U.S. 341, 83 S.Ct. 1246 (1963).

cartel. The defense asserted in *Silver* would effectively have given the NYSE members the power to cartelize all aspects of the stock brokerage market.[17]

Allegations of concerted refusals by accreditation or standard-setting associations often arise in complex areas in which the court has little competence to determine whether the standard setting is really "objective" or reasonable. In such circumstances the court is often forced to look at motive. For example, Wilk v. American Medical Ass'n [18] involved "Principle 3" of the AMA Principles of Medical Ethics, which states that "a physician should practice a method of healing founded on a scientific basis; and he should not voluntarily professionally associate with anyone who violates this principle." Wilk was a chiropractor who claimed that physicians, acting under Principle 3, concertedly refused to give chiropractors access to medical educational facilities and hospitals, and refused to refer patients to them. The Seventh Circuit applied the rule of reason but minimized any inquiry into the question whether the physicians' disapproval of chiropractors was well-founded. Rather, it held that the plaintiff should have the initial burden of showing that Principle 3 restricted competition. If so, then the defendant physicians would have to show:

> (1) that they genuinely entertained a concern for what they perceive as scientific method in the care of each person with whom they have entered a doctor-patient relationship; (2) that this concern is objectively reasonable; (3) that this concern has been the dominant motivating factor in defendants' promulgation of Principle 3 and in the conduct intended to implement it; and (4) that this concern for scientific method in patient care could not have been adequately satisfied in a manner less restrictive of competition.

 WESTLAW REFERENCES

concerted /3 refus** /3 deal /p efficien**
di joint venture

---

17. There was some history of the NYSE warning or disciplining members for competing too intensely. Brief for United States as Amicus Curiae 37–41, Silver v. NYSE, Oct. Term 1962, #10. See also Pacific Stationery & Printing Co. v. Northwest Wholesale Stationers, Inc. 715 F.2d 1393 (9th Cir. 1983).

Under *Silver* a disciplined member of a joint venture is entitled to notice and to be presented with an explanation for the action taken. How much due process he must have beyond that point is unclear. See Zuckerman v. Yount, 362 F.Supp. 858 (N.D.Ill.1973), holding that the hearing record must contain a reasonable justification for the disciplinary action taken; but see Crimmins v. Amer. Stock Exch., 346 F.Supp. 1256 (S.D.N.Y. 1972), holding that there is no right to counsel in such disciplinary hearings.

18. 719 F.2d 207, 213, 227 (7th Cir. 1983), certiorari denied, ___ U.S. ___, 104 S.Ct. 2398 (1984). The District of Columbia Circuit has adopted the reasoning of the Seventh Circuit. Kreuzer v. American Academy of Periodontology, 735 F.2d 1479 (D.C.Cir. 1984). For an argument that professional licensing and regulation is efficient because it reduces customer search costs, see Leland, Quacks, Lemons, and Licensing: A Theory of Minimum Quality Standards, 87 J.Pol.Econ. 1328 (1979).

§ 10.4 Unilateral Refusals to Deal

In U.S. v. Colgate Co.[1] the Supreme Court reiterated the ancient common law doctrine that "[i]n the absence of any purpose to create or maintain a monopoly" a private trader may freely "exercise his own independent discretion as to parties with whom he will deal." The rule is good law, and the Supreme Court has repeated it as recently as 1980.[2]

The *Colgate* doctrine of refusal to deal contains two explicit exceptions. First, the decision not to deal must be "independent." The doctrine does not apply to concerted refusals, which are discussed in the previous sections. Second, the refusal must occur "[i]n the absence of any purpose to create or maintain a monopoly." If a unilateral refusal to deal is ever illegal, it is when the refusal is undertaken by a monopolist, or by someone who hopes by the refusal to become one.

For example, in Lorain Journal Co. v. U.S.[3] the Supreme Court condemned a monopoly newspaper's refusal to sell newspaper advertising to customers who also purchased advertising on a nearby radio station. Although the Court characterized this as an "attempt" to monopolize it is clear that the scheme required that *Lorain Journal* be a monopolist to begin with, or else anyone who wanted to buy both radio and newspaper advertising would have bought the newspaper advertising from a competitor. More properly, *Lorain Journal* was trying to force the radio station out of business in order to protect its local advertising monopoly from erosion.[4]

However, in Official Airline Guides, Inc. v. FTC[5] the Second Circuit held that a simple refusal to deal by a monopoly publisher of commuter flight schedules was not illegal. The plaintiff had to show not only that the defendant was a monopolist who refused to deal, but also some exclusionary act or intent to restrain competition, or to entrench or enlarge its monopoly.[6]

§ 10.4

1. 250 U.S. 300, 307, 39 S.Ct. 465, 468 (1919).

2. Reeves, Inc. v. Stake, 447 U.S. 429, 100 S.Ct. 2271 (1980); and see Burdett Sound, Inc. v. Altec Corp., 515 F.2d 1245, 1249 (5th Cir. 1975): "[I]t is simply not an antitrust violation for a manufacturer to contract with a new distributor, and as a consequence, to terminate his relationship with a former distributor, even if the effect of the new contract is to seriously damage the former distributor's business."

3. 342 U.S. 143, 72 S.Ct. 181 (1951). See § 5.6 above.

4. See also Otter Tail Power Co. v. U.S., 410 U.S. 366, 93 S.Ct. 1022 (1973), rehearing denied, 411 U.S. 910, 93 S.Ct. 1523 (1973), on remand, 360 F.Supp. 451 (1973), judgment affirmed, 417 U.S. 901, 94 S.Ct. 2594 (1974), where the Court applied similar analysis to a statutory monopolist; and see Eastman Kodak Co. v. Southern Photo Materials Co., 273 U.S. 359, 47 S.Ct. 400 (1927).

5. 630 F.2d 920 (2d Cir. 1980), cert. denied, 450 U.S. 917, 101 S.Ct. 1362 (1981). See also Paschall v. Kansas City Star Co., 727 F.2d 692 (8th Cir. 1984), discussed in § 5.6 above.

6. In General Motors Corp., 99 F.T.C. 464, 580 (1982), however, the Commission suggested in dicta that a monopolist may not refuse to deal if the result is to

A broad rule condemning refusals to deal by the monopolist would prevent a monopolist from achieving cost savings through vertical integration. More fundamentally, a monopolist's simple refusal to deal is not necessarily the kind of "exclusionary practice" that warrants condemnation under § 2 of the Sherman Act. If a monopoly manufacturer sells to 50 retailers, and then arbitrarily cuts one of them off, the retail market will remain competitive. There is no plausible way that such a refusal can result in lower output or higher prices. Absent any showing that the refusal will create a second monopoly in the retail market, it should be legal. Even when the refusal does create a second monopoly, the argument that the refusal is anticompetitive is weak.[7]

A practice that is legal for the monopolist should also be legal for the nonmonopolist. Unilateral refusals to deal by the nonmonopolist are illegal, if at all, because they are part of some other antitrust violation. In many of the important antitrust cases discussed elsewhere in this book, the plaintiff's claimed injury resulted from the defendant's unilateral refusal to deal. For example, in Continental T.V., Inc. v. GTE Sylvania, Inc.,[8] which established that vertically imposed territorial restrictions would be governed by a rule of reason, the plaintiff was a terminated retailer. Likewise, in many cases alleging illegal tying,[9] exclusive dealing,[10] or mergers [11] the plaintiff claims that, as a result of an antitrust violation, the defendant refused to deal with it, or forced others to do so. In such cases the refusal to deal is generally a mere detail in the court's evaluation of the substantive offense, although it may be important in the determination of the plaintiff's standing or the computation of damages.

 WESTLAW REFERENCES
synopsis,digest(monopol*** unilateral** /s refus*** /2 deal sell)

---

deny the victim access to a unique or scarce product or resource.

7. See § 7.2 above; and see 3 P. Areeda & D. Turner, Antitrust Law ¶ 736 (1978).

8. 433 U.S. 36, 97 S.Ct. 2549 (1977), on remand, 461 F.Supp. 1046 (1978), judgment affirmed, 694 F.2d 1132 (9th Cir. 1982).

9. See Heatransfer Corp. v. Volkswagenwerk, A.G., 553 F.2d 964 (5th Cir. 1977), cert. denied, 434 U.S. 1087, 98 S.Ct. 1282 (1978).

10. For example, Barnosky Oils, Inc. v. Union Oil Co., 665 F.2d 74 (6th Cir. 1981), on remand, 582 F.Supp. 1332 (1984).

11. See *Heatransfer*, note 9 above.

CHAPTER 11

MERGERS OF COMPETITORS

Table of Sections

§ 11.1 Introduction: The Problem of Mergers

A merger occurs when two firms that had been separate come under common ownership. The word "merger" has a broader meaning in federal antitrust law than in state corporation law.[1] In many cases a "merger" for antitrust purposes is merely the purchase by one firm of some or all of the assets of another firm. A merger of corporations can occur when one corporation buys some or all of another corporation's shares. The antitrust laws also use the word "merger" to describe a consolidation: two original corporations cease to exist and a new corporation is formed that owns the assets of the two former corporations.

Today the means by which a merger occurs is largely irrelevant to its legality under the antitrust laws. This was not always so. Before § 7 of the Clayton Act was amended in 1950 the statute

§ 11.1

1. See H. Henn, & J. Alexander, The Law of Corporations 979–88 (3d ed. 1983).

applied to stock acquisitions but not asset acquisitions. The result was that stock acquisitions came under the relatively strict test imposed by § 7, which condemns mergers that "may ＊ ＊ ＊ substantially ＊ ＊ ＊ lessen competition, or ＊ ＊ ＊ tend to create a monopoly." Asset acquisitions came under the less restrictive test of § 1 of the Sherman Act, or, if the acquisition produced a monopoly, § 2 of the Sherman Act.[2]

Before 1980 § 7 of the Clayton Act applied only to corporations. It has now been amended to refer to all "persons," whether incorporated or not.

A "horizontal" merger occurs when one firm acquires another firm that manufactures the same product or a close substitute, *and* both firms operate in the same geographic market. In short, the firms were actual competitors before the merger occurred. If the two firms were not actual competitors before the merger, then the merger will be treated either as "vertical" or "conglomerate" depending on the relationship between the firms. These kinds of mergers are discussed in chapters 7 & 12, respectively.

Because the horizontal merger involves two firms in the same market, it produces two consequences that do not flow from vertical or conglomerate mergers: 1) after the merger the relevant market has one firm less than before; 2) the post-merger firm has a larger market share than either of the partners had before the merger. Horizontal mergers may facilitate collusion by reducing the number of firms in a market. They can also create opportunities for price leadership or other forms of oligopoly behavior. Finally, horizontal mergers may increase the market power of the post-merger firm. Any of these would yield reduced output and higher consumer prices, and are therefore appropriate concerns of merger policy. In fact, however, the level of concentration at which collusion becomes a problem is significantly lower than the level of concentration required for the market to contain a single-firm monopolist. Since merger policy is designed to avert both, the standard in the area of marginal legality is concerned chiefly with identifying markets conducive to express or tacit collusion. Necessarily, such a standard will also condemn a merger that creates a single-firm monopolist.

If mergers produced no beneficial consequences, but only anticompetitive ones, we could justifiably condemn all of them under a *per se* rule. Most mergers are legal, however. They are permitted because mergers can increase the efficiency of firms by enabling them to

2. See U.S. v. Columbia Steel Co., 334 U.S. 495, 68 S.Ct. 1107 (1948), which applied the Sherman Act to an asset acquisition. The court noted that the "public policy announced by § 7 of the Clayton Act" should be applied to an asset acquisition that achieved the "same economic results" as a stock acquisition. 334 U.S. at 507 n.7, 68 S.Ct. at 1114. However, it went on to uphold the merger under Sherman Act standards.

attain minimum optimal scale (MOS) [3] more rapidly then they could by internal growth, and by permitting them to acquire productive assets more quickly and without the social cost that internal growth plus the bankruptcy of some firms might entail.

Economies of scale can be broadly grouped into two kinds: economies of plant size, and various multi-plant economies. Generally a horizontal merger does not increase plant size, but rather increases the number of plants that are controlled by a single management. This suggests that a merger will not often decrease the costs of operating a single plant,[4] but it may yield certain multi-plant economies. These can be substantial. For example, it may be cheaper per unit to purchase 1,000,000 units of some raw material at a time rather than 200,000. Further, the costs per unit of research and development decrease as the number of units a firm produces increase. A 30-second television commercial costs as much for a small firm as for a large one, and a one-page grocery store advertisement in a newspaper costs the same, whether it represents the offerings of a single store or of a 100 store chain. In general, the more a firm spends on mass media advertising, the more economy it can achieve from large size.

Large horizontal size may also make various forms of vertical integration possible. For example, a large grocery chain with hundreds of retail stores may be able to own its own farms and dairies and operate its own warehouses. This would not be feasible for a single-store firm, which would have to rely on the market.

The kinds of efficiencies that can be achieved by horizontal merger vary immensely depending on the industry. They are largely a function of the technology and distribution systems of a particular industry. Some industries, such as retail grocers, banks, and trucking companies, may be able to reduce costs substantially and improve consumer welfare by horizontal mergers. Others, such as delicatessens and small French restaurants, may work more efficiently as single-store operations.[5]

Horizontal mergers can create other efficiencies than decreased costs of production or distribution. For example, if horizontal mergers are legal, independent businessmen have a "parachute" that they can use if their business does poorly or if they want to retire. Too

---

3. See the discussion of MOS in § 1.4.

4. However, substantial empirical evidence suggests that mergers can also create single plant economies, by permitting longer production runs and increased specialization within each plant. For example, if two ball bearing manufacturers merge, the post-merger firm will be able to make all bearings of one type in one plant, those of a second type

in a second plant, etc. See F.M. Scherer, Industrial Market Structure and Economic Performance 133 (2d ed. 1980).

5. For a good discussion of the different scale economies available in various industries, see F.M. Scherer, Id. at 81–150. A good discussion of the relationship between scale economies and the law of mergers is Y. Brozen, Concentration, Mergers, and Public Policy (1983).

strong a rule against horizontal mergers may make a small business difficult to sell, particularly if a larger business can be run more efficiently and the small business is languishing as a result. The knowledge that someone can sell out to a larger firm can actually encourage entry into a particular market.

The most difficult problem in determining an appropriate merger policy is that the field of mergers cannot be divided into mergers that encourage collusion or increase market power on the one hand, and mergers that create efficiency on the other. Most mergers do both of these things at the same time. To be sure, there are cases at the extremes where we can confidently predict that the efficiency produced by a particular merger far outweighs the predictable danger of collusion or monopolization, or vice-versa. The majority of legally questionable mergers, however, produce ambiguous results.

 WESTLAW REFERENCES
di merger
di consolidation

§ 11.2 Efficiency and Merger Policy

Courts and antitrust commentators have recognized for some time that horizontal mergers can simultaneously facilitate collusion or enlarge market power, and create substantial efficiencies. They have considered three different positions concerning the relationship between efficiency and the legality of mergers:

1) mergers should be evaluated for their effect on market power or likelihood of collusion, and efficiency considerations should be largely irrelevant;

2) mergers that create substantial efficiencies should be legal, or there should be at least a limited "efficiency defense" in certain merger cases;

3) mergers should be condemned *because* they create efficiencies, in order to protect competitors of the post-merger firm.

The merger policy of the Warren Court in the 1960's adopted the third proposal: it condemned mergers *because* they created certain efficiencies. For example, in Brown Shoe Co. v. United States the Supreme Court held that a horizontal merger between competing retailers of shoes was illegal because the large, post-merger firm would be able to undersell its competitors. The Court concluded that Congress desired "to promote competition through the protection of viable, small, locally owned businesses," and the creation of a large company with lower costs would frustrate this goal. "Congress appreciated that occasional higher costs and prices might result from the maintenance of fragmented industries and markets," the Supreme Court acknowledged, but it "resolved these competing considerations in favor of decentralization." [1]

The district court in *Brown Shoe* had been even more explicit about its reasons for condemning the merger:

> [I]ndependent retailers of shoes are having a harder and harder time in competing with company-owned and company-controlled retail outlets. National advertising by large concerns has increased their brand name acceptability and retail stores handling the brand named shoes have a definite advertising advantage. Company-owned and company-controlled retail stores have definite advantages in buying and credit; they have further advantages in advertising, insurance, inventory control * * * and price control. These advantages result in lower prices or in higher quality for the same price and the independent retailer can no longer compete * * *[2]

Brown Shoe's critics have attacked the opinion for protecting competitors at the expense of consumers.[3] The identification of antitrust's protected class presents a value question, however, not a question of fact. Furthermore, any such critique must come to terms with the relatively clear legislative history of the 1950 Celler-Kefauver Amendments to § 7. The *Brown* opinion read it correctly. In 1950 protection of the "viability" of small businesses who were being "gobbled up" by larger companies was much more on Congress's mind than low consumer prices or high product quality.[4]

Brown Shoe and successor cases such as *Von's Grocery* [5] can be criticized, however, not for the goals they chose but for their efficacy in achieving them. *Von's Grocery* involved a merger between the third largest and the sixth largest grocery chains in greater Los Angeles. The market was unconcentrated, however, and the combined share of these two chains was 7.5% of sales. Both chains were family owned and operated. The largest firm in the market, which was not a party to the merger, had a market share of only 8%. The market exhibited a "trend" toward concentration with many individual stores being purchased by chains, suggesting that the larger chains were able to undersell the smaller chains and the individual mom-and-pop grocers.

If a medium-sized chain is prevented from acquiring existing stores, it likely will respond by building new stores of its own, particularly if expansion will strengthen its position vis-a-vis larger chains. The result will be that very small chains or single store

§ 11.2

1. 370 U.S. 294, 344, 82 S.Ct. 1502, 1534 (1962).

2. U.S. v. Brown Shoe Co., 179 F.Supp. 721, 738 (E.D.Mo.1959).

3. See R. Bork, The Antitrust Paradox: A Policy at War With Itself 198–216 (1978).

4. See Bok, Section 7 of the Clayton Act and the Merging of Law and Economics, 74 Harv.L.Rev. 226, 234 (1960); Hovenkamp, Distributive Justice and the Antitrust Laws, 51 Geo.Wash.L.Rev. 1, 23–27 (1982).

5. U.S. v. Von's Grocery Co., 384 U.S. 270, 86 S.Ct. 1478 (1966).

companies will find themselves unable to compete with larger firms, and unable to sell their stores to competitors. Not only will they lose the power to compete, but they might also lose most of the value of their most substantial capital asset—their stores.[6] It is therefore far from clear that the rule of *Brown Shoe* and *Von's Grocery* gave small businesses the kind of protection that Congress had in mind.

The rule that mergers should be condemned because they create efficiency has been implicitly abandoned.[7] The opposite position is that mergers should be legal when they create substantial efficiencies—or alternatively, that there should be an "efficiency defense" in merger cases. Such a rule has been discussed frequently but never adopted by courts.

The best argument for an "efficiency defense" in merger cases comes from Professor Williamson,[8] and is illustrated by the graph in Figure One. The graph illustrates a merger that gives the post-merger firm measurably more market power than it had before the merger. As a result, the firm reduces output from Q_1 to Q_2 on the graph, and increases price from P_1 to P_2. Triangle A_1 represents the monopoly "deadweight loss" created by this increase in market power.[9]

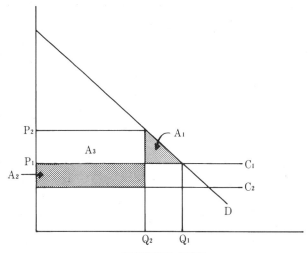

FIGURE ONE

6. See R. Posner, Antitrust Law: An Economic Perspective 105 (1976).

7. Perhaps it has been explicitly abandoned if the plaintiff is a private party seeking damages. See Brunswick Corp. v. Pueblo Bowl-O-Mat, Inc., 429 U.S. 477, 97 S.Ct. 690 (1977), cert. denied, 429 U.S. 1090, 97 S.Ct. 1099 (1977), and the discussion below in § 14.5.

8. Williamson, Economies as an Antitrust Defense: the Welfare Trade-Offs, 58 Amer.Econ.Rev. 18 (1968); see also, Williamson, Economies as an Antitrust Defense Revisited, 125 U.Pa.L.Rev. 699

(1977); Muris, The Efficiency Defense Under Section 7 of the Clayton Act, 30 Case West.Res.L.Rev. 381 (1980); Fisher & Lande, Efficiency Considerations in Merger Enforcement, 71 Calif.L.Rev. 1580 (1983); Rogers, The Limited Case For An Efficiency Defense in Horizontal Mergers, 58 Tulane L.Rev. 503 (1983); Hovenkamp, Merger Actions for Damages, 35 Hastings L.J. (1984); 4 P. Areeda & D. Turner, Antitrust Law ¶¶ 939–962 (1980).

9. See the discussion of the social cost of monopoly in § 1.3.

At the same time, however, the merger produces measurable economies, which show up as a reduction in the firm's costs from C_1 to C_2. Rectangle A_2 represents efficiency gains that will result from these economies. If A_2 is larger than A_1 the merger produces a *net* efficiency gain, even though it permits the firm to raise its price above its marginal cost. Furthermore, A_2 is often larger than A_1. The efficiency gains illustrated by A_2 are spread over the entire output of the post-merger firm. The deadweight losses in A_1 are spread over only the reduction in output. If the post-merger firm reduced its output by 10%, each of the 90% of units still being produced would contribute to the efficiency gains; the deadweight loss, however, would accrue over only the 10% reduction.

Williamson concluded that in a market with average elasticities of demand and supply, a merger that produced "nontrivial" economies of 1.2% would be efficient, even if it resulted in a price increase of 10%.[10]

Williamson's analysis is vulnerable to some criticism. First, his description of triangle A_1 in the figure as the efficiency costs of a merger probably understates the true social cost. Rectangles A_2 plus A_3 represent potential monopoly profits to the post-merger firm. A profit-maximizing firm will be willing to spend substantial resources in an effort to acquire or retain a certain amount of monopoly power.[11] If a particular merger will give a firm $1,000,000 in additional monopoly profits, the firm will spend up to $1,000,000 in order to accomplish the merger and then retain its monopoly position. It could spend this money in highly inefficient ways, such as espionage, predatory pricing against a potential take-over target, or vexatious litigation. At the extreme, $A_2 + A_3$ are not increased profits to the post-merger firm at all, but funds inefficiently spent in order to give the firm its market position.

The second problem with Williamson's analysis is more ideological than economic. Williamson is willing to balance an absolute output reduction and price increase against any efficiency saving. Suppose that two firms selling widgets at a competitive price of $1.00 merge. As a result of the merger the post-merger firm has enough market power to reduce output and increase the price of widgets to $1.05. In addition, the firm's marginal costs drop from $1.00 per widget to 95¢ per widget. In this case the efficiency gains, which are measured across all widgets produced, will probably be larger than the deadweight loss from monopoly pricing, which is measured across only the reduction in output. However, the merger results in an *actual* output reduction and an *actual* price increase for consumers. Although the overall effect of the merger is efficient, all the benefits of

10. Note 8, 58 Amer.Econ.Rev. at 22–23.

11. See § 1.3 above.

the increased efficiency accrue to the post-merger firm in the form of higher profits.[12] Such a merger rule would undoubtedly be politically unacceptable, even though the rule promotes efficiency.

The third and perhaps most substantial problem with Williamson's proposal is that courts are simply not capable of making the kinds of measurements that his analysis would require. Efficiencies, Judge Posner has written, are an "intractable subject for litigation." [13] Courts are not up to measuring marginal costs or elasticities of supply or demand with anything approaching the precision required by such an "efficiency defense." Our knowledge that mergers can produce both economies and monopoly pricing is fairly secure. However, quantifying either of these in a particular merger case is impossible.

The 1984 Justice Department Merger Guidelines take a more pragmatic approach to the problem of dealing with post-merger efficiencies. Under the Guidelines the DOJ will not accept a general efficiency defense in merger cases. However, it will consider "clear and convincing evidence that a merger will achieve . . . efficiencies." The department lists qualifying efficiencies as including, but not limited to, "achieving economies of scale, better integration of production facilities, plant specialization, lower transportation costs, and similar efficiencies relating to specific manufacturing, servicing, or distribution operations of the merging firms." However, the Department notes that it will "reject claims of efficiencies if equivalent or comparable savings can reasonably be achieved by the parties through other means." [14]

To date, an "efficiency defense" has not played an important part in merger law. Most mergers found illegal under current law probably create efficiencies. They are condemned, however, because no court is capable of balancing the increase in market power or the potential for collusion against the economies achieved. Judges must necessarily make decisions based on the information they can obtain and understand. When a merger involves companies having a small share of the market they infer that the potential for monopolistic pricing or collusion is trivial; therefore, the merger must be calculated to increase the efficiency of the post-merger firm. If the merger involves firms sufficiently large that the threat to competitive pricing is significant, however, then the alternative explanation of monopoly or collusion and the difficulty of measuring any resulting efficiencies warrant condemnation.[15]

---

12. Eventually, absent effective exclusion, the higher profits will attract new entry and prices will drop to the competitive level.

13. Posner, note 6 above, at 112.

14. 49 Fed.Reg. 26,823, 26,834 (1984). For a similar proposal, see P. Areeda &

D. Turner, note 8 above. The Guidelines are discussed more fully in §§ 11.4–11.6 below.

15. See United States v. Philadelphia National Bank, 374 U.S. 321, 370, 83 S.Ct. 1715, 1745 (1963), where the Court rejected a defense that a merger that

WESTLAW REFERENCES
digest(efficien** /p merger)

§ 11.3 Concentration, Markets Shares, and Prima Facie Illegality

The prevailing concern of merger law today is not to protect small businesses from more efficient rivals but to deter oligopolistic pricing or express collusion. Since many mergers have a significant but unmeasurable potential to create efficiencies, an ideal antitrust policy would condemn mergers when the risk of oligopoly pricing or collusion is substantial and approve them when such risks are minimal.

Economists generally agree that there is a relationship between the size and number of firms in a market and the likelihood of collusion. They disagree over a wide range about the relevant numbers. Furthermore, markets differ greatly from each other. One market containing six firms might be much more susceptible to collusion than another, depending on a number of factors—ease of entry; the degree of standardization or uniformity in the product; the way the product is marketed, whether by relatively large infrequent orders or frequent small purchases; the opportunities for secret price-cutting; and differences in size and efficiency among the incumbent firms.

However, courts have tried to develop more-or-less unitary market share rules for prima facie illegality that apply in all industries with a given level of concentration. Then they use non-market share considerations such as those listed above as mitigating or aggravating factors on a case-by-case basis. This approach was approved by the Supreme Court in U.S. v. Philadelphia Nat. Bank.[1]

In the 1960's and 1970's courts and the Department of Justice (DOJ) most often looked at the "four-firm concentration ratio" (CR4) to determine the degree of danger present in a particular market. The CR4 is computed by adding the market shares of the four largest firms in the market. Thus a market in which the four largest firms have market shares of 30%, 20%, 15%, and 10% has a CR4 of 75%.[2] Such a market was considered highly concentrated, and any merger in that market would be given close scrutiny. If the CR4 was much smaller, such as 25%, then a merger involving firms of somewhat larger market shares might still be legal. Under the original Merger

lessened competition in one market should be approved because it increased competition in a different market.

§ 11.3

1. 374 U.S. 321, 355–66, 83 S.Ct. 1715, 1737–43 (1963). The Court compared market share percentages in merger cases in a wide variety of industries and concluded that the percentages in the case before it (combined market share more than 30%) "raise an inference that the effect of the contemplated merger of appellees may be substantially to lessen competition * * *." Id. at 365, 83 S.Ct. at 1742.

2. Some economists prefer the 8-firm concentration ratio (CR8), which is the sum of the market shares of the eight largest firms. Courts, however, have used the CR4 almost exclusively.

Guidelines issued by the DOJ [3] a merger of two firms of 4% market share each was presumptively illegal in a highly concentrated market (CR4 greater than 75%). If the market was less concentrated, mergers involving firms of 5% each were presumptively illegal. These Guidelines, issued in 1968, were substantially more tolerant of mergers than Supreme Court case law, which had condemned mergers in unconcentrated markets of firms whose combined post-merger market share was less than 8%.[4]

Economists differ greatly on questions about how market concentration must be measured, how concentrated a market must be before close scrutiny of mergers is appropriate, and how large the parties must be before the danger to competition is substantial. At one extreme are Supreme Court cases condemning mergers of small firms in unconcentrated markets. At the other extreme is Judge Bork's suggestion that mergers are not likely to be harmful unless the combined share of the post-merger firm is 60% or so.[5] In the middle is a vague consensus that a market in which the CR4 exceeds 75% is conducive to collusion, and that a market in which the CR4 is less than 40% or so is a "safe harbor" in which most mergers should be legal. Likewise there is a very vague consensus that if the CR4 is 75% or higher, a merger in which the combined market share of the post-merger firm exceeds 12% should be illegal. The figures mentioned here, however, are only generalizations from a variety of economists whose opinions vary across a wide range.[6] Courts have gravitated toward the same numbers, although there is no unanimity among the judges either.[7]

 WESTLAW REFERENCES
"four-firm concentration ratio" "4-firm test"

§ 11.4 The 1984 Merger Guidelines and the Herfindahl-Hirschman Index

In 1982 the DOJ issued a new set of Guidelines for its merger enforcement policy. The Guidelines were amended and reissued in

3. U.S. Dep't of Justice Merger Guidelines, reprinted in 1 Trade Reg. Rep. (CCH) ¶ 4430 (1968).

4. For example, in U.S. v. Von's Grocery Co., 384 U.S. 270, 86 S.Ct. 1478 (1966), the Supreme Court condemned a merger in which the combined market share of the merging firms was 7.5% and the CR4 was 24.4%. Likewise, in U.S. v. Pabst Brewing Co., 384 U.S. 546, 86 S.Ct. 1665 (1966), the Court condemned a merger in which the firm's combined market share was only 4.5%, and the CR4 was less than 30%.

5. See R. Bork, The Antitrust Paradox: A Policy at War With Itself 221 (1978).

6. See, for example, 4 P. Areeda & D. Turner, Antitrust Law ¶ 910d (1980); G. Stigler, The Organization of Industry 58–59 (1983 ed.); for a truly agnostic conclusion, see F.M. Scherer, Industrial Market Structure and Economic Performance 295 (2d ed. 1980).

7. For a helpful table of recent cases, indicating the market shares of the company, the market structure, and the decision, see 4 P. Areeda & D. Turner, Antitrust Law ¶ 909b (1980).

1984.[1] The Guidelines are only "guidelines" and do not absolutely bind the Department. Nor, of course, is any court or Congress bound to follow them.

One of the most significant contributions of the 1984 Guidelines was their abandonment of the CR4 measure of market structure. In its place the 1984 Guidelines use the Herfindahl-Hirschman Index.[2] The Herfindahl-Hirschman Index (HHI) as used in the Guidelines is the sum of the squares of every firm in the relevant market. For example, if a market has 3 firms each with a market share of 25%, 1 firm of 15% and 1 firm of 10%, the HHI would be $25^2 + 25^2 + 25^2 + 15^2 + 10^2 = 2200$. Such a market (which has a CR4 of 90%) is considered highly concentrated under the 1984 Guidelines, which so regard any market with an HHI greater than 1800.

Most economists believe that the HHI describes market structure and dangers of anticompetitive activity more accurately than the CR4 does. For example, the CR4 fails to account for distribution of market shares among the four largest firms. A market in which the four largest firms each have a 20% share has a CR4 of 80%. A market in which the largest firm has 77% and firms 2, 3 and 4 each have 1% also has a CR4 of 80%. The danger of anticompetitive behavior is significantly greater in the second market than the first, however. A market with four equally sized, equally efficient firms may behave quite competitively. An industry with one giant and several pygmies, however, will be conducive to "price leadership," a form of oligopolistic pricing in which the largest firm sets a supracompetitive price and the smaller firms, fearful of retaliation, follow with their own supracompetitive price. In the above example, the largest firm even has a large enough market share to be guilty of illegal monopolization. The HHI acknowledges that markets with the same CR4 may exhibit widely different degrees of competition. The HHI of the market containing four 20% firms will be around 1700 or 1800, depending on the size of the remaining firms. In the case of the market containing one 77% firm and three 1% firms, the HHI will be around 6000.[3]

§ 11.4

1. 49 Fed.Reg. 26,823 (1984). Problems of market definition under the 1984 Guidelines are discussed above in § 3.6.

2. For the history and early use of the Index, see Hirschman, The Paternity of an Index, 54 Amer.Econ.Rev. 761 (1964); Stigler, A Theory of Oligopoly, 72 J.Pol.Econ. 44 (1964).

3. Some empirical studies suggest that likelihood and success of collusion in a market varies with HHI. Marvel, Competition and Price Levels in the Retail Gasoline Market, 60 Rev.Econ.Statistics 252 (1978). However, other studies suggest that the HHI is no more reliable than the CR4. See Cohen & Sullivan, The Herfindahl-Hirschman Index and the New Antitrust Merger Guidelines: Concentrating on Concentration, 62 Texas L.Rev. 453, 490 (1983).

There has been a healthy debate among economists over whether "single firm dominance" or "level of concentration" is the most important factor in making a market conducive to collusion. Earlier empirical studies suggested a positive correlation between the level of concentration in an industry and the amount of monopoly profits. For exam-

The HHI also does a better job than the CR4 of accounting for
size disparities between the merging firms. If two firms with 20%
market shares merge, the result will be a firm with a 40% market
share. The same result will obtain from a merger of a 38% firm with
a 2% firm. Most economists agree, however, that the first merger
will have a more serious impact on competition than the second. The
first one may double the size of the dominant (or second largest) firm
in the market. The second merger will merely make a large firm
marginally larger. The CR4 accounts for the result only haphazardly, depending on whether one or both of the merging firms are
among the four largest in the industry. The HHI accounts for the
difference rather precisely: the first merger increases the market's
HHI by 800 points, while the second increases the HHI by only 152
points.[4]

Finally, the HHI can be used to establish "safe harbors"—relatively unconcentrated industries in which mergers will not ordinarily
be challenged. By accounting for all firms in the market (rather than
the top four) the HHI can give a measure of total market concentration that indicates to the policy maker whether mergers are likely to
be a problem in a particular industry.[5] The 1984 Guidelines indicate
that the DOJ will not challenge any merger in an industry in which
the post-merger HHI is less than 1000, "except in extraordinary
circumstances."[6]

Use of the HHI presents some difficulties, however. First, computation of the CR4 required measurement of only the four largest
firms in the market. The HHI theoretically requires measurement of
every firm in the market. The other side, of course, is that the HHI
claims to be a more reliable indicator of overall market concentration
because it measures every firm. Furthermore, the error that results
from miscalculation is very small with respect to the smaller firms in

ple, Bain, Relation of Profit Rate to Industry Concentration: American Manufacturing, 1936–1940, 65 Q.J.Econ. 293
(1951). However, later economists argued that by using the CR8 as his index
of concentration, Bain ignored the fact
that asymmetry of firm size within the
market may have much more influence
than concentration itself on the amount
of monopoly pricing. See Kwoka,
Large-Firm Dominance and Price/Cost
Margins in Manufacturing Industries, 44
S.Econ.J. 183 (1977). Other aspects of
the debate are summarized in Pautler, A
Review of the Economic Basis for
Broad-Based Horizontal-Merger Policy,
28 Antitrust Bull. 571 (1983). The HHI
can be viewed as a "compromise" index
of concentration, which seeks to account
for *both* the absolute level of market
concentration and the extent of single
firm dominance within the market.

4. To calculate the *increase* in HHI
produced by a merger, take the product
of the market shares of the merging
firms (as whole numbers) and multiply
by two. Thus a merger of a 20% firm
with a 15% firm produces an HHI increase of 600. Do you see why this is
so? Before the merger the two firms
represented 20^2 plus 15^2 HHI points.
After the merger, however, they represent $(20 + 15)^2$ HHI points. The square
of a binomial $(A + B)$ equals $A^2 + 2AB
+ B^2$. The 2AB represents the increase.

5. See Posner, Oligopoly and the Antitrust Laws: A Suggested Approach, 21
Stan.L.Rev. 1562, 1602–1603 (1969); Cal-
kins, The New Merger Guidelines and
the Herfindahl-Hirschman Index, 71
Cal.L.Rev. 402, 419 (1983).

6. 49 Fed.Reg. at 26,823, 26,831
(1984).

the market. A 5% firm, for example, adds only 25 HHI points, and a 1% firm adds only 1 point. Since the relevant threshold concentration under the HHI is around 1000, an error in the measurement of a small firm makes little difference. For most purposes fringe firms with a market share of 2% or less may be ignored.

A more substantial problem with the HHI is that an error in measuring the market share of a large firm will distort the measurement substantially. For example, assume that a market contains four firms with market shares of 35%, 15%, 10% and 10%. The CR4 is 70% and the HHI will be around 1700, depending on the size of the other firms in the market. Suppose, however, that the size of the largest firm is erroneously measured as 40%. In that case the four-firm concentration ratio goes to 75%—not a dramatic difference. The HHI, however, jumps to about 2100, and that difference is quite substantial. In fact, a 5 point error in the measurement of the largest firm has about the same impact on the HHI as a 5% error in the measurement of all three of the other firms in the CR4. For this reason precise and careful market definition and share computation is essential to a court relying on the HHI, especially with respect to the largest firms in the market.

 WESTLAW REFERENCES
(guideline /5 merger /5 1982) herfindahl-hirschman

§ 11.5 Market Share Thresholds Under the 1984 DOJ Guidelines

The Guidelines rely heavily on industrial organization theory to establish some prima facie indicators of when the DOJ will challenge a particular merger. In brief, the DOJ regards any market in which the *post*-merger HHI is below 1000 as "unconcentrated, having the equivalent of at least 10 equally sized firms." The DOJ is "unlikely" to challenge mergers falling in this region.

If the post-merger HHI falls between 1000 and 1800, the DOJ is unlikely to challenge a merger that produces an HHI increase of less than 100 points. If the increase is greater than 100 points, however, the DOJ is more likely to challenge the merger, depending on the presence of other factors, which are discussed below in § 11.6.

The DOJ will challenge most mergers in which the post-merger HHI is greater than 1800 and the merger adds more than 100 points to the HHI. If the increase is less than 100 but more than 50 points, the DOJ may challenge the merger depending on the post-merger concentration of the market, the size of the resulting increase in concentration, and the presence or absence of the non-market share factors.

In a market with an HHI above 1800 a dominant firm likely would be prohibited from acquiring any but the smallest of competitors. For example, if a firm with a 30% market share acquired a firm with a 2% share, the increase in HHI would be 120. The DOJ would probably challenge the merger.

 WESTLAW REFERENCES

merger /p unconcentrated concentrat*** /p (department /2 justice) d.o.j.

§ 11.6   Non-Market Share Factors

The following are the most significant factors other than market share that can be relevant in evaluating the competitive effect of a horizontal merger. Here, existing law is compared with the position taken in the 1984 DOJ Merger Guidelines.

Barriers to New Entry

A barrier to entry is some factor in a market that makes the cost of doing business higher for a new entrant than it is for established firms.[1] If barriers to entry are completely absent mergers are not likely to result in supracompetitive pricing: as soon as incumbents increase their price to monopoly levels the market will be flooded with new rivals that will drive the price back to marginal cost. The 1984 DOJ Merger Guidelines give great weight to the absence of entry barriers in the relevant market: "If entry into a market is so easy that existing competitors could not succeed in raising price for any significant period of time, the Department is unlikely to challenge mergers in that market."[2]

Perhaps more appropriately, the DOJ indicates that firms that can easily and economically shift to manufacturing the relevant product, or that can easily ship it into the relevant geographic market, ought to be included in the relevant market to begin with. If that is done, then analysis of entry barriers is partly accounted for in market definition.[3] Of course, entry barriers exclude not only outsiders

---

§ 11.6

1. See Demsetz, Barriers To Entry, 72 Amer.Econ.Rev. 47 (1982).

2. 49 Fed.Reg. at 26,832. Although it is too early to predict the general influence of the 1984 DOJ Merger Guidelines on judicial decisions, this particular passage of the Guidelines had a very powerful impact on one panel of the Second Circuit. In U.S. v. Waste Management, Inc., 743 F.2d 976 (2d Cir.1984), the court held that a horizontal merger challenged by the Justice Department itself did not violate Section 7 because barriers to entry in the industry—solid waste disposal—were very low. The combined market share of the merging firms was 48.8%, which the court acknowledged to be prima facie illegal under U.S. v. Philadelphia National Bank, 374 U.S. 321, 364–366, 83 S.Ct. 1715, 1742–1743 (1963). See § 11.3 above. The court then admitted that the Supreme Court has never held that evidence of low entry barriers could be used to rebut a showing of prima facie illegality. Nevertheless, in this instance the entry barriers were so outrageously low that people had been known to enter the market at issue by working out of their homes. Citing the DOJ's own Guidelines against it, the court concluded that if the Department "routinely considers ease of entry as relevant to determining the competitive impact of a merger, it may not argue to a court addressing the same issue that ease of entry is irrelevant."

3. This is particularly true of the approach to market definition taken in the

already in business and sitting on the "edge" of the market, but also firms that do not even exist at the time a merger is evaluated. For that reason, not all entry barrier factors can be considered in the market definition itself.

The Supreme Court has sometimes cited high entry barriers as a rationale for condemning a particular merger,[4] but has seldom cited low entry barriers as a reason for approving one. The decision in *Von's Grocery*,[5] for example, has been strongly criticized for ignoring the fact that entry barriers in the retail grocery business were extremely low. As a result monopolistic pricing in that market was unlikely.[6] However, this criticism itself overlooks the fact that monopoly pricing was not the perceived evil of the merger in *Von's Grocery*. The perceived evil was the greater efficiency of the post-merger firm, which would force smaller grocers to go out of business or merge themselves. Superior efficiency is the world's greatest entry barrier, except perhaps for governmental entry restrictions. Few things make entry into a market more difficult than an incumbent's superior ability to produce a good product and sell it at a low price.

Any merger policy that places a high value on economic efficiency and consumer welfare must designate as "barriers to entry" only those things that permit incumbent firms to engage in monopoly pricing while keeping outsiders from entering the market. Economies of scale, an "entry barrier" often cited in Supreme Court merger jurisprudence, should generally not be considered an entry barrier at all. The burden of diseconomies of scale falls not specifically on the new firm, but on the inefficiently small firm. Furthermore, a policy that condemns mergers when barriers to entry are high, and then designates economies of scale as a barrier to entry, is calculated to condemn mergers *because* they produce scale economies. Such a policy could prevent firms from achieving MOS in the most efficient way. More appropriate candidates as entry barriers include state and federal regulations restricting entry, which were cited in some of the bank merger cases; the higher cost of capital to new entrants for whom business risks are higher; or access to scarce, non-duplicable resources.[7]

1984 Merger Guidelines, of hypothesizing a "small but significant and nontransitory" price increase and considering how many firms could enter. 49 Fed. Reg. at 26,829, 26,832. The result of very high entry barriers (which would permit incumbent firms to increase price) would be that certain outside firms would not be included in the relevant market. See § 3.6 above.

4. For example, U.S. v. Phillipsburg Nat. Bank & Trust Co., 399 U.S. 350, 368–69, 90 S.Ct. 2035, 2045–46 (1970), citing state banking regulations that restrict entry as warranting condemnation of a horizontal merger. See also, FTC v. Procter & Gamble Co., 386 U.S. 568, 579, 87 S.Ct. 1224, 1230 (1967), discussed in § 12.4 below.

5. U.S. v. Von's Grocery Co., 384 U.S. 270, 86 S.Ct. 1478 (1966).

6. See R. Posner, Antitrust Law: An Economic Perspective 106 (1976).

7. See 4 P. Areeda & D. Turner, Antitrust Law ¶ 917 (1980).

Adequacy of Irreplaceable Raw Materials

In United States v. General Dynamics Corp.[8] the Supreme Court considered a merger of two coal producers. The acquiring firm produced 6.5% and the acquired firm 4.4% of the coal in one of the relevant markets chosen by the government. The acquired firm owned only 1% of the coal *reserves* in the market, however, and virtually all known reserves were already committed. The Supreme Court refused to condemn the merger, citing among other factors the disparity between the acquired firm's current production and its much more limited potential for future production, as indicated by its depleted reserves.

Many scarce natural resources such as coal, oil, and copper are in a practical sense irreplaceable, and often most of the known reserves that can be profitably produced at current market prices are already owned by other firms. If a firm is running out of such reserves its market share of current production may overstate its position as a continuing force in the market. The Supreme Court found in *General Dynamics* that, although the acquired firm was currently producing more than 4% of the coal in the market, its reserves were depleted and there was no "possibility of acquiring more * * *." The percentage of the acquired firm's *reserves* probably reflected its strength in the market much more accurately than the percentage of current output.

Some caution is in order, however. A firm with only 1% of the world's sand could probably produce 100% of the world's silicone chips for computers from now until eternity. Any blanket rule that a firm's irreplaceable reserves rather than its current output be used in estimating market share would cut far too broadly. The court should find initially that a firm's reserve holdings are irreplaceable and depleted, and that as a result its output will decline substantially in only a few years.

Excess Capacity

Excess capacity has occasionally been treated by courts as a "non-market share" factor to be used in assessing the effects of a merger. Excess capacity held by a firm's competitors will confine the firm's ability to increase price. As soon as it does so, the competitors will respond with an output increase. If market share is properly defined, however, it will include the excess capacity held by competitors in the relevant market, and its presence will show up in the merging firm's market share percentages.[9]

Degree of Product Homogeneity

The entire notion of "market share" in the economist's competition model rests on the premise that all competing firms produce

8. 415 U.S. 486, 94 S.Ct. 1186 (1974).   9. See § 3.2 above.

identical products—that is, consumers are unable to differentiate among them. In the real world many manufactured products within a relevant market are distinguishable. Although Baldwin and Steinway are competitors in the market for pianos, their products are nevertheless different and many customers prefer one to the other.

A high degree of product differentiation in a market, especially in markets dominated by custom made products, makes oligopolistic coordination and even explicit price fixing more difficult to achieve.[10] A difficult question for merger policy is how product differentiation should be accounted for in estimating the anticompetitive consequences of a merger. First, although product differentiation makes price fixing or tacit collusion more difficult, it does not make it impossible. The second *American Tobacco*[11] case and the more recent FTC proceeding against the ready-to-eat breakfast cereal manufacturers[12] both suggest that tacit collusion can occur in markets in which product differentiation in the eyes of consumers is large.

Antitrust policy makers have tended to ignore product heterogeneity as a "mitigating factor" in merger law, largely because so little is known about the relationship between the degree of homogeneity and the likelihood of collusion. The 1984 DOJ Guidelines concede that product differentiation is "arguably relevant in all cases." Nevertheless, the lack of any reliable index of homogeneity and collusion substantially limits the usefulness of such information. As a result, information about product differentiation "will be taken into account only in relatively extreme cases where both identification and effect are more certain." The Department ambiguously concludes that it will be "more likely" to challenge a merger in a market with a completely fungible product. On the other hand, "when the relevant product is very heterogeneous or sold subject to complex . . . options" the DOJ is "less likely" to challenge the merger. In other instances the degree of product homogeneity will be ignored.

Marketing and Sales Methods

Some pricing methods are more conducive to price leadership or price fixing than others. The new Merger Guidelines have been criticized for considering all markets to be "auction" markets, in which every seller competes for every buyer and the buyers have

10. See F.M. Scherer, Industrial Market Structure and Economic Performance 200 (2d ed. 1980): "With perfect [product] homogeneity, there remains only one dimension along which rivalrous actions and counteractions can take place: price. In such a case, oligopolists have a particularly easy task of coordinating their behavior * * * When products are heterogeneously differentiated, the terms of rivalry become multidimensional, and the coordination problem grows in complexity by leaps and bounds."

11. Amer. Tobacco Co. v. U.S., 328 U.S. 781, 66 S.Ct. 1125 (1946).

12. In re Kellogg Co., 99 F.T.C. 8 (1982). See § 4.3 above.

complete, easily available information about the offerings of competing sellers.[13]

The amount of competition in a market varies with the way price information flows. A Chicago physician may have a great deal of market power in the Chicago market, even though there are several competitors in her specialty. Often people in need of emergency surgery find comparison shopping very expensive. Since many customers are likely to enter this market only once, the seller does not need to worry about pricing her product low enough to keep the buyer.

At the other extreme is a market like the New York Stock Exchange or the Chicago Board of Trade, where every buyer has virtually complete information about the offering price of every seller, and vice-versa. If the market price of IBM stock is 230, a seller who offers his shares at 232 will be unlikely to make the sale.

The Merger Guidelines do consider some market characteristics in evaluating the anticompetitive potential of a merger. The Guidelines note, for example, that collusion is much more likely in markets in which orders are "frequent, regular and small relative to * * * total output." Sellers are encouraged to collude when detailed, prospective information about prices is available to all of them. The Guidelines simply note that the DOJ will be "more likely" to challenge a merger in a market exhibiting such characteristics.[14]

The Significance of a "Trend" Towards Concentration

In *Brown Shoe* [15] and *Von's Grocery* [16] the Supreme Court cited an industry-wide trend toward concentration as a rationale for condemning the mergers. If the court approved these mergers, it reasoned, it would be forced to approve other similar mergers in the future. This "domino theory" has been relied on by courts to condemn dozens of mergers.

The significance for merger policy of a "trend" toward concentration in the relevant market has been hotly debated by antitrust scholars.[17] The 1984 DOJ Guidelines ignore it, even though it is a well established element in Supreme Court antimerger policy.

13. Harris & Jorde, Market Definition in the Merger Guidelines: Implications for Antitrust Enforcement, 71 Calif.L.Rev. 464, 476–79 (1983). The criticism was directed at the 1982 Guidelines. The 1984 Guidelines are generally unresponsive to the criticism.

14. 49 Fed.Reg. at 26,833.

15. Brown Shoe Co. v. U.S., 370 U.S. 294, 346, 82 S.Ct. 1502, 1535 (1962).

16. U.S. v. Von's Grocery Co., 384 U.S. 270, 277, 86 S.Ct. 1478, 1482 (1966).

17. Supporting condemnation of mergers in markets exhibiting a trend toward concentration: Bok, Section 7 of the Clayton Act and the Merging of Law and Economics, 74 Harv.L.Rev. 226, 310 (1960); opposing it: R. Bork, The Antitrust Paradox: A Policy at War With Itself 205–206 (1978); See generally, Y. Brozen, Concentration, Mergers, and Public Policy (1982).

What does a "trend" toward concentration indicate? Most of the time it indicates that larger firms have developed economies of scale. Suppose, for example, that a market contains 50 firms, each with 2% of the market and having costs of $4.00 per unit. Two firms merge and achieve economies that reduce the costs of the post-merger firm to $3.60. What will happen next? The larger firm with the lower costs is likely to expand output. The smaller competitors will lose business unless they can achieve the economies themselves, and the quickest way is by merger. The industry will exhibit a "trend" toward concentration (and merger) until it reaches a new equilibrium in which all firms have achieved the available economies.

Any rule that identifies such a trend toward concentration as justifying condemnation of mergers is probably calculated to protect small businesses at the expense of consumers. This almost certainly explains the Supreme Court's citation of a trend toward concentration in *Brown Shoe* and *Von's Grocery*. In his *Von's Grocery* dissent Justice Stewart criticized the majority for trying to use Clayton § 7 to "roll back the supermarket revolution." [18] Grocers were merging because multi-store companies were achieving economies in buying, advertising and other forms of coordination that were generally not available to smaller chains or individual stores.

The irony of using a "trend" toward concentration to condemn a merger under these circumstances is that the rule often damages the fortunes of the very small businesses it was designed to protect. If multi-store economies are substantial in the grocery business, firms will procure additional stores. If they cannot acquire existing stores they probably will build new ones of their own. The result will be that small operators will still have to face the more efficient operation of their bigger competitors but will have no easy way of exiting the market when things go bad. The "trend" toward concentration that the Court cited should have been used to support, rather than condemn, the mergers at issue.

 WESTLAW REFERENCES

Barriers to New Entry

(department /2 justice) d.o.j. /p merger /5 guideline /p
    barrier /5 entry

Adequacy of Irreplaceable Raw Materials

(raw scarce natural +1 material resource mineral) coal oil
    copper /50 merger % digest(railroad)

Excess Capacity

"excess capacity" /p merger

---

18. 384 U.S. at 288, 86 S.Ct. at 1488: "[T]he [majority's] opinion is hardly more than a requiem for the so-called "Mom and Pop" grocery stores * * * that are now economically and technologically obsolete in many parts of the country."

§ 11.7 When Is a Merger Horizontal?

A merger is strictly "horizontal" only if 1) the two firms involved produce the same product (i.e., consumers cannot distinguish between the products of the two firms, or are completely insensitive to the differences); and 2) the firms operate in the same geographic market.

As you might guess, the real world contains no perfectly horizontal mergers. Identical gasoline stations across the street from each other are not exactly in the same market: one will be more attractive to west-bound traffic, the other to east-bound traffic. Nevertheless, a merger between them would almost certainly be treated as "horizontal" for antitrust purposes.

Drawing the line between horizontal and non-horizontal mergers is difficult, however. Courts characterize a merger as "horizontal" only after they have decided that the merger partners are in the same product and geographic markets. If they are not they characterize the competition between them as merely "potential" and the merger as "conglomerate." [1]

The following mergers have been characterized as "horizontal": a merger 1) of a metal can manufacturer and a glass bottle manufacturer; 2) of a company that strip-mined coal and a company that deep-mined coal; 3) of a company that manufactured dry table wines and a company that manufactured sweet, fruity wines; 4) of a firm that manufactured heavy steel products and a firm that manufactured light steel products; 5) of a grocery chain whose stores were located in northeast Los Angeles and a grocery chain whose stores were located in southwest Los Angeles.[2]

It is difficult to generalize about the degree of competition that existed between these pairs of merger partners. In some cases, such as *Continental Can*, cross elasticity of demand between the cans and bottles was high for some customers. The court found that beer bottlers were very sensitive to price and would have responded to a small price increase in cans by switching to bottles, or vice-versa.[3] On the other hand, there were other customers who strongly preferred bottles to cans, and for whom the price of bottles would have to go very high before they would consider cans to be satisfactory substitutes.

§ 11.7

1. Potential competition mergers are discussed in the following chapter.

2. U.S. v. Continental Can Co., 378 U.S. 441, 84 S.Ct. 1738 (1964); U.S. v. General Dynamics Corp., 415 U.S. 486, 94 S.Ct. 1186 (1974); In re Coca-Cola Bottling Co., 93 F.T.C. 110 (1979); U.S. v. Columbia Steel Co., 334 U.S. 495, 68 S.Ct. 1107 (1948); U.S. v. Von's Grocery Co., 384 U.S. 270, 86 S.Ct. 1478 (1966).

3. 378 U.S. at 451–52, 84 S.Ct. at 1744.

Courts sometimes look at elasticity of supply when determining the extent to which two companies operate in the same relevant market. For example, U.S. v. Aluminum Co. of America (Rome Cable) involved the acquisition of a company that made copper and aluminum conductor by a much larger firm that made only aluminum conductor. The district court had found that aluminum and copper conductor should be placed in the same market because "there is complete manufacturing interchangeability between copper and aluminum, and manufacturers constantly review their product lines and 'switch readily from one * * * metal to another in accordance with market conditions.' "[4] The Supreme Court reversed, looking largely at demand conditions to hold that aluminum and copper conductor were separate products. The Court was probably wrong; the competition between aluminum and copper conductor was substantial, if the district court finding was correct.

In monopoly cases the defendant frequently argues that the relevant market should be larger than the market alleged by the plaintiff. The effect will be to make the defendant's market share smaller. This is not necessarily so in horizontal merger cases, however. The defendant will argue for a large market if the result will be to make the relevant market appear less concentrated and the post-merger firm's market share appear smaller. For example, if a defendant manufacturer of men's cowboy boots acquired a manufacturer of women's cowboy boots, the defendant might argue that the relevant market should be all "footwear." The result would be to place more manufacturers in the relevant market and perhaps make it appear less concentrated, and also to lower the relative market shares of the two merging firms.

The defendant might also try to make the market much smaller, however—so small, in fact, that the merger would not appear horizontal at all, but conglomerate. For example, the defendant might argue that men's cowboy boots and women's cowboy boots are really different markets. Therefore the merger should be treated as conglomerate and given the much more lenient potential competition standard. The ideal market definition for the defendant would be "men's footwear" in one market and "women's footwear" in another. In that case the market would appear unconcentrated and the merging firms' market share small, *and* the merger would be treated as conglomerate rather than horizontal.[5]

Ideally, a court capable of making the proper measurements would establish a sliding scale that would evaluate the competitive impact of a merger in proportion to the closeness of competition between the two firms. Unfortunately, courts are not capable of

4. 377 U.S. 271, 285, 84 S.Ct. 1283, 1291–92 (1964) (J. Stewart, dissenting). See § 3.4 above for a more complete discussion of elasticity of supply.

5. This is essentially the position that the defendant argued for in the *Alcoa* (*Rome Cable*) case. Id.

such precise measurement. They have tended to divide all mergers of competitors into two kinds: "horizontal" and "conglomerate." Once the court has characterized a merger as "horizontal," the fact that the firms make different products, or sell them in substantially different geographic markets, is largely irrelevant. In *Von's Grocery*, for example, the court defined the relevant market as greater Los Angeles and simply added up the market shares of the two grocery chains who were parties to the merger. Once the merger had been classified as horizontal, it was no longer important that virtually all of Von's stores were in the southwest part of the city and all the Shopping Bag stores in the northeast. Surely such a merger did not eliminate as much competition as a merger between two grocery chains all of whose stores were across the street from each other. In fact, Los Angeles was 70 or 80 miles wide, but the lower court found that the average shopper would drive only 10 minutes to buy groceries. The only pairs of Von's and Shopping Bag stores that actually competed with each other were a few pairs toward the middle of the city.[6] The Supreme Court's established framework left it only two alternatives, however: it could have looked at elasticity of supply and considered the likelihood that each chain would have built stores in the other chain's area in response to the second chain's price increase. In that case it would have treated the merger as "conglomerate" and evaluated it under the potential competition doctrine. The alternative was to ignore the fact that the two chains had stores in different sections of town and treat the merger as purely horizontal.

The Supreme Court's analysis in U.S. v. Columbia Steel Co.[7] was more convincing. The government challenged United States Steel Corp.'s acquisition of Consolidated Steel as an illegal horizontal merger. Both companies manufactured "steel," but the defendants alleged that United States Steel fabricated heavy steel products, while Consolidated specialized in lighter products. The bidding record of the two companies bore this out. United States Steel bid on approximately 2,400 jobs, while Consolidated bid on about 6,400 jobs. Each was successful about one-third of the time. However, the two companies had bid on the same job only 166 times.[8] Clearly, with respect to those 166 bids the two firms were "competitors." About 8500 jobs, however, were bid by only one of the firms. The court found no "substantial" competition between the firms and dismissed the complaint.

The court in such a situation has two choices. Assuming elasticity of supply in the market is high (that is, that United States Steel

---

6. Von's Grocery, 384 U.S. at 295–96, 86 S.Ct. at 1492–93. (J. Stewart, dissenting). Justice Stewart concluded that the Von's and Shopping Bag stores actually in competition with each other accounted for "slightly less than 1% of the total grocery store sales in the area."

7. 334 U.S. 495, 68 S.Ct. 1107 (1948).

8. 334 U.S. at 515 n. 13, 68 S.Ct. at 1118.

easily could have produced Consolidated's products out of its existing capacity, and vice-versa), the court can look at the entire output of each company and treat the acquisition as a conglomerate, or potential competition, merger. The alternative is to examine the 166 projects on which both companies bid, and try to define some "market" that described them. In that case the relevant market would represent a trivial percentage of the output of the two firms. Furthermore, the joint-bid projects might not define an area having sufficiently low elasticities of supply and demand to be considered a relevant market for the purpose of merger law.

 WESTLAW REFERENCES
250k20(9)

§ 11.8   The "Failing Company" Defense

The failing company defense exonerates a merger that would otherwise be illegal under § 7. The legislative history of the 1950 Celler-Kefauver Amendments to § 7 makes clear that Congress intended some kind of exemption for acquisitions of "failing" companies.[1] However, the legislative history gives little guidance on the important questions of how "failing company" should be defined and what the scope of the defense ought to be.

The failing company defense was probably designed to protect the creditors, owners or stockholders, and employees of small businesses. In that case, the defense is more concerned with distributive justice than with efficiency. However, the defense does a poor job of achieving its objective. To be sure, the failing company defense can be beneficial to a small, "failing company" acquired by a larger firm and saved from bankruptcy. However, the failing company defense can seriously injure a small business that competes with a failing company acquired by a more efficient firm. The merger at issue in Brunswick Corp. v. Pueblo Bowl-O-Mat, Inc.[2] was a good candidate for the failing company defense,[3] although the Supreme Court never reached that issue. The plaintiff was a relatively small bowling alley operator. Its competitor was also a small operator who was in deep financial trouble. The competitor was acquired by Brunswick Corp., one of the giants in the industry. The acquisition saved the failing company that was acquired, but it injured the (equally small) plaintiff, who then faced a much more formidable competitor than it had before.

§ 11.8

1. S.Rep. No. 1775, 81st Cong., 2d Sess. 7 (1950). See Laurenza, Section 7 of the Clayton Act and the Failing Company: An Updated Perspective. 65 Va.L. Rev. 947 (1979).

2. 429 U.S. 477, 97 S.Ct. 690 (1977). See § 14.5 below.

3. See Areeda, Antitrust Violations Without Damage Recoveries, 89 Harv.L. Rev. 1127 (1976).

The acquisition of a failing company sometimes injures competing small businesses, but it can be harmful to consumer welfare as well. For example, suppose that a market contains four firms, each with 25% of the market, one of which is failing. If the failing company were permitted to close its doors, its customers would probably turn to the remaining three firms in roughly equal numbers. In that case the failure would create a market with three firms, each with about 33% of the market. Under the "failing company" defense, however, one of the three firms will be permitted to acquire the failing firm— and that will leave a market in which one firm has about 50% of the market and the other two have 25% each. Such a market is more conducive to oligopolistic behavior than a market of three equally-sized firms.

The failing company doctrine is sometimes defended as efficient because it tends to keep in production facilities that would otherwise be shut down. However, many failing firms are reorganized in bankruptcy and their assets continue to be productive. About the only consistent exception is when the market contains a great deal of excess capacity and the assets are highly specialized. In that case, however, no competing firm is likely to want them.

The failing company defense is well established in antitrust case law, although a qualifying "failing company" has been found only a few times.[4] Citizen Publishing Co. v. U.S. assessed the requirement that before the failing company defense can be used the defendant must show 1) that the acquired firm is almost certain to go bankrupt and cannot be reorganized successfully; and 2) that no less anticompetitive acquisition (i.e., by a smaller competitor or a noncompetitor) is available as an alternative.[5] The 1984 Merger Guidelines generally adopt this position:

> The Department is unlikely to challenge an anticompetitive merger in which one of the merging firms is allegedly failing when: (1) the allegedly failing firm probably would be unable to meet its financial obligations in the near future; 2) it probably would not be able to reorganize successfully under Chapter 11 of the Bankruptcy Act; and (3) it has made unsuccessful good faith efforts to elicit reasonable alternative offers of acquisition of the failing firm that would both keep it in the market and pose a less severe danger to competition than does the proposed merger.[6]

4. See U.S. v. Black & Decker Mfg. Co., 430 F.Supp. 729, 778–781 (D.Md. 1976); U.S. v. M.P.M., 397 F.Supp. 78, 96 (D.Colo.1975).

5. 394 U.S. 131, 138, 89 S.Ct. 927, 931 (1969). The Newspaper Preservation Act, 15 U.S.C.A. §§ 1801–1804, permits "joint operating agreements" between two newspapers in the same city, and contains a weaker version of the "failing company" requirement. In order to enter into a JOA, the parties must show that at least one of the two newspapers "is in probable danger of financial failure * * *." See Committee for an Independent P–I v. Hearst Corp., 704 F.2d 467 (9th Cir.), cert. denied ___ U.S. ___, 104 S.Ct. 236 (1983).

6. 49 Fed.Reg. at 26,837.

In addition to the failing company defense, the DOJ also acknowledges a "failing division" defense, which might arise when a multidivisional firm decides to abandon a single, unprofitable market. Although the content of the "failing division" defense is not entirely clear, the Guidelines require a showing that the corporation from which the allegedly failing division was acquired would have liquidated the division in the near future had it not been sold. In addition, the defense must meet the same requirements respecting prospective purchasers as are assessed by the failing company defense.[7] The Guidelines give no precedent in either case law or legislative history for a "failing division" defense. Therefore the "defense" should be regarded as no more than a prediction about the Department's future exercises of prosecutorial discretion.

 WESTLAW REFERENCES
"failing company" /5 defense

§ 11.9   Partial Acquisitions and Acquisitions "Solely for Investment"

§ 7 of the Clayton Act condemns the acquisition of the "whole or any part" of the stock or assets of another firm if the requisite anticompetitive effects result. However, the section does "not apply to persons purchasing * * * stock solely for investment * * *."

The antitrust laws are concerned with the effects of certain practices on competition, not with the ownership of corporations. Legal "control" of a corporation should therefore not necessarily be the threshold for considering partial acquisitions under the Clayton Act, and the Supreme Court has said as much.[1] As a general rule a person has legal control of a corporation if he owns and votes 50% or more of its shares. Realistically, however, ownership of far less than 50% will enable someone to have effective control of a corporation. In the case of a large corporation, ownership of 15% to 20% of the shares by one person could make him an enormous shareholder with tremendous influence in the buying, selling, entry and exit decisions of the corporation—particularly if all other shareholders were substantially smaller. The Supreme Court has not wasted much time deciding whether one company owned enough shares to have legal "control" of another company. More often than not, it has assumed control when the percentage of shares held was substantial. In U.S. v. E.I. du Pont de Nemours & Co.,[2] for example, it assumed that

7. Id.

§ 11.9

1. Denver & Rio Grande West. R.R. v. U.S., 387 U.S. 485, 501, 87 S.Ct. 1754, 1763 (1967).

2. 353 U.S. 586, 77 S.Ct. 872 (1957). See also U.S. v. General Dynamics Corp., 415 U.S. 486, 94 S.Ct. 1186 (1974), where the acquiring firm owned 34% of the acquired firm's shares, but the parties agreed that there was "effective control."

duPont had substantial influence on General Motors' buying decisions even though duPont owned only 23% of GM's shares.

Competition can be threatened, however, even if the acquiring firm's interest is so small that it has no influence at all over the acquired firm's decisions. Suppose that firms A and B are competitors and A acquires 15% of the shares of B. Clearly the competitive game has acquired a new twist. Under the rules of competition A would like nothing better than to force B out of the market through A's greater efficiency. As a result of the partial acquisition, however, A suddenly has a strong financial interest in B's welfare. The risks of tacit or explicit collusion may increase dramatically.

There is one additional good reason for carefully scrutinizing stock acquisitions of less than a controlling interest. Granted that there is no "control," there is also no opportunity for the creation of efficiency. Mergers, you will recall, receive rather complex rule of reason treatment because they pose serious dangers of noncompetitive behavior on the one side, but have the potential to create substantial economies on the other. If A acquires 15% of the shares of its competitor B, A may not have enough equity to "control" B. Neither, however, will the firms have common management or other bases for obtaining the kinds of economies that make mergers socially valuable. In this case, the potential for social harm may be somewhat attenuated because the ownership interest is small—but the potential for social good has disappeared altogether. That rationale, as the discussion in chapter four suggests, has often been used to justify application of a rule of *per se* illegality.

Here a *per se* rule is not appropriate, however, because § 7 contains an explicit exemption for "persons purchasing * * * stock solely for investment and not using the same by voting or otherwise to bring about * * * the substantial lessening of competition." The exemption appears to give the fact finder the difficult job of determining whether a purchaser's motive was "solely for investment." The courts, however, have leaned toward a different position: if the purchase has a measurable anticompetitive effect, then it will not be considered "solely for investment," regardless of the subjective intent of the purchaser.[3] The result is that the "solely for investment" exception is really not much of an exception at all. Any stock purchase may be challenged on the grounds that it may substantially lessen competition. If it does so, then the "solely for investment" exception will not apply. If it does not substantially lessen competition, then the merger is not illegal in the first place. The exemption of acquisitions solely for investment has done nothing to simplify judicial evaluation of partial acquisitions.[4]

3. See, for example, Gulf & West. Indus. v. A & P, 476 F.2d 687, 693 (2d Cir. 1973).

4. Areeda & Turner, however, propose a presumptive rule of thumb exempting 5% holdings for investment purposes. 5 P. Areeda & D. Turner, Antitrust Law ¶ 1203d (1980).

The problems presented by partial asset acquisitions are different than those presented by partial stock acquisitions. First, asset exchanges are the very heart of a market economy. If Xerox Corp. buys a Ford truck to make its deliveries, Xerox has acquired an "asset" from the Ford Motor Company. Obviously, firms, even competitors, exchange assets routinely as part of their business. The vast majority of such asset acquisitions pose no antitrust problems, particularly if they are purchases from the inventory of another firm. Antitrust policy becomes concerned with partial asset acquisitions when the asset that changes hands represents a measurable and relatively permanent transfer of market share or productive capacity from one firm to another.[5]

Even here, however, partial asset acquisitions deserve somewhat different antitrust treatment than partial stock acquisitions. For example, if A purchases an unused plant from its competitor B, that purchase would not give A a continuing interest in B's welfare. In fact, a substantial asset acquisition might not affect competition very much at all. Suppose that A and B are the only competitors in a market. A owns two plants and B three. If A purchases one of B's plants the result will be that A owns three plants and B two, and market concentration may be about the same after the acquisition as it was before. If A had purchased 33% of B's shares, however, the effect on competition would probably be substantial.

An efficient market demands relatively free exchange of productive assets among competitors. In general, the more specialized the assets the more essential it becomes that the assets can be purchased by a competitor. If a firm finds itself with more trucks than it needs it may be able to sell them to a variety of other firms. However, if a business uses a specialized machine to grind optical lenses, the only available buyer may be another firm that makes similar lenses. If a company using a large, specialized plant or piece of equipment puts it on the market, the highest bidder, or perhaps the only bidder, is likely to be a competitor. Any rule that forbids too many such transactions could cause a great amount of social waste.

The effect on competition of *total* asset acquisitions, however, is generally about the same as that of total stock acquisitions. For example, if A's rival operates only one plant, A purchases it and the rival exits from the market, the transaction is likely to be as anticompetitive as a merger between the two firms. In fact, this was a common mechanism by which firms avoided application of § 7 before its 1950 Amendments, when the statute applied only to acquisitions of stock.[6]

---

5. Id at ¶ 1202a.

6. See Thatcher Mfg. Co. v. FTC, 272 U.S. 554, 560, 47 S.Ct. 175, 178 (1926).

Once again, the difficult problem for the policy maker is where to draw the line between legal and illegal asset acquisitions. One answer is that § 7 condemns only those acquisitions which "may * * * substantially * * * lessen competition." The trouble with that solution, however, is that analysis of whether an acquisition lessens competition requires an expensive study of the relevant markets and the competitive position of the firms involved.

Nevertheless, no shorter analysis has yet appeared that will effectively separate harmless from dangerous asset acquisitions. In general, if the asset acquisition appears on its face not to affect industrial concentration or the market share of its buyer, the acquisition will be treated as outside the scope of § 7. If it does tend to enlarge the market share or productive capacity of the acquiring firm, or if it increases concentration in the industry, then its effects on competition must be assessed.[7]

 WESTLAW REFERENCES
partial "solely for investment" /5 acquisition

---

7. Certain asset acquisitions may tend to increase industrial concentration or give the acquiring firm a larger market share even though the asset acquisition itself does not increase productive capacity. Acquisition of a trademark, for example, would fall into this category. § 7 should apply. U.S. v. Lever Bros. Co., 216 F.Supp. 887, 889 (S.D. N.Y.1963).

CHAPTER 12

CONGLOMERATE MERGERS

Table of Sections

§ 12.1 Introduction: Competition and Conglomerate Mergers

A merger that is neither horizontal nor vertical is generally called "conglomerate." Although the word "conglomerate" implies the union of completely unrelated products or activities, antitrust law has been relatively unconcerned with so-called "pure" or "true" conglomerate mergers. Most of the conglomerate mergers subject to antitrust scrutiny are between firms that stand in a relatively close market relationship to each other. For example, mergers between firms that manufacture the same product but sell it in different geographic markets are called "market extension" mergers. Mergers between firms that sell different products that are somehow identified or related to each other are called "product extension" mergers.

A small amount of evidence, not particularly convincing, suggests that Congress intended to include conglomerate mergers in the coverage of amended § 7 of the Clayton Act.[1] Whatever Congress intended, the reach of § 7 to such mergers is now clearly established. Courts have generally interpreted § 7 as being concerned with mergers that threaten "competition," however, and not with mere size as such (although courts have occasionally come close to condemning

§ 12.1

1. See Brodley, Potential Competition Mergers: A Structural Synthesis, 87 Yale L.J. 1, 43–44 (1977).

mere size). Injury to competition is unlikely unless a particular kind of market relationship exists between the merging firms, or between the post-merger firm and its customers or competitors.

 WESTLAW REFERENCES
"market extension merger"
"product extension merger"

§ 12.2   Conglomerate Mergers and Efficiency

In general, the closer the market relationship between two firms, the greater the efficiencies that can be obtained by merger. By definition, conglomerate mergers involve firms that are not competitors and that do not have a significant buyer-seller relationship with each other. As a result the efficiencies available from conglomerate mergers are usually not as large as the efficiencies that can be obtained from horizontal mergers that enable the post-merger firm to attain minimum optimal size, or vertical mergers that permit substantial savings in distribution.

Nevertheless, conglomerate mergers can yield efficiencies. The nature of the efficiencies that can be obtained from conglomerate mergers varies with the relationship between the merging firms. For example, if the two firms produce related, complimentary products that are commonly purchased together, such as laundry soap and bleach, the post-merger firm might be able to distribute the two products together more cheaply than two independent firms could each distribute them before.

Likewise, product extension mergers can enable a firm to save money on advertising, by working two related products into the same advertisement. Further, name recognition derived from advertising can sometimes be spread to additional products. For example, a firm such as Procter & Gamble may spend a great deal of money obtaining recognition of its name for a half dozen related household cleaning products. Once consumer recognition is established, however, P & G might easily be able to add a seventh product to the list. The benefits of past advertising that has created a favorable impression of the first six products in the minds of consumers will spread to the seventh product as well, often at little additional cost.

Similar efficiencies can accrue from market extension mergers. If firms selling the same product in different geographic areas merge, the post-merger firm might be able to coordinate buying of materials, marketing, transportation, and production itself much more efficiently than each firm alone could do.

In addition are several scale economies that are available to larger or diversified firms. Research and development, particularly of the "pure" sort, can have spillover benefits into a number of areas that might be unrelated in the market.[1] Likewise, larger firms can hire their own economists, statisticians, lawyers and other specialists, while smaller firms must buy these services in the marketplace. In short, certain economies can be achieved by "pure" size, regardless of whether the products of the merging firms are related.

Finally, the conglomerate firm can often raise capital internally, without relying on the market. An independent firm short of money must generally enter the capital market, disclose information to outsider lenders or equity buyers, and permit outsiders to evaluate the risks and rewards of investment. Further, the firm must incur all the transaction costs that dealing on the capital market entails. The conglomerate, on the other hand, is likely to be operating in some areas that need capital and in others that are producing large amounts of revenue. It may be able to internalize the entire process of financing new development, simply by shifting money from one division to another.[2]

Courts have long recognized that conglomerate mergers can create efficiency. They have not always been sympathetic, however. The post-merger firm's increased efficiency has sometimes become the rationale for condemning, rather than upholding, a merger. For example, in FTC v. Procter & Gamble Co., the Supreme Court condemned a merger between a major producer of household detergents and cleansers and a major producer of household liquid bleach. One of the reasons the Court cited was that Procter & Gamble could take advantage of "volume discounts" in advertising and therefore market bleach more cheaply than competing bleach producers could.[3] Likewise in Allis-Chalmers Mfg. Co. v. White Consolidated Indus.[4] the Third Circuit condemned a merger between a company that made electrical equipment and a company that made rolling mills, used in the manufacture of steel. The rolling mills required fairly elaborate electric hook-ups, and generally a purchaser of a rolling mill needed to obtain its electrical hook-up from a different seller. The merger enabled the post-merger firm to become "the only company capable of designing, producing and installing a complete metal rolling mill." The creation of a company that could deliver the entire package, the

§ 12.2

1. See Nelson, The Simple Economics of Basic Scientific Research, 67 J.Pol. Econ. 297 (Jun.1959). The "Nelson hypothesis" is that research and development is more profitable for diversified firms than for more homogeneous ones.

2. For the same reason, firms often diversify to reduce risk. For example, they might develop some high profit areas that are quite vulnerable to economic recession, but buy "insurance" by investing in other areas that, while less profitable in the peaks, are relatively

more secure in bad economic times. See F.M. Scherer, Industrial Market Structure and Economic Performance 105–107 (2d ed. 1980). For a more complete analysis of the kinds of efficiency that can be achieved by conglomeration, see Y. Brozen, Concentration, Mergers, and Public Policy 350–58 (1982).

3. 386 U.S. 568, 579, 87 S.Ct. 1224, 1230 (1967).

4. 414 F.2d 506, 515–518 (3d Cir. 1969), cert. denied, 396 U.S. 1009, 90 S.Ct. 567 (1970).

court concluded, "would raise higher the already significant barriers to the entry of others into the various segments of the metal rolling mill market." Clearly the "entry barrier" that the Court had in mind was the post-merger firm's increased efficiency. Nothing is a more effective barrier to entry than a firm's capacity to produce a high quality product at a low price, or to provide improved service to its customers.

Today, courts are less likely to condemn a merger merely because it increases the efficiency of the post-merger firm. On the other hand, neither is there any generalized "efficiency defense" in conglomerate merger cases. Although economists can produce dozens of reasons why conglomerate mergers produce efficiency, measurement of the cost savings that result from a particular merger is virtually impossible, certainly in litigation.[5]

Rather, antitrust law searches for a way to identify those mergers that threaten competition. These are condemned, in spite of the fact that they may produce significant economies. Mergers that are unlikely to increase the market power of the post-merger firm and that will probably not facilitate collusion, oligopoly behavior or inefficient exclusionary practices are generally left alone.

 WESTLAW REFERENCES
synopsis,headnote("conglomerate merger")

§ 12.3   Perceived Dangers to Competition

Courts have perceived two broad categories of dangers to competition from conglomerate mergers. First, the conglomerate merger, like the horizontal merger, may facilitate collusion or oligopoly pricing by eliminating *potential* (rather than actual) competition between the merging firms. Most of the case law condemning product extension and market extension mergers relies on this rationale, which is discussed below in § 12.4.

Second, conglomerate mergers have been condemned because courts believed they would facilitate inefficient exclusionary practices directed at outsiders, such as reciprocity, tying or predatory pricing. The risk that a conglomerate merger will increase the likelihood of such practices is usually more imagined than real. Nevertheless, the precedent for condemning conglomerate mergers on these grounds is well established.

Reciprocity

Reciprocity, or reciprocal dealing, occurs when Firm A buys from Firm B and Firm B buys from Firm A. Most reciprocity is purely

5. See the discussion of the efficiency defense in horizontal merger cases in § 11.2 above.

fortuitous, or at least noncontractual. Firms commonly consider it "good business" to buy from their customers when they have the opportunity, provided that price and quality are competitive. For example, if Bethlehem Steel Corp. provides Ford Motor Company with steel, executives at Bethlehem are likely to buy trucks from Ford.

Reciprocity itself can be efficient. Sometimes it reduces direct operating costs—such as when Firm A can deliver a truckload of material to Firm B's plant and return with a load of B's product rather than with an empty truck. Reciprocity can also reduce transaction costs and uncertainty costs by reducing the number of outside firms with which a company deals.

Courts have termed reciprocity "coercive" when a firm refuses to buy from others who refuse to buy from it. Such coercive dealing has been analogized to tying arrangements and has been condemned under both § 5 of the FTC Act [1] and § 1 of the Sherman Act. [2]

Mergers can facilitate two different varieties of reciprocity. First, a merger of two firms often increases the amount of reciprocal dealings that the two firms have with each other. For example, if a truck manufacturer purchases its own steel mill, the manufacturer likely will obtain its steel from the steel mill, and the steel mill will obtain its trucks from its parent truck plant. In such a case the two firms stand in a buyer-supplier relationship with each other, and the union should be analyzed as a vertical merger.

The second kind of reciprocity exists between the post-merger firm and other buyers or suppliers who were not a party to the merger. Conglomerate mergers generally increase the potential for reciprocity because the post-merger firm sells in more markets than it did before the merger. As a result there are a greater number of possible avenues through which reciprocity can occur.

In FTC v. Consolidated Foods Corp. [3] the Supreme Court condemned a merger under § 7 on the theory that the merger facilitated reciprocity. Consolidated Foods operated food processing plants as well as wholesale and retail food stores. It acquired Gentry Inc., which manufactured dehydrated onion and garlic that were commonly used in processed food. During the ten years following the acquisition, Consolidated frequently urged its suppliers of processed food to purchase their dehydrated onion and garlic from Gentry. The Court held "at the outset that the 'reciprocity' made possible by such an acquisition is one of the congeries of anticompetitive practices at which the antitrust laws are aimed."

§ 12.3

1. See California Packing Corp., 25 F.T.C. 379 (1937).

2. See U.S. v. General Dynamics Corp., 258 F.Supp. 36, 65–67 (S.D.N.Y. 1966). See § 8.11 above.

3. 380 U.S. 592, 594, 85 S.Ct. 1220, 1221–22 (1965).

Justice Douglas rejected the view that post-acquisition evidence of actual, coercive reciprocity was necessary to condemn a merger on this ground. Such a rule would permit acquisitions to "go forward willy-nilly, the parties biding their time until reciprocity was allowed fully to bloom." No one "acquiring a company with reciprocal buying opportunities is entitled to a 'free trial' period." Rather, the acquisition can be condemned immediately if there is a "probability" that reciprocity will occur. Then Justice Douglas concluded:

> We do not go so far as to say that any acquisition, no matter how small, violates § 7 if there is a probability of reciprocal buying. Some situations may amount only to *de minimis*. But where, as here, the acquisition is of a company that commands a substantial share of the market, a finding of probability of reciprocal buying by the Commission * * * should be honored if there is substantial evidence to support it.[4]

Consolidated Foods appears to hold that if reciprocal buying is "probable," and if the acquired company "commands a substantial share of the market," the merger is illegal under § 7. This standard would condemn almost any merger in which substantial reciprocity is likely to occur, and lower courts have generally interpreted the standard this way.[5]

The *Consolidated Foods* standard condemns reciprocity-facilitating mergers before it is clear that reciprocity will occur, or whether it will be anticompetitive when it does occur. As noted above, reciprocity is often efficient. Further, actual reciprocity that is anticompetitive can be reached under § 1 of the Sherman Act.

Economically, reciprocity functions in much the same way as the tying arrangement.[6] A firm cannot enlarge its monopoly profits by nondiscriminatory reciprocity. For example, if a firm is already selling widgets at their profit-maximizing price it cannot increase its profits by forcing customers to sell it gidgets in return at less than the competitive price. The customers will treat the loss on gidgets as an increase in the price of widgets.

On the other hand, reciprocity can and often does facilitate price discrimination. Suppose that a firm with a certain amount of market power has been selling widgets at $3.00 but has a chance to fill a very

---

4. Id. at 598–600, 85 S.Ct. at 1224–25.

5. See 5 P. Areeda & D. Turner, Antitrust Law ¶ 1130a (1980): "We know of no case approving * * * a merger creating a probability of substantial reciprocity. The few cases dealing with the subject are unequivocally otherwise." Occasionally, however, firms have defended an acquisition successfully by showing that they had a rigid policy against reciprocal buying. See U.S. v. Int'l Tel. & Tel. Corp., 306 F.Supp. 766 (D.Conn.1969). If a company can point to a history of taking competitive bids for all relevant purchases, and of accepting the lowest bid, then reciprocity will be merely fortuitous. See Bauer, Challenging Conglomerate Mergers Under Section 7 of the Clayton Act: Today's Law and Tomorrow's Legislation, 58 B.U.L.Rev. 199, 231 (1978). Today the government rarely challenges mergers under the reciprocity theory.

6. See § 8.11 above.

large order at a price of $2.80. If it is prevented by customer outrage or the Robinson-Patman Act from making the sale at $2.80, it might agree with the large buyer to a $3.00 price but purchase something from the large buyer in return, paying a supracompetitive price. This type of reciprocity is common, and often buyers and sellers use it to "get together" on a price. It generally facilitates transactions and is procompetitive.

Reciprocity agreements can also be used to avoid statutory price regulation.[7] For example, Firm A might sell a price-regulated product to Firm B at the regulated price but buy something from Firm B in return. The reciprocal product would be priced at more than or less than the competitive price, depending on the relationship between the regulated firm's price and Firm A's profit-maximizing price in the regulated product.

Reciprocity is also an important mechanism by which cartel members "cheat" on the cartel—by selling at the cartel price but buying something from the customer at a supracompetitive price. The result encourages the break-up of the cartel.

Whether any particular instance of reciprocity is efficient depends on the situation. Reciprocity that facilitates price discrimination, for example, may result in larger output and more total consumer satisfaction than would result from nondiscriminatory monopoly pricing. On the other hand, reciprocity may frustrate a regulatory agency's efforts to prevent a price-regulated monopolist from charging a monopoly price.

When a court scrutinizes reciprocity under the Sherman Act, it can balance the efficiency effects of a particular reciprocity agreement against any competitive injury. The Clayton § 7 standard, which condemns a merger because of its potential for reciprocity, preempts the opportunity for this kind of case-by-case analysis. Furthermore, it ignores the fact that the merger itself may create substantial efficiencies. The standard assessed in *Consolidated Foods* condemns *all* instances of "substantial" reciprocity that will "probably" occur. Firms generally have been able to defend only by showing that reciprocity would not occur—not by showing that there are compensating efficiencies or that reciprocity, if it occurs, will not be anticompetitive.

The doctrine of *Consolidated Foods* was formulated at a time when the Supreme Court believed that tying arrangements contained almost no potential for good and were certain to cause harm. They responded with a virtual *per se* rule.[8] Justice Douglas' broad observation that reciprocity is one of the "congeries of anticompetitive

7. Tying arrangements can be used for the same purpose. See § 8.6 above.

8. See Northern Pacif. Rwy. Co. v. U.S., 356 U.S. 1, 6, 78 S.Ct. 514, 518 (1958).

practices at which the antitrust laws are aimed" reveals the same attitude toward reciprocity agreements.[9]

Leverage and Tie-ins

Conglomerate mergers can sometimes facilitate tying arrangements. A film manufacturer's merger with a film processor, for example, might make it easier for the firm to tie film processing to film sales.

Once again, the important question for the antitrust policymaker is, Why § 7? Both § 3 of the Clayton Act and § 1 of the Sherman Act reach actual tying arrangements with substantial overdeterrence to spare. Should a merger be condemned simply because it increases the probability that a firm will engage in tying?

Areeda and Turner suggest that certain "subtle" tying arrangements might be beyond the reach of Clayton § 3 or Sherman § 1.[10] If that is true, the problem lies with the law of tying arrangements, not with the law of mergers. Any rule that condemns a merger, probably efficient, because a tying arrangement not reachable by either Clayton § 3 or Sherman § 1 is "likely" to occur, is outrageously overdeterrent.

Strategic Pricing and Entry Deterrence

A firm generally cannot "finance" predatory pricing in one market by raising prices in another market. A profit-maximizing firm will already be selling in each market at its profit-maximizing price for that market.[11] However, predatory behavior may be more rewarding for the multi-market seller. By predating a rival into submission in one market, for example, the firm can "send a message" to competitors in other markets.[12] Thus a dominant firm selling in three different geographic or product markets might predate against a rival in one market and at the same time warn competitors in the other two markets that they should not cut prices. Predatory pricing might be more rational in such a case, because the predator could reap post-predation monopoly profits in three different markets instead of one.

Courts have occasionally cited the possibility of predatory pricing as a reason for condemning a merger. In general, the theory has not been the one outlined above. Rather they have suggested that the merger introduced into the market a giant firm with a deep pocket that could afford extended periods of loss selling.[13]

9. *Consolidated Foods*, 380 U.S. at 594, 85 S.Ct. at 1221.

10. See 5 P. Areeda & D. Turner, Antitrust Law ¶ 1134c (1980).

11. See § 6.12 above.

12. See Salop, Strategic Entry Deterrence, 69 Amer.Econ.Rev. 335, 337 (1979).

13. See Reynolds Metals Co. v. FTC, 309 F.2d 223, 229–230 (D.C.Cir.1962); U.S. v. Alum. Co. (Cupples), 233 F.Supp. 718, 727 (E.D.Mo.1964), affirmed mem., 382 U.S. 12, 86 S.Ct. 24 (1965); and see

Both these theories stretch § 7 liability much too far. *All* mergers produce a firm that is larger after the merger than before. Likewise, by definition all conglomerate mergers increase the number of markets in which the post-merger firm sells. If the predatory pricing rationale is not to become a *per se* rule against mergers, some principled way must be found for determining when the dangers of predatory pricing or other price-related strategic behavior are sufficient to warrant condemnation.

Most economists today believe that true predatory pricing is quite rare. No empirical data obtained to date suggests that predation by multi-market firms is unusually common. To be sure, one result of any merger can be a price reduction. Most of the time, however, the price reduction results from the merger's increased efficiency, not from its predation.[14] To condemn a merger too quickly on the grounds that it might facilitate predatory pricing would undermine the most central goal of the antitrust laws—high quality and low consumer prices. If predatory pricing occurs, it can be condemned under the more appropriate standards of § 2 of the Sherman Act.

 WESTLAW REFERENCES
Reciprocity
reciproc*** /p coercive

Strategic Pricing and Entry Deterrence
predat*** /5 pric*** /p merger

§ 12.4 Mergers of Potential Competitors

Most conglomerate mergers, particularly the product extension and market extension types, are analyzed under two versions of the "potential competition" doctrine.

"Potential" competition is a misnomer. Potential competition is really actual competition assessed from the supply side rather than the demand side. As chapter three indicated, a firm's market power is limited by two things: consumer response to a price increase *and* new entry by competitors in search of higher profits. A firm's knowledge that its price increase will flood the market with new sellers is competition just as "actual" as its knowledge that a price increase will cost a loss of many customers.

The separate standard for potential competition mergers developed at a time when antitrust policy makers equated "competition" with a large number of firms in a market. Within that paradigm "competition" did not exist in a market with only one producer, even

Purex Corp. v. Procter & Gamble Co., 596 F.2d 881, 887–88 (9th Cir. 1979), appeal after remand, 664 F.2d 1105 (9th Cir. 1981), cert. denied, 456 U.S. 983, 102 S.Ct. 2256 (1982).

14. See Hovenkamp, Merger Actions for Damages, 35 Hastings L.J. (1984).

though the producer had absolutely no power to price at above marginal cost without causing substantial new entry. Today antitrust law has generally adopted the economist's more useful definition of competition as that set of market conditions that drives prices toward marginal cost. The "potential competition" doctrine survives as a relic of an earlier era.[1]

The potential competition merger is best viewed as a form of horizontal merger. It is condemned because of its tendency to facilitate oligopolistic pricing or collusion in the post-merger market. The chief difference between the potential competition merger and the conventional horizontal merger is that the former focuses almost exclusively on elasticity of supply. The cross-elasticity of demand between the products produced by the merging firms is sufficiently low that they are regarded as being in separate relevant markets.

The Supreme Court first applied the term "potential competition" to a merger in U.S. v. El Paso Natural Gas Co.[2] The case illustrates the imperceptible distinction that often exists between "actual" and "potential" competition. El Paso was the only out-of-state supplier of natural gas to California, and it sold more than 50% of the gas consumed in the state. In 1956 El Paso began acquiring the stock of Pacific Northwest, a natural gas company that had bid to make sales into California but had never actually sold gas there. El Paso and Pacific Northwest had often competed for California contracts, however, and El Paso had occasionally revised a bid downward in order to retain customers who had gotten more favorable offers from Pacific Northwest. The Court condemned the merger, observing that "unsuccessful bidders are no less competitors than the successful one," and that the "presence of two or more suppliers" gave the buyers a choice, even though only one of the suppliers could ultimately be chosen.

A natural gas pipeline serving a single city is generally a natural monopoly. That is, the market is most efficiently served at any given time by a single supplier. The market itself is "contestable," however. Dozens of suppliers could offer bids for the opportunity to build the pipeline, and if there were true competition among the bidders, the resulting price would be competitive. El Paso had simply won all past bids. For future bids El Paso still had to contend with the competition of Pacific Northwest, until the merger eliminated Pacific Northwest as a competitor. Pacific Northwest was an "actual"

§ 12.4

1. For some insights into the two meanings of "competition" see D. Dewey, Monopoly in Economics and Law (1959); Mason, Monopoly in Law and Economics, 47 Yale L.J. 34 (1937); and see Hovenkamp, Book Review, 33 Hastings L.J. 755, 762 (1982).

2. 376 U.S. 651, 84 S.Ct. 1044 (1964). In the same year the Supreme Court held that the potential competition doctrine would apply to a joint venture between noncompetitors. U.S. v. Penn-Olin Chem. Co., 378 U.S. 158, 84 S.Ct. 1710 (1964). Joint ventures and competition are discussed in § 4.3 above.

competitor, even though it was not making any sales into the California market.

El Paso Natural Gas is an easy case, because in franchise bidding situations the distinction between elasticity of demand and elasticity of supply virtually evaporates. Whether we regard Pacific Northwest's competition as "actual" or "potential" is purely semantic. The court treated the acquisition as a horizontal merger.

A more typical potential competition case is FTC v. Procter & Gamble Co.,[3] in which the Supreme Court condemned P&G's acquisition of Clorox. P&G manufactured a wide variety of household products including cleansers and detergents, but not bleach. Clorox manufactured only bleach. In spite of evidence that P&G never intended to enter the bleach market on its own, the Court found that P&G was the "most likely entrant" into the market. Its acquisition of Clorox, however, foreclosed any possibility of *de novo* entry. Furthermore, the bleach market itself was concentrated, with Clorox controlling 50% of the national market, and the top two firms together controlling 65%.[4]

The Supreme Court did not clarify the theory of potential competition in the *P&G* case. Justice Douglas was more concerned with the possibility that the post-merger firm would obtain advertising discounts and injure competitors by its lower costs than any likelihood that the merger would facilitate collusion among bleach producers. Such collusion, of course, would be a benefit, not a detriment, to other bleach firms in the market. It would injure consumers, who would either pay a higher price for bleach, or else find a less satisfactory substitute.

The Supreme Court articulated a more complete theory of potential competition mergers in 1973, in U.S. v. Falstaff Brewing Co.[5] The government challenged a merger between Falstaff, the nation's fourth largest brewer, which made no sales in New England, and Narragansett, the largest regional brewer in New England, having about 20% of that market.

The government pleaded that Falstaff was a potential entrant into the New England market. Had it entered that market *de novo*, or else by a "toe-hold" acquisition of a smaller firm in the New England market, the result would have been increased competition. The district court dismissed the complaint, finding that Falstaff would never have entered the market unless it could have acquired an important brewer with an established distribution network.

---

3. 386 U.S. 568, 87 S.Ct. 1224 (1967).

4. However, there were some 200 smaller producers, many of whom undoubtedly could have increased output in response to a price increase.

5. 410 U.S. 526, 93 S.Ct. 1096 (1973), mandate conformed to, 383 F.Supp. 1020 (1974).

The Supreme Court reversed but rejected the theory offered by the government. The important factor, concluded the Court, was not whether Falstaff subjectively planned to enter the New England market, but whether beer producers in the New England market *believed* that Falstaff was a potential entrant and behaved more competitively in order to deter its entry.

This "perceived potential entrant" doctrine as formulated in *Falstaff* begins with a "target" market that is highly concentrated and conducive to monopolistic or oligopolistic pricing. The tendency of the incumbent sellers to raise prices is restrained, however, by the presence of a large and capable firm poised on the "edge" of the market,[6] eager to enter should the market appear profitable enough. Thus the perceived potential entrant's presence has the effect of keeping prices lower and output higher than they would otherwise be.

The restraint on pricing disappears, however, if the large firm on the edge of the market acquires one of the larger firms within the market. The target market will still be conducive to oligopoly pricing, but now there is no longer a firm on the edge of the market, threatening to enter if prices rise too high. As a result output in the target market may be reduced and prices will rise. If the theory is correct, such a merger clearly would fall within the language of § 7 condemning mergers the effect of which "may be substantially to lessen competition   *   *   * ."

The plausibility of the perceived potential entrant doctrine is controversial, however. The doctrine rests on a complex theory of "limit pricing." Under the theory, the firms within the market charge a price lower than their short-run profit-maximizing price in order to deter the entry of the firm sitting on the edge of the market. Whether such a limit pricing strategy is profitable for an incumbent with market power is debatable. In this case, however, the limit pricing is carried out not by a unitary monopolist but by a small group of firms in a concentrated market. In *Falstaff*, for example, the acquired firm was the leading seller of beer in New England; however, it still had only 20% of the market. Absent an express agreement, coordination of a "limit price" among five or more sellers seems all but impossible.[7]

That hurdle aside, the perceived potential entrant theory applies only to relatively well-defined conditions. First, the target market must be concentrated and must appear conducive to monopolistic or oligopolistic pricing. Second, the acquiring firm must either be the only perceived potential entrant, or else the number of perceived

---

6. A firm on the "edge" of the market can be either a maker of a related or complimentary product, as in the *P&G* case; or else it can be the seller of the same product in a different geographic market, as in the *Falstaff* case.

7. See G. Stigler, The Organization of Industry 20–22 (1983 ed.); for a somewhat less pessimistic view, see 5 P. Areeda & D. Turner, Antitrust Law ¶ 1120 (1980).

potential entrants must be sufficiently small that the elimination of the acquiring firm will affect pricing in the market. Finally, the merger itself must not increase competition within the target market significantly, or else the doctrine would be counterproductive.

If a market is already behaving competitively, the presence of a potential entrant will have no effect on output and pricing in the market. Courts generally have been consistent in requiring that the target market be highly concentrated before the perceived potential entrant doctrine will apply.[8] However, high concentration alone is not necessarily conducive to new entry. The market might be a natural monopoly, or it might have room for only two or three firms of minimum optimal scale (MOS). In that case it might be unrealistic to expect an outsider to enter the market *de novo*.

A market is conducive to monopoly or oligopoly pricing only if it contains substantial barriers to entry. If entry is easy and a new entrant can operate as cheaply as an incumbent, any monopoly price will result in competitive entry. Entry barriers in potential competition cases present a paradox, however. They must be present, or else the market will perform competitively and the presence of any potential entrant will be irrelevant. However, an acquiring firm cannot itself be barred by the entry barriers, or it could not reasonably be perceived as a potential entrant. For example, if local law permitted only three banks in a community and three already existed, no outside bank could be a perceived potential entrant. It would have to enter, if at all, by acquiring one of the three banks already in the market.[9]

In Tenneco, Inc. v. FTC [10] the Second Circuit refused to condemn a merger between Tenneco, a large manufacturer of auto parts, which did not manufacture automobile shock absorbers, and Monroe, a leading shock absorber manufacturer. The court found "substantial" barriers to entry in the replacement shock absorber market, the most significant of which it identified as "economies of scale." Minimum efficient scale for a plant in the industry was 6,000,000 units annually, which was about 10% of annual total sales. The court also identified as barriers "the need for technology and marketing skills peculiar to the industry" and high start-up costs that would result from the "significant time lag" between a firm's decision to build a plant and its attainment of a profitable share of the market.

The court found that Tenneco had actively considered entering the shock absorber market but would not enter *de novo* because start-up costs were too high in proportion to earnings during the early years. In short, the entry barriers may have explained why the target

8. See U.S. v. Marine Bancorporation, 418 U.S. 602, 630–31, 94 S.Ct. 2856, 2874–75 (1974).

9. See Marine Bancorporation, 418 U.S. at 628, 94 S.Ct. at 2873.

10. 689 F.2d 346 (2d Cir. 1982).

market was not performing competitively, but they also excluded Tenneco from consideration as a potential entrant.[11]

The perceived potential entrant doctrine makes sense only if the number of potential entrants is limited. If a market contains three firms but a dozen are sitting on the edge, the elimination by merger of one of the firms on the edge will not affect performance in the market. In the *Procter & Gamble* case the Supreme Court based its holding in part on a finding that "the number of potential entrants was not so large that the elimination of one would be insignificant."[12]

The Court provided no guidelines, however, for determining how few potential entrants there must be, or how likely it must be that any or all of them would enter in response to a price increase. Some scholars regard this kind of measurement as far beyond the capacity of any court. Judge Posner, for example, concluded that there "is no practical method of ranking, even crudely, the potential competitors in a market for the purpose of identifying a set of most likely or most feared entrants."[13] Simply to say that the doctrine applies only to the "most likely" *de novo* entrant will not do—for as soon as the "most likely" entrant is eliminated by merger, another most likely entrant will take its place.

About the best a court can do is compare the target market before and after the merger. In some cases, it might try to determine whether the acquiring firm did in fact restrain prices before the merger took place, and whether any similar firm was restraining them after the merger occurred. Simply stating the phenomenon that needs measurement, however, suggests how difficult the measurement is. For this reason Areeda and Turner suggest a presumptive rule permitting the merger if the number of perceived potential entrants exceeds three, and that the presumption should be conclusive if the number of perceived potential entrants exceeds six.[14]

Finally, a merger should not be condemned on potential competition grounds if the merger substantially increases actual competition in the target market. This often happens when the acquired company is not the dominant firm in the market. Suppose that an oligopolistic market contains four firms with market shares of 50%, 25%, 15%, and 10%. The market is clearly conducive to price leadership;

11. For a case finding both high entry barriers and a likely entrant see Yamaha Motor Co., Ltd. v. FTC, 657 F.2d 971 (8th Cir. 1981), cert. denied, 456 U.S. 915, 102 S.Ct. 1768 (1982). The court found high entry barriers in the relevant market (small outboard boat motors), but it also found that the acquiring firm was well established in other markets around the world. For an incorrect application of the theory see Mercantile Texas Corp. v. Bd. of Governors, 638 F.2d 1255, 1268 (5th Cir. 1981),

approving a finding that the acquiring firm could be a potential entrant because "no significant barriers to entry existed in the target market." In that case, however, the target market would have been performing competitively before the merger occurred.

12. 386 U.S. at 581, 87 S.Ct. at 1231.

13. R. Posner, Antitrust Law: An Economic Perspective 122–23 (1976).

14. 5 P. Areeda & D. Turner, Antitrust Law ¶ 1123b (1980).

furthermore, the supracompetitive pricing might be restrained by the perceived presence of a large firm on the edge of the market. The market could behave less competitively if the outside firm acquired the largest firm in the market. But what if it acquired one of the smaller firms? In U.S. v. Marine Bancorporation, Inc. the Supreme Court approved a market extension merger between a bank in Seattle, Washington, and another bank in Spokane, across the state. The Spokane bank controlled less than 18% of the target market. Their merger might have eliminated a perceived potential entrant; however, the trial judge concluded that the merger would "substantially" *increase* actual competition in the Spokane banking market.[15]

This situation should be distinguished from the one in the *Philadelphia Bank* case, where the Supreme Court rejected the defense that a horizontal merger that lessened competition in one market (small loans) increased competition in another market (large loans).[16] In *Marine Bancorporation* the government alleged a lessening of "potential" competition in the Spokane banking market, but the court found an increase of actual competition in the same market. Given the elusive nature of the potential competition doctrine, any merger shown to increase actual competition substantially should be approved on that ground alone, and the potential competition doctrine forgotten.

The perceived potential entrant doctrine discussed above condemns certain mergers when the acquiring firm was perceived by incumbents in the target market to be a likely entrant. The theory has a weaker variation which has never been approved by the Supreme Court, although it has been used by a few circuit courts. The "actual potential entrant" doctrine holds that even though a merger has no current effect on competition in the target market, it should be condemned because the acquiring firm could and probably would have come into the target market in a more competitive way, such as by *de novo* entry or by a "toe-hold" acquisition of a smaller firm. This alternative method of entry would have increased competition.

The actual potential entrant doctrine does some violence to the plain language of § 7, which appears to condemn mergers only when they "may substantially lessen competition." The actual potential entrant doctrine condemns a merger because it fails to increase competition, not because it damages existing competition in any way. In *Falstaff* the Supreme Court left "for another day" the question whether § 7 should condemn a merger that would "leave competition in the marketplace exactly as it was, neither hurt nor helped," and that could be challenged only "on grounds that the company could,

15. 418 U.S. 602, 616, 94 S.Ct. 2856, 2867 (1974).

16. U.S. v. Philadelphia Nat. Bank, 374 U.S. 321, 83 S.Ct. 1715 (1963).

but did not, enter *de novo* or through a 'toe-hold' acquisition
* * * ." [17]

In *Marine Bancorporation* the Supreme Court declined a second opportunity to adopt the actual potential entrant doctrine. It held that at the very least the government must show that the suggested alternative method of entry was feasible and that, if used, would have produced "deconcentration of [the target] market or other significant procompetitive effects." [18]

Since *Marine Bancorporation*, some circuit courts appear to have made the requirements even stricter. For example, in BOC Int'l Ltd. (British Oxygen) v. FTC [19] the Second Circuit required a showing of a "reasonable probability" that the acquiring firm would have entered the market anyway in the "near future," whether by acquisition of a smaller firm (a "toe hold" acquisition) or by *de novo* entry. The Fourth Circuit has gone even further, holding that entry of the outside firm by an alternative and more competitive route must appear "certain." [20]

It strains credulity to think that courts can reliably make these kinds of findings. Many stock market analysts would give anything for the ability to predict when and how a particular firm was going to enter a new market. Yet fact finders are asked to determine, generally without access to reliable subjective evidence, whether it was "certain," merely "probable," or "uncertain" whether a firm would have entered a new market by another route had it not entered by merger. [21] Further, the rule sensibly applies only after the court has determined that the *perceived* potential entrant doctrine does not apply—that is, that the firms operating in the target market had not behaved more competitively because they feared entry by the acquiring firm. The actual potential entrant doctrine should join shared monopoly [22] and predatory price discrimination [23] in the scrapheap of defunct antitrust theories. [24]

---

17. U.S. v. Falstaff Brewing Corp., 410 U.S. 526, 537, 93 S.Ct. 1096, 1103 (1973), mandate conformed to, 383 F.Supp. 1020 (1974).

18. 418 U.S. at 633, 94 S.Ct. at 2875.

19. 557 F.2d 24, 29 (2d Cir. 1977).

20. FTC v. Atlantic Richfield Co., 549 F.2d 289, 295 (4th Cir. 1977).

21. Areeda & Turner propose a complex rule for establishing the likelihood that a particular firm would have entered the market by means other than the merger. Under their proposal the plaintiff could obtain a presumption of probable entry by showing the acquiring firm's "proximity" to the market, its ability to raise needed capital, and the absence of legal barriers to entry. The

defendant could then rebut by showing that, under the plaintiff's criteria, a large number of firms were "probable" entrants. The plaintiff would then have to show that the acquiring firm was much more likely than these other firms to enter the market. See 5 P. Areeda & D. Turner, Antitrust Law ¶¶ 1121–1123 (1980).

22. See § 4.2 above.

23. See § 6.12 above.

24. The actual potential competition doctrine has been used to condemn some mergers, however. See Yamaha Motor Co. v. FTC, 657 F.2d 971, 977–78 (8th Cir. 1981), cert. denied, 456 U.S. 915, 102 S.Ct. 1768 (1982).

WESTLAW REFERENCES

digest(potential + 1 competit! entrant)

potential + 1 competit! entrant /p target /p merger

§ 12.5   Conglomerate Mergers and the DOJ Guidelines

Commentators have criticized the judicial standards for conglomerate mergers as confusing, ambiguous, often irrelevant to the competitive results of the acquisition, and impossible for courts to apply.[1] Courts have responded to the criticism by assessing formidable evidentiary requirements which often have frustrated both the government and private plaintiffs.

The 1984 DOJ Merger Guidelines are significant for conglomerate merger law for several reasons. First, they reiterate that the government still regards certain product extension and market extension mergers as anticompetitive. Second, they offer simplified standards for evaluating potential competition mergers. Third, they ignore virtually all rationales for condemning conglomerate mergers except potential competition. Reciprocity is never mentioned.

The Department is not likely to challenge a potential competition merger if the HHI in the target market is below 1800.[2] Nor will it challenge a potential competition merger if entry into the target market is easy. If there are more than three perceived potential entrants, the DOJ will be unlikely to challenge the merger. Elimination of one potential entrant in that case would not affect competition in the market.

The 1984 Merger Guidelines purport to treat all potential competition mergers under "a single structural analysis analogous to that applied to horizontal mergers."[3] They generally avoid separate doctrines for "perceived" and "actual" potential competition. Nevertheless, the Guidelines note one important distinction between perceived and actual potential entrants. Under the Guidelines the actual potential entrant doctrine continues to have "independent importance" because often entry-deterrent "limit" pricing will not be feasible for the firms in the market. In cases where limit pricing will not work a merger can be condemned, if at all, only under the actual potential entrant doctrine.

Whether the 1984 Guidelines will simplify the law of potential competition mergers remains to be seen. There are some reasons for pessimism, however. Even under the new Guidelines the DOJ appears willing to attempt certain predictions that will be extraordinarily difficult to make in court. For example, the Guidelines indicate

§ 12.5

1. See Brodley, Potential Competition Mergers: A Structural Synthesis, 87 Yale L.J. 1 (1977).

2. For a description of the Herfindahl-Hirschman Index (HHI) and its use see § 11.4 above.

3. 49 Fed. Reg. at 26,834.

that the DOJ is likely to attack a merger if the likelihood of "actual entry by the acquiring firm" was "particularly strong." The Guidelines do not say, however, how strong "particularly strong" is, or how the DOJ will attempt to establish such a likelihood.[4]

4. For criticism of the 1982 Guidelines' lack of clarity in identifying a likely entrant see Brodley, Potential Competition Under the Merger Guidelines, 71 Calif.L.Rev. 376, 389–401 (1983). The 1984 Guidelines have not been responsive to the criticism.

CHAPTER 13

PRICE DISCRIMINATION AND THE ROBINSON–PATMAN ACT

Table of Sections

§ 13.1   Introduction: Price Discrimination

Price discrimination occurs when a firm makes two sales at two different rates of return. More technically, two sales are discriminatory when they have different ratios of price to marginal cost. Discriminatory pricing must be distinguished from differential pricing, which occurs whenever the same product is sold to two buyers at different prices. The sale of the same product at two different prices can be nondiscriminatory if the price difference is proportional to the different marginal costs of serving two different customers. Likewise, two sales at the same price can be economically discriminatory if marginal costs for the two sales are different. For example, a seller who charges the same delivered price to a buyer one mile away and another buyer 100 miles away is price discriminating if it costs the seller more to transport the product 100 miles than to transport it a mile.

The buyer who pays the lower price or produces the lower rate of return to the seller is called the "favored" purchaser. The buyer who gives the seller the higher rate of return or who pays the higher price is called the "disfavored" purchaser. If the favored purchaser is paying a competitive price (marginal cost), the disfavored purchaser must be paying a price higher than marginal cost, and which may produce a certain amount of monopoly profits to the seller.

 WESTLAW REFERENCES
83k62.13 /p discriminat! /3 pric*** /s define* definition mean occur!

§ 13.2   Price Discrimination and Competition

Price discrimination would not occur in a perfectly competitive market in equilibrium. Any disfavored purchaser (that is, a purchaser asked to pay a price above marginal cost) would walk away from that seller and find someone willing to sell at the competitive price. In such a hypothetical market all sales would be made at marginal cost.

In the real world such markets do not exist, however. Markets are in constant flux; they are shocked daily by wars, famines, fads, elections, and the weather. No one has complete knowledge of all market conditions at any given time and as a result sporadic price discrimination is a daily occurrence in even the most competitive markets. One day a farmer may sell corn for $4.00 a bushel. During the night news breaks about a particularly large harvest in a different state and several buyers decide to postpone their purchases. The first buyer who comes to the farmer in the morning and the farmer himself may not know of the news, and they will complete a sale at $4.00. Later in the day, however, the second and third customers walk away. Eventually the farmer learns that the market price has dropped to $3.70. He sells to the next customer at that price. He has discriminated between two purchasers on the same day; however, this is an absolutely common occurrence in the most competitive of markets. It happens even in the stock market, where information about market prices can be obtained very cheaply. Nevertheless, prices fluctuate hourly in a way that bears little relation to the marginal costs of the sellers.

Competitive markets change constantly not only through time, but also in space. Suppose that firm A sells in three cities. In one of them a competitor opens a new plant and the immediate result is a large supply in that city in relationship to the demand. The price in that city will drop first, and the price in the other two cities will drop some time later. During the interval firm A will sell its output in different cities at two different prices, in response to the local market conditions. Likewise, if there is a sudden surge of demand in one city the immediate result will be a price increase in that city, and the price increase will encourage more of the product to flow into that city until the balance between supply and demand is restored once again. Competitive markets *tend* toward an equilibrium in which all sales are made at marginal cost. In the process of arriving at that equilibrium, however, a certain amount of price discrimination is essential. The low price in Chicago and the high price in St. Louis will cause goods to flow from Chicago to St. Louis until the balance is once again restored. If a seller is forbidden from raising price in response to increased demand in St. Louis, unless she also raises prices in Chicago where demand has not increased, the result will be shortages in one city and surpluses in the other.

The kind of price discrimination characteristic of competitive markets is usually termed *sporadic* because it varies daily and is often unpredictable. One day a particular buyer will be favored, the next day disfavored. *Persistent* price discrimination, on the other hand, occurs when a seller systematically divides customers into classes and obtains different rates of return from them. Persistent price discrimination requires the seller to have market power.

The complete absence of sporadic price discrimination in a market, far from being a sign of competition, is usually a signal that the market is cartelized. When sellers fix prices the first thing they are concerned about is "concessions"—the result of hard competitive bargaining between individual buyers and sellers that is reflected in slightly different prices or other terms for each negotiated transaction. The nature of a cartel is to require all sales within a certain category to be made on the same terms. The result is generally a rigid price structure.[1] Thus *sporadic* price discrimination is generally consistent with competition on the merits, and inconsistent with cartelization.[2]

 WESTLAW REFERENCES
pric***   /3   discriminat!   /s   competit!   /3   market
pric***   /3   discriminat!   /s   sporadic continued persistent
market   /s   carteliz!

§ 13.3   Price Discrimination and the Monopolist: Perfect Price Discrimination

Sporadic price discrimination is an everyday occurrence in competitive markets. However, persistent price discrimination requires that a seller (or group of sellers) have market power. Price discrimination is persistent when a seller or group of sellers establish a policy of obtaining a higher rate of return from some customers than from others. In a competitive market disfavored purchasers will simply seek out a different seller willing to sell to them at the competitive price.[1]

§ 13.2

1. See § 4.1 above.

2. See § 4.2 above. However, evidence of systematic, persistent price discrimination in a market with multiple sellers likewise suggests a cartel. See

R. Posner, Antitrust Law: An Economic Perspective 62–65 (1976).

§ 13.3

1. However, persistent price discrimination may be a result of rents rather than market power in the high profit

All markets contain different customers who place different values on a seller's product. Both braces and bridge supports are made of steel, for example, but orthodontists may be willing to pay much more than bridge builders for a pound of steel. The ideal situation for a seller is to be able to sell every unit to every customer at the customer's reservation price, which is the maximum amount that customer is willing to pay. This is *perfect* price discrimination.

Figure One illustrates the difference between competitive pricing, nondiscriminatory monopoly pricing, and perfect price discrimination. The figure shows the demand curve, marginal cost and marginal revenue curves of a seller with market power. In a perfectly competitive market a seller would produce $Q_{(c)}$ output and sell at price $P_{(c)}$—the point at which its marginal cost curve crosses the demand curve. Output beyond that point could not be sold at a price sufficient to cover the additional costs. In a perfectly competitive market triangle 1–3–6 is consumers' surplus: the excess value that accrues to consumers because they are able to purchase the product at a lower price than the value they place on it.[2]

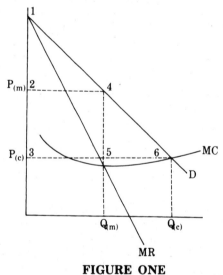

FIGURE ONE

The monopolist, however, will reduce its output to $Q_{(m)}$, where its marginal cost and marginal revenue curves intersect, and sell at price $P_{(m)}$, which is its nondiscriminatory profit-maximizing price. $P_{(m)}$ is the price that will maximize the seller's profits if the seller is unable to price discriminate. The output reduction from $Q_{(c)}$ to $Q_{(m)}$ causes the traditional deadweight loss of monopoly, equal to the area of triangle 4–5–6. Consumers' surplus is reduced to the area of triangle 1–2–4. Rectangle 2–3–5–4 has traditionally been thought of as monopoly profits.[3]

market. For the distinction between monopoly profits and rents see § 3.7 above.

2. See § 1.1 above.

3. But see § 1.3 above.

Even the monopolist charging its nondiscriminatory profit-maximizing price does not make all the money theoretically possible from its position. First, the monopolist loses sales to customers located between points 4 and 6 on the demand curve in Figure One. Any sale that can be made at price $P_{(c)}$ or higher is profitable to the seller. In reducing output to the profit-maximizing level the monopolist foregoes these profitable sales. Second, high preference customers, located between points 1 and 4 on the demand curve, have reservation prices even higher than $P_{(m)}$.

If the monopolist can identify and charge each customer its reservation price, the monopolist will be able to capture these profits as well. Under such a scheme customers located on the demand curve near point 6 will pay a price approaching the competitive price (which is nevertheless profitable). On the other hand, customers located near point 1 on the graph will pay a price that could be far higher than the nondiscriminatory profit-maximizing price.[4]

Perfect price discrimination has two important results. First, the area of traditional monopoly profits, or producers' surplus, is increased to all of triangle 1–3–6. Everything that would be consumers' surplus in a competitive market may become monopoly profits under perfect price discrimination. Second, output under perfect price discrimination is restored to $Q_{(c)}$, the same as under perfect competition. For this reason perfect price discrimination is just as efficient as perfect competition, even though one result of perfect price discrimination is that customers are far poorer and the seller far richer.[5]

 WESTLAW REFERENCES
perfect /s pric*** /3 discriminat!

§ 13.4 Imperfect Price Discrimination

Perfect price discrimination never exists in the real world. The costs of determining each customer's reservation price and structuring the market to enable the seller to charge that price would be prohibitive. About the best most sellers can do is identify and segregate two or three groups of customers who place different values on the product, and price discriminate among these groups. Furthermore, any price discrimination scheme can be frustrated by arbitrage. Arbitrage occurs when favored purchasers resell the product to disfavored purchasers at some price that is profitable to

4. See Hovenkamp, Market Power and Secondary-Line Differential Pricing, 71 Geo.L.J. 1157, 1162–66 (1983).

5. That is, perfect price discrimination is as efficient as perfect competi-

tion, provided that it costs the seller nothing to engage in price discrimination.

the favored purchasers but less than the disfavored purchasers were asked to pay.

Arbitrage generally works only when the discriminatory prices are also different prices. For example, if buyers one mile and 100 miles from the seller pay the same delivered price, there is likely price discrimination in favor of the more remote purchaser. However, that purchaser will not be able to resell the product to the disfavored purchaser because the higher costs that occasioned the price discrimination have already been sunk and there is no "spread" in the price between the two purchasers. On the other hand, if one buyer pays $1.00 for salt and another buyer pays $1.10, arbitrage may be possible. In this case the first buyer might resell the salt to the second buyer at some price between $1.00 and $1.10.[1] Before arbitrage will work, however, the transaction costs of the arbitrage must be less than the price difference. The favored and disfavored purchasers must find each other, negotiate an arbitrage price and perhaps reship the product from the favored purchaser's location to the disfavored purchaser's location. If the costs of these maneuvers in the above example exceed 10¢, arbitrage will not occur.

In perfect price discrimination output is restored to the competitive level. The same thing is not true of imperfect price discrimination. In fact, sometimes output under imperfect price discrimination is actually smaller than output under nondiscriminatory monopoly pricing.[2] Suppose that a monopolist has marginal costs of $1.00 per unit and a profit-maximizing price of $1.50. In studying the market the monopolist has managed to identify three groups of customers who have different reservation prices. One group, the marginal customers, are willing to pay $1.00 but no more. A second group, the medium preference customers, are willing to pay $1.50. A third group, high preference purchasers, are willing to pay any amount up to $2.00. Sales to all three groups will be profitable, but will the seller make all three sets of sales? Perhaps not. Although the medium preference group is willing to pay $1.50, it may be difficult to segregate them from the low preference customers. Furthermore, the middle group may be quite cost conscious: they will opt for the $1.00 version of the product if it is available. In this case the seller may decide that he will make more money if he offers the product only in $1.50 and $2.00 versions and forgets about the relatively unprofitable group of marginal buyers. In short, the seller may price discriminate, but only *within* the group of customers who are willing

§ 13.4

1. If there are several favored buyers they will compete with each other to make arbitrage sales to disfavored buyers. The competition will drive the arbitrage price down to the sum of the price paid by the favored buyers plus the transaction costs of the arbitrage.

2. See J. Robinson, The Economics of Imperfect Competition 188–95 (1933).

to pay the profit-maximizing price or higher. In this case output will be no higher than under nondiscriminatory monopoly pricing.[3]

 WESTLAW REFERENCES
arbitrage   /s   transaction community

§ 13.5   Price Discrimination and Antitrust Policy

All forms of persistent price discrimination transfer wealth away from consumers and toward sellers. If antitrust policy should be concerned with such wealth transfers, then price discrimination necessarily presents an antitrust problem.

The question is more complex if economic efficiency is the exclusive goal of the federal antitrust laws. Some commentators have argued that price discrimination should not be an antitrust concern because it does not produce losses in output as other monopolistic practices do.[1] As the preceding sections indicate, however, only perfect price discrimination maintains output at the competitive level. Under imperfect price discrimination output is always somewhat lower.

Further, *all* price discrimination—even perfect price discrimination—can generate substantial social losses. The efficiency losses from price discrimination are of two kinds, analogous to the efficiency losses that can result from all forms of monopoly. One is the deadweight loss caused by reduction in output. Since all imperfect price discrimination results in output at less than the competitive level, and all real world price discrimination is imperfect, it necessarily follows that persistent price discrimination produces a certain amount of deadweight loss.

The second kind of social loss comes from exclusionary practices: the actions that the price-discriminating monopolist takes in order to obtain or maintain its market power. Just as any other monopolist, the price discriminating monopolist must deter competitive entry into its high profit markets (that is, the markets containing the disfavored purchasers). The social cost of exclusionary practices varies with the activity; however, many such practices are inefficient.[2] There is a presumptive reason for thinking that the cost of exclusionary practices are higher for the price discriminating monopolist than for the monopolist who does not discriminate. A monopolist will price discriminate only if the discrimination is more profitable than nondiscriminatory pricing. Since the profit potential is larger, the discrimi-

---

3. See Hovenkamp, Market Power and Secondary Line Differential Pricing, 71 Geo.L.J. 1157, 1167–71 (1983).

§ 13.5

1. For example, R. Bork, The Antitrust Paradox: A Policy at War With Itself 394–98 (1978).

2. See § 1.3 above on the social costs of monopoly.

nating monopolist will be willing to spend more on exclusionary practices.

Finally, imperfect price discrimination produces one large social cost in addition to both the monopoly deadweight loss and the cost of the exclusionary practices. In order to price discriminate the monopolist must undergo the expense of identifying different groups of customers who have different reservation prices, segregating them, perhaps creating different distribution systems, and disguising the product in such a way as to prevent arbitrage. All these efforts are pure social loss.

As a result, even an antitrust policy based exclusively on efficiency should be concerned about persistent price discrimination.[3]

  WESTLAW REFERENCES
social /3 loss cost /s pric*** /3 discriminat!

§ 13.6   The Robinson-Patman Act and Price Discrimination

An antitrust policy against persistent price discrimination can be justified on purely economic grounds. An economic justification for the peculiar approach to price discrimination taken by the Robinson-Patman Act, however, is somewhat harder to find.

§ 2 of the Clayton Act, amended in 1936 by the Robinson-Patman Act, makes it "unlawful for any person * * * to discriminate in price between different purchasers of commodities of like grade and quality * * * where the effect * * * may be substantially to lessen competition or tend to create a monopoly * * * ."[1]

Welfare losses caused by price discrimination were not on the mind of Congress in 1936. Rather, they were concerned that small businesses, particularly small retailers, were rapidly losing market share to large "chain stores" that were able both to underbuy and undersell the small operators.[2] This Congressional concern with small business welfare has substantially colored judicial interpretation of the Act. For example, a small business is injured by a larger firm's lower price whether or not the lower price results from true economic price discrimination by a firm with market power. *Low*

---

3. However, see § 8.8 above for an argument that price discrimination accomplished by means of variable proportion tying arrangements should generally be legal, particularly in the franchise setting. See also R. Posner, The Robinson-Patman Act: Federal Regulation of Price Differences 10–12 (1976).

§ 13.6

1. 15 U.S.C.A. § 13(a).

2. The Bill originally proposed was entitled the "Wholesale Grocers' Protec-

tion Act." See Hansen, Robinson-Patman Law: A Review and Analysis, 51 Fordham L.Rev. 1113, 1123 (1983); see also Federal Trade Commission, Final Report on the Chain-Store Investigation, S. Doc., No. 4, 74th Cong., 1st Sess. (1935). For a more detailed account of the statute and its legislative history see F.M. Rowe, Price Discrimination Under the Robinson-Patman Act (1962); and see § 2.4 above.

prices, not discriminatory prices, are the chief evil condemned by the Act. For that reason the Robinson-Patman Act cannot be understood as designed to encourage allocative efficiency or to maximize consumer welfare. It was designed to protect small businesses from larger, more efficient businesses. A necessary result is higher consumer prices.

A statute is not bad, however, simply because it manifests a distributive rather than an efficiency concern and requires consumers to pay the bill. Many statutes do that, and one function of the legislative process is to protect people whom the free market protects poorly. Rather, criticism of the Robinson-Patman Act focuses on two things. First, although the Act was designed to protect small business, it has not done so very well. Often small businesses have run afoul of the act. For example, the statute has been applied against cooperatives of small businesses designed to enable members to purchase (and therefore to resell) at a lower price, so they could compete more effectively with larger stores.[3]

Secondly, while the Robinson-Patman Act is quite hostile toward competition it is nevertheless disguised as an antitrust law. Furthermore, its inconsistencies with the other antitrust laws are so substantial that businesses have often complained that they can comply with the Robinson-Patman Act only by violating the other antitrust laws, or vice-versa. The Supreme Court has responded by trying to interpret the Act so as to make it consistent with the other antitrust laws.[4] The result, however, has done some violence to the Robinson-Patman Act and its legislative history.

The Act is frequently called a "price discrimination" statute, but that is a misnomer. The Act directly condemns price *differences*, and only indirectly and haphazardly reaches economic discrimination.[5] For example, two sales at the same price can be discriminatory if marginal costs are different. Two sales at the same price do not violate the Robinson-Patman Act.[6] On the other side, sales at two different prices are nondiscriminatory if the price difference is proportional to the difference in marginal costs of servicing the two customers. However, a pair of sales at different prices makes out a *prima facie* case under the Robinson-Patman Act. Although the Act

3. See Mid-South Distrib. v. FTC, 287 F.2d 512 (5th Cir. 1961), cert. denied, 368 U.S. 838, 82 S.Ct. 36 (1961); Standard Motor Prod., Inc. v. FTC, 265 F.2d 674 (2d Cir. 1959), cert. denied, 361 U.S. 826, 80 S.Ct. 73 (1959).

4. Great A. & P. Tea Co. v. FTC, 440 U.S. 69, 80 n.13, 99 S.Ct. 925, 933 (1979); U.S. v. United States Gypsum Co., 438 U.S. 422, 458, 98 S.Ct. 2864, 2884 (1978), appeal after remand, 600 F.2d 414 (3d Cir. 1979), cert. denied, 444 U.S. 884, 100 S.Ct. 175 (1979).

5. See Falls City Indus., Inc. v. Vanco Beverage, Inc., 460 U.S. 428, 103 S.Ct. 1282, 1293 n. 10 (1983), on remand, 705 F.2d 463 (7th Cir. 1983); FTC v. Anheuser-Busch, Inc., 363 U.S. 536, 549, 80 S.Ct. 1267, 1274 (1960): "[A] price discrimination within the meaning of [the statute] is merely a price difference."

6. See Carroll v. Protection Maritime Ins. Co., Ltd., 512 F.2d 4 (1st Cir. 1975).

does contain an affirmative "cost justification" defense that permits a defendant to show that sales at different prices were nondiscriminatory, the defense has been so narrowly construed that it is almost impossible to use. It has not rescued many defendants.

The Robinson-Patman Act has done an extraordinarily poor job of identifying those forms of price discrimination that most economists consider to be inefficient. At the same time it has often been used to condemn efficient practices that were really evidence of healthy competition. The Act has been widely castigated by critics who see it as doing far more harm than good to the competitive process. The Department of Justice has not enforced the Act since 1977,[7] and the Federal Trade Commission has all but abandoned it as well.

The Robinson-Patman Act includes two offenses that are very different from each other, although both are covered by the same statutory language. "Primary-line" differential pricing is really a form of predatory pricing directed at the defendant's competitors. It is treated in § 6.12 above.

"Secondary-line" price discrimination, on the other hand, is the sort of persistent price discrimination engaged in by a monopolist. The perceived victims of secondary-line discrimination are the seller's disfavored purchasers, who are also generally the plaintiffs in private, secondary-line actions.[8] The theory of injury is generally that the defendant's lower price sales to the plaintiff's competitor (the favored purchaser) placed the plaintiff at a competitive disadvantage and caused it to lose business.[9] This theory necessarily requires the plaintiff to show that he competes with the favored purchaser.

As the discussion in § 13.3 suggests, persistent price discrimination cannot occur unless the seller has market power. However, the Robinson-Patman Act does not require a showing of the defendant's market power. This failure, plus the fact that the "cost justification" defense has been very narrowly construed, has yielded a large amount of overdeterrence.[10] Many defendants condemned by the Act were not monopolists engaged in true price discrimination at all. Their differential prices were either nondiscriminatory or else part of the normal give-and-take of the competitive market process.[11]

7. See U.S. Dep't of Justice, Report on the Robinson-Patman Act (1977); and see Hansen, note 2 above, at 1174–86. Among the most clever critiques of the statute is Baxter, A Parable, 23 Stan.L. Rev. 973 (1971).

8. The statute also recognizes so-called "third-line" and "fourth-line" injury, which occur further down the distributional chain. See Perkins v. Standard Oil Co. of California, 395 U.S. 642, 89 S.Ct. 1871 (1969); F.M. Rowe, Price Discrimination Under the Robinson-Patman Act 195–205 (1962).

9. See, for example, J. Truett Payne Co. v. Chrysler Motor Corp., 451 U.S. 557, 101 S.Ct. 1923 (1981), on remand, 670 F.2d 575 (5th Cir.), rehearing denied, 677 F.2d 117 (11th Cir.), cert. denied, 459 U.S. 908, 103 S.Ct. 212 (1982); Edward J. Sweeney & Sons, Inc. v. Texaco, Inc., 637 F.2d 105 (3d Cir. 1980), cert. denied, 451 U.S. 911, 101 S.Ct. 1981 (1981).

10. See Hovenkamp, Market Power and Secondary-Line Differential Pricing, 71 Geo.L.J. 1157 (1983).

11. For example, see FTC v. Morton Salt Co., 334 U.S. 37, 68 S.Ct. 822 (1948),

The Robinson-Patman Act is a morass of technical requirements that often hide or subvert its basic purpose. Elaboration of these is beyond the scope of this discussion.[12] Knowledge of a few details is helpful, however. Unlike the Sherman Act, which applies to all transactions "affecting commerce" up to Congress's full constitutional power, the Robinson-Patman Act requires the seller to be "engaged in" interstate commerce and that one of the discriminatory sales itself be made in interstate commerce.[13] The statute expressly applies to sales, not to leases, even though price discrimination is as common in leasing as it is in sales. Perhaps more importantly, the statute applies only to the sale of "commodities," and therefore ignores business services. This limitation is particularly irrational because price discrimination in service markets is much more prevalent than in the sale of goods. For example, a patient walking into a doctor's office is likely to have very poor information about the price that the doctor charges other people for various procedures. Furthermore, the doctor need not worry about arbitrage: the favored patient cannot resell the service to a disfavored patient.

In order to fall within the statute the different sales at different prices must be of products of "like grade and quality." The requirement has given rise to substantial litigation. Physical differences between two items will often take them out of the "like grade and quality" requirement, and they can freely be sold at different prices provided the differences are recognized and appreciated by consumers.[14] The courts have consistently held, however, that mere differences in the way a product is packaged or advertised will not defeat the requirement. Thus if a producer manufactures and sells a high-priced "name brand" which is advertised, and a chemically identical but unadvertised "house brand" at a lower price, the two sales may violate the statute, even though the seller may have incurred substantial advertising costs for the name brand but not for the house brand.[15]

§ 2(a) of the Act applies to "indirect" as well as "direct" price discrimination. "Indirect" discrimination refers to a seller's provision of different services to different customers—for example, if the seller gives the favored buyer better credit terms, delivery, stocking or storage, advertising, brokerage allowances, return privileges, or other favorable terms that put one buyer in a better position than

---

where there was no allegation that the defendant was a monopolist in the sale of table salt; and see, U.S. v. Borden Co., 370 U.S. 460, 82 S.Ct. 1309 (1962), where the defendant was in intense competition.

12. See the works by F.M. Rowe and Hansen, note 2 above.

13. Cliff Food Stores v. Kroger, 417 F.2d 203 (5th Cir. 1969).

14. But see Bruce's Juices v. Amer. Can. Co., 87 F.Supp. 985, 987 (S.D.Fla. 1949), modified, 190 F.2d 73 (5th Cir. 1951), cert. dismissed, 342 U.S. 875, 72 S.Ct. 165 (1951), holding that a small difference in the shape of cans sold to consumers was irrelevant, because both "gave substantially identical performance."

15. FTC v. Borden Co., 383 U.S. 637, 86 S.Ct. 1092 (1966).

another. Such discriminations are legal, however, if they are "functionally available" to all buyers, even though some buyers did not take advantage of them.

When courts analyze such "indirect" discrimination they look from the buyer's point of view, not the seller's. Thus if a seller provides delivery of carload lots at one rate, but requires smaller buyers to pay a higher delivery rate, courts will not begin by looking at the seller's costs. Rather they will ask whether the carload lot buyer effectively obtained the commodity at a lower price. If so, the burden shifts to the defendant seller to show that the lower price delivery was "cost justified."

The Act explicitly accounts for the fact that some customers require different services than others. For example, § 2(c) prohibits sellers from giving buyers allowances in lieu of brokerage or commission fees unless the services for which the fees would ordinarily be due were actually performed. However, the Supreme Court once held it illegal for a broker to reduce his commission in order to bring the parties together, if the result was a discriminatorily low-priced sale.[16] § 2(d) of the Act permits a seller to give "allowances" to buyers who perform certain services themselves, such as promotion, handling or hauling, which the seller would otherwise perform. The statute requires that the allowances be made available "on proportionally equal terms to all other customers competing in the distribution of such products or commodities." § 2(e) of the statute prohibits a seller from furnishing facilities or services to a buyer for processing, handling or resale of the commodity unless it makes the facilities available to all buyers on proportionally equal terms.

The statute requires two different sales to two different purchasers at two different prices. One sale and an offer to sell at a higher or lower price is not a violation of the Act. The two sales must be consummated within a reasonable time of each other. Whether a parent and its subsidiary, or affiliated corporations, are two "different" purchasers has perplexed the court, but recent cases suggest that closely related corporations are not "different" and therefore differential sales to them do not violate the statute.[17]

Sales to agencies of the federal government are exempt from the statute. In 1983, however, the Supreme Court decided that the Act applies when the low price sale is made to a state or local government agency, if the agency resells the commodity in competition with the disfavored purchasers. The Supreme Court assumed without decid-

---

16. FTC v. Henry Broch & Co., 363 U.S. 166, 80 S.Ct. 1158 (1960).

17. See Parrish v. Cox, 586 F.2d 9 (6th Cir. 1978); Brown v. Hansen Pub., 556 F.2d 969 (9th Cir. 1977). The Supreme Court's decision in Copperweld Corp. v. Independence Tube Corp., —

U.S. —, 104 S.Ct. 2731 (1984), may have laid the issue to rest. In *Copperweld* the Supreme Court held that a parent and its wholly-owned subsidiary could not be "conspiring entities" under § 1 of the Sherman Act. See § 4.2, n.1 above.

ing that a sale to a state or local government agency for internal consumption is exempt.[18]

§ 2(f) of the statute makes it illegal for a *buyer* "knowingly to induce or receive a discrimination in price which is prohibited" by the Act. For many years § 2(f) was interpreted to mean that a large buyer could not put undue pressure on a seller to grant the buyer a discount not given to other, smaller buyers. In such cases the buyer was viewed as the violator, and the seller a more-or-less innocent victim.[19] The Congress which passed the Robinson-Patman Act was actually more concerned about pressure to discriminate from large buyers than from sellers: the statute was substantially directed at the buying practices of large chain stores. In Great Atlantic & Pacific Tea Co. v. FTC (A & P),[20] however, the Supreme Court held that a buyer could not violate § 2(f) unless he actually received "a discrimination in price which is prohibited * * * ." That is, a buyer cannot violate the statute unless the seller is violating it as well. If the seller had a good faith belief that it was only "meeting competition," then the seller could assert one of the affirmative defenses recognized by the Act and discussed below. In that case the buyer could not be in violation either, even though the seller incorrectly believed he was meeting competition because the buyer provided false information.

The *A & P* holding undermined much of the original Congressional intent in passing the Robinson-Patman Act.[21] For example, if many small grocers were buying milk at $1.50 a gallon and a large chain store suddenly announced that it would like to make a large purchase at $1.35, the chain store would probably be condemned under the intent of the Act's framers, if the effect was that some seller sold to the chain store at $1.35 while selling to other stores at $1.50. Under the *A & P* holding, however, if the chain requested competitive bidding for a large purchase and received a low bid of $1.35, its purchase at that price would not violate the statute even though the seller also sold to other, smaller stores at $1.50. The bidding seller could raise the "meeting competition" defense. Since the seller did not violate the Act, the buyer could not be violating it either.

The Robinson-Patman Act contains two affirmative defenses, both of which become relevant only after the plaintiff has made out a *prima facie* case. In both the defendant has the burden of proof.[22]

18. Jefferson County Pharmaceutical Ass'n, Inc. v. Abbott Laboratories, 460 U.S. 150, 103 S.Ct. 1011 (1983), rehearing denied ___ U.S. ___, 103 S.Ct. 1808 (1983), on remand, 709 F.2d 8 (5th Cir. 1983).

19. FTC v. Fred Meyer, Inc., 390 U.S. 341, 88 S.Ct. 904 (1968).

20. 440 U.S. 69, 99 S.Ct. 925 (1979).

21. See Justice Marshall's dissent. Id. at 86, 99 S.Ct. at 935.

22. For discussion and criticism, see Kuenzel & Schiffres, Making Sense of Robinson-Patman: The Need to Revitalize its Affirmative Defenses, 62 Va.L. Rev. 1211 (1976); Standridge, An Analysis of the Cost Justification Defense Un-

The "cost justification" defense of § 2(a) of the Act provides "that nothing herein contained shall prevent [price] differentials which make only due allowance for differences in the cost of manufacture, sale, or delivery" of commodities. The defense has the potential to turn the Act at least halfway into a true economic price discrimination statute. Under it differential prices would not be condemned if the differences were in direct proportion to the differences in marginal costs of serving two customers.

The cost justification defense has not saved many defendants from liability, however. It has been so rigidly construed by courts that it virtually requires the defendant to show affirmatively that lower prices to a particular purchaser were proportional to the lower marginal costs of serving that purchaser.[23] The Supreme Court has rejected defendants' expensive, detailed cost studies, because they did not divide purchasers into sufficiently homogenous categories or did not account for every aspect of cost difference.[24] The ironic result has been to force many sellers to engage in true economic discrimination by charging the same price to different groups of buyers, even though the costs of serving them differ. Pricing in proportion to cost would threaten them with Robinson-Patman liability; however, they can avoid liability by charging all buyers the same price.[25]

Different buyers invariably impose different marginal costs on a seller. A customer who tries on three pairs of shoes before he makes a purchase is more expensive to serve than a customer who purchases the first pair. When goods are delivered the differences can become even more pronounced. The delivery agent may have to walk up a flight of steps in one location but not in another. One location may be slightly further away or be surrounded by congested traffic. These things and others can make it more costly to deliver products to one buyer than to another. About the best any seller can do is find a rational scheme for grouping buyers according to the

der Section 2(a) of the Robinson-Patman Act, 9 Rutgers-Camden L.J. 219 (1978).

23. Actually, under the statute *marginal* cost may be the incorrect measure. The defense applies only to lower prices that reflect savings in the "cost of manufacture, sale, or delivery * * * ." The FTC once held that a return on capital was not an applicable "cost" saving within the meaning of the statute. See Thompson Prod., Inc., 55 F.T.C. 1252, 1265–66 (1959). Likewise, where average total cost is higher than marginal cost and disfavored purchasers are charged a price sufficient to cover average total cost, a seller will probably not be able to "cost justify" an additional sale made at short-run marginal cost. That is, all relevant costs will have to be averaged over all customers to whom they apply. See Standard Oil Co., 49 F.T.C. 923, 942 (1953), reversed on other grounds, 233 F.2d 649 (7th Cir. 1956), affirmed, 355 U.S. 396, 78 S.Ct. 369 (1958).

24. See U.S. v. Borden Co., 370 U.S. 460, 82 S.Ct. 1309 (1962); however, cost studies met the requirements of the cost justification defense in FTC v. Standard Motor Prod., Inc., 371 F.2d 613 (2d Cir. 1967); Morton v. National Dairy Prods. Corp., 414 F.2d 403 (3d Cir. 1969), cert. denied, 396 U.S. 1006, 90 S.Ct. 560 (1970).

25. See Adelman, The Consistency of the Robinson-Patman Act, 6 Stan.L.Rev. 3 (1953).

costs that they impose on the seller. The cost justification defense can do no more.

Furthermore, in a competitive market no seller could long get away with charging a higher price if the price did not reflect the higher costs of serving certain classes of customers. As a result a market power requirement, rather than a "cost justification" defense with the burden on the defendant, would be a much more satisfactory way of initially determining whether differential prices were really discriminatory.[26]

§ 2(b) of the Robinson-Patman Act also permits a defendant to rebut a *prima facie* case of violation by showing that his lower price "was made in good faith to meet an equally low price of a competitor * * *." This "meeting competition" defense has traditionally required the seller to have actual knowledge that a particular competitor had offered a lower price on an identical or similar product. For example, if a seller had been selling widgets to X at $2.00, but learned that a competitor had offered X widgets at $1.80, then the seller could match the $1.80 offer rather than lose the sale.

In FTC v. A.E. Staley Mfg. Co.[27] the Supreme Court held that the "meeting competition" defense could be raised only by someone who had "first-hand" knowledge of an actual offer of a lower price from an actual competitor. If such an offer did not exist, the seller could not raise the meeting competition defense. *Staley* therefore suggested that it was a seller's responsibility to "investigate or verify" any information about a lower-price offer from a competitor.[28] Additionally, *Staley* held that a seller could not "meet" a competitor's general price structure or schedule, but could "meet competition" only on a transaction-by-transaction basis.

In U.S. v. United States Gypsum Co.[29] the defendants, who were competitors, were charged with illegally exchanging information about resale prices. The defense raised was that the sellers needed

---

26. Even with its market power established, however, a defendant should still be permitted to cost justify sales at different prices. That is, market power is a *prerequisite* for persistent price discrimination, but it is not proof of persistent price discrimination. See Hovenkamp, note 10 above at 1176.

27. 324 U.S. 746, 65 S.Ct. 971 (1945).

28. See Id. at 758–59, 65 S.Ct. at 977. The defendants in *Staley* had made their low price sales "in response to verbal information received from salesmen, brokers, or intending purchasers, without supporting evidence, to the effect that in each case one or more competitors had granted or offered to grant like

discriminations." In affirming the FTC's decision that this information was not good enough to sustain the "good faith" meeting competition defense, the Court cited an "entire lack of a showing of diligence * * * to verify the reports * * * or to learn of the existence of facts which would lead a reasonable and prudent person to believe that the granting of a lower price would in fact be meeting the equally low price of a competitor." Id.

29. 438 U.S. 422, 98 S.Ct. 2864 (1978), appeal after remand, 600 F.2d 414 (3d Cir. 1979), cert. denied, 444 U.S. 884, 100 S.Ct. 175 (1979).

to "investigate or verify" rumored lower price bids from competitors, and the only way they could do so was to ask the competitor.

The defense raised in the *Gypsum* case illustrates the anticompetitive potential of the Robinson-Patman Act. A great deal of law under § 1 of the Sherman Act forbids price information exchanges among competitors, if the exchange influences price.[30] In *Gypsum* the defendants presented what appeared to be a bona fide defense: in order to comply with the "meeting competition" defense of the Robinson-Patman Act they were obliged to verify that a competitor had in fact given a lower bid to a particular customer. In short, compliance with the Robinson-Patman Act required violation of the Sherman Act.[31] The Supreme Court, holding that the policies of the Robinson-Patman Act must be harmonized with the policies of the Sherman Act,[32] held that "meeting competition" required only "good faith," not actual knowledge. Under *Gypsum* a seller is entitled to believe a customer if the customer says "I can get it cheaper from your competitor," and the seller has no particular reason to doubt the customer's word. If later it turns out that the customer was lying or mistaken, the seller will not be held liable, provided that he acted in good faith.

Another element of the *Staley* holding was substantially undermined in Falls City Industries, Inc v. Vanco Beverage, Inc.,[33] when the Supreme Court unanimously decided that a seller could meet the lower general price structure in a different market, without necessarily meeting competition on a customer-by-customer or sale-by-sale basis. The Supreme Court found "no evidence that Congress intended to limit the availability of [the meeting competition defense] to customer-specific responses." Rather Congress "intended to allow reasonable pricing responses on an area-specific basis where competitive circumstances warrant them."

Whether this new broader application of the "meeting competition" defense will carve a significant hole in Robinson-Patman enforcement remains to be seen. The potential is present. *All* sales are made at a price calculated by the seller to "meet competition." Even the absolute monopolist cannot charge an infinite price for its product. When the monopolist calculates its profit-maximizing price as $2.00, it has concluded that at a price of $2.10 too many customers

---

30. For example, U.S. v. Container Corp. of America, 393 U.S. 333, 89 S.Ct. 510 (1969), discussed above in § 4.3.

31. The Robinson-Patman Act may facilitate express or tacit collusion in other, more subtle ways. For example, cartel members "cheat" on the cartel by making discriminatorily low-priced sales to certain large purchasers. If enough cartel members cheat, the cartel will fall apart. Robinson-Patman enforcement

by buyers in an oligopoly or cartelized market can actually help the cartel or oligopoly protect itself from cheating. See § 4.2 above.

32. *Gypsum*, 438 U.S. at 458, 98 S.Ct. at 2884.

33. 460 U.S. 428, 103 S.Ct. 1282 (1983), on remand 705 F.2d 463 (7th Cir. 1983).

will purchase something else instead. More to the point, why would a seller who has just sold 50 gallons of milk to one store for $1.50 per gallon agree to sell 1,000 gallons of milk to another store for $1.35? Any reasonable seller would do so for only one reason: if he refuses the buyer may look elsewhere. Since the seller has calculated that he can profitably make the larger sale at the lower price, he will generally suspect that someone else could do it as well. The Supreme Court's suggestion in *Vanco Beverage* that the "very purpose" of the meeting competition defense "is to permit a seller to treat different competitive situations differently" makes good economic sense. It also substantially undermines the Robinson-Patman Act.

 WESTLAW REFERENCES

robinson-patman   /15   critic! problem concern

robinson-patman   /15   primary-line   /3   pric***

robinson-patman   /p   engaged   /5   "interstate commerce"   /s   discriminat!

robinson-patman   /s   "like grade and quality"

robinson-patman   /s   2(f)   /s   discriminat!

robinson-patman   /p   "cost justification"   /s   defense

robinson-patman   /p   meet***   +2   competition   /s   defense

CHAPTER 14

PRIVATE ENFORCEMENT

Table of Sections

§ 14.1 Introduction: § 4 of the Clayton Act

§ 4 of the Clayton Act provides that "Any person injured in his business or property by reason of anything forbidden in the antitrust laws may sue * * * and shall recover three-fold the damages * * * sustained and * * * a reasonable attorney's fee." 15 U.S.C.A. § 15.

The simplicity of § 4's language belies the complexity of the many questions it has raised, and that have been answered only by litigation. One problem with the statute is its unrealistic breadth. In a market economy (and the entire world, ideology notwithstanding, participates in the market to some degree) a simple price fixing agreement has effects that injure everyone. Witness the impact of the OPEC cartel, which resulted in higher prices not only of petroleum, but of everything that required energy for its manufacture—industrial products, agricultural products, even other natural resources. The result threw several national economies into disarray.[1]

The difference between a large cartel like OPEC and a small price fixing conspiracy among manufacturers of cardboard boxes is merely

---

§ 14.1

1. See Int'l Ass'n of Machinists v. OPEC, 649 F.2d 1354 (9th Cir. 1981), cert. denied, 454 U.S. 1163, 102 S.Ct. 1036 (1982). See Hovenkamp, Can A Foreign Sovereign be an Antitrust Defendant? 32 Syracuse L.Rev. 879 (1981).

one of degree, not of nature. By its language § 4 appears to give a cause of action to every person who is financially injured by a cartel or overcharging monopolist. Courts have generally taken the position that the statute cannot be as broad as it purports to be, however, and they have devised ways to limit its scope. Chief among these limitations are various standing requirements, the "antitrust injury" doctrine, and the indirect purchaser rule established in Illinois Brick Co. v. Illinois.[2]

Although private antitrust actions were filed soon after the passage of the Sherman Act, the number of such cases was not large until the 1950's. The number grew rapidly during the 1960's and exploded in the 1970's. Recently the number has leveled off somewhat. However, the private antitrust action continues to be the principal mechanism by which the antitrust laws are enforced. In the last decade over 90% of all antitrust cases were brought by private plaintiffs.[3]

 WESTLAW REFERENCES
caption(15 & "persons injured")

§ 14.2 Permissible Plaintiffs—Who Should Enforce the Antitrust Laws?

Clayton § 4 requires a plaintiff to be a "person," which includes natural persons, corporations, and unincorporated associations recognized by federal, state or foreign law. Municipalities, states and foreign governments are all permissible plaintiffs—although foreign governments, as well as the United States seeking damages for its own injuries, are limited to actual rather than treble damages.[1]

§ 4 also requires the plaintiff to show injury to its "business or property." Most private plaintiffs have alleged injury to some business interest that they owned. They therefore claimed injury to both their "business" *and* their "property." In Reiter v. Sonotone Corp.,[2] however, the Supreme Court granted a damages action to a retail consumer who allegedly paid a higher price for a product because of a price fixing conspiracy. The consumer was injured in her "proper-

---

2. 431 U.S. 720, 97 S.Ct. 2061 (1977), rehearing denied, 434 U.S. 881, 98 S.Ct. 243 (1977), discussed below in § 14.4.

3. See Posner, A Statistical Study of Antitrust Enforcement, 13 J.L. & Econ. 365 (1970). Data since 1970 are summarized in 46 Antitrust & Trade Reg. Rprt. (BNA) 360 (Mar. 1, 1984). For a classification of private filings in the first half of the century see Clark, The Treble Damage Bonanza: New Doctrines of Damages in Private Antitrust Suits, 52 Mich.L.Rev. 363 (1954). For a detailed

analysis of the kinds of private antitrust cases filed in a single district during the 1970's, see National Econ. Research Assoc., Inc., Statistical Analysis of Private Antitrust Litigation: Final Report (1979).

§ 14.2

1. Pub. L. No. 97–393, 96 Stat. 1964 (1982), codified at 15 U.S.C.A. § 15a.

2. 442 U.S. 330, 99 S.Ct. 2326 (1979), on remand, 602 F.2d 179 (8th Cir. 1979).

ty" but not in her business. Today the term "property" in § 4 is nearly co-extensive with the common law concept: property is anything in which a person claims a legally recognized ownership interest. In *Reiter* the Supreme Court suggested only personal injuries as not included in § 4's concept of "business or property." It did not explain how an antitrust violation might cause personal injuries.[3]

The concept of "business or property" has sometimes been construed narrowly by lower courts. For example, in Reibert v. Atlantic Richfield Co.[4] the Tenth Circuit held that an employee discharged in the wake of a personnel consolidation brought about by a merger had no cause of action under Clayton § 7, because employment was not "business or property" within the meaning of § 4. A job is clearly a legally recognized property interest, however, and other courts have granted standing when the target of the antitrust violation was the labor market itself.[5] Employee termination does not usually support a damages action under the antitrust laws—but the lack of a "business or property" interest has nothing to do with the denial of standing.

The scope of "business or property" under § 4 is not unlimited. For example, one of the most problematic of plaintiffs is the unestablished business—the person who was denied an opportunity ever to compete in the first place.

Any policy of promoting competition through private antitrust enforcement must protect entry into markets. Furthermore, the prospective entrant is often an easier target than the incumbent, for the prospective entrant has fewer unrecoverable sunk costs and is in a better position to consider alternative markets. For that reason many practices such as strategic exclusionary behavior[6] are directed primarily at new entrants or prospective entrants.

Nevertheless, a person who merely wishes to enter a new field has not clearly suffered injury to business or property when an incumbent lowers its prices or engages in some other exclusionary

3. Suppose, however, that firms with good safety records are excluded from a project by an illegal boycott; as a result, firms with poorer safety records participate, and someone is killed. See Hamman v. U.S., 267 F.Supp. 420, 432 (D. Mont.1967), denying treble damages under Clayton § 4 under this theory for loss of consortium. The court held that loss of consortium was not injury to "business or property" under § 4, even though state law recognized a property right in consortium. See also In re Multidistrict Vehicle Air Pollution, M.D.L., 481 F.2d 122 (9th Cir. 1973), cert. denied, 414 U.S. 1045, 94 S.Ct. 551 (1973), on remand, 367 F.Supp. 1298 (1973), rehearing denied, 414 U.S. 1148, 94 S.Ct. 905 (1974), judgment affirmed, 538 F.2d 231 (9th Cir. 1976), involving a claim by farmers that a conspiracy among automobile manufacturers to delay development of auto emission controls resulted in increased air pollution and a decline in agricultural production.

4. 471 F.2d 727 (10th Cir. 1973), cert. denied, 411 U.S. 938, 93 S.Ct. 1900 (1973), rehearing denied, 412 U.S. 914, 93 S.Ct. 2289 (1973).

5. See Tugboat, Inc. v. Mobile Towing Co., 534 F.2d 1172 (5th Cir. 1976), rehearing denied, 540 F.2d 1085 (5th Cir. 1976).

6. See § 6.9 above.

practice. Courts often insist that the prospective entrant have obtained some kind of property interest, have some sunk costs or other commitment to entry before the requisite "injury" can be inferred. Occasionally they have found the plaintiff's clear intent to enter a certain market to be sufficient. More often they have required something else, such as contracts with prospective purchasers, a commitment of financing, or substantial funds spent in marketing research or advertising. In general, the more the unestablished business has at stake in a certain market, the more likely the court will find injury to business or property.[7]

Courts also generally require that the injured business or property belong to the plaintiff and not to someone else. Occasionally, however, ownership of a particular property interest is ambiguous. In Hawaii v. Standard Oil Co. of California,[8] for example, the Supreme Court held that a state could not assert a damages claim for economic injuries to its citizens, or for injury to its general economy, if it was not itself a purchaser or competitor of the defendant. § 4 did not authorize a state's use of the common law doctrine of *parens patriae*, under which a governmental entity could bring an action asserting injuries to citizens within its protection. Since the citizens themselves had causes of action, the Court reasoned, any damages action brought by the State asserting the same injuries, or some more general injury to the state's economy, would yield duplicative recoveries.[9]

The term "duplicative recovery" merits analysis, for courts often have used it to deny standing to a particular class of plaintiffs. The term implies that an antitrust violation produces some identifiable total amount of injury, and that under § 4 the defendant's liability cannot exceed three times that amount.

However, most antitrust violations produce no such easily demarcated "pool" of injuries. Many produce ripples whose injurious effects in the economy are endless. Courts generally use the term "duplicative recovery" only to suggest that a certain amount of liability seems like too much, measured by some standard of common sense or fairness that has not been articulated. Injury is always measured by the plaintiff's losses, not by the defendant's gains, and there is no natural correlation between the amount of injury an

---

7. See Neumann v. Vidal, 710 F.2d 856 (D.C.Cir.1983); Hayes v. Solomon, 597 F.2d 958, 973 (5th Cir. 1979), cert. denied, 444 U.S. 1078, 100 S.Ct. 1028 (1980); Note, Unestablished Businesses and Treble Damage Recovery Under Section Four of the Clayton Act, 49 U.Chi.L.Rev. 1076 (1982).

8. 405 U.S. 251, 92 S.Ct. 885 (1972).

9. § 4 was subsequently amended to permit *parens patriae* actions by states attorneys general on behalf of natural persons residing in the state. 15 U.S. C.A. § 15c. See Kintner, Griffin & Goldston, The Hart-Scott-Rodino Antitrust Improvements Act of 1976: An Analysis, 46 Geo.Wash.L.Rev. 1 (1977); Note, Parens Patriae Actions on Behalf of Indirect Purchasers: Do They Survive *Illinois Brick*?, 34 Hastings L.J. 179 (1982).

antitrust violation causes and its profitability to the violator. Consider an unsuccessful predatory pricing scheme which produces substantial losses for both the predator and its victims. During the period of predatory sales consumers may actually be benefitted by lower prices, at least over the short run. Competitors, however, are injured. Some may be driven from business, thereby injuring suppliers with long-term contracts, employees and their dues-collecting unions, customers, creditors, landlords and federal, state and local governments which stand to lose tax revenues. To decide that the failing competitor ought to have a cause of action against the predator, but that the landlord, the victim's employees or the state seeking lost taxes should not, may be reasonable. But the problem is not "duplicative recovery." There is no pool of unjust earnings that will be overdrawn; nor is there any relationship between the amount of the defendant's illegal gain and the injuries to the various victims. Each victim has its own distinct injury. The competitor, who probably has a cause of action, will be able to recover for its lost profits and perhaps for the loss of its business. It will not recover for the injuries to its employees, however, nor those to the state treasury. Recovery by all these victims would not be "duplicative," but it would yield a large amount of damages—more than many defendants would be capable of paying, and probably more than Congress envisioned when it passed § 4.

The only coherent meaning of "duplicative recovery" is recovery by one person for injuries sustained by another person who has also been able to recover. For example, if a private party obtained redress for its injuries and later a state suing as *parens patriae* obtained damages for the same injury, the two recoveries would arguably be duplicative. The term "duplicative recovery" may therefore have some meaning in the context of the indirect purchaser rule, discussed in § 14.4 below. Under the rule a direct purchaser is permitted to recover the entire monopoly overcharge, even though most of the overcharge may have been passed along to the direct purchaser's customers. Some state antitrust laws, however, permit indirect purchaser lawsuits. Suppose that an indirect purchaser recovers for its own passed-on injuries after the defendant has already paid the direct purchaser an amount sufficient to cover the injuries of direct and indirect purchasers all the way down the distribution chain. In this instance recovery is arguably duplicative.[10]

Many classes of persons do not have standing to bring an action under § 4, even though they have suffered injuries to their business or property, and even though their recovery would not be "duplicative" of a recovery by someone else. Some decision must be made about the amount of antitrust enforcement that the law should

10. See Hovenkamp, State Antitrust in the Federal Scheme, 57 Ind.L.J. 375 (1983).

permit. That decision is essentially a function of the basic purpose of the antitrust laws. If the exclusive purpose of the antitrust laws is to maximize the efficiency of the market system of allocating resources, the optimal level of enforcement will leave the largest amount of social wealth intact after all costs of violations, enforcement and penalties are paid.

Private enforcement is subject to the law of diminishing returns— the more there is, the less deterrence will be obtained per enforcement dollar. If a rule that gave direct purchasers a treble-damages action for cartel overcharges deterred 90% of price fixing, then any rule that additionally gave a cause of action to indirect purchasers, creditors, or employees could not do more than deter the remaining 10%. However, lawsuits by these injured persons would be just as costly to litigate as lawsuits by direct purchasers. Furthermore, there are many more indirect purchasers than there are direct purchasers, so they might file many more lawsuits. The amount of increased allocative efficiency in the form of deterrence of price fixing would be relatively low in proportion to the costs of litigation. A perfect deterrence system designed to maximize social wealth would locate that point at which the marginal cost of an additional quantum of enforcement is equal to its marginal value. If every dollar in increased litigation costs produced by a broader standing rule—perhaps a rule giving an action to indirect purchasers—yielded only 75¢ in efficiency gains, then the rule is a bad one and should be abandoned.[11]

This theoretical conclusion does not help us very much to determine the proper range of permissible plaintiffs in the real world, although it does suggest some guidelines. As a premise, enforcement rules should maximize the amount of deterrence of inefficient practices that can be obtained per enforcement dollar. The premise suggests 1) that enforcement rights (standing) should be granted first to those who can discover violations most accurately and readily, and whose incentive to bring an action is high; 2) that the rights should be given first to those for whom litigation costs will be smallest; 3) that denial of standing is most appropriate when we can point to injured persons other than the plaintiff who better fit the criteria in (1) and (2) above.

The Clayton Act's provision of mandatory treble damages plus attorney's fees to prevailing plaintiffs has put extraordinary pressure on courts to develop intelligible limits on antitrust standing. These statutory provisions encourage litigation by people for whom the amount of recovery discounted by the probability of success would otherwise be marginal. The incentive to sue is further increased by

---

11. Too broad a rule might deter companies from engaging in efficient, marginally legal practices that might nevertheless be open to challenge. See K. Elzinga & W. Breit, The Antitrust Penalties: A Study in Law and Economics 7–16 (1976).

the availability of procedural devices such as class actions, which give potential plaintiffs a more favorable balance between the expected recovery and the costs of pursuing an action.

Unfortunately, intelligibie limits on standing have never emerged, and the law of standing in antitrust cases is haphazard and inconsistent. One reason is that neither Congress nor the courts has articulated a rationale for private enforcement. The above framework suggests that the purpose of private enforcement is to maximize social wealth. However, courts have generally analyzed antitrust standing requirements in terms of compensation to victims. Once a court permits compensation rather than deterrence as a permissible objective of private antitrust enforcement, then the door is opened to many rationales that are even more difficult to quantify than allocative efficiency itself—such as justice, fairness, or the preservation of opportunities for small business.

WESTLAW REFERENCES

person /s association corporat*** government**
    natural /p clayton /5 4

synopsis,digest(injur** /s business property /p clayton /5 4)

business entrant entry /12 anticipat*** future new potential
    prospective unestablished /p clayton /5 4

business property /p "duplicative recovery" "parens patriae" /p
    clayton /5 4

265k28(1.4) +p clayton /5 4

265k28(1.6) +p clayton /5 4

§ 14.3   Permissible Plaintiffs—Judicially Developed Rules of Standing

Courts have identified certain favored and disfavored classes of antitrust plaintiffs under Clayton § 4. Favored plaintiffs include customers and competitors of the violator. Disfavored plaintiffs include nonpurchasers, potential competitors and employees of the violator, and stockholders, creditors, landlords, and employees of victims. Standing is sometimes denied to people in the favored categories and sometimes granted to those in the disfavored categories. As a general rule, however, customers and competitors are the preferred antitrust plaintiffs.

Unfortunately, judicial rules of standing have not been articulated as clearly as the previous paragraph suggests. Rather than identifying preferred classes as such, courts have taken a more conceptual approach, borrowed from various causation doctrines of tort law. The prevailing tests for plaintiff standing in private antitrust damages actions are the "direct injury" test, which purports to measure whether the relationship between the defendant's violation and the plaintiff's injury was "direct" or "indirect"; and the "target-area" test, which tries to identify a class of persons who should be protected from a particular antitrust violation. Both tests have involved courts in an endless cycle of verbal games, and neither has produced a reliable set of predictive tools calculated to give consistent results.

The "direct injury" test originated in Loeb v. Eastman Kodak Co.[1] The court denied standing to a stockholder in a corporation allegedly victimized by an antitrust violation. The holding was based on two rationales. First, the stockholder's injury was only an "indirect" consequence of the antitrust violation; the direct consequence was the injury to the corporation itself. Second, the court concluded that § 7 of the Sherman Act (Clayton § 4's predecessor) was not intended by Congress to "multiply suits" by conferring standing on thousands of stockholders "when their wrongs could have been equally well and far more economically redressed by a single suit in the name of the corporation."

Measure of the "directness" of an injury, as courts knew from their experience in tort law, would yield complicated metaphysical problems and no clear predictive rule.[2] At the extremes it is perhaps easy to characterize an injury as "direct" or "indirect"—but in the middle are hundreds of cases in which the plaintiff's injury is clear but the chain of events between the act and the injury contains several, sometimes improbable links. The Loeb court's alternative observation—that the corporation is a more efficient enforcer than its individual stockholders and should have the same information and incentives to sue—was much more sensible. However, Loeb became known for its "indirect injury" language, and courts have often relied on it to deny standing to the employees, franchisors, landlords and stockholders of victims, as well as to people in several other categories.[3]

The "target area" test was designed to eliminate some of the uncertainties of the direct injury test. As the Ninth Circuit formulated the test in Conference of Studio Unions v. Loews, Inc.,[4] the plaintiff must "show that he is within that area of the economy which is endangered by a breakdown of competitive conditions in a particular industry." The court then held that a labor union and its members were not the target of an alleged conspiracy between major motion picture producers and a second union to drive smaller motion picture companies out of business.

§ 14.3

1. 183 F. 704, 709 (3d Cir. 1910).

2. See Hovenkamp, Pragmatic Realism and Proximate Cause in America, 3 J.Legal History 3 (1982).

3. See, e.g., Solinger v. A&M Records, Inc., 718 F.2d 298 (9th Cir.1983) (shareholder); Jones v. Ford Motor Co., 599 F.2d 394 (10th Cir. 1979) (employee); Billy Baxter, Inc. v. Coca-Cola Co., 431 F.2d 183 (2d Cir. 1970), cert. denied,

401 U.S. 923, 191 S.Ct. 877 (1971) (franchisor); Southaven Land Co., Inc. v. Malone & Hyde, Inc., 715 F.2d 1079 (6th Cir. 1983) (landlord). For an excellent discussion of the cases and some of the difficulties see Berger & Bernstein, An Analytical Framework for Antitrust Standing, 86 Yale L.J. 809 (1977).

4. 193 F.2d 51, 54–55 (9th Cir. 1951), cert. denied, 342 U.S. 919, 72 S.Ct. 367 (1952).

The target area test has proved just as problematic as the direct injury test. If standing under the target area test is limited to the defendant's *intended* victims, then the range of potential plaintiffs is often very small. However, if standing is expanded to include all persons whose injury is "foreseeable," then the target area test will often be unduly broad: it is certainly foreseeable that when a firm is driven out of business its employees and their union, its creditors, stockholders, suppliers and landlord will all be injured. All of these participate to some degree in that part of the economy that is threatened by the violation.[5]

The problem of employees' standing illustrates some of the ambiguity in judicially created standing rules. Courts have consistently denied standing to employees who claimed they lost their jobs because of their employer's illegal output reduction schemes, such as price fixing, or because their employer was the victim of a competitor's violation. Courts found either that the injury was too "remote" under the direct injury test, or else that the employees were not in the "target area" that merited statutory protection.[6]

In 1982 circuit courts considered a somewhat different employee standing question—the employee who alleges that he lost his job because he refused to participate in his own employer's intentional antitrust violation. In Bichan v. Chemetron Corp.[7] the Seventh Circuit denied standing under both the indirect injury and target area theories, holding that an action should be granted "to those who, as consumers or competitors, suffer immediate injuries with respect to their business or property," and denied to those "whose injuries were more indirectly caused by the antitrust conduct." In this case, which involved an alleged price fixing conspiracy, the target of the violation was the conspirator's customers, not its employees.

Bichan's loss of employment was arguably an "indirect" result of the antitrust violation. He was also not the "target" of a price fixing conspiracy. But did the two tests, both correctly employed, produce the correct result? An employee terminated because he refused to participate in an antitrust violation could be a highly efficient enforc-

5. Some circuits have developed alternatives to the "indirect injury" and "target area tests." For example, the Sixth Circuit's "zone of interests" test, also borrowed from tort law, seeks to determine whether the plaintiff's injury "arguably comes within the zone of interests protected by the [antitrust] laws." Malamud v. Sinclair Oil Co., 521 F.2d 1142, 1152 (6th Cir. 1975). The test tracks the antitrust injury doctrine, which is discussed below in § 14.5. The Third Circuit uses a "balancing test comprised of many constant and variable factors" because there is "no talismanic test capable of resolving all § 4 standing problems." Bravman v. Bassett Furn. Indus., Inc., 552 F.2d 90, 99 (3d Cir. 1977), cert. denied, 434 U.S. 823, 98 S.Ct. 69 (1977). In Blue Shield of Virginia v. McCready, 457 U.S. 465, 102 S.Ct. 2540, 2547 n. 12 (1982), the Supreme Court expressly refused to "evaluate the relative utility of any of these possibly conflicting approaches toward the problem of remote antitrust injury."

6. See 2 P. Areeda & D. Turner, Antitrust Law ¶¶ 338–339 (1978).

7. 681 F.2d 514, 517–20 (7th Cir. 1982), cert. denied, 460 U.S. 1016, 103 S.Ct. 1261 (1983).

er of the antitrust laws. He certainly has the motivation. More importantly, he has better knowledge than almost any potential plaintiff of the fact of the violation. If the cartel is successful it will never be detected by consumers, the preferred plaintiffs. Giving a plaintiff in Bichan's position the right to sue brings evidence of the existence of a cartel into the open at an early stage, before it has had a chance to cause significant harm.[8]

Both the direct injury and target area tests for standing give a strong preference to consumers who suffer overcharge injuries or competitors injured by exclusionary practices. Occasionally courts even suggest that standing should be limited to these two classes of plaintiffs. The Supreme Court rejected that view in Blue Shield of Virginia v. McCready,[9] when it granted standing to a health insurance purchaser who alleged that the insurance provider conspired with psychiatrists to exclude psychologists from the health policy's coverage. McCready alleged that the exclusion forced her to pay for her own psychologist's services separately.

The intended victims of the alleged conspiracy were clearly the psychologists. However, the defendant easily could foresee that any exclusion of psychologists from policy coverage would also injure purchasers of psychologists' services. Thus although Ms. McCready was not the "target" of the antitrust conspiracy her injury was plainly foreseeable.

Undeniably a boycott against a group of employees foreseeably would injure the employees' labor union. In *McCready* the Supreme Court did not purport either to overrule or even to distinguish *Loew's*, however. Rather, it expressly found that plaintiff McCready was "within that area of the economy" that had been endangered by the "breakdown of competitive conditions" that resulted from the alleged violation. The Court appeared to add only one restriction to a broad rule granting standing to all plaintiffs whose injury was both foreseeable and not *de minimis*—that the injury suffered by the plaintiff be "inextricably intertwined with the injury the conspirators sought to inflict on psychologists * * * ." [10]

The Court's "inextricably interwined" language is ambiguous, however, and not well designed to achieve consistency in standing cases. A stockholder's injuries are inextricably intertwined with the demise of the corporation in which he owns shares. The terminated employee of an antitrust victim suffers injuries that are inextricably interwined with those suffered by his employer. The *McCready* case

8. The Ninth Circuit granted standing in a similar case in Ostrofe v. H.S. Crocker Co., Inc., 670 F.2d 1378 (9th Cir. 1982), vacated and remanded, 101 U.S. 1007, 103 S.Ct. 1244 (1983), affirmed on remand, 740 F.2d 739 (9th Cir.1984). See Comment, Discharged Employees: Should They Have Antitrust Standing Under Section Four of the Clayton Act?, 34 Hastings L.J. 839 (1983).

9. 457 U.S. 465, 102 S.Ct. 2540 (1982).

10. Id. at 484, 102 S.Ct. at 2551.

did little to clarify the law of antitrust standing, except to reaffirm that sometimes (we don't know when) persons who are not the target of the violator may be antitrust plaintiffs. Furthermore, the Supreme Court overlooked the fact that another group of potential plaintiffs, the psychologists, were the direct target of the alleged conspiracy. Certainly they knew that the defendant had excluded them from its insurance coverage, and they had a strong incentive to sue.[11] Ms. McCready was only the second-best plaintiff.

A few months later the Court backtracked from the *McCready* opinion in Associated General Contractors of California, Inc. v. California State Council of Carpenters,[12] in which it denied standing to a labor union which alleged that defendant employers coerced various members of the plaintiff into dealing with nonunion firms and thereby "restrained the business activities of the unions."

In holding that the union had not been "injured in its business or property," the Court acknowledged that the defendant employers' alleged coercion was aimed at labor unions. However, in this case the court could find no link between the quality of competition in the target market (construction contracts) and the welfare of the labor unions.

After two important Supreme Court decisions in 1982 and 1983 the law of standing in private antitrust actions remains unclear. None of the generalized, conceptual tests adequately predicts whether a particular plaintiff will be granted standing.[13]

A more useful, functional approach would be to divide plaintiff classes into categories. Consumers and competitors of the violator presumptively should be granted standing. Other classes, such as landlords, employees, stockholders, and creditors of victims, presumptively should be denied standing. In all close cases the court should first determine whether there is another highly motivated group of potential plaintiffs in a position to enforce the antitrust laws more efficiently. Second, the court should make sure that the plaintiff at hand truly has been a victim of "antitrust injury"—that is, that it stands to gain from the improvement of competition in the market in which the alleged violation occurred.[14] Finally, the court should consider whether the particular plaintiff is in a unique position to discover an antitrust violation earlier than other potential plaintiffs

11. In fact, the psychologists had sued. See Va. Academy of Clinical Psychologists v. Blue Shield of Va., 624 F.2d 476 (4th Cir. 1980), on remand, 501 F.Supp. 1232 (1980), cert. denied, 450 U.S. 916, 101 S.Ct. 1360 (1981).

12. 459 U.S. 519, 103 S.Ct. 897 (1983).

13. For some of the difficulties of applying *McCready* and *Associated*

General Contractors to questions of standing, see Crimpers Promotions Inc. v. Home Box Office, Inc., 724 F.2d 290 (2d Cir. 1983), cert. denied, — U.S. —, 104 S.Ct. 3536 (1984).

14. See § 14.5 below.

would. In that case, granting standing could minimize the duration, and thus the social cost, of antitrust violations.

 WESTLAW REFERENCES

standing /p "direct injury" /p (clayton /5 4) (private /6 antitrust)

standing /p "target area" /p (clayton /5 4) (private /6 antitrust)

standing /s creditor employee landlord s****holder /p (clayton /5 4) (private /6 antitrust)

standing /p intertwin*** second-best /p (clayton /5 4) (private /6 antitrust)

§ 14.4 The Indirect Purchaser Rule

In Hanover Shoe, Inc. v. United Shoe Machinery Corp.[1] the Supreme Court held that a direct purchaser from a monopolist could claim the entire monopoly overcharge as damages, even though the purchaser passed most of the overcharge on to its customers. The Court acknowledged that much of a monopoly overcharge is passed down the distribution chain and absorbed by the consumer. However, lawsuits by indirect purchaser consumers would be impractical. There might be thousands of such purchasers, each with only a "tiny stake in a lawsuit."

A decade later in Illinois Brick Co. v. Illinois[2] the Supreme Court followed *Hanover Shoe* in deciding that since the direct purchaser has an action for the entire monopoly overcharge, the indirect purchaser should have none—even though the indirect purchaser could show that part of the overcharge had been passed on and that it had been injured as a result.

A monopoly overcharge at the top of a distribution chain generally results in higher prices at every level below. For example, if production of aluminum is monopolized or cartelized, fabricators of aluminum cookware will pay higher prices for aluminum. In most cases they will absorb part of these increased costs themselves and pass part along to cookware wholesalers. The wholesalers will charge higher prices to the retail stores, and the stores will do it once again to retail consumers. Every person at every stage in the chain likely will be poorer as a result of the monopoly price at the top.

Theoretically one can calculate the percentage of any overcharge that a firm at one distributional level will pass on to those at the next level. However, the computation requires knowledge of the prevail-

§ 14.4

1. 392 U.S. 481, 88 S.Ct. 2224 (1968).

2. 431 U.S. 720, 97 S.Ct. 2061 (1977), rehearing denied, 434 U.S. 881, 98 S.Ct. 243 (1977). The indirect purchaser rule applies with equal force to sellers who deal indirectly with a monopsonist or buyer's cartel. See Zinser v. Continental Grain Co., 660 F.2d 754 (10th Cir. 1981), cert. denied, 455 U.S. 941, 102 S.Ct. 1434 (1982).

ing elasticities of supply and demand, and obtaining that information is beyond the technical competence of courts.[3] If courts could make such measurements they would be able to measure such attributes as market power directly, without the need to define relevant markets and market shares.

Nevertheless, examination of the relationship between demand elasticities and pass-on can provide some guidance about the proper scope of the indirect purchaser rule. For simplicity we consider only demand elasticities and ignore elasticity of supply. We also assume that any monopoly overcharge is spread over an entire relevant market and has absolutely no effect on possible substitute products in a different market. These assumptions distort our pictures of the real world. However, without them the analysis would be complicated enormously.[4]

Finally, we assume that the cartelized product is a variable cost item to all firms in the distribution chain. If the cartelized product is a fixed cost item to a particular firm—for example, if a pizza parlor pays a monopoly price for its delivery truck—the monopoly overcharge will not show up in the firm's short-run marginal cost curve, which includes only variable costs. In a competitive market, in which prices are driven to marginal cost, a pizza parlor that paid a monopoly price for a delivery truck might have to absorb the entire monopoly overcharge itself. If the monopoly overcharge was in anchovies, however, the marginal cost of any pizza with anchovies would rise.[5] Further, if the cartelized product is a fixed cost item, it is less likely that all purchasers in an affected market will buy it. For example, if manufacturers make their plants out of bricks, and the lifetime of a plant is fifty years, a cartel would have to function for fifty years before every manufacturer in the market fell victim to it. If it existed for only three or four years, as most cartels do, it would have imposed higher costs on only a small percentage of the firms in the market. These firms would have to compete with other firms that were not subject to the cartel.

3. For the relevant formulas, see Landes & Posner, Should Indirect Purchasers Have Standing to Sue Under the Antitrust Laws? An Economic Analysis of the Rule of *Illinois Brick*, 46 U.Chi. L.Rev. 602 (1979).

4. For some suggestions about how courts should deal with pass-on problems in real world markets see Harris & Sullivan, Passing on the Monopoly Overcharge: A Comprehensive Policy Analysis, 128 U.Pa.L.Rev. 269 (1979); Landes & Posner, The Economics of Passing On: A Reply to Harris and Sullivan, 128 U.Pa.L.Rev. 1274 (1980).

5. See Harris & Sullivan, Id. at 279–81. The discussion also assumes that each firm uses a rigid proportion of the cartelized product. This is not always the case: a pizza parlor might respond to a monopoly price increase in anchovies by putting fewer anchovies and more cheese on its pizzas. Likewise, a price-regulated utility might be entitled to pass on to its customers the full amount of any cartel overcharge. However, in response to a cartel price increase in oil, the utility might begin burning less oil and more coal. These possibilities make pass-on much more difficult to calculate. See Cooter, Passing on the Monopoly Overcharge: A Further Comment on Economic Theory, 129 U.Pa.L.Rev. 1523 (1981).

Figures One, Two, and Three illustrate the pass-on problem in three different markets. In each MC represents the marginal cost curve faced by every firm in the market when it purchases the product at a competitive price. MC′ is the higher marginal cost curve each firm faces because of a cartel or monopoly operating at a higher level in the distribution chain.

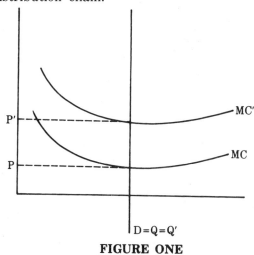

FIGURE ONE

In Figure One the market demand curve is perfectly inelastic—that is, exactly the same number of sales will be made in the entire market when price = MC′ as when price = MC. (Remember, in a competitive market price always tends toward marginal cost.) In such a market a firm could pass on 100% of the overcharge and continue producing at the same rate as it did before the cartel came into existence. It would not be injured by the cartel.

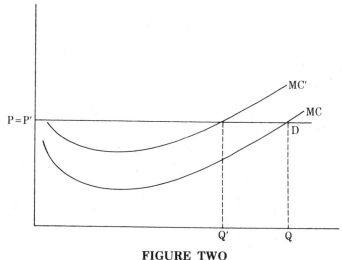

FIGURE TWO

Figure Two illustrates the situation of a single firm whose demand is perfectly elastic: if the price rose by a fractional amount demand would fall to zero.[6] In that case the firm will respond to the cartel price increase by reducing output from Q to Q'. However, it will continue to charge the same price, effectively absorbing the entire monopoly overcharge. None would be passed on to consumers.

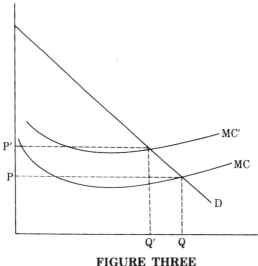

FIGURE THREE

Most real world markets are of the type illustrated in Figure Three. The market demand curve slopes downward, and each firm in the market tends to produce at a level at which its marginal cost equals the market price. When marginal cost is MC, market output is Q and price is P. When the firms must pay a cartel price for a variable cost item, however, their marginal costs rise to MC', output is reduced to Q' and price rises to P'. The reduction in output produces lost profits to the firms, while the increase in price represents that part of the overcharge that is passed on to consumers. Other consumers are injured because they substitute a different product.

Occasionally the demand conditions facing a particular firm resemble Figure One more than Figure Three. Suppose that a direct purchaser executes a 10-year contract to sell 1000 widgets per year at a price 10% higher than its costs. A year later the firm's supplier enters into a cartel and raises the price of an input to monopoly levels. In that case the direct purchaser can pass on the entire monopoly overcharge for purchases under that contract. In fact, the firm will actually make money from its supplier's cartel. Suppose that before the cartel came into existence the firm's costs were $100. It resold the widgets at $100 + 10%, or $110. As a result of the cartel the firm's costs rise to $120. Now it can sell the widgets at

6. Figure Two illustrates the unlikely situation that would occur if a single perfect competitor paid a monopoly overcharge for a product, while all other competitors in the same market bought the product at a competitive price.

$120 + 10%, or $132. The direct purchaser's profits increase from $10 per widget to $12 per widget.

Courts have generally recognized an exception to *Illinois Brick* for *fixed-quantity, fixed-mark-up* contracts that existed *before* the cartel price took effect. Indirect purchasers buying under such contracts can show that the entire monopoly overcharge was passed on to them; hence they should have the action for damages. It follows that the direct purchaser should not have a damages action for purchases and resales made under such contracts.[7]

One caution, however: this exception to the *Illinois Brick* rule applies only when the pre-existing contract is fixed *both* as to mark-up and quantity. If an indirect purchaser has a simple "cost-plus" contract, such as a requirements contract, it will respond to the cartel price increase by reducing the amount it purchases. In that case the direct purchaser will lose profits, and the indirect purchaser's losses will be less than if it were bound to purchase a set quantity. The injury will be shared by the direct purchaser and the indirect purchaser. Some courts have erroneously held that an exception to *Illinois Brick* exists for the "functional equivalent" of a cost-plus contract— usually a rigid formula that the direct purchaser always uses in computing the resale price.[8] Although such a rigid formula satisfies the "fixed-cost" part of the cost-plus contract exception described above, it fails to satisfy the "fixed-quantity" part. Invariably, demand will be reduced when the price rises, and the direct purchaser will make fewer sales. Courts should abandon the notion of a "functional equivalent" to a cost-plus contract, unless they should happen to encounter a formula that dictates *both* mark-up and quantity.

A second important exception to the *Illinois Brick* rule is indirect purchaser actions seeking only an injunction. The measurement difficulties discussed above apply only to calculation of the *amount* of a particular purchaser's damages. The fact of damages can be inferred. Likewise, there is no chance of duplicative recovery: it costs a defendant no more to comply with 10 identical injunctions than to comply with one. Lower courts generally have held that an indirect purchaser may seek an injunction against a cartel.[9]

7. In re Beef Industry Antitrust Litigation, 600 F.2d 1148 (5th Cir. 1979), cert. denied, 449 U.S. 905, 101 S.Ct. 280 (1980), on remand, 542 F.Supp. 1122 (1982), judgment affirmed, 710 F.2d 216 (5th Cir. 1983), rehearing denied, 716 F.2d 901 (5th Cir. 1983), cert. denied, ___ U.S. ___, 104 S.Ct. 1326 (1984); Comment, A Legal and Economic Analysis of the Cost-Plus Contract Exception in *Hanover Shoe* and *Illinois Brick*, 47 U.Chi.L.Rev. 743 (1980).

8. See *Beef*, Id., 600 F.2d at 1165. The plaintiffs were unable to prove that a rigid formula was in fact used, however, and eventually their claim was dismissed. See 710 F.2d 216 (5th Cir. 1983), rehearing denied, 716 F.2d 901 (5th Cir. 1983), cert. denied, ___ U.S. ___, 104 S.Ct. 1326 (1984).

9. Mid-West Paper Products Co. v. Continental Group, Inc., 596 F.2d 573, 589–94 (3d Cir. 1979).

Finally, an exception which is really no exception at all involves a middleman who is really part of the antitrust conspiracy. Suppose a cartel member sells to A, who resells to B, but A is also part of the price fixing conspiracy. B is not really an indirect purchaser, but a direct one. He should have a damages action.[10] One result of such a rule is that indirect purchasers are encouraged to name their direct sellers as co-defendants in order to avoid dismissal at an early stage of the litigation.

Is the indirect purchaser rule a good one? Commentators have argued both sides with great vehemence.[11] Several states responded to *Illinois Brick* by amending their own antitrust statutes to allow damages actions by indirect purchasers.[12] Congress has repeatedly considered legislation that would have done the same, although none has passed.

Attitudes toward the rule track basic ideology very closely. Commentators who believe that antitrust enforcement should be concerned exclusively with efficiency support *Illinois Brick*. Commentators who believe that antitrust should be concerned with full compensation to victims tend to disapprove. Both positions are ideologically consistent. Permitting indirect purchaser actions would magnify the costs of litigation and probably result in overdeterrence.[13] However, the *Illinois Brick* rule clearly deprives injured parties of their claim to damages. In short, the most fundamental evaluation of the indirect purchaser rule rests not on price theory or empirical data, but on basic values.

Remotely related to the indirect purchaser is the buyer injured by "umbrella pricing" made possible by someone else's antitrust violation. Suppose that X, Y & Z fix the price of widgets at $1.50. The competitive price is $1.00. X, Y & Z control 85% of the market and Q, who is not part of the conspiracy, controls the other 15%.

The cartel will create a price "umbrella" under which Q will be able to raise his price to some level just under $1.50 and sell all it can produce.[14] Suppose that P buys widgets from Q at $1.45. Clearly P

---

10. See Arizona v. Shamrock Foods Co., 729 F.2d 1208 (9th Cir.1984); Florida Power Corp. v. Granlund, 78 F.R.D. 441 (M.D.Fla. 1978). Courts apply a similar analysis when the direct purchaser is wholly owned or controlled by the cartel member. Royal Printing Co. v. Kimberly-Clark Corp., 621 F.2d 323 (9th Cir. 1980).

11. See notes 3 and 4 above.

12. See Hovenkamp, State Antitrust in the Federal Scheme, 57 Ind.L.J. 375 (1983).

13. However, in certain cases recognition of indirect purchaser actions actually may result in underdeterrence.

Suppose that the minimum monetary injury a person must suffer before he would bother with a lawsuit is $100. If a direct purchaser were able to have the entire damages action, he could claim $1000 in damages. However, he sold to two distributors who sold to 12 stores, each of whom sold to 50 customers. No one's net injury exceeds $50. Unless a consumer class action is practicable, the defendant might never be sued at all.

14. See § 4.1 above. Eventually the fringe may grow so large that its presence will undermine the cartel. Further, the existence of the fringe performs one valuable social function even while the

has been injured by the cartel. P has no cause of action against Q, for Q has done nothing illegal. Instead P sues X, Y & Z, claiming that their cartel caused P's overcharge injuries.

In Mid-West Paper Products Co. v. Continental Group, Inc.[15] the Third Circuit rejected such a theory as speculative. It then analogized the umbrella claim to the indirect purchaser rule and concluded that computation of damages would present problems analogous to those in computing pass-on in indirect purchaser actions. In the *Beef Industry* [16] antitrust litigation, however, the Fifth Circuit permitted "inverted umbrella" sellers to recover from a buyer's cartel which depressed the wholesale price of beef.

Although some courts have compared umbrella actions with indirect purchaser actions, the similarities between the two are not substantial. Both may yield a form of "duplicative" recovery, but the two forms are quite different from each other. Indirect purchaser damages actions may yield duplicative recoveries when a defendant is forced to pay overcharge damages twice—once to the direct purchaser for the full overcharge and a second time to the indirect purchaser for the passed-on overcharge. The umbrella action, on the other hand, yields a duplicative recovery because the umbrella plaintiff is seeking to recover monies that never accrued to the defendants, but rather to a non-conspiring competitor.

Further, although courts have suggested the contrary, computation of overcharge injuries from umbrella pricing need be no more difficult than computation of overcharge injuries in direct purchaser actions. Assuming that X, Y, Z and Q all operate in the same market and produce fungible products, they would have the same competitive price. A direct purchaser from X, Y or Z would have to show the difference between the competitive price and the price he actually paid. A purchaser from noncartel member Q would have to show precisely the same thing. The fact that Q may have charged a lower price than the cartel will not complicate computation: P will merely be able to recover the difference between the competitive price—which is the same for Q as it is for X, Y, and Z—and the price Q actually charged.

Denial of umbrella actions may be the appropriate rule. However, the rule rests not on the premise that the damages are unusually difficult to compute, or that the plaintiff will recover profits that never accrued to the defendants. Rather, it should rest on the premise that if direct purchaser actions for treble damages provide

cartel exists. The existence of any fringe, no matter how inefficient, will reduce the cartel's profit-maximizing price. See Note, Standing At the Fringe: Antitrust Damages and the Fringe Producer, 35 Stan.L.Rev. 763, 773 (1983).

15. 596 F.2d 573, 583–87 (3d Cir. 1979). See also Calif. v. Standard Oil Co., 691 F.2d 1335 (9th Cir. 1982), cert. denied, — U.S. —, 104 S.Ct. 972 (1984).

16. See note 7 above.

sufficient deterrence, recognition of umbrella actions would result in overdeterrence.[17]

 WESTLAW REFERENCES

"indirect purchaser" /p damages /p overcharg*** pass***

"indirect purchaser" /p damages /p cost-plus (fix*** +1 mark quantity) ("functional equivalent")

"indirect purchaser" /p enjoin*** injuncti**

umbrella /2 anti-competiti** claim invert*** pric***

"hanover shoe" /s "united shoe" (392 +3 481)

"illinois brick" /s 431 +3 720

---

§ 14.5   Antitrust Injury

In the 1970's federal antitrust policy underwent a comprehensive ideological transformation. Perhaps no legal doctrine displays that change more transparently than the "antitrust injury" rule of Brunswick Corp. v. Pueblo Bowl-O-Mat, Inc.[1] The potential of the antitrust injury doctrine is still not completely realized, and there is no telling how far the Supreme Court will push it.

In *Brunswick* a firm challenged the merger of two of its competitors under § 7 of the Clayton Act. The plaintiff owned several bowling alleys and the defendant was a major national manufacturer of bowling equipment and an owner of several alleys. It sold bowling equipment to independent alleys on credit, and sometimes acquired independent alleys that were in financial trouble. Over a ten-year period the defendant had taken over several defaulting alleys that competed with the plaintiff. Most of these acquired alleys would probably have gone out of business if they had not been acquired by Brunswick. The plaintiff claimed that its market share would have increased had the competing alleys been permitted to go out of business.

The plaintiff's theory of action reaches the heart of the debate about whom the antitrust laws should protect: competition and consumers, or competitors. Horizontal mergers have the capacity to cause two different kinds of injury. First, mergers can facilitate monopolistic or collusive pricing by increasing concentration in the market. Consumers will pay higher prices; however, the post-merger firm's output reduction and price increase will benefit other firms already in the market, which probably will be able to charge higher prices under the "umbrella" created by the larger, post-merger firm.

---

17. See Landes, Optimal Sanctions for Antitrust Violations, 50 U.Chi.L.Rev. 652, 668 n. 30 (1983). For an argument that actions by umbrella purchasers would not result in overdeterrence and should be permitted, see Blair & Maurer, Umbrella Pricing and Antitrust Standing: An Economic Analysis, 1982 Utah L.Rev. 763.

§ 14.5

1. 429 U.S. 477, 97 S.Ct. 690 (1977).

Second, mergers can increase the efficiency of the merging partners. Increased efficiency benefits consumers but invariably injures
competitors. The plaintiff in *Brunswick* formerly had a languishing,
spiritless rival. After the merger it faced a rejuvenated and aggressive competitor. Whether or not the merger was illegal, the plaintiff's injury was caused by the post-merger firm's increased efficiency, not by the market's increased proclivity toward monopoly pricing.

In denying recovery the Supreme Court observed that many
antitrust violations could cause "losses which are of no concern to the
antitrust laws." In order to recover a plaintiff must show not only
that an antitrust law has been violated and the plaintiff injured. It
must also show "*antitrust* injury, which is to say injury of the type
the antitrust laws were intended to prevent and that flows from that
which makes defendants' acts unlawful." Such an injury should
"reflect the anticompetitive effect * * * of the violation
* * *."[2]

The antitrust injury doctrine applies only to private antitrust
actions. The *Brunswick* Court contrasted the "prophylactic" nature
of Clayton § 7 with the "remedial" nature of § 4, the provision
authorizing private damages actions. § 7 was designed to reach
mergers while the danger to competition was in its "incipiency," and
somewhat uncertain.[3] § 4, however, requires a private plaintiff to
show monetary injury. Since the merger contains two different
potentials for injury—one from the post-merger firm's increased
market power and the other from its increased efficiency—it becomes
important for the plaintiff to identify how it was injured.

Brunswick's contrast of § 7's prophylactic reach with the remedial nature of § 4 suggested that the antitrust injury doctrine applied
only to mergers, not to other antitrust violations.[4] In J. Truett Payne
Co. v. Chrysler Motor Corp.,[5] however, the Supreme Court applied the
doctrine to a private action alleging illegal price discrimination under
the Robinson-Patman Act.

The Robinson-Patman Act contains the same prophylactic language as Clayton § 7—it condemns price discrimination which "may
* * * substantially * * * lessen competition or tend to create
a monopoly * * *." But what about antitrust violations whose
immediate injury is much more apparent, such as *per se* violations of
§ 1 of the Sherman Act? At least one circuit has decided that "the
case will be quite rare in which a *per se* violation of the Sherman Act

2. Id. at 489, 97 S.Ct. at 697.

3. See §§ 7.3 & 11.3 above.

4. See Engine Specialties, Inc. v.
Bombardier Ltd., 605 F.2d 1 (1st Cir.
1979), on rehearing, 615 F.2d 575 (1st
Cir. 1980), cert. denied, 446 U.S. 983, 100
S.Ct. 2964 (1980), rehearing denied, 449
U.S. 893, 101 S.Ct. 259 (1980).

5. 451 U.S. 557, 101 S.Ct. 1923 (1981),
on remand, 670 F.2d 575 (5th Cir. 1982),
rehearing denied, 677 F.2d 117 (11th Cir.
1982), cert. denied, 459 U.S. 908, 103
S.Ct. 212 (1982). See Hovenkamp, Market Power and Secondary-Line Differential Pricing, 71 Geo.L.J. 1157 (1983).

does not cause [antitrust] injury." Therefore antitrust injury should be presumed in such cases.[6] In Blue Shield of Virginia v. McCready the Supreme Court came close to agreeing. It found that the plaintiff, who was not the target of an alleged concerted refusal to deal but whose injury was a necessary byproduct, had suffered antitrust injury.[7]

Any rule presuming antitrust injury in *per se* cases must be used carefully, for even *per se* violations can create efficiencies. For example, a joint venture of physicians which includes an agreement about the maximum fees the physicians will charge might be condemned as price fixing under the *per se* rule.[8] If the physicians were sued by a competitor who was injured because she had to compete with the defendants' lower fees, however, the defendants should prevail under *Brunswick*. The plaintiff was not injured by price fixing but by the increased efficiency that resulted from the joint venture.

Many practices illegal under the antitrust laws produce compensating efficiencies. Courts condemn them either because the anticompetitive effects are clear, while the efficiencies are ambiguous and incapable of measurement, or else because the anticompetitive effects appear to outweigh the efficiencies. Mergers and joint ventures in particular may simultaneously create efficiencies and increase the market power of the participating firms. Vertical integration, whether by contract or by merger, has an even greater capacity to produce efficiencies, and an even smaller potential to be anticompetitive.[9]

Increased market power creates a social cost while increased efficiency creates a social gain. Both, however, can impose private losses. To characterize a certain practice as "efficient" is not to conclude that the practice benefits everyone, but only that the benefits are greater than the injuries.[10] As a general rule increased market power injures purchasers while it benefits competitors. However, increased efficiency benefits purchasers while it injures competitors or potential competitors.

Private plaintiffs are generally not concerned with the social cost or value of a particular practice. They sue in order to vindicate their own private losses. Substantive liability under the antitrust laws is

---

6. Lee-Moore Oil Co. v. Union Oil of California, 599 F.2d 1299, 1303 (4th Cir. 1979). However, see Murphy Tugboat Co. v. Crowley, 454 F.Supp. 847, 851–52 (N.D.Cal.1978), holding that the antitrust injury doctrine applies to all suits for treble damages.

7. 457 U.S. 465, 102 S.Ct. 2540, 2549 (1982). See § 14.3 above.

8. See Arizona v. Maricopa County Medical Society, 457 U.S. 332, 102 S.Ct. 2466 (1982). See § 4.4 above.

9. See §§ 4.3, 11.2, & 7.2 above.

10. This is because the standard for efficiency in antitrust policy is not Pareto efficiency, but potential Pareto, or Kalder-Hicks efficiency. See Hovenkamp, Distributive Justice and the Antitrust Laws, 51 Geo.Wash.L.Rev. 1, 8–12 (1982); and see § 2.3 above.

often based on a rather tentative prediction that the net effect of the condemned practice will be a social cost. The private plaintiff seeking damages, however, must show *how* it was injured. If the antitrust laws are not to be grossly overdeterrent, enforcement must be calculated to compensate for the social costs of the defendant's acts, not to remedy private injuries caused by increased efficiency. Any other rule would deter firms from engaging in practices whose potential for efficiency is clear but whose legality is ambiguous.[11]

 WESTLAW REFERENCES

"antitrust injury" /p (clayton /5 4 7) "joint venture" merg***
"antitrust injury" /s how incipien** manner "per se"
brunswick /s bowl-o-mat (97 +3 690)

§ 14.6 Contribution Among Joint Violators

Contribution is the right of one guilty defendant to force other participants in the same offense to pay a share of the damages award. Many states have adopted contribution rules for tort law, either by statute or by common law rule.[1] In Texas Industries., Inc. v. Radcliff Materials, Inc.,[2] however, the Supreme Court decided that neither the antitrust statutes nor the federal common law implied a right to contribution in federal antitrust cases. The current antitrust rule, therefore, is that a single defendant may have to pay the entire damages award, even though several co-conspirators participated in the violation that caused the plaintiff's injury.

The wisdom of a contribution rule in antitrust has been controversial, with a fair amount of literature on both sides of the question.[3] This debate has been rendered moot by the *Texas Industries* decision, at least temporarily. Congress continues to consider contribution legislation, however, and thus the issue deserves at least brief consideration.

The current rule of no contribution injects a certain amount of arbitrariness into private enforcement of the antitrust laws. Theoretically, at the plaintiff's whim one defendant can be held liable for far more than treble the damages that it caused. Another, equally at fault, goes away free. This has prompted arguments that a no contribution rule is overdeterrent, because under it a single firm may be liable for very large damages. The answer, of course, is an argument that a no contribution rule is really underdeterrent, because some firms known to be guilty will not have to pay anything.

---

11. See Hovenkamp, Merger Actions For Damages, 35 Hastings L.J. (1984).

§ 14.6

1. See W. Keeton, D. Dobbs, R. Keeton & D. Owen, Prosser & Keeton on Torts § 50 (5th ed. 1984).

2. 451 U.S. 630, 101 S.Ct. 2061 (1981).

3. See Polinsky & Shavell, Contribution and Claim Reduction Among Antitrust Defendants: An Economic Analysis, 33 Stan.L.Rev. 447 (1981).

Both of the above judgments can be made only after the fact, however. At the time a firm decides whether to commit an antitrust violation it does not know whether it will have to pay damages for an injury actually caused by a co-conspirator, or whether the co-conspirator will have to pay. However, a no contribution rule may distort antitrust enforcement to the disadvantage of some potential defendants and the advantage of others. For example, if plaintiffs generally sue the largest available defendant rather than the smaller ones, the effect of a no contribution rule would be overdeterrence with respect to large firms and underdeterrence with respect to small ones. To date, however, there is no convincing evidence that the no contribution rule systematically favors any identifiable groups of potential defendants.

However, the no contribution rule of *Texas Industries* reduces the overall costs of antitrust enforcement by encouraging defendants to settle before trial.[4] For example, suppose that X, Y, and Z are co-conspirators sued by P. X, Y, and Z predict that if P wins it will collect $6,000,000 in damages, and that P's chances of winning are 50%. For each defendant the expected liability is $1,000,000 (one-third of 50% of $6,000,000). The value of P's expected award is $3,000,000.

If X settles with P for $1,000,000 the law of claim reduction provides that P's future award will be reduced by that amount, to $5,000,000. P still has a 50% chance of winning. Now the expected liability of Y and Z is $1,250,000 (each has a 50% chance of paying the $5,000,000 judgment, and there is a 50% chance that it will have to be paid). The first settlor comes out better than the two other firms.

The second settlor will come out second best. The expected liability to firms Y and Z is $1,250,000 each. P's expected recovery is $2,500,000 ($5,000,000 discounted by the 50% chance it will lose). Now suppose that Y settles for $1,250,000. If P later recovers from Z, the $5,000,000 will be reduced to $3,750,000 to reflect the settlement with Y. Z's expected liability is $1,875,000.

The result will be a race among the parties to settle. The eagerness of the defendants to settle first may yield higher settlements than would occur otherwise. In the example above, for instance, the first settlor will pay $1,000,000, while the second settlor can expect to pay $1,250,000. The firms will bid against each other to be the first settlor, and the initial settlement may well be more than $1,000,000. Once the first defendant has settled, the remaining defendants will bid against each other for the right to settle next.

A contribution rule, depending on its type, can discourage defendants from settling. In the same case, suppose that X settles early for $1,000,000, leaving P with a 50% chance of recovering $5,000,000

---

4. See Easterbrook, Landes & Posner, Contribution Among Antitrust Defendants: A Legal and Economic Analysis, 23 J.L. & Econ. 331 (1980).

from Y and Z. If Y ends up paying a $5,000,000 damages award, Y will have a cause of action against Z for $2,000,000 and against X for $1,000,000 (that is, for an amount such that the total payment of all three defendants is the same.) In this case Y's and Z's expected loss is $1,000,000 each, after discounting for the 50% likelihood of P's success. X, however, is in a less fortunate position. The $1,000,000 already paid is sunk costs that it is certain to lose. Its expected additional losses are $500,000, giving it expected total losses of $1,500,000. A contribution rule that does not create a special incentive for early settlement can make early settlors worse off (disregarding litigation costs) than nonsettlors. Thus any contribution rule that does not create an exception for early settlors is calculated to increase the costs of private antitrust enforcement.[5]

Finally, any right of contribution in antitrust cases will impose one additional social cost—the cost of litigating the contribution claims themselves. If its guilt has not been established in a prior proceeding to which it was a party, a defendant in a contribution case may still defend on the merits. A formula will still have to be developed for computing the relative liability of each co-conspirator. One possibility, for example, is liability in proportion to market share. However, such a rule would force the parties to a contribution case to determine a relevant market and calculate each co-defendant's share of it, even though this determination may not have been made in the earlier proceeding.

Most arguments for a right of contribution in antitrust rest on the lack of fairness or justice in any rule that forces one guilty party to pay for the offenses of another party who is equally guilty. If consumer welfare and efficiency are the principle goals of antitrust, however, the current rule of no right of contribution among antitrust defendants may be a good one, for it achieves the same total level of deterrence and reduces litigation costs.

 WESTLAW REFERENCES
contribution /p damages /p antitrust co-conspirator co-defendant

---

5. The incentive to settle can be restored by a contribution rule that frees any settling defendant from future contribution liability. Some states apply such rules to torts defendants who settle in good faith. See West's Ann.Calif. Code Civ.Proc. § 877. This is in effect a no contribution rule for good faith settlors.

APPENDIX A

WESTLAW REFERENCES

Analysis

The WESTLAW System

WESTLAW is a computer-assisted legal research service of West Publishing Company. WESTLAW is accessible through several alternative public communications networks. The materials available from WESTLAW are contained in databases stored at a central computer in St. Paul, Minnesota.

The WESTLAW user sends a query, or message, to the computer where it is processed and documents are identified that satisfy the search request. The text of the retrieved documents is then stored on magnetic disks and transmitted to the user. The data moves through a telecommunication network. The user sees the documents on a video display terminal. When the documents appear on the terminal the user can decide whether or not further research is desired. If another search is necessary, the query may be recalled for editing, or an entirely new query may be sent to the computer.

379

Documents displayed on the terminal may be printed out or, on some terminals, the text may be stored on its own magnetic disks.

In addition to the extensive state and federal case law libraries to which the preformulated queries in this hornbook are primarily addressed, WESTLAW provides access to many specialized libraries. For example, WESTLAW contains separate topical databases for areas of federal law such as tax, patents, copyrights, securities, bankruptcy, communications, labor, first amendment constitutional law, military justice, admiralty, and government contracts. A topical database of especial interest to readers of this treatise containing federal antitrust and business regulation documents has also been created. WESTLAW also includes the text of the United States Code and the Code of Federal Regulations, the Federal Register, West's INSTA–CITE™, Shepard's® Citations, *Black's Law Dictionary*, and many other legal sources.

Improving Legal Research with WESTLAW

Traditional legal research begins with the examination of texts, treatises, case digests, encyclopedias, citators, annotated law reports, looseleaf services, and periodicals. These secondary sources of the law provide compilations and summaries of authoritative material contained in primary legal sources. The goal of legal research is to analyze and interpret these primary sources.

In their familiar printed form, such primary sources appear in the state and regional reporters, federal reporters, and in statutory codes and administrative materials. In WESTLAW, these documents are extensively represented in electronic databases, or libraries.

WESTLAW permits access to the many cases that do not get indexed or digested into manual systems of secondary legal sources. With WESTLAW it is possible to index any significant term or combination of terms in an almost unlimited variety of grammatical relationships with other terms by formulating a query composed of those terms.

WESTLAW queries may be made as broad or as specific as desired, depending upon the context of the legal issue to be researched. WESTLAW queries add a dynamic aspect to this treatise. Since new cases are continuously being added to the WESTLAW databases as they are decided by the courts, the addition of queries provides a type of self-contained updating service to the publication. Since a query may be addressed to the entire range of cases contained in the database designated for a search—from the earliest decisions to the most recent—the search results obtained from WESTLAW reflect the most current law available on any given issue.

In addition, WESTLAW queries augment the customary role of footnotes to the treatise text by directing the user to a wider range of supporting authorities.　Readers may use the preformulated queries supplied in this edition "as is" or formulate their own queries in order to retrieve cases relevant to the points of law discussed in the text.

Query Formulation: (a) What a WESTLAW Query Is

The query is a message to WESTLAW.　It instructs the computer to retrieve documents containing terms in the grammatical relationships specified by the query.　The terms in a query are made up of words and/or numbers that pinpoint the legal issue to be researched.

An example of the kind of preformulated queries that appear in this publication is reproduced below.　The queries corresponding to each section of the text appear at the end of the section.

　　potential　+1　competit! entrant　/p　target　/p　merger

The query is taken from chapter 12, section 12.4.　The query, or question, that is directed to WESTLAW appears at the end of the section of the text.　This query is asking WESTLAW to find documents containing the term POTENTIAL followed within one term by either a form of COMPETITION or the term ENTRANT, within the same paragraph as the term TARGET, and within the same paragraph as the term MERGER.

This query illustrates what a standard request to WESTLAW looks like—words or numbers describing an issue, tied together by connectors.　These connectors tell WESTLAW in what relationships the terms must appear.　WESTLAW will retrieve all documents from the database that contain the terms appearing in those relationships.

The material that follows explains the methods by which WESTLAW queries are formulated, and shows how users of *Economics and Federal Antitrust Law* can employ the preformulated queries in this publication in their research of antitrust law.　In addition, there are instructions that will enable readers to modify their queries to fit the particular needs of their research.

Query Formulation: (b) Proximity Connectors

Proximity connectors allow search terms to be ordered so that relevant documents will be retrieved from WESTLAW.　The connectors and their meanings appear below.

Space (or).　A space between search terms means "or".　Leaving a space between the query terms MONOPOLY and OLIGOPOLY

　　monopoly oligopoly

instructs the computer to retrieve documents that contain either the word MONOPOLY or the word OLIGOPOLY (or both).

& (and) or (ampersand).　The & symbol means "and".　Placing the & between two terms instructs the computer to retrieve documents that contain both of the terms.　The terms on either side may

be in reverse order. For example, if the & is inserted between the terms MERGER and EFFICIENCY

    merger & efficiency

the computer will retrieve documents containing both the word MERGER and the word EFFICIENCY in the same document. In any such retrieved document, the word MERGER may either precede or follow the word EFFICIENCY. The & may be placed between groups of alternative terms. For example, placing the & between MERGER or CONSOLIDATION and EFFICIENCY or PROFICIEN-CY

    merger consolidation & efficiency proficiency

instructs the computer to retrieve documents in which the terms MERGER or CONSOLIDATION (or both) and EFFICIENCY or PROFICIENCY (or both) appear in the same document.

/p (same paragraph). The /p symbol means "within the same paragraph." It requires that terms to the left of the /p appear within the same paragraph as terms to the right of the connector. For example, placing a /p between the terms INTENT and EX-CLUDE

    intent /p exclude

will instruct the computer to retrieve documents in which INTENT and EXCLUDE occur in the same paragraph. The terms on each side of the /p may appear in the document in any order within the paragraph. As with &, the /p connector may be placed between groups of alternative terms. Thus, the query

    intent motivation /p exclude prevent

will command the retrieval of all documents in which the words INTENT or MOTIVATION (or both) occur in the same paragraph as the words EXCLUDE or PREVENT (or both).

/s (same sentence). The /s symbol requires that one or more search terms on each side of the /s appear in the same sentence. If a /s is placed between the words PREDATORY and PRICING

    predatory /s pricing

the computer is instructed to retrieve documents that have the word PREDATORY and the word PRICING in the same sentence, without regard to which of these words occurs first in the sentence.

The /s may be placed between groups of alternative terms. Adding the terms ANTICOMPETITIVE and CHARGES to the above example

    predatory anticompetitive /s pricing charges

instructs the computer to retrieve documents with either the words PREDATORY or ANTICOMPETITIVE (or both) within the same sentence as either the word PRICING or CHARGES (or both) regardless of which terms appear first.

+s (precedes within sentence). The +s symbol requires that one or more terms to the left of the +s precede one or more terms to the right of the +s within the same sentence. The query

    express +s agreement

instructs the computer to retrieve all documents in which the word EXPRESS precedes the term AGREEMENT in the same sentence. The +s connector, like the other connectors, may be used between groups of alternative terms. Thus, the query

    express tacit +s agreement collusion

instructs the computer to retrieve all documents in which either the word EXPRESS or TACIT (or both), precedes the terms AGREEMENT or COLLUSION (or both) in the same sentence.

/n (numerical proximity—within n words). The /n symbol means "within n words," where n represents any whole number between 1 and 255, inclusive. It requires that terms to the left of the /n appear within the designated number of words as terms to the right of the connector. For example, placing a /4 between the terms EXCLUSIONARY and PRACTICE

    exclusionary /4 practice

instructs the computer to retrieve all documents in which the term EXCLUSIONARY occurs within four words of the term PRACTICE. Numerical proximities may also be used between groups of alternative search terms. In addition, the + symbol may be used to require that terms to the left of the numerical proximity symbol precede the terms to the right of the symbol. Thus, placing the +2 symbol between the words HORIZONTAL or VERTICAL and MERGER

    horizontal vertical +2 merger

instructs the computer to retrieve cases in which the words HORIZONTAL or VERTICAL occur within two words preceeding the word MERGER.

"_____" (quotation marks/phrase). The "_____" (quotation marks/phrase) symbol can be thought of as the most restrictive grammatical connector. Placing terms within quotation marks instructs the computer to retrieve all documents in which the terms appear in the precise proximity (i.e., contiguousness) and order that they have within the quotation marks. For example, placing the following terms within quotation marks

    "market power"

instructs the computer to retrieve all documents in which the term MARKET appears adjacent to, and precedes, the term POWER.

This technique of query formulation is effective when used to search legal terms of art, legal concepts, or legal entities that occur together as multiple terms. Some examples are: "per se", "clayton act" and "four-firm concentration ratio."

% (exclusion). The % symbol means "but not." It instructs the computer to exclude documents that contain terms appearing after

the % symbol. For example, to retrieve documents containing the terms WITNESS and TESTIMONY within the same sentence, but not the term EXPERT within the same sentence as TESTIMONY, the following query would be used:

```
witness  /s  testimony  %  expert  /s  testimony
```

Query Formulation: (c) The TRAC Method

The acronym "TRAC" is a convenient mnemonic device for a systematic approach to query formulation on WESTLAW. "TRAC" stands for Terms, Roots, Alternatives, and Connectors. This step-by-step method is explained below.

T Terms. After determining the legal issue that is to be researched, the first step in query formulation is to select the key terms from the issue that will be used as search terms in the query. Words, numbers, and various other symbols may be used as search terms.

The goal in choosing search terms is to select the most unique terms for the issue. In selecting such terms it is frequently helpful to imagine how the terms might appear in the language of the documents that will be searched by the query. Moreover, it is necessary to consider the grammatical and editorial structure of the document. This involves a consideration of how the writer of the document (i.e., judge or headnote and synopsis writer) has worded both the factual and legal components of the issue involved in the case.

Although traditional book research generally starts with a consideration of the general legal concepts under which particular problems are subsumed, WESTLAW research starts with a consideration of specific terms that are likely to appear in documents that have addressed those problems. This is so because documents are retrieved from WESTLAW on the basis of the terms they contain. Accordingly, the more precisely terms that will single out the desired documents can be identified, the more relevant the search results will be.

R Root Expansion (!) and Universal Character (*). When constructing queries it is necessary to consider various forms of the search terms that are selected. Derivative forms of words should be anticipated due to the variety of ways in which the language in a document may be worded. There are two devices available on WESTLAW for automatically generating alternative forms of search terms in a query. One device is an unlimited root expansion. Placement of the ! symbol at the end of the root term generates other forms containing the root. For example, attaching the ! symbol to the root term MONOPOL in the following query:

```
monopol!  /16  "rule of reason"
```

instructs the computer to generate the words MONOPOLY, MONOP-
OLIES, MONOPOLIST, MONOPOLISTIC, and MONOPOLIZATION
as search terms for the query. This saves time and space that would
otherwise be consumed in typing each of the alternative words in the
query.

The other device permits the generation of all possible characters
from a designated part of a term. This is done by placing one or
more * symbols at the location in the term where the universal
character is desired. For example, placing three * symbols on the
root REFUS in the following query

refus *** /4 deal

instructs the computer to generate all forms of the root term with up
to three additional characters. Thus, the words REFUSE, RE-
FUSES, REFUSED, REFUSAL, and REFUSING would be generated
by this query. The * symbol may also be embedded inside of a term
as in the following query:

standing /s s****holder /p "clayton act"

This will generate the alternative terms STOCKHOLDER and
SHAREHOLDER without the need to enter both synonymous terms.

WESTLAW automatically generates standard plural forms for
search terms (e.g., the endings –s –es and –ies) so it is generally
unnecessary to use the root expansion devices to obtain plural forms
of search terms.

A Alternative Terms. Once the initial search terms have been
selected for a query, it is important to consider synonyms, antonyms,
and other alternatives for the search terms. The nature of the legal
issue will determine which terms are desirable.

Note that a space, which means "or" in WESTLAW, should be left
between search terms and their alternatives.

C Connectors. The next step in query formulation is to consider
the appropriate grammatical context in which the search terms will
appear.

Place one of the proximity connectors discussed earlier between
the search terms and their alternatives to instruct the computer to
retrieve documents containing those search terms in the specified
proximity.

Query Formulation: (d) General Principles of Query Formulation

The art of query formulation is the heart of WESTLAW research.
Although the researcher can gain technical skills by using the terminal, there is no strictly mechanical procedure for formulating queries.
One must first comprehend the meaning of the legal issue to be
researched before beginning a search on WESTLAW. Then the user
will need to supply imagination, insight, and legal comprehension
with knowledge of the capabilities of WESTLAW to formulate a

useful query. Effective query formulation requires an alternative way of thinking about the legal research process.

Using WESTLAW is a constant balancing between generating too many documents and missing important documents. In general, it is better to look through a reasonable number of irrelevant documents than it is to be too restrictive and miss important material. The researcher should take into consideration at the initial query formulation stage what he or she will do if too many, or not enough documents are retrieved. Thought should be given as to how the query might be narrowed or the search broadened, and what can be done if the initial search retrieves zero documents.

Some issues by their very nature will require more lengthy queries than others; however, it is best to strive for efficiency in structuring the query. Look for unique search terms that will eliminate the need for a lengthy query. Keep in mind that WESTLAW is literal. Consider all possible alternative terms. Remember that searching is done by syntactic structure and not by legal concepts.

Always keep in mind the parameters of the system as to date and database content. Especially consider inherent limitations of the computer. It doesn't think, create, or make analogies. The researcher must do that for the computer. All that the computer does is look for the terms in the documents in relationships specified by the query. The researcher should know what he or she is looking for, at least to the extent of knowing how the terms are likely to show up in relevant documents.

The *WESTLAW Reference Manual* should be consulted for more information on query formulation and WESTLAW commands. The *Reference Manual* is updated periodically to reflect new enhancements of WESTLAW. It provides detailed and comprehensive instructions on all aspects of the WESTLAW system and offers numerous illustrative examples on the proper format for various types of queries. Material contained in the *Reference Manual* enables the user to benefit from all of the system's capabilities in an effective and efficient manner.

Search Techniques: (a) Field Searching

Documents in WESTLAW are divided into separate sections called fields. The computer can be instructed to search for terms within designated fields. This technique is known as field searching. The fields available for WESTLAW case law databases are described below.

Title Field. The title field contains the title of the case (e.g., *Bigelow v. RKO Radio Pictures, Inc.*).

Citation Field. The citation field contains the citation of the case (e.g., 66 S.Ct. 574).

Court Field. The court field contains abbreviations that allow searches for case law to be restricted to particular states, districts, or courts.

Judge Field. The judge field contains the names of judges or justices who wrote either an individual or a majority opinion.

Synopsis Field. The synopsis field contains the synopsis of the case, prepared by West editors.

Topic Field. The topic field contains the West Digest Topic name and number, the Key Number, and the text of the Key line for each digest paragraph.

Digest Field. The digest field contains digest paragraphs prepared by West editors. It includes headnotes, corresponding Digest Topics and Key Numbers, the title and citation of the case, courts, and year of decision.

Headnote Field. The headnote field contains the language of the headnotes, exclusive of the Digest Topic and Key Number lines and case identification information.

Opinion Field. The opinion field contains the text of the case, court and docket numbers, names of attorneys appearing in the case, and judges participating in the decision.

The format for a query that will instruct the computer to search for terms only within specified fields consists of the field name followed by a set of parentheses containing the search terms and proximity connectors, if any. For example, to retrieve the case appearing at 66 S.Ct. 574, the citation field, followed by a set of parentheses containing the volume and page numbers of the citation separated by the +3 connector may be used:

    citation(66 +3 574)

Correspondingly, to retrieve the case entitled *Bigelow v. RKO Radio Pictures, Inc.*, the title field, followed by a set of parentheses containing the names of the title separated by the & connector may be used:

    title(bigelow & "rko radio")

Terms may be searched in clusters of fields by joining any number of field names by commas. One application of this technique is to search for terms in the combined synopsis and digest fields. This technique is illustrated below:

    synopsis,digest (monopol! unilateral** /p refus*** /2 deal sell)

In this example, the descriptive terms in the query are searched in the synopsis and digest fields simultaneously.

Field Browsing

In reviewing the documents that have been retrieved in a search, the user may instruct the computer only to display specified fields. This technique is known as field browsing. When a search has been completed, enter the command: f. You will then view a list of the fields available for browsing. Enter the corresponding number to view WESTLAW document displays limited to the selected field(s).

The *WESTLAW Reference Manual* should be consulted for further instruction on using WESTLAW fields for searching or browsing.

Search Techniques: (b) Date Restrictions

Queries may be restricted to retrieve documents appearing before, after, or on a specified date, or within a range of dates. The date restriction format consists of the word DATE followed by the appropriate restriction(s) within parentheses. The words BEFORE and AFTER may be used to designate the desired date relationships. Alternatively, the abbreviations BEF and AFT, or the symbols $<$ and $>$ may be used. Moreover, the month and day and year may be spelled out (e.g., January 1, 1984) or they may be abbreviated as follows: 1–1–84, or 1/1/84. The date restriction is joined to the rest of the query by the & proximity connector. For example, to retrieve documents decided or issued after March 23, 1966 that discuss cost justification under the Robinson-Patman Act, any of the following formats can be used:

```
robinson-patman  /p  "cost justification"  /s  defense  &  date(after 3/23/66)

robinson-patman  /p  "cost justification"  /s  defense  &  date(aft march 23,
   1966)

robinson-patman  /p  "cost justification"  /s  defense  &  date( > 3–23–66)
```

To retrieve documents decided after March 23, 1966 and before February 22, 1979 the following format could be used:

```
robinson-patman  /p  "cost justification"  /s  defense  &  date(aft mar 23, 1966
   and bef feb 22, 1979)
```

Search Techniques: (c) Digest Topic and Key Number Searching

Searches may be performed using West Digest Topic and Key Numbers as search terms. When this strategy is used, the search term consists of a West Digest Topic Number followed by the letter k, (or the ☞ symbol available on WALT keyboards), followed by a Key Number classified as a subheading under the Digest Topic and Key Number. For example, to retrieve cases that contain the Digest Topic classification for Monopolies (Digest Topic Number 265) and Key Number for Injunctions as a remedy to prevent or restrain unlawful combinations (Key Number 24(7)), the following queries could be used:

```
265k24(7)
```

or

```
265☞24(7)
```

A complete list of Digest Topics and their numerical equivalents appears in the *WESTLAW Reference Manual* and is also available on-line in the WESTLAW Database Directory.

Using WESTLAW as a Citator

Legal Research frequently entails finding decisions that apply to specific sections of statutes, or to other court decisions. WESTLAW can be used to retrieve documents that contain citations or reference to such authority. Because citation styles are not always uniform, special care must be taken to identify variant forms of citations.

Retrieving Cases that Cite Code and Statute Sections

Court decisions that cite to sections of codes or statutes are retrievable by including the section number in the query. For example, to retrieve cases that cite section 13(f) of the Robinson-Patman Act, 15 U.S.C. 13, the following query could be used:

    headnote(15 +5 13(f))

Because the headnotes to decisions published in West Reporters cite statutory references, it is useful to use the headnote field to find case law citations to specific statutory sections. When searching documents that may not contain headnotes, simply omit the headnote field restriction. Unless the statutory section has a unique citation number such that the number is unlikely to appear as anything other than the citation, add descriptive terms to the citation as in this example:

    15 +5 13(f) & induc*** /s price /3 discriminat***

Search techniques similar to those described above can be used to find citations to sections of the Code of Federal Regulations or documents contained in the Federal Register.

Retrieving Cases that Cite Other Court Decisions

WESTLAW can be used as a citator of other court decisions if the title of the decision, its citation, or both, are known. When only the title of the case is known, use the following format:

    bigelow /5 "rko radio"

This query instructs the computer to retrieve all documents that have cited the case of *Bigelow v. RKO Radio Pictures, Inc.* The /5 numerical connector requires that the word BIGELOW occur within five words of the phrase "RKO RADIO".

If the citation of the case is known, a query may be constructed that will retrieve documents that have cited the case. This is done by using the numbers of the citation as search terms in the query. For example, to retrieve cases that have cited to *Bigelow* by its citation, 66 S.Ct. 574, use the following format:

    66 /3 574

If both the citation and the case title are known, the following formats may be used:

    bigelow /5 "rko radio" /15 66 /3 574

or

    bigelow /15 66 /3 574

In the first example above the computer is instructed to retrieve all documents that contain the terms BIGELOW, "RKO RADIO", 66 and

574 within the number of words designated by the numerical connectors separating each term. This query would retrieve all documents that contain the full citation: *Bigelow v. RKO Radio Pictures, Inc.*, 66 S.Ct. 574. The query in the second example above could be used if the name of only one party was known.

The date restriction may be utilized to retrieve documents that cite cases within a given year, range of years, or before or after a given date. For example, for cases citing *Bigelow* in 1976, this query could be used:

    bigelow /5 "rko radio" & date(1976)

Shepard's® Citations on WESTLAW

From any point in WESTLAW, case citations may be entered to retrieve Shepard's listings for those citations. To enter a citation to be Shepardized, the following format is used:

    sh 392 u.s. 481

or

    sh 392 us 481

or

    sh392us481

When the citation is entered, Shepard's listings for the citation will be displayed. To shepardize a citation it is not necessary to be in the same database as that of the citation. For example, a Supreme Court citation may be entered from the Pacific Reporter database.

West's INSTA–CITE™

INSTA–CITE, West Publishing Company's case history system, allows users to quickly verify the accuracy of case citations and the validity of decisions. It contains prior and subsequent case histories in sequential listings, parallel citations and precedential treatment.

Some examples of the kind of direct case history provided by INSTA–CITE are: "affirmed," "certiorari denied," "decision reversed and remanded," and "judgment vacated." A complete list of INSTA–CITE case history and precedential treatment notations appears in the *WESTLAW Reference Manual*.

An example of an INSTA–CITE reference from this hornbook appears below. The format for instaciting a case citation consists of the letters IC followed by the citation, with or without spaces and periods:

    ic 431 u.s. 720

or

    ic 431 us 720

or

    ic 431us720

Black's Law Dictionary

WESTLAW contains an on-line version of *Black's Law Dictionary*. The dictionary incorporates definitions of terms and phrases of English and American law.

Along with the preformulated queries in this publication appear references to *Black's Law Dictionary* for many important terms in antitrust law. The format of such demands is as follows:

di cartel

The command consists of letters DI followed by the term to be defined. To see the definition of a phrase, enter the letters DI followed by the phrase (without quotation marks):

di parens patriae

If the precise spelling of a term to be defined is not known, or a list of dictionary terms is desired, a truncated form of the words may be entered with the root expansion symbol (!) attached to it:

di mono!

This example will produce a list of all dictionary terms that begin with the root MONO. From the list of terms, a number corresponding to the desired term can be entered to obtain the appropriate definition. For example, to see the *Black's* definition of MONOPSONY, enter the number which precedes that term in the list.

WESTLAW Antitrust Databases

This section discusses the WESTLAW Antitrust databases, in which the preformulated queries in this publication have been designed to be used. The component databases of the topical antitrust and business regulation database include case law databases, relevant sections of the United States Code, Code of Federal Regulations, and Federal Register, decisions of the Federal Trade Commission, and Texts and Periodicals.

The case law databases consist of cases from the National Reporter System. Cases in WESTLAW are in "full text plus." That is, they include the court's decision enhanced by a synopsis of the decision and headnotes stating the legal propositions for which the decision stands. The headnotes are classified to West's Key Number classification system.

Judicial decisions on antitrust matters are available in all WESTLAW case law databases. Special topical databases limited to the antitrust decisions of the federal courts are also available and are identified with the prefix FABR. Opinions of the United States Supreme Court are found with the identifier SCT or FABR–SCT; U.S. Courts of Appeals decisions are found with the identifier CTA or FABR–CTA; the indentifier for U.S. District Court opinions is DCT or FABR–DCT; and all federal cases are available with the identifier ALLFEDS or FABR–CS.

WESTLAW has individual state databases containing decisions from specific states and the District of Columbia. The database identifier for an individual state database consists of the state's postal abbreviation followed by a hyphen and the letters CS (e.g., MN–CS for Minnesota cases).

In addition to case law, WESTLAW has many other documents available of interest to antitrust law researchers. The Sherman Act, Clayton Act, Robinson-Patman Act and other relevant portions of the U.S. Code are available in either the United States Code database (USC) or in FABR–USC where sections of the U.S. Code relating specifically to antitrust law are gathered.

Antitrust Law related federal administrative regulations contained in the Code of Federal Regulations can be found in either the CFR or FABR–CFR databases. Proposed regulations placed in the Federal Register can be found in databases identified FR or FABR– FR.

Decisions of the Federal Trade Commission (F.T.C.) that are reported in *Federal Trade Commission Decisions and Reports* are available on WESTLAW in the database identified FABR–FTC. Although the available fields differ somewhat, the search techniques described for case law databases will apply to F.T.C. decisions, and many of the preformulated queries in this book will retrieve valuable results in this database.

Finally, selected scholarly articles from over 150 law review, bar association, and American Bar Association publications (including the A.B.A.'s *Antitrust Law Journal*) are available. Use the comprehensive Texts and Periodicals database (NTP), the Federal database (FTP), the Multi-state database (MTP) or the Antitrust Texts and Periodicals database (FABR–TP) for this research. The identifier for the *Antitrust Law Journal* is ANTITRLJ.

WESTLAW Hornbook Queries: (a) Query Format

The queries that appear in this publication are intended to be illustrative. They are approximately as general as the material in the Hornbook text to which they correspond.

Although all of the queries in this publication reflect proper format for use with WESTLAW, there is seldom only one "correct" way to formulate a query for a particular problem. This is so even though some techniques are clearly better than others. Therefore, the queries reflect a wide range of alternative ways that queries may be structured for effective research. Such variances in query style reflect the great flexibility that the WESTLAW system affords its users in formulating search strategies.

For some research problems, it may be necessary to make a series of refinements to the queries such as the addition of search terms or the substitution of different grammatical connectors, to adequately fit the particular needs of the individual researcher's problem. The responsibility remains with the researcher to "fine tune" the WESTLAW queries in accordance with his or her own research requirements. The primary usefulness of the preformulated queries in this hornbook is in providing users with a foundation upon which further query construction can be built.

Individual queries in this hornbook may retrieve from one to over a hundred cases, depending on the database to which they are addressed. If a query does not retrieve any cases in a given database, it is because there are no documents in that database which satisfy the proximity requirements of the query. In this situtaion, to search another database with the same query, enter the letter S followed by the initials DB, followed by the new database identifier. Thus, if a query was initially addressed to the FABR–DCT (District Courts) database, but retrieved no documents, the user could then search the FABR–CTA (Courts of Appeals) database with the same query by entering the following command:

    s db fabr-cta

This command instructs WESTLAW to search the Courts of Appeals database of antitrust law documents with the same query that was previously used in the District Courts database.

The maximum number of cases retrieved by a query in any given database will vary, depending on a variety of factors, including the relative generality of the search terms and proximity connectors, the frequency of litigation or discussion of the issue in the courts and administrative bodies, and the number of documents comprising the database.

WESTLAW Hornbook Queries: (b) Textual Illustrations

This section explains how the queries provided in this treatise may be used in researching actual problems in antitrust law that a practitioner might encounter. Examples from the text of this edition have been selected to illustrate how the queries can be expanded, restricted, or altered to meet the specific needs of the reader's research.

A segment of the text from Chapter 6, section 6.5, of *Economics and Federal Antitust Law* appears below. The selection has been edited slightly and the footnotes omitted.

§ 6.5 "Dangerous Probability" and Market Power

Courts have expressed concern that the attempt [to monopolize] offense can be used anticompetitively to condemn "unfair" business conduct when there is little likelihood of monopoly. For some courts this means that the plaintiff in an attempt case must show that the defendant has a certain amount of market power. Others have rejected the requirement, arguing that it virtually destroys the distinction between the offense of attempt and completed monopolization. Most courts, however, require a plaintiff to establish a dangerous probability that the defendant could have monopolized some identifiable market. This market generally need not be defined as precisely as it must be in monopolization cases. Further, a substantially lower market share will support an attempt case than a monopolization case.

Courts that have tried to produce a generalized formula for market power in attempt cases probably have been wasting their time. The market power requirements in attempt cases vary with the conduct alleged to be an attempt. A firm that seeks to create a monopoly by dynamiting its compeitor's plants does not need market power—only a saboteur and a match. The same thing generally applies to other kinds of conduct that have been held to be an attempt to monopolize, such as bad faith litigation or patent fraud.* * *

Thus it is impossible to generalize: some attempts to monopolize require the defendant to have substantial market power, while others do not. Further, the success of a particular attempt scheme sometimes depends not on the defendant's market power, but on its relatively large market share. * * *

In all cases it is important to remember that the attempt offense is designed to reach conduct likely to create a monopoly. In the debate over market power requirements in attempt cases some courts seem to have lost sight of this. A few courts have assessed what appears to be a universal market power requirement. Others have dispensed with the requirement and in the process have permitted plaintiffs to prove an attempt without showing a dangerous probability of success. The attempt offense was not designed to condemn the exercise of present market power. Nor was it designed, however, to condemn conduct unlikely to give the defendant to monopoly. At the very least a plaintiff should be required to identify some market in which the defendant's activities, if allowed to run their course, plausibly would have generated a monopoly.

The text of this section discusses the need to prove defendant's market power in attempted monopolization cases. In order to retrieve douments discussing this point of law the following preformulated query is given as a suggested search strategy on WESTLAW:

attempt** /p "dangerous probability of success" /21 "market power"

A page of a case that was retrieved from the FABR–CTA (U.S. Courts of Appeals) database by this query appears below:

R 1 OF 12   P 31 OF 43   FABR–CTA T

627 F.2d 919

To understand the reason for requiring proof of dangerous probability of success, one must keep in mind the central purpose of the **attempt** offense to discourage unilateral activity that poses a threat to competition and that, if left alone, could result in the acquisition of monopoly power. P. Areeda & D. Turner, supra, at 312. The focus must be on the danger to competition posed by the activity and by the actor. It is apparent that each situation will present different problems that mandate a flexible approach toward the "mix" of conduct, actor, and market conditions that make up the offense. In some cases of clearly exclusionary conduct, the conduct itself, along with the exclusionary intent that can be inferred from it, poses such a danger to competition that it may be condemned regardless of the **market**

power of the actor. In a sense, the conduct carries an inherent **"dangerous probability of success."** Such clearly exclusionary behavior, even though it poses no immediate measurable danger to the market, presents the potential for mischief. To the extent that such conduct inevitably harms competition, there is little reason to tolerate it.

On the other hand, in circumstances involving ambiguous conduct, the requisite degree of danger may not exist in the absence of appreciable market power because market power increases the potential for harm. What may be legal for the company lacking substantial market power may be illegal for the firm with such power. And where the conduct is ambiguous, the market power of the firm may help clarify the intent of the actor.

The query can be used to search in other case law databases. For example, to search in the U.S. District Courts database with the same query, enter the command:

s db fabr-dct

This instructs the computer to search the database of antitrust law cases of the District Courts with the same query used in the previous search. A headnote from a document retrieved from the FABR–DCT database with the preformulated query from section 6.5 of the text appears below:

R 1 OF 16 P 14 OF 84 FABR–DCT T

421 F.Supp. 274.

265 k12(1.3)

MONOPOLIES

k. Monopolization; monopoly power.

D.C.Cal.1976.

In an action alleging attempt to monopolize, determination of "relevant market" becomes necessary only when it is essential to prove defendant's dangerous probability of success by showing of market power. Sherman Anti-Trust Act, s2, 15 U.S.C.A. s 2. Id.

General Communications Engineering, Inc. v. Motorola Communications & Electronics, Inc.,

421 F.Supp. 274.

A portion of the text from Chapter 8, section 8.3 of the treatise is reproduced below:

§ 8.3 Tie-ins, Market Power, and the Per Se Rule

* * *

Courts generally presume market power, however, when the tying product is patented or copyrighted, and some courts give the same presumption when the tying product is trademarked. In most cases courts regard the presumption as rebuttable. Many patents confer absolutely no market power on their owners, and often patented products are not even marketable at their cost of production. Likewise, any group of words or symbols can be copyrighted.

The rule creating a presumption of market power in such cases overlooks the fact that in a world of brand-specific products almost everything except fungibles is protected at least to a certain extent by a patent, copyright or trademark. These are the mechanisms by which consumers distinguish among brands. More often than not the patent or trademark makes a product "distinguishable" but confers little or no measureable market power upon its owner. Automobiles, stereo equipment, home computers, watches, fast food franchises, clothing and canned food are all likely to be patented, trademarked or copyrighted, but all are sold in arguably competitive markets. The economic case for "presuming" sufficient market power to coerce consumer acceptance of an unwanted tied product simply because the tying product is patented, copyrighted, or trademarked is very weak.

* * *

This part of the text discusses illegal tie-ins or tying arrangements where the defendant uses its patent, copyright, or trademark on one product to coerce buyers into taking a second product as well. Accordingly, the following preformulated query is provided as a suggested search:

digest(tie tying   /p   patent** copyright** trademark**)

A headnote from a case retrieved by this query in the FABR–CTA database is set out below:

R   1   OF   41   P   11   OF   46   FABR–CTA   T

448 F.2d 43

265 k17(2.5)

MONOPOLIES

k.   Restrictions on buying competitors' goods: tying agreements.

C.A.Cal.1971.

One cannot immunize tie-in from antitrust laws by simply stamping a trademark symbol on tied product, at least where tied product is not itself product represented by the trademark. Sherman Anti-Trust Act, s 1, 15 U.S.C.A. s 1; Lanham Trade-Mark Act, ss 5, 45, 15 U.S. C.A. ss 1055, 1127. Id.

Siegel v. Chicken Delight Inc.,

448 F.2d 43, certiorari denied 92 S.Ct. 1172, 405 U.S. 955, 31 L.Ed.2d 232, and 92 S.Ct. 1173, 405 U.S. 955, 31 L.Ed.2d 232.

The query can be altered to meet the needs of individual researchers. For example, a practioner may wish to find cases involving this issue only in the context of patented products. In this situation, the preformulated query shown above can be modified to retrieve documents relevant to the more specific issue by editing the query as follows:

digest(tie tying   /p   patent**)

A headnote from the first case retrieved by the modified query from the FABR–CTA database appears below:

R   1   OF   18   P   5   OF   55   FABR–CTA   T

512 F.2d 993

(3)

265 k21.1(2)

MONOPOLIES

k.   Licenses and royalties.

C.A.Cal.1975.

Label licensing program whereby holder or patent relating to use of epoxy material as backing for wearing parts of gyrating crushing machines sold unpatented epoxy backing material with a "can label" license authorizing use of contents in practice of the patent constituted a tying arrangement in violation of the Sherman Act and, consequently, misuse of patent where patent holder never issued a direct license, had consistent program of bringing patent infringement suits against all other sellers of epoxy resin for use as backing material for crushers and, in so doing, effectively dried up any source of supply which crusher users might look to expect for patent holder and its licensees. Sherman Anti-Trust Act, s 1, 15 U.S.C.A. s 1.

Rex Chainbelt Inc. v. Harco Products, Inc.

512 F.2d 993

Ranking Documents Retrieved on WESTLAW: Age and Term Options

Documents retrieved by a query can be ordered in either of two ways. One way is to order documents by their dates, with the most recent documents displayed first. This is ranking by AGE. Using the AGE option is suggested when the user's highest priority is to retrieve the most recent decisions from a search.

Alternatively, documents can be ranked by the frequency of appearance of query terms. This is ranking by TERMS. When a search is performed with the TERMS option, the cases containing the greatest number of different search terms will be displayed first.

When a database is accessed by entering a database identifier, WESTLAW responds with a screen requesting that the query be entered. At this point the user may select which type of ranking, AGE or TERMS, is desired.

The queries offered in this hornbook were formulated and tested for relevancy with use of the TERMS option. Accordingly, in certain instances use of the AGE option with the preformulated queries may display less relevant, yet more recent cases, first.

Conclusion

This appendix has reviewed methods that can be used to obtain the most effective legal research in antitrust law possible. Herbert Hovenkamp's *Economics and Federal Antitrust Law* combines the familiar treatise publication with a powerful and easily accessed computerized law library. The WESTLAW references at the end of each section of the treatise text provide a basic framework upon which the lawyer can structure additional research on WESTLAW. The queries may be used as provided or they may be tailored to meet the needs of researcher's specific problems. The power and flexibility of WESTLAW affords users of this publication a unique opportunity to greatly enhance their access to and understanding of antitrust law.

*

Table of Cases

References are to Pages

Table of Statutes

*

Index

COST—Cont'd
Average fixed cost, defined, 10.
Average variable cost, defined, 10–11.
Fixed cost, defined, 10.
Information costs, 14, 195.
Long-run average cost, 28–29.
Marginal cost, defined, 10–11.
Social cost, defined, 19.
Sunk costs, 13.
Variable cost, defined, 10.

DELIVERED PRICING
See Basing Point Pricing.

DETERRENCE
Overdeterrence, social cost of, 109, 120, 166–168.
Underdeterrence, social cost of, 166–167.

DIVISION OF TERRITORIES, HORIZONTAL, 115–116
See, also, Cartels.

DUAL DISTRIBUTION
See Vertical Nonprice Restraints.

ECONOMIC ANALYSIS, POSITIVE AND NORMATIVE, 44–45

ECONOMIES OF SCALE
Generally, 2, 24–35.
Minimum Optimal Scale (MOS), 27–31, 97–98, 112, 141–142, 177–179, 195, 208, 211, 294, 306, 332.
Multiplant economies, 26.

EFFICIENCY
Allocative, 41–42, 45–49, 375.
And marginal cost, 13.
And mergers. See Mergers.
And monopoly, 19–24.
Pareto-efficiency, 46–47, 375n.
Potential Pareto-efficiency, 46–48, 375n.
Productive, 45, 47.
"X-efficiency," 24.

ELASTICITY
Cross elasticity of demand, 62–66, 328–329.
Of demand, 6, 9, 17, 57–58, 60, 367.
Of supply, 7, 9, 60–61, 66–70, 328–329, 367.
Market and firm elasticities distinguished, 9–10, 57–58.

EQUILIBRIUM, COMPETITIVE, 3–5, 7–8

EXCESS CAPACITY
Generally, 7.
Market definition and, 66–67.
Mergers and. See Mergers.

EXCESS CAPACITY—Cont'd
Predatory pricing and, 182–184.

EXCLUSIVE DEALING
Generally, 241–246.
Economic efficiency and, 242–243.
Foreclosure theory, 241–242.
Free riding and, 244.
Market uncertainty and, 243.
Merger Guidelines (1984) and, 246.
Per se rule and, 245–246.
Price discrimination and, 243n.
Robinson-Patman Act and, 244n.
Rule of reason and, 246.
Tie-ins compared, 242.

FEDERAL TRADE COMMISSION (FTC) ACT, § 5
Basing point pricing and, 105–106.
Legislative History, 51.
Predatory pricing and, 186n.
Requirement of agreement, 107–109.
Tacit collusion and, 107–109.

FREE RIDER PROBLEMS
Exclusive dealing and, 244.
Joint ventures and, 114–116, 131.
Refusals to deal and, 277–278.
Resale price maintenance and, 252–258.
Vertical restrictions and, 252–258.

HERFINDAHL–HIRSCHMAN INDEX
See Merger Guidelines, Dept. of Justice.

***ILLINOIS BRICK* RULE**
See Indirect Purchaser Rule.

INDIRECT PURCHASER RULE
See Private Enforcement.

INDUSTRIAL ORGANIZATION, 24–36

INFORMATION EXCHANGES, PRICE, 101, 116–120

INNOVATION, 22
And monopoly, 23.

JOINT VENTURES
Generally, 110–124.
Advertising and, 115–116.
Efficiency and, 113–114, 120–124.
Free rider problems and, 113–116.
Price setting and, 111–113.

LEGISLATIVE HISTORY OF ANTITRUST LAWS, 50–54

LIMIT PRICING, 331
See, also, Predatory Pricing.

†